The Intellectual History of Europe

Also by Friedrich Heer

THE MEDIEVAL WORLD

FRIEDRICH HEER

THE INTELLECTUAL
HISTORY OF EUROPE

Translation by Jonathan Steinberg

THE WORLD PUBLISHING COMPANY
CLEVELAND AND NEW YORK

Published by The World Publishing Company
2231 West 110th Street, Cleveland, Ohio 44102

Published simultaneously in Canada by Nelson, Foster & Scott Ltd.

Library of Congress Catalog Card Number: 66–23090

FIRST EDITION

CONTENTS

Translator's Preface   vii

Foreword   1

Abbreviations   6

1 The Anxious Beginning: Eastern Domination (Second to Fifth Centuries)   7

2 From Boethius to Eriugena (Sixth to Ninth Centuries)   25

3 The Tenth Century   47

4 The Revolution from Rome (Eleventh Century)   70

5 The Birth of History (Twelfth Century)   80

6 The World of the Three Rings: The Mediterranean Foundations of Western Europe   95

7 'Left Wing' and 'Right Wing' Popular Religious Movements (Thirteenth Century)   111

8 The Hour of Aquinas (1225–74)   141

9 The Revolt Against the Curial *Universum* (1282–1348)   158

10 The First German Movement in Its European Setting (1270–1350)   172

11 The New Age of Salvation (Fifteenth Century)   184

12 Dante to Machiavelli: Italy's Political Humanism (1300–1527)   198

13 The Second German Movement: Between East and West; Luther and Maximos the Greek (Sixteenth Century)   218

14 The Rise and Fall of the Spanish Spirit   254

15 Italy of the Counter Reformation (1527–1870)   289

16 From Calvin to Descartes and Pascal (1490–1661/2)   315

CONTENTS

17 England: The Counterweight to Europe   348

18 France (1650–1794): The Potentialities of Europe   382

19 The Inner Kingdom: Germany (1601–1800)   409

20 The Nineteenth Century (1789–1945)   448

    Notes   477

    Index   547

TRANSLATOR'S PREFACE

THE preparation of the English edition of Friedrich Heer's great work presented certain peculiar difficulties. It may help the reader to find his way through the volume to know what they were, because, in a sense, they are problems which confront the reader as much as the translator. To begin with, Professor Heer rejects the purely linear, chronological idea of history. He believes that great historical ideas have a radial influence, which cannot be described or analysed by a mere recitation of their historical genesis and development. As a result, he has developed in his own thinking an unusual and provocative treatment of the connections. The book is in a certain sense circular in construction, because the great ideas and great works which it discusses continue to exist, interweave and interpenetrate each other in different ages and in different ways. The modern reader who has a copy of Augustine's *City of God* on his book-shelf along with Kant's *Critique of Pure Reason* is in a very real way a contemporary of both Augustine and Kant. Professor Heer's book is, therefore, no less contemporary in its significance than the works which it discusses. To help the reader to adapt his thinking, the epilogue from the German edition has become the introduction to the English one. There Professor Heer outlines several fundamental, radial themes, which he sees as the vital determinants of the inner struggle of the European spirit.

A second difficulty arose from the fact that this volume is only a part of a much larger corpus, the entire series of works which Professor Heer has written. It spreads out in several directions, not all of which are treated with complete thoroughness in this book, because Professor Heer has already devoted other works to the problems in question. In the course of time, the English-speaking reader will, it is to be hoped, be able to follow up the germinal and provocative ideas in this volume by reading the translations of other works by Professor Heer.

A third difficulty was that of selection. Professor Heer believes passionately that ideas are explosive and must be taken extremely seriously. Ideas, he argues, are often dynamite, and those of us who follow the explosion of European ideas in Asia and Africa will find it hard to deny his thesis. The effect of ideas varies from age to age and from country to country. The various nations of the world are not all living in exactly the same period from the point of view of the history of ideas. This means that it is extremely difficult to know how much space ought to be given to the analysis of a given idea within the body of this work, and the American or British reader may well find that the treatment of certain concepts which he considers vital is much briefer than the treatment of others whose efficacy in other areas may be unknown to him. This is both a necessary evil and the great value of this work, that its selection and arrangement are so extraordinary and unusual.

It may also help the reader to appreciate the purposes of the author to remember, as he reads, that this book was written in Vienna at the height of the Cold War. While Professor Heer struggled for clarity and for an open mind, Russian troops still occupied sections of his native city. The Nazis had already arrested him and destroyed his papers. The Russians arrested him in 1946 by mistake. He had to begin again from scratch in an atmosphere of physical discomfort and intellectual despair. His struggle to retain an open mind in divided Austria and his relentless determination to uncover some pattern in the tragedy of Europe give this book its inner dynamism. Professor Heer believes with the deepest sincerity that only through open discussion, free of slogans and petrified conceptions, can we of the twentieth century confront the great movements of our age. This dispute must be a real discussion in which we listen to one another, and it must be informed, so that we know what we and our opponents are actually saying. As Europe struggles to overcome its divisions and to confront the non-European world, Professor Heer's book offers us new perspectives on our past and new directions for our future.

Finally, I cannot close this preface without expressing my thanks to Professor Heer whose friendly assistance and kind co-operation have greatly eased my task.

Christ's College, Cambridge   JONATHAN STEINBERG

The Intellectual History of Europe

FOREWORD

THE history of Europe's great ideas is not linear. The most significant of them lie like overlapping rings across the spiritual map of Europe. In this Foreword, I want to outline a group of themes, which seem to me to recur throughout European history and to emphasize their contemporary relevance. If the reader sees them first in their modern guise, he will, perhaps, more readily recognize them when they appear in the discussion to follow. The Foreword is consequently a kind of guide to the book and not an exposition of the themes as such. By presenting them schematically, I want to underline their importance and also their continuity throughout Europe's past.

(1) There has always been a struggle between 'above' and 'below' in Europe's inner history. The 'upper' culture of Christianity, educated humanism and rationalism has struggled against a 'lower' culture of the masses. This cultural 'underground' included both the deeper levels of the individual personality and the customs, manners and faith of the people. During the nineteenth century which really means the era that ended for Europe in 1945 this struggle entered a new phase. For the first time, movements from below broke the surface of the upper culture. Whether these movements were rationalist or irrationalist, spiritualist or naturalist, they were marked by great fanaticism and enthusiasm. Their leaders were determined to create a new salvation from the midst of the people or from the depths of the human ego. Until the nineteenth century, such attempts had been limited to certain areas, groups and persons. The most important sign of this phase was the totality of the new spirit's claims. In the era of the old kings and fathers, this spirit had broken out explosively in a few volcanic natures (Francis of Assisi, Joan of Arc, the Hussites, the Lollards, Luther, Munzer). It now became the driving power in the movements of the Enthusiasts, inspired democrats, political and national communities of salvation all with their charismatic or demonic leaders.

(2) The tolerant legislation of many European governments between the French Revolution and the Second World War helped these movements to emerge from the depths of the people. Witches were no longer officially burned and religious dissenters were no longer publicly persecuted. When the new popular movements came out into the open, the most remarkable and exciting fact of all European intellectual history was unconsciously brought to light: despite a persecution lasting 1,000 years not one 'heretical' idea, philosophy,

1

or conviction had been exterminated. At the very height of the eighteenth century, all the sects and heresies were present in the old places and areas where they had first appeared: Barcelona, Toulouse, Naples, Florence, Milan, Basle, Strasbourg, Amsterdam, London, Cracow, Prague, Venice, Lyons, Geneva. Persecution by the orthodox and the secular rulers had only succeeded in pushing heretical movements underground or in forcing them to put on disguises. Repression often turned religious into secular movements, especially where sects were forbidden to carry on theological education. In other cases, they became narrow, fanatical political movements. But they all survived. The fate of Spain and Russia, where suppression from the fifteenth to the twentieth century was most thoroughly carried out, and the oppression of the free churches in Germany afford instructive examples.

(3) The civil war between the upper and lower cultures which resulted in all parts of Europe would have been milder if orthodoxies and the ruling systems had dared to enter into an open 'dialogue with the enemy'. The awareness that no one can possess 'truth' or 'have' God in his fist was only gained after much bloodshed. Many men had to suffer before the rulers, priests and politicians of the West accepted the fact that many are called to a life of truth but few are chosen to bear witness to it.

(4) The anxiety of the persecutors and the persecuted, of oppressors and oppressed, and the increasing split between East and West, have led to Europe's collapse within a global civil war. In this atmosphere of anxiety and tension, conditions are right for the formation of monastic, aggressive, Caesaro-papist grand churches like those which conquered and occupied Europe in the age which followed the death of Constantine.

(5) The European orthodoxies will regain a genuine strength of spirit only when they stop timidly peering about for their actual and alleged opponents and consider instead their own genuine questions and problematic positions. For Catholicism this would mean a resumption of a dialogue broken off in the fourth century. For Protestantism this would mean the courage to face the reality of dissolution of doctrine and questioning in regard to Christ, the old ecclesiastical tradition, the theses of Luther and the early Reformation, and last but not least the exciting questions of the Higher Criticism and research of the nineteenth century. André Gide's observation that 'Catholics are not fond of the truth' contains a worthwhile admonition for all orthodoxies and confessions.

(6) The secular philosophies and intellectual systems of our day are theologies of laymen. As surrogate theologies of nonconformist circles, they are intrinsically committed to a discussion with the theologies of orthodoxy. The idealist, pantheistic, gnostic, existentialist, materialistic and spiritualist systems of our age, each in its own way, have tried to bring the Christian intellectual heritage into a debate with the non-Christian experiences of peoples, continents and persons, of undergrounds and ideological superstructures, which heretofore had not been sufficiently considered in the inner European dialogue.

(7) The works of the poets and artists are spiritual games played in space as well as time. They add their weight to the play of the philosophers and theologians, and act as mediators of invaluable experiences, structures, contents, forms and materials.

(8) The incipient dialogue about 'spirit' and matter and space and time cannot be pursued without the help of poets and artists.

(9) The hasty syntheses of the natural sciences and the humanities, of theology and philosophy, so popular nowadays in certain circles, enjoy a mere pseudo-life under totalitarian pressure. The most significant scientists themselves refer, often unconsciously, to old intellectual traditions. Heisenberg's 'uncertainty principle' is an expression of a typical German-Protestant irrationalism. Einstein's unified theory of the relations of space, time, energy and matter (1953) has its home in the world of the Three Rings and the *Ars Magna* of Raymond Lull. Einstein may well have been one of the fathers of a new baroque synthesis.

(10) Christian and anti-Christian systems can always be deduced from every significant theological and philosophical system. Aristotle, Aquinas, Descartes, Kant and Marx were theistic and atheistic at the same time. The most orthodox thinkers, the church fathers of philosophy and theology, all contain their opposite in themselves. Hence they turn out to be powerful promoters of heresies while they were consciously defending orthodoxy. A good deal of the nonconformist systems of thought and belief prevailing in Europe can be traced back to Paul, Augustine, Scotus and Eckhart.

(11) How much are the European thinkers responsible for the consequences of their ideas? It hardly seems fair to blame a thinker because others have drawn destructive consequences from his system. On the other hand, men are responsible for their thoughts as well as their deeds. An intellectual history of Europe, moreover, is conceivable only if we believe in a true, concrete connection among all its thinkers. This implies responsibility, the guilt of all thinkers (a metaphysical guilt that is not to be prosecuted or judged by any court of this earth). Spirit is the most dangerous thing which exists and Nietzsche was right when he considered himself 'dynamite'. When the old-fashioned guardians of orthodoxy burned a heretic, they knew what they were doing and why. They realized that the spirit is explosive and treated it far more realistically from their point of view than the pseudo-liberal babblers and advocates of tolerance in the nineteenth century. We cannot condemn the inquisitors' concern about the right spirit and the consequences of movements without that spirit but only the means and methods which they applied to oppose them. The obvious fact that no thinker of consequence can predict or accept in advance the results of his thoughts is extremely disquieting. We cannot turn away from this terrible problem either, just because it disturbs our peace of mind. We must face it even though we cannot solve it. The solution has to be looked for in the bright breadth, in the abysmal depth and in the love of the infinitely merciful God. It is a part of the mysteries of the economy of

salvation. A man who believes in grace has no option. He must tell of the disgraces which the thinking man (a unit of many spirits, bodies, opposites!) prepares for himself and his sons.

(12) Consideration of this reality leads directly to the problem of spiritual discipline. *Monachatus non est pietas* (Monasticism is not true piety) is a fundamental thesis of the modern age. The acceptance of the proposition has unleashed the spirit from all bonds. Arbitrariness, lack of discipline, and base impertinence have characterized European thinkers and moulders of the spirit for a long time. They have become impotent. European intellectuals cannot rule because they cannot rule themselves. The high play of the spirit cannot be indulged in moodily and voluptuously; the exercise of the spirit demands strong self-discipline. An attribute of this self-discipline is a loving openness to all the experiences of society. The open spirit will understand the interests of the natural sciences. It will undertake a strenuous inquiry into all European traditions and hear the 'voices of the age'. Above all, the open spirit requires self-control, self-criticism, self-supervision, self-discipline. The intellectuals and all those concerned with the spirit have no choice. Either they discipline themselves or they will be disciplined by new and different powers. The facts of the last thirty years in Europe are undeniable. It has been child's play to suppress the intellectuals in Europe's totalitarian states. Overnight, intelligentsia, professors, theologians, artists and poets were co-ordinated, supervised and disciplined by this or that totalitarian system or pressure group. It is better that this discipline be imposed entirely by the pressure of one's own conscience. Creative and spiritual men must realize that there is an ultimate and decisive difference between genius and holiness. Men must learn to recognize the human and the divine spheres. Nothing would do the average intellectual more good than a little reverence for the genuine monk. Such reverence is a recognition of the indestructible independence of the spirit. Without a degree of asceticism no spiritual activity can prosper. This asceticism should be a characteristic of the new 'monk' who lives in the world and is open to it. It is the image and reflection of that other, higher asceticism in which everything (human) is given to receive everything (divine). This sacred exchange is not ridiculous, as intellectuals for five hundred years have pretended. It must become our model. In the future the European spirit will be worth as much as its representatives are prepared to give, to sacrifice, to serve. They must be ready to receive from above and from below, from past, present, and future. They must sense what is in the air. They must respond to the spirit which bloweth where it listeth.

The book which follows is thus an essay between yesterday and tomorrow, between the old and the new. It attempts to single out certain lines of force and to isolate certain fixed points which have been decisive in the spiritual history of Europe. Its first goal, the short term objective, is to try to translate the spiritual vocabulary of old Europe and those spiritual experiences deposited in it, into a language which the scientist can use and the layman can understand. I have scrupulously attempted to avoid judging the ideas discussed from a partisan point of view, although I have my own views, which I have tried to indicate as such. In theme and content, this work is no more than an essay.

22 April 1953
Vienna

F.H.

ABBREVIATIONS USED IN THIS VOLUME

AKG	Archiv für Kultur-Geschichte
AL	Archiv für Liturgie-Wissenschaft
ALKM	Archiv für Liturgie und Kirchengeschichte des Mittelalters
AUM	Archiv für Urkundenforschung
BRG	Bibl. rer. Germ.
DVJ	Deutsche Vierteljahrsschrift für Literaturwissenschaft und Geistesgeschichte
Hist.Jb.	Historisches Jahrbuch der Görres-Gesellschaft
HV	Historische Vierteljahrsschrift
HZ	Historische Zeitschrift
JHI	Journal of the History of Ideas
MIOG	Mitteilungen des Instituts für österreichische Geschichtsforschung
NA	Neues Archiv der Gesellschaft für ältere deutsche Geschichtskunde
PG	Migne, *Patrologia Graeca*
PL	Migne, *Patrologia Latina*
SB	Sitzungsbericht (Proceedings of an academic congress)
ZfdA	Zeitschrift für deutsches Altertum
ZKG	Zeitschrift für Kirchengeschichte
ZRG	Zeitschrift der Savigny Stiftung für Rechtsgeschichte
Z.K.Theol.	Zeitschrift für katholische Theologie

1

THE ANXIOUS BEGINNING
Eastern Domination
(Second to Fifth Centuries)

THE idea of Europe was first conceived in the eastern half of the late Roman Empire. Initially, the term was used merely to denote a difference. Dio Cassius observed in AD 199 that there was a sharp distinction between the 'Europeans', the Roman troops from the West, and the 'Syrians', the Orientals, in C. Septimius Severus' army. Even as late as the turn of the fifth century, the *Historia Augusta* used the terms *res europeenses* and *europeenses exercitus* interchangeably.[1] At the beginning, 'Europe' meant armies and solid, political structures. The 'East' stood for a swirling, converging, fusing and redividing amalgam of religious movements, philosophical ideas, political experiments and ethnic peculiarities. The East was a congeries of the peoples, nations and empires of the area. From the second to the fifth centuries, the Christian communities emerged from this welter of ideas, institutions and peoples. And that division of 'Church' and 'heresies' which had determined spiritual events down to our own days was born during the same three centuries.

At the beginning, the early Christian communities were deeply aware of the inner unity of all human existence. Although conversion tended to shatter the sense of brotherhood with all mankind, it could not entirely obscure the link with the past. Not even the justified fear of reverting to heathen cults could suppress the commonly accepted idea that Christ had been foreshadowed in the gods. He was merely the 'true Orpheus' (on the ceilings of the *cubicula* in the catacombs), the true Logos (St John's prologue); in him, as the *logos spermatikos*, the whole human race participated.[2] The philosophers of antiquity were regarded as thoroughly Christian.[3] Christian teaching perfected the wisdom of the Greek thinkers.[4] Clement of Alexandria and Origen, and after them the three great Cappadocians, Basil of Caesarea, Gregory of Nyssa and Gregory Nazianzen, were the first spokesmen of that Christian humanism which through Jerome, Abélard, Petrarch, Erasmus, Budé and Leibniz, down to the nineteenth century, celebrated the ultimate union in holiness of heathen and Christian antiquity and wisdom.[5]

Had the new age of Christ finally done away with all the star-gods and god-states of ancient Asia?[6] What of the world empire itself? Would Christian intellectuals succeed where Rome's greatest poets had failed? Would they achieve mastery of the Empire and its thinkers?[7] Had the great work of tradition been achieved without the slightest gap or seam down all its length? On the surface it appeared to have done so. *Traditio*, however, usually meant the secret transmission of a mystery, a treasure of arcane revelations, within the closed circle of a ritual community.[8] Thus, Paul who put the language of the ancient mystery-cults into the service of Christ, especially in the Epistles to the Ephesians and Colossians, necessarily accepted a considerable amount of pagan ritual.[9] Similarly the return of the Christ-emperor in the Apocalypse was set in the sacral-political framework of a cosmic circus performance, because the assumption of the throne by a late Roman emperor usually began with a circus. The horses of the four riders of the Apocalypse wore the colours of four teams of the circus.[10]

The roots of Christianity stretched deep into the soil of the cosmos of late antiquity. Christian catacombs lay peacefully by the side of their heathen neighbours, grave for grave, cult for cult, word for word. Table manners, the gestures of prayer, funeral feasts, every use and abuse during three hundred years were shared by Christians and heathens alike.[11] The same manifestations of decadence in the martyrologies and grave symbolism of the Christians can be found in the heathen political and erotic language of the times. The love duel of the late Hellenistic *novella* turned into the martyr's combat.[12]

From the second to the fifth centuries, the Christians in the world of the Roman imperium were in a tragic situation. They were far less endangered and threatened by the sporadic, localized and intermittent outbreaks of persecution (rich as these were in doctrinal and disciplinary consequences) than by living naturally in the non-Christian world.[13] It was not their remoteness and separation but their intimacy and proximity with the life around them which was the threat. After all, they breathed the air of the great cities and lived the lives of the pagan *gentes*. How could they preserve their own identity? In the course of this inescapable internal struggle, their thinking was subjected to such conflicts and strains that many of the protective devices and defensive barricades which they set up still stand today.[14] Here we encounter a basic law of intellectual history: whenever the thinking of a religious, political or social group is forced into a corner by some specific historical circumstance, usually in a life and death struggle, the shock of this experience creates a psychological block which can prevent further thinking in the given traumatic area for centuries afterward. In other words, whole complexes of ideas and impressions are simply blotted out. This blocking occurs whether it is the inner or outer existence of the group which is threatened. Christianity in the late classical world was threatened with absorption into the environment in which it lived and by which it was permeated. The threat continued not for years but for centuries. In its fight against other cults, often closely akin to it in much of their thought and feeling, in its struggle with the philosophical intellectualism or refinements of Greek culture, Christianity was forced from the beginning to concentrate itself into small, individual, local groups. It simply had to find a way to assert itself in the hand-to-hand struggle against popular mysticism, learned gnosticism or the philosophy of the Hellenic schools. This conflict, conducted by individuals and groups on their own, each in a different situation, in a different local, intellectual and social relationship to its 'alien' environment, was the basis of the heresies. As early as the second century, Hegesippus, that 'strictly logical, consequential, historically-minded'[15] man, reported that heresies had broken out in strength immediately after the passing of the Apostles and the first generation. In the time of Ignatius of Antioch it was already a title of special praise for a Christian community to be free from heresy.[16] Irenaeus (*circa* 202) declared that the number of apostates and heretics was past all reckoning.

'For there must be also heresies among you.'[17] 'No one can set up a heresy who is not of fervent spirit and possessed of natural gifts designed and created by God.'[18] 'Do not suppose, brethren, that heresies could have arisen from men of little spirit. It takes great men to make heresies.'[19] *Magni homines ...* this is our first encounter with the 'great man' in the intellectual history of Europe; he appears as a mighty mind, discovering, inventing, *making* heresies. But in the consciousness of Christians the truth expressed here was largely obscured by the anxieties of daily experience. 'Heresies' sprang up on all sides. There were a hundred differing truths about, for and against, God and Christ. Where was the one pure doctrine, the one indivisible truth? These embattled Christians were in no position to realize that the Church and the heresies are bound up together, and that Christianity's mysterious growth, in the shadow of the Spirit, toward self-knowledge and self-assertion as 'the Church', depends upon releasing heresies from her own womb.[20] All human thought exists in a complex dialectial relationship with its given historical and social environment. This subtle interpenetration accounts for the bitterness of intellectual struggles. What could still pass as thoroughly orthodox in the late first century was no longer so in the third.[21] Something which the Church, the bearer of tradition and the guardian of the Christian inheritance, had found useful enough in its fight against some sect, philosophical tendency or political movement in the second century might be revealed in the fourth as a heresy. In Luther's time certain ideas could still be included within the sphere of Catholicism which were unacceptable after the Council of Trent.

The Church grows by constantly releasing new and old heresies from within herself. A heresy is no more than an attempt to solve all the intellectual and religious difficulties of a given time at once. These attempts are necessarily made from within the constricted area of a specific historical situation with its own particular outlook and its own particular fears. Experiments with non-Christian ideas and systems of thought to test their durability within the Christian framework have often occurred. The Church depends on the heresies and the heresies on the Church. They constrict, condemn and confirm each other. Each determines the other's appearance. The Church is always tempted to commit itself to some temporally conditioned position, in fact, a heresy – a part-solution, a part-definition. The temptation for the heresies is the desire to be the whole, to *be* the Church. If they surrender to their temptations, the necessary spiritual wrestling between them becomes a struggle for power. Both the Church and the heresies always run the risk of petrifying in the given defensive posture of a particular historical moment and of losing their living fluidity. They forget that the human mind is relative and dialectic. If it is taxed beyond its natural limits it gives one answer and swings at once to the opposite extreme.

European theology was born in the work of the second century apologists, in Christian gnosis, and in the schools of the Alexandrian catechism. This curious prologue was the beginning of European intellectual history.[22] In the recklessness of its drive to conceptualize the Godhead and cosmos, Christ and Christian existence, this early theology threatened to dissolve Christianity into rationalism, a mechanistic theory of nature and spiritualistic speculation: i.e., into morality, culture and education. The thought processes of these theologians were to provide Europe's humanists, moralists, atheists, Bible critics and naturalists with all the material they needed to transform Christianity into an ethic of the inner life.

These theologians were all cultivated men of the world of late antiquity. They had been formed by their schools, society and political culture. They were, in fact, unacquainted with the inner life of a young Church struggling to find and assert itself. Naturally they grasped the intellectual content of Christianity in the only way they could, with the ideas and conceptions which the civilization of their world so readily supplied. The case of Justin is a good example.

Plato and stoicism were the sources of Justin's thought and Christian theology, and ethics in Europe would be unthinkable without them.* Justin's pupil, Tatian, the Syrian, reacted against this dissolution of the substance of Christianity in philosophy and idealism. Tatian was a barbarian, a man of the *menu peuple*, of the lower class. He was torn between a craving for culture and a radical longing to sever every tie that might link God with the world or spirit with matter. Logically enough, he finished as a sectarian but his *Harmony of the Gospels* (translated, among other languages, into Gothic) had an influence far beyond the bounds of the ancient world.

At the beginning of the second century, a wave of popular uprisings began which violently attacked the theological and philosophical speculations of the educated, the concentration of power in the hands of the bishops and the centralism of the imperial government. These movements were propelled both by local passions and hostilities and by the powerful eschatological hopes of the early Christians. Perhaps, the most important driving force in these outbursts was fear. The common people were afraid that the learned men and the rulers were about to steal their Saviour and that he was going to be theorized away, dissolved into a series of abstractions. These anxieties expressed themselves in that extraordinary radicalism which popular movements often generate. The first of these was the heresy of the Phrygians, or Montanism, which broke out

*Nietzsche very perceptively remarked that Christianity was 'Platonism for the people'.

in the second century. Montanism was a movement of enthusiasts, the Montanists were men of an individualistic and prophetic caste of mind who rejected the ecclesiastic hierarchy, officialdom and scholastic theology. Their movement spread like a roaring prairie fire. By the middle of the second century Montanism had already covered much of the Mediterranean area.* In Africa, Donatism arose out of similar grievances. The higher African clergy, who were politically easygoing and tolerant, collided head on with the people's implacable hostility to Rome. Donatism became the first Christian group in the history of the Church against which a Christian state took legal action. It was not to be the last.

The strongest of these folk movements of the second century rallied round Marcion, a man of the Far East, and the darling of contemporary spiritualists from Harnack to Buonaiuti. 'What broke his heart was the failure of the Christian community to understand the uniqueness of the Gospel.[23] Marcion, who had many of Luther's characteristics, was born in Sinope in Pontus, which was at the time dominated by pious legalists, ritually scrupulous Jewish Christians and churchmen. His father, the Bishop of Sinope, was its ruler. We know relatively little about his life except that he was a sea captain for a time and that he founded an opposition Church in Rome. His Church rejected the evil God of the world of his ancestors and of the grim legalism of the Old Testament. That God had become the demonic world ruler of the 'Catholic Church'. Marcion discovered his new God of love, pity and forgiveness, between the lines of *his* own Gospel of St Luke. A profound religious experience of the 'new God' turned Marcion into a radical critic of the Bible. He became the founder of the spiritualistic view of history. The 'pure Gospel' was to be cleansed of all the Jewish 'falsifications' introduced by Peter and the other Apostles. The evil world and the visible Church would continue, he felt, until the end of time to persecute the Church of the spirit, the Church of the truly redeemed, of the inwardly pious and loving. Yet the truth and the consolation of the Spirit were only to be found among these victims of persecution.†

Marcion was the first example in European intellectual history of that specifically European father complex which has led to so many significant rebellions of sons against paternal authority and the world of the fathers and kings. All the institutions of Western society, the monasteries, courts, universities and cities have been scarred by such rebellions. The embittered attempts to replace the world of the fathers by a world of brothers has been a major theme of European development. Despite the fact that Marcion's teaching has survived only in the attacks made on it by his great opponent, Tertullian, Marcion has exerted a powerful and lasting influence on the

*It reached as far as Lyons by the end of the century, and brought that extraordinary city the first of a long series of religious, intellectual and political movements of dissent. Lyons was to be from then on a centre for every sort of nonconformism and heresy.
†cf. the spiritualistic view of history of the Fraticelli, Franck, G. Arnold and Goethe.

development of a great many of the ideologies of resistance to authority of the succeeding centuries. This form of transmission has sufficed to preserve the explosive power of many of his ideas.

Although Marcion was no gnostic, he could not avoid a certain amount of gnostic speculation seeping into his doctrines. No intellectual in the second century could have failed to absorb a certain amount of gnosticism, if only because it was so widespread.[24] For gnosticism was as much an attitude of a social class as it was a metaphysical doctrine. In a world which had renounced the traditions and authority of the great patrician families, the gnostic theology offered a means of self-assertion to an alienated aristocracy. The ancient *polis* of Athens was no more. The Attic tragedy of the fifth century had not been able to save its old gods. The citizens of Rome, the Senate and the senators, the patricians and the plebeians of the Republic's heroic age, had lost their political rights and their share in the government.[25] The world empire had become overgrown with bureaucratic corruption and caprice. The honorable citizenry of the *polis* had been degraded to the level of an urban proletariat. The very will, let alone the power, to change this state of affairs had disappeared. Nothing remained but the inner kingdom.

All educated people, Christians included, of the Hellenic *oikoumene* were fascinated by gnosis, neoplatonism and stoicism, because each of these views of the universe promised to restore the sovereignty of the noble and virile mind over matter. The world was to be subjugated by contemplative penetration into the ultimate depths of the Godhead. Given the secret knowledge of the gods and the world revealed thereby, the noble and cultivated man could always penetrate the confusions of time and place by applying the proper technique of intellectual discipline. Beyond the restraints of social misery and political circumstance he could plunge himself into 'true being'. Liberation, redemption and self-fulfilment were the products of thought, knowledge and self-discipline. This *élite* of knowers and spiritual men all over the civilized world formed an invisible community of *friends*. As 'friends of God' and 'friends of man', they had to defend themselves vigilantly and suspiciously against the masses, the uneducated artisans, materialists, slaves, barbarians, and devotees of monstrous and inhuman cults.

The early Christian thinkers belonged, heart and soul, to this world-wide community. They thought in its terms and expressed its attitudes. The traditional distinction between pagan gnosticism and the so-called Christian gnosticism of Clement of Alexandria and Origen is a gross over-simplification. Distinctions certainly existed, but they were far from clear. Pagan gnostic schools and Christian ones mingled freely.[26] The intercourse between them was complicated and confusing. Pagan philosophers became Christian apologists. Christian bishops developed thoroughly immanentist views of the world from which Christ had either been banished or reduced to secondary importance. Ideas and men moved in and out of different groups. It is absolutely necessary to be aware of this background if the ideas and development of the great Christian thinkers, Tertullian, Origen and Augustine are ever to be understood. This anxious, swirling, variegated world was the one which moulded them and through them much of later Christianity.

This pagan-Christian cultural world was both universal and yet restricted in the narrowest sense to places and persons, to the ethnic qualities and particular genius of an individual. It was wracked by never ending quarrels of 'schools', professors and theologians. These circles were united only in contempt for the masses whom they regarded as sunk in superstition. Generally, they tended to deny both the Trinity and the divine-human nature of Christ. They hated personal, existential *and* philosophical interpretations of sin. The incarnation, suffering and the necessarily historical character of creation were repellent to them.

The other side of the early church was represented by the African Tertullian (*circa* AD 200) the first great theologian of the West. As an African he resented Rome, and he bore the grudges of a member of the oppressed classes against the cultural world of those at the top. A spiritualist and materialist at the same time, he initiated that peculiar thousand-year alliance between prophetic, Utopian, ascetic enthusiasts and mechanistic materialists. His compatriot Arnobius was to be a direct inspiration for Lamettrie and Condillac. Pure spirit cleaved to pure nature, and this union created the fascination of dualism. Tertullian was the first to coin those brilliant, seductive and perilous antitheses. Their pathos and rhetoric have intoxicated intellectuals of every later century. It is hard to say how far they represent 'literature', existential thought, or essential faith. Tertullian was a radical spiritualist and the creator of the historical vision of the 'middle ages' (*tempus medium* of sin and mediocrity) and of the third kingdom of the Holy Spirit.[27] He anticipated in many respects the tragic mood of Pascal and Kierkegaard. What, he cried, had Athens and Jerusalem, the philosopher and Christian, in common?[28] The philosophers were the patriarchs of the heretics.[29] Tertullian had really become a 'heretic' long before he accepted Montanism, because his radical separation between 'pure spirit' and the evil, sensual world made any reconciliation between the real and ideal worlds impossible. He saw Catholicism as a foul compromise, and opposed it by founding a counter-church. Yet like so many extreme ascetics, Tertullian clung with glowing sensuality to the world and its wisdom, so that to attain the final state of perfection he had to condemn the world as rationalist, sensual and materialist. His desperate pride drove him again and again into the very arms of the stoics and philosophers whom he abused. As an extreme individualist, as an African opponent of the Roman state, as a lawyer and, not least, as a member of that intelligentsia which was partly at home in all the intellectual and religious systems of the age, but never entirely so,[30] he developed into an early Christian advocate of religious freedom for all schools of thought.[31] There is no doubt that before Constantine and Theodosius, Christian intellectuals were united with their pagan brethren, their minds still free of the pleasures and promises of power.

Clement of Alexandria and Origen bore striking witness to this alliance.[32] With them the city re-emerged as one of the focal points of Europe's inner history. To demonstrate how important the city has been to Europe's intellectual development, one need only think of the extraordinarily powerful ideas and images associated with Rome, Aachen, Frankfurt, Paris, Toulouse, Venice, Padua, Florence, Oxford, London, Salamanca, Alcala, Brussels, Amsterdam, Basle, Berlin, St Petersburg and Vienna. This history of cities as intellectual centres and strongholds began in Alexandria, where pagan, Jewish and Christian gnosis were all at home. The city was feared as much by pagan and Christian emperors because of its rebellions as by bishops of Rome and patriarchs of Constantinople for its heresies. This then was the setting in which Clement and Origen attempted to purify the simply Christian faith into a philosophy of pure spirit. For them, the highest good was not faith (*pistis*) but knowledge (*gnosis*). The Christian-stoic sage was resigned as God is;* he is wise as God is wise – 'a god sojourning in the flesh';[33] he performs perfectly good works. He rises at will above the limits of space and time to God, to enjoy, behold and understand him in unending peace and exaltation. These were more than mere intellectual delusions of grandeur. They were strong enough to sustain Origen through a life of persecution, privation and consuming activity. His terrifying career led eventually to self-castration and to the prisons of Decius, where in AD 254 as a result of his sufferings he died.[34] Origen was the culmination of the free, Greek spirit. He was determined to understand everything, even to the uttermost mysteries of the Godhead, and, having attained this ultimate wisdom, to stare transfixed in blessed contemplation of God: *amor dei intellectualis*. Meister Eckhart and Spinoza were very close to Origen. The intoxication of the baroque, with its attempt to arrive at scientific certainty of God through mathematics, especially geometry, revived his cause.† During the course of his life, because of his experiences in the struggle with various bishops and heresy tribunals, Origen became the first master of the art of Nicodemism which was to reappear often in Western intellectual history. He did not say all that he thought, and much that he said was purposely disguised. It was possible to interpret his ideas in the sense of the 'primitive' faith of the masses and their organizations. Origen himself was an extreme individualist. He had no more sympathy for Church and state than for the 'historical Christ'[35] and the 'unspiritual' faith of the common people. With Plotinus and other Neoplatonists, Origen believed that God is pure spirit, an insubstantial monad.[36] His task in life was to reinterpret both Old and New Testaments spiritually by means of allegory, which would, of course,

---

*Perhaps the nearest equivalent to the notion of apathy in Christian stoicism is the German mystics' use of *gelassen*.

†Erasmus edited his works at Basle in 1536. The greater part of them, indeed, was lost. Most of what remains has been subjected to later revision to make it orthodox and has been thoroughly mishandled. We only have the Latin version of Rufinus. Yet the boldness of his thought can still be heard speaking from this 'Fragment of the First *Summa*'.

be comprehensible and available only to those few civilized gnostics who could recognize in it the doctrine of the spirit. Since God is wholly transcendent, man is wholly free, i.e., he can at any time rise to self-mastery through reason and asceticism.

Origen taught that there are many worlds which arise and disappear in the course of time. The world's history was a process of education in which the Logos drew men on to the knowledge of God. At last all things would be gathered in and God would be all in all.[37] Christ was merely a secondary god, entirely subordinate to *the* Godhead. He was an exemplary teacher, enlightener and ethical instructor of mankind, but his Gospel was no more than an earthly doctrine of salvation and thus impermanent. Like the Apostles Peter and Paul, it possessed only a very small part of the whole truth.[38] One day it would be taken up into the eternal Gospel.[39]

The Emperor Justinian had Origen condemned as a heretic at the Fifth Ecumenical Council in 533.[40] Violent conflicts raged about him in the late third and fourth centuries. Even in the sixth century, Origenists were still gaining considerable ground in Palestine. The spiritualist monks, who were his most radical partisans, were finally defeated and driven from Jerusalem, and it is fascinating to speculate about their fate. Did they wander westward to Spain? Did they withdraw further into the East? We do not know. Although Origenism as a particular party within the Church was effectively eradicated, the influence of his ideas was pervasive. All the leading theologians of the Eastern Church were to some extent Origenists: Arians and Pelagians alike based themselves on him. The spiritualism of the West, from Eriugena in the ninth century to the idealist philosophers in the nineteenth, is part of the legacy of this man.

'Origenism and Arianism were, fundamentally, attempts to give the Gospel a theological form capable of satisfying the natural perceptions of contemporary pagan intellectuals.'[41] Origen and Arius strove to reconcile the Greek mind and the intelligentsia of the Hellenic East with Christianity. They began by subordinating Christ to the paternal Godhead as understood by Platonists and gnostics. Next they divided him into a gnostic Christ – merely one of the many emanations of the Godhead – and an historical Christ of entirely secondary significance. Arianism could count on the political support of the emperors after Constantine. The tottering Empire needed unitary faith, something that was, as far as possible, just a philosophy, a generally valid spiritual doctrine, which could be adopted by all confessions. By 313, in the Milan 'Edict of Tolerance', Constantine was evidently working toward a union of all creeds, i.e., pagan, Jewish and Christian – under the *summa divinitas*, the highest Godhead, who sits upon the throne of heaven (*in sede caelesti*).[42]

It is misleading to ask whether Constantine ever really became a Christian, or whether his acceptance of the Christian God was 'sincere'. The very phrasing of such a question presupposes later developments when Christianity and paganism had grown away from each other. Just as the 'pagan' philosophers and Christian theologians lived together within a single co-ordinated system, in one and the same dualistic, Neoplatonic world of thought, so Constantine was able to subordinate the old gods and the New Christ-god. Within the same political and religious sphere of reality, it was easy for him to turn the sun-star of Apollo $\frac{P}{X}$ into the monogram of Christ.[43] The invincible sun-god Helios (*sol invictus, sol justitiae*) was present to him throughout the battles and triumphs of life as Christ the King. His relationship to this God was blunt and simple. Like all the European soldiers, army leaders, dukes and kings of the following thousand years, Constantine served his God as the divine representative on earth.[44] The functions of the gods of old in the political commonwealth of men had always been concrete. Their presence assured the well-being, health, peace and safety of the state. It is not easy for those for whom Christ, *the* Christ, has dissolved into an 'idea' to realize this. One of many available examples of this realistic and concrete attitude toward Christ the King is the account which has survived of the mosaic on the great triumphal arch in the Basilica of St Peter which he founded in Rome.* In it Constantine, holding the Church of St Peter in his hand, said to Christ: 'Because under You, the Leader-God, the world has risen triumphant to a new aeon, Constantine the Victor has raised this temple to You.'[45] An act of state had been transacted between *Constantinus Victor* and Christ, the *Sol Invictus*. *Konstantinos Helios*, upon whom the 'most high God' had laid the task of winning and securing salvation, peace and justice for his subjects, was, as a matter of course, worthy to take part, as bishop (*koinos episkopos*) in the counsels of Christian bishops concerning the Church. The pagan Constantine regarded himself as their co-bishop, because the *cura exteriorum et interiorum* (as Gregory I was later to define the office of bishop) had been laid upon him by his God: the task of caring for the safety, body and soul, of the people of his state. By his side, as friends and advisers, stood Eusebius and Bishop Hosius of Cordoba in Spain. Hosius presided at the Council of Nicea and acted as a mediator between Arius and the Patriarch Alexander, but in the bitter and confusing struggles which followed Constantine's death, Hosius was eventually forced to accept Arianism.

Eusebius of Caesarea followed an easier path. This 'herald of Byzantinism'[46] proclaimed Constantine as the new Moses and the new Augustus. The one God, enthroned as the mighty King, sat in his heavenly palace with his royal court around him.[47] On earth he was represented by Constantine.[48] The foundations were laid at that time for the development of Byzantine court ceremonial which was finally fixed in the time of Constantine Porphyrogenetos.

*Constantine built a great many large churches after his conversion to Christianity, none of which have survived in their original form, although a good deal is known about them. For a brief description of the Basilica of St Peter, the reader is referred to Nikolaus Pevsner's *An Outline of European Architecture*, Jubilee Edition, Baltimore, Maryland, Penguin Books, 1960, p. 19.

Eusebius can be seen as the father of the political theology of Byzantium, Aachen and Moscow. He was a Greek monotheist and a disciple of Origen and Arius, not a mere political opportunist. The formula that was to move the world – one God, one Emperor, one land, one faith – had its roots both in Jewish monotheism and in the political facts and the intellectual world of the Greek-Hellenic *oikoumene*.[49] Eusebius was, as a court prelate, an influential and many-sided person. He was interested in philology and history, wrote a great deal and was active in political matters. His basic attitudes were absolutely typical of the East. He disliked, for example, the Apocalypse which thereafter was banished from aristocratic and palace culture for many centuries. It became instead the dream book of the folkish visionaries. The divine monarchy and the Emperor's monarchy were so closely bound together because the dual universe of Origenist Neoplatonism had completely subordinated Christ to the one God.[50] Thus, the Emperor, the 'new Christ'[51] came forward as a brother to help Christ in the battle to win the whole world back to God. The Greek mind simply balked at the divinity of the historical Jesus. Both Origen, whom Eusebius defended in a lively apologia, and Arius, because of whom Eusebius was condemned by the Council of Antioch, subordinated Christ to the one Father-God. This supreme Father-God was a vital political foundation stone for the authority of the late Roman emperors. As often occurs in history, the political demands of those in power coincided with a deeply rooted fundamental attitude of a large group. Eusebius signed the creed of Nicea against Arius under compulsion, but in his *Ecclesiastical History* he blandly omitted to mention Arius' condemnation, the most important event of the whole period.

Under Constantine's sons and first successors, Christendom fell apart into East and West. The first decisive event occurred as early as AD 340. Athanasius fled to Rome during the terror of Constantinus. The bishops and theologians of the West, Pope Liberius of Rome, Lucifer of Cagliari, Eusebius of Vercelli, Hilary of Poitiers, and Ambrose of Milan, took up the fight against the Arian emperors of the East. This resistance of the Western bishops created the West as a self-conscious unity. The West emerged in the battle for the 'freedom of the Church', the mystery of the Trinity and the divine and human nature of Christ. 'By rejecting the mystery (of Christ and the Trinity), Arius necessarily denied the legitimacy of the society which had arisen to be the steward of that mystery'.[52] That society was the Roman Church. The Church attained its independence by rescuing the mystery of the Trinity and the God-man, Christ, from the clutches of the Greek theologians and emperors.

With an impetus at once political and religious, vigorous missionaries brought Arian-imperial Christianity to the neighbouring barbarian peoples. Through the conversion of Germanic tribes to Arianism, the first step was taken in the conversion of the Slav world to Byzantine Christianity. 'On the Danube frontier, from Vienna to Belgrade (Singindnum) and Sofia (Sardica),

in the middle of the fourth century, the spiritual destiny of the Roman world
was decided.'[53]

The episcopate in this border-land between two worlds was fantastically
imperialist and Arian. It followed the emperor about, as a political department, from province to province, from battlefield to battlefield, from synod
to synod. Against this overwhelmingly powerful enemy, with all the political
and cultural strength of Christian-pagan late antiquity behind it, Europe took
shape. In southern France, Spain, Italy and North Africa, the simple folk
rallied to the faith under the leadership of the bishops. A strange alliance was
forged between the lower classes, who were not willing to let their Redeemer-
God be argued away by learned Greek clerks, and Roman aristocrats, men of
the upper bureaucracy. The assistance of the Africans, who hated Eastern
domination, helped to consolidate the alliance. The struggle against the East
which continued until the twelfth century was an extremely bitter one. It
produced a profound aversion among the most influential circles in Western
Christendom to pagan culture, science and philosophy. The religious and
political struggles over the uniqueness of the son of God and the mystery of
the Trinity were waged against the immensely superior intellectual culture of
the Greek world and the equally superior military and political power of the
East. Culture, learning and science belonged to the rich and all-too-eloquent
Byzantine court prelates, men who lived on familiar terms with pagan intelligentsia. Western bitterness, therefore, was fed by an acute sense of inferiority. The hatred of the West for all things from the East continued to
burn, fanned by the struggle over images in the eighth century, throughout
the following seven hundred years. In the East, the grievances of the common
people found expression only in the fractiousness of the monks. In the West,
they found leadership and genuine expression in the works of the great
patrician bishops.

When the Emperor Constantius II wanted to force Arianism upon the
Synod of Arles and the Council of Milan, he banished Hilary of Poitiers to
Phrygia, one of many such banishments to the East. The spiritual climate of
the Greek world was supposed to break this man of the West. There he learned
to speak Greek but continued to affirm the dogma of the Trinity in silence. He
was deeply influenced by Origenist allegory but remained essentially Western
in outlook. When he finally returned to his native country, he reverted at once
to his original position and proceeded to organize a purge of Arian bishops at
the Council of Paris (361–2?). Political positions, Christian dogma and the
new Western self-consciousness fused in Hilary's efforts to support his theological positions with careful historical accounts of the actual events upon
which they depended. For the East the historical Christ had no convincing
force; for the West, the historical fact was the very proof of God.

During this epoch, Ambrose, the Governor of Liguria and Emilia, was
elected Bishop of Milan. The people of Milan saw nothing unusual in the
selection of an unbaptized aristocrat for a Church office. To them, the virtues

of Christianity and those of a Roman man of virtue were quite indistinguishable. Both his election and his controversy in 384 with the pagan Governor of Rome, Symmachus, over the removal of the altar of the Goddess of Victory showed how closely pagan and Christian agreed in their conceptions of the one world.[54] Neither Ambrose nor Symmachus had any notion of tolerance. The safety and stability of the *polis* were bound up with the practice of the cult. The correct sacred, political, public and legal performance of divine service was, as a result, not something about which one could be tolerant.[55] The two celebrated letters to the thirteen-year-old Valentinian II expressed succinctly the whole programme of the Roman Church, which had already emerged as successor to the *imperium* as guardian of *salus, pax et securitas*. Ambrose, the popular leader, was the precursor of the Pataria and Gregory VII. He was both a Roman statesman and a bishop at the same time. His funeral orations were masterpieces of the late ancient sense of life and of Latin style. No one felt that there was any inconsistency in the idea of a man who was at one and the same time a popular leader, a Roman orator and a Christian bishop. It was perfectly natural that the Bishop spoke freely of Cicero and stoicism.[56] When Milan was threatened by imperial troops under orders from an Arian emperor, Ambrose led his people in a vigil in their churches night and day, singing and reciting psalms. His preaching occasionally struck a communist note.[57] Property was theft. It was God's will that the land should belong to all. Like modern socialists, he distinguished between ownership for use and ownership for profit.

This solidarity with his people gave him the strength to confront Theodosius and compel him to make public penance.[58] The act was of great importance. A Roman bishop had for the first time compelled the holder of the world's highest office to accept his own sinfulness. Thus, in AD 390 the foundation of the European right of resistance was laid; without the stoic-Christian-natural *jus rebellandi*, Europe's inner history is unthinkable. Despite their differences, however, Ambrose and the Spaniard Theodosius were fundamentally in agreement with each other on many points. Both believed in the rebirth of Rome and the Roman Empire;[59] Claudian and Rutilius Namatianus in the necessity for a return of power, rebirth and growth through the mastery of evils.[60] Both Christian and pagan accepted without qualification those organic, cosmological formulae of renewal so characteristic of the united world of the 'Theodosian Renaissance'.[61]

One great bridge still remained between the intellectual worlds of East and West, St Jerome,[62] the idol and model of all European humanists from the twelfth to the sixteenth century.* He was an irritable, scholarly man, filled with the intellectual riches of antiquity. Jerome was born into an aristocratic Dalmatian family and at the age of twelve he came to Rome where he spent eight years absorbing the lavish humanist culture of the age. Pope Liberius baptized the young man when he was twenty. He travelled widely in Gaul and

*Erasmus edited his works in Basle between 1516 and 1520.

spent some time at Trier, after which, in 374, he travelled through the Syrian desert. Jerome's combination of the grand tour and a penitential pilgrimage became a model for more than a thousand years. His cult of friendship and his quarrelsome scholarship had all the characteristics of later academic life, and the letter-writing humanists, living in a round of literary feuds and visits to their friends, rightly honoured him as their patriarch. Jerome was ordained a priest in Antioch in 380. He learned Hebrew from a Jewish convert and did his biblical studies under Gregory Nazianzen. Then, commissioned by the Spanish humanist, Pope Damasus, he undertook his celebrated revision of the Bible. Jerome lived out his last thirty-five years in ascetic retirement at Bethlehem, but always and everywhere, in Rome, in Constantinople, in the desert of the Thebaïd and Nitria, he remained a humanist. Even in the desert, Cicero was nearer to him than Christ.[63]

One hundred and twenty-two letters of Jerome's have been preserved. In them he cited Horace, Juvenal and Lucian. His letters were an ironical commentary on the world of late antiquity, which he both loved and hated. He pilloried the vices of Roman society in his *Libellus de Custodi Virginitatis*, and described the ostentatiousness of the Christian nobility in words borrowed from Ammianus Marcellinus' description of the pagan Roman patricians.[64] He mocked the Roman clergy as a 'Senate of the Pharisees'. When his friend, the Pope, died, he was deprived of his one protection against the hatred of the envious and the objects of his criticism.[65] But it was not really for any of these reasons that he could not return to the West. Jerome's malaise was a symptom of a profound change which had taken place in the West. In reality Jerome could never go home. To begin with, he had become an Origenist, if not in dogma, as Rufinus claimed, then in spirit. Jerome belonged entirely to the fluctuating, flowing and ambivalent world of Christian-pagan culture and the Hellenist intelligentsia. It was part of his nature and he could not escape it.

Jerome's great legacy to the West was philological discipline. In his translation and editing of the Bible, he championed the *graeca fides* of the New Testament and the *hebraica veritas* of the Old. His hagiographical and biographical writings, *De Viris Illustribus*, moulded literature up to the seventeenth century. Jerome left the West another legacy, less obvious, but no less important. He was the first great churchman to cultivate noble and virtuous women, and thus the founder of the Western tradition of feminine culture. In Jerome's relationship to the noble ladies Paula and Eustochium, whom he had brought to the monastery in Bethlehem, the later role of the woman as the repository of the spirit was foreshadowed. The nuns of the imperial house in the age of Otto, Héloïse and Abélard, Petrarch and Laura, Francis de Sales and Jeanne Françoise de Chantal, *humanisme dévot* and its secular off-shoots in French society of the seventeenth and eighteenth centuries, and Theresa of Avila were spiritual descendants of St Jerome, Paula and Eustochium.

The real founder of Western Christianity was an African, St Augustine. He rejected Rome not for its sins, as had St Jerome, but for itself. He turned from Rome precisely because he understood its greatness. Nothing could be further from the classical learning than Augustine's famous remark, 'the tears of a single woman are worth more to me than all the emotions of the Roman people'.[66] It may well have been that Augustine resented Rome initially because he was a Berber, one of those who did not belong, but later he rejected it because his concerns lay elsewhere, 'I care to know only God and the soul, and nothing more.'[67] This spirit tore apart the unified world of Christian-pagan antiquity. Although he honoured Romulus and the race of the Romans, justly renowned for the *virtus* of a Scaevola, a Scipio, a Fabricius,[68] he did not believe in the Constantian conversion and the Theodosian Renaissance. Augustine followed the hard road trodden by the company of Christ from Abel to the world's end. He believed in the little band of elect, travelling through the night of persecution, and thus he became the chief inspiration of the spiritualist interpretation of history from the eleventh to the nineteenth century. His fifteen books concerning the Trinity, which were written between 398 and 416, became the basis of all Western theology.[69] His doctrine of God's relationship to the individual, to mankind, to the world, to nature and to history, was an attack on the Hellenic East. Augustine hardly knew Greek. For him, the East was the home of all heresies, of all the intellectual difficulties and trials of faith which he bore in his own breast.

The staggering breadth of Augustine's experience is the explanation of his enormous influence on orthodox and nonconformist thinking during the ensuing fifteen hundred years. He became an inexhaustible source of ideas for every direction and grouping in later Christianity, largely because virtually everything could be found somewhere in his work: the defence of reason (*De Ordine*, ii, ix, xxvi) and of authority (*Contra Ep. Manichei*, v, vi): of free will (*De Libero Arbitrio*, PL, xxxii, 221) and of predestination in its harshest form. Augustine praised pagan philosophers, especially Plato and the Neo-platonists (*De Civ. Dei*, viii), upon whom he was entirely dependent for the very core of his doctrine of God. Yet he considered human wisdom worthless because God's illumination and grace were the only things which men needed. On the one hand, he praised the universe and creation as a unique and marvellous work of God, whose beauty lay in its variety; but, on the other hand, he was constantly dismayed by the wretchedness of the life of man. He saw the world both as a place of beauty and a vale of tears. Mankind was glorious and noble, but simultaneously a 'mass of sin, corruption, wrath, self-destruction (*perditionis*)' (Enchiridion, xxvi f.).

Augustine always ran the risk of committing himself to some position dependent upon, limited by, imprisoned within, time. The aged battle-scarred pastor gathered himself together once more in AD 426-7, and compiled his two books of *Retractationes*, allotting to his own writings their permanent place in the scheme of history, and providing corrections and self-criticism. This work laid the foundations of strict intellectual precision for post-Roman

Europe – and hence for the scientific spirit characteristic of Western Europe. It also served as an excellent manual for appreciating Augustine's breadth of thought. His catholicity set its stamp upon his own and upon all post-Augustinian thought in Europe until Bossuet and Voltaire.

A Mediterranean, a 'Roman', a sane world had begun to emerge. Its ideology was realistic humanism. Its close-knit social relationships, and its stout commonsense resisted the devouring whirlpools of the East. It refused to deny the world and rejected anarchical individualism and Eastern arrogance of spirit. All things were good, because God was good. Evil was only an absence (*defectus boni*), and had no substance of its own.[70] God was present in all things, and had given men many powerful aids in their struggle for salvation: beauty, order and goodness. The whole nature of the cosmos had been directed towards God.*

Western Europe's ontology, its fundamental optimism and its spirit of adventure are the mere echoes of Augustine's great 'yes' to the universe. Despite nine years of Manichaeanism and constant temptation by the East, Augustine fought his way through to an affirmation of the world and matter. The foundations of the cosmos were sound and whole; but man was unsound and always in danger. Despite all his great gifts, he inclined constantly towards evil. He could easily be seduced by mind, by goodness, by the flesh or by power. To cure himself he needed the assistance of a community. Next Augustine decided that the post-Constantinian *imperium* was not that community; nor was it the Christendom which had been sucked into the confusion of its orbit of power. Bitterly he enumerated eighty-eight heresies, from Simon Magus to Pelagius, which were gnawing away the heart of Christianity.[71] The only protection against this temporal and eternal suicide was the Church; her tradition and authority were the only bearers of reason, knowledge and faith.[72] 'I would not believe the Gospel if the authority of the Roman Church did not urge me to do so.'[73] For there were many gospels: gnostic, half-gnostic, pagan and Christian. There were nearly as many such gospels as there were cities and schools of wisdom in the Hellenic *oikoumene*. Among these highly personal gospels he reckoned not only the noisy proclamations of salvation of the Donatists, but also the arrogant wisdom of the Greek theologians.[74]

Augustine was the spokesman of the provincial people of Latin Christendom. He had always defended that people's faith and certainty of salvation. In his last great fight against Pelagius, Augustine won his greatest victory, and suffered his most far-reaching defeat![75] In the heat of that struggle, like a dormant fever, his African inheritance and manichaean infection flared up again. He began to preach total human helplessness. An awful and incomprehensible grace would be granted by a terrible God. His opponents eagerly seized the chance to quote Augustine (*De Libero Arbitrio*) against Augustine! The grand catholicity which harboured Luther and Erasmus side by side

*The religious and metaphysical order reflected the still extant political order of Rome, especially in the provinces, where it had survived.

within the heart and mind and conscience of this one man had been smashed. To save himself and his age, despite its and his own contradictions and conflicts, he turned to seek refuge within the *Ecclesia*. 'There could', he asserted, be 'no salvation outside the Church'.[76] He asked for imperial legislation to help him against the heretics, but in 408 he wrote to the Proconsul Donatus: 'We beseech your Excellency, do not have them killed.' The *Ecclesia* had already become in his eyes the kingdom of Christ and of the heavens.* The Church was composed of a series of free communities of citizens. Certain men, before and after Christ, within and without the people of Israel could and did belong. This embattled association of little groups struggled to live 'through this evil, wicked, perilous age ... amid the persecutions of the world and the favours of God'. It drew ever nearer to the last persecution which was to come upon it at the end of the world's history.[77] This then was Augustine's famous *Civitas Dei*. It has been variously understood. Medieval Germans translated it as 'God's State' in the Carolingian religious political tradition of the holy empire. The post-Tridentine Catholic understood it as the papal Church arrayed against the other Christian confessions. For Augustine himself, it signified a triple denial and a triple assertion:

(1) It was the denial of the Christian empire, as it had been proclaimed by Eusebius, and of the rest of the court theology, Arian and orthodox, of East and West.[78]

(2) It was the rejection of an authoritarian kingdom of God, as again in the East it had been conceived by Origen and Dionysius the Areopagite in a blaze of hierarchical Neoplatonism.

(3) It was a negation of that rigid, self-assured identification of the here-and-now Church with the kingdom of God to which the European bishops were being driven in the battle for 'their' Church against the Arian emperors.

On the positive side, the *Civitas Dei* was for Augustine the community of the friends of God. It was, secondly, a family and, thirdly, a citizenry of God ceaselessly working to reform and renew the external Church.[79]

The political side of this *Ecclesia-Civitas-Dei* was the heritage of the sacred, political humanism of the ancient *polis* and *urbs*. It reflected the community of the city-state, with its dead, its saints, its gods and its cult. Its laws formed one sacred area, (cf. the medieval cities, guilds and corporations). This closed community lived according to authority and according to reason.[80] It expressed itself in a free, sober rationalism whose strength was constantly renewed from its irrational substructure. This rationalism accepted its literal substructure and absorbed peacefully the city cults of graves, relics and shrines. It had a firm foundation in the irrational and was resistant to various kinds of mysticism. This political humanism was social,[81] but not in our sense of that word because our societies have arisen in reaction against their own

*This was directed against the Chiliasts. It is to be found in that twentieth book of *De Civitate Dei*, which Otto of Freising was later to use as the model for his Carolingian imperial theology.

sacral substructure. It is not surprising that they have, consequently, fallen prey to technicians, manipulators and organizers.

Augustine joined monastic spirituality to the political humanism of the *polis*. For him, the true Christian was a monk who was also a priest, a pastor and a teacher. 'It was the example of the monks which had provoked the spiritual crisis which led to his moral enfranchisement.'[82] Through his monastic rule, probably intended for nuns,[83] through his monastic foundations at Tagaste and Hippo, through the monastic life which he led, as bishop, with his own clergy, Augustine founded Western monasticism and Western monastic spirituality: a spirit drawn from the fire of the Trinity, disciplined through poverty, obedience and abstinence.

The history of Western Europe is the history of how the spirit of Augustine *in itself* ever rebellious, intellectualist, spiritualist and enlightened, broke away from monastic discipline to embrace the liberties of the independent *animus inordinatus*; how the *Ecclesia*, considered as the 'free community of God's citizens', left the shelter of the political humanism of the ancient world, the *polis* and *urbs* which constituted the unit of salvation for the Mediterranean peoples, and fell into the grip of new political entities (emperor and pope) and of new, unstable classes of society (the new nobility, the princes, the new bourgeoisie, the proletariat of letters, the workers). Thus were set free once more those disintegratory forces of the ancient world which Augustine had fused together within the catholicity of his own personality as a thinker and a man of prayer. The heritage of Augustine, the conqueror of Pelgaius, passed to Augustine, the father of Western European enlightenment and of every intellectual rebellion in our history.[84]

2

FROM BOETHIUS TO ERIUGENA
(Sixth to Ninth Centuries)

THE great decisions of the fourth and early fifth centuries were to be decisive for the development of Western Europe. While the East debated the dogma of the Trinity and the doctrine of the two natures of Christ, the Roman papacy struggled to protect those mysteries of the Faith against gnostics, Arians and early Byzantine absolutists. An alliance was made between Western bishops and the masses of the people. It was this alliance which made it possible for the Western bishops to attack the two greatest problems inherited from the ancient world: the heresies, and the rejection of the world implied by the notion of authority inherent in Hellenic ethics and the wisdom of the Greeks. While the heresies were an expression of the violence of the internal struggles of the Church, the inherited Hellenic idea of authority had its roots in the aristrocratic, urban society of the ancient Greeks. The learning and the 'liberal arts' of that society were part of an attempt to support the rule of the upper classes in the *Polis*. Thus, Greek learning made a sharp distinction between knowledge and experience, the liberal and the illiberal arts, in short, between the culture of the nobility and the wisdom of the common people. If the new alliance of Church and people was to survive, the Hellenic notion of authority would have to undergo a transformation. During the following centuries, the secular and religious aristocracy of the barbarian peoples, who had become Europe's new masters, began to see the political possibilities of this inheritance from the Greeks.

The gradual spread of these ideas to the West was accelerated by the encroachment of Byzantine power and by the rise of Islam. Byzantine Christianity and Islam were very close to each other, and medieval, Western Christendom was nervously aware of the seductively fascinating power of the Islamic and Byzantine hemisphere. The failure of the West to confront Islam and Byzantium with greater poise and less violence was a symptom of its own difficult internal situation. It knew that it was not yet equal to a great reappraisal of its Christian-pagan heritage of theology and philosophy, much as it needed to do it; neither did it feel called upon, nor equipped, to undertake the equally necessary dialogue between the 'upper world' and the 'under world', between the culture of the rulers and the suppressed pagan culture of the people. For more than a thousand years, authority and tradition were to act as surgical clamps, holding together the edges of the gaping wounds.

Fortunately for the West, the collision with the Eastern Church and Islam was not head on. There was a buffer zone between Constantinople and Rome, just as there was between the world of antique culture and popular tradition. The buffer was the monasterys which provided a link between the competing religions and classes. This vital function was first performed by the monasteries in southern Italy, North Africa, the south of France, Spain and the British Isles; and later in the north of France, southern and central Germany and the north of Italy. Among the monasteries we must reckon the monastic communities of priests, colleges of canons, and the schools connected with the episcopal sees.[1]

Italy's spirituality and political humanism was, therefore, a kind of residue, crystallized out of a mixture of Greek, Roman, Etruscan and indigenous elements in antiquity, supplemented by Goths, Lombard, Franks, neo-Greeks and Arabs. Long before the fall of the Roman Empire, the area had become a gigantic melting pot. Victorious Romans could be tolerant, and they easily accepted Virgil, the son of Celtic peasants and Horace, the son of an Apulian freedman. This may, perhaps, have been the beginning of the long inter-penetration of ideas between victors and vanquished which did so much to determine the evolution of Italian civilization. From the fifth to the nineteenth centuries, Italy was under foreign masters. In the process of accepting and resisting them, the Italians developed that special and characteristic sense of pure speech, pure doctrine, and pure form, and created Roman and Canon Law. Their thought and culture was a resistance movement, a political act of *fuorusciti*, a form of outer and inner emigration. Italian monasteries were set up against the heathen peasantry, the dug-in-and-rooted *pagani*, the German nobility, and the outlandish foreign bishops. Italian towns, set up against the German nobility and the bishops, were secular monasteries, which by their cult of Roman law and their academic culture resisted the impure speech and customs of the disgusting barbarians. Of 150 Germanic words in the vocabulary of literary Italian, there is not one which is concerned with things of the mind![2] Yet, side by side with this purist, ascetic and spiritual exclusiveness, we find an equally strong capacity for assimilation. By the twelfth century, after 700 years of struggle, the absorption of the Lombard and Frankish lords was completed. In the succeeding centuries German, French, English and Spanish bishops, theologians, officials and scholars were miraculously transformed into *Italian* humanists and curial politicians, Italian university professors and diplomats.

The period of the fourth to the sixth centuries already had its cultural ambassadors and political agents who operated between Byzantium and Rome, between classical culture and the barbarians: the late Roman masters of rhetoric.[3] Using the sacred formulae of Virgil, Ovid, Horace and the Bible, they hailed and celebrated the renewers of Rome after its long decline, first Constantine, Theodosius and Stilicho, then in succession the Frankish and Gothic kings and finally the popes and the Roman city consuls. The whole ideology of the Renaissance was first communicated to European consciousness by these humanists. They developed the idea of the middle age of sin, of decay in spiritual discipline, decline in the power of Roman virtue and the Roman state. Yet all had not been lost. Christ (or Stilicho, or Pope Damasus, or Theodoric) had appeared to renew the cosmos.[4] Rome would have a new birth through the intervention of whichever barbarian king the rhetorician happened to be celebrating. (Baptism had of course made the barbarian a Roman.) The same bizarre mixture of classic and Christian ideas can be seen in Novatian, who used Virgil's picture of Etna in eruption to depict the Christian hell.[5] He too proclaimed the advent of 'heaven on earth' through the 'rebirth of *mores* and of culture'.[6] Culture meant the seven liberal arts. Like the kingdoms of the world, the arts bloom and fade only to be brought to new birth. The Italian masters of grammar and rhetoric clung to purity of language as the one and only guarantee of culture, but at the same time paid tribute to Frankish counts[7] and German grammarians as men who had awakened literary studies from the grave.[8]

There is a temptation to dismiss all the high-sounding rhetoric of these pagan-Christian *literati* as historically of no account and to ignore their attempt to collaborate with their conquerors. It is easy to forget these men living in the midst of the fear-ridden world of Roman towns and famine-stricken masses of people,[9] that world whose despair comes down to us today monumentally expressed in the Lenten liturgy of the Roman Church. But to do this is to block the way to an understanding of Italian humanism, of Dante, and more immediately of that characteristic movement of reform whose principal exponents were Boethius, Cassiodorus, Benedict of Nursia and Gregory the Great. The European importance of these men is proof of the degree of leverage exerted by this specifically Italian self-assertion.

The men who developed this great reform movement were practically all members of the same family. Boethi were a branch of the ancient, noble and renowned family of the Anicii. Benedict was probably a direct descendant of the Anicii. The mother and father of Gregory I, Silvia and Gordianus, also belonged to it. The scanty contemporary records give no direct information on the ancestry of Cassiodorus, but his descent from an old family of important public servants and diplomats placed him within the narrow ancestral circle of patrician and senatorial families who fought for every movement of renewal, renaissance or revolt in Rome from the fifth century onwards. This strong familial element was the first example of a fundamental characteristic of Europe's spiritual history: over and over again, through the centuries, there have always been individual aristocratic clans, families of ecclesiastical and secular noblemen, families of well-born doctors, astrologers, humanists, heretics, upon whom, from sixth-century Rome to eighteenth-century Weimar, as upon a series of isolated cells, the substance and structure of conscious culture and spirituality has rested. Boethius, Cassiodorus, Benedict and Gregory the Great represented four possible, but related, reactions of this world of the Roman aristocracy. To take a personal stand in politics, in the Church, in monasticism or in philosophy meant, on Italian soil, to undertake a policy of political alliances, of monastic reform, of missionary activity in the Church and of a renewal of the one, holy and ancient wisdom and culture.

Boethius was marked by profound distrust and reserve towards the new powers in the world. Although he held the highest offices in the state, he was essentially an opponent of the Gothic régime. He was a Christian; an educated, cultivated Christian, like so many of the nobility of the next millennium and a half, but his personality had been formed by pre-Christian and extra-Christian influences. Boethius was soberly aware of the threat to the cultural treasure received from antiquity, which was the very substance of his own thought, the spiritual blood which he set out to defend by a vast work of translation. Plato and Aristotle were to be translated whole and entire, but none of the Fathers of the Church. This selection reveals how completely Boethius reflected his classical traditions.

There was tragic grandeur in his death at the hands of Theodoric. Boethius defended a Senator accused of treacherous dealings with the Byzantine emperor and did so on traditional Roman grounds. He in turn was condemned to die, which he accepted despite the obvious injustice. While in prison he spent his time writing *De Consolatione Philosophiae*: 'Consolation through the love of wisdom.' *Fatum* and *providentia* are, he argued, one and the same.[10] The Godhead – God – is the good; out of goodness he created the world; by goodness he governs it. There is no such thing as real evil; evil does not exist. Virtue is always rewarded, vice punished with an iron rigidity. The law which governs the universe is as hard as iron. Wisdom teaches men to understand the blows of fate, which only seem to be unjust but are in fact a part of providence and the ordering of the world. Thus, stoicism and an open Platonism, capable of a Christian interpretation, characterized the thinking of this personality. Boethius's great work has been published more often in succeeding centuries than any other books except the Bible and the *Imitation of Christ*. One reason for its importance was the fact that it contained the first satisfactory definition of the individual: *Persona est naturae rationabilis individua substantia*. But the deeper reason for its phenomenal popularity maintained throughout a thousand years, lay in the profound longing in educated men throughout the succeeding millennium for a reasonable interpretation of the world. They wanted to believe in a universe firmly constructed according to a clear, luminous system of law, and yet open to the wisdom both of the pagan and the Christian fathers of old.

The death of Boethius convinced those in Rome who were akin to him – in blood, culture or party – that the conscious personal stand which had to be made could no longer take the form of his kind of isolation. His pupil and friend Cassiodorus drew the logical conclusions.[11] As Theodoric's leading statesman and as the only stable point of reference through the changing succession of Gothic régimes, he strove to incorporate the Goths into the one, ancient, holy Roman order of things. Theodoric's first task, Cassiodorus believed, was to renew the unity of law and custom and culture. In that famous collection of letters and documents, the *Variae* of 537, is to be found the complete governmental and cultural programme of a medieval prince. Theodoric was expected to renew Rome, 'the holy City of Rome' – holy, now, in the Christian, the pagan and the native Germanic sense. The Goths were the Gaeti, allies and kin of the true old Romans. Thus it was their obligation to re-establish Rome, the *civitas litterarum*.

The Gothic kingdom went down before the victorious Justinian. Cassiodorus and his Roman Catholic noble kinsmen now faced a new problem. Should they place themselves at the disposal of the new Emperor of the Romans? Their decision to resist Justinian was one of the most momentous events in European history. It preserved the Italian spirit at this early stage of its development from absorption by Byzantine civilization. It must never be forgotten how near Italy came to disappearing during the sixth, seventh and eighth centuries. Eastern Christianity had a firm foothold in Ravenna, and the Eastern empire was politically very strong. The East exerted great influence in the Greek areas of southern Italy, in the Basilian monasteries, among the hermits and the prophets and the Neoplatonic cultural theologians. It was Cassiodorus's political humanism, Benedict's new world of monasticism and Gregory I's expansion into the West (southern France, Spain and England) which preserved Italy's inner independence.

In 526 work began at Ravenna on San Vitale, the beginning of the vast Byzantine building programme which was to make Ravenna into Justinian's sacred fortress.[11a] In 529 Justinian closed the last Neoplatonic school in his empire.[12] He saw himself as God's representative, as Emperor (pope), leader of the Church, and theologian. He deprived pagans, heretics and Jews of their civil rights. As head of the Church, he decided what it was to profess and subjected it entirely to his decrees. Children who did not recognize the four ecumenical councils (Nicea, I Constantinople, Ephesus and Chalcedon) could be disinherited by their parents. Women guilty of heresy received no dowries.[13] With the help of a high official, Julianus Argentarius, and an ambitious bishop, Maximian, the God-Emperor began to show the West what the sacred *imperium* demanded of its subjects.* San Vitale, built in opposition to Theodoric's splendid royal chapel (Sant'Apollinare Nuovo, built that same year, 526), introduced Western Europe to the images of the sacred emperor and his imperial court. These images represented his power. During the fourth and fifth centuries, the majority of the Eastern bishops had already accepted the cult of the emperor's image. At the inauguration of a régime, each city would receive the sacred image of the new ruler and carry it to the market place, where it would be set up. Even in the time of Gregory the Great, imperial images were still found in Roman churches.[14] In the central act of the state liturgy, the kingdoms of heaven and earth were welded

*This term was applied to all Western Europeans as late as the twelfth century.

together, and in the great mosaics in Ravenna this union was symbolically portrayed. Justinian, robed as a royal priest, can be seen bearing the golden paten with the Eucharistic bread. Theodora, his wife, holds the chalice with the blood of Christ and, standing with Justinian as his forbears, are Abel, Abraham and Melchisedech. As the new Moses[15] and as a high priest or even Christ himself, the emperor presents the sacrificial gifts to the Father on behalf of his people. The claims of such a state liturgy were enormous. The house of God was reduced to a mere annexe to the imperial palace. The emperor's divinity was proclaimed. In order to support such ambitious claims, the emperor relied on his powerful imperial bishops.[16] The Byzantine imperial organization remained the standard one for centuries. Quite early it began to produce the earliest manifestations of a totalitarian bureaucracy, the *quaesitors*.[17] Within this system, the bishops were entirely subordinate to the emperor, but enjoyed higher rank than any other group in the hierarchy. They nominated municipal administrators so that the city was both imperial and episcopal. The bishop did all the work of construction and renovation, supervised the sacral-political renaissance, and built fortifications, waterworks, bridges, warehouses and public baths. The bishop supervised weights and measures; he was, in fact, judge and ruler of the city.* Byzantium's leading spokesman in the West, Archbishop Maximian of Ravenna, built Sant' Apollinare in Classe as a visible demonstration of the power of this Byzantine state episcopacy.[18] It was a distinctly anti-Roman gesture since St Apollinaris was St Peter's contemporary, friend and rival.

The fundamental premise upon which the Byzantine imperial hierarchy was based was the monophysite conception of God. His representative, the emperor (with his bishops) governed the universal world of cities through his religious-political liturgy. The perfect expression of that liturgy was the domed church, built upon the octagon. The holy gnostic number eight had been taken to convey the sacred sign of cosmic perfection.[19] Overarching and overmastering mankind, these domed churches reminded men that they were ordained to be subjects. They were raw stones for a mosaic work, and their place was determined by God.† The imperial deity, enthroned in the spiritual centre of the golden dome, had absorbed the glorified Christ into himself.[20] Justinian firmly rejected any sort of theology of suffering. The total state can never afford to permit the existence of such a gap in its closed world.

By contrast, Theodoric built his church, St Martin, as an expression of the search for union with Rome and the primitive Church. Similarly, the cautious reconstruction undertaken at Sant'Apollinare Nuovo by Maximian's western-minded successor, Angellus, reflected the Roman concept of the basilica, that first temple of European freedom and democracy, of *Romanità* and its political humanism. From the fifth to the fifteenth century, it served as the proper

---

*One must remember that for the Byzantine civilization the city was the only cultural unit. Monasteries were merely heavenly cities on earth.

†cf. the idea of the saints as 'stones in the Heavenly Jerusalem'.

assembly hall of the civic people, for the election of popes and bishops and municipal bodies, and as a setting for political oratory and agitation. Gregory VII the Pataria with Sant'Ambrogio in Milan, Florentine political humanism in the fourteenth and fifteenth centuries, Savonarola and Machiavelli were all at home in the basilica. Between Leo the Great and Gregory the Great, the Roman basilica became the refuge of the city state. It stood for the *polis*, which knew no subjects but required the *consensus*, the lawful assent of the people. The people was a community in which account was taken of each individual, a community to be led along the ancient triumphal way. All its acts were responsibly performed in the full light of day and before the face of God. In the basilica the *Christus praesens* appealed for the assent and recognition of those who believed in him. It seemed perfectly natural that the assent of the people should be required for the election of popes and bishops.

Justinian's imperial deity, on the other hand, reduced everything to itself, and Byzantine theology left no place for the individual human being. Men in the flesh were nothing, according to Byzantine theology, but all in all once their spirits ascend into the hierarchical cosmos of the dome of God. Such a concept of God and man was as unacceptable to Theodoric's chancellor as was Justinian's political programme – inseparably bound up with it – for the re-acquisition of rebellious Europe.[21] *Gothorum laus est civilitas custodita.*[22] Although Cassiodorus realized that the Gothic kings were no longer able to protect *civilitas* (the archetype of all Italian *civiltà*) he rejected the idea that the Eastern emperor should replace them. Unable to serve Justinian politically, he retired to Squillace to found a hermitage and monastery. There he hoped to preserve the civic, personal, Roman, humanist culture, which the Goths could not and Dostinian would not protect. Prayer, manual work, reading, sacred and secular study, constituted the programme. His basic theses were: 'Philosophy is a consideration of death';[23] the soul of man is rational and immortal; its temple is the body, 'set up for contemplation of eternal and rational things' – *ad res supernas et rationabiles intuendas*. This was the beginning of Europe's dualism.

To protect this world of work, reason and the individual against the totalitarianism of the East was the task of Benedict of Nursia.[24] The patricians and senators of Rome sent him their sons to be educated. By the seventh century, according to a Bull of Pope Sabinian, 40,000 persons were being educated at Benedictine cloisters.[25] Seven times in the twenty-four hours of the day, the bells of the cloister were rung. Time was measured by the daily round and space by the boundaries of the monastery as a civic unit. Its structure of government determined the nature of the community; its system of labour allotted men their calling. In these monasteries, the monks became the first Europeans. *Benedict's Rule was the first constitutional charter of Western Europe.* The Rule began with a firm rejection of itinerant, prophetical, spirit-ridden Eastern monasticism. Benedict set up his new monasticism in the very midst of Byzantium's political power. His infant order was surrounded and threatened by wandering monks and the grandiose, Basilian monastic culture. Through this direct confrontation with the East the West achieved its initial self-consciousness. Benedict's monastery was Rome, Rome creatively withdrawn into herself. Benedict's monastery was a renewed and purified Rome. It was a Rome returned to manual labour, chastity, prayer and obedience.

This daily round was a far more important thing for the intellectual constitution of Europe than many thousands of books written in the post-Benedictine age; far more important, too, than the somewhat over-rated intellectual activity of the Benedictines of the early middle ages. It is difficult to overestimate the contribution of this orderly existence to the development of Western ideas. Its regularity and discipline fostered a rationalism which was confined within the multiple limits of this earth. The daily round produced a matter-of-fact attitude which rejected spiritualist enthusiasm and work for its own sake. Work was a means and not an end, as it later developed in Calvinist workhouses and poorhouses, the counter-monasteries of the modern world. We need only compare this apportionment of the day with our own: eight to sixteen hours of mechanized work, and the rest – an inorganic hodgepodge devoted to food, luxuries and the pursuit of pleasure. The crux of the changeover from the Benedictine culture of old Europe to what followed it was neatly expressed by Pascal in a famous sentence: 'All the ills of man stem from his inability to be still in his own room.'[26] For the Benedictine, it was possible, to be still; still in spirit and in body, for his *stabilatas loci*, the ordering of his time and his environment, gave him strength both for *otium* and *negotium*, for leisure and for work.

Benedict's Rule was a creative distillation of the classical city state. Ancient Rome was in its basic pattern. This agricultural *familia* under an all-embracing paternal authority culminated in the *Magna Charta* of the father. The Abbot administered the monastic community as the heir of patricians, senators, consuls and the first fathers of primitive Rome.[27] In important matters, he had to consult the whole community; he had to hear the opinions of each one, down to the youngest monk. In lesser matters, he was to consult with a few of the elders, but he alone bore the responsibility and had to make the decisions. Let him give his monks no ground for just murmuring: here we have *in nuce* the European right to resist, as it was later understood in the high middle ages by monks battling for the control of monasteries.

'See how all the lands of Europe are delivered over to barbarian rule; cities destroyed, strongholds razed to the ground, provinces depopulated. There is no one to till the earth; servers of idols rage at will, winning power by murdering true believers; and even priests, who should be doing penance in dust and ashes, yearn for empty honours and glorify themselves by the use of new, worldly, pagan words.'[28] Gregory I saw a people shattered by centuries of invasion, collapsing in a chaos of famine and pestilence, oppression and heresy. Italian humanists, right up to the nineteenth century, were to imitate the portrayal of the *terra*, the land and the people, which can be found in his *Dialogues* in the vernacular of 593–4. Here was the recurrent equation: the Germanic peoples are invaders, barbarians, pagans, heretics; the foes of the pure Roman faith, of pure Latin speech, of all morality and culture.[29] The sufferings of Rome, of the Italian people and of the Roman Church during these centuries of the great migrations were being welded together into a single sacral-political formula, a single world-view.[30] Henceforth Theodoric was the heretic; henceforth it was the duty of monks, humanists, churchmen and politicians to liberate Italy from the shame of foreign occupation, from the Gothic, from the middle ages and the bad emperors, and to lead her back to her ancient purity. Gregory sought aid in Byzantium, where he spent the years between 579 and 586 as the legate of Pope Pelagius II. He wanted the emperor to be the 'lord of free men',[31] and his *imperium* to be the protection of each man's freedom.[32] But he found no protection there, nor freedom for his country and his people. After this he turned first to inner meditation and then towards the West. He never broke directly with Byzantium, but did something else perhaps more significant. He wrote the life of his kinsman, Benedict of Nursia, and placed it as a solemn protocol in the second book of his *Dialogues*. There would be no documentary source of Benedict's life, had Gregory not seen it as a symbol of the goal toward which he now began to move – to save Italy by her own strength. This high Roman official, politician, soldier and leader of men now set about organizing the rich territories of the Roman Church into an orderly system of social welfare to relieve the wretched masses of the people. Long before this he had given away his own goods and turned his Roman palace into a monastery. He knew that this was not enough. In the long run, it would only be possible to protect his people's spiritual health and earthly survival, the Roman Church's pure doctrine and Rome's sacred tradition, in an alliance with the barbarians. Hence the conversion of the Arian Lombards and the mission to the Angles and Saxons. The conversion of King Ethelbert and his people took place in 597. On the feast of Christmas, at Dorovernum, at Canterbury, they left the political-religious service of their former gods for the service of Christ the King and St Peter in Rome. By this act Gregory finally tipped the scales in favour of the West. His intervention on behalf of Recared in Spain and against the Hellenist intelligentsia in Gaul may be reckoned as mere episodes, whereas the conversion of England led to the Anglo-Irish missions in central Europe, to the alliance of the popes with the Franks and finally to the coronation in Rome of Charlemagne.

During the following centuries, a historical justification for this new direction in church policy was worked out. It was the famous 'Donation of Constantine', which would appear to have been written in the Lateran school of the eighth or ninth centuries and was an attempt to make the new direction both legitimate and consonant with Roman tradition. We know now that the culture, law and learning of late antiquity persisted in Italy after the fifth century. Schools of writing continued to maintain themselves (there is evidence of one in Verona, going back to the sixth century). Both hagiography and hymnology display evidence of the classical tradition, as does the cultivation of letters by the bishops of eighth and ninth century Milan.[33] The bearers of tradition were the episcopal cities, especially Rome, whose school of the Lateran flourished in the seventh and eighth centuries and which, in the ninth, practically became the basis of Carolingian musical culture.

The schools not only preserved the traditions of antiquity. They transformed them into sacred, saving formulae. These formulae in turn expressed a set of fundamentally defensive attitudes which become intricately associated with the spirit of the Roman Church: nothing new was good; no salvation could come from the barbarians; every innovater was a heretic, a rebel, a barbarian. The Rome of Luther's time reacted to the German heretic in exactly the same way. Just as the patricians and nobles, schoolmen and theologians of the seventh, eighth and ninth centuries rejected all change, so did their successors in the sixteenth century. The men of the early Roman schools saw their only hope in rediscovery of the 'old', in a 'renewal' of learning, of the pure customs of old Rome, of her speech, her law, of the whole *ordo*, the whole realm of salvation which was the *orbis Romanus*. Classical thought of this kind contained no concept of development. It could not conceive of the centuries of growth of the alliance between the Roman papacy with the Western barbarians. It was the great break with the Eastern Roman Empire only in terms of a *status* which had been destroyed. It could not think historically. All of these characteristics become part of the essential fabric of the Roman Church, and in part account for its rigid adherence to conservative, classical principles.

This papally-sponsored *renovatio* in the *ecclesia romana* had another equally important effect. It brought about an historically momentous alliance between the 'Roman Bishop' and the faith of the masses of His people, on the one hand and a union of the holy *polis* of God, humanism and the reform movement in the monasteries on the other. This juncture of dissimilar forces was an entirely unique and extraordinary product of the general condition of things in the early middle ages. It was the fundamental pre-condition for the rise and triumph of scholasticism as a Roman, civic, humanist system of authoritarian thought. It was also the basis of the alliance of the great force of Western humanism with the Roman Church from the fourteenth to the eighteenth century, and the absolute rejection, on the part of both of them, of all eastern, German reformations. Law, order, culture, humanity and salvation were only to be found in the Holy City. The basilicas, Roman and Constantinian, of the fourth and fifth centuries were the presentation in architecture and mosaic of this union: the simultaneous presence of the heavenly Jerusalem and the eternal Rome. Within the city walls which surrounded this Roman world[34] the Roman Bishop reigned as lord of the city, king, *vicarius Christi* and representative of God.* Even in the Rome of the early middle ages, the official encouragement of the

---

*cf. Ignatius.

arts, the restoration of the city, the maintenance of the Church's treasures and relics formed an essential part of the papal régime.[35] The maintenance of Rome was *the* renaissance: it is only necessary to look at the *Liber Pontificalis* to see what value the Popes themselves attached to this work of renewing the world by restoring Rome. Pope Leo the Great (440–61) appears there as the great renovator after the ravage of the Vandals.[36] In the case of each pope in turn, note is taken, in sacral-political formulae, of the acquisition of new ecclesiastical treasures and liturgical objects, the upkeep of the martyrs' tombs, the restoration of the old churches and of the city of Rome.

The great renovations of the popes were based on the assumption of a close unity between the ecclesiastical community and Roman patrician families, which went back to the days of St Peter. The *cathedra Petri*, his episcopal chair, was the *Sedia Gestatoria* of a Roman senator of the imperial age,[37] probably that of Cornelius Pudens, in whose houses the early Christians of Rome found a strong protection, as so many later nonconformists were to do in the castles and palaces of noble lords. There are many permanent memorials to this alliance. Many of the great Roman basilicas were erected within the boundaries of patrician estates and seem to have been regarded as a part of the villa itself.[38] There is, in addition, a famous statue of St Peter as a Roman senator. We can, perhaps, see further evidence in the arrangements of graves. As late as 390, by which time Christianity had already become the state religion, pagan altars and pagan graves continued to be placed within the environs of the Basilica of St Peter.[39] Certainly, the church of St Peter in its golden age from the fourth century until its destruction by the Saracens in 846, reflected the close relationship between the church and the patricians. This architectural power-house, beyond the reach of our imaginations now in its gold and silver and diamonds, its silken curtains gleaming in the light of a hundred lamps, fascinated the barbarians. As the house of Christ and Peter and Constantine (as shown in the mosaic in the apse), it was a constitutional monument to the new world view of the *ecclesia romana*. In the mosaic of Constantine's apse, the Church defined itself to the faithful: *Justitiae sedes, fidei domus aula pudoris. Haec est quam cernis pietas quam possidet omnis.*[40] The seat of divine, cosmic and earthly order and law; the house – palace – of faith, in which salvation is preserved; *aula* of Roman virtue (*pudoris*); the Church claimed it all. If the beholder were 'pious' (like *pius* Aeneas), he would be able to see it all here. The work of *renovatio* of the popes from the fourth century on was the maintenance of this house of salvation, honoured even by the barbarians through all the devastation and warfare and chaos of the terrible years. The momentous historic effect radiated by this 'golden house' upon the peoples of the 'wandering of the nations' is past all reckoning; it united Theodoric, the Franks, and the Anglo-Saxons to Rome. In 846 the Lombards and Franks and Friesians and Anglo-Saxons swarmed to Rome, 'To St Peter', to defend it against the Saracens.[41] It was the life's work of the Roman popes and their Roman patriciate to maintain and renew this house.

Another element in the renaissance was the 'rebirth of the sciences'[42] through the revival of the schools. The official lives of the popes never fail to make the claim that each was an educated man – *litteratus*.[43] How else could they have defended the one, pure teaching and ancient sacred culture against the barbarians? During the middle of the ninth century, John the Deacon wrote his famous *Life of Gregory the Great* for Pope John VIII. It was a typical picture of the Roman papal renaissance.[44] Gregory the Great had renewed Christianity and ancient Roman culture and protected them against the uncultured barbarians. The *Vita* defended the cultural primacy of Rome against the Carolingian renaissance. Rome alone was the true cradle of culture. France was a land of louts and barbarians, who despoiled whatever they touched. Charlemagne had brought the light of Roman civilization to France, but only because he had been blessed and taught by the Roman pope. If the Franks were ever to behave properly, they would simply have to come back to Rome, to the sources of pure faith, pure thought and pure culture.

The Popes and the Italian humanists were also agreed about the need for renovation of *the whole* of Rome. There was, after all, only *one* sacred *antiquitas*: this had always been Rome's daily experience. The Christian saint sat enthroned in the pagan temple. In the tenth century a humanist like Eugenius Vulgarius took over the whole Stoic conception of renaissance and cyclic recurrence and applied it to Pope Sergius III, whom he called *gloria mundi* and *causarum reparator*.[45] This Roman city of God was also present in the Benedictine monasteries. The Popes took these monasteries under their protection, reformed them, and in turn received powerful support from them in their own great battles. The architecture of Cluny was, for example, an attempt to renew the Roman Constantinian basilica of the fourth century which was regarded as the symbol of the Church at its best. Similarly, Desiderius called Gregory VII Romulus and Augustus, when in the eleventh century he proclaimed the renaissance of Monte Cassino. The College of Cardinals was the Roman Senate risen from the dead. The reform of the monasteries, of ecclesiastical discipline, of the Church and of learning and culture was conceived as one single task.

The problem was quite different when the Roman Church attempted to exert its influence in areas where there was no such tradition. For more than four centuries, Southern France, Spain and the British Isles were the scene of a bitter struggle. Slowly the Roman, Augustinian, Benedictine spirit carried the day against powerful forces of a different nature: forces belonging to the folk world, to the world of Hellenist culture (in the cities of Spain and Southern France), of the African *literati*, of monks from Asia Minor and of Greek spiritualist theologians.[46] These forces were nourished by the emigration composed of a number of heterogeneous elements which fled before the Vandals, the Arabs and the Byzantine State. Out of this mixed society, the initial elements were fused for the extreme conservatism typical of Spain, for the free-thinking, Albigensian, Huguenot, republican southern France, and for

Pelagian England. There is hardly a feature of the spiritual geography of those countries today which was not moulded at that time.

Augustine's last battle, against Pelagius, reveals to us much of the inner condition of the Western world of the day. The 'man of the sea', Morgan, (Pelagius in Latin) a British monk, probably of Irish origin, like Toland, Tindall and Joyce, played a brilliant role in the best Roman society at the beginning of the fifth century. He went busily to and fro between the palaces of the Anicii Probi, the clan to which Boethius, Benedict and Gregory belonged. When Demetrias, a young noblewoman of the same family, entered a monastery, this gifted intellectual and moral rigorist wrote a letter to her from Africa in 412. In it he expounded his entire personal philosophy.[47] Human nature was essentially good and could do good on its own. The virtuous lives of the pagan philosophers demonstrated that a good life did not depend exclusively on Christian revelation or doctrine. This was precisely what the old patrician families of Rome had always believed, and Pelagius became their spokesman. The will of man was wholly free: 'There is, I say, in (well-born) souls a certain natural holiness which enthroned at the pinnacle of the castle of the soul,* passes its free judgment upon good and evil.' 'God has created man as the lord of all creatures; through reason and intelligence man can know God. Even in face of God, I, as a man, am entirely free.' 'I do not obey God, I agree with him. I follow him because of my own conviction, not because I have to.'† Goodness could obviously only come from within oneself. Faith, too, was an act of allegiance. Since both goodness and faith were acts of will, men should train themselves to exercise their wills properly and to act well. They should learn temperance, contempt for death, introspection, and a searching awareness of their own thoughts, for thought was 'the source of life and the origin of sin.' Europe's first 'spiritual exercises' originated in a system of thought which combined the human wisdom of the ancients and the aristocratic and popular self-consciousness of the early Western world. In his commentary on the Epistle to the Romans, Pelagius asserted that, strictly speaking, there was no Original Sin. All men were free to follow the example of Adam and his sin, or the example of Christ. Sin was not inborn, sin in our souls was merely 'a guest, a stranger within a stranger'.

Pelagius gave open expression to what was already the mental attitude of wide circles in Roman society and in the Hellenist city-culture of the western Mediterranean. It also suited the natural, earthy self-consciousness of the new peoples who, between the fifth and twelfth centuries, very slowly crossed the threshold, first into the Christian cult and only later into a Christian manner of existence and a Christian understanding of the world. Pelagius was met by waves of sympathy flowing from all sides. Though Augustine and the Africans immediately became his bitter opponents, Pelagius, now a refugee from the

---

*In arce animi praesidens – cf. Plotinus, Eckhart & Theresa of Avila.

†How near and yet how far is this great philosophical 'I' of the European spirit from the 'I' of the heart in Augustine.

Goths, found enthusiastic support, and not only in Eastern Christendom where Bishop John of Jerusalem became his protector. His clear ethical rationalism made a great impression on the Greek Pope Zosimus, and it was only under pressure from the Emperor and from Africa that the Pope had him condemned in the *Tractoria*. This act was greeted with violent opposition; numerous bishops, with the Patriarch of Aquileia at their head, and later eighteen bishops of Southern Italy, formed an unambiguous pro-Pelagian party.

Whereas in Italy, thanks to Augustine, Pelagianism was superficially beaten down, it spread with headlong speed both in the East and in southern France, Spain, Britain and Ireland. Southern France was launched into a century and a half of struggle between Augustinianism and a somewhat more moderate Pelagianism. Cassian and his monks at St Victor, near the Greek town of Marseilles, and the Abbot Faustus of Lérins became spokesmen of what has been called 'semi-Pelagianism'. Eastern monks and all those who had been trained in the East simply could not accept the doctrine of grace found in the later, anti-Pelagian Augustine. The whole Gallican Church split. The centre of the struggle was at Lérins, the nursery of southern French monasticism, where Augustinian, Eastern-spiritual, Hellenist and folk currents mingled. Thanks to Caesarius, Bishop of Arles, a compromise was struck between the semi-Pelagians and the moderate Augustinians, during the fourth decade of the sixth century. The reconciliation was based on the classical definition of the nature of Catholic doctrine, formulated by Vincent of Lérins: 'In this, the Roman Church, we must, above all things, take care that we hold fast to that which has been believed everywhere, always, by all. For it is this which is really and truly Catholic.' Catholicism thus became the democratic-authoritarian faith of the community of the Roman world, united in space and time, and represented by Rome and the monasteries. Ironically Vincent arrived at this classical delimitation of Catholicism in the course of a semi-Pelagian pamphlet directed against Augustine, whom he regarded as an innovator and disturber of the peace and orthodoxy of the Catholic world.[48] How symbolic of the tremendous lability and the precarious situation of Catholic Western Europe!

Up to the time of the Albigensian wars, Spain formed a single spiritual unit with the south of France. The provincial Hellenism of the later Roman Empire was strong in both countries. During the early middle ages, while both countries were strongly influenced by Augustinian and Benedictine doctrines, Pachomius, Basil, Cassian and many other *émigrés* from the East began to introduce a monasticism of a much more spiritualist temper.[49] Spain, which in modern times was to compel so many of her best minds to emigrate, was the refuge of *émigrés* seeking a home during those centuries. Later, poised between Europe and Africa, between Rome, Geneva, Wittenberg and London, Spain was to bleed to death in the battle for pure orthodoxy. In the early middle ages wave after wave of unbelievers and heretics poured across her frontiers. The Italian jibe that 'Spaniard means heretic' seemed ironically justified. Pelagianism was merely the first in a long and tragic series of heretical conflicts. More passionately than any other Roman province, Spain had believed in the *imperium*.[50] She was the first country to raise a shrine to the deified Emperor Augustus, and the first to embark upon that cult of the martyrs and saints which was really a form of state patriotism. Spain had given up her foremost intellects to Rome: Seneca and his nephews, Lucian, Martial and Quintilian, and the great Emperors: Trajan, Hadrian and Theodosius. They were followed in the early middle ages by Pope Damasus, the poet Prudentius, the historian Orosius and Isidore of Seville. During the first five hundred years of the Christian era Spain supplied the genius of the Empire and the Church.

Spain also gave Western Europe the first heretic who was ever put to death by the state – Priscillian executed in 385 at Trier. Priscillian's thinking had been moulded by the rhetorician Elpidius and Agape, a noblewoman. Their ideas, strongly Neoplatonist and gnostic, had been brought to them from the East by Marcus of Memphis. Priscillian was, as a result, a rigorous dualist. His teaching spread quickly among the Hellenist intelligentsia of Spain and southern France. It rejected matter, marriage and everything sensual as the work of the devil. It denied the Resurrection and appealed to a kind of spiritualist rationalism which had already been widely disseminated by the Arians. The country was divided between Arian Goths and disunited sects of Catholics until 589. Spanish orthodoxy arose out of this constant, embittered struggle against the 'thousand-headed hydra of heresy'. Prudentius's world-famous psychomachia, the struggle of the virtues and vices for the possession of man – a basic concept in Christian anthropology up to the sixteenth century – was directed at the Priscillianists. It is possible that the Athanasian Creed was also produced by the anti-Priscillian theology of fifth-century Spain. In 561 the Synod of Braga finally condemned Priscillian's teaching but soon afterwards the spiritual realm of Spain was shaken by a fresh series of struggles.

During the breathing spell before the conquest of Spain by Islam in 711 and before the new nonconformist movements flared up afresh, Isidore of Seville (d. 636) published his studies in grammar, history, the natural sciences and the Bible. It was Western Europe's first encyclopaedia. His father was a Roman of the provinces; his mother probably an Arian Goth. Their son tried to unite the magical lore of Mediterranean antiquity and of the Germanic peoples in his derivation of words. In his etymologies, collection of sayings and Biblical allegories, Isidore aimed at establishing the true name of everything. 'In him, aids to the memory and comfort for the soul are all entwined together, or simply belong together as do word and sense, name and meaning, idea and substance.'[51] It was this magical tradition which Isidore transmitted to the North. It flowed into the development of Carolingian humanism, and the wisdom of Alcuin and Rhabanus Maurus! Boniface, the apostle of Germany,[52] was to meet a martyr's death in Friesland with Isidore's book of *Synonyma* clasped, as protection and shield, in his arms.[53]

Isidore of Seville was an important inspiration for the age which followed. His preoccupation with the magical significance of words suited the ideas and attitudes of the Carolingian humanists. They were also concerned with words and formulae, books and images, and their particular interests in a significant sense continued to determine Europe's ways of thought up to the twelfth and thirteenth centuries. A book was something rare and holy. It was a gift of kings or popes, or a dowry brought to a monastery. It was fitting that gold and silver should adorn book bindings. The magical patterns of its initials which united Germanic, Celtic and ancient oriental forms were the visible evidences of the sacred formulae within, which bound its contents together.

After four hundred years of fighting, the Franks had conquered what is, today, Western Europe. Charlemagne's empire represented the peak, the watershed and the moment of crisis in this development. Since he wanted to unite his conquered peoples spiritually, he had no choice but to subject them to his Carolingian imperial Church. The much discussed Carolingian 'educational and cultural legislation' was an essential part of this process. The creation of academies and universities was never an end in itself, as later humanists have often preferred to believe. The object was the total subjection of the Arian, pagan, or superficially evangelized nations, to the *one* God-King, Christ, and his representative on earth, Charlemagne. The cult, the Mass, the Roman liturgy, the imperial-ecclesiastical Latin language and the authority of *sapientia* were the tools. *Sapientia* in Carolingian humanism united the secular poets, philosophers and natural scientists of antiquity with the Bible and the Christian Fathers. Their ideas were all of equal validity as juridical-sacral citations. Through careful citation of authority, a theory of government was hammered out by the *émigrés* from Italy, Spain, Ireland and England who gradually collected at Charlemagne's court. This theory was constructed to defend the political order of the realm against Rome, Constantinople and the heresies. Charlemagne lavished abbeys, lands and titles on these foreigners, but, like the French philosophers at the court of Frederick the Great, like the Westerners at the courts of Peter the Great and Catherine, they remained aliens. Their ideas had no real roots in the native soil of the kingdoms in which they lived. They had no connection with the culture or mentality of the peoples subjected to their rule.

In 799, Charlemagne was glorified in song as the 'worshipful summit of Europe'.[54] Charlemagne had erected a new order in Europe. The props of the new order were the men he had collected. There was a kind of rough division of labour among the various nationalities. The Anglo-Saxons were largely occupied with subjecting the various peoples. Charlemagne used the Spanish *émigrés* for the struggle with Byzantium. Alcuin, master of the school at York, summoned by Charlemagne to Aix, completed the work of Boniface: the organization of the Carolingian imperial Church as a closed order of thought, prayer, service of God and one's lord. He opposed the individualistic missions and rejected the oriental-spiritual cast of the Irish 'monastery bishops', as well

as the numerous and disunited kinds of Christianity and ecclesiastical life –
Gallo-Roman, Celtic-Germanic – found among the peoples between the Ebro,
the Danube and the Elbe. The Anglo-Saxon emissaries who followed Alcuin
into the service of Charlemagne were remarkable men, great organizers and
gifted, sober politicians.

In the two preceding centuries, the Anglo-Saxons had been moulded in the
Augustinian and Benedictine schools of Rome and Lérins. They defeated the
powerful culture of Irish monasticism. This victory was important, not because
of the – rightly disputed – intellectual achievements and cultural level of Ireland in the sixth to eighth centuries,[55] but because of the colossal unity which
existed between the indigenous, ancestral culture of the country and the
monastic schools of Clonard, Clonmacnoise and Bangor. Irish monks were
the heirs and successors of the *Filid*, the pagan schools of poets, and they fused
their own Christian treasure with the ancestral culture of the Celts. It is they
who committed to writing the epic *Tain Bo Cualgne*.[56] Like the twelfth century
redaction of the *Nibelungenlied* by the 'Carolingian world', it reflected the importance of these monastic branches of the tribe as centres of its government.
The abbot was chosen from the clan to which the founder belonged, and exercised episcopal and juridical rights over a whole diocese. The Celtic monks of
the school of Columbanus derived their monastic system and pattern of
spirituality from the East. Rapidly they spread their foundations in France,
Flanders, southwest Germany and northern Italy. This was the seed of that
central European monasticism, with its deep roots in the local folk-culture,
which was so often to arouse the anger of reformers, humanists and spiritualists during the next thousand years. At first the Carolingian government had
no hold there at all; it could obtain one only when its own men were in possession of the episcopal sees and the abbot's thrones. These were the men around
Alcuin, the famous Carolingian humanists and court academicians.[57] All the
renaissance formulae in the *Liber Pontificalis*, which we have already noted,
reappeared. The Carolingian humanists connected the 'rebirth of the arts and
sciences', the purification of the sacred texts, of the liturgy, of the chant and
cult of the Church with the reform of the monasteries, the restoration of
crumbling structures and the rebirth of the Church.

In the service of the King of Heaven, with these trusty followers behind him,
Charlemagne plunged into the battle against the errors that had crept into
books.[58] Rome was to provide pure texts: the pure sacramentary of Gregory
the Great, pure texts of the Bible, pure texts of the Church's law, of the Fathers,
of Gregory the Great and the Benedictine Rule, a Latin grammar, and the
architecture of Vitruvius. It was as the protector of orthodoxy, of pure doctrine, pure language, piety and science reborn, that Charlemagne thought
himself capable of resisting the manifold nonconformists, folk-cultures and
heresies arrayed against him. At this point, he was confronted by the Spanish
emigration. The peculiar dialectic of spiritual history made itself felt once
again in the two inter-related but separate effects of this emigration. Although,

on the one hand, it spread a leaven of heretical and near-heretical ideas throughout the south-west of his empire, it also provided support for his campaign against Byzantium.[59] The Spaniards became invaluable court theologians under the leadership of Theodulf of Orleans. Their work was reserved to orthodoxy exclusively for the Western Empire and to make the East heretical by definition.

For over a hundred years the Byzantine Empire had been shaken by the image controversy. After 726, when Emperor Leo III condemned 'the worship of images as idolatry', the spirit of Origen and of Eastern spiritualist intellectualism seemed to be invincible. In the political sphere it was supported by the desire to arrive at a political, religious and cultural agreement with Islam. The relations of the Byzantine Emperors with Islam during these first centuries were excellent; the Emperor Theophilos was neither the first nor the last to honour Arab-Hellenist culture. On the other hand, sympathy, admiration and veneration for Byzantine government, the culture of Byzantine society and Byzantine official art were plentiful throughout the Arab-Hellenist world from Spain to Bagdad. There was, however, one constant source of scandal, mockery and enmity: the superstition and idolatry of the masses of the people of Byzantium, their inordinate veneration of the saints and devotion to images. A purge was a necessity. It could serve as a gesture of political and religious conciliation to Islam and its fanatical monotheism. The Byzantine theologians found the way to bring about this purge in their distinction between the adoration of images, which was condemned, and the veneration of images, which was acceptable. Drawing their arguments from the creation and the incarnation, they distinguished between the image and what the image represents. At the Council of Nicea in 787, the last to be recognized by both Eastern and Western Christendom as an ecumenical council, they achieved a condemnation of iconoclasm as heresy.[60] The hour of the Spanish *émigrés* had come.

The Spaniards had been deeply imbued with Islamic monotheism and Eastern spiritualism. They turned emphatically against the error of the Byzantines. In Charlemagne's official memorandum against Nicea, the *Libri Carolini*, the Byzantines were condemned as fetishist and pagan: 'To worship none but God, to glorify Him alone, thus rings out the voice of the awful trumpet of Holy Scripture.'[61] The sentence was formulated by Theodulf. It was the very essence of the Koran. It had an additional political significance. Charlemagne could not tolerate variety in his empire. There must be one Lord in heaven and on earth. Christ was completely absorbed into God the Father. The service which this strictly unitarian God required was one which could be taught in solid doctrine and practised in a strictly controlled cult. Charlemagne was mistrustful of the manifold cults of the saints. They were all too often linked to tribe and kindred, clan and brotherhood. Such cults had been influential in Merovingian Gaul[62] and among all his subject peoples. Hence his chilly reserve about the veneration of any saints who were not his! This was the famous rationalism of Charlemagne.

Charlemagne set out to be the successor of Constantine. His cathedral church was modelled on Ravenna, Constantinople, Jerusalem and Rome. It testifies eloquently to his conception of his role.[63] Over a period of twenty years the court theologians had been preparing for this assumption of power. The 'orthodox council' of Frankfurt in 794 accused the emperors of the East of wanting to 'reign with God' and be themselves 'divine'.[64] The more closely the world of the Carolingian court resembled Byzantium, the more bitter this invective was to become.

There was a second aspect of the Spanish emigration and infiltration of the Carolingian Empire, very closely connected with the first, or orthodox aspect. This was the movement which we may call Spanish adoptionism. It had its roots in the same Arian, Eastern, Islamic soil as the overweening unitarianism and quasi-Monophysitism of the Carolingian court theologians. Christ was God and nothing but God. The Carolingian gospel of lordship and mastery had been ordered by Charlemagne from his clergy. Naturally it said nothing about the suffering Christ, nor about the people and their miseries. It frankly proclaimed, as Alcuin asserted, a 'doctrine of the sword'. This 'heresy' really consisted of older Spanish tendencies in a more emphatic form. It led to a violent conflict between Elipand, the Bishop of Toledo, and Migetius, who had developed an historical interpretation of the Trinity similar to that of Joachim of Flora: Migetius taught that the Father became incarnate in David, the Son in Jesus, the Holy Ghost in Paul. Elipand replied by declaring that Christ's human nature did not participate in the Godhead. Bishop Felix of Urgel, who supported Elipand, understood Elipand's idea of adoption of the man Christ by God to mean a legal, master-servant relationship. The imperial Bishop Eberhard of Bamberg in the twelfth century worked out a similar interpretation for very much the same reasons. The concern of both was with the absolute transcendence of God. Felix differed from Eberhard, however, by his emphasis on the apostolic calling of humanity. Like Gerhoh of Reichersberg, Eberhard's great opponent, Felix believed that we have all, like Christ, been adopted as God's sons and received the same grace as he. The conflict spread rapidly and Rome and Aix were brought into it. After his condemnation as a heretic in 792, Felix fled to Arab territory, probably to Toledo which was still in Moorish hands.* Upon the intervention of several bishops, the matter was again brought before Charlemagne. As 'external bishop' of his 'orthodox' imperial Church the Emperor heard the case at the Council of Frankfurt in 793–4. Once again Felix was condemned, and once again there was episcopal intervention on his behalf. This time it was from Leidrad of Lyons. At Aix, in the spring of 800, Felix finally submitted to Alcuin and was placed in the custody of his protector Leidrad. After Felix died in 813, Agobard of Lyons, Leidrad's successor, found among his possessions a tract reaffirming the old heresy. In the meantime, a Carolingian mission had secured

*The frontiers between the Islamic and Christian worlds were much more fluid at that time than we usually think. This was also true of theology and spirituality.

the return to orthodoxy of practically the whole of Christian Spain. Alcuin proudly reported to Bishop Arno of Salzburg the conversion of twenty thousand dissidents. Missionary work meant in Carolingian terms the transfer from a false culture, from an heretical or pagan religious-political allegiance, to the true service of God the King and his representative, Charlemagne. A sincere political decision and a consistent willingness to learn and accept the pure form of doctrine were required.[65] The Lord's Prayer and the Creed were the sacred formulae by which the transfer was made from the 'kingdom of darkness' into the 'kingdom of light'. In the last years of his life, Alcuin began to realize that being a Christian meant something more. The rationalistic legalism of this kind of service and mere faithfulness to God and the Emperor could no longer help the old man in his terror of death and hell. The age of Louis the Pious had begun.

Charlemagne's empire fell apart under his sons. The rationalism which characterized it disintegrated too. Its intellectual assurance had rested on the self-confidence of the régime. The imperial commonwealth, forcibly united by Alcuin's semi-Pelagianism and Charlemagne's system of Church government, split into its natural geographical units and hereditary spheres of interest. This disintegration of rationalism has been a marked and recurrent aspect of Europe's intellectual history. The unitarian intellectualism of the Spanish *émigrés* began to turn into a revolutionary type of enlightened spiritualism. The high humanism of the Irish-Scottish group produced a number of completely un-Christian speculations. A few of its representatives arrived at an extreme form of Augustinian asceticism in their search for a living God.[66] Behind the variety of these positions lay the necessary reaction of the spirit – of the Christian conscience and of intellectual consciousness – against the weight of Charlemagne's powerful régime. It was a reaction comparable, in its momentous and far-reaching effects, to the resistance which broke out on all sides to the sacral régime of Louis XIV.

Charlemagne and Alcuin had triumphantly proclaimed that their empire was the stronghold of orthodoxy, of the pure doctrine of Christ, of true culture and justice. The reality looked very different. The various nations were held together with difficulty amid constant wars and insurrections. The masses of the people, sunk in paganism, offered sacrifices to the spirits of the grove, spring and seed. The clergy lived in the midst of this pagan, barbarian world.[67] Some may have joined in the animal sacrifices. As late as 757, priests had practised such rites, and some may well have reverted to their older habits.[68] We know definitely that the clergy often gave the sacraments to the unbaptized. If they belonged to the higher clergy, they lived a life of warfare, hunting and revelry in the ancient style of pagan feastings and banquetings. The lower clergy shared the life of the superficially Christianized people, sometimes even as vassals without free status. The conditions of Charlemagne's court, of his family and entourage were equally unsatisfactory. Here too, as a matter of course, the higher clergy lived worldly lives. Very few were ordained priests and even Alcuin remained a deacon. Angilbert[69] and Einhard remained lay-men even when they became abbots. The Church and her treasures, the ordering of spiritual things, of culture and of cult, were all under the domina-tion of a set of extremely worldly lords.

God and the world, spirit and nature, power and law were apparently hope-lessly entangled when the men who came after Charlemagne began to sort things out. Since Charlemagne wanted to do everything and Alcuin wanted to know everything, considerable damage had been done to the theories of evil and grace. The inevitable reaction began. At the school of Fulda, for example, Bruun (Candidus), laid stress on the almighty power of God and grounded his proof of his existence upon it:[70] God is that super-power (as Eriugena was to say, super-God) who rules over all things, all creatures, all men. Ratramnus of Corbie aimed at an even more clear-cut position. In the work commissioned by Charles the Bald, he took up the position of the later Augustine in regard to predestination, and taught the omnipotence of grace and a strict pre-determination of all good and evil. His opponent in the same monastery, Paschasius Radbertus, made himself the spokesman of the younger Augustine. Their dispute over the nature of the Eucharist gave rise to the great division of the cosmos into nature and super-nature which was to be elaborated in scholasticism from the twelfth century onwards.

The humanists living at the imperial court and in the monastic schools who had mourned the decline of learning after the time of Charlemagne hailed its rebirth under the Third Charles, Charles the Bald: thus Walafried Strabo, Lupus of Ferrières and Wandalbert of Prüm. Heiric of Auxerre, for example, despite his concentrated, almost nominalist reverence for Augustine,[71] could use these words to describe the culture of Charles the Bald's empire: well may Greece mourn, for the culture of the Byzantine Empire has departed to the empire of Charles, thanks especially to the men from Ireland![72] An ornate court humanism began to take shape. Its fixed formulae were to persist until the eighteenth century. It devoted itself to the application of quotations from antiquity and from the Bible to the production of rhetorical culture. This classicism, so often overrated, was almost always the opponent of scientific progress and often of religious renewal. It was always chained to the protec-tion of some prince or bishop, or monastic school or academy.

The emigration of the Irish to the court of Charles the Bald resembled in some ways the earlier Spanish movement to the court of Charlemagne. Its effect was very different. The pseudo-cosmos of the spiritual world of Charles' court would be destroyed by it. The Irish world was full of ideas which did not fit the Carolingian medieval, religio-political cosmos. The Irish abbot-bishops, who occasionally controlled South German monasteries during the fifth, sixth and seventh centuries, had violently rejected the rigid, Bonifacian, Franco-Roman organization of Central Europe within the Frankish imperial Church.[73] In the curtain-raiser to the 'Copernican question', the holy man Virgil, later Archbishop of Salzburg and previously Abbot of Aghadoe near Dublin, proposed, with the support of Augustine's hints about the antipodes,[74] that there might possibly be 'another world and other men beneath the earth'. Pope Zacharias commanded Boniface in 748 to compel him to recant under pain of excommunication.[75]

The greatest figure in the Irish emigration was Eriugena. His influence was to run in many channels throughout the entire middle ages. John Scotus (Eriugena) had been strongly affected by Augustine and Boethius, but in the course of work on a polemic against Godesalc's doctrine of predestination, which had been commissioned by Hincmar of Rheims, he became more and more committed to Neoplatonism. Eriugena's haughty Neoplatonic rationalism was the absolute antithesis of Godesalc's ardent faith, the product of the anguished soul of a man of the people.[76] Charles the Bald then summoned Eriugena to the court school of Paris, where he began to translate the works of Dionysius Areopagite from a manuscript presented to Louis the Pious by the Greek Emperor. There is extraordinary irony, in view of the later history of the University of Paris, in the fact that its first major scholastic undertaking should have been a Greek text translated by a Neoplatonist.[77]

The peculiar power, the inner meaning and goal of his thought arose out of the unusual combination of traditions from which he drew his ideas. In order to defend the interests of Charles the Bald's state ideology, Eriugena united the Greek doctrine of deification (as in Clement, Origen and Dionysius) with Celtic-Germanic beliefs regarding rebirth and return. For years people believed that Eriugena lived in a vacuum in an age without any intellectual activity. We know that this was not so. He was very much a man of his time. There is evidence for this in the close kinship between his great work and the *Liber de Rectoribus Christianis*, the first great medieval 'Mirror of Princes'. Eriguena was accused of heresy by Pope Nicholas I and Archbishop Hincmar of Rheims. He was safe in Paris until the death of Charles the Bald. Then he disappeared. According to later sources, he was summoned by Alfred the Great to the new school at Oxford. If so, the road he travelled from Paris to Oxford might be compared to that of Roger Bacon and Thomas Hobbes.

3

THE TENTH CENTURY

EUROPE'S THOUSAND YEARS OF UNITY

EUROPEAN intellectual development has been a story of bitter and continuing conflict, but there were enormous areas within European civilization in which there was agreement and harmony. For over a thousand years, life in Europe had certain characteristic common features. All over Europe people did certain kinds of things in the same way and despite the differences there was also a remarkable degree of unity in form and spirit.[1] The foundations of European civilization reach back into a pre-history which unites Europe with Africa and Asia; foundations which remained essentially unchanged until the nineteenth century and which lived on in the culture and mentality of the people. Upon this base rested a governmental system which was aristocratic and urban.[2] We might express it briefly by saying that Europe's thousand years were a thousand years of domination by the nobility. That nobility produced the great houses, imperial, royal, princely and noble. It claimed to have sprung from the race of the gods, and its members emerged from the matrix of the collective human substratum as the first 'egos'. They became the first complete men, fully Christian and personal. Throughout these thousand years they possessed the posts of leadership in the Church[3] (episcopal sees, canonries, abbacies and chapters), in society and in the universities and academies. The lord's household, with its own economy,[4] was a sociological, political, economic, mercantile, ethical and religious unit. As such, it was the model for the peasant's household and the bourgeois household as well. The father[5] was supreme authority. He was master of the house, head of the family, director of internal and external economic relations and cultural life, both in work and in holiday-making. In all its essentials, the father's authority was a model of the noble household. What is often overlooked is that this rulers' world implied the continuation of slavery in Christendom.* Until the middle of the nineteenth century,[6] slavery continued to exist or at least find defenders all over western European Christendom.[7]

The millennium was characterized by unity of the whole of society, that is, by unity in government and also in economics and technology.[8] Lewis Mumford rightly speaks[9] of an 'eo-technical' phase in Europe lasting from 1000 till 1750 and in some places till 1850. It is important to grasp this truth: for a

---

*In this connection, Leo XIII's Encyclical to the Brazilian bishops on the occasion of the legal abolition of slavery (*In Plurimis*, 5 May 1888) merits attention.

thousand years European man employed the same media, within the same technical and economic order, to apprehend the world of things.[10] Economic life in Europe from the eighth to the nineteenth century assumed a very limited number of typical forms. The only deviations from the usual patterns were found in the eastern border-zone and in enclaves in the Mediterranean countries. Agriculture was generally, although by no means everywhere, based on the seignorial rights of the nobility under whose protection Europe's peasantry usually tilled the soil in the three-field system. In a few Mediterranean areas the ancient two-field system continued. 'For nearly a millennium and a half, until the eighteenth and in some places halfway through the nineteenth century, the manor and the village, in their relationship to each other, determined the structure of life in the lowland areas ... In peasant ownership and village organization we first encounter that distinctively rational order of things which underlies specifically European rationality, Europe's greatness and her danger throughout her history.'[11] This was the European household organization. It was rational and orderly, but it was not free of irrational elements. In part, its rational arrangements were sustained and given direction by forces which grew out of the irrational substratum. The underground in the peasant's world was not far from the surface. The rational arrangements of his life and work drew nourishment from the substance of *civilisation traditionnelle*,[12] of folk-culture.

In the midst of the country and the landed estates stood the town, under the rule at first of its bishop or prince. In Italy, at a very early stage, it began to include the nobility among its citizenry[13] and in 'considerable portions of southern Europe',[14] to embrace town and country alike as *civitas*. Within its shelter and protection, its security and freedom, the town developed the type of the European citizen. The European town, as *urbs diis hominibusque communis*, was the primal image of the European world view. It saw itself as a cosmos, cherishing heaven and earth and man and beast within its own order. Along with the castle and the noble's court, the town was the fortress of European conformism and orthodoxy but at the same time the refuge of European nonconformists, heretics and outsiders. The town sheltered the proletariat of letters, a homeless intelligentsia of wanderers, scholars, *goliards*, *vagantes*, banished teachers, professors and pastors, whom we see passing in uninterrupted procession from the eighth century to the nineteenth.[15]

The unity of government and of economic organization in old Europe, J. Burckhardt's 'Alteuropa', of its nobility and its urban citizenry, rested upon the unity of its intellectual leadership. Whether we see it first taking shape in the monasteries, cathedral schools and chapters, or later in the medieval universities, curias and courts of law; whether its representative embodiment was the regular or the secular monk, the humanist of the twelfth or the fifteenth century, the canonist and the legist, the cultivated courtier, the Catholic baroque scholar or the Lutheran professor, one thing is clear: there was an unbroken line of development from Lupus of Ferrières's 'lettered cleric' in the ninth century to the educated man and scholar of the eighteenth and nineteenth centuries. Similarly, the *simplex sacerdos*, the raw barbarian servile priest was the intellectual forbear of the uneducated layman of the nineteenth century. This contrast remains a continuous feature of Europe's inner development, and it was always felt by both sides.

The cultural world of old Europe was a closed world of grand forms. Its heritage of culture, science and faith rested on this one sacred, ancient pattern,[16] which it passed on to posterity with the primal authority of the first fathers.[17] It was the 'model, *paradeigma, exemplum*,[18] for every renaissance and for every conservative revolution. Membership in the world of nobility and culture imposed a duty of education and self-education. Aristotle, Plato, Plotinus and Proclus, Cicero, Seneca, Virgil, Ovid, Horace, Plutarch and Sallust, Hippocrates and Galen, Euclid, Vitruvius and Ptolemy, the Fathers of the Church from Augustine to Thomas and Suarez and the orthodox Protestants were accepted as the consecrated means to education. The external world was government by the grace of the archetypal emperor, the Godhead as First Mover. What remained was to construct the interior and inferior world in accordance with these external models and archetypes. This is the basic meaning of the tenacious determination to hold on to the high arts of rhetoric and to the precious vocabulary of classical Latin. E. R. Curtis[19] has assembled an overwhelming abundance of material illustrating this thousand year continuity in Europe's scholastic and literary culture. The sacred language – Latin in this case – was the safeguard of man's store of culture, science and faith. Latin protected it from the sacrilegious gaze and grasp of the inferior masses and preserved it in the hands of those who were the lawful bearers of culture, science and pure faith. From the eleventh century to the eighteenth, translation of the Holy Scriptures into the language of the people and discussion of scholarly subjects or production of lofty poetry in the vulgar tongue, the speech of the common people, was liable to count as heresy, dissent and rebellion, a sign of revolt against the one, ancient and Christian authoritative order of things. In this sense, Roman Catholic bans on the Bible, from the thirteenth to the nineteenth century (1893 was the year this ban was finally removed), were of a piece with the fight against heresy. Around 1750 it slowly began to be customary in Germany to give lectures in the language of the country, but until 1850 Latin was the European language among scholars, clerics and court poets, and in Hungary the language of official life as well. Even today many lectures in Catholic theological faculties in Europe are given in Latin.

There was a political and social unity in the order of government, and an intellectual unity in education and culture. This larger unity included all revolutionary and nonconformist movements within itself in an interplay of thesis and antithesis. It was unavoidable that the dialectical struggle of union and unity involved Europe's life of faith, its religions and confessions.

This inner unity was not denied but asserted by the spectacle of a thousand years of heresies, religious wars and persecutions of nonconformists. There was a deep inner harmony, and intense interplay, often in the furthest depths of their beings, between orthodoxies and heresies; between church and anti-church, saint and sectarian.[20] Thomist scholasticism is unthinkable without Islam, without Jewish enlightenment, Franciscan spiritualism and Averroist intellectualism. Luther, Calvin, Erasmus, Ignatius of Loyola and Theresa of Avila all belong together. Tridentine and Protestant theology in the seventeenth century, Catholic pietism and Protestant spiritualism in the eighteenth, were intimately tied to each other. All were based upon the series of constitutions, religio-political in character, of state and imperial Church from Charlemagne to Joseph II. Their maxim, *cuius regio ejus religio*, 'He who lives within my system of law and salvation must be an adherent of my faith', found its classic basis in Lactantius (*De Ira Dei*, VIII): *Ita fit, ut religio et majestas et honor metu constet. Metus autem non est, ubi nullus irascitur.* In effect, this doctrine meant that a rigid system of political rule, preferably in the hand of one ruler embodying the world-sustaining wrath of divine majesty, was the only guarantee of the maintenance and protection of society, true knowledge and true faith. For Charlemagne, empire and Church were identical,[21] as they were for Otto the Great, the 'Lord's annointed', as they were for Frederick I when he called upon his believers to 'be obedient to God and to us' (*ad obediendum Deo et nobis*)[22] as they were for all the Catholic, Lutheran, Calvinist, Anglican and enlightened Church lords from the sixteenth to the nineteenth century.

Almost at once Europe fell apart into a number of individual sacral kingdoms, each anxiously preoccupied with its own autonomy. These windowless monads were full of windows in practice, and were all founded upon one common ground. Together they formed that established state of harmony in old Europe to which Leibniz bore retrospective testimony and which Clausewitz, accepting Leibniz's account of it, admired. As we watch the violent struggles and debates which scarred Europe's intellectual history, we shall do well to remember that they have their setting within the security of the aristocratic-bourgeois governmental order of these thousand years.

The hereditary aristocratic structure of this world secured it despite a state of perpetual tension, struggle and war. It also produced that typical aristocratic tolerance which provided common ground for Athenian citizens and Persian lords, for medieval nobles and their Moslem peers, and for aristocratic Christian theologians and the good pagans, Plato, Aristotle, Avicenna and Confucius.[23]

This higher culture, this culture of the grand form, would not have survived without the solid underpinning of the ancient underground which took shape at the dawn of history. The great movements in Europe's intellectual history throughout these thousand years would be unintelligible without an awareness of the constant debate and struggle between the upper level and the lower. It was from contact with the underground that spiritually creative thought received its secret, indefinable and yet determining character. We learn of such contacts in the form of childhood experiences, conversions, dreams, visions, etc., in the lives of men such as Anselm of Canterbury, Roger Bacon, Paracelsus, Luther, Pascal, Descartes, Kant and Mach. Unfortunately, little research has as yet been done on this problem. Every intellectually important figure was in some sort of contact with the submerged, non-rational culture of the people. In each case there must have been a creative flow between the rational, humanist language of form and the pre-rational underground. We know virtually nothing about this despite the fact that it is here that we must seek the roots of the systems they constructed and the mould which shaped their basic ideas and their pictures of the world.

The most alert representatives of the higher culture, from the end of the period of antiquity until the nineteenth century, lived in a state of perpetual anxiety lest the world relapse into barbarism and fall away from culture and good manners. They were always afraid that knowledge, the arts and pure doctrine would be lost.[24] In their fear, they forged chains with which they shackled those formative forces of life and kept them in a state of repression. They permitted any change to proceed to a certain point only and no further. Long before Vico, this fear had ripened into a positive reaction, associated with political revolutionary movements. The guardians of the Grand Form were largely responsible for the fact that each of the great cultural nations had fallen, or was in danger of falling, into two nations, the rulers and the ruled (this occurred in England and France as early as the sixteenth century). The positive reaction took the form of an acceptance of the underground into the upper world, giving it a place in government, or in a proclamation of the sovereignty of the underground itself after the revolution.

This anxiety was justified. Mankind is hundreds of thousands of years old, and those hundreds of thousands of years have stamped certain basic patterns upon its substance which survive even the severest shocks. Nothing is so hard to change as the creature most prone to change, man.[25] Thus it should not astonish us when we see attitudes of mind and patterns of thought emerging in the nineteenth and twentieth centuries which politicians, theologians and humanists who trust in superficial appearances were certain had long been conquered. European higher culture was an island culture, something carried on in strongholds – monasteries, cities, schools – by a few hundred families. The history of European Christianity teaches us that even religion and faith, the strongest forces of change in the world, need many centuries to achieve a superficial conversion and thousands of years if they are to enter into the very heart of the structure of society and re-shape it.

The Europe of pre-history, of early history, of non-historical history, which is today making its presence felt anew, was deeply united with Africa,[26] that 'storehouse of primitive community life', and with Asia.[27] This has been especially stressed by Madariaga, a Spaniard. Spain is in many ways related to Russia and the Slavonic East, because all three were the bridges linking us with those storehouses. The non-European areas of traditional society were first broken into and violently destroyed in this century by European forces and the peasant uprisings and explosive revolutions have been the response to the ruthless and sudden demolition of delicate and ancient social and individual ways of life. Anyone wishing to see this European-African unity in one glance need only compare the figure of Christ the King carved by negroes of the Ivory Coast for the new Cathedral in Coventry with German figures of Christ the King from the tenth to the thirteenth century; or the magnificent cock in the 'Denial of Peter' from the Belgian Congo shown in the missionary exhibition in Rome in 1951 with the ancient bronze cock in St Peter's.[28] He will see for himself that this is all *one* world.

The migration of the Beaker people at the end of the Neolithic period (*circa* 1900–1800 BC), from eastern Spain over western and central Europe to England on the one hand and to Hungary and Poland on the other, with a second branch spreading across Italy into the Danube countries, may serve as a prototype of all those vast migratory movements within which the static relationships of primitive society persisted. A migration of beakers and brooches, of salt and amber, gold and copper and iron; a migration of sagas, legends and tales, of gods, saints and cults; a migration of herdsmen and farmers, warriors and traders, of peoples. The wandering of the nations from the fifth century BC to the tenth AD was only an echo of this great primitive migration within which mankind lived and maintained itself. The ancient tradition of wandering was slowly restricted until the absolutist state of the eighteenth and nineteenth centuries began to put an end to it by force. Maria Theresa, for example, prohibited pilgrimages to Compostela, but the wandering continued: craftsmen, stone-carvers, masons, weavers, monks, missionaries, humanists, pilgrims, heretics, crusaders: Syrians, Irish and Scots, Jews.[29] The people – the simple peasants, the little people – went wandering through the thousand years to Santiago, Aix, Tours, Rome, Einsiedeln. Drontheim, Canterbury and so on, visiting their 'fathers' and 'mothers'. G. Schreiber[30] has demonstrated in numerous studies of the sacral landscape and sacral culture of Europe the immense significance of these journeys. The people carried its own cults and its own saints and it elected them itself in the process of popular canonization against which Alexander III protested in vain. It spread its wealth of sagas, culture and lore throughout the length and breadth of Europe. There was a Bavarian peasant from Gaden, near Waging, who died in 1866 – the year when Austria, the foremost power in old Europe, collapsed at Königsgrätz – who went three times on pilgrimage to Rome, twice to Jerusalem and once to Compostela.[31]

Pilgrimage and migration formed the medium through which the various movements of religion and reform, conformist and, more especially, nonconformist, spread with such furious speed. These wanderings are part of the explanation of the phenomena of Albigensianism and Waldensianism, of the Franciscans, the Hussites and the various forms of Protestantism.

After the end of the eighteenth century, the old folk culture began to decline.

By the middle of the nineteenth century it was disintegrating rapidly.[32] At the same time the higher culture of the old Europe began to wither, as if it could not survive without its roots in the lower culture. The joint decline of both cultures is a remarkable phenomenon. Despite the bitter struggle to repress the spiritual, religious and political movements which grew out of the soil of folk-culture, the high culture was tied to the low by a mysterious alliance. It fed and depended upon the people. Europe's Christianity stood only so long as Europe's genuine paganisms continued.

For ten thousand years the European village [33] formed a social, economic, and communal unity,[34] a highly complicated organism within which the living and the dead, the two sexes and the different generations, divided between them their work and leisure, their distress and joys, their spiritual welfare and disaster. Thousands of years of intercourse with life and death, in one fearful crisis after another, created a society whose adaptibility and powers of resistance to the severest hardships are reminiscent of those rafts, built without nails and at home amid the great waves, on which prehistoric peoples sailed the seas of the world and Heyerdahl of the *Kon-Tiki* after them. This closed world was built upon a sense of identity[35] in which nature and man, God and the world, spirit and matter were conceived as a single unity. This was the broad foundation of the mysticism, sacramentalism, magic and technology of our folk-materialism (not to be confused with the spiritualist materialism of the late enlighteners of the eighteenth and nineteenth centuries). There was a highly complex 'domestic architecture'[36] in which a cult with manifold usages of rite and law regulated the common life of man and wife, the members of the family and the village (clan) community. Every thing and every animal – every article of clothing, weapon or agricultural tool – had its magical juridical function to fulfil in the house. Each house was a unit of sacral space, organizing correct co-operation between the living and the dead, storing up and administering spiritual welfare through the medium of the festal calendar.

There was a division of labour between the generations. The elders withdrew from the primary physical activities of manual labour and procreation. They exercised a certain juridical function and were the bearers of tradition, the *encyclopédie orale*.[37] An encyclopaedia represents the consolidated knowledge of a closed world; this 'oral encyclopaedia' possessed a higher degree of verbal fidelity than the written encyclopaedias of the sixth to the eighteenth century. It transmitted the heritage of law, saga, epic and song from one generation to the next,[38] linking them together with formulas of words and songs – *incantare* – which had a binding force of their own. 'Children pipe as old men sing.' The new generation had to live what had been lived and sung before it. Hence the incalculable significance of the dead. There was an unbroken continuity between Christian belief in immortality and pagan belief in the after-life. As late as 1940 and 1942, primitive death customs (money for the journey) survived in the Cluniac south of France. The Christian cult of the dead from the eighth to the eighteenth century – grave furniture, memorial rolls and books, innumerable secular and spiritual brotherhoods, associations and guilds, the whole of old Europe's magnificent life of comradeship – was simply the living cultivation of this inter-relationship which lay at the basis of folk-culture. The company of the dead was an age group within the company of the living. Life in the beyond was a direct continuation of life on earth. There is plenty of evidence for this in customs of popular piety throughout Europe,[39] and in Christian visions from the ninth to the nineteenth century, where, for instance, saintly imperial bishops are present at sacral banquets in the company of Christ the King. The dead often emerge in life to give news about the Beyond, which is an inexhaustible storehouse of power and strength. They confer fruitfulness upon corn, cattle and mankind, dispensing health, victory, blessing, weal and woe.

Everything in this *civilisation traditionnelle* was ambivalent. Good and evil, salvation and damnation, death and life, God and the devil were always simply the two sides of a single power. Linguistic research reveals this ambivalence many times over. It persisted in the thousand years of the middle ages. In Romanesque symbolism the lion, for example, stood both for Christ and for the devil. It was inherent in the wrath of God and the saints, whose power determined good and evil and whose favour therefore must somehow be obtained so that they would not show themselves ungracious.*

When archaic society first began to socialize nature,[40] to divide the land according to a social scheme and to work it in a regular system of ploughing and stock-raising, it included the supernatural from the start. Not, as has often been supposed, in order to obtain control over it by magical practices, but in order to enter into pacts and periodical alliances with it. Nature and super-nature[41] were not opposed terms but comprised a single note of existence. Life in both was divided into the same units – household, family, village, tribal community – and regulated by a festal cult dependent upon the festal calendar. This festal calendar united the community and culture of the people with the higher culture of court and city. It was the strongest of the links between the upper world and the underworld, and without it there would have been no old Europe.[42] Emperors and kings, bishops and abbots, and all the great lords were concerned not only to celebrate *their* feasts, the feasts which belonged to their ecclesiastical and courtly order of things, but to take part in the festal rites of the people. German traditional law and German preachers required that the emperor *sul mit den kegeln spieln*, that is play with the illegitimate children of his lower class subjects on the first of May, the high day of the people's sacerdotal May King. Varagnac gives splendid examples from French history:[43] Francis I fought mock battles with his nobles on the *Jour des Rois*; Louis XIV lit the St John's fire in the Place de Grève; Fallières, President of the Republic, received the Carnival Queen in the Elysée.

For a long time the European man, Christian and pagan, felt no need to make any verbal distinctions within this single sphere of reality. The word

*cf. Paracelsus, Böhme, Baader and the German idealists.

supernaturalis, which first appeared in translations of the Pseudo-Dionysius, only acquired a wider currency in the thirteenth century[44] when this one world was already beginning to fall apart. Today primitive Negroes and Indians still regard matter as a white man's invention.[45]

The festal calendar, understood as a cosmic ordering of things, gave household, family and village their place in the *oikoumene*, the sacred order for interdependence. Men, animals and things were entirely interdependent. Since everything was in a state of constant danger, from war, famine, pestilence and evil influences of all kinds, it was up to each member of the community – man, animal or thing – to play his part within the right order of things, in his own proper field of service toward all others. A most beautiful description of this archaic communal interdependence is to be found in the works of Hildegard of Bingen in the twelfth century. *Ordo* is the name which the middle ages, from Sedelius Scotus to the nineteenth century, gave to this interplay of all things. The *ordo* of the scholastics, Leibniz's 'pre-established' harmony, the 'magical idealism' of German romanticism, are all only attenuated reflections of this sacred order in which every member, in work and leisure, in technology and in cult, was responsible for every other member of his sacral group.

The *ordo* was reflected in the sacred character of courts of law and the holiness of their findings. In 1478 the Bishop of Lausanne began legal proceedings against caterpillars, which ended with the caterpillars being laid under the ban of the Church. In the sixteenth century, the lawyer Bartholomew de Chasserée won fame by his brilliant conduct of the defence in the famous rat case at Autun.[46] In 1928, in a little village in lower Austria, a legal action was brought against a toad. In 1951 and 1952, witches were still being persecuted in southern and northern Germany.[47] The 'wicked enemy', the 'evil-doer' – man, animal, thing (for example, a sword falling from the wall) or element – must be banned, or exorcized, or eliminated, by due process of law. He, or it, was always guilty of a 'breach of the peace'; he or it deliberately chose to break the peace, the artificial order which archaic society and its folk-culture had been creating for tens of thousands of years. The persecution of sectarians, heretics and innovators of all sorts, which has so characterized Europe's spiritual history, has its roots in the anxiety of a closed society about the destruction of its sacral order. (This anxiety was the popular equivalent of the humanist's fear of a relapse into barbarism.) The ecclesiastical and state Inquisitions of the thirteenth to eighteenth centuries arose because the natural inquisition of primitive society, with its basis in family, household, clan and village, was no longer regarded as adequate, or, alternatively, because it refused to take its orders from above. This natural inquisition mercilessly rooted out and banished from its midst all who did not adapt themselves to its pattern of life, work and ritual.

All of this occurred on the most fundamental level. It was the sustaining force in European conservatism, a force which, under pressure from innovators at the top, was constantly provoked to bloody revolts. Archaic society always fought under the banners of return to the old order, for the ancient law, for the primitive Church, and for return to Adam and Eve. The peasant revolt was almost always conservative in essence. It was natural that men reacted violently to attempts to change their ways of life, because their ways were the right, traditional and sacred ways. All their activities and ways of behaviour, ideas and feelings were determined by the principle of right usage – a custom, *consuetudo, habitude*. The most important element in this fundamental reality of custom was that of *répétition malgré les échecs*, the steady re-assumption and repetition of old forms of work, technique, thought and prayer despite innumerable crises, disillusionments and catastrophes. Hence this closed society required a mighty faith in order to maintain its tradition. It had to ensure a perpetual rebirth of its ancestral father, of his mind and activity, his words, life and personality, who in turn guaranteed the continuation of the stream of sacred, saving life. It possessed certain significant means to this end. The culture of its working life was based upon a grasp of the earth and the world of things. Often it used tools which remained practically unchanged from the classical age to the nineteenth century, as can be seen in the *Musée des Antiquités Nationales* in Paris.[48] Constant repetition of the same work created the rhythm of life, a rhythm expressed in a perpetual repetition of the same ritual actions. The same songs, the same prayers (endlessly lengthy litanies, and prayers for the different hours of the day), sustained the spiritual and festal culture of the people. At the feast – something which included eating, drinking, song and sometimes dancing as well – the crises of life (birth, adolescence, marriage and death) and of the annual cycle (winter and summer solstice, seed-time and harvest) were mastered through communion with the dead. The dead sat at table with the living, and their power and example were invoked there in song and story.

In saga and legend, in epic and myth,[49] drawing on the experience of a thousand years of history, the world of archaic thought condensed, crystallized and particularized its knowledge and wisdom. It developed a few definite themes, motifs and persons who were the bearers of salvation, the heroes and saints.* Thought – like singing and saying, like working and holiday-making – meant a process of repetition, a rebirth of that exemplar who lived before us, of the words in which he dispensed salvation, the deeds in which he won it, the life which he lived. The cult of heroes and saints – veneration for a holy *antiquitas*, for *viri illustres*, for the authorities – acted as another unifying link between the folk-culture and the higher culture.[50] Both high and low civilizations were equally pre-occupied with the necessity for defence against innovators, 'who have a different spirit, who do not drink at the banquet with us, nor sing with us, nor pray with us, nor think with us, nor work with us in that one and only sacred form which is right for these things'.

*Pope Alexander III wrote to the Swedes that they were not to canonize people who had died in their cups and at the festive board. (cf. Heer, *Aufgang Europas*, 1949, Commentary, pp. 208 f.)

Humanist doctors of medicine fought as savagely against innovators who refused to swear upon *their* sacred books, as did scholastic scientists against those whose researches led them to lay hand or thought upon the Untouchables; orthodox theologians battled against innovators in the faith as ferociously as learned poets and philosophers against unlearned bards and thinkers.

Throughout this European millennium, the world of archaic thought and communal culture was defended and preserved in the folk-culture of the village, in pre-Reformation monasticism, in the clergy and in the old aristocracy. Together they fought against reform and against foreign ways, defending themselves fiercely against invasion from above and outside. There is an abundance of evidence in European folklore that pagan festal customs, cults of the dead, ways of resorting to the other world in legal matters, primitive magic and techniques, persisted in the villages of many parts of Europe until the middle of the nineteenth and often into the twentieth century.[51] The Merseburg incantations, in their ninth-century wording, were in use near Vienna about 1930, and at about the same time, a procession at Maria in Lavant included the sacrificial ram which excavations show to have been offered in sacrifice at that very spot three thousand years ago. Various games and customs at different seasons of the year, Masonic lodges, initiation rites (like those practised a century ago by French seafarers),[52] preserved, in a reduced form, the festal calendar and festal culture which lasted until the new mechanical techniques and ways of work broke up the ancient concept of the world.

The people and the old aristocracy were united, in addition, by the monastery, which sheltered the scion of the nobility and the culture of the people alike. In the ninth century we find a Carolingian canon forbidding nuns *minileodos scribere vel mittere*, to write or send *minne*, love songs.[53] Reformers throughout the succeeding centuries, from the reforming Synod of Sutri in 1059 to Ricci's Synod of Pistoia during the eighteenth century, battled in vain against the worldly culture of holidays and festivals practised by monasteries and clergy of the old school. No saint, no pope, no king or emperor, no council (including Trent) succeeded in making any serious impression on this continuity. Bishop Gunther of Bamberg in the eleventh century[54] was the first poet (*Dichter*, meaning finder-and-preserver) of heroic song in the German tongue to be known by name. Bishops of Salzburg in the baroque period[55] devoted themselves to the same festal culture as the imperial bishops under Charlemagne. Otto and the house of Hohenstaufen went to war surrounded by a host of singers, dancers, tumblers and soothsayers.[56] Walter Mape, Walter of Châtillon and the *Golias Apocalypse*[57] satirized the worldliness, drink and revelry in the monasteries and amongst the clergy in the twelfth century. This worldliness was later attacked by Petrarch, Erasmus and all reformers and men of the spiritual party down to the nineteenth century.

The monasteries of the old school preserved within themselves the life and thought, the actions and sufferings of the ancient people. Folk-art, in contrast to the court art of the higher culture, found a home in the monasteries.[58] Under their protection, primitive animal-forms and conjuring of demons were preserved in Romanesque ornament and the columns of animals of Moissac and Toulouse. The painted glass of the eighteenth and nineteenth centuries continued to serve as an abbreviated ritual sign language, often expressing the whole story of redemption in a few definite symbols of saving significance.

Pilgrimage,[59] the cult of popular saints, the liturgy of the dead (i.e., reception into the realm of salvation) and all the rich multiplicity of ritual blessing combined to unite the people, its monasteries and its priests. Down to the nineteenth century, the priests, as *simplices sacerdotes*, were as one with the people as Russian popes. The people's clergy resisted the intellectual book-culture of higher theology. A hundred reforming synods were not enough to impose literacy upon this priesthood; literacy meant foreign scriptures and theology and a foreign world of thought. During the very golden age of scholasticism (1260–1310), a council held in 1260 in the Cologne of Albert and Eckhart laid down the rule that all clerics must be able to read and to sing Mass. In 1311 a council at Ravenna restricted this requirement to canons. In 1268 a council held in London ordered the Archdeacon of each English diocese to ensure that all priests were sufficiently taught so that they could understand the canon of the Mass and the rite of Baptism.[60]

The old nobility exercised considerable influence on monastic culture through *their* churches, occupied by *their* priests (often enough not freemen, and dedicated to the priesthood by their lords), and through *their* monasteries. Their clergy served the living members of the family and ensured the salvation of its dead. This was done within the framework of a strict, legal contract with the saints, with whom the transfer agreement, the *traditio*, was directly and personally concluded. Throughout the thousand years the old nobility, its bishops and its monasteries, stubbornly resisted the young nobility, the bearers of reform, of new forms of spirituality, piety and humanity. The old nobility was bound up within the folk-culture and mentality of the archaic community and it looked upon the young nobility as renegades and deserters. It persecuted their reforming bishops and reforming monasteries, their new orders and new religious habits, their new missions, new words, new preaching and new songs.

Let me illustrate this point by citing three examples of the thousand-year domination of the old nobility over *their* Church.* Between the eighth and tenth centuries the nobles were successful in winning the blessing of their Church for duelling, an essential element in their code of honour and their social structure. The Church was forced to accept such activities and to teach that duelling and the other forms of ordeal which originated in pagan folk-

*It was partially broken in France at the Revolution, in Germany in 1803, in Eastern Europe not till the coming of the People's Democracies in 1945; in Spain and South America, it remains to this day.

culture were divine judgments. The priests blessed the elements employed in the ordeals, the water and the fire, the iron, the ploughshare, the cauldron for the boiling water test, the bread and cheese for the consecrated morsel test, the shield and weapon for the duellists. Where possible, trial by ordeal or combat took place in the church itself.[61] The whole cosmos of archaic society was thus present in the people's church of the old nobility.

After this blessing upon single combat came the nobility's greatest success: the sanctification of war. Their tribal warfare was reborn as the holy war or crusade. Since the concept of war was an essential part of the world of great lords, their church had to accept it and justify it. It has taken over a thousand years for the Church to free itself from the baronial attitude toward war, and this liberation has only become apparent after the Second World War and the advent of the atomic bomb. The Church now repudiates the holy war with a vehemence almost equal to its former approval. The Byzantine emperors, court theologians and intellectuals always regarded this particular manifesta-tion of Western barbarism with horror and amazement. Yet it was not until 1918, while the empire collapsed around his ears, that His Apostolic Majesty, the Emperor Charles I of Austria, was able to release his officers from the *duty* of duelling. Officers of the Catholic empire whose Christian consciences forbade them to duel, had, prior to 1918, been obliged to quit the service.

After the First World War, at the very gates of Vienna, a priest was dis-missed from his post because he dared to preach against the *jus primae noctis* (the right to the first night with every newly-married peasant woman on the manor) which had been claimed by the lord who was his ecclesiastical patron. Generally speaking, within that ancient world, the 'right' was quite willingly accorded to the nobility by their people. To the peasant, it meant an influx of divine strength from the holy blood of great lords, the blood of so many holy ones of the ancient world. In this way he was in communion with them as he was with his dead through feast and solemnity and with material things, elements and nature through his work.

Archaic society was the substructure of European civilization. Western culture, technology and religion had roots in its great unities, connections, identities and relationships. It maintained itself down to the nineteenth century by a network of inter-relationships. Visible and invisible threads tied folk-culture, the monasteries, the towns, the ancient nobility, the companies, fraternities and guilds together. This world and the world above; nature and supernature; God and man; freedom and fate; perception and reason; life and death; soul and body; inanimate and animate; individual and collective; 'I, thou and it' all formed a series of dialectical identities. In the matter-of-fact popular view of things this meant a system of unions and alliances which needed to be renewed, strengthened and reaffirmed through the ritual and rhythm of the cults of feast and holiday, or working life and of the dead. In the majority of cases, European popular speech (and for a long time the people's languages were, in a sense, only dialects of the one common language of archaic society and its people) had no words at all for these dualities and mental distinctions.

These problematical questions belonged to the foreign world of the higher culture. They lacked words for them, because their own problems and questions lay elsewhere. Only towards the end of the fourteenth century, relatively late in European history, did the seamless universe begin to tear apart. The people's speech began to be used in theology and philosophy. For a long while, vernacular poetry (saga and legend, song and epic), in close connection with customary law, was the expression of this folk-wisdom and its conception of cosmos and chaos. A truly comprehensive intellectual history of Europe would have to bring to light the struggle between these two worlds throughout our European millennium. It would have to reunite what history has arbitrarily divided and study both cultures as one: Alcuin's semi-Pelagian court philosophy, and the Song of Hildebrand and Hadubrand; the pomp and circumstance of the humanism of Lupus of Ferrières,[62] and Godescalc's doctrine of grace; Hugh of St Victor's humanist cosmos and the Nibelungenlied; the fairy stories and the spiritualist philosophy of the eighteenth century.

The struggle between the two cultures generally assumed three forms:

(a) An open battle on the part of the higher culture and its governmental order against the folk-culture, which could never be entirely vanquished. The higher culture hurled its prohibitions and enactments of councils, curias, parliaments, universities, academies and faculties against the upthrust and undertow from below. Such definite acts from above were historically clear-cut events occurring at particular moments, and they often provoked rebellion from below (peasants' revolts, heretics' wars, etc.).

(b) Parallel with this state of open conflict, a manifold process of assimilation and accommodation took place. The dress, fashions, architecture, music and dance of the aristocracy and the towns sank down to the level of the people, but so did thoughts, ideas and mental attitudes. Distortion of these ideas occurred frequently and produced bizarre responses among the people. Revolutions and heresies often arose out of misunderstandings of words, concepts, ideas and emotions. Mutilation of an idea often had a strange power to unleash explosive forces in the lower sphere. The migrations along the roads of Europe transmitted the ideas from group to group. The people scavenged in the palace of culture built by those who ruled them and picked up bits of theologies and ideologies and scraps of systems of thought and belief.

(c) Within the great creative personalities a constant psychological dialogue went on between the two worlds. Dreams, visions and childhood experiences of the lower culture fused with their philosophical and theological systems. At the same time, the personal underground of the subconscious mind fed their conscious work from below. At its deepest level their intention was always reconciliation: reconciliation of the upper world, the world of order and government, with the lower world; reconciliation of time (something imposed from above) and eternity, which flows along in the time in flux, time asleep.[63]

SAECULUM OBSCURUM

'The cities are depopulated, the monasteries ruined and burned, the country reduced to servitude. As the first men lived without law or fear of God, abandoned to their passions, so now every man does what seems good in his own eyes, despising laws, human and divine, and the commands of the Church. The strong oppress the weak; the world is full of violence against the poor and of the plunder of ecclesiastical goods. Men devour one another like the fishes in the sea.'[64]

The Synod of Troslé (909) described the collapse of the Carolingian order in these words. In 991, at the Council of Saint-Basle de Verzy, 'the French bishops openly declared their belief in the bankruptcy of the Papacy'.[65] 'We seem to be witnessing the coming of Antichrist, for this is the apostasy of which the apostle speaks—not merely of nations, but even of Churches.'[66] The death of John VIII, whom we encountered earlier as a Pope of renaissance and world-renewal celebrated by John the Deacon, may be taken as a symbol of the breaking of the wave of barbarism over Europe.[67] He had fought a desperate battle against the Saracens and the inroads of anarchy; now his kinsman gave him poison to drink, and beat out his brains with a hammer, because he took too long to die. The papacy seemed to be going down in ruins among the factional quarrels of the Roman aristocracy. In the ghastly 'Corpse Synod' of 897, Pope Stephen VI brought the disinterred body of his predecessor Formosus to trial. Theodora, a virago with all the strength of a Michelangelo Sybil, and her daughters Theodora and Marozia, ruled Rome. The Saracens sacked St Peter's in 846, and so made an end to the Golden Rome of the fourth to ninth centuries. Then, from their stronghold at Fraxinetum in Provence (which Otto the Great captured in 972), they overran and plundered Italy, southern and central Europe as far as St Gall (Pontresina – Pons Sarracenorum). The Hungarians, pouring in from the southeast, swooped down on central Europe and between 899 and 955 got as far as Burgundy and Champagne. The north and northwest, and all the coasts of France, had long been the prey of the Normans, who at last, in 911, settled in France. In all this devastation, the legitimate heirs of Carolingian Christendom took part in full measure. Otto the Great, in a feud with Duke Gilbert, laid Flanders to waste in 939, in 946 Louis and Otto ruthlessly plundered every place which they passed through in their war with each other. Benedict, the monk of Monte Soracte, lamented the new fall of Rome. After the sack by Otto I, King of the Saxons, Rome lay in the dust, ravaged and put to shame. There was a general collapse of the monasteries of Romania. The spiritual and secular nobility, bishops, abbots and laymen, vied with each other, according to the denunciations of Odilo of Cluny,[68] in enmity and ambition, in lust and avarice and rapacity. There was misery among the peasantry (portrayed in the *Miracula Sancti Benedicti*), starvation[69] and peasants' revolts. The life and death struggle between the free peasantry and the robber lords which had been going on from the seventh century assumed catastrophic proportions. The small property owner was rapidly dying out. As early as the eighth century in one small area in Salzburg alone 137 small properties were absorbed into twenty-one ecclesiastical, twelve ducal and seventeen absentee-owned estates. The defeat of the peasant transformed him into the villein, the bond-slave, the crop-eared boor. He was shorn of his hair, the sacred badge of freedom, (*G'scherter* is the word for him in Austria to this day) and thus rendered unfit for religious education and hence for any intellectual cultivation from above.* In effect, the peasant was forcibly enclosed within the archaic world. The defeat of the free world of work, the world of free craftsmen and labourers, sealed the victory of the *artes liberales* and the rhetorical school culture. It brought about the rejection of experimentation, physical exploration and research into nature for more than five hundred years. From now on, in whole areas of Europe, the subject people of the land – *servus*, *rusticus*, knave, barbarian, heretic (the equation goes back to Bernard of Clairvaux) – were to live in a half-wild state with their beasts in the reed and mud huts where St Vincent was to find them in the seventeenth century and Rousseau and Marie Antoinette to discover them in the eighteenth.

As early as the eighth and ninth centuries, the peasants began to form secret societies, the fraternities of the archaic world. Armed with the people's only weapon: terror (ambush and the knife in the dark), they made war upon the nobility.[70] Peasants' risings and revolts were so numerous that the chroniclers did not consider it worthwhile to record them. A peasant revolt did not belong within their literary tradition, which was devoted to the acts of the great world of lordly rule. Many were recorded in other ways and we know that there were peasants' risings in Normandy in 997, in Brittany in 1008, and in Saxony, Friesland, Holland and France throughout the eleventh century. A hundred years after the Normandy rising, Wace celebrated it in song, a sort of peasant 'Marseillaise', crying out for equality and liberty.[71] The France of Richelieu was still convulsed by similar peasant risings.

Organization of these risings was entirely in the hands of those characteristic fraternities of the archaic world. Studies in French and German folklore have revealed that they existed well into the eighteenth century. There were associations of fighting men, associations for cult and festivity, associations of age-groups and whole villages. At an early date certain Christian values began to penetrate these basically pagan societies, bound together by cult and oath. The peasants began to speak of the natural equality of all men and to call for the return to the free state of Adam. Such ideas were immediately denounced as heretical by the rulers and were conveniently exaggerated to

*Even where we find isolated instances of free peasants, their freedom was narrowly restricted. At best, they belonged only to the king and to no one else.

justify repression. As in Spain today, the ruling classes of the tenth and eleventh centuries tended to regard any demand from below as rebellion against the divinely ordained order of things. Yet the charge of heresy was not entirely baseless. The very frequency with which the charge was made is suggestive. It was as heretics that the Bishop of Orléans, Hugh de Noeriis, suppressed the 'hooded men' in 1166.[72]

The battle of the Stedinger against the Archbishop of Bremen is another example of the link between heresy and peasant rebellions. The trouble began when these peasant frontiersmen refused to pay their tribute. Several decades of negotiation and dispute followed, during which the Stedinger proved themselves to be masters of guerilla warfare and delaying tactics. Finally, the inner resistance latent in the folk-culture broke out in armed, external revolt, and for five years (1229–34), an extremely bitter war was waged. After the ignominious defeat of 1229 of the episcopal army, a synod, held in Bremen by Archbishop Gerhard II of Lippe in 1230, declared that the Stedingers were heretics, because they 'despise the Church's overlordship and her sacraments, have no regard for the Church's teaching, attack and kill the clergy, plunder and burn monasteries and churches, break oaths, put the Body of the Lord to such shameful uses as cannot be expressed in words, consult evil spirits concerning the future, make waxen images, follow the counsels of women sooth-sayers, and perform other abominable works of darkness'.[73] In March 1232 the Emperor Frederick II entrusted the Inquisition in Bremen to the Dominicans. In October the Bull of Gregory IX appeared which, after a penetrating analysis of the heresy, proclaimed a crusade against the Stedingers. In May 1234 the crusading army, under the command of the Duke of Brabant and the Counts of Holland, Guelderland, Lippe and Cleves, crushed the Stedingers in a battle which lacked none of the atrocious characteristics of civil and revolutionary war. The whole of the upper world of Europe (see, for example, Matthew Paris) hailed this victory of the Cross over the powers of darkness.

The revolt of the Stedinger is instructive and unusual because the original sources give such a complete picture of archaic folk-culture intermingled with the political grievances. The practices of the Stedingers were to be found among the people right down to the nineteenth century: magical practices with the Host;[74] ritual communication with the dead, with spirits; the great part played by women as mediators between the two worlds.[75] The resistance of the people to the clergy and bishops provoked a crisis on this occasion. It was an expression of their hatred for their masters, which burst out again and again in the numerous murders of bishops, abbots and clerics during the middle ages, often performed with deliberate, i.e., ritual, cruelty. But their revolt also reflected the conscious claim of a cultic community to be self-sufficient. The village felt able to carry out its own functions in house, clan and village through its own fathers, elders, women and children. It did not need an alien priest. The unimportance of the priestly functions for the peasantry can be seen in the fact that such things are totally ignored in the whole body of folk-literature in saga and song.[76] The enormous success of the heretical proclamation by Waldensians, Wyclif, Hus, the *Schwärmer* and the Protestants of the 'royal priesthood' of every 'free Christian man' can certainly be attributed in part to this basic attitude of the peasant villagers.

The tenth century was a crucial watershed. That dark century, *saeculum obscurum*, when alien peoples (Hungarians, Normans, Arabs) broke in from without, and forces of native origin erupted powerfully from below, laid the real foundations of Europe. It might well be called the first century of modern Europe. The veneer of civilization under the Carolingian régime was shattered and the kind of life which was thrust up by these tribes and peoples became terrifyingly visible. These noble families were as untamed as in the days of Gregory of Tours, when Frankish tradition traced the holy and life-giving House of the Merovingians to a union of men with sea-monsters.[77] The wretchedness of the people had grown worse, and it became desperately clear that they had never really been converted. They had not even been touched by Augustine's or Alcuin's *De Catechizandis Rudibus*. Education and scholarship collapsed in its artificial strongholds. The ferocity of this onslaught from below and from without aroused powerful forces of positive reaction.

From the fourth century on, classical civilization and the Christian had begun to go through a peculiar process of distillation and reduction. This process had continued during the ensuing five centuries and in the tenth century, the last period of the great migration of the peoples, the final, decisive concentration of that heritage began. Only those elements of ancient civilization and the Christian faith managed to survive which had genuine powers of endurance. Cluny embarked upon its work of education among the nobility of France, Burgundy and northern Spain. Through its festal liturgy and its cult of the dead it drew more and more noble families into its sphere of influence. Its doctrine and discipline began to fashion the first prototypes of a Christian nobility and thus to make certain that at least one social class was truly converted. For centuries thereafter the nobility remained the only group in society which had completely accepted Christianity. It always remained the class in which that influence was strongest and hence it played a special role in initiating all the movements of reform. This Christianization of the nobility slowly affected sections of the spiritual nobility. The bishops began to develop the idea of the Peace of God and a great wave of building followed even before the end of the tenth century.

The Peace of God movement, starting in the north of France and spreading through the whole of post-Carolingian Europe, was an extraordinary combination of elements of archaic society and of the new Christian and ecclesiastical order. The world had turned into a dreary, unsanctified waste where neither house nor field nor churchyard had remained. Men turned for help to the festal calendar and chose particular times and seasons hallowed by sacred history. They began to fence in little areas of peace. Certain privileged areas, market-places, towns and monasteries, were placed under the protection of particularly powerful saints and the people bore the holy relics into the sanctuaries.

The saints of the Merovingian and Carolingian lines often contributed more as dead men to the building up of a peaceful order, than ever they had as living rulers. One requirement of this peace was the existence of enclosed areas, sheltering and assuring the presence of holiness and safety. Toward the end of the tenth century, as a necessary organic development, people began to build again. The shattered churches and monasteries had to be renewed, a duty which lay upon kings, abbots and bishops.[78] The cathedrals of the empire, which were to set a precedent for the succeeding thousand years, arose. The twelfth and thirteenth century restorations adhered closely to the pattern they were given in the days of Otto. At last genuine construction was possible; not strange, religio-political imitations of Byzantine, Eastern or Roman models, but something authentic. Building was begun by the Christianized elements of the nobility and hurried on by the depth of their anxiety about the end of the world.

Although scholarship has destroyed the legend of a general expectation of the end of the world in AD 1000, it does not deny the fact that the tenth century was a period in which the strength of Western eschatology as a driving force in history and the minds of men became clear. Sheer primitive terror of the end which characterized the age of the invasions ripened into a strong, constructive fear of God. This creative metamorphosis was the result of many forces: of the work of Cluny, of the monastic reform in southern Italy, of the Peace of God movement in northern France, of the wave of building in Germany and of the renaissance, under Otto, of the Carolingian Empire. Fear and hope focused upon the Last Things and an authentic sense of historical realities, something which distinguishes Otto's founding of the Empire from that of Charlemagne, slowly emerged. Significantly women now became the bearers of culture and civilization, and to some extent of the empire itself, for example, the abbesses of Otto's Saxony or the Empress Theophano. The so-called feminine traits in Otto III mirrored the fact that women were the first to attain the new Christian cultural type.

Hrotsvith, the poetess of the Ottonian renaissance, lived wholly in terms of the Christian hope of regeneration.[79] She saw Christ as the (Germanic) World-King, coming in the world-fire to renew the cosmos. For the first time, the old German *muspilli*, the Song of the World-Fire, successfully united folkish, pagan and Christian feeling. The new combination was to form an alloy fit to satisfy the minds of men. Although Hrotsvith belonged to a world of closed societies in which the principle of the renewal of usage and custom was sacrosanct, she dared for the first time to denounce an ancient, holy order of things as *mala consuetudo*. Secure in the Ottonian, Christian Order, she was able to expose the bad old ways, opposed to the progress and enlightenment of Christ. This was her attitude to the culture, the *cultus* of the old pagan Romans.[80] The Ottonian King and Emperor had been ritually established by his coronation in a mixture of pagan folk-custom, the ideas of antiquity and of Christianity. To Hrotsvith, he was the mediator between God and men and the lord-protector of the Church. She called him 'our Solomon' and 'David' who excelled all previous emperors by his *pietas* (a quiet but significant repudiation of Charlemagne). He conquered for Christ the pagan peoples who dwelt outside the Holy Empire, as he had been commanded to do in the coronation service. He established the one true order of peace, the *pax ecclesiae*.

In the eyes of the men who served the Ottonian emperors, the renewal of the imperial office by the coronation in Rome in 962 had made Otto I the new Charlemagne, the new Theodosius and Constantine. The renewal of the *ecclesia* – 'Christendom' – of Churches and monasteries, the renewal of education and culture, and the reconstruction of economic life were intimately connected with the wars against, and missions to, the heathen.[81] All the old renaissance formulas of Carolingian court humanism were now applied to Otto.[82] His followers opposed Byzantium emphatically and resisted the Moslem East which they considered to be very closely linked to it.[83] In 967, in this 'heroic century of the idea of Rome',[84] Pope John XII hailed Otto I as the King who had restored 'Rome, the head of the cosmos, and the universal Church' to her former status in the world.[85]

For all their inner and outer similarities, there was a great difference between the ostentatious humanism of late antiquity and the Carolingian age, and the Ottonian renewal of empire, world and cosmos. Regensburg or Bamberg were, to be sure, hailed as the second Athens, and the renaissance of the *res publica* of some monastery was often celebrated in pompous classical phrases. The abbot was called a consul, the monks senators. Groups of Italian humanists attached to Ratther of Verona or Gunzo of Novara compared each other with the brightest stars of the ancient intellectual firmament. Gerbert was set beside Boethius and Cicero. Nevertheless, the orientation, the outlook and policies of the Ottonian emperors were entirely different. They opposed ancient pagan Rome and were hostile to gilded Byzantium. They erected and extended the empire in missionary struggles with the Slavonic East. Magdeburg, with its relics (e.g., the lance of St Maurice) became the 'capital of the German East'.[86] 'The distance from Würzburg to Bamberg is the measure of the expansion of the German Empire to the east between the middle of the eighth and the beginning of the eleventh century.'[87] This bishopric of Bamberg, founded by the Emperor Henry II, was to be 'a valuable strong-point, consolidating the gains made so far and protecting the flanks of the advance. It was a further stage in the eastward progress of the Slav policy which had already been developed, in a series of far-reaching plans, by Otto I.'[88] A network of churches and monasteries, of property and privilege, was to control the pagan Slavonic East. Benedict VII had already founded S. Alessio on the Aventine as a Slavonic missionary institute.

This work of *cultura Christi*[89] of service to God, empire and Church, was not to be entrusted to the self-interest of secular lords. Local lords would very quickly rob their emperor of any possible successes he might have in his Eastern policy of settlement.* Instead, the Ottonian emperors employed their imperial bishops. These men, the successors of Byzantine imperial bishops and of Roman bishops of the type of Ambrose, were not invented by Otto the Great but under him for the first time they assumed their special character as princes of the empire. They were ardent reformers and were very like the new bishops after the Council of Trent. From Sigebert of Gembloux in the twelfth century[90] to Nicholas of Cusa in the fifteenth and Leibniz at the threshold of the eighteenth, men have looked with justified admiration at this type of *pastor clarissimus*. One of the best of his type was Notker of Liège.[91] Surrounded by his retinue and household, by his great *familia* of knights and by a multitude of men of high rank in the Church and the world, 'there on his throne sits the Bishop of Liège, powerfully wielding the two swords (of secular and spiritual jurisdiction), at once a great king and a great priest'. These imperial bishops, noble in body and soul (their *Vitae* speak in the same breath of their *sanctitas* and their *nobilitas*) were the men who conducted the policies of the empire, and ran the Eastern mission. They were always accompanied by court humanists, singers, *jongleurs* and strolling folk. Their courts were the nurseries of the heroic epic of the Nibelungen, sung in praise of their ancestors and of the *Vitae* which celebrated their holy predecessors in the episcopal sees. They built the empire's cathedrals. But they failed in their policy and missions in the East. In the end they were too weak militarily and spiritually to carry it out.

The short life of Otto III (983–1002) which fell during this period illustrates another difference between Ottonian and Carolingian civilization. During Otto's reign, the melting down of the elements of the classical world, of the archaic folk-world and of Christianity which fused to form the West received an important new element. Otto was the heir of the Carolingians but also of the Greeks. He was hailed as Charlemagne and Louis the Pious, Theodosius and Constantine. In his programme for 'renewing the Empire of the Romans' – *renovatio imperii Romanorum* – he was the heir of their blood, their spirit, their policies and their piety, all of which he bore within himself. The worlds of his father and his mother, Byzantium and Aix, Eastern reform. Italian humanism and ancestral statecraft were at war in him. In his early youth he was fired with an ambition to excel in his mother's world, Byzantium. In his famous correspondence with his tutor Gerbert, he begged him to awaken Greek culture in him so that he could learn to understand the ancient wisdom and culture of which he, as Emperor, was the rightful heir. Gerbert replied: 'Ours, ours is the Roman Empire ... You are ours! Emperor and Augustus of the Romans, sprung from Greek imperial blood, towering over the Greeks by the might of your Empire, ruling over the Romans by right of inheritance, and excelling both by your inborn and acquired culture (*ingenio et eloquentia*).'[92]

Gerbert of Aurillac was the man whom Otto III made Pope Sylvester. He

*The Slavonic aversion to the 'German God' may well have arisen initially from the hatred felt by the Eastern nobility for the alien Germanic missionaries.

was to co-operate with Otto, the 'new Constantine', in restoring the primitive Church and he assured the Emperor that he himself owed all his culture to the three Ottos. In fact he came from another world, the world of southern France and Spain. It was an area of Greek and Arab culture, which was to take powerful and determinative hold on Europe's inner history a century and a half later. In the Ottonian empire and in Rome, Gerbert was a foreign body. Western Christendom later condemned him, and quite rightly, as a sorcerer. After all, he came from that mysterious borderland where Europe confronted paganism, Islam and magic. The young Emperor, too, appeared as a foreign body to the Romans despite, indeed even because of, his concern for Rome, 'our royal city', despite his relations with Italian humanists like Leo of Vercelli and spiritual, ascetical reformers like Nilus and Romuald. Otto III must have been clearly aware of this, which may explain his constant urge to justify and re-justify his origin and his claim to power. He could never be sufficiently endowed with sacred power: hence the tremendous emphasis on the cult and veneration of his dead friend and helper, St Adalbert. He sought to obtain from St Adalbert the same thing which he sought from 'Saint' Charlemagne. Thietmar reported that Otto secretly had the bones of Charlemagne dug up, and took the cross from his neck and some of his clothes. The son needed the sacred power of the father (Charlemagne) and of the great friend of God (Adalbert). He needed the holy monks to give him the power of prayer, sacrifice and asceticism for his colossal task, which was nothing less than subjugating the hereditary power of race to the service of Christ the King. In co-operation with Gerbert, he liberated the Eastern lands from the domination of the Carolingian imperial Church. He gave the Poles and Hungarians an independent national ecclesiastical constitution and thereby confirmed their national existences. In the world of Charlemagne, such a deed would have been parricide: to let men who were *fideles*, believers, slip from the one and only empire-Church! As Dawson rightly says: 'The unity of Christendom was no longer conceived as the unity of an imperialist autocracy, a kind of Germanic Tsardom, but as a society of free peoples under the presidence of the Roman Pope and Emperor.'[93]

In Otto III Louis the Pious rose again, striving for a new authentic Christianity against his father, Charlemagne. Like Louis, whose sons rebelled, Otto also had to pay dearly for his bold undertaking. He was like so many other spirituals – thoroughly enlightened. He exposed the Donation of Constantine as forgery, and had no regard for the Roman citizen's medieval, mystical faith in Rome, in the sense of the *mirabilia mundi* and Cola di Rienzo. His plan for the world was extremely rational in its clarity and simplicity.

Otto intended to give the peoples of the East to Christ the King, of whom he himself was the foremost servant: *Servus Jesu Christi et apostolorum et Romanorum Imperator Augustus*. This was an imitation of the Pope's proudest title: *Servus Servorum Dei*. He was the first servant of Christ and the Apostles, and as the Apostle-Emperor he wanted to reign in Rome not in Aix. Together with the Pope, his revered friend and only true father, he wanted to rule over a new Christendom in which all the realms would serve God. In this conception, Otto anticipated Gregory VII and Innocent III, and beyond them, Maximilian I and Charles V. It was fantastic in its unhistorical and therefore anti-historical rationalism.* The urge to plan on a vast scale without regard to a host of actual historical conditions links Otto III intimately with Frederick II Hohenstaufen and Frederick II of Prussia. Spiritualist rationalism of this sort does not necessarily exclude all awareness of political realities. When the young Emperor withdrew Poland and Hungary from the German Church, he may well have been aware that the interior resources of that Church simply were not adequate to the great task of Christianizing the Slavonic East. The collapse of the Salzburg mission to Bohemia and Moravia pointed out the weaknesses. It was also for this reason that Russia and the Balkans fell to Byzantium. The inner feebleness of the German Church was revealed in the poverty of its achievement in evangelizing the Slavs and other alien peoples within the Empire. It made little progress with the Serbs, Wends, Lithuanians, Letts and Esthonians. Even in the eighteenth century there were still strong pagan islands around Berlin, in Lusatia and in Saxony. When the East rose at last, when Hus, Luther, revolutionary pietism and enthusiasm burst out, the German Church completely collapsed, and all the forces of the old Slav world were liberated.

*In the muddled world of historical fact nothing is quite as fantastic as pure rationalism!

4

THE REVOLUTION FROM ROME

(Eleventh Century)

THE most momentous of all the actions and movements of modern European history was the Gregorian Reform.* From this reform sprang the curial Papacy and the national states, the reforming nobility, the crusading movement, humane urban civilization, scholasticism, modern European mysticism and the spiritualism, philosophical rationalism and philosophical materialism of the last few centuries. Europe's theology and philosophy of history and all the reformations and revolutions of the thirteenth to the nineteenth centuries were profoundly dependent upon the Gregorian movement.[1]

The mixture of classical, folk-archaic and Christian elements in western Europe between the fifth and tenth centuries could only be integrated by a mighty purge. The symbiotic growth of various complex institutions had to be crushed, if Europe was to resist the East and the mighty pressures exerted by it. The pre-Gregorian West was helpless against the seductive power of the East. While the West was struggling with the internal problems left by the collapse of Carolingian hegemony and slowly rebuilding under the Ottonine emperors, important events were taking place in the East. In 860 the Russians first successfully attacked Byzantium. In 988 Prince Vladimir married the Byzantine Princess Anna and was baptized. Russia began to imitate Byzantium and to become its heir. Under Yaroslav the Wise (1016–54), the critical years of German domination over the Papacy, Byzantine Russia achieved an early pinnacle of culture and power. The German King Conrad II and his ally, Knut the Great, were lured into an alliance with Yaroslav against Poland, which was to be the Original Sin of Germany's political history. It undermined the power of Poland, western Europe's sea wall against Russia, Byzantium and Turkey.

At the same time Byzantium itself began to develop fresh and significant energies in political, intellectual and religious life. In 1045 a college of philosophy and law was founded at Constantinople. The monastic, highly intellectualized mysticism of Simeon (1025–92) suggests that the Byzantine spiritual

*Only a brief outline is given in this chapter for two reasons: first, because some of its aspects have already been thoroughly discussed in my other works (*Aufgang Europas* and *Die Tragödie des Heiligen Reiches*, with their accompanying commentaries, Vienna, Stuttgart, 1949, 1953, and various essays); secondly, and more important, because I shall be constantly referring to it throughout the rest of this book.

revival was more than mere political ambition or ideological preparation for a fresh campaign in the sphere of foreign policy. By its history and traditions Byzantium was the master of cultural and matrimonial politics. It subverted the surrounding world by the travels of its monks and humanists and the marriages* of its women. Byzantium was a nightmare which haunted the minds of the early Gregorian reformers.

A third threat to the West was Islam. During the eighth, ninth and tenth centuries, Spain developed a cultural power and splendour against which the West simply could not compete. Especially during the reign of Abdarrachaman III, theology, philosophy and mystical science flourished. In the followin century, Avicenna, who died in 1037, and Gebirol-Avicebron continued to enrich the speculative life of Spain. By the eleventh century, its magnetic power must have been tremendously strong. The suppression of the 'Visigothic' Mozarabic liturgy in 1071 and 1090 was undoubtedly a desperate counter-attack by the Church. The omniscient, blurred and misty erudition of an Alcuin, the superficial humanism of a Lupus of Ferrières, the cosmic speculations of an Eriugena were incapable of resisting the East or Islam. The totalitarian monism of imperial state theology and of pantheistic intellectualism were too seductive.

Obviously, certain spiritual lines would have to be drawn. If an outward stand was to be made, inner freedom was necessary. Hence, there had to be a line between the spiritual and the secular. The clerical Church must be freed from blood (the archaic society) and from soil (imperial domination of the Church). Otto III, as the Apostle-Emperor, had taken the title and hierarchical position of St Paul, who according to a widespread tradition stood higher than St Peter.[2] *Servus Jesu Christi*, the servant of Christ, was St Paul's name for himself, and it was 'as a second St Paul' that the Emperor accepted the call to cleanse the Augean stable at Rome. In a Bull of 980, the Emperor was called the guardian of the Holy Spirit.[3] He led and protected the Church and Christendom. He appointed popes and bishops and advanced the reformation of the monasteries.[4] As a reincarnation of Charlemagne, Otto the Great and Otto III, the Emperor Henry III exercised the same office. His proclamations, the manifestoes of his principles and policies, adopted the sacred, political formulas of Otto I's chancellery. The high point of imperial domination over the Church came at Sutri in 1046 when the Emperor, as Vicar of God and Head of the Church[5] deposed three popes and appointed a new one of his own. At first he was unopposed, because he was the leader of that movement of monastic reform which was fighting, in the name of the Holy Spirit, against the 'old world of sin'.[6] As Protector of Cluny, and in alliance with the Peace of God movement in Aquitaine, Henry gave his Empire peace as a union of the law and grace. He granted freedom to the reformed monasteries by releasing them from their servitude to the bishops and nobility of the old world and taking them under the protection of his Empire and (his) Church. It was a lofty

*cf. the similar penetration-by-marriage of Germany by Russia in the nineteenth century.

and perilous undertaking to protect the Holy Spirit and to carry out the condemnation of the old world, one which was entirely beyond the power of young Henry IV, who was both badly educated and advised. He was a son of the old world who simply did not understand one word of the new language. It was no wonder that he succumbed to Gregory VII, the 'new father'.

The man who began the papal revolution was Humbert, Cardinal of Silva Candida, a son of that Burgundian land which, during the next thousand years, was to be the home of so many conservative and revolutionary spiritualists: Bernard of Clairvaux, the mystics of the fourteenth and fifteenth centuries, Poiret, Rousseau and Albert Schweitzer. Humbert exposed the Carolingian and Ottonian imperial Church as a lie. The German emperors, he argued, had violated the Church of God with their simoniac clergy, their liturgy and their bishops. Freedom for the Holy Spirit[7] and the Church implied the liberation of the clergy from their unworthy servitude to secular lords, from whom they purchased spiritual offices (simony). The Church, now established as a Church of the clergy, was to be freed from the secular empire. The election of bishops and popes was reserved strictly to the clergy which, for the first time, constituted a clerical class in contrast to everything secular.

Every successful revolution creates a new language. New words and slogans bring into focus problems which men have ignored or regarded as unimportant. A good example of this process is what Humbert and his reforming movement did to simony. They took the professional ecclesiastical reformer's technical term for the sale of spiritual offices and made it the battle cry of a revolution which tore the whole of the Carolingian world to pieces. Simony became the name for the adulterous cohabitation of empire and Church under the German emperors, simoniac the word for most of the imperial bishops and higher clergy of the old world. Their consecrations were invalid, the sacraments they administered were without effect. Peter Damian,[8] the great leader of the conservative revolution, the partner, friend and opponent of Humbert and Gregory VII, maintained the unconditional objectivity and validity of sacraments and consecrations administered in the correct form – as did the whole of the middle ages with him. Humbert denied it. For him the sacraments and consecrations of simonists were empty signs. In other words, he declared the grace-bearing activity of 98 per cent of existing bishops and priests invalid. What Humbert wanted was a purely spiritual Church, freed by the Holy Spirit from bondage to the world, the world which had eaten its way deep into the very heart of the Church. His devastating criticism of the secularized Church and his denial of the objectivity of the sacraments were to inspire every left-wing reformer, heretic and spiritualist from the twelfth century on.

If Humbert was to establish his own orthodoxy, and impose the standard of his own true spirituality upon the Church, he had to be extremely careful with his own more radical followers. The reform movement could easily get out of hand, once it had really begun to split all the entities hitherto regarded as indivisible. What would be left after nature and supernature, God and the world, spirit and matter had been completely severed? Hence his battle with Berengar of Tours, whom he forced to recant despite the sympathy and protection of Damian and Gregory VII. Berengar, like Humbert himself was a spiritual descendant of Augustine, the radical spiritualist Augustine, and like Humbert (at least in his doctrine of the unity of the Church) a follower of Eriugena. Again like Humbert, he battled against the popular conception of the unity of God and the world, of spirit and nature. The difference was that Humbert was concerned with the purity of the spiritual Church and Berengar was concerned with the purity of concepts. Berengar viewed with horror the vulgar notion of communion current amongst the uneducated clergy and uninstructed laity. People believed that they were really and literally devouring the flesh and blood of Christ. Berengar denied the belief vigorously and asserted that the material substance of wine and bread were absolutely distinct from the spiritual meaning of the sacrament. The one was mere matter and the other pure spirit. In effect he denied the union of God and the world as expressed in the mystery of the Sacrament. Since he denied that the wine and bread were changed into the blood and flesh of Christ, they became mere signs, a remembrance of Christ who instituted the Sacrament of the altar as his memorial.

The intimate connection between Berengar's intellectual spiritualism and the political spiritualism of Humbert is obvious. The difference between them was, however, vital. If Humbert's Church of the spirit, his Roman Church, did not truly dispense salvation, it could not survive. Berengar's thought threatened the Roman Church with destruction by attacking its most valuable attribute. The hands of its priests had to give God literally to each of its believers in the administration of the Sacrament of the altar. The capacity to offer the Sacrifice of Christ was the exclusive guarantee of the power of saving grace, without which the Church of Rome had no claim against the three ancient realms of salvation: Byzantium, the powerful German emperors, and the salvation system of archaic society. Humbert drew up a formula of belief which he forced Berengar to swear: after the consecration, the bread and wine are the true body and blood of the Lord. This final, decisive, victory of 1079 was the end of decades of struggle.

In 1054, in Hagia Sophia, Humbert had excommunicated Cearularius, the Patriarch of Constantinople. This was *the* schism, *the* break between East and West! Violent, fanatical, partisan and unfair, like all great fighters, Humbert championed the superior purity and spirituality of unleavened bread against the Greeks who clung to the leavened bread of the ancients.[9] The split between East and West led to the transformation of Western Eucharistic doctrine from a spiritual to a Christological concept[10] and thus to a new kind of Eucharistic devotion outside the Mass.[11] It is important to remember how precariously the Western Eucharistic doctrine stood. The ancient kingdoms and all the archaic sacraments binding God and the world had been destroyed by the new spiritualism. The new sacraments of the Roman clerical church were not yet firmly rooted in popular consciousness.* It is understandable that Humbert regarded the Byzantine doctrine of the Eucharist as *preuma* or 'pure spirit' with bitter hostility. He charged that Byzantium had been spiritually conquered by Islam. This was how Humbert saw its spiritualist monotheism, its identification of God and the emperor and its indifference to the passion of the Son of God. For all its obvious injustice, the rebuke contained a kernel of profound truth. East Rome's political monotheism was spiritually very near to Islam. Moreover, Byzantine influences had permeated the West through work of the Spanish *émigrés* in the Carolingian empire. Significantly, Christopher Dawson has called the Ottonian, Salic empire of the tenth and early eleventh centuries 'a kind of Germanic Tsardom',[12] and Rosenstock-Huessy argues that the danger of Western Christendom's becoming a caliphate during this eleventh century was very real.[13]

Humbert realized this. As soon as he returned from Constantinople, he began his struggle with the Carolingian empire by attacking it on the fundamental level of premise and axiom. This was the reason that this first revolution in the West was so effective and so much the model for all succeeding revolutions. Only at the end were its opponents able to set up tenuous ideologies against it. The papal revolutionaries established their own new principles and basic axioms. In his polemical works, Humbert rarely attacked the individual emperors, even the Carolingians. It was the Ottonian *system* of domination over the Church that was the essential evil. Its source was the Carolingian liturgy and sanctified social order. In 1059, at the reform Council of Sutri, Humbert officially exposed the Carolingian Church as the primary instigator of ecclesiastical sin. The councils of the Carolingian Church in 794 and 797 gave the monks licence for that lavish eating and drinking which was their ruin.[14] The sacred culture of feasting and carousing, the *Minnetrinken* of archaic society and the medieval monastic clans, was denounced as a foul practice. With the agreement of all the Roman-Gregorian reformers, Humbert then began his onslaught on the Carolingian liturgy. Humbert and the new Romans wanted to revive golden Rome, the golden St Peter's of the fourth to eighth centuries, and to make it what Leo the Great, the victor over the Huns, had meant when he called the Roman Church 'a holy stock, an elect people, a priestly and royal citizenship (*civitas*), raised by the See of Peter to be the head of the world'.[15] This golden Rome, pure and holy, had been shamefully degraded, because the barbarians and the German emperors had ruined the liturgy.

Instinctively Humbert and Gregory VII recognized that it was here that the 'wicked middle age' had made its most important inroad into the heart of the Church. The Roman liturgy of the fourth to sixth centuries was an expression of the victory won by the *Kyrios Christus* over the *Kyrios Nero*. The *domus aurea*, the earthly Emperor-God's golden house, had been conquered by the

*It was St Thomas Aquinas' Corpus Christi hymn and his *Summa Contra Gentes* that first achieved a real consolidation of Humbert's revolution.

Word spoken by the God-Emperor Christ. Arrayed in the might of the Roman emperor's sacred colours,[16] Christ, the high priest, had assumed the emperor's place. But, in the eyes of the reformers, this Roman liturgy had been degraded by the barbarian emperors and made into *their* liturgy – a pretentious glorification of their own holy majesty. In their exaltation of themselves, they dared to use the royal psalms of the Old Testament. This accusation had a certain basis in fact. Charlemagne had entrusted the revision of the *Sacramentarium Gregorianum* to Alcuin,[17] and further reforms were introduced into his edition of it by Paulus Diaconus, and later on by Helisachar, the chancellor of Louis the Pious. The German emperors – the Ottos and the early Salic emperors – tried to impose their imperial liturgy on Rome. Charlemagne had planned to bind his empire together with liturgical bonds:[18] Christ the holy King, as Judge, Guardian of Peace, King of Peace in the liturgy of Advent and Christmas, was to direct the subject peoples into the way of *fides* – political-religious allegiance to Charlemagne, the King.

Byzantine glorification of the role of the king had been introduced into Europe by the Franks. Theodolf of Orleans, for example, was the author of that imperial salute, the *Gloria Laus et Honor*.[19] The warrior spirit of the Franks found the Roman breviary deplorably lacking in good solid selections from the Books of Maccabees. The Roman liturgy was gradually perverted into a ritual homage to barbarian emperors and kings and their sacred laws of blood and race. Humbert and Gregory wanted to purify and restore it to the classical simplicity of old Rome.[20] It was no longer to serve the Holy Emperor, but St Peter. The emperor was not the only opponent. The Humbert-Gregory front soon faced the terrible antagonism of the archaic, tribal culture of the clerical aristocracy. The imperial and princely bishops, Manasses of Rheims and the German hierarchy, bitterly opposed Gregory's attempts to liberate them from blood and soil, from principality and power. These were men for whom the pomp and splendour of the liturgy was a proclamation and celebration of their own empire – (*riche*). With bitter irony Humbert explained to them that it is not the art of singing which makes a good priest, but 'a good life'.[21]

As representatives of the Roman Renaissance in its struggle against the barbarians, Humbert and Gregory proceeded to solidify the position of the Roman pope. In 1046 Pope Clement II proclaimed himself the successor of the early Roman Pope Clement I. For the next hundred years, till Lucius II (1144–5), each reforming pope celebrated in himself the rebirth of a pope of the primitive Roman Church, whose name he bore. It was a counter-demonstration against the reborn Charleses and Ottos, and the Hohenstaufen Fredericks. This self-proclamation was one of the most remarkable demonstrations in history.[22] It gave the Christian rebirth its setting within the realm of grace, the clerical *civitas*, and denied the sacral-political rebirth within the archaic community and in the emperor's *sacrum imperium*. Their campaign was not confined to the names of the emperors. Gregory VII stripped the ancient community of *all* its sacred names – i.e., of all the bases of its law and its very existence – and transferred them to his own empire of grace. Otto III had sought to regard himself as a new Paul. Gregory, the Pauline Pope, was the first to put Paul side by side with Peter on his coins (as later popes did on their seals).[23] Henceforward the Roman Church was the Church of Peter and Paul, the presence on earth of the power of God, of law and of the spirit.

Gregory was able to achieve his initial success in this colossal 'expropriation of the Expropriators', to use Marx's phrase, only because he himself was *filius fabri*, a man of the common people who was at the deepest level both bound to and estranged from the magical bonds of that people. Damian described his great friend as 'a holy Satan', a union of extreme opposites. Like the magicians of archaic society, Gregory tells us that he heard every thought in the mind of Odilo of Cluny, though travelling far behind him on the road.[24] He was a wizard of the ancient world when he laid upon the Emperor Henry IV the ban of his bulls of excommunication and deposition: 'Victory do we take from his weapons; not only in the spirit do we bind him, but even in this natural world ...'[25] 'No (sacred) power in battle shall he have, nor any victory, to the end of his days.' To his contemporaries this act seemed demonic. Gregory stripped the sacred power from the old world with the old world's own weapons. When that world had recourse to its saints, Gregory confronted it with his holy patrons and protectors, Peter and Paul, and solemnly declared that there had been in all history very few truly holy kings and emperors. History was a record of endless persecution of the true Church of God by the evil sovereigns of the world. Hrotsvith, the Ottonian nun, had timidly hinted at the idea of *mala consuetudo*; now it became the ideology of a revolution. Five thousand years of 'evil custom', declared Anselm of Lucca, 'cannot turn injustice into justice'.[26] The whole outlook of archaic society and its medieval heirs was mortally wounded by this blow. The 'good, old law' was stripped of its power to save.

Only a few years before, the 'holy emperor' had been deposing unholy popes. Now Gregory declared that any priest, the very least of clerics in the lowest degree of orders in the new spiritual Church of spiritual men, possessed more saving power than all the kings and emperors on earth.[27] A later canonist, Hugo Hostiensis, was to establish that the dignity of a priest was precisely $7,644\frac{1}{2}$ times higher than that of a king, for such is the proportion, by Ptolemy's reckoning, between the sun and the moon. It was vain henceforth for the emperors to array themselves in the sun-mantle, and – as did Frederick I and Frederick II – to have their propagandists hail them as the true sun and the invincible sun. The ban and the solemn excommunications of Gregory VII reduced Henry IV, the 'holy Emperor by blood and by rite' to the naked man of sin. The de-sacralization of the ancient ruling power formed the definitive basis for Europe's great dualities. It set Church and state, religious and secular, materialist and spiritualist against each other. At the same time, it created a polarized field of tension in which the liberties of modern Europe, heirs of the *libertas ecclesiae*, found room to grow. The violence of this attack led, in turn, to the fifty-year battle over Investiture between the pope and the Salic emperors. The gregorian reform was, in a sense, a triumph over the East.[28] The remarkable document of 1075 known as the *Dictatus Papae*, records that 'the Pope alone shall bear the imperial insignia'. 'All princes shall kiss the Pope's foot.' 'He alone shall be spoken of by name in the liturgical prayer of all churches.' 'He can depose Emperors.' None can judge him.' 'Every Pope is sanctified by the merits of St Peter.' 'The Pope can himself, without a synod, condemn bishops.' *Unicum nomen est papae.* 'The Pope is the one representative of God on earth; he bears the keys of heaven and hell.'

These world-shattering propositions were directed not only against Constantinople and Aix[29] but against all hitherto self-sufficient saviour-rulers of the archaic world. The secular nobility, in communion with all their comrades living and dead, had also dispensed salvation, each in his own realm, *riche* or *regnum*. If modern Europe* was to be created as a union of secular and spiritual realms (*regna*) under the patronage of the pope, the bishops had to be detached from the governmental order of the ancient folk-community and the clergy from the world of their kindred and from the ties of marriage, blood and soil. Like all revolutionaries, Gregory was not afraid of such a utopian undertaking, even if it involved centuries of protracted struggle. The behaviour of the bishops of the period after the Council of Trent indicates that as late as the seventeenth and eighteenth centuries very little progress had been made. But the foundation was laid, in principle, by the imposition of celibacy upon the clergy. The demand that the secular clergy, and not only the small band of universally admired ascetics, should lead a purely spiritual life appeared to the ancient world as unnatural, even monstrous. Gregory was forced, in order to carry it out, to burden his renovated papacy with a series of highly perilous alliances. He supported the radical, popular movement of the *Pataria* in Milan, the enemy of all 'great, rich lords' who attempted to make an adulterous union between the world and the priesthood, and adopted the revolutionary spiritualism of the later Augustine, and the no less revolutionary rationalism of the dialecticians associated with Berengar of Tours.

The consequences of Gregorian celibacy for Europe's spiritual history were far-reaching. A special realm of the spirit was detached from the world. An entirely new field of tension was created in which pioneers of the mind and of the heart were to set about constructing a new set of relationships between God and the world and between man and woman. A new kind of purely intellectual labour was made possible, out of which the pure research and pure science of a later age was to grow. At the same time a remarkable culture of the heart evolved. Not only were priests and nuns new men and women in a literal sense, but all men and women were related in a new, spiritual way. Whereas the archaic world had regarded marriage and sex entirely in terms of legal status, the post-Gregorian Church spoke of spiritual and sacramental

*It was the reforming popes who began again to speak of Europe!

union.* Love was possible outside of marriage, and there were marriages of the spirit like those of Abélard and Héloïse, or Francis de Sales and Jeanne Françoise de Chantal. The single man, who lived a life of celibacy, resisted nature and the world and the tension generated by this resistance was inherently creative.

Gregory and his successors won the support of only one genuine ally, the young nobility. As a result, this nobility was the first to reap for itself the fruits of the quarrel. It rejected its old fathers for its new father, the pope, and by handing over to him its (reformed) monasteries, it went on to receive an education. For the first time, a thoroughly reformed, coherent class took shape, which expressed its ripening self-consciousness in the new religious orders: Cistercians (1098), Premonstratensians (1120), Carthusians and Carmelites. In the secular world the courtly culture of the Christian knight of the twelfth and thirteenth centuries began to emerge. The knight received the consecration and anointing which were formerly reserved for king and emperor. He was the new king and emperor, who built himself a kingdom of grace in monastery and court (Gottfried of Strasbourg's *minne-grotte*). From 1096 on, he waged the new wars, the crusades, against Islam in the East and in Spain, against Byzantium, against the Albigensian heretics, against primitive peasant leagues (the Stedingers) and pagans (Prussians). He lived the new life (Dante's *Vita Nuova*).

The iron law of the spiritual dialectic was to bind Europe for the next thousand years in the tension of spirit and matter. Gregory VII won his final personal victory while suffering his last defeat. His last words, while he lay dying, after fleeing from Rome, denied the claims of the kings of the ancients. 'I have loved righteousness and hated injustice,' he said, 'therefore, I die in Exile.' The psalmist of the Old Testament had sung: 'Thou hast loved justice and hated iniquity, therefore God the Lord anoints thee with the oil of salvation.' The psalm belonged to the old world. The king or bishop of the psalmist was the man blessed with the power of grace, who achieved earthly and heavenly dominion, saving power and victory. Heaven and earth were united in a single, continuous order of law and fate. Gregory's last words spoke of the new world: heaven and earth confronting one another. The servant of God could triumph on earth only in persecution and death.

From the late eleventh century until the thirteenth century, all the symbols of power (throne, crown, royal robe), the rites and formulas, and the wordly status of emperor and king were transferred to the papal Church. Innocent III sat as judge upon the kings of the earth, as once Otto the Great and Henry III had upon popes. Imperial law was broken by canon law; the Papal University suppressed the emperor's palace and monastic schools; scholasticism triumphed over the symbolic, universal lore of the old world. In the long run, there were other consequences for Europe. The cities of Italy and the kingdoms of

*The reformed Church's canon law began immediately, right from the twelfth century, to fulminate against the concept of marriage as a legal instrument between families.

France, England, Hungary and Spain became western Europe, grouped with the *Curia* against Germany, which now became the new Eastern Empire. The 'Empire' and German thought suffered a blow from which it never recovered. For seven hundred years German political life was to be subjected to peculiar strains and tensions arising from the shattering defeat of the emperor. German thought, from Otto of Freising via Nicholas of Cusa to Leibniz, Kant and Hegel, never managed to get over the fall of the holy emperor.[30] Attempts to restore the emperor were made, and in the years immediately following the Investiture dispute the Hohenstaufens strove to renew the 'Holy Empire' of Charles and the Ottonians. Walther von der Vogelweide spoke for huge sections of the population when he expressed his hatred of the pope 'who perverts the right order of things'. Wolfram von Eschenbach sought in the kingdom of the Holy Grail a way of reconciling the ancient royalty of blood with the new spiritual order. Gottfried of Strasbourg sneered both at the imperial and at the ecclesiastical order of salvation. They were lies and pretence. Hildegard of Bingen foresaw the utter collapse of the papal Church. German poetry manifested deep suspicion of this new Rome. From the twelfth to the nineteenth century it practically ignored the pope. Nor would it acknowledge the holy man, a priest, the new father of the new world, now liberated from the dominion of race. The West accepted him: *padre, mon père*, Father. The ultimate rejection of Gregory VII by the German world was its refusal to call the new Gregorian priest its father.

5

THE BIRTH OF HISTORY
(Twelfth Century)

THE twelfth century was the first century of modern European historical thinking. Rupert of Deutz, Hugh of St Victor, Anselm of Havelberg, Hildegard of Bingen, Ekbert of Schönau, Gerhoh of Reichersberg, Otto of Freising, Joachim of Flora appeared at the same time, a phenomenon which was unparalleled until the nineteenth century. Creative historical thinking occurs only in times of crisis. When men find the standards of the past no longer valid, and when they are uncertain or fearful of the future, they turn to history. They seek to understand what has happened, while searching for an idea of what may happen. Thucydides and Augustine, Otto of Freising and Hegel all belong to such periods. Thucydides was confronted with the ruins of the old Athenian democracy and the Attic *polis*; Augustine experienced the collapse of the Roman Empire; Otto of Freising sought an explanation for the decline of the Carolingian empire, and Hegel confronted the end of a thousand years of Carolingian-Christian humanism which stretched from the *Veni Creator Spiritus* of Rhabanus Maurus to the re-creation of that hymn by another poet of the Main valley, Goethe.

The historical thinking of the twelfth century grew out of western Europe's attainment of self-consciousness. The challenge of Byzantium, Islam and Hellenism and the challenge made by Gregory to the old pattern of unity between kingdom and priesthood in the *ecclesia* were the formative influences in this growth. Naturally enough, the meaning and value of the old empire and the old Church were the crucial questions for the historians of the twelfth century. The polemical literature of the investiture dispute had for the first time consciously thrown open all the fundamental questions concerning the medieval world, and in a sense the historiography of the twelfth century was a late flowering of German Carolingian symbolist theology. From the beginning it had very little hope of survival in a world increasingly dominated by the anti-historical prejudices of the scholastic theologians.* After the thirteenth century there was no innately European historical thinking until the enlightenment.† The history of the Church and the heresies, and the *renovatio* and *rinascita* of Manetti and the renaissance philosophers must be regarded as

---

*Bonaventure alone made an attempt to salvage the concrete individual event.

†It is significant that Lessing, and Herder after him, chose the twelfth century as a starting-point.

marginal. The Jesuit's *ratio studiorum*, the influence of which extended far beyond any confessional boundaries, allotted only a modest place to history, beside rhetoric among the fine arts. In order to define the particular standpoint of this twelfth century historical thinking it would be useful to establish what it was *not*, to see what fields of thought were not included in it, and to examine those authors and works, which, although closely related, do not, in fact, belong to the category of historical writing with which we are concerned here.

First, there was the sphere occupied by the chronicles, among which were works as diverse as the old world chronicles in the style of Ekkehard of Aura, the royal chronicle of Cologne, and the Italian city chronicles. In all these a new world proclaimed its consciousness of its surroundings. Certain traits in the chronicles were reminiscent of Orosius and Augustine and of Tychonius's exigesis of the Apocalypse, and others reflected current medieval views on the subject of Antichrist. This kind of historical writing formed a genus of its own.

A sub-species of the chronicle was the regional history. The historical works of such a man as Ordericus Vitalis, which were products of the spirit of the Norman State, belong in this rubric. John of Salisbury's history of the popes, and the increasing flood of *vitae* of secular personalities, for example, the life of Louis vi by Suger of Saint-Denis, of Boso's life of Alexander iii, although unmistakably animated by particular points of view and political tendencies, can not be compared with Otto of Freising's portrait of Frederick, or the figure of Francis of Assisi as seen by the Fraticelli. The crucial difference was that in the biographies by Friesing and the Fraticelli one person's life-story was treated as part of a co-ordinated pattern, symbolizing an idea within an interpretation of world history. They contained a comprehensive ideological programme with a specific vision of the universe.

There was yet a third group which is harder to grasp and define. It began with that category of writings which Martin Buber, in his *Moses*, calls 'historical legends'. It included Geoffrey of Monmouth's genealogical construction of the Arthurian cycle, Godfrey of Viterbo's *Pantheon*, and led straight on through the Passau *Anonymous* into the rich world of late medieval and humanist genealogical poetic history.[1] In these genealogical constructions the whole of world history, known or invented, from Noah to Alexander the Great and from Caesar and the early Celtic princes to Charlemagne, was used to fulfil a specific purpose. It cannot be denied that they reveal a closed, self-contained vision of history, but it was not historical thinking in the sense used here. Western Europe, under England's leadership, arrived very rapidly at historical writing of a realistic and often astonishingly critical kind, but, by contrast, the Germans, and a few Italians, began to *think* history. They were deeply stirred by the collapse of the holy empire and the encounter with the world of the Eastern Church. The English, then, wrote history. Their young Norman State was on the upward grade. The Germans and Italians *thought* history, because they had to work out the riddles of their own collapse and oppression, and of their encounters with the spiritual world of the East.

The historical thinking of the twelfth century was a philosophy of history. It borrowed the tools of symbolist theology, and used concepts reaching back to Augustine. The patristic doctrine of the four-fold sense of scripture often appeared in Carolingian theology in the simplified form of an allegorical interpretation of holy writ.[2] The way led through *littera* and *vox*, through the letter, to the spiritual significance. The historical events of the Old and New Testaments were believed to have more than one meaning. They were figures and primal images of realities in a moral sense and contained truths about the meaning of salvation. The great historians of the twelfth century believed that there was no such thing as a history of a particular nation, kingdom or historical personage; there was only the history of the world. One thing in which, from its beginning to its end, all history was involved. This world history was seen under two aspects. On the one hand it was a vast process of development and enlightenment. God and Christ were the great pedagogues, educating man through the Holy Ghost to the fullness of the age of Christ. On the other, it was an unceasing battle, as Tychonius had already shown, between the *corpus Christi* and the *corpus diaboli*, as in Augustine, between the *civitas Dei* and the *civitas diaboli*.

The historical thinking of the twelfth century, as was that of Bossuet and Voltaire, was built upon Augustine. Universal use was made of his images and concepts, and Otto of Freising modelled the eighth and last book of his Chronicle of the World upon the twentieth to twenty-second books of the *De Civitate Dei*. Nevertheless, the twelfth century historians were not strictly Augustinian. Just as the great builders of the middle ages (Charlemagne is only one example) used the buildings of antiquity as quarries, taking from them stones with which to construct their own cathedrals, churches and palaces, the intellectuals and scholars used Augustine. His works produced the materials for all the great movements during the middle ages. In the Carolingian conception the *civitas Dei* was identified with Christendom united in *regnum* and *sacerdotium*, with the emperor its highest lord, protector and shield. The idea of the papal *imperium*, regarding the pope as the supreme ruler of Christendom, was a branch of the same ideology.

The abiding concerns of this historical thinking were as conservative as its conclusions were revolutionary. Rupert of Deutz, Hugh of St Victor, Ekbert of Schönau, Gerhoh of Reichersberg, Hildegard of Bingen and Otto of Freising were aiming at a comprehensive restoration of the ancient world, or more concretely, at a restoration of the ancient unity of God and the world. They examined the available facsimiles of this unity, the *regnum* and *sacerdotium* in the one *ecclesia*, and found that, as a result of the struggle over investiture, the political foundations of this unity had been badly shaken. When they attempted to clarify the situation, as often happens in history, the clarification, interpretation and vindication of an old world was the way to a new reality.

The basic ideas in their historical thinking were first to be found in Rupert of Deutz's works, *De Trinitate et Operibus Ejus*, *De Victoria Verbi Dei*, and *De Glorificatione Trinitatis et Processione S. Spiritus*. World history was considered as an unfolding of the Trinity, especially of the Holy Ghost. For Rupert, the third 'reign' was the *imperium pietatis*, the empire of Christ, which had overcome the four empires of the world. Even the *regnum Romanorum* would at last give place to the *regnum aeternum*, the reign of Christ. *Princeps mundi diabolus*. Rupert devoted a whole chapter to proving that the kingdoms of men are a fiction, *simulata* as he called them. The only true *imperium* over cosmos, nature and man belongs to the Emperor Christ. Rupert transformed the difficult, ambiguous, earthly and political concept of empire into a liturgical concept of *imperium*, but it would be a mistake to describe Rupert simply as a spiritualist. There was a German folk-quality about his revival of patristic theology with its emphasis on creation, incarnation and the grace-bearing value of all created things. Everything was, under certain circumstances, a sacrament.*

Hugh of St Victor died in Paris in 1141. He was probably, by origin, a member of the German nobility, who had become a monk. He was the representative historical thinker of his age. For him, world history was a work of grace, the narrative of God's triumphs in history. The massive religio-political interpretation which the earlier imperial theology had put upon Augustine's *civitas Dei* constituted the basis of this thought. Political history was the story of the spread of the Kingdom of God. Every single earthly event had its meaning within the framework of the story of redemption. Six epochs and three ages of the world were the stages in the progress of the Kingdom of God in history. Christ, the exemplar, the pattern of creation, had appeared in the midst of these ages. This conception of progress was a source of trouble for Hugh, and, indeed, for others of the same period. Was progress a perpetual renaissance, a *renovatio imperii*, a constant process of return to the same original sources, or was there a real growth, a development in which the beginnings were surpassed? Were new things always to be regarded as evil, heretical and sinful innovations? Neither Hugh nor his disciple, Otto of Freising, were entirely clear on this point. On the one hand, he was bound to the Augustinian sense and pathos of eternity. It is possible that Augustine's most powerful experience was that of the *Deus immutabilis*, the unalterable God, not subject to any of the fluctuations and changes which affect empires and persons. Similarly, for Hugh, every *mutatio* in history was a decline from the *stabilitas* of paradise. Things and men change because they are affected by sin, and have thus lost their static condition of perfection. On the other hand, Hugh subscribed to a different, sharply defined idea of progress. Even measured by earthly kingdoms, world history was ripening to the fullness of the stature of Christ. This is evident in his idea of a *status excellentior*: different kingdoms, persons and men of various classes all live at the same time; but one is chosen

*The number seven had not yet been fixed.

from amongst them to be the bearer of progress. The only earthly kingdom which is of importance is that *imperium* which is the bearer of the Kingdom of God.*

Hugh paid no attention to the Investiture dispute. His ideal was a harmonious co-operation of laity and clergy in the one Church, under the leadership of the spiritual power. By consecration and anointing the earthly kingdom could be changed into that *corpus Christi* which Christ, the warrior King, leads forth to his battles and victories. The emperor may play a role in this vision of the world, but he is not necessary to it. Hugh believed that there had been a movement from East to West in world history,† and that the *novus ordo*, a monastic renewal of the Church as the image of the Heavenly Jerusalem,[3] would usher in the truly new age. Although Hugh put the idea of the *novus ordo* to use in a conservative cause, others like Joachim of Flora and Anselm of Havelberg, were to release the latent explosive power inherent in it, with extraordinary results for later history.

Hugh's ultimate concern, which drove him to write, was the threat to theology. The old, patristic, Carolingian theology was endangered by the rationalistic thought of early French scholasticism. The exigencies of this defence compelled him to a consideration of history which was, for him, simply the history of redemption, and his theological speculations were very often no more than veiled historical reflection. Throughout this century, things rooted in the needs of the day motivated historical thinking. Among the German clergy, the after-effects of the Investiture dispute led to a restless search for sacred law. The question of the true status of the empire within the history of redemption acted as a powerful stimulus to thought and forced men to a reconsideration of things. As is often true in history, the simple, almost primitive thinkers achieved the clearest expression of the problems of the age. The plainest defence of the historic rights and unique status of the old empire and its imperial Church within the framework of world history appeared not in the great work of the imperial Bishop Otto of Freising, but in the anti-Catharist sermons sent by the Rhineland cleric Ekbert of Schönau to his boyhood friend and schoolfellow, Rainald of Dassel.

In Catharism, Ekbert, Canon of Bonn, had seen the manifestation of a kind of spiritualism which rejected the whole secular, religious and historical order of the old empire and the old Church. Worse, it aimed at exposing them as deceits of the devil. For these heretics, with their strict dualism, any understanding of the union of God and the world in the Sacraments, in the Church, in the imperial episcopal hierarchy or in the *sacrum imperium*, was wholly impossible. They were spiritualists for whom history – the history of salvation – was always crypto-history, the secret history of the lives and work of a few *illuminati*. They were champions and martyrs of pure doctrine who bore

---

*This was the point of departure for Otto of Freising.

†An Augustinian idea, which reappears in Otto of Freising, of the migration of kingdoms and cultures from East to West in the path of the sun.

"the light of faith"* through the darkness of a world history which had fallen prey to the evil one. As a challenge to the Cathars, Ekbert developed the historical outlook of the German imperial clergy. His object, as he repeatedly affirmed, was to establish the uninterrupted continuity and legitimacy of the imperial Church within the framework of the universal Church. He placed enormous value upon the conversion of Germany by direct disciples of St Peter and St Paul, and the dominant role of Charlemagne, patron of the imperial house of Otto and the Hohenstaufen and canonized, as a matter of high politics, by order of Frederick I.† For Ekbert, Charlemagne had been the steward of the Church, its patron, and also its great teacher, the truest missionary of the Christian faith. The one *fides*, imposed by Charlemagne with sword and Gospel, was, Ekbert insisted, the *fides* of St Peter and of all Roman emperors and kings down to the Roman Emperor Frederick and the French King Louis. In relation to this religious and political conception of fealty, the Cathars were not only guilty of heresy but also of treason.

In reality, the Cathars' main attack had not been against the empire but against the Church. They sought to produce historical evidence that the Catholic bishops and popes had long ago lost the apostolic succession through the corruption of their morals and their abandonment of the pure doctrine of the Gospel. The Catholic Church was no longer the bearer of salvation – the true meaning of history – but an adulterous association of simoniac bishops, superstitious doctrines and worldly and criminal lords. The bishop's consecrations were invalid, the cathedrals and churches unhallowed, the whole life of the Church an empty outward semblance, devoid of any interior, historically authentic power of grace or justification. They denied Europe's understanding of itself and reduced the significance of its history to the account of a continual process of decay. The Cathars were the precursors of the Italian humanist critics of the middle ages (the concept of the *tempus medium* came from the spiritualist Tertullian) and the whole decline-and-fall ideology of the Protestant sectarians – Weigel, Franck, Gottfried Arnold, and later Lessing, Gibbon and so on down to Harnack. They were all descendants of these spiritualists, against whom Ekbert of Schönau, a cleric of the Hohenstaufen Empire, endeavoured to array proof of the continuity of grace in empire and Church.

The Cathars, described by Bernard of Clairvaux, and again by Ekbert, as scum of the earth, *genus vile et rusticum*, hiding from the light in the cellars of Cologne, were not the only ones who pronounced this condemnation upon European history. The heretical spiritualists had great and legitimate forbears. The reformers who had preceded and surrounded Gregory VII and Humbert of Silva Candida, had already stripped the empire of its saving significance and

*Men of the age of enlightenment would say, the light of pure reason; humanists, the light of true classical learning and culture.

†Voltaire, for equally political reasons, condemned Charlemagne as part of his campaign for the desacralization of the Bourbon *roi thaumaturge*.

rights. They had thus branded the history of the West with the character of decay and decline. In order to avoid any contact with the desacralized and accursed *imperium* of the Germans, the reformers had created a new concept of Christendom, that of a single Christian Europe, This entity included all European *regna* subordinate to the pope and was supposed to include the Christian East as well. Urban II gave expression to it, when he appealed to the Byzantine Emperor Alexius for support for his crusade: *Id mihi et universae Christianae rei publicae jucundissimum fore.* Such a sweeping claim merely provoked the inevitable counter-attack from the imperial theologians. Petrus Crassus in his defence of Henry IV, branded Gregory VII as 'the enemy of all Christendom', *totius Christianitatis hostis.* Almost as a by-product of the struggle, a new idea of Europe was forged. One can see it in the words of the message to Henry V after the Concordat of Worms with which Calixtus II deplored the heavy damage done to the faithful of Europe by the long feud between Church and empire: *Quantum diuturna ecclesiae imperiique discordia Europae fidelibus intulerit detrimentum'* – Europe had become *Christianitas,* a synonym for the faith. Under such circumstances the task of defending the historical position of the empire became almost impossible.

Gerhoh of Reichersberg was another *homo simplex,* as the French scholastics disdainfully called the German theologians. He too was uncertain about the sacred significance of the old empire and of world history. There is no space here to go into all the waverings and hesitations of his vision of the world and its history, as mirrored, for instance, in his *Libri Tres de Investigatione Antichristi,* his *Tractatus de Schismaticis,* his famous commentary on Psalm LXIV or his *Liber de Edificio Dei.* By the time of Frederick I, Gerhoh had arrived at a more optimistic conception of history than his earlier view that the *Imperium* and the empires of the world would succumb to a maelstrom of war and inner decay. Now he declared that the *Imperium* would exist until the end of time. His kings and emperors emerged from unhallowed darkness. They were no longer enemies of God and at odds with the course of history. These modifications followed the political evolution of their author. He was in turn a champion of ecclesiastical reform and of the higher secular clergy and finally changed from a passionate adherent of the Gregorian party to a peaceable supporter of the policy of compromise between the emperor and the pope.

His enormous significance in relation to the historical thinking of the age, and his extraordinary effect on succeeding centuries, however, were less the result of his optimism than of his expression of a closed system of historical pessimism. In his *De Quarta Vigilia Noctis,* we can find the decadence theory in its classic pattern. According to the decadence theory, world history is one long process of decline. In the dark night of barbarism, unbelief and moral ruin (later on the starting point was to be pure civilization and classical culture) the light of faith (later of pure morality, culture and reason) is held aloft only by a few individual heroes. This was the orthodox version of the

Cathar vision of history. There were, however, important differences between the Cathar's account and the orthodox one.

Gerhoh believed that the black night of barbarism was periodically broken by the night-watches of his individual saints and heroes. In the first watch of the night, the age of Christ, the beginning of the new age, the Apostles watched and did battle and were victorious until 'the empires of the world were subjected to the *Imperium Christi*'. The second watch was kept by the Church, battling against the great heretics of the early centuries. The third was an inner struggle against the *corruptio morum*.* This watch lasted from Gregory I to Gregory VII. The fourth watch began after Gregory VII and included the whole modern age up to the Day of Judgment. During this time, the worst threat to Christendom was that of internal disintegration. Ambition, avarice and lust for power had seduced the popes, and Christ was about to abandon the ship of the Church, which seemed ready to sink in the tempest of the world. During this fourth vigil it was not so much the popes who kept watch as the *beati pauperes spiritu*, the poor and humble in the Holy Spirit. Gerhoh bitterly reproached the popes with their desire for wealth and power and pointed to the example of the 'poor man Christ' and the 'poor man Peter'. Gerhoh's thinking provided an important link between the historical ideas of the Gregorian reformers and the left-wing heretical sects. This Bavarian provost's vision of history was to have considerable influence in the growth of Franciscan spiritualism in the thirteenth and fourteenth centuries. Through them, the decadence theory of history passed into renaissance historiography and thus on to the present.

The doctrine of decadence was also important for Hildegard of Bingen, but much more important for this extraordinary personality was the ancient German vision of the world with its union of God and nature, God and the world, the empire and the Church, the person and the liturgical community. Her life's work is unintelligible without some grasp of that old pre-dualist world. Hildegard of Bingen was probably a member of the noble house of Bermersheim, whose nephews Archbishop Arnold I of Trier and Provost Wezelin of St Andrew's at Cologne were leading members of the imperial clergy. Unfortunately, there is no critical edition of her works, so that we are still not in a position to make an accurate judgment of their genesis or their influence in twelfth-century Germany. The corpus of her collected letters, as it stands, is an intricate mixture of fact and fiction, genuine material and typical twelfth-century monastic invention.[4]

Certain features are clear enough for a preliminary study. For Hildegard, world history was the history both of the macrocosm and the microcosm. It was the account of the santification and purification of the individual elements of nature and of the large units of political and social life. To bring them back to their first perfection was Christ's deed, and the deed of the *Corpus Christi*, the *Ecclesia*. The *Ecclesia* was Christendom, not the Church of the clergy or

*How clearly one can trace the line of development down to Harnack!

the laity. The process of purgation and purification included wind and weather, herb and animal as well as *regnum* and *sacerdotium* and all the degrees of secular and clerical society of her day. In the course of five ages of the world, the omnipotent God disciplines and educates mankind to a state of inner and outer maturity. Hildegard used great symbols drawn from the visual arts of the Gothic period to portray these ages: the age of the fiery hound (crude power), of the tawny lion (the agonies of war), of the dun horse (frivolity and luxury), of the black swine (corruption and schism), and, last of all, the grey wolf (the age of Antichrist). Swarms of heretics, following closely upon each other, each deadlier than the last, were to sweep down upon the lands of Christendom. Empire and imperial throne would collapse because of the *desidia*, the culpable weakness of the Emperor.* The princes and kings of the West would then assert their independence, and the fall of the papal Church would follow. Priests and people were to achieve religious independence, reducing the pope's domination to Rome and its immediate environs ... Every country would take over the ordering of its own *religio* and *fides*. After the downfall of the empire and papacy, Hildegard looked forward to a glorious last age of the cosmos before the Final Judgment, but it was her vision of general collapse which had real historical influence. Around 1220 Gebeno of Eberbach gathered these visions together in his *Pentachronon*, and in this readily accessible form they became known throughout the middle ages and through all Europe as far as Iceland. The *Magdeburg Centuriatori*, the sixteenth-century spokesman of the Protestant ideology of history, were to appeal to Hildegard as a key witness for the Lutheran Reformation.

Otto of Freising is the best-edited and most frequently consulted historical thinker of the twelfth century. He was a remarkable man, a member of the Salic and Hohenstaufen royal families, a bishop of the empire, and a Cistercian at the same time. His historical study was prompted by one vital question: the *gravis questio de regni ac sacerdotii justitia dissensio*, the search for the meaning, in terms of grace and justice, of the great conflict between emperor and Church. The decline of the empire corresponded to the rise of the Church. In an attempt to make sense of this fact, Otto developed his vision of history from various basic concepts of Augustine's. The *regni mundi*, the ancient kingdoms of the world were declining. Gradually, *paulatim* (this Augustinian idea is particularly important), interrupted by setbacks yet still continuing, the *civitas Dei* rose upwards like the sun. This progress is matched by a progress in the *civitas terrena* – a progressive worsening, in three stages: *primus miser, secundus miserior, tertius miserrimus.*

The three-stage law in world history appeared again in Anselm of Havelberg and Joachim, and continued to influence historical thinking down to Hegel and Comte and beyond. In Otto of Freising's version, before Christ the *civitas Christi* existed on the first level under the rule of the Old Testament and

* *Desidia* was a key propaganda word in Hohenstaufen imperial documents, and held a pre-eminent place in the *Ludus de Antichristo*.

in the pagan world which was closely connected with it. Like his master Abélard, Otto stressed the intimate connection of pagan antiquity, e.g., Plato and Seneca, with pre-Christian Judaism. This was the imperfect *status humilis* of foreshadowing types and images. In the second stage the middle ages, which lasted from Christ to the present day, the *status medius seu mediocris*, flesh and spirit, the secular state and the divine state are all intermingled. The third stage, the age of the future is the eschatological consummation, *tertius status perfectus*. A trans-historical age will come after the end of the world.

Although Otto was powerfully affected by the new French intellectualism and rationalism, he was less concerned with the cosmological speculations which fascinated Rupert of Deutz and Hildegard than with the formal Parisian disputations. He was sympathetic to the new spirituality of the reforming orders and interested in Parisian arguments, but he was at heart neither a scholastic nor a modern monk. Cistercian though he was, he kept deliberately clear of Bernard of Clairvaux. He remained a German nobleman and a cleric of the empire. In his *Gesta Friderici*, he painted a glowing picture of the world brought into harmony, returned to the days of Charlemagne and the Ottos, the days before the Investiture dispute. Theological and eschatological historical speculations were, however, far less important than the *renovatio imperii*, the work of his nephew Frederick I. The theorist and historian surrendered to an overwhelming political reality. Otto of Freising's position as a bishop in the empire was very plainly a limitation on the development of his speculative historical thought.

The greatest of all the German historical thinkers of the twelfth century, Anselm of Havelberg, held almost the same position in the empire as Otto. Its effect was utterly different. Anselm faced and solved problems through his position which no static life (that of a Benedictine monk, for instance) could ever have raised for him, and his spiritual growth followed his outer activities. As an imperial ambassador and chargé d'affaires, he became familiar with the colourful variety of the world, and the violent contrasts which he saw everywhere moved him to consider the meaning of the differences and contrasts within the Church, the question of the Holy Spirit's guidance of the Church, and the possibility of development and genuine inner progress. As the Emperor Lothar's ambassador to Byzantium in 1135, he disputed with Nicetas the most important difference between East and West: their differing forms of the confession of Faith, the *filioque* phrase. The debate revolved around the nature of the Holy Spirit, the *Pneuma* and his penetration of the world.

The East's pneumatic doctrine of the Spirit and the flourishing development of its monastic life, especially in the Basilian monasteries, excited Anselm enormously. He must often have felt challenged and attracted. Another problem which had begun to move the historical speculation of western theologians may well have been emphasized for Anselm by the multiplicity of Eastern religious life. In the West, the new Orders, the Cistercians and Premonstratensians, and the other foundations such as the Canons Regular, had sprung into vivid activity and were forcing consideration of the same question: how can God tolerate all this multiplicity, division and contrast within one Church and one Christendom?[5] The violent conflicts and disputes between the old orders and the new, and among the new orders themselves, gave rise to an abundant literature of controversy in many ways strangely anticipatory of post-Reformation arguments. Anselm was a Premonstratensian, an aristo-cratic Order, which had begun a staggering enterprise of renovation in the semi-pagan East. It engaged in missionary and pastoral work, mainly serving the low Churches, which provoked strong hostile pressure from the old-style orders. The necessity of justifying a new kind of activity and a new kind of monastic existence in the Church before the eyes of Byzantium and of the older world of Western Europe forced Anselm to develop his historical thought.

His travels opened his eyes to the exciting variety and the prismatic con-trasts of the world. There was Rome – he knew it well; there was Byzantium; there was the old Carolingian West; finally, there was his poor, barbarian Havelberg, his bishopric, to which he could return all too seldom. Barely wrested from paganism, it was a strange twilight zone between East and West, between pagan and Christian. It is well known to us in Otto of Bamberg's descriptions of missionary journeys in his *Vitae*. The peculiar course of Anselm's life made this much-travelled man the theologian of development, of progress, of the right of novelty in the Church. The very idea of a history of dogma was revolutionary. It was so revolutionary that it has never even approached respectability. The Church has always regarded heresy and innovation as more or less synonymous. In 1950, an encyclical of Pius XII warned theologians against the 'spirit of novelty'. Few people have managed to scale the wall which Platonic, Aristotelian, anti-historical thought has always represented. A second, equally solid barrier to historical or develop-mental conceptions of the faith has been the strongly-felt experience, charac-teristic of Augustine and late antiquity generally, of the *Deus incommutabilis* who planted the Church as a rock in the changing swirl of things. In this, the East confirmed the West. According to Nicetas, as Anselm reports him, the Gospels leave no room at all for development of the truths of faith.

Anselm's most important ideas on history are found in his 'three books of dialogues'.[6] History is a magnificent educative work on the part of God, who teaches mankind through the truth, which is Christ, and the Holy Spirit, the *auctor et doctor veritatis*. With indescribable patience, *paulatim quasi furtim*, gradually and as though by stealth, God leads men through image, sign and sacrament from the idolatry of paganism to the Law of the Old Testament and then to the Gospel. As each age is conquered in turn, God partly sup-presses its religious rites and customs and partly adapts them. Gradually, in accordance with man's weakness, he reveals the full truth of the Faith. Men are afflicted with blindness. God could not, then, in earlier ages, burden them beyond measure; *paedagogice et medicinaliter* he brings them up to the fullness of the age of Christ. The Greek patristic vision – Christ as teacher and healer – came to life again in Anselm and dispersed the medieval vision of Christ as the war-lord and warrior King, leading his men into the battle of world history. Anselm slowly realized that religious rites and customs change and adapt themselves according to the progress of the age. Unity and stability in this process of change are provided in the Church, from Adam to the end of time. But Christ has entrusted much to his Church which has still to come to maturity. In due time, the Holy Spirit teaches it all that the Son still keeps hidden.

In place of the one dominant historical concept of the middle ages, that of *restoratio, reformatio*, Anselm set up that of *instauratio*, conscious pioneering. The Church of today, he argued, is capable of grasping more than in the days of the Apostles. *Quae tunc soli apostoli non potuerunt portare, ea nunc simul portat Ecclesia.*[7] Its knowledge of the Faith, present only implicitly in the Gospels, unfolds under the guidance of the Holy Spirit. According to Anselm, the councils of the Church actually progressed in the Faith and perfected the dogma. Mankind is taught by the Holy Spirit through variety and difference. The new orders are examples of the unfolding of the truth. For the first time, Anselm argued that the process of change was something positive. The idea, indeed, was already to be found in Augustine, but now the dynamic power within it was really released. Through the Holy Ghost, all Christian peoples have a part in this progress. The new is necessary to sustain and develop what was valuable in the old. In *novae religiones*, in new orders, the Church renews its youth like the eagle. No one, declares Anselm, should be amazed that the Church looks and is different in the three ages of the world: *ante legem, sub lege, sub gratia*. It is its glory that is adorned with variety *diversarum religionum et actionum*.

Anselm must have been fully conscious of the revolutionary potentialities of his historical thought, because he tried to limit its dangers. At one point, for example, he says that the development of dogma came to an end with the great councils of the Patristic age, but there are many other passages in which he accepts the consequences of his view of history, and speaks of the enlightening and instructing activity of the Holy Spirit going on continuously until the end of time. The imperial bishop in him occasionally flinched, and his hesitation is only too easy to understand. Speculation concerning the Holy Spirit covers every element of religious thought and feeling which was to disturb the old European community in the course of the succeeding centuries.

Since the time when Lessing discovered Joachim of Flora, no historical thinker before Vico and Hegel has been the object of so much attention as the Abbot of Corazzo. The long chain of research in Germany from Friederich and Denifle to Grundmann, Dempf, Benz and Huck, and in the Western world from Renan to Fournier, Tocco, Anitchkof, Buonaiuti, Foberti, Tondelli and Reeves is impressive proof of this.[8] Yet we are still only at the beginning of an interpretation of Joachim. Not lack of materials for research but the wide radius of his influence has swallowed up the man himself and his personal work. There is the pseudo-Joachim of the commentaries on Isaiah and Jeremiah and of the innumerable prophecies circulating among the common people, the shield and progenitor of the great spiritualist movements of the thirteenth and fourteenth centuries, and later of the reforming and humanist spiritualism of fifteenth-to nineteenth-century Europe. The words of wisdom attributed to him concerning the end of the old order in Europe in apocalyptic collapse, and the approach of the new age of the Holy Spirit have thrilled men's minds and influenced the religious feeling and thought of Europe more than any earlier historical thinker, except Augustine.

Augustine was the inspiration of the real Joachim. Joachim's doctrine of the three ages of the world, his ideology of decline and progress (*gradatim*), his interpretation of the Sacraments and his concept of the Church are unambiguously Augustinian, in particular the revolutionary Augustine of extreme spiritualism and exaggerated eschatology. The Spirit overwhelms and demolishes the signs and structures of the old world. The husks of the political kingdoms of this world, of the clerical Church of the sacramental dispensation, fall away. The first empire of the old covenant signed with fear – the world of the Old Testament before the time of Christ the King, the *rex regum* of the romanesque age and the Hohenstaufen emperors have been conquered. The second stage of the world, the clerical Church, under the sign of the rule of a regulated *fides*, the obligation of Faith, is withering away. The Third Empire of *caritas*, the new Church of the Spirit, is rising. In effect Joachim turned eschatology into a historical category, one which is already beginning. The final state of illumination, expected and announced by Rupert of Deutz, Hildegard, Otto of Freising and Anselm of Havelberg, is immediately at hand. It stands at the doors; it is historically visible already.

Most of Joachim's ideas can be found in the tradition of German symbolism and there may well have been personal ties between Joachim's Southern Italian Greek world and the German world. Rupert of Deutz spent years at Monte Cassino, and Anselm of Havelberg died as Archbishop of Ravenna.[9] Joachim's use of this tradition was what made him so remarkable. He liberated the revolutionary chain of ideas immanent in these German historical thinkers, and let their innate power circulate widely. His work directly affected the last great struggles of the Holy Empire of the Hohenstaufen and the establishment of the papal Church as an *imperium*. It encouraged the beginning of the grand campaign waged by the Italian Fraticelli and later by the massed spiritualist forces of Europe against the Curial successor to the ancient *Romanum Imperium*. The Gregorian spiritualists of the eleventh century had profaned the Carolingian-German, Ottonian-Salian *Sacrum Imperium*. They had exposed it as unhallowed and in conflict with the march of history. The Alexandrines of the twelfth century, like John of Salisbury and Boso, had imitated them; now the heir and successor of that empire, the papal

Church, shared the fate of its predecessors. It was condemned by spiritual men. Rome, the clerical Church, was that Babylon whose fall the world awaited and which was to be accomplished by the Holy Spirit.

Joachim himself, certainly, did not go so far. His thoughts cannot be reduced to a consistent, logical system; he had the elasticity and flexibility of the older symbolism. He saw the transition from the second stage to the third as something growing in secret. The clerical Church, still laden with elements of the old Covenant was being subverted by the new order. Slowly, silently, and steadily, the new would thrust its way through the old, until the time would come when it would openly throw off the shell. His much discussed and variously interpreted *spiritualis intelligentsia* always tries to discern some redeeming element in every phenomenon of the old order. No empire, no emperor, no sacrificial offering, however fleshly, was altogether evil or devoid of redemptive meaning in his eyes. Every great thing in the past pointed forward and helped to prepare the advent of the new age of the Spirit, the age of love and freedom. The personal gentleness and the peaceful tolerant spirit of this Abbot of the new Cistercian age are beyond question. His dearest ecclesiastical aim was the reconciliation of East and West, (not the reunion of the Eastern Church with the Western); his dearest political aim, the protection of his beloved *populus latinus*, the people of his Italy, from invasion by the lords of other lands and oppression by their feudal overlords.

His historical thought, taken by itself, has been a great reservoir for all revolutionary spiritualists. Its central aim was to demolish the static concepts of the old, established order of things. He made constant and repeated attempts to grasp the dynamic concepts of progress, change and newness, and to justify them as part of the history of redemption. What we have said about Anselm is even more true of Joachim. He was not concerned with the traditional idea of *reformatio* nor with maintaining the old world. He wanted to overcome it. John was good, John was great – but he was redeemed by 'Elias'. The Spirit's baptism of fire will do away with the baptism of water. The sacrifices of the first stage and the Sacraments of the second will disappear. Joachim demanded that the papal Church recognize his *spiritualis ordo*, and thereby fulfil and perfect itself in the third stage. There must be a *transire*, a crossing-over. Joachim employed the mystical experience of inner conversion and turned it into a historical category to explain the passage from one age of the world to the next: *oportet mutari vitam, quia mutari necesse est statum mundi.*[10]

Peter still reigned, but beside him stood John, who was to survive him. Within the papal Church the spiritual Church of the future was secretly at work. The twelfth century was over, and with it an entire age. It was the end of the middle ages, the half-way kingdom of God and the world, flesh and spirit, lying between the first and the second earthly paradise, Tertullian's *tempus medium*, the German symbolists' *status mediocris*. It was the knell of that intermingled world whose sign was king and emperor anointed with an Old

Testament unction, and whose popes were their rivals and successors. Twelfth century historical thinking began while the old world of the *sacrum imperium* was falling to pieces. The Church was beginning to regard itself as the only *imperium Romanum*, and the kings of the West, the *reguli* whom the empire declared devoid of the power of grace, were beginning to set up their *regna* as autonomous realms of grace. Twelfth-century historiography began as a last attempt to justify the old world, and ended in spiritualist criticism and the dissolution of all the forces of that world. The *Imperium* and *Ecclesia* were both denied saving power. They could no longer defend *pax et securitas, fides, timor et amor*, nor sustain the cosmic order and the peace of human society. Their real power over men had been abolished. It was relatively unimportant whether they could maintain their external structure and position. As the new Emperor of the Spirit,* Joachim addressed himself to 'all believers in Christ'.[11]

Terror of the barbarians, to which the clergy of the old Church succumbed, was to usher in the age of the Holy Spirit. Joachim wanted to prepare for it with a monastic state[12] consisting of lay and clerical communities, reminiscent of Mount Athos, of Campanella's City of the Sun and of Newman's New University (the fraternity of scholars at the Dublin Oratory of St Paul). The spiritual interpretation of history gave birth to a political Utopia. 'God, who once gave the spirit of prophecy to the prophets, gave me the spirit of understanding (*spiritum intelligentiae*), so that I am able, in the Spirit of God, to understand most clearly all the secrets of Holy Scripture, even as the holy prophets understood them when formerly they gave forth these writings in the Spirit of God.'[13] At the dawn of the age of the Holy Spirit, the new spiritual man, the successor of the ordained man, was to begin his reign. The man of the spirit, the spiritualist reformer, humanist scholar, and finally the enlightened gentlemen of the eighteenth-century republic, were the later stages in the evolution of the *ecclesia spiritualis*. The status of the *Deus immutabilis* was replaced by the *processus* of the *Spiritus Sanctus*. Europe was on the move.

*cf. the old imperial patents, Gottfried of Strasbourg's manifesto to 'the new lovers', and Dante's song of the coronation of the new man with the (imperial) crown and the papal mitre.

THE WORLD OF THE THREE RINGS

The Mediterranean Foundations of Western Europe

'THE perfect human being would be of East Persian stock; in faith, Arabian; by education, Iraqi (Babylonian); a Hebrew in subtlety, a Christian in conduct; pious as a Syrian monk; in knowledge of the sciences, a Greek; in interpretation of mysteries, an Indian; lastly, and above all, a Sûfi in his spiritual life.'[1]

On the threshold of our 'high Middle ages', this was the ideal of the enlightened Islamic intelligentsia, heirs of the Hellenist *oikoumene* with its syncretist, tolerant and cultured cosmos. As opposed to the super-orthodoxy of theology and the pedantry of professional scholarship, the *adab's* idea of an educated man included culture, good conduct, wit, *bon sens*, discretion; the cultivated man of the world was at home everywhere from Spain to Bagdad. In the role of *katib* (scribe, *clerc*, secretary, educated man) he served as doctor, poet, astrologer, statesman and historian in all the courts of the princes of that Islamic world which he savoured in his wanderings and travels.

The ideas of Hellenist late antiquity, its religious speculations and its philosophical theses, were very much alive in this Islamic cosmos. During the twelfth century they flowed into western Europe in broad, discernible streams through Spain and southern France, through Venice-Byzantium, and through southern Italy and Sicily. To the western European knight, the Arabian nobleman was the image of the good pagan, supreme in culture and courtly breeding. To the Paris theologian, the Islamic philosopher was the man who possessed the pure text of Aristotle. But not everyone greeted the Moslem influence with joy. Among the radical nonconformists, the reaction was very different indeed. In those circles men spoke sneeringly of the 'three imposters' (Moses, Christ and Mohammed) and this attitude became characteristic of the nonconformists from the thirteenth century to Lessing's parable of the Three Rings.[2] The 'three imposters' was a distortion of a common saying of Mohammed's popular among the Moslem intellectuals, that the Old Testament, the Gospel and the Koran were the three aspects of one word of God. The bitterness which underlay the idea of the 'three impostors' suggests the intense confusion of the West in the face of the challenge of Islam.

Moslem civilization was superior to that of post-Gregorian Europe in every way, and Europe knew it. It reacted violently. The condemnation of the Mozarabic liturgy in Spain, for suspected collaborationism in 1071 and 1090 was the first stage.[3] The Crusades, the Albigensian war, the Inquisition, the Mendicant orders and scholasticism were further developments in this campaign. The Emperor, Henry IV, had to be defeated for the sake of greater Europe. His semi-barbarian halfway Empire, with its Carolingian heritage and its half-colonized Eastern territories, was intellectually, religiously and politically inadequate to meet such a challenge.

Islam was a Christian sect of the world of late Hellenism.[4] It had been enriched in the course of its rise and expansion by a complex mixture of Arabic folk-culture and Persian and Far Eastern elements. Its precursors were the Jewish-Christian sects and those Syrian Christian thinkers who had struggled to preserve the reality of the Trinity in an atmosphere of Eastern monotheism.[5] It is typical of that world that Alfarabi and Avicenna studied medicine under Syrian Christian physicians.

Mohammed's desire was to save his people from hell, through 'perfect devotion to God' (Islam). The one God, Allah, had absorbed into himself the star-gods of the Arabs and Semites and established himself as the Lord of destiny (*dahr*) and the Creator of heaven and earth. Between the creation of the world and its judgment, he schools his believers in preparation for his heavenly kingdom. Man's life is a process of testing by God, but he can be helped by the prophet and the saints. Satan waits on the side to tempt man. The one God casts down the gods of Persia and Greece in holy war (*jihad*).[6] The sword is the key to heaven and hell.* The earth is divided into the world of true faith, culture and humanity (*dâr-al-Islâm*) and the hostile, uncultured, uncultivated world of infidels (*dâr-al-harb*). (The equivalent Christian concepts were the Byzantine *eremos*, desert, and the Carolingian liturgical *gentes*.) Between these two worlds there can be no peace.

Within 100 years (632–732) Islam had conquered the world from Spain to Persia. By the beginning of the eighth century the form of its ritual was fixed, and by the end of that century its dogma. After that anything new was either *bid'ah* an evil innovation, heresy or *kufr* (infidelity). 'The greater part of my community will never cling to error.' Mohammed's definition of the catholicity of his doctrine, remarkably similar to that of Vincent of Lérins, gave the Muslim a deep inner certainty, and established Islam as a closed world of revelation, law, culture and society. The closed world of Islam collapsed for ever in 1918. It lasted precisely as long as its great rivals, the post-Carolingian sacred empire, represented by old Austria, and the post-Byzantine sacred empire, represented by Russia. The historic significance of this fact cannot be overemphasized. Ever since the days of Constantine and his Arian descendants, the Balkan peninsula had been the field on which the three empires did battle. It was very appropriate that their final agony should have begun on

---

*cf. the eleventh-century French *Song of Roland*, and Spanish *catolicismo de cimitarra*, scimitar-Catholicism'.

that same ground, in a place like Sarajevo. In this last of old Europe's holy wars they all went down together – the tsar and the emperor (each with his double-headed eagle) and the sultan-caliph with his mosque of Hagia Sophia in Constantinople.*

The Islamic cosmos was static. Mastery of its laws meant exact knowledge of Heaven (conceived either as a sphere or as a pyramid) and Hell: eight beatitudes, eight names of paradise, eight forms of praise of its spherical construction.† The cosmos was clear, precisely defined and intelligible. The Islamic Faith reflected its orderliness. Each individual was allotted his place in the beyond by an absolute predestination. Man was able to act without regard to metaphysical consequences.[7] Although he was supposed to follow the good, it made very little difference if he did so. His entire life, from the cradle to the grave, was secretly contained in the Koran and the Sunna (religious custom). Everything of real importance had already been said by Mohammed. Piety meant trusting wholly in God and reciting the prescribed prayers, in silence, humility and poverty. Riches were dangerous; the world was transitory; it was wise to renounce it.[8]

There was no practical difference between Church and state. The Lord of Heaven and Hell was lord of both. There was the state treasury of Allah and the army of Allah.[9] Every law came from him, and jurisprudence was knowledge of the practical laws of religion'. Secular and spiritual power were identical. Before God all men, as believers, were equal, although there would always be a strict hierarchy of rank in the social order.[10] As in Byzantine feudalism, vassals were bound to the sovereign alone.[11] Questions of etiquette and ceremony were very important and quarrels over precedence and rank, like those in Byzantium and Spain, were common. Since the earthly order had been ordained by God, questions of ceremony or etiquette could never be disregarded. Hence there was no such thing as social or political progress. Over the centuries, the divine empire of Islam slowly turned to stone. The same applied to theology and poetry; innovation was the ultimate sin.[12] The holy language, Arabic, the language of paradise and the chosen people (al-Fârâbi, d. 950), was made the object of a cult. That most beautiful, most perfect, most human and most god-like of languages has been chosen to be the bearer of God's last message to man.‡ The lords of Islamic feudal society

*This is also the context for the little-regarded prologue which was played out in Africa: the last of the Pharaohs, the imperial god Gaki Sherotsho of Kaffa (whom his people could never see) was defeated by the 'Napoleon of Ethiopia', the Emperor Menelik II of Abyssinia, and kept a prisoner for twenty-two years, riveted to his slaves with a silver chain. There exists one photograph of this last of Africa's god-kings, taken by the Imperial Austrian envoy Friedrich Julius Beiber, who penetrated to his presence in 1888. It has transmitted to the twentieth century the majestic features of a captive emperor-god.

†cf. the octagon in Byzantium and Aix; and, for the precise delineation of hell, Dante, who owed much to Islam.

‡After the fall of Byzantium in 1453, this Eastern cult of language was brought to the West by the Greek emigrants.

found this humanist culture of the word congenial, while the people clung desperately to the concept of the *mujaddid* who comes in every century to bring old decayed sciences and arts to a new life.[13] The new life which he brought could only be a rebirth of the past, a renaissance of holy antiquity. On the periphery of society, the ascetic holy man, the wise fool, was allowed by custom to criticize society. Using a traditional vocabulary, the holy man would berate the caliph,[14] and the caliph, although he was a god-king,[15] would listen and weep. The king then repented, did penance and dismissed a few corrupt officials (as in the Spanish world). Nothing changed.

'My community will split into seventy-three *firaq* (heresies), of which only one will be saved.' This apocryphal saying of Mohammed expressed the great anxiety of the closed world of Islam. Moslem society hardened into petrified rigidity because of a deep-rooted fear of disintegration. It was frightened of political-religious parties, sects and pre-Islamic paganism. The Greek Hellenist spirit, its sciences and rationalism threatened to absorb it. Mystical tendencies[16] might devour it from within. As early as the second half of the eighth century a wave of unorthodox feeling swept through the Islamic intelligentsia. Manichean and Zoroastrian influences were at work shattering the 'true faith'.* By the end of the seventh century the language of love poetry had won mastery over the sacred language.[17] A high courtly culture played carelessly among holy things. Poets praised their ladies as paradise on earth. Frivolity and a deep (sin-conscious) religious sense were often combined in the same men (e.g., Waddâh-al-Yaman, *circa* 700). It was not until the late ninth century that the Koran finally defeated the rich poetry of humanism.[18] The renowned Abû'l Alâ'al Mâs arrî (d. 1058) seems to have been the last poet of any standing who dared occasionally to vie with the Koran.

The struggle with secular humanist culture, with the courtly poetry of Arabia, Spain and Persia, involved a small advance section of Islamic orthodoxy. The mentality and ways of thinking of the masses were like a flood pushing against the wall of orthodoxy. They yearned for redemption and assurance. They turned the Koran into a book of divine magic and Mohammed into a wonder-worker, which originally he was not. They created a cult of saints through 'folk canonization' and exalted both the living and the dead.[19] Orthodox theology was not equal to the demands of the masses, because unlike medieval Catholicism, otherwise so similar to it, Islam possessed no hierarchical system of government, and because its potentialities for growth were limited by a strict traditionalism (*salafiyyah*) and a speculative, rational theology (*kalam*). Although after 1100 'a philosophy proper to Islam really began',[20] it was never more than a struggle between conservative and liberal tendencies among the *mu'tazilah*, who were by definition removed from affairs of the world. The great decisions which influenced world history and the inner history of western Europe had already been made in the eighth,

*Faint ripples from this wave were brought by Felix of Urgel, Agobard of Lyons and Claudius of Turin, to the Carolingian empire.

ninth and tenth centuries. The struggles between Islamic orthodoxy and sectarian philosophies presented western Europe with a unique spectacle which at that stage of its growth it was unable to understand. Many years were to pass before Europe was fit to intervene. During the eighth and ninth centuries, Islam went through a period of conflict very much like the struggles of the early Christian Church. Neoplatonism, gnostic wisdom and Aristotelian rationalism threatened Islamic orthodoxy as it had early Christianity. In the very midst of Europe's emergence, the West suddenly faced again all those terrifying difficulties, conflicts and potentialities of the Christendom of late antiquity, which had mercifully been forgotten. The dead had risen from the dust to bedevil Islam's intellectual heirs in western European Christendom from the eleventh to fifteenth centuries.[21]

The parallel growth and interior kinship between Christianity and Islam are particularly evident in two ways: in Islam, as in Christendom, the process of discovering its own orthodoxy involved the rejection as heresy of much which had originally been legitimate opinion within the Faith. 'Innovation' is often older than the 'old' which triumphs over it![22] Islam was, secondly, no more successful than Christendom in harbouring the whole treasure of its Faith within one state Church. It soon split into three main confessions, Sunnites, Shiites, Kharajites and numerous nonconformist sects. Under cover of the one Faith, the one God, the one realm of law, cult and culture, the Islamic élite disintegrated. It dissolved into a swarm of independent seekers after God, doubters and sceptics. Radical Neoplatonism was formulated for the first time. A radical Aristotelianism, which became very important for the West, was developed. Al-Kindî (d. 873), al-Fârâbi (d. 950), Avicenna (d. 1037), Avempace (d. 1138) and Averroes (Ibn Ruschd, d. 1198) embarked on a critical examination aimed at discovering the real Aristotle. The Faith and revelation of Islam began to turn into secular wisdom and rationalist philosophy. Knowledge of salvation was threatened with extinction by cultural and scientific knowledge. Many of the thinkers of the eighth to eleventh centuries were branded and persecuted as heretics and atheists. Their lives were often long emigrations, from Spain to North Africa and Egypt, to Syria, to Bagdad and Persia. Often enough they died in banishment, or were poisoned, assassinated or officially executed. Their works were burned, banned and suppressed often as late as the nineteenth century.

For over three hundred years there was a real possibility that Islam would crumble and return to the elements from which it came. The anxiety of Mohammedan orthodoxy is as comprehensible as the fear of Christian orthodoxy in the early Church. Ironically the aims of many of the persecuted philosophers were for the most part deeply orthodox and catholic. Like the *diasozein ta phainomata* (Clement of Alexandria), they were looking for the reconciliation of revelation and philosophy, of faith and rational knowledge. Even Averroes' often-condemned 'double truth' was no more than a legitimate effort to discover deeper levels of meaning behind the literal sense of the

Koran. Islam's great philosophy, the exegesis of Aristotle *and* of the Koran, had a great deal in common with emergent scholasticism in western Europe. Both aimed at the great reconciliation of faith and knowledge. Both wanted to expound revelation in a true interpretation.[23] The profound orthodoxy of *will* in these philosophers led to their search for a 'catholic concordance', a harmonizing of opposites (apparent and real). The results of their research were often far from orthodox. The great thinkers of Islam were masters of Nicodemism; and in this too they set an example to western Europe.[24] Knowledge and wisdom are too strong for the masses, who can only take milk. The wise man must disguise his higher knowledge in conformism, not only to save his own life but also to preserve the precious purity of the higher doctrine. Out of many elements a *disciplina arcani* arose, a wariness in the expression of philosophical and religious thought, a kind of double-talk. Orthodoxy was not entirely fooled and often rallied to a violent counter-attack on it.*

The dissolution of revelation in philosophy and the dissolution of God in natural law led the orthodox theologians to extreme formulations. Some of them were prepared to deny causality and to assert that the world continues to exist only because of a constantly renewed, arbitrary intervention of God. Such a rejection of 'worldly common sense', as in the baroque period (in Pascal, Malebranche and Hume) is ultimately self-destructive. It inevitably provokes a swing to the opposite extreme of rationalism, because it insists on an intolerable relationship between faith and knowledge and asserts that such a relationship is normal. Islamic orthodoxy managed to reconcile the con-flicting claims only after a painful struggle with Sufiism which lasted from the eighth to the eleventh century. What could not be accorded to totalitarian reason began to be allowed to totalitarian faith. The Sufis were mystical spiritualists who had been affected by Neoplatonism and gnosis. They ack-nowledged God alone as reality. Only through becoming divine, they argued, can man become real.[25] By a threefold path of abnegation, by ceasing to exist as an individual (*fanâ*)† man rises to a 'meeting with the Friend', God. In the end, the love and knowledge of God are one; the purified soul is idea and reason and beauty.[26] Islamic orthodoxy taught the exact opposite of this doctrine. It defended the absolute transcendence and unapproachable remote-ness of the Allah of the Koran and denied the possibility of such a mystical union of God and man, which was all too reminiscent of Neoplatonism and Eastern Christian mysticism. Although certain groups on the extreme left wing of this spiritual movement denied both cult and law, an historically significant convergence of orthodoxy and Sufiism took place. Upon this

---

*The accusation against Joachim of Flora was that he secretly promulgated his doctrine. In the thirteenth century, at Paris, secret and private lectures were forbidden. During the time of Bernard of Clairvaux, a principal accusation against heretics and nonconformists was that they worked secretly and taught in concealment.

†cf. Eckhart and the German mystics.

surprising *entente* the profoundly personal elements in Islam are based to this day. During the tenth century Sufiism was the strongest inner force within the life of the people, despite the violent opposition of official theologians and legists of all schools, to whom this 'religion of the heart' represented an undermining of the sacred political order of government in the Islamic world. In 1045 the Sufi leader al-Kushairî wrote his famous *Risâla*, intended to bridge the gulf between official theology and the mystically-inspired piety of Sufiism. By the end of the eleventh century official theology had been forced to give grudging recognition to this emotional movement, but the compromise was precarious.

A good example of the fragility of the alliance between Sufiism and orthodoxy can be seen in the life and work of the movement's greatest thinker al-Ghazâlî (Algazel), the Pascal of Islam. As an intellectual and a member of Islam's Hellenist intelligentsia, he was always enticed by its freethinking wisdom. As a man, he struggled to gain faith by making the religion of law into a religion of the heart, but religion based on the experience of the soul's inner light frightened him with its prospect of secular immanence. Caught in this dilemma, he eventually denied causality. A denial of this sort is always an avowal of a profound inner conflict, of a soul trapped in an historical situation with no way out. Al-Ghazâlî became a living contradiction, believer and pessimistic sceptic at the same time, and ended in a state of exhausted resignation so characteristic of many intellectuals in the Islamic theocracies of the twelfth to the nineteenth centuries.[27] They were educated men; they lived in big cities, where the contrasts of daily life were only too apparent. They knew that they were badly ruled and that the history of their theocratic church-states was one long process of corruption from beginning to end. The history of the Islamic law, for instance, in theory and practice, was the history of the uninterrupted collapse of theocratic principles, unable to triumph over reality. As the contrast between theory and reality became greater and greater, cynicism and scepticism grew apace. Al-Ghazâlî expressed the general disillusionment of these spiritually creative men. He accepted the framework of power as it actually existed, although it was out of harmony with God and the law, simply in order to avoid even greater chaos.[28] During the ensuing centuries, political thinking was stamped by an even more extreme type of despair and resignation. The Kadi Ibn Jamâa of Damascus (d. 1333) declared that 'the ruler has a right to reign until another stronger than he drives him from power and reigns in his stead'. The similarity between the outspoken cynicism of this idea and the political theories of Byzantium or the European Baroque (Machiavelli, Bodin and Hobbes) is striking.[29]

Arabic Islam which stood at the doors of Europe in Spain, North Africa and Sicily, was in fact already baroque by the twelfth century. It was intricate and over-ripe. For 300 years its inner existence had been in a precarious balance. Hellenist thought, Persian dualism, religious and political parties, spiritualist sects and Aristotelian philosophies had pulled at it. Quite unexpectedly the military expeditions of the Western European and Spanish nobility, who conquered Spain between 1000 and 1492, began to threaten it from the outside. Yet even the successive wars could not halt the Islamic mind in its assiduous quest for its own spiritual treasures.

Throughout these centuries, the vital link between East and West was provided by the Mediterranean Jews. Jewish sects had been present in Islam at its cradle, and followed it on its career of conquest. As doctors, interpreters, astrologers, traders, they combined Hellenist, Jewish and Islamic thought.[30] From the end of the eleventh century onwards they brought this amalgam to Europe, while at the same time their own religious and philosophical thought had been stirred by Cabalism, Neoplatonism and Aristotle. Aquinas, Siger and Eckhart were inheritors of this complex legacy.[31] Jews were great travellers. Ibn Ezra (Abraham Judaeus) was born in Toledo about 1090. We know that he was in Rome in 1140, in Salerno in 1141, in Verona in 1145, in Lucca in 1148, in Béziers in 1156, in London in 1158, in Narbonne in 1160, and died, probably in Calahorra, in 1167. A Spanish Jew, a translator from Arabic into Hebrew, he was one of the greatest biblical commentators of the middle ages, a forerunner of the modern Bible criticism (and much admired by Spinoza!). In the course of his travels among the Jews of western Europe, he disseminated a propaganda of enlightenment, the rationalistic, scientific approach which Islam and Judaism had created in Spain. His compatriot and co-religionist Pedro Alfonso (d. 1110) became physician to King Alfonso VI of Castile. After being converted, he spent a period in England as court physician to Henry I. His thirty-three tales (*disciplina clericalis*) were translated into several vernacular tongues and became a bridge between the folklores of East and West (and a source for Chaucer, Shakespeare, etc.).[32] He also wrote a tract against the Jews, and helped to foster the anti-Jewish trend, the literature of which was to alter the destiny of Spain. In 1096, 1099 and 1146, in connection with the Crusades, the first of western Europe's pogroms took place in the Rhineland,[33] and many of the journeys of the Jews were attempts to escape persecution. Maimonides died in 1204 in Old Cairo, having fled from Spain. Two Jewish travellers of the twelfth century, Benjamin of Tudela and Petahiah of Regensburg, described the journeys they made through the whole of Europe and the Near East to the other side of the Euphrates.

Eleventh-century Jewish thought reached its peak in Spain, in the Neoplatonism of Ibn Gebirol (Avicebron, Avencebrol) and in Ibn Pakuda, whose *Guide to the Duties of the Heart* was his most famous work. It is singularly appropriate to use their Arabic names, (Arabic *ibn*, Jewish *ben*) because in a very real sense they were sons of Arabic thought and its religious disintegration. Ibn Pakuda was the herald of an inner ethic transcending all external convention and morality. He was not only the most important ethical thinker of the middle ages, but also the forerunner of a new ethic in western Europe, which asserted the independence of the individual against all the old powers and authorities. Church and society were merely externals. In a sense, Ibn

Pakuda wrote the foreword to Abélard's *scito te impsum* which was to appear a few decades later. Thus at the beginning of the great movement of Jewish thought in the high middle ages there was an exaltation of inwardness. Its significant contemporaries were the great poets Moses Ibn Ezra and Jehudah Halevy. Halevy (1085–1140) has been the most influential poet in Israel since biblical times. Many of his poems have found a place in the Jewish liturgy. By the twelfth century, hundreds of years of contact had resulted in so thorough an integration of the Arabic and Hellenist heritage into Western Mediterranean Jewry that the latter in a sense summarized both Eastern and Western Islam. Their culture was a glorious achievement of richness and breadth.[34]

The religious and intellectual energies of Judaism were concentrated in three centres from which they radiated into western Europe: Salerno, southern France and Spain. Salerno was the intellectual centre for the whole of southern Italy. It is probable that its famous school of medicine goes back to Jewish origins.[35] Salerno was also the home of the greatest of the Talmudists, Isaac ben Melchisedech. Southern France, whose spiritual soil was soaked in Hellenist, Spanish, Arian* and Manichaean influences, possessed Jewish colonies in the twelfth century which contained notable schools of translators (the Tibbon family at Montpellier) and doctors.[36] Working at the same period in Spain was Ibn Suhr (1091–4/1161–2) perhaps Islam's greatest clinical practitioner, the son of six generations of doctors. He was an empiricist, in contrast to most Islamic physicians, and a friend of Averroes. Arabic-Islamic, Christian and Jewish Spain formed in effect a single unit with southern France.

At the same period Abraham ben David of Posquières, his son Isaac the Blind and the latter's pupil Asriel ben Menahem, founded Cabalism. The cabala whose roots go back to Babylonian, Hellenist and early Jewish times, is a Jewish gnosis. Out of the ineffable infinite Godhead, which is pure nothingness, the worlds emanate in manifold gradation; around God's throne are grouped numbers and primal forms, the first revelation of nothingness (*En-Soph*, the limitless) is the primal man, Adam Kadmon. This Jewish gnosis in western Europe was the godfather of all the natural philosophies from Chartres via Reuchlin and Mirandola to Paracelsus and the age of the Baroque. Alongside this intellectualist mysticism, and often bound to it by the closest personal links, exact thought and exact science, so characteristic of the middle age from Bacon to Goethe, developed. During the same period (late eleventh and twelfth centuries), the broad cultural area of Spain and Provence became the home of early Jewish critical philology and biblical science, and in Toledo in 1168, Abraham ben David Halevi dared for the first time to unite revelation and Aristotle.

Maimonides (d. 1204) completed the triumph of Aristotle in Jewish thought. After him, down to the nineteenth century (note the analogy with develop-

*Toulouse was visigothic from 419 to 507.

ments inside Christianity), Jewish philosophy revolved around the perpetual debate between Aristotelians, Neoplatonists and mystics (cabalists). Like his great contemporary, Averroes, in Islam, with whom he often engaged in polemical disputes, Maimonides wrote in the holy language of the East, Arabic. Like Averroes again, he desired to reconcile faith and knowledge. Both of them were physicians. Maimonides and Averroes were the great champions of medicine and of the physicians against the humanists. This was the beginning of nearly 800 years of struggle between physicians and scientists who believed in a naturally-constituted determinism and humanists who defended the Creator God, freedom, and the indestructible image of God in man.[37] To understand Maimonides' highly individual rationalism, both his medical experience and its expression in many-sided written works must be studied. His writings had a broad scientific range. He wrote a scientific consideration of the problem of sexuality, an explanation of prophetic visions as psychic experience, and an analysis of Jewish customs and Law in terms of comparative folklore. As the son of seven generations of practising physicians, he knew the worth of practical knowledge, knowledge which was independent of faith and of theology.[38] He was a serene intellectualist, the great 'enlightener', the bulwark of enlightened Jewry throughout the next half-millennium. He made himself intellectually independent and set Aristotle above the authority of the fathers, and very soon he was persecuted by Jewish orthodoxy and excommunicated. In southern France the Jews asked and received the help of Catholic Inquisitors against him. This treason of the orthodox Jews was an alliance of the two old worlds against invasion. But it was not to this episode that Maimonides owed his vast influence on history and upon scholasticism, St Thomas, Eckhart, Cusa, Leone Ebreo, Spinoza and Kant, but to his open philosophy. His thinking was open to God and to faith, ready to render to faith the things of faith and to knowledge the things of knowledge. Maimonides, like Kant, wrote for men who had lost their faith by becoming involved in 'false' philosophy. He was convinced that faith could be regained through true knowledge of the mutual relationships between faith and reason. He argued that God cannot be defined (cf. Augustine: *Si comprehendis, non est Deus*), nor grasped in concepts. What one needs instead is a 'negative theology', carefully expressing all that God is not. By this method Maimonides made room for the recognition of God's creation of the world and for the establishment of free will, and at the same time room for the thought and knowledge of man at work in the world. Maimonides was well aware that his 'open rationalism' had sprung from deep, irrational sources and that it required considerable tension to maintain it. In this formulation, it became the basis of scholasticism.

Ubique sunt Hebraei; 'there are Jews everywhere', wrote the chronicler in the early thirteenth century. As early as the twelfth century, powerful 'Jewish propaganda'[39] had called into being an abundance of Christian polemical writing (Rupert of Deutz, Abélard, Peter the Venerable, Peter of Blois, Wibert of Nogent, and many others). The Abbot of Westminster, Gilbert Crispin (d. 1117) spoke in courteous and light-hearted terms of a discussion he had with a learned Jew of Mainz who had come to England on business. In the course of the twelfth century, England, France and Spain provided a whole series of accounts of such discussions.[40] Public discussions between Jews and Christian theologians were forbidden in Paris in 1208, in Trier in 1223, and by Gregory IX in 1231, but still they took place in Paris in 1240 in the presence of Louis IX and in Barcelona in 1263 before James I of Aragon, – i.e., on both occasions under royal protection. The turmoil and the absence of self-assurance afflicting western Europe were apparent in the wide differences of tone to be found in these discussions. Some belaboured and abused the Jews with all the ritual paraphernalia of ancient anathemas as *gens prava atque perversa*; others (such as Crispin, Anselm of Canterbury, and Peter the Venerable) maintained a realistic and open tone. The twelfth century was the century of great public debates: between 'new religions' (meaning new Orders, such as Cistercians, Cluniacs and Premonstratensians), between theologians of East and West, and between Catholic theologians and heretics. In later periods the sword, the Inquisition and the university decided such matters.

This twelfth-century Mediterranean world was kept open by the practice of travelling. Not only Jews and Crusaders travelled. Secular and clerical laws imposed expiatory pilgrimages as a form of punishment. Many towns kept lists of pilgrimages, graded according to difficulty.[41] Multiple lines of communication, of whose abundance we had till recently no idea, ran between northern Italy, Byzantium, Rome and Sicily.[42] Post-Gregorian Italy in the aftermath of the struggle against the German empire established new economic, political and cultural connections with the Byzantine and Islamic East. This was the age of the rise of Venice, Pisa and Genoa. The 'mysterious infiltration into the West' of 'numerous examples of Greek handwriting'[43] is thus easily explained. In 1112 the Archbishop of Milan, Petrus Chrysolanus, held a debate with Eustratus of Nicea. In 1136 Anselm of Havelberg, Moses of Bergamo, Burgundio of Pisa and Jacob of Venice took part in theological disputations in Constantinople before John II Comnenos.[44] They were full-scale discussions between East and West. Disputations of this kind were part of the solid structure of Byzantine and Arabic courtly humanist culture. Pisa, then at the pinnacle of its political and military power, was in a position to supply the West with middlemen: diplomats, merchants, traders and translators. Among them were Burgundio of Pisa, the brothers Hugo Etherius and Leo the Tuscan, and Stephen of Antioch. We have already spoken of Salerno. In Naples, the city of Frederick II and young Thomas Aquinas, the East was at the very doors. There were rich monastic libraries of Greek Basilian monks, and the Greek and Arab-Islamic populations were tolerated and protected in southern Italy by the Norman Kingdom.[45] The court of William I and Roger II (protector of the Arab scientist al-Idrisi) at Palermo was the centre of the

Sicilian group of translators consulted by Abélard of Bath, John of Salisbury, Peter and William of Blois. Henry Aristippos of Catania translated Plato's *Menon* and *Phaedo*, for the ultimate benefit of Petrarch, Salutati and Nicholas of Cusa.

The Popes (Innocent III, Eugene III, Alexander III), cardinals, bishops and kings of this seething twelfth century were on the hunt for translators and translations.[46] The hunger and thirst for knowledge and culture meant that the West after its great victories in the eleventh century, was beginning to feel strong enough to wrestle with the heritage of the East. It dared to receive it and go out to meet it. The centre of the 'World of the Three Rings' was Toledo. This fateful Spanish city, under Moorish rule from 712 to 1085, had already produced numerous influential men; among these were Bishop Elipand, who encouraged Felix of Urgel, and Archbishop Raimund I (1126–51), who made great efforts to mediate between East and West and between old and new. Twelfth-century Toledo still spoke Arabic. There Jews and Moors and Spaniards, both Islamic and Christian, could be found living side by side.[47]

With the help of his Archdeacon, Gundissalvi, a converted Jew, Raimund inaugurated a translation school which acted like a magnet on the élite of western Europe.[48] From England came Abélard of Bath, western Europe's 'first natural scientist', and Walter of Malvern, whose family originally came from the Burgundy-Lorraine area which had been mediating Arab astrology, astronomy and natural science as early as the tenth and eleventh centuries.[49] Then came Robert of Chester and Michael Scotus. From Spain, John of Seville and Hugo of Santalla; from the land of Jerome and the Bogomils came Hermann of Dalmatia; from Flanders Henry Bate and Rudolf of Bruges; from southern France Armengaud, Jacob Anatoli, Moses ibn Tibbon, Jacob ben Mahir; from Italy, among others, Plato of Tivoli, Gerhard of Cremona, Aristippus of Catania, Salio of Padua and John of Brescia.* In the Sicilian schools there had been a preponderance of translations from the Greek. In Toledo the main effort was directed toward Arabic, the Arabic Aristotle, the Neoplatonists, Averroes and Avicenna, and occasionally the scientific and astrological-astronomical writings of the Islamic world.

An enormous gulf separated this early scholastic intelligentsia in Toledo, Pisa, Venice and Palermo from the German East. We need only compare these arguing, translating, Islamic-Jewish-Christian humanists, physicians and theologians, with their delight in anything strange and alien, and Helmold's Chronicle of the Slavs. It was a cold and ruthless story, which Helmold told, a tale of bloody massacres, deportations and forced conversions of Slavs beyond the Elbe. The destruction of this 'other world' was carried out in a crusade of colonization. Its object was the elimination of the Slavonic neighbour-peoples. Helmold died in 1177. In the same year, after twenty

---

*It is interesting to note in passing that virtually every region or area represented in the school at Toledo was later to become a centre of European heresy. This is another example of the persistence of heretical ideas in certain, definable geographic areas.

years of conflict with the Italian cities and the Citizen Pope Alexander III, the Emperor Frederick I made his peace with the West. The Pope, a wise Sienese jurist, was afraid that the split between western Europe and eastern Germany might become permanent. The two great growing processes in twelfth-century Europe were moving in diametrically opposite directions. The north and east German settlements were forever thrusting outwards. Ferociously they pushed into the barbarian eastern lands of the 'unholy Slavs', as though fleeing the interior world of the West. Meanwhile, the West's intellectual and emotional movement was in danger of drowning in the materialist and idealist sea of Greek and Arab civilization.

At this stage a remarkable process of integration began, starting in the second half of the twelfth century. It was this process which brought about the comparatively close-knit unity in the world of the high middle ages. The dangerous 'open positions' in Spain, southern France, Sicily and Naples were abandoned, or rather, repudiated. The Crusade in Spain, the Albigensian War, the Inquisition, and the collapse of the Norman-Hohenstaufen enlightened régimes and courtly culture, are all part of the same process. Western Europe, still overloaded with intellectual and cultural spoils, concentrated its forces in a gravitational centre represented roughly by the area covering Paris, Oxford, Brussels, Cologne and Basle. The first transformer, the first to take the strain between East and West, between the archaic folk-society and the new intellectual and spiritual high culture, was twelfth-century France.[50]

Two men stand out in this process of self-recognition, Bernard of Clairvaux and Abélard. As a Burgundian, Bernard was poised between Germany and France. As master of the Second Crusade and founder of western Europe's mystique of the heart, he bore the conflict between the old and the new, Christ the King of armies and the 'sweet heart of Jesus', within his own breast. He called himself the 'chimera of the century', and there was something mysterious in the way he condemned Abélard, a man who stood for the same things intellectually which Bernard represented emotionally. Abélard was the father of scholasticism. He rationalized theology and transformed it from a sacramental meditation on the mysteries of salvation into a rational system of ascertainable propositions. As an ethical thinker, he replaced the social, class-morality of the old aristocratic community, bound up with ideas of blood and honour, by an ethic of the mind – *scito te ipsum*. As spiritual friend and director of Héloïse's nuns, he revealed to them the 'new life' of the intellectual, spiritual man. He subjected the whole of the old régime – bishops, nobles, abbots, and their men – to the criterion of his own spiritual reason. By virtue of his position as a lecturer at Paris, this 'Celtic genius' had all Europe for his audience. At the same time and in the same area (Paris, London, Canterbury and Chartres), John of Salisbury began his intellectual life as a student. During a long and active life he was secretary to Thomas Becket, an opponent of Barbarossa and Henry II of England, and a publicist in the service of Pope

Alexander III. His letters were the first newspapers, linking Italy with France and England with Germany (Cologne). His *Polycraticus*, the new Europe's first statement of political theory, was the product of his life as an *émigré* and member of a resistance, of his spiritual consciousness, and of his first-hand knowledge of the courts and political usages of western Europe.

Chartres, lying on the route from Spain to Paris, was an immensely old, numinous place and a holy centre of archaic society. On the foundations of its Celtic and Roman temple, the Cathedral of Our Lady was built, with the strong enchantments of its coloured glass and its spell-binding figures of prophets and saints.[51] It became a centre of peace pilgrimages and the building movement, and its Neoplatonist school was a twelfth-century forerunner of the University of Paris. The school of Chartres was western Europe's elementary school of speculation. All the cosmologies of the twelfth to eighteenth centuries, as well as magical-naturalist humanism and rationalistic theology were first worked out there. It is well to bear in mind the magical substratum in Chartres. It had deep ties with the Spanish and Arab world, but it was also strongly influenced by the fanciful and magical traditions of its Celtic surroundings.[52] 'Chartres' stood for *intellectibilitas*, a word invented there by Clarenbaldus. *Intellectibilitas* meant a perception of God, the cosmos, nature and man, which was to be attained by the understanding. 'To engage in theology means to philosophize.' The Breton brothers, William and Thierry of Chartres, were the founders of this Neoplatonist school of cosmic interpretation, which virtually reduced God to numbers and geometrical figures, and creation to an automatic process. Duhèm is by no means wrong to suggest: 'Neither Descartes nor Laplace went further than Thierry in bold and sweeping rationalism.'[53] 'We are able to see more, and further' than pagan or Christian antiquity, said William. Thierry proceeded to explain the Trinity by means of geometrical symbols. The being of the Son was a geometrical polygon and the procession of the Holy Ghost from the Father and the Son was an expression of love between 'Unity' and 'Likeness of Unity', exactly like the unions between natural objects in chemistry and mechanics. In the Neoplatonic natural philosophy of his friend Bernardus Silvestris (*de mundi universitate*), essential Christian elements were entirely eliminated. Nature beseeched *nous*, the divine World-Spirit, to give form to its chaos. The world-soul, as an emanation of divine reason, did so and imposed form on matter. William of Conches, referred to in English manuscripts as Shelley, developed a similar cosmology in his world-philosophy (*De Philosophia Mundi*). He was a pupil of Bernard of Chartres, and was later accused of heresy because his allegorical and moralizing explanations of the ancient gods could be too easily applied to the Christian God and his saints.

These developments at Chartres could not have occurred without the world of the Three Rings and its infiltration of Spain and Provence. Thierry sent his pupil Hermann of Carinthia to Spain on a mission of research (1138–42), where he did a considerable amount of translating from Arabic. Together with Robert of Chester (Anglicus, Ostiensis) he completed the first translation of the Koran, a work commissioned by the Abbot of Cluny, Peter the Venerable, Abélard's patron. In his *Experimentarius*, William worked from an Arabic treatise on astronomy translated by his friend Hermann. The influence of the various Arabic texts in the school of Chartres produced unexpected results. By the time the open tradition of thought and the curious mixture of Neoplatonist, Christian and Arab ideas, which made up the core of Chartres' attitudes, reached the second and third generation, it had very often turned into orthodoxy. Some of the men of the later generations made a considerable contribution to the formation of orthodoxy by engaging in energetic controversies with heretics. They never entirely rejected their ancient heritage.

The celebrated Alanus ab Insulis (of Lille), who died in 1202 in 'heresy-infected' Montpellier, was trained by Bernardus Silvestris. Typically he saw Christ and Socrates standing peacefully side by side,[54] while Dame Nature complained that man had deviated from her ways and given himself to disordered love.* According to Alanus man was created in the Palace of Nature, a description still employed by Milton, and it is possible to argue that the allegory and cult of nature of a later epoch began here. Although Alanus belonged to the same world as the Cathars, Albigensians, Waldensians, Jews and Muslims he wrote passionate attacks on them. Another descendant of the first generation of Chartres was Nicholas of Amiens, who tried to clarify the geometrical and arithmetical speculations of Thierry and Bernardus Silvestris and build an arithmetical theology. He adopted the schematic form of Euclidean geometry, and deduced theological propositions from definitions, postulates and axioms. The object of this was *theologia more geometrico demonstrata*, a clear, rational construction according to the archetype of (divine) numbers and the pattern of arithmetic and geometry.[55]

The world of Chartres produced the Gothic cathedrals in their purest form. They were 'like Jerusalem coming down out of heaven'.[56] On one level, they were the creations of the French kings and the spiritual administrators at St Denis and Rheims. Yet they had roots deep in the archaic world of Celtic society and its magical experiences. The East played an important role.† Their basic measurements mirrored the speculations of Arab gnostics. Their masterful treatment of matter reflected the dualist heresies which had to be overcome. Their cult of light, 'the longing to see the Host',[57] was a continuation of the optical preoccupations of Spanish Arab mystics and physicians. The superb buildings were the earliest attempts to synthesize all these heterogeneous elements and they were, as a result, strangely fragile. Centuries were to pass before all the elements expressed in their stones could be sorted out and assimilated, and even then only by returning to Chartres for a further

*Was this a protest against asceticism, or the widespread contemporary sodomy?

†The concept of the Holy Grail, which was introduced at this time, also came from the East, probably from Persia. It was originally conceived as the cure of the Cosmos and seems to have appeared in France at the time of the emergence of the Albigensians and Waldensians.

examination. The return to Chartres became marked during the fifteenth century, but continued for two centuries thereafter.[58] Nicholas of Cusa borrowed whole passages *verbatim* from Thierry for his *De Docta Ignorantia*. The inclusion of Bernardus Silvestris in Vincent of Beauvais' encyclopaedia of the middle ages gave him the widest possible dissemination in Avignon, Paris, Heidelberg, Pavia and England. William of Conches was read throughout Europe right into the seventeenth century, especially in baroque Germany (Heilbronn, Melk, Vienna). The important work of Alanus ab Insulis, the *Anticlaudian*, was published in Basle in 1536, in Venice in 1582, in Antwerp in 1625. A considerable part of the pantheism and nature cult of the renaissance and baroque was historically connected with the literary products of the cosmologists of Chartres. It was an inheritance from the 'World of the Three Rings' in the last of the open centuries.

7

'LEFT-WING' AND 'RIGHT-WING'
POPULAR RELIGIOUS MOVEMENTS

(Thirteenth Century)

AT the very summit and watershed of the high middle ages, the Fourth Lateran Council opened on 11 November – in the year 1215. The greatest pope of the age, Innocent III, painted an alarming picture of the Church dissolving in a sea of heresy. He demanded a thorough reform of the Church.[1]

The success of popular movements – religious, political and social – like the Waldensians, Franciscans, Albigensians, Dominicans, and later Hussites and 'evangelicals' was explosive. One can ask why the storm suddenly broke out at this particular moment; or equally, one may ask what forces managed to hold back the outbreak so long. Of the two questions, I find the latter more engaging. It is clear that every element of an outbreak was already there in Europe, locked up and latent, from late antiquity to the nineteenth century. The Carolingian State Church had superficially christianized the masses of central Europe without really touching their archaic culture. Carolingian open theology had decked itself out with the wisdom of the Fathers, but collapsed with unfailing regularity whenever it faced any real challenge. The Mediterranean area, within the Toledo-Toulouse-Lyons-Milan-Naples line, had stuck to Syrian and Greek, Arian and gnostic patterns of thought, in effect those of the Christian intelligentsia of late antiquity. The thinkers of the South were contemptuous of the *ecclesia carnalis*, the physical Church of the ecclesiastical lords, bishops and abbots who were usually foreigners anyway. They were receptive to the intellectual ideas of Spanish-Arabic Islam and its strict dualism in religion. Criticism from above (nobles, physicians, judges, rich burghers) was joined by criticism from below: from the people, who did not understand Church theology and its Latin system of government, who complained about the unchristian lives of the (higher) clergy, and who sought *their* Gospel, their *Christ*. The high Nicodemism of the nonconformist monks, humanists and scholars, was echoed by a low Nicodemism, a mass of custom, taboos, confederations and rituals by which people succeeded for thousands of years in preserving their way of life and thought against the Church's system of government. On particular occasions, in rituals of birth and death, of carnival and revolution, it manifested itself in visible signs.

This was the world into which the spiritual reforming movement and the Gregorian revolution burst.[2] Humbert of Silva Candida, Peter Damian and

Gregory VII emerged as the critics of a Church gone worldly. In the twelfth century, Bernard of Clairvaux, Gerhoh of Reichersberg, Hildegard of Bingen, Elisabeth of Schönau, John of Salisbury continued this criticism.[3] The monk Nigel Wireker (d. *circa* 1200) brought a mass of accusations against the clergy of England and France. Gilbert the Belgian (*De Superfluitate Clericorum*) attacked the lust for power and gold to be found in monasteries of the old school: one abbot lavished attention on a sick sparrow-hawk, and kept five kinds of wine and four legal advisers while the poor starved at his palace gates.[4] Nivard of Ghent made the strongest of all attacks on monasticism, personified in his *Ysengrimus* (*circa* 1148) by the gluttonous stupid Monk Wolf. Walter of Lille, the friend of John of Salisbury, one of the outstanding poets and humanists of the twelfth century, wrote almost half his songs against the corruption of the higher clergy; it was the same story of the poor going cold and hungry while the monks caroused in their palatial monasteries. Like Walter von der Vogelweide and a dozen or two other writers, he coupled this with attacks on Rome and the cupidity and ambition of the *Curia*; everything in Rome was for sale, from pope to porter.

Three features of all this polemic are important: first, wide circles of Europe in the twelfth century had lost confidence in the highest authorities in the Church – the pope and bishops; second, the discrediting of monasticism as a Christian form of life,* led historically to the destruction of the sociological bases of the communal religious life; third, the Gregorian reform itself had stimulated this criticism of the worldly Church and kept it alive. Gregory VII had made an alliance with the Pataria and stirred up the people against simoniac bishops and abbots.[5]

One arm of the great religious movement so prominent in the twelfth century was formed of wandering preachers, calling for repentance, poverty and an apostolic life in imitation of Christ. They often appealed to the anti-clerical and anti-monastic instincts of the people, but more significantly they carried the Gospel to the people. As early as 1030 heretical groups in Milan preferred to be burned rather than recant, because they recognized the Gospel as the one and only revelation and authority.[6] By the twelfth century the orthodox wandering preachers, 'the new Apostles', as Abélard disparagingly called them, men like Norbert of Xanten and Robert of Arbrissel, could no longer hold their own against the numerous heretical preachers like Tanchelm in Zeeland, Eudo of Stella in Brittany, Peter of Bruys and Henry of Lausanne, who in their struggle against the worldly Church went as far as the rejection of the sacraments and the Eucharist.[7]

From the eleventh century onwards heresies arose among individual thinkers, theologians and philosophers, which then took hold, first among the nobility and citizenry of the Mediterranean lands, then among the wandering poor, and last among the vassal peasantry bound to the soil. The right-wing Christian revival movements tried to win a legitimate place in the Church,

*cf. Erasmus, *Monachatus non est pietas*.

while the moderately radical left-wing groups were pushed to the border-lines of orthodoxy by episcopal opposition. We now know that there was much more co-existence between these groups than was formerly thought. This era was, after all, three centuries before the Council of Trent, and a hundred years before the rigid influence of Thomism was felt. The border area between the archaic community of old Europe and the Hellenist intelligentsia of the Mediterranean was evidently quite large. This is why all sorts of ancient heresies, superstitions, astrological and gnostic speculations and very old pagan rites existed so unaltered within the broad scope of the Church right down to the turn of the twentieth century. It remained for the huge monolithic state churches (secular or otherwise) to stamp out these nonconformist trends. The existence of the border zone helps to explain the Church's famous uncertainty with regard to Luther, as well as its less commonly known uncertainty in the twelfth century. In this period of the Church's growing self-discovery and self-knowledge, it tended to lump together right-wing and left-wing movements within Christianity – even Catholic Christianity – along with movements of altogether non-Christian origin, to label them all as heresy, and to persecute and suppress them all alike. The Waldensians, Albigensians and Franciscans may serve to illustrate this state of affairs.

In Lyons, that ancient centre of Greek thought, Christian culture and heresy, citizen Peter Waldo commissioned a poor student, Bernard Ydros, to translate the Gospels and other writings into French. Next, he got Etienne d'Anse the grammarian (later a Canon of Lyons) to translate the Gospels into the *langue romane*. A Christian lay movement, the 'Poor Men of Lyons', began to grow up around Peter, in which reading of the Bible and literal imitation of Christ were the main activities. Faced with increasingly bitter opposition from the Archbishop of Lyons, Jean de Belles-Mains,* they rose first in revolt and then took to heresy. They revived all the ideas of Agobard of Lyons and Claudius of Turin. The Waldensians were against honouring the saints and praying for the dead (which put them against the whole of the old world and its vital solidarity). Any kind of external cult was idolatry. They would rather pray in a stable or a bare room than a church. Away with the bishops' cathedrals!† For them, the Church was invented by Pope Sylvester in that Constantinian era which had ruined everything. Along with the Roman priesthood, the Waldensians rejected the Roman Mass. They celebrated the Mass in full as the Lord's Supper only on Maundy Thursday; otherwise they held only commemorative services. The vernacular Bible, vernacular prayers and songs, a communal life in fraternities,‡ schools of their own and well-organized missionary work and propaganda brought about a rapid spread of

---

*Right down to the nineteenth century such courtly names were still commonly borne by the aristocratic representatives of the French Church.

†Francis's crib was in part a reply to this 'stable' challenge.

‡cf. the Franciscans and 'Jacobins', i.e., Dominicans, who were the forerunners of the Jacobins of 1789!

Waldensianism in Italy, southern France and Spain. Their violent anti-clerical and anti-Roman preaching, with its *écrasez l'infâme* motif, led them into coalition with the Cathars, and soon their ideology was to a great extent influenced by this other, more powerful, intellectual movement.

Not until the late eighteenth century, after six hundred years of persecution, could the Waldensians obtain their civic and religious freedom. Their history illustrates the way in which a spiritual movement could be forced to become both more radical and more spiritual by its opposition. The Waldensian heresy was a religious movement starting from old European orthodoxy, which was pushed out of it into the border zones. This process, especially so in later history, turned such groups into secular and political organizations as well. Deprived of its places of worship and its schools, a spiritual resistance movement soon tends to turn into a secular intellectual one, and then not infrequently, into political resistance. Waldensian districts, communities and families, with an admixture of the remnants of the Cathars, provided both the regional hereditary and the intellectual basis for the Huguenots, the men of the Enlightenment and the revolutionaries of 1789.[8]

The Cathars (Albigensians), who also flourished on the ancient fertile soil of southern France and Spain, were much more manifestly a movement from the East. Their doctrine was made up of pre-Christian, non-Christian, anti-Christian and early Christian elements, and, as a reaction to the Crusades, the adherents of such ideas once again tried to undermine and conquer western Europe. The hatred of the Cathars for Rome was the eternal hatred of the Eastern Church for the unchristian, unspiritual West. The West's violent response was a measure of the extremity of its anxiety.[9] The Crusades played a crucial role in the history of the movement and it is to that phenomenon that we must now turn our attention.

Recent research into the Crusades[10] has arrived at the conclusion that, while they were many other things as well, they were first and foremost a series of bitter quarrels, inspired by deadly hatred, between Eastern and Western Christendom.[11] They started with a misunderstanding at the outset. Emperor Alexis's appeal to Pope Urban II for West European mercenary troops, in the tense atmosphere of the eleventh century, was misinterpreted as a summons to conquer Jerusalem and the Holy Land. To the Greeks, the Crusaders were superstitious barbarians. They felt, by contrast, a profound unity between themselves and Hellenist-Arab culture. The conquest of Constantinople set the ultimate seal on the sundering of two worlds.[12] The history of the Holy Land, with its struggles between Orthodox (Easterns) and Latins for the holy places (churches and monasteries) provides a visible documentation of the cleavage. In this field, it was the Franciscans who confronted the Eastern Church as champions of the West. They were western Europe's answer to the spirituality of the East.

While the struggle for mastery between West and East followed its headlong, convulsive course, a type of Neomanichaean gnosis, weirdly arrayed in the guise of a Christian church, was seeping into western Europe from the Balkans.[13] Bogomilism, the movement of the 'Friends of God', arose in the early years of the tenth century in the first kingdom of Bulgaria. By the first half of the twelfth century it was powerful in Constantinople itself, and began to crop up in northern Italy and southern France as Patarenism and Catharism. 'The pure gospel' of the Bogomils was a disguise for an anti-Christian system of thought which saw no value whatever in earthly life. They taught that the devil was lord of the world and of the power-Churches of Rome and Byzantium and their cults (especially the sign of the cross).

Bogomilism was born of the encounter between the subject masses of the Slav peoples and certain Eastern gnostic sects, the Paulicians and Messalians. It was a product of the gulf between the ruling caste and the people and between the prelates and the lower clergy. The Byzantine state itself unintentionally fostered its development, by deporting the Paulicians to Thrace in the late ninth century.* In the year 1200 the learned, cultured Greek goldsmith Aristodios (Rastudije) was banished from Split by Archbishop Bernard.[14] Aristodios became the founder of the Bogomil Church of Bosnia, which flourished as an intermediary between Western and Eastern Manichaeism until the fifteenth century and was then rapidly absorbed into Islam, to which, like Arianism and Spanish Adoptionism, it was deeply akin in some of its features. The last Bogomil clan in a Herzegovinian village is supposed to have gone over to Islam in 1867.[15] In twelfth-century western Europe, Bulgar (Bugres, Boulgres, Bugares) was a synonym for Cathar.

Between 1150 and 1250 sixteen Catharist Churches, i.e., national Churches and Churches of émigrés organized as national groups, have been identified. There were six in Italy: the largest was in Lombardy (Ecclesia de Concorresco), and the most cultured in Florence, maintaining a famous school at Poggibonsi. There were six in the East: in Constantinople, one for Latins and one for Greeks.† There were four Churches in France, The most radical Church of them all (dualist and Manichaean), the Dalmatian Ecclesia Druguciae, was the doctrinal source for the ideas of the Cathars of southern France. The doctrine naturally varied in its details, because it was composed of the ideas of ultra-spiritual individualists, with an admixture of local traditions and various gnostic influences. As a whole it revealed a taut internal consistency. It is remarkable that early Christian gnostics (like Marcion and Origen) and sectaries (e.g. Tertullian's speculations concerning Adam) should so perfectly reflect the mentality of the common people over a thousand years later. The Cathars believed that the whole world was in decay. A good God could not have created such an appalling world.‡ Thus there must be both a good and an

---

*cf. the methods used by the Carolingian Church under Charlemagne and Alcuin.

†In 1167 the heretic Bishop of Constantinople, Nicetas, presided over a great Cathar Council at Saint-Felix de Caraman.

‡This certainly must have been the experience of the menu peuple in their daily round of unspeakable sufferings: see the medieval chronicles.

evil God.* Hell is not eternal (is not life here a hell on earth?); man must go through purgatory on earth; anything from eight to sixteen rebirths may be necessary before a man is wholly pure. 'The Pure', *cathari*, were to be present at the cradles of all later movements of purists, purifiers, radical and revolutionary spiritualists. Their tormented yearning to be made clean can be discerned, for instance, in Calvin's theocracy, in the 'language purifying' societies, and in Robespierre. A high percentage of the names which were to recur among France's intellectual élite from the sixteenth to the nineteenth century were originally the names of prominent Cathars.

The first purification applied to the Bible; the Old Testament was subjected to a severe critical process, leaving only thirteen prophets, the five Books of Solomon and the Psalms as genuine.† Christ was not God; he and Mary were exalted spirits, and possessed only the appearance of bodies.[17] There was no incarnation, no need for redemption. All the evil and distress of the human race stemmed from its lack of knowledge. Blinded by Satan, it adored him, the dark God, under the name of Jehovah, Baal, Jupiter, the God of the Church of this world, and thus enslaved itself to him more and more. Man was delivered by true knowledge of his origins and his end, which was knowledge of the true, good God. Christ was the teacher who brought this liberating knowledge into the world. As the Cathar, Fabre de Pech-Hermer, declared: *Deus tamquam filium suum misit Christum in mundum praedicare nomen Dei.*[18] After Christ's death, Satan created a Satanic Church, the Whore of Babylon, the Roman Church, which persecuted the Pure, the true, apostolic followers of Christ. The struggle between the two Churches was the struggle between God and Satan. (This was the point of departure for the Franciscan spirituals, and many revolutionary spiritualists after them.) In their great propaganda-battle against the 'basilica of Satan', 'the Whore', the 'Roman Church', the Cathars created all the slogans used by radical anti-clericalism from the thirteenth to the nineteenth century.

The judgment passed on the Bible and on the worldly Church implied a radical attitude to the established order of things and inevitably led to the rejection of all existing political authority. Kings and princes were servants of the devil, slaves of the lord of this world; hence they had no right to pass judgment on 'heretics'. The Waldensians held that God had entrusted the persecution of heretics to the secular government under the Old Testament, but no longer under the New. This was the birth of European tolerance. Out of the very intolerance with which ultra-spiritual nonconformists abjured secular government as a godless thing, the foundations of tolerance of dissent were constructed. Secular law fell to the ground along with secular government. The Cathars rejected oaths and the death-penalty, and declared that all war

---

*The Monarchians, on the other hand, taught that the one God created both good and evil; cf., at a later date, Boehme.

†cf. at a later date Richard Simon, Bayle, and the English seventeenth and eighteenth century freethinkers.

was murder, whereas the Catholics sought to justify both as legitimate means of 'defending the social order'.[19] The Bogomil Church of Bosnia gave glorious proof of the nobility of its office as a peacemaker between king and nobles, Catholics, Hungarians and Turks from the twelfth to the fifteenth century.[20]

Total rejection of the world implied the separation from it of each individual. The *perfecti* abstained from 'flesh' – marriage, and the eating of meat, eggs and milk. They considered animal life sacred, because it was possible for the souls of men to dwell in brutes. (There was a reflection of this idea in Francis's love of animals). Some of them lived in severely ascetic convents (not unlike those planned by Augustine, who was, after all, an ex-Manichaean), under the discipline of a president (abbot). Their life was one of poverty and unremitting missionary zeal. Their preaching and exegesis of the Gospel (they referred almost exclusively to the New Testament) were far superior to the Catholic preaching given to the people. Their translations of the Bible and their vernacular religious literature had practically no competition. The 'noble' and 'perfect' man was expected to die by his own hand. Among various methods in use, the *endura*, death by starvation, was often preferred. This marked the entry into western Europe of approval of suicide, later to be reinforced in the renaissance of Stoicism. In Toulouse, within that crucial area of southern France, during the twelfth and thirteenth centuries, many of the *perfecti* actually died such deaths.

The 'Church of the Pure' fascinated both the intellectual and the common folk because of its radicalism. It possessed a cult which impartial research has established as duplicating in many essential features and even in trifling details, the cult of early pre-Constantinian Christianity.[21] The great drama of the extermination of the Cathars in the Albigensian wars of 1208 to 1228 has, therefore, great historical significance. The world of western Europe, growing steadily more European and more medieval, was here confronted with a world of thought, cult and religious practice which in its fanatical, uncompromising radicalism, its enthusiasm and its medley of early Christian and gnostic elements, was startlingly reminiscent of those chaotic centuries – second, third and fourth – when Europe was born. The background of this drama was the encircling world of Hellenist-Arab and Byzantine intellectual culture.

The one all-inclusive sacrament of the 'Pure' was the *consolamentum*, the conferring of the Holy Spirit by the Perfect upon the Believers who thus became perfect. By the *consolamentum*, each received back his own Holy Spirit, which he had left behind in paradise when the angels fell (a basic theme running through many theories of spirit and genius since the sixteenth century). This imparting of the spirit had to be preceded by at least a year's catechumenate, a time of testing and of penance. The *consolamentum* was baptism of the spirit, confirmation, priestly ordination and the extreme unction, all in one. Washing of hands, baptism of spirit and fire, adoration of the *Perfecti* by the faithful, the *traditio* of the Creed, the Gospels and the Lord's Prayer comprised a liturgy of early Christian character and of solemn, awful majesty. The

Roman Liturgy of today has preserved elements of this only in its baptismal and paschal liturgy. The neophyte was hailed as 'a living stone in the temple of God' (cf. the Templars) and a 'disciple of Jesus Christ', and as 'a church of God', solemnly initiated into the Lord's Prayer. 'Dost thou entrust thyself to God and to the Gospel?' Vows of terrible solemnity constituted the response to this question in the baptismal interrogation; the candidate obligated himself, if need be, to martyrdom. In this connection, the *consolamentum* also represented the power given by Christ to His Church of binding and loosing; it bestowed forgiveness for all sin. Through the *consolamentum*, the neophyte received the power to perform all the works of Christ, including loving his enemies.*

The Cathars celebrated communion with thanksgiving, blessing of the bread, Eucharist and a common meal, in the same way as the early Church about the middle of the third century, before the *agape*, the love-feast, had been separated from the *coena Domini*, the Lord's supper. There were also some points pecular to this liturgy (which closed with the kiss of peace): the *melioramentum*, in which the faithful knelt in reverence before the *perfecti*, invoking the Holy Spirit; and the *apparelliamentum*, in which the whole community publicly confessed its sins each month before one of the *perfecti*. Like their doctrine, their liturgy showed a mingling of early Christian elements from the time of Tertullian and Origen and of Egyptian and Persian influences.

This majestic liturgy of the spirit – an entirely commemorative ceremonial, wholly free of any notion of communion between heaven and earth, constituted the backbone of the Cathars' fanatical warfare against the Catholic Sacraments.[22] *Sacramentum altaris nichil est; – missa, et sacrificium nichil valent.*[23] The first expression of European nihilism was a form of total spiritualism. In its earliest formulation, it claimed that there could be no binding together of God, the Spirit, and the stuff of this world. The Catholic Mass, Sacraments, rites and dogmas must be fables and deceits. The Cathars conducted a campaign of ridicule against them, directed especially against the veneration of the Cross and of images and saints. At the centre of their attack was the Mass. They claimed that it had been invented as late as the fourth century under Pope Sylvester, by priests and cardinals whose aims were to ensure their own domination over the Church and to wring money out of the faithful! In this charge, the Cathars were quite consistent, and their connection with the pre-Constantinian age found its appropriate outlet in hatred of Constantine.

In their great war against the godless, unspiritual, diabolical, *stupid* Sacraments, cults and dogmas of the Roman Church, the Cathars' radical spiritualism combined with the common people's massive materialism. This momentous alliance persisted even into the twentieth century. Iconoclasm and hatred of rich monasteries and prelates worked together. It is worth remembering

---

*These rites were described by Tertullian, *De Pudicitia*, XIII, 7, and we know that Agobard of Lyons was the owner of the great Tertullian codex.

that they were prefigured in the clamorous propaganda of Clunic art in Moissac and in Toulouse,[24] and the Cluniac portrayals of 'lust' and 'ambition' and 'lady world'. The barbarism thus let loose must not obscure the great intellectual force of the doctrines. 'The Pure' knew that they were in possession of the true knowledge, the true doctrine and the true liturgy of the Holy Spirit. They regarded their final triumph over the liturgy of the devil and its horrible mixture of divine and earthly things as inevitable. This is the key to that amazing demonstration thought up by Eleanor, wife of Count Raymund VI of Toulouse: while the pope said Mass in his chapel in Rome, in that very place she performed a solemn *melioramentum*.

There was also a good deal going on in the North, the area comprising the north of France, Flanders, the lower Rhineland and Burgundy, which from now on was to make such constantly fruitful contributions to Europe's spiritual history. In Cologne and on the Rhine, Ekbert of Schönau and Hildegard of Bingen, summoned to the aid of a helpless higher clergy, preached and argued against the heretics.[25] In the north of France, the disciples of Peter of Bruys taught that the churches should be destroyed. True Christians needed no sacred buildings, since 'God is everywhere and hears everything, and will listen to all who deserve it'. The places of pilgrimage and other holy places, where there were gatherings of people from all lands, were the centres of heresy. In Vézelay, where Bernard of Clairvaux initiated the third Crusade, citizens were arrested in 1167 because they denied the Sacraments, the Roman Church, and the need to build such an enormous and costly church. The brother of Louis VII, Bishop Henry of Beauvais, later Archbishop of Rheims, while journeying through Flanders in 1162, was horror-struck by the multitude of heretics; some of them, rich lords and burghers, even tried to buy toleration from him with money.

The great conflict which was to change European history broke out in southern France, where by the middle of the twelfth century the great masses of the people had been won over to Catharism and Waldensianism. Under the protection of the cities* which enjoyed considerable freedom, and of the nobles, especially the Counts of Toulouse, the Cathars were free to practise their cult, to preach, to missionize, to hold great councils.[26] The fact that the majority of the great nobles were also patrons of rich abbeys, led to a good deal of political conflict with the bishops and prelates. The lesser nobility quarrelled with monasteries and bishops over the division of tithes. These quarrels undoubtedly made a contribution to the establishment of a nobility of heretics. Innocent III blamed the rich, simoniac prelates of the south for the rise and spread of heresy.[27] A ruthless struggle for mastery between secular and spiritual lords had been going on for a long time and the petty gentry were threatened by the wealth of the great ecclesiastical estates. There was more to the movement than mere class struggle. The Cathars became the pattern and model of the fronde and of all reformist, enlightened and political

*Montpellier, for instance, was recognized as a republic by the King of Aragon in 1204.

resistance among the nobility down to nineteenth-century Russia because a new nobility had at last emerged. These men were the first products of the active religious movement, both right and left, of Cluny, of the Crusades and of Arabic-Spanish culture. Like their Huguenot heirs and successors they were genuinely zealous missionaries of their new Faith. The movement was supported by famous ladies of the noblest society such as Blance de Laurac,[28] and there were nuns of the most exalted families who received the *consolamentum*. The list of heretical leaders rings with great names: the lords of Montesquieu, Sabatier and Mazerolles, the counts of Foix and Montréal.[29]

The ancient Church was impotent against the Cathars. The *perfecti* constituted an élite of an unique type. They wandered as missionaries all over the area encompassing Spain, northern France and Lombardy. They travelled as physicians, bankers, merchants and pedlars. They made their appeal alike to the great nobles and to the workers on the land (vassals of the monasteries). They visited them in the fields, organized and educated the youth of the common people, both boys and girls, in the cloth-making factories. Abbots and canons, monks and parish priests were in open sympathy with the heretics. The bishops were descended from the same families as the heretics' most powerful patrons. The failure of both Bernard of Clairvaux and of Dominic in their preaching proved that the two sides spoke totally different languages.

Innocent III finally resolved upon a Roman solution. He proclaimed a Crusade against the Albigensians and promised the nobles of northern France the goods and properties of the heretics. King Philip Augustus of France was to gain dominion over their lands. The King's response to this revolutionary papal step was slow and doubtful. He reminded the impatiently bellicose Pope of the legal issue. It was not such a simple matter for the Pope to promise the Crusaders the Albigensians' goods.[30] If we call Charlemagne's Saxon wars the first, the murderous conflict which wrested southern France from the East was he second major battle of Europe's growth. It lasted from 1208 to 1228, and ended with the land laid waste and the sects gone underground. The free-thinking secular culture of the troubadours was totally annihilated. The struggle began and ended with two religio-political acts of state: in 1209, before the Lion Porch of Saint Gilles, Count Raymund VI of Toulouse, the greatest lord of the land, did public penance for his encouragement of the heresy; and on 12 April 1229, at the great door of Notre-Dame in Paris, his son Raymund VII swore allegiance to the King of France, in the presence of cardinals, legates and bishops and under the images of Christ the King and Mary, Queen of Heaven, who had their domain at the portal of their heavenly palace, the Cathedral.

The two sides which had fought each other so bitterly for twenty years were, of course, intimately connected. There were Catholic nobles in the Catharist political party, many of whom had fought bravely in the Crusade of 1212 against the Arabs, in the famous battle of Las Navas de Tolosa. In the Albigensian Crusade, many men in the Catholic army of northern France were killed by comrades with whom they had fought side by side only a year before. King Peter of Aragon, the Lord of Astarac, and many others besides, fell in battle with the invaders from the North.[31] At the same time, in the immediate entourage of the Count de Montfort, leader of the Crusade, there were actually heretic priests![32] In addition, one Catholic reform movement, the Dominicans, actually tried to win over and subdue the heretics by using their own means and methods. Durandus of Huesca with his 'Catholic poor men' and Dominic the Spaniard, with his convent of new converts at Prouille,[33] had obviously been influenced by their opponents. The Dominican Order had to construct a firm and rigid theology to fight off the poisons of the East, and the aggressive position which it took in later scholasticism reflected its anxiety-ridden origins in this troubled time. The physical organization of Dominic's new order was an obvious imitation of the Cathars' Church, with its *perfecti* and 'believers'.

Neither St Bernard's preaching, nor the Cistercian missions, nor the papal legates, nor Dominic himself could alter the desperate situation in the South. The last free and fluid exchange between East and West there took place in 1204 at Carcassonne: a public dispute between Cathars and Catholics, with a court of thirteen Albigensians and thirteen Catholics to supervise the conduct of this expression of religious democracy. This was no way to achieve conversion or incorporation into the Catholic Church's religio-political realm of salvation. Both sides remained unchanged. On the very eve of the war, on 26 January 1205, Innocent III wrote to Pierre de Castelnau, his plenipotentiary for the reconversion of the South, who wanted to give up and go back to his monastery: 'Action', wrote the Pope, 'is of more value than contemplation.'[34] This hair-raising dictum was far more momentous than the Magna Charta in England ten years later. It marked the final and definitive establishment of western Europe, and its Church as the Roman Church. What Leo the Great, Benedict of Nursia, Gregory I and the Gregorian Reforms had begun was completed under Innocent III. After a thousand years of hesitation the lines of communication to Byzantium and the world of the Eastern Fathers were cut. The Catholic Church came to recognize itself. Henceforth there was only the Roman Church. This was the final rejection of the East, and it led eventually to the Inquisition and ecclesiastical discipline. The Church had decided to rule the world through alliances with ruling princes, no longer with the *one* emperor or king, and to defend its realm of salvation through universities, monasteries and holy wars.* The victory of Roman over Greek was the victory of the *fides* and *pietas* over the free, fluid religious intellectuality and speculativeness of the Hellenist East.

German idealism, the heir of Eastern spirituality, argued that the Greeks were much more religious than the Romans, and identified religion with

---

*Trent and the Counter-Reformation merely renewed the alliance with the lords of northern France against the Albigensians, just as, at the same period, the Baroque was renewing Chartres.

religiosity, religious genius and insight. This judgment was an expression of a Hellenist renaissance which reflected Germany's intellectual kinship with the East, but it forgot that Roman *religio* was a paternal order of things embracing home and court, city and state in the service of the gods. 'To listen with strict attentiveness and then act accordingly sums up Roman religion.'[35]

Fides, faith, was a treaty with the gods, who protected the state so long as it remained bound to them in true service. Law and cult, state and religion belonged together in the closest unity.[36] Rome deserved and obtained dominion over the world because the Roman state was the most religious in the world.[37] *Do, ut des* – 'I give to thee, O God, that I may receive good measure from thee again.' The ultimate basis of security in archaic society had been transformed into state service and divine service within a strict system of sacred law. The state, the guardian of the cosmic weal, collapsed if it did not correctly honour its gods.[38] Augustus inherited from his 'father', Caesar, the lofty mission[39] of restoring and re-establishing the ancient, holy, Roman *religio*, and he ruthlessly suppressed all the libertine, anarchist cults of the East which had invaded it.[40] Roman authority, *auctoritas*,[41] was the office of the 'father', the defence of the sacred, saving realm of the state against innovations – which meant, against orgiastic, disruptive types of religiosity from the East. This anti-Eastern authority was reborn in the father-figures of the abbots and the popes.

Gregory VII regarded himself, historically and logically, as a reincarnation of Scipio, Caesar and Augustus. This 'holy Roman Father' strove to make the Christian kings and princes of Spain and England, Brittany and Denmark, Saxony, Bohemia, Hungary, Dalmatia, Croatia, Serbia and Russia (1075!) his vassals, by subjecting them to the sovereignty of St Peter.[42] His object was to bring all Europe into the sheltering bosom of a religious and political system of salvation and peace. As successors of the Roman emperors, the Roman popes defend the *right* universal order in religion and politics. One of their most important moves was to set up the Inquisition. The 'pagan' Diocletian had persecuted the Manichaeans with fire and sword. Justinian, Charlemagne, Robert the Pious in France,[43] Henry II and Louis VII, all at various times had revived the ancient laws against heretics. By systematic heresy-hunting, the Inquisition was inaugurated by the pact between Lucius III and Frederick I at Verona in 1183. The Inquisition was a welcome instrument of royal absolutism. Between the end of the twelfth and the end of the thirteenth century, it was the chosen means of delivering western Europe from Eastern infiltration, of suppressing eruptions from the primitive underground, and, in general, of reducing Christianity to Roman *religio*.

After the defeat of the Albigensians, the Inquisition was set up with headquarters at Toulouse. Every woman over twelve and every man over fourteen was required to abjure heresy. No one was allowed to possess either an Old or a New Testament, either in the vernacular or in Latin. The only books permitted were the Psalter, the Breviary and the Little Office of the Blessed Virgin Mary (all in Latin). The Synod of Toulouse in 1229 was the start of those

Roman Catholic prohibitions and restrictions[44] on Bible-reading in the vernacular which were to play an ominous role in Europe's spiritual history. Toulouse was followed by Tarragona in 1234 and Oxford in 1408. In 1559, Paul IV made the use of the Bible in the vernacular dependent upon permission from the Roman Inquisition. This rule was modified in 1564 to allow the individual to obtain this permission from his own bishop. Despite the Tridentine rule, Sixtus V and Clement VIII continued to demand the authorization of the Roman Inquisition. In 1757 Benedict XIV declared that approved translations of the Bible could be freely read by all. Yet in 1836 Gregory XVI reasserted the rule of Clement VIII, and it was not until 1897, in the midst of the disappearance of the older order in Europe, that Leo XIII made Benedict XIV's concession, freed from all restrictive conditions, into the law of the Church.

In 1229 the University of Toulouse was founded to help combat heretics. It bore an ancient Roman motto: *Pravos extirpat et doctor et ignis et ensis.*[45] Henceforth there was to be a *militant* learning, and learned professors wielding the sword and the flaming torch embarked on a campaign of extermination. Violent opposition was provoked and for a time the Dominicans were driven from Toulouse. In 1242 there was a massacre of Inquisitors and the bishops made appeals for moderation and equity. In the end the Inquisition succeeded in imposing an outward peace upon the country.

In 1246, after five years of fighting, came the fall of the Castle of the Grail, Montségur, the centre of Albigensian resistance. There delegates from Spain, from the North and from Italy had been accustomed to meet their brethren from the South. The secret police of the Inquisition, the *exploratores*, tracked the heretics into the undeground and found out where secret heretical societies met in woods, stables and country houses, very much like the *église du désert* in the same area in the eighteenth century. In time, the heretics began to congregate in certain kinds of occupations, and from then on, where heretics were to be found, they were usually in weaving, manufacturing, medicine or peddling. Within the close and narrow compass of Spain, the introduction of the Inquisition led to the establishment of two Spains:[46] freedom-loving, nonconformist, democratic Franciscan Spain,[47] with its centre in Catalonia, the stronghold of considerable groups of Spanish and French Cathars and Italian Waldensians; and royal, absolutist Castilian Spain, where Ferdinand the Saint carried faggots to the stake upon his own shoulders.

In the North, during the first half of the thirteenth century, the Inquisition carried on a struggle against rich and influential heretics in Champagne, Burgundy and Flanders; in Rouen, Rheims, Bourges, Tours and Sens. 'There are heretics everywhere' complained the chroniclers. The ominous figure of Robert le Bougre, the Inquisitor, haunted France. His own name meant 'heretic' and eventually he disappeared in a royal prison. In 1210 a cell was discovered in the University of Paris, where the followers of Amalric of Bena (d. 1206) were busily constructing a spiritual doctrine based on Eriugena and Eastern gnosis. The Holy Spirit becomes daily incarnate in us, they believed, to prepare for his coming and his kingdom. Those who are in the Holy Spirit no longer need faith, for they live in the Spirit by love and knowledge. Along with this free spirit there were certain pantheistic features: *Omnia unum, quia quicquid est, est Deus.* Similar to the doctrine of Amalric were those of David of Dinant and Maurice of Spain, also at the University of Paris. Around 1250 Antwerp became an important headquarters of heresy, a meeting place of many different kinds of heretics from North, South, East and West. This Venice of the North, like the Serenissima itself, later became a publishing centre for European nonconformism between the sixteenth and eighteenth centuries. As early as the thirteenth century a system of wires spread out, stretching over the Rhine and the Alps and northern Italy which connected the two cities and both soon became throbbing arterial centres of European spiritualism.

Despite the fearful blows rained upon it – twenty years of war and thirty of Inquisition – heresy was not extinguished in the south of France.[48] The second half of the thirteenth century witnessed a new, secret resurgence in the very midst of persecution. Nobility and clergy (including a Benedictine abbot), monks, episcopal officials, canons, and a multitude of jurists, professors of law, physicians and merchants, were recorded in the registers of the Inquisition. Several officials from northern France, who had been brought south to fight the Cathars, ended by joining them. In the cities of Limoux, Albi, Cordes and Castres, the heretics still formed more or less powerful parties. In Carcassonne between 1280 and 1291 successful attacks were made on the Inquisitorial archives. It was not unusual to see Catholic bishops and heretical town councils stand together in profound hostility to the Inquisition. It was this land of southern France which, late in the thirteenth century and again in the fourteenth, was to give shelter to the Franciscan Spirituals and to carry on their fight against Rome.

A well-organized emigration movement had led many of the *perfecti* out of southern France into Italy.[49] A whole system of collectors of funds (*quaestores*), agents (*nuncii haereticorum*) and guides through strange and unfriendly areas (*ductores haereticorum*) was organized to provide safety and security on the road and at necessary halts. The journey usually ended in one or other of the rich and respectable heretical churches of Italy. The rising cities of Italy were the bastions of such groups. In their attempts to extend their rights against bishops, cathedral chapters, abbots and the Ghibelline nobility they sought whatever assistance they could get. Alliances between imperialists and heretics took place in many cities during the thirteenth century. Serious disturbances often followed. Milan, the Emilia, Florence and Tuscany were governed from time to time by Cathars and Waldensians.[50] Rome itself had powerful heretical families (that of the Senator Brancaleone, for instance);[51] and most of the nobility in sympathy with the Hohenstaufen became protectors of heretics as part of their battle with the popes.

The whole country was in a state of turmoil, civil war and religious unrest.

'Free thinkers' from the Arabic-Spanish 'world of the three rings' declared that all three religions, Christian, Jewish and Muslim, were lies.[52] The flagellants vacillated between enthusiasm and anarchy. Peace had been forgotten and the people were hounded by fear and ruined by the war between the emperors and the popes. Soon no one would be able to tell who or what was to be regarded as orthodox or heretical. Many of the Inquisitors were formerly fanatical heretics, such as the famous Raynier Sacconi. His fellow-Inquisitor, St Peter Martyr, who was a member of an heretical family,[53] was murdered by heretics. One of his numerous opponents, a man involved in his murder, was a Franciscan. The murderer himself, Carino, died a holy death in the Dominican priory at Forli where the prior was the murdered man's brother, and in the popular mind the cult of the murderer coalesced with that of the victim.[54] In the last third of the thirteenth century, when Armanno Pungilupo died in 1269, he was at first venerated in the cathedral of Ferrara as a saint, and lay in state before an altar already raised in his honour. In 1300 his beatification process ended in a trial before the Inquisition. The Catholic 'saint' was revealed as an heretical leader, his images were destroyed and the altar and body burned.[55] This is an example of the extraordinarily highly-developed Nicodemism which persisted in Italy down to the nineteenth century. Under pressure from foreign occupying powers and foreign Inquisitors, ideas tended to burrow deeper and deeper under ambiguous symbols, hiding their secret wisdom behind an orthodox façade.

The Franciscan movement emerged out of this confused world[56] of heretics, city states and wretched common people. Although after more than a century of struggle the ruling system of the old world subdued it, a constant succession of heretical or quasi-heretical movements continued to grow out of the Franciscan Order. Bitterness over the defeat of their master and the suppression of their most sacred concerns created a resentment which proved to be one of the most fruitful and dynamic elements in Europe's intellectual history.

There were Franciscans, or Franciscans in spirit, presiding over the cradle of every revolution down to 1789. The Franciscan spirit was to fling itself against Thomist authoritarian thought for five centuries. The first victory was, however, its most impressive. It was the first time that a movement from below had burst into the open. Some of the deepest forces of mind and soul in the people penetrated the Christianity of the ruling system of the old world. Nothing else can adequately explain the swift growth of the movement. The Franciscans alone of all the heretical popular movements eventually flowed into orthodoxy.[57] Only the Franciscans transformed the basic realities of the lives of the people of Italy in the middle ages into significant Christian terms. Franciscan poverty and humility made virtues of the hunger, starvation and misery of the masses. The curse was made into a blessing; the terrible Byzantine *Pantokrator* and German divine King – represented by the foreign bishops – became the King of Grace, the Saviour of the poor. Unofficial recognition was given to the Franciscan doctrine of poverty by Innocent III in 1210. The approbation of the rule of the Order by Honorius III in 1223 marked the triumph of the poor men's movements in Italy after two hundred years of dramatically varying fortunes.

Archaic society, with all its internal safeguards, was already seriously threatened, if not already destroyed in Italy and western Europe by the development of great cities and trade.[58] By the middle of the thirteenth century Florence possessed eighty great banking houses, while Flanders, Italy and northern France contained the first large scale industries (wool and weaving). Florence, Venice and Milan were all cities of more than 100,000 inhabitants.[59] The life of the masses in these cities was wretched and insecure. Jacob of Vitry in the early years of the thirteenth century described the great city as a Babylonian monster, a pitiless lion, tearing and devouring all things.[60] Its outward face was war, its inward, terror. Heretics naturally realized that the cities were their true homes. The *menu peuple* were stirred to their very depths by the spiritual chaos and disorder and by their misery. Suddenly Francis came and taught them to sanctify their poverty and their entirely concrete lack of holiness (a matter of no concern either to their secular or to their spiritual lords). He taught them to understand it, bear it and transform it spiritually.

The Waldensians had already made an attempt at Christian living in the unhallowed city, organizing themselves on the model of the city's own institutions, its communes and guilds. They had formed brotherhoods (*fraternitas*), bound by common friendship (*amicitia communis*) – a new kind of kinship tie, not of blood but of the faith and civic membership (friend kinsman). Each brotherhood was under the leadership of twelve *majores*, like the twelve *majores* of the civic community and was modelled on the confederation of citizens in a town. The inner affinity between the early Waldensians and the early Franciscans was much greater and the contacts more numerous than is generally admitted.[61] When the persecution reached the limits of endurance, large groups of Waldensians sought refuge in the Franciscan communities now rapidly springing up. The unholiness of country life was as great as that of the towns. In Italy the lords were often strangers, not sprung from the *populus latinus* which Joachim of Flora had loved so passionately. The thirteenth century Franciscans supported the people in their reaction against the number of the taxes and tributes imposed upon them,[62] but they also tried to build up a new society to guard against the great fear of the common people, the fear of losing the life of salvation. For the first time since Roman antiquity men spoke again of hallowing the land and the life of the land. Franciscan antifeudalism was thus the product both of urban and of rural influences.

What Francis produced was a new people of God, a people of poor brethren with a father chosen by him in defiance of all the dominating fathers of the old world. First he rejected his bodily father: 'Listen all of you, and understand. Up to now I have called Pietro Bernardone my father, but as I am now resolved to serve God, I gave him back the money about which he was so perturbed, as well as the clothes I wore which belonged to him, and from now on I will say:

"Our Father who art in Heaven" instead of "my father Pietro Bernardone".'

The legend of the Three Companions described this liturgical act of renunciation with a grand flourish – renunciation of his former father, his possessions and his clothes.* Stripped of his own clothes, the naked Francis was wrapped in the bishop's cloak. Although Francis was never ordained, he had come of age in God and was arrayed with the gifts and garments of the clergy. It was now his priestly office to convert the people to Christ by preaching to them a union of co-operation and solidarity with all creatures. The new brotherhood – with nature, with the animals, with all 'poor men' – was built upon a new fatherhood. 'Give your coat to your poor brother.'[63] This brotherhood was a revolution. It implicitly rejected all the terrible 'fathers' of the old world – the terrifying divine King, the alien emperors, kings and overlords, and all the sinful fathers who were the hereditary lords of land and city. Where did Francis find his new father? In the Roman Pope. Innocent III was in a position to spread the mantle of his protection over Francis because Gregory VII had already declared himself to be the new father. No doubt he was equally eager to secure Francis as a useful weapon against the 'pure' and the 'purely spiritual' and the endless philosophizings of the East.

Francis, the father of the Italian people, was a valuable ally of his father, the Pope. Francis embraced the Son of God in the crib, in the person of every poor man, of each of our neighbours, fellows and brothers, and in 1223 he constructed the first visual representation of the birth of Christ for the church at Greccio.[64] This historic act, rightly given a monumental position in Giotto's series of paintings, was thoroughly repellent to the East, and almost as unpleasant to the Church of the lords and their cathedrals. God was near now – near enough to be held and touched. He had to be as near as that, because he was received and held by every one of our brother men. In Byzantine Ravenna, the Eastern emperor and imperial bishop had effaced the images of the passion of Christ; the Eastern Church had been more categorical still, rejecting the *filioque*, the procession of the Holy Spirit from the Father *and* the Son. Now Francis, 'our holy father Francis', took God into his arms in the form of a child, and carried the dove of the Holy Spirit out to all lands and to all his fellow men. His *Laude*, his new Canticle of the Sun, supplanted the old *sol invictus* of the divine Constantinian sun-king. He sang the praise of God through all creation. Instead of the cosmic mantle of the emperor and the hierarchical mantle of the 'prince of the Church', he was clothed in God himself. Gregory VII had rediscovered St Paul, Christendom's first master of the Spirit and the Pauline injunction 'put on the new man, clothe yourselves with Christ', was now fulfilled in Francis. On Mount Alverna, Francis displayed the marks of Christ's wounds.[65]

The East might have forgiven the West a hundred hostile councils, but this

*The struggles in councils and elsewhere among the various ranks of society and the new orders for the dress 'appropriate to their state' shows how important clothes were in that society.

was intolerable.[66] To the East, Christ was the Divine Man; his cross was the triumphal emblem of the victor. No tears dimmed the heroism of his sufferings (often likened to those of Hercules). The flesh of Christ in the Eucharist was 'the bread of immortality'. Man's goal was to be transformed into that divine, spiritual body – itself wholly transformed by the Spirit of God – as the relics of the saints had already been. This view had been accepted by the ancient Carolingian-German medieval world, and Rupert of Deutz had agreed with John Damascene.[67] By contrast, Augustine coined the confession of the West: *Per Christum hominem ad Christum Deum*, through Christ the Man to Christ the God. This was the formula taken up by the Cistercians; and in Hagia Sophia, in the ultimate rejection of Byzantium, Humbert of Silva Candida had given the Eucharistic basis of this Western view: the closeness of Christ's approach to men in the Host.

Francis was bolder still. He picked him up in his arms, as a child, and by assuming the stigmata he put on the outward form of Christ.[68] It was the birth of the new imitation of Christ. To be a Christian now meant to do as Christ did, to suffer as he suffered, to love him and live in him, in obedience to the new father and in the service of the brethren. This alliance between the Roman Pope Innocent III and Francis, the son of the Italian people, had deep foundations on both sides. In the Franciscan crib the *filioque* was safe for the first time. It showed how the Spirit of God was born in God the Son, and thus it was also the basis of the emancipation of Italian art from Byzantium. Every representation of the crib from then on was a *trionfo* over the East. Stigmatics arose again and again after Francis's day but never in the East. By these marks Francis outshone all the most ancient and most venerable tombs of saints and sees of patriarchs in all the East. His stigmata proved that the true *auctoritas*, the power of the new holy Father, resided in Rome.

As the 'new Christ', Francis sacrificed his life, his work, and his order to the new Father, the Pope. The consummation of his sacrifice and his crucifixion was his consent to the Pope's mutilation of his Order, which robbed it of its poverty and its total dedication to the love of one's enemies. This was the most profound spiritual drama in the history of the West, and the greatest of its tragedies, because it was the most genuine. Francis wanted his Order to be entirely poor and to serve. All the brothers were to work, and so transform the curse of work into a blessing. They were all to learn some craft and not turn to study. In 1220 he ordered that the house of studies in Bologna – founded by the Provincial, Pietro Staccia, formerly a Bolognese lawyer of some repute – should be destroyed. 'You are trying to destroy my Order. It is my wish and desire that my brethren shall, according to the example of Jesus Christ, beg rather than study.' Francis cursed Staccia, and even toward the end of his life he still hesitated to lift the curse. He had an unconquerable mistrust of the intelligentsia, who were susceptible to the temptations of the world and of the (Eastern) love of the Spirit. In the end, Francis consented to the complete destruction of his Order from within: study, the abolition of poverty, the full incorporation of the Order in the structure of the old régime, that system of domination which he and the Christ Child had conquered and annulled.

Francis of Assisi saw the vices of his city, and of the city in general, as *orgoglio e cupidigia*, pride and avarice, and he knew that they dwelt in his own breast too. Against them he set poverty and humility. How could his new gospel hope for disciples, if he did not conquer himself? The temptation to rise in rebellion was always latent in Francis right up to the end of his life, hidden under endless fresh acts of obedience. There was another threat, no less dangerous: Francis was, on his mother's side, a son and kinsman of heretical Provence. He had received many 'heretics' into his Order and had even modelled his preaching and doctrine on their evangelical life. Even a modern Franciscan like Agostino Gemelli[69] admits that 'Francis understood their principles and morality'. 'He took everything which these false teachers had set up in opposition to Rome, and found a solution for it within his obedience to Rome.' Francis could not but feel a justified foreboding that his Order, which had grown into a European movement within the space of a few years, might easily disintegrate once more into the elements which it had succeeded in binding together: Humiliati, Waldensians and converted heretics of all kinds.

This fear was mirrored in his Testament, in its striving for total obedience. There he declared: 'I will have recourse to the priests, even though they should persecute me (*che, se mi movessero persecuzione, voglio ricorrere a loro mede-simi*); I accept them as my masters (*gli tengo per miei signori*), because they alone consecrate the body and blood of Christ and give it to other men.[70] The sacred power possessed by these new lords had broken the sacred powers of the old hereditary and tribal structure. Although Francis recognized himself as their son, bound to them in obedience, he was painfully aware of his own vocation: 'After the Lord had given me the care of the brethren, and there was none to show me what I should do, He, the Highest, revealed to me that I must live according to the rule of the Holy Gospel' (*ma lo stesso Altissimo mi rivelò, che dovessi vivere secondo la forma del Santo Vangelo*), in absolute poverty and by manual labour. 'And I worked with my hands, and still wish to work; and it is my firm will that all the other brothers should do some manual labour.' *Mi rivelò il Signore*: 'The Lord revealed to me'; poverty, labour, and the preaching of peace. 'I strictly command by holy obedience that all the brethren should beware of asking for any letters of privilege from the Court at Rome ... (not even) to escape open persecution.' Finally, Francis submitted himself in obedience to the Superiors of the Order; but the Testament itself was to be published everywhere together with the Rule of the Order. 'And to all my brethren I strictly command that they shall make no gloss to the Rule, but keep it even as it was given to me by God!' As early as 1223, when Honorius III approved the Rule, he struck out the all-important clause concerning poverty. In 1230, Gregory IX (*Quo Elongati*) declared that the Testament was not binding unless ratified by the chapter of the Order. In many places, the victorious majority actually burned the Testament, occasionally, on the head of a spiritual.[71] Bonaventure never so much as breathed a word of it.

The Order began to split even while Francis was alive. There was a small circle of companions who adhered closely to him and who joined him on his endless wanderings. It was this circle which produced all the most important testimonies and sources of his life and intentions, such as the *Second Life* by Thomas of Celano, and the *Three Companions* (*Tria Sociorum*). Following his death came a century of bitter struggle for control of the Order, in which it was the Conventuals, as they were later to be called,* who were victorious. As a result the Order became like other orders. It had monasteries and possessions, houses of study and professors; and only a limited and conditional devotion to the service of peace.

The Conventuals at once took steps to eradicate all memory of Francis and his revolutionary programme for renewing the world. Thus between 1260 and 1263 the General Chapter of the Order decided that the General, Giovanni da Fidanza (Bonaventure) was to write an official biography of St Francis. After it appeared, all the written sources deriving from his immediate circle were sought out and destroyed. They did not come to light again until the old order of things was breaking up at the end of the nineteenth century. Most of the records which survived were found in the archives of convents of Franciscan nuns, to whom the persecuted companions of Francis had consigned them for safe keeping.

This monstrous destruction – the mutilation of the Order in contradiction to the mission of its founder – was never fully accepted by any of the more alert spirits, regardless of the party, current or movement in the Order to which they might belong. There were many possible degrees of reaction, ranging from silent, unexpressed resistance to open rebellion. By the end of the thirteenth century the Order had split into Conventuals, radical Spirituals and moderate Spirituals. In the first half of the fourteenth century it seemed on the point of collapsing altogether and disintegrating into heretical groups.[72] It began the fifteenth century in a stronger condition, but soon split into a number of different groups in the struggle between Observants (who wanted to return to St Francis), Conventuals and neutrals.[73] But it would be a mistake to take a wholly negative view of these severe conflicts within the Order. They were all emanations from a single stream which gushed out in so full a flood that one channel simply could not contain it. Right and left Franciscans and even the best minds of the broad centre were often related, as they themselves knew.

It is precisely because Franciscanism was so rich in internal tensions and contradictions that it was capable of becoming the strongest of all Christian movements. The movement fertilized Western European folk culture, humanism from Petrarch to Erasmus, and poetry from Dante to Rabelais and on to Gerard Manley Hopkins. Because of its resistance to the old world of race, divine kingship and princes of the Church, and also because of the deep wound

*The conformists who came to terms with the old world and its régime of power.

inflicted on it at its birth, the Order produced such projections as the 'Third Kingdom' of the Spirituals, the scientific Utopianism of Roger Bacon, the philosophical dialectic of Duns Scotus and the 'nominalism' of Ockham, one of Luther's spiritual teachers. The authors of the Magdeburg Centuries and all the revolutionary spiritualists down to the nineteenth century looked on Francis as their progenitor.

Francis himself knew what his mission was. It is best expressed by the commemoration which follows immediately after the consecration in the Roman Mass: *Unde et memores, Domine, nos servi tui, sed et plebs tua sancta* ... It was as 'the servant of God' and 'the chosen people' that Francis saw himself and his Order. He had been called to the service of establishing the new age of Christ. This was God's democracy! Yet how Roman it was. Francis bore the wounds of our Lord. Was he not the new Christ, reborn to usher in the Kingdom of God in this age? The immediate circle of his companions began to see him as, at least, the herald of God, the new evangelist, John the Baptist, the new David and Elijah, or as a seraph.[74] Like a second Christ, he had taken his own people, his Friars Minor, out of the world with its racial structure of blood, honour, soil and hereditary sacred powers, and made them into 'the holy company of the last age' and 'a new humanity'. Even in Bonaventure's official life of Francis there is an echo, in the prologue, of this historic sense of being the new 'people of God' and the bearers of a new age, in which Francis appears as John and as Elias, and as the angel of the Apocalypse bearing the sign of the living God. The victory of the conformist majority led to the outlawing of this sense of historic mission, which was consequently forced to ally itself with Joachimism and scientific Utopianism. It flared up again as revolutionary spiritualism which condemned not only the sin-bound ancient world but its sin-bound emperor and pope to be consumed by the fire of the Holy Spirit.

In 1241 an abbot of Joachim of Flora's Order fled to the house of the Friars Minor in Pisa[75] and consigned to their keeping the writings of Joachim. He feared that his own monastery was about to be destroyed by the Antichrist Emperor Frederick II. The Pisan Minorities made a synthesis of Joachim's eschatology and their own, applying Joachim's third order to themselves. Thus Francis was made into the spearhead of the 'third Kingdom' of the Holy Spirit. An intermingling of Joachimite enthusiasm and historicism with the radicalism of the Franciscan Spirituals took place under pressure from the German feudal lords in Italy. The fusion solidified in a common fear of Frederick II and a common love of the 'Italian people', the *populus latinus*. The whole Order closed its ranks for the last time in that fear of the Last Things and hope of a new age, which throughout the middle ages were but two expressions of one sense of the meaning of history. They were united in resistance to the terrifying apparition of the Emperor, who had set the crown of the world upon his own head in Jerusalem. Through the words of his Chancellor, he had assumed all those holy titles – Lord of the World, Anointed of the

Spirit, Bearer of the New Reign of Peace and Justice[76] which, the Spirituals felt, were appropriate only to Francis and the Roman Catholics to Christ and to the pope. The laity of Italy in the Third Order of St Francis organized political resistance to the new god-man.[77] St Rose of Viterbo preached in the streets and squares against Frederick II and for 'the freedom of Church and commune'. This was the spirit of the Pataria, and it was also a foretaste of Joan of Arc, who would never have arisen without the Franciscan movement.[78]

As early as 1228, and again in 1239 the 'Holy Emperor' was excommunicated by the pope. In 1245 the Council of Lyons declared the Emperor deposed as a heretic! In vain his ambassador appealed over the head of the Pope to a general council – thus heralding, on his side, the advent of the new European age in which kings and their national councils built up their kingdoms independently of, or in opposition to, the pope. The 'Holy Emperor' had to fall, the first victim of the new age. The agents of his fall were the nations. It was at Lyons that the representatives of Christendom appeared as nations for the first time.[79] They were aided by French scholasticism and by the popular movements in France and Italy. Pope Urban IV, in alliance with the French and with Guelph scholasticism, completed the work of Gregory VII.[80] This momentous collapse of the powers of the ancient racial world and its sacred order of men laid the foundation for the executions of Charles I of England and Louis XVI. It had been undermined by the Franciscan revolution, which had proclaimed Christ the sole King of Heaven and earth. Despite their fusion of the Joachimite and the primitive Franciscan sense of history, the Spirituals were still within the Roman Church when they anathematized Emperor Frederick as Antichrist.

Ten years after Lyons, in 1255 and again in 1260, the Church condemned Gerardino of Borgo San Donnino, the Friar Minor of Pisa.[81] 1260 was the year which the Joachimite Spirituals had expected to be the first of the new age of the Holy Spirit. The Emperor was dead ,and yet the new age of freedom, poverty and love had not come. On the contrary St Francis's Order was being firmly riveted into the structure and system of the old world. Such members of the Order as dared to remember St Francis's Testament, and his summons to unconditional poverty and peace, were persecuted. The Spiritual movement now entered a third stage. Its centres of gravity were Provence, Tuscany and the Roman Marches. Its allies came from the religious movement among the laity and Catholic reformist elements. An ever-increasing influx of radicals out of the Waldensian and Albigensian underground joined it. Gerard had already interpreted Joachim of Flora's work as the 'eternal gospel' (*evengelium aeternum*) by which he meant a revolutionary abolition of the whole of the old bodily order both in the Church and in the world.

Meanwhile Peter John Olivi, the son of John Olivi of Languedoc, had entered the Order at Béziers, a notorious centre of heresy, and had begun to work out the Spirituals' vision of history.* In his letter to the sons of Charles

*Olivi died in 1298 burdened with many ecclesiastical condemnations in Narbonne, the ancient centre of Spanish, Arab, Jewish and Albigensian intellectualism.

II of Naples and a little later in his book of sermons on the Apocalypse, the course of world history is divided into three ages of salvation: the kingdoms of the Father, of the Son and of the Holy Spirit.[82] Olivi wrote that there are always sufferings and persecution when a new age painfully struggles to break through. The 'third Kingdom' of the Holy Spirit had been introduced by the Church of the Spirituals, he argued, and the Roman Church, by persecuting it, was showing itself to be Antichrist.[83] Like many sectarians of the period, Olivi believed that the Church had not always been corrupt. Its decline did not stretch back to the days of Constantine, as the Cathars taught, but only began when the Church had become corporeal and given in to the greedy popes, feudal bishops and ignorant, worldly clergy. Since then, the Church had become the new Babylon; enslaved by lust for power and pride in its possessions, it had trampled Francis, the poor man, under foot. It would have to give place to him, for Francis was the 'new man', the *novus dux*, and his Rule the new gospel. His Church was the ark of the elect in this last age. Francis was the angel of the Apocalypse bearing the sign of the living God; he was the second Christ with the fullness of spiritual power, the leader of the new humanity and the standard-bearer of the Spirituals, who were to bring about the fulfilment of time.

This view of history and of the glory of suffering was imbued with a profound exaltation because of its eschatological conviction. As the thirteenth century wore on, the persecutions increased in ferocity and the optimism of Olivi was darkened. The Spirituals began to say that as true Christ bearers, they were re-living the passion of Christ. They were the true Church, whose life flowers in secret while its blood flows in public, and the Roman Church had finally and conclusively revealed itself as Antichrist. In southern France and Catalonia, the Beguines, the Spirituals and large groups of the common people began to build a cult of Olivi, in which he was venerated along with, and often more than, Francis as the spiritual leader of the last age. The Spirituals put to death by the Inquisition had their cult as martyrs in the Mass and the martyrology. The four Friars Minor executed in Marseilles in 1318 under John XXII were especially exalted in this cult as 'Catholics and glorious martyrs'. The existence of faith in the Church of the Spirit and of a cult of these 'witnesses to the truth' among Beguinages, Minorite friaries and lay groups in Provence during the fourteenth and fifteenth centuries prepared the soil and climate there for the emergence of the Illuminati, Huguenots and sceptics hundreds of years later.

On Italian soil, this same awareness of the end of the world in Fra Dolcino's theology of history developed into a highly characteristic combination of eschatology and social utopianism.[84] The hope of his apostolic sect, once reform had been rejected by the papal Church, was that the great renewal of the world, the Church and the social order would come through a new emperor of the House of Aragon. The year 1300 (Boniface VIII's Holy Year) was to see the beginning of the great renewal of all things. This movement around

Fra Dolcino was the model for the flight of the Spirituals (Michael Cesena and Ockham) to the Emperor Ludwig of Bavaria, and it anticipated some of the ideas of Wyclif, Jerome of Prague and Hus. Its political utopianism was descended from the line stretching from Joachim to the Franciscans and continued down to Campanella and Vico. In the later thirteenth century the Spirituals found shelter at the Angevin court in Naples, where they began to explore the possibility of a new political alliance. The way led through the people to popular revolt and ultimately to scientific utopianism, social reform and state power. Its slogan was: 'Down with the pope! Down with the priests! Long live the emperor (or the king), who strikes down the priests!' Society had become the object of their efforts and the source of their hopes. They saw in social reform the opportunity to provide a substitute for that return to Francis which the Order had rejected and that reform of the whole Church which had been nipped in the bud.

Another possibility was missionary work.[85] A new kind of crusade seemed particularly appropriate to the disciples of St Francis. The debate with the East had been sharpened by Francis, and his drama of the crib and stigmatization was carried by the Franciscans to Russia, the Near East, India and China. John of Plano Carpini went to Karakorum, to the Great Khan of the Tartars. Soon there were Franciscans on the Volga (in Sarai), in Persia, India and China. The missionaries were often Spirituals, for whom there was no longer any place in their home in old Europe. They carried out Abélard's desire to escape the pressure of the monastic, tribal system of the old world and to flee to the furthest lands of paganism where it would be possible to live as a Christian. Despite Gemelli's cautious observation that it is not known whether these missionaries were Conventuals or Spirituals,[86] it is undeniable that the first exodus of Franciscan missionaries, the model for the others, occurred precisely in the decade when the Spirituals were being most violently persecuted.[87] We also know that Waldensians and Cathars seem to have followed the Franciscans or even accompanied them. Angelo Clareno, the historian of the persecuted Church of the Spirit, went with Franciscans on the mission to Armenia in 1299 and it is very unlikely that his travelling companions would have been Conventuals. It seems reasonable to believe that the general disillusionment of the Spirituals at the end of the thirteenth century would have resulted in missionary work. Men like Roger Bacon and Ramon Lull were always fascinated by the accounts of the travels of their brethren.[88] The relationship between the retreat into missionary work and the escape into nature which characterized the work of Bacon and Lull suggests that both Franciscan monastery at Hyrèes near Toulon which had been the spiritual disillusion.

Franciscan science had modest beginnings. One of its first centres was the Franciscan monastery at Hyères near Toulon which had been the spiritual home of Joachimism in Provence. There Hugo of Digne, the brother of Douceline the seer and foundress of the Beguines of Marseilles, gathered to-

gether notaries, judges, physicians and 'educated men', who came to his cell
for biblical exegesis and common study of the works of Joachim of Flora.[89]
These enthusiastic and religious laymen began to waken the interest of the
Spirituals in the natural sciences. Peter John Olivi was a scientist as well as a
theologian of history. Alone in his period he asserted that higher knowledge
arises out of sense-perception. His theory of impetus and his idea of the inertia
of matter were the first steps towards modern mechanics.[90] Before him, and for
long after him, the middle ages refused to accept the meaning of motion. It
was something imperfect and evil, as evil as progress in history; both were
contradictions of the one, unmoving, beautiful, perfect, good God. Olivi was
able to accept such ideas because Franciscan spirituality was in several respects
not medieval. Franciscan ideas on science were based on the intellectual climate of the 'World of the Three Rings'. The profane analysis of nature and the
attack on the divinity of the emperor were two expressions of an assault on
archaic society. The new man, the man of the spirit, understood all things.
Hence he could and did assail nature itself, taking hold of it by experiment.

This represented a three-fold conscious protest: intellectually against
Thomist scholasticism, which built a wall of authoritative thought in defence
of the inviolable *ordo* of the cosmos; politically against the curial Church and
its régime of power, which suppressed the poverty movement; and spiritually
against all unintellectual, uneducated men and powers who were devoid of
true knowledge and whose faith had not been purified. Ockham was the
embodiment of the political protest, Bacon and Arnold of Villanova of the
scientific. Ramon Lull strove to reconcile the two opposing worlds.

In Roger Bacon, the Spirituals' prophetical enthusiasm turned toward
science, as a means by which the true initiate, the man filled with the Holy
Spirit, could set about renewing the world.[91] This English friar, who sacrificed
his patrimony in the cause of science, was laughed at by the Spanish students
at Oxford on account of his studies, and imprisoned by the Conventual
Superiors of his Order. The Arab-Jewish-Christian South was for Bacon the
land of that universal science which brought salvation. There flourished
mathematics, astrology, bible criticism (the purification of corrupt texts!),
philology, true theology and natural science. In every branch of knowledge
summoned by this Franciscan encyclopedist to the service of salvation – in his
Opus Tertium, Opus Minus, or *Compendium Studii Philosophiae* – Arab-Jewish
'fathers' were cited; the *Summa Philosophiae** cited the testimony of more than
thirty Islamic and Jewish scholars.

Bacon sought to produce a universal knowledge as a means to help the
missions. He had read accounts of the Franciscan missions by William of
Rubruck and he called upon his Pope to explore the whole earth.† His Pope,

*Not that of Grosseteste, the man who won Bacon for the Order of St Francis, but his
own – probably written by a disciple.

†Bacon drew a map of the world (now lost), showing the sea route from Spain to India,
which came down, via Peter d'Ailly, to Columbus.

Guido of Foulques, had led a long life as a layman in the heretic South, as a soldier, a lawyer and as secretary to St Louis. He had first become a priest after the death of his wife, afterwards Archbishop of Narbonne and, in 1265, Pope Clement IV. He commanded Bacon, against the orders of his Franciscan Superiors, to send him a secret account of his discoveries. All Bacon's works were hastily formulated letters to his 'angelic Pope', from whom he hoped for the renewal of the Church, the purification of the sciences and the liberation of theology.[92] The sciences, especially the natural sciences in statesmanship, the art of war, progress or lengthening of the span of human life, were useful because they gave Christendom the wisdom and the will to confront the intellectual and moral world of paganism.[93] It was better to convert unbelievers through wisdom and true knowledge, than to resort to civil wars and the savagery of unlearned men (*laicalis ruditas*) which at best could achieve only problematic and transitory successes.[94] Bacon was well aware of the insecurity of the victories won by the Albigensian wars and the Inquisition, and hated Parisian scholasticism, so falsely sure of itself and of its triumph. It had defeated his lord and master Francis, and was puffed up with pride in the perfection of its knowledge, whereas, it was, in reality, far below the South in matters of intellect and godliness.[95]

Bacon's criticism of his time, and his programme of scientific and theological reform conditioned each other. Judging by external appearances, and by the degree of activity in the universities, he wrote, we are living in an age of great learning; in fact, however, everything is in a state of corruption, ignorance and ruin.[96] The source of this corruption is in the head, in Rome. The *Curia* has been perverted by the laws of the Roman emperors and by secular Roman law (a typical accusation of the Spirituals). Rome is ruled by pride, avarice, envy, lust and gluttony (*superbia, avaritia, invidia, luxuria, gula*). All the Orders, new ones included, are involved in this decay. *Totus clerus vacat superbiae, luxuriae et avaritiae.* In Paris and Oxford and everywhere else the clergy quarrel and stir up laymen in wars and feuds and all kinds of vice. The laity too are corrupt, and keep faith (*fides*) with their princes no longer.[97] The Christians are morally inferior to the pagan thinkers, and this is why they lag behind them in the world of thought and discovery. 'Many wise men, basing themselves on salutary prophecies, have believed ... that it is in our age that Antichrist will come. Hence it is necessary that evil shall be rooted out, so that God's chosen ones (*electi Dei*) may appear.'[98]

Bacon believed that the great purification of Christendom would certainly be achieved. What was uncertain were the means God would use: a pope, a prince (as a rod of divine correction, as with the Joachimites and Fraticelli), or a persecution of the corrupt Church by Tartars, Saracens or other Eastern peoples. Bacon's science was intended to contribute to this purification. He believed that the reason for the present corrupt condition of things was that true science, the wisdom of God, had been defiled by men. This defilement (a basic idea among cleansers after the time of Humbert and Gregory VII) was literal and spiritual.* Paris was the home of the seven deadly sins of theology, where men were devoted entirely to mere philosophy and to verbal quibbles, while neglecting the natural sciences. Paris, moreover, stubbornly insisted on expounding a corrupt text of the Bible, which made it impossible to penetrate to the spiritual meaning of Scripture.[99] Bible criticism, ancient philology and the study of language had an eschatological significance, because a single word of the Bible might well contain the key to the history of the Church and the stages of her development from the beginning to the end.[100]

Bacon wanted to know when the end of time would come, and to accelerate its coming through the great process of purification. He invoked the help not only of the Spiritual's view of history, to which he constantly made direct reference, but also of natural science. *Natura est instrumentum divinae operationis.* To the devoted researcher, forgetful of self, nature is the key to the mysteries of time and history, of the Church and of God. Even astrology, which, from the thirteenth century onwards, transposed the historical prophecies of the Spirituals into the realm of science, could provide information about the course of history and the duration of the religions of the world – including the *secta Christi*.[101] In this way, a formidable and successful enemy of the Christian mind, the astrology of the ancient and of the Arabic Jewish worlds, was allowed a new lease of life in western Europe. From the twelfth century to the eighteenth atheist astrologers cast the horoscope of Christianity, as of all other sects, and stated in precise terms the seasons of its flourishing and of its decay. Spengler and Nietzsche belong to this tradition. Bacon's intention was to apply it, along with his interpretation of the Apocalypse, to work out the date of the fall of Islam and to use astronomy, to reform the calendar. He loudly bewailed the lack of learning in the early Church, which made it unable to carry out this reform: even today, pagan philosophers laugh at the ignorant Christians, who do not even know how to tell the time.

To Bacon all true men of knowledge, wisdom and scientific research were spirituals, men of the spirit, and had been victims of persecution since the days of the early Church. World history was the story of their *passio*,[102] and his own life (a strange caricature of the *passio* of Francis, Olivi and Angelo Clareno) was that of a man of the spirit, a discoverer, striving in vain to rescue a sinful world from the darkness of ignorance. Spiritual reform set the stage for the beginning of the Enlightenment and the Franciscan revolt turned into a humanist attempt to reform the world.† Spiritual, scientific optimism was the result of eschatological expectation. All science should take the form of an exposition of the Scriptures, and by thus cultivating Holy Writ the Church would return to the holiness of early Christianity. Universal peace would descend upon the Church and the world. It was 'by the grace of God' that the modern

---

*He mentions sodomite perversions among Parisian theologians and professors in *Beatus Franciscus*.

†Later many Franciscans were to be remarkably open towards humanism, the Jesuits and the Enlightenment. Mersenne, for example, was a Minim, a neo-Franciscan.

burning glass had been constructed.[103] *Dei gratia*: the miracle of technics was set up against the magical world of archaic society, whose singing-spells and ordeals and hallowings Bacon listed. In a letter on the secret works of art and nature and the unreality of magic, he declared that art came from the hand of God.[104] Bacon was not a scientist in the modern sense; he made very few experiments.[105] *Experimentum* meant at this period a magical process, an attempt at sorcery, and hence a temptation.[106] The boundary line between Bacon's natural science and sorcery or magic was not clear. If deer, eagles and snakes prolong their lives by the use of herbs and stones, he asked, why should man be forbidden the discovery of an elixir of life?[107] His vision of a world of technology contained rudderless ships, automobiles, aeroplanes, little magical devices for escaping from prison, for attaching people to oneself, or for walking on water. It was a mixture of magic, technology with a magical character, and Franciscan mastery of the world. Any Spiritual could work the miracles of Francis himself, if he had the spirit of the master. The seer gazes at Utopia: the realm wherein the *homo spiritualis* is, through the spirit of God, master of nature and the things of nature.

Arnold of Villanova, Bacon's disciple, was born in Catalonia about 1238, the year in which Bacon was deprived of papal protection and disappeared into prison. Arnold was protected against persecution and the Inquisition by the kings and popes upon whom he attended as physician. He was the embodiment of Bacon's dream of universal knowledge. He got his degree at Naples, and then moved about between Barcelona, Montpellier, Paris and Rome, working as a physician, alchemist, astrologer, diplomat, social reformer and historian-theologian. He translated works from Arabic into Latin and was rooted in that world of the Three Rings which Bacon had constantly in mind. Like all the Spirituals, he was both anticlerical and anti-Thomist and was the author of the famous *Sword of Truth against the Thomists*. He endeavoured to save the Spirituals' vision for orthodoxy, and hoped, like Bacon, for a total renewal of this outworn cosmos, of man, of the elements, of the Church and of society, through an angelic pope.[108] Midway between Hildegard of Bingen, to whom he referred, and Paracelsus (who relied on Bacon), Arnold aimed at an all-embracing art of medicine, a universal chemistry which would rejuvenate and spiritualize man and thus conduct him into the third Kingdom of the Holy Spirit. The Franciscan renewal of the world was to be accomplished by science. He inveighed against the worldly Church of the clergy which was the embodiment of Antichrist, and later ages returned to his ideas for ammunition.[109]

Ramon Lull, the Franciscan Tertiary (1253–1315), was also a Catalan and a representative of this Franciscan Baroque enlightenment. Like Francis and Ignatius, he set out to conquer the world for Christ. 'At the Roman *Curia*, in the lecture halls of the Sorbonne, in councils and in the courts of princes in France and Germany, in the streets and squares of north African towns, possibly in Asia too',[110] this all-knowing, all-believing man went on his way, learning and teaching. The spell cast by Lull upon Nicholas of Cusa, Pico and Bessarion, on Giordano Bruno, Gassendi and Leibniz, his wide dissemination in Germany,[111] and his influence in Spain to this day, rest on his truly Franciscan reconciliation of the world of the Three Rings with Christianity. He combined enlightenment and faith, mysticism and rationalism, folk-culture and the life of the intelligentsia. Lull belonged to the open world of the twelfth century and to the bold rationalism of Chartres, Alan of Lille and Nicholas of Amiens. His life suggests what might have come of that world if it had not been destroyed. Lull's vision of the 'Noble Art' on Mount Randa in 1272 resembles Francis's experience on Mount Alverna, Descartes's dream, and Ernst Mach's moment in the meadow. He believed that he had seen the mystery of being and grasped it: there exists a logical universal science, with first principles, or basic words, which, combined together, make it possible to demonstrate every truth in every branch of knowledge, and in Faith itself. In the archaic world, it had been the emperor, who held the Holy Spirit in his hand and who controlled it. Then the Gregorian popes had claimed the right to exclusive dominion over the Spirit. Now the *homo spiritualis* the man of the spirit (and soon it would only be he) suddenly seized the power of binding the spirit (*ligare intellectum*).

Every system of pan-logic and universal knowledge, from Alcuin to Marx, has sought converts. The Crusades had failed, so there was only the *ars magna* to convert the unbelievers. Science was to serve the missions. Lull learned Arabic, and, in the spirit of Bacon, demanded that academies be founded in Western Christendom in which Arabic, Hebrew and Greek should form the basis of study. The schools of translation which had existed since the twelfth century in Toledo, Sicily and Provence would be extended and made legitimate. His own studies and spirituality made him 'the brilliant lover of his enemy, Islam'.[112] He longed to continue the discussions which used to take place in the East in the world of the Three Rings. In his *Libro del Gentil* which first appeared in Arabic at Majorca 1272–3, a Jew, a Muslim and a Christian explain the superiority of their faith to a pagan. In the *Liber Sancto Spiritu* (Montpellier, 1276–8), there is a debate between a Greek and a Latin in the presence of a Muslim; in the *Liber Tartari et Christiani* (Rome, 1285), the Tartar interrogates a Jew, a Muslim and a Christian. The Christians show a respect for their opponents, and for religions akin to their own, which implies that they are 'enlightened' and know the human and religious values they possess.

Like Bacon, who was anxious that young boys should be taught the meaning of his scientific method, Lull was deeply concerned with education. Even a child should be given a glimpse of the world of Christians, Jews and Muslims (*Liber Doctrinae Puerilis*, written in 1274–5 for his son, Dominic). Indeed, the whole of Western Christendom needs to be re-educated, so that its eyes may be opened to the beauty of foreign worlds. In his educational novel, *Blanquerna*, he described Barbary, Tartary, Abyssinia, Turkey and Georgia, and gave the first European account of a journey through the Sudan. The Eastern missions were to be balanced by a religious and scientific education of the West. Lull translated the Spirituals' programme of world renewal into the language of a fervently religious lay intelligentsia. While other reformers pinned their hopes on universal and national councils, Lull considered the possibility of an international court and a kind of League of Nations.[113] Like Bacon, Lull believed that uniting of the world must be the work of an angelic pope, who appears in the novel and becomes its spokesman.

All his life Lull hesitated between the Dominican and Franciscan Orders; he longed to reconcile the intellectuality of the one with the love of the other. But his 'impetus' – to borrow a concept of Olivi's – was Spiritual-Franciscan. He was horrified by the University of Paris. Towards the end of his century (1297–8) he was certain that it would dissolve in a welter of atheist, 'Averroist', intellectualism. Although Lull's anti-Averroist writings include a great deal of Thomist Aristotelianism, his love of the people is unmistakably Franciscan. He was one of the greatest of medieval vernacular authors (comparable with his contemporary, Eckhart), and was a master of his beloved Catalan. The gentle spiritual mysticism of later Arabic Sufiism (to which he himself made reference) mingled in him with Francis's love of children, the people and his enemies. The world of opposites was to be reconciled. Hence he was the forerunner of Nicholas of Cusa, of Leibniz and the baroque *mathesis universalis*.

8

THE HOUR OF AQUINAS (1225-74)

THOMAS of Aquinas lived in Naples and his life links the schools of Frederick II and the beginnings of the Angevins, the span between Averroist Naples and the Neoplatonic pantheism of a later age. The Guelph papacy subdued the 'holy Emperor' while Thomas was alive. Prophetical spiritualism had been defeated but not destroyed and the vicious struggle among the mendicant orders continued to rage. The universities as heirs to the debates once held before meditative Islamic princes had become open arenas for all sorts of Christian and non-Christian forces. Finally, Thomas was born into a world of rising, Mediterranean, 'enlightened' princes, and it is to these new powers which we must first turn.[1]

The culture of the court of Frederick II can only be understood in the context of the world of the Three Rings. Men like Roger Bacon, Arnold of Villanova and Lull found their princely equivalents in Alfonso the Learned, Dinis of Portugal and Frederick II. Alfonso the Learned* was heir and governor of Murcia.[2] He founded a comprehensive school for Christian, Jewish and Islamic children under the mastership of Mohammed al-Riquiti and at Seville he established a Latin-Arabic college for Islamic and Christian physicians and teachers. His father, Ferdinand the Saint, had also been concerned with the transmission of oriental learning to Christendom: the Koran, the Talmud, the Cabbala. Alfonso continued his work and expanded it to include scientific and systematic treatments of astronomy (the revised Toledo Tables of 1272), alchemy and legislation. His Spanish statute book, *Las Siete Partidas*, vestiges of which were still in force in 1819 in the State of Louisiana, contained Europe's first educational legislation.[3] Another enlightened Mediterranean prince was Dinis of Portugal (1279–1325), who in 1290 founded the University of Lisbon, transferred to Coimbra in 1308. Dinis commissioned numerous translations from Spanish, Latin and Arabic into the vernacular, was himself a poet, and carried out the typical improvement programme of such rulers: canal-building, development of agriculture and encouragement of foreign trade. For Dinis and Alfonso, politics and culture were two aspects of the same policy. Theirs was the spirit of the enlightened despots, and it was said of Alfonso, for example, that 'had he been consulted at the creation of the world, things would have been arranged much better'. Alfonso, a Hohenstaufen on

---

*Alfonso x, *El Sabio*: 'the Wise' is a mistranslation.

141

his mother's side and an imperial candidate in 1254, was an alien in his domain, and resembles in a more than coincidental way Frederick II Hohenstaufen, Frederick II of Prussia, Peter the Great and Stalin.

The Emperor Frederick II 'terrified his age'. He was 'the marvellous maker of changes' (*immutator mirabilis*), the very embodiment of the new technical intellect. There was something appalling about this new quest for power. It seized indifferently upon the world of nature and upon human material – a phrase from a later age here, for the first time, strictly applicable – upon animals and upon things. *Coaequare naturam*: 'rivalling nature' was the main intention of this 'most experienced artist in all the mechanical arts'.[4] What a contrast to the sense of reverent awe in Thomas, for whom there is only one *artifex peritus*, God. The Emperor questioned Michael Scotus[5] to find out in *which* heaven it is that God is enthroned in all his divine majesty. He wanted to seize Heaven, earth and Hell in his grasp, to enter them in one comprehensive inventory, and to fix his own true place – that of sacred majesty, disposing absolutely over God's kingdom on earth and its justice and peace. There were two origins and bases of imperial world government: divine providence, and the inflexible natural necessity of the fallen and sinful state of the world.[6] The psalmist marvelled 'Thou hast ordered all things in measure and number and weight' but the Emperor said 'I am lord of the world'.[7] God, who for Bernard and Abélard had been the searcher of hearts (*scrutator cordis*) was now to be replaced by the Emperor. Using the science of physiognomy brought to him out of the East by Michael Scotus, he gauged the inner nature of 'his' men from the outward proportions of their face.[8]

The Emperor made exhaustive use of the enormous adaptibility of human material and employed astrologers, mathematicians, engineers (for engines of war, fortifications and canals), poets, jurists, travellers and explorers, philosophers and professors. He regularly collected 'cultural material' from the world of the Three Rings; around 1240 he sent a number of philosophical questions to scholars of the Islamic world, and got answers back from Ibn Sabin, amongst others. Ibn Sabin, a heretic, had been persecuted by Islamic orthodoxy throughout Spain and Africa and died by his own hand in Mecca in 1270. The importance of Sabin for the Emperor was that he quoted freely from Plato, Socrates, the Psalms, the New Testament and the Koran. The Emperor, whose own reading included Maimonides and Averroes, was delighted. His famous scepticism and atheism were really no more than a certain freedom of phrase and expression characteristic of such a court and type of society.

The essential point about Frederick was not his alleged atheism but his far more revolutionary conception of knowledge and wisdom as means to power. Knowledge was a tool for changing the world, purging it by law, and improving it by experiment. He flatly denied the scriptural *fides ex auditu*, 'Faith comes by (right) hearing', and asserted instead *fides enim certa non provenit ex auditu*.[9] Only the sure results of observation are reliable – observation of the flight of the falcon, of artificial fertilization, of the diseases of horses and of men. Men and horses were to be cared for and treated on the same hygienic principles. Economic, military, scientific and political interests combined to produce an outlook strongly reminiscent of the Spirituals' scientific Utopianism.[10]

Animals and men were simultaneously taken out of their magical context in the archaic cosmos and subjected to the process of experiment. Frederick's choice of appropriate objects included chickens, doves, dogs, horses, camels and 'his' falcons. This 'noble' bird was considered especially suitable for his various experiments. Salimbene, the Spiritual, reported that the Emperor had men dissected alive in order to study the processes of digestion and sleep, and described other terrifying experiments which could easily have been carried out in concentration camps. The Emperor once drowned a man in a wine-barrel to see whether the soul dies with the body.[11] The things of this sort credited to the 'damned and diabolical' Emperor, whether true or not, certainly reflected his consuming desire for universal knowledge for the sake of universal power. He established the first chair of anatomy at Salerno, and supplied it with corpses. He founded at Naples what was probably the first modern state university[12] and in its charter he promised 'his' professors high honours, dignities and financial rewards, 'his' students cheap lodgings, rich stipends and assured careers.[13] Frederick collected a group of Catalans, Irishmen and Bolognese at his imperial and absolutist university which soon became a fortress against *curial* Bologna. In 1225, in his battle with Bologna, Frederick dissolved its university, intending to transfer it in its entirety to Naples. Although he forbade his subjects to attend foreign schools, his absolutist educational policy broke down in practice, even earlier than his Empire, mainly because it encountered energetic resistance in university circles throughout Europe. Frederick could only conceive of a university, especially his own, as an *instrumentum regni*.[14]

At this court where the first substantial translations of Averroes were made, between 1227 and 1230, and in the thoroughly Averroist and libertine climate of this state university, young Thomas Aquinas received his first impressions. He was so profoundly shocked by what he saw that he never mentioned the Emperor in any of his works. For Thomas, as for Gregory VII, the Emperor had lost the *unicum nomen*, and he dedicated his portrayal of the just king to one of the *Curia's* petty vassals.[15] Yet, in the deepest sense, all of Thomas's work was directed against that figure whose name he never uttered. Ten years after Frederick was deposed at Lyons, Thomas wrote the sacral hymn of the New Kingdom, the sequel to *Corpus Christi*. In 1268, Frederick's heir, Conradin, was beheaded in Naples, and thus the last traces of spell-binding power which that house could hold for Thomas were extinguished. Thomas, who believed in the aristocratic principle, was a kinsman of the Hohenstaufen, and by law, as a son of the lords of Aquino, their subject. At last he was free to produce his greatest works in the years which followed, 1269–72.

As school-learning, scholasticism was bound up with the universities.[16] These institutions were becoming increasingly political places where rivalry between the popes, kings and city states of the free world of the West was manifest, and where constant battles between chancellors, professors, students and citizens occurred. The universities represented western Europe's discovery of itself and were the heirs of the discussions which took place in court society and among the intelligentsia in the world of the Three Rings. Universities were founded to reflect every shade of disagreement and rivalry in the political and religious struggles of the time. The school at Arezzo was a Ghibelline foundation. When the Guelphs came to power there, their opponents started a new Ghibelline *studium* at Siena. During his fight with Thomas Becket over the sovereignty of the Church, Henry II promoted Oxford to the status of *studium generale*, and compelled all English clerics abroad to return to England on pain of losing their benefices. Cambridge came into existence as a result of an exodus of students and professors from Oxford and Paris in the first quarter of the thirteenth century. Montpellier achieved the rank of University after a bitter battle with the bishop. In Italy, several cities founded their universities. Padua was formed by secession from Bologna and continued for centuries, under the patronage of Venice, to be an outpost of Averroism. These Italian universities were practically independent of papal control; they had no *studium* in theology; their students modelled their organizations on the civic fraternities and guilds.[17] Valencia, Salamanca and Coimbra were royal creations, intended for the cultivation of a native intelligentsia for state service. A school was an important political asset in terms both of Church and state; Prague and Leipzig, and the foundations of the Reformation period, are evidence of this. During the Hundred Years War, both English and French founded their universities for political propaganda in France: Poitiers in 1431, Caen in 1437, Bordeaux in 1441.[18]

The university, the birthplace of Thomist scholasticism, thus represented a remarkable interplay of extreme freedom and extreme repression. It was designed to capture the free-floating intellectuals, roaming at will through castles and courts, cities and market-places. They could be found everywhere and pinned down nowhere. The university was designed to collect and supervise this intelligentsia at certain definite 'strong places' – strongholds, and it had from the beginning an inquisitorial significance. Most universities were created at the same time as the Inquisition. The first papal university was Toulouse, founded in 1229 for the pacification of the Cathars, and, as part of his penance, Count Raymund the heretic had to provide the means for it.[19] The professors of this remote university advertised it throughout the length and breadth of Western Christendom, and its students were given lectures on Aristotle's works on the natural sciences, which were still banned in Paris![20] As in every living organism, the interrelation between progress and reaction was highly complex.

The University of Paris,[21] a combined product of the abbey schools of

Sainte-Geneviève and Saint-Victor and the Cathedral school of Notre-Dame, which had been given privileged status in 1200 by Philip Augustus, was now at the start of a long period of growth pursued under conditions of constant friction and conflict, first with the Bishop of Paris (supported by the Pope) and later with every ecclesiastical, royal and papal authority in existence. Its moment of triumph came at the Council of Constance (1414–18) when it stood alone in Europe, a political power without a rival, the judge of popes, the counsellor of kings, the leader of the democratic Conciliar movement. It maintained its supremacy until 1499, when Louis XII rode into it in armed force, to break its resistance and abolish its right to strike. This remarkable accumulation of political power in its hands was the culmination of a process of growth in its intellectual powers, which had already taken place. During the thirteenth century, the University had made Paris Europe's *patria*, the true home of all civilized minds. Victor Hugo could still call upon it in 1870 when German canons thundered at its gates. In 1252, the year in which Innocent IV's bull *Ad Extirpandos* ordained the use of torture to extract confessions from heretics, Thomas came to Paris.

The situation of the University in the first half of the century had grown critical. Chartres had become completely defenceless against the world of the Three Rings, and, as a result, through the teaching of Amalric of Bène (near Chartres) and David of Dinant (who wrote in French), the University of Paris had been saturated with a kind of glittering pantheism. Its speculations concerning God and the world, man and nature, and faith and knowledge, mingled in a mystical baroque confusion. During the years 1210–15 the pantheist doctrines and the writings of Aristotle on natural philosophy had been banned.* In 1217 the Dominicans came to Paris, and in 1229 the Franciscans. Both represented a disturbing element for the old school of theology which still clung to the Carolingian mixture of Augustinian and Neoplatonic elements, with a cautious adoption here and there of an Aristotelian formula.

It is no wonder that this mixture of theology and philosophy, with its allegorical speculations and vague compromises, failed to hold any attractions for the younger generation in religious and intellectual life, with their striving for sharp distinctions and differentiations. Religious enthusiasts flocked into the mendicant Orders, those with worldly ambitions made for the law *studium*, and the intellectuals went to the faculty of arts. The year Thomas arrived in Paris, the mendicant Orders were expelled from the University. During the course of the struggle which lasted nearly a decade the University had grown more and more nationalist,† with the Sorbonne prominent as the mainstay of the secular clergy against the Orders and against (papal) internationalism. As early as 1219, Honorius III had repressed the *studium* of Roman Law at the

---

*There was as yet no distinction between Aristotle and the Neoplatonic apocrypha attached to him.

†It was as a revolutionary and outsider that, in 1270, Thomas was condemned by the University.

University of Paris, because the majority of clerics wanted to study law instead of theology. But the result of this prohibition was the unwelcome one of diverting the current into the faculty of arts. Between 1210 and 1240, there were numerous complaints that in Paris theology had become the handmaid of philosophy and the natural sciences.[22] The 'lower' faculty of the Seven Liberal Arts, regarded as the Cinderella of the University, was a 'preliminary philosophical course' obligatory for all. Its members had ambitions to compete with the higher levels, and the lay Masters of Arts were youngish men for the most part. They made up the 'nations', membership in which did not continue during the higher courses, and had considerable influence in university politics. Since theology was closed to them, they were naturally bent on achieving a systematic philosophy on the basis of natural science and pure reason.

Bacon was a Master of Arts at Paris from about 1240 to 1247; Albert the Great may have been a Master there from 1242 to 1248. By 1243 practically the whole of Averroes' philosophical work was available in Latin. In 1245 Aristotle was condemned once more in Toulouse. Siger arrived in Paris between 1255 and 1260. In 1257 Bonaventure became Master of the Order of St Francis. Somewhere between 1260 and 1265 came the rise in Paris of 'heretical Aristotelianism'.[23] During the following years, Siger was lecturing at Paris on natural science and Thomas on philosophy and theology.

The enormous attraction exercised by Averroes' purely secularist and immanentist philosophy (as understood by these Averroists) had a multiplicity of causes. Paris was the wealthy capital of the Western world, but side by side with the higher clergy, who lived like lords, there was a proletarian lower clergy; and, in addition, an intellecual proletariat described, for instance, by Walter of Lille. Hungry, filthy, without a roof over their heads or light for their work, the students of Paris led lives of utter wretchedness, painted by John of Auville in his *Architrenius*.[24] These students – *vagantes*, *Goliards* (Bernard of Clairvaux called Abélard a *Goliard*!) – had no prospect of continuing their studies unless they joined one of the Orders; no hope of a benefice without family influence. It is they who listened to the new gospel of the faculty of arts. Man must suffice for himself. As often happens, a peculiar secret alliance developed between rich and poor.[25] A secular public of rich burghers and high officials, with a craving both for material goods and for culture, joined with the Masters of Arts to form a new, free-floating intelligentsia.[26]

This world, and its intellectual interests, was portrayed by Jean de Meung, around 1277, in the *Roman de la Rose*, which became a kind of encyclopaedia for his enlightened public. Like Gottfried of Strasbourg, he was avowedly writing for the bourgeois[27], and like his public De Meung, the translator of Vegetius's *De Re Militari*, the letters of Abélard and Héloïse, and a characteristic selection of Giraldus Cambrensis's marvellous tales of Ireland, was anticlerical, cynical and anti-spiritualist. He liked both *liberté* and libertinism. Poverty, whether secular or spiritual, was something evil and pedantic: *Trop* *est povretez laide chose.* Theology was fable; sin was whatever runs contrary to nature, 'the Goddess Nature' of Allan of Lille, whom De Meung cited. 'The Goddess Nature had turned maid-of-all-work and sunk to rank promiscuity,' as Curtius points out, 'her ordering of the life of love soon became an obscene travesty of itself.'[28] Humility and abstinence were 'anti-natural' vices! The *Roman de la Rose* was a praise of 'free love,* and the apotheosis of the intellect as the divine element in man, and of labour. Cain, the fratricide, appeared as the symbol of labour, industry and civic life. This was a gnostic tradition which may be compared with the extolling of Original Sin and of work by the German Idealists. But we should not be distracted by the mere libertinism. What lay behind it was a sombre vision of the world: the universe was a mechanism, like a watch. Man's life was determined by iron necessity and fate dependent upon the stars and the laws of nature (the *dira necessitas* of Frederick II and the Cathars); there is neither freedom nor personal individuality.

A diagrammatic, one-dimensional exegesis of Aristotle, eschewing all excursions into metaphysics as unscientific, provided the foundation of De Meung's hierarchical philosophy of society, in which the professor of arts and his henchman, the philosophically educated man (*clericus*), were hailed as the world's highest-ranking class, and one which the stupid fools of the great lords desired in vain to press into their own service.

In 1277, the whole, 'free-thinking' Parisian world, Siger and Thomas along with it, was condemned by Bishop Tempier of Paris in 219 theses. In them the Bishop testified that Thomas was not really very far from his great opponent, Siger. Both Chancellor Pierre Dubois, who planned to combine their teachings in one universal text-book, and Dante, who has Thomas praise Siger in heaven, realized this too. According to Agostino Nifo, Siger was also a pupil of Albert the Great.[29] Albert was the forefather of that 'first German movement' which ran through Eckhart to Nicholas of Cusa and on to the pansophism and science of the Baroque period; Albert the Neoplatonist, whose circle of interests was dangerously wide and dangerously open, 'open' in the same sense as the old pre-scholastic world, could not fail (unconsciously and unwillingly) to drive the greatest of his pupils in the direction of Averroism. In his 'Neoplatonizing, eclectic Aristotelianism'[30] God and nature, man and spirit still flowed through and into each other in the old Carolingian way.

In 1256, commissioned by Pope Alexander IV, Albert produced a small work against Averroes in defence of the immortality of the individual soul (*De Unitate Intellectus*).[31] The Pope was dismayed by the rising wave of Averroism sweeping over Paris and Naples, and Albert did indeed endeavour to define the position of the natural sciences within the Christian intellectual cosmos. He wanted to arrive at once (like Paracelsus and Schelling) at a 'perfect natural science'[32] (*scientiam naturalem perfectam*). His mind was a seemingly inexhaustible fountain, fruitful from contact with Averroes and

---

*Accusations of homosexuality were frequently made at this period against the University of Paris.

Maimonides and filled with the spirit of his native Germany. He was an alchemist and an astrologer, a researcher into North Sea fauna; he quoted Homer and Plato, observed the diseases of horses and hawks and wrote a description of the tooth of a whale. He was, in short, a universal genius in the Carolingian, cultural, humanist sense, and stood intellectually between Rhabanus Maurus and Goethe. Albert had neither the ability nor the desire to provide an answer for Thomas and Siger. They demanded a clear-cut intellectual division between God and the world, faith and knowledge, theology and philosophy. For Siger, the Master of Arts, it was the need for clarity in intellectual matters which was uppermost while, for Thomas, it was the need for clarity in both intellectual and religious matters. Both found in Averroes an Aristotle stripped of all Platonism and mystery, the *maestro di color' che sanno* in Dante's words. Aristotle was pure reason, scientific method, an intellectual system capable of explaining practically everything naturally and reasonably if only one were willing to submit to the sway of its deductive processes and laws of thought.

Between 1265 and 1270, under Bonaventure's leadership, the great Franciscan reaction against Thomas and Siger, against right and left-wing Aristotelianism alike, began. 'The conflict between Thomas and the Friars Minor was to have incalculable consequences in history.'[33] To summarize it, as is usually done in histories of philosophy, as a fight between Franciscan Augustinianism and Dominican Aristotelianism does less than justice to this major battle, which has continued to rage down to our own day. Ultimately two attitudes to the world confronted each other here, one strongly emotional, with its emphasis on the will and union of love with God, and the other rational and intellectual, desiring to take hold of God and the world by thought. Aristotelianism was condemned at Paris in 1270 and 1277; in 1272 Thomas had to leave Paris, a heretic, persecuted by the Franciscans; in 1273 Bonaventure delivered his incendiary series of lectures in Paris against Aristotle and Thomas, *Collationes in Hexaemeron.*[34] Bonaventure expressed all the immeasurable bitterness of his Order (the *whole* of the Order) over the world's defeat of Francis. Some of this bitterness, strong though unconscious, may have arisen because of the paltry results of the great compromise with the world. Study had been admitted into the Order but of what use was it? Instead of serving the imitation of Christ and of Francis, it led to intellectual pride and philosophical explanations of the world which practically dispensed with God. The hatred of the Spirituals, the fears of the conservative Franciscans and the uneasiness of the Paris theologians, who knew that Siger and Thomas were denouncing their old-fashioned theology for its unscientific character and its failure to give either God or the world their due (e.g., William of Saint-Amour and Gerhard of Abbeville) joined forces.

A few breathless years of triumph followed. In 1274, Thomas and Bonaventure died, followed in 1280 by Albert the Great, who had already proclaimed Thomas's tremendous victory. The opponents of Aristotle and Thomas saw it

coming, and in face of the advancing tidal wave of victorious Thomism a
united front of all its opponents was formed behind a neo-Augustinian system
which included everyone from Scotus to Ockham.[35] Its policy in the intellectual struggle was to out-play Thomas at his own game, to expose even his
clear-cut separation between theology and philosophy, God and the world,
faith and knowledge, as just another messy compromise which did justice
neither to faith nor to knowledge, neither to God (Scotus) nor man (Ockham).
Bonaventure, the 'grand old man' of the old open world, had never gone that
far, although he was not averse to borrowing from Aristotle on a limited
scale. His cosmos, a sacramental, hierarchial order in which the heavenly
powers, man, and the other creatures all intercommunicated was the last
sunset-blaze of German symbolist theology, as embodied in the twelfth-century Victorines. Creatureliness meant being involved in the processes of history. Bonaventure at least made an effort to save the aspirations of the
Spirituals for the Order and for the Church. His defence of Joachim contained
the last genuine contribution to the theology of history between the twelfth
century and the twentieth. Thomas's reply was vigorous. The surmises of
Joachim – the 'unscientific' (rudis) Joachim – about the course of history were,
he asserted, marred by the same confusions as Bonaventure's theological
sermons.[36] World history belonged entirely to God; man could no more prove
and expound it by his own ratio than he could understand the beginning of the
world in time. The history of creation was not susceptible to philosophical
proof but could only be accepted by faith as revelation, a thesis he developed in
his *De Aeternitate Mundi Contra Murmurantes* which was directed against the
Franciscan theologians.

By 1255 Aristotle had conquered the faculty of arts. All his known works
had become required reading,[37] Siger of Brabant, who came from the centre of
Northern Nonconformity,* became one of the most radical interpreters of
Aristotle. Like most of the professors and students (the intelligentsia who
formed De Meung's public) he was an Averroist from his very first appearance
on the scene. For him, Aristotle taught a wholly immanentist philosophy. He
accused Thomas and Albert of not understanding Aristotle, or, alternatively,
of exploiting him in the service of their own philosophical-theological systems
of compromise. Pure reason, as contained in Aristotle[38] and expounded by
Averroes, knew nothing of providence or freedom of the will. Reason could
only affirm the (uncreated) eternity of the world and the unity of the human
intellect in all men; hence there was no personal immortal soul. The thirteen
Averroist doctrines condemned by Bishop Tempier in 1270 were reducible to
these four basic principles. Siger, a skilled Nicodemist in the concealment of
his ultimate personal convictions, declared that religion was necessary for the
mass of people but not for those who are truly educated – men whom he, in
conscious and characteristic affinity to the Franciscan Spirituals, called
prophets. Dogmas held good for faith, but natural reason often taught the

*Louvain was later to be the birthplace of Jansenism.

reverse of them. 'We are not here concerned with miracles of God; we have now to treat naturally of natural things.'[39]

Siger accepted the Aristotelian doctrine of cycles. Everything repeats itself in vast historical cycles – everything, including philosophical teaching, laws and religions. There is no such thing as providence, he argued. God does not know contingent events. It is only through a chain of subordinate causes that the world stands, very remotely, in a relationship of dependence to God. The machine which is the world is almost entirely autonomous in its functioning, merely receiving on its periphery some guidance from the stars – the heavenly intelligences. Time, matter and motion are eternal. It is only individuals who are transitory, and they possess in common only *one* intellectual soul, *anima intellectiva*. Freedom of the will, strictly speaking, is an empty phrase. Good means whatever is beneficial and useful to the human race; evil means whatever damages it. Lack of insight and reason leads man to perform evil actions; but in the last analysis he is always under the strict compulsion of necessity. He has to act the way he does.[40]

With mathematical clarity Siger the Great, as one manuscript calls him, deduced from Aristotle a closed, rationalist view of the universe in which theologians were no more than poets (*De Aeternitate Mundi*). The condemnation of 1277 included the following additional propositions: theology is based upon fables; it teaches nothing essential or true; the wise of *this* world are the only true thinkers.[41] This mechanistic view of the world produced a type of political thought which cleared the way for the new absolutist state. Pierre Dubois reported hearing Siger lecture on a sentence from the *Politics* of Aristotle: 'It is far better that a state should be ruled by just laws than by valiant men.'[42] The offices in such a state would be held by a bureaucracy rather than an hereditary aristocracy!

Siger was a many-sided man. There is a certain playful quality in his intellect and in his answers to the various impossible and ultra-daring questions in his *Impossibilia*.[43] There is also the pathos of the never-resting brain. He expressed this feeling in the closing words of the *De Aeternitate Mundi*: 'Watch, study and read, so that the doubt which yet remains to you may spur you on once again to study and to read: for life without enquiry is death and a dishonorable grave.' The play, the doubt, and intensity of mind is reminiscent of Descartes.* He was a very controversial figure, and, as Thomas charged, often discussed his unchristian ideas with students and the people. Despite his importance in the history of Europe, we know very little about him, and although new specimens of Siger's works and transcripts of his lectures are coming to light every year, the outlines of his personality and work remain hazy. We know that he was politically active and may well have contributed to what Torco described as the growing lack of faith among the people of Paris.[44] We know with some certainty that he led a faction in the University, the 'Siger

---

*It would be fascinating to investigate the extent to which Siger, Calvin and Descartes, who were all from Picardy, were influenced by the traditions of secularized Catharist thought.

Party' (*pars Sigeri*), which agitated in the elections for the rector in 1271.[45] If he was active in other aspects of the intellectual and religious life of Paris, it is not surprising that his doctrines were vulgarized and mixed up with every anticlerical, atheistic or spiritualist idea.

These were years of great ferment at the University. Secular clergy, members of the mendicant orders and theologians of the faculty openly called each other heretics and antichrists in their lectures, disputations, sermons and books. The Franciscans were fighting the Dominicans: Peckham and Bonaventure versus Thomas.[46] The Orders themselves were split. There was an old school of Dominicans fearful that theology would be crushed by the new philosophy, and there were young Franciscans who were sympathetic to Thomas. The contemporary accounts, and especially the 219 theses of 1277, make it quite clear that this tumultuous world harboured more than an Averroist movement.* There were also powerful currents of thought from Catharist, Waldensian, free-thinking, gnostic and indigenous archaic communities and sects. On 6 December 1276, the Cardinal Legate Simon de Brion threatened excommunication to all clerics and students who *inter alia*, mocked at Jesus and Mary during the Mass itself and played dice on the altar.[47] The condemnation of 1277 gave an important place to the *De Amore* of Andreas Capellanus,[48] in whose work, the wisdom of the Templars, that jealously-guarded secret doctrine, was revealed. Later the tradition of the Templars influenced the *dolce stil nuovo* and produced in Italy's noble and educated classes a profound anticlericalism.[49] Templar wisdom was a direct inheritance from the Cathars and bore striking witness to the strength of the Catharist movement, even after its suppression.

The 219 Theses themselves were a mirror of this ferment and contained propositions of unusual explosive force:[50] 'Nothing is to be believed unless it is self-evident or can be explained by what is self-evident.' 'We can know God in His essence in this mortal life.' (The basis of idealism.) Bishop Tempier included in his condemnation a number of Neoplatonic and Aristotelian propositions about the heavenly bodies, the world soul, etc. These are followed by the assertions: 'It is impossible for a man to be produced out of filth (*putrefactio*), by the influence of the stars' entering into the humus as it does into the seed of generation.' 'Nothing happens freely, everything is determined. The soul dies with the body.' 'In all his actions, man always follows the strongest of his impulses.' (cf. Hobbes and Spinoza.) 'There is no difference between men and animals.' (cf. Frederick II.) 'Happiness is to be found only in this life, not in another.' 'No good remains to man after death.' 'Ecstasies and visions are only events of nature.' 'Natural law prohibits the killing of all irrational creatures and animals.' (cf. the Cathars.) 'The Christian revelation and its authority hinder free learning.' (*Quod lex christiana impedit addiscere*.) 'There are fables and false statements in the Christian religion as in other religions.'

*Despite its condemnation and the decree of 1276 against private lecturing, Averroist lectures continued to propogate its doctrines in secret.

'Theological treatises are based on fables.' '*The Trinity is a fiction.*' 'There is no sense in praying.' 'There is no need to go to confession, except for appearances' sake.' 'No care should be expended on the burial of the dead.'* 'Continence is not essentially a virtue.' 'Complete sexual abstinence is the ruin of body, mind and virtue!' 'Humility, when it consists in a person's not displaying what he has but despising and humiliating himself, is not a virtue.'† 'There is no resurrection, no heaven and no hell.' In these condemned propositions, one can see the faithful reproduction of an entire corpus of heretical thought, and get a glimpse of the intellectual turmoil of the period.

When Thomas died on his way from Naples to the Council of Lyons, the Rector Alberic and members of the faculty of arts sent messages of condolence. The members of the theological faculty, which hated and feared Thomas, not only refused to express any regret but began to plan their revenge. In 1277 they tried to include Thomas in the condemnation of Averroism. They were men of the old European world and it was that world which Thomas, by drawing a clear line of division between philosophical, natural theology and revelation, had threatened to destroy. In defiance of the Fathers of the Church, Eastern and Western (and their modern successors), Thomas declared that reason cannot establish the truth of the Trinity, the creation of the world in time, original sin, the Incarnation, the Sacraments, Purgatory, the resurrection of the body nor the 'last things'. Thomas blasted the venerable historical theories of the German Empire and wiped out the cycles of the Italian Spiritualists. Even the victory of Christianity was a miracle. Thomism was a kind of creative renunciation and self-limitation.

The *Summa contra Gentiles* was begun about 1259 and would appear to have been completed during the years 1269 to 1272, in Paris.[51] The *Quaestiones Quodlibetales*, which belong to the same period, were public replies to questions raised by members of a lecturer's own public, or by his opponents, with which the professors used to deal on certain feast days.[52] These two works offer the best opportunity to approach Thomas's own view of the situation of the Church and his relation to it. In the *Quodlibetales*, Thomas showed that he was acutely aware of the perils facing Christianity which had, he saw, been overrun with heresy, error and unbelief. 'As the strength of the spiritual building (of the Church) depends on true belief, so the strength of the devil's building results from false belief.' *Firmitas diabolici aedificii*: every heresy which had ever surged into the world since the time of Marcion was still present in its most virulent form. Thomas then moved to defend the unique character of the Scriptures against those who tried to assimilate them to poetry and literature (*fictiones poeticae*), and to consider whether saints legally canonized by the Church might after all be in hell.[53] He turned to the type of

*Indifference to the dead is a link between the Cathers and Islam, and the modern successors of both.

†Here began the long battle against humility which proceeded via Spinoza and Kant to Nietzsche.

revolutionary spiritualism which rejected the Incarnation, the Eucharist and all external Sacraments.[54] He had already seen a great deal of this sort of spiritualism in Italy and in both the *Summa Contra Gentiles* and *Quodlibetales*, he attacked its denial of the after-life and heaven, its doubts and questions about sexual intercourse and marriage, its condemnations of wealth and rich clothing and its glorification of poverty.[55]

Thomas was a southern man, and the 'World of the Three Rings' had taught him that all the powerful heresies of his own day originated in one way or another from the time of the Fathers. That is why Thomas rightly called the Cathars of his own day Manichees and the Spiritualists Pelagians. The heretical conceptions of his own era were no different from those of Arius, Marcion and Origen, whom he frequently cited.[56] Nor was it coincidental that Thomas resurrected Tertullian the Berber in an attempt to subdue that other Berber, Augustine.[57] Thomas has been accused of 're-interpretation' and 'tactful corrections' of Augustine, but that was not really the point.[58] Thomas realized, as his critics have not, that Augustine was a genius of dangerously inexhaustible fertility, that there were many meanings and levels in Augustine, and that orthodoxy and heresy alike drew their arguments from him. Thomas saw Augustine as the fountain-head of Franciscan revolutionary spiritualism and wherever he engaged in combat with Franciscanism, he was – circumspectly, respectfully, but firmly – challenging Augustine. Augustine's highly personal and Platonic doctrine of the penetration of the divine light into man, the illumination of the Spirit of God, could be made to support every arbitrary position held by any self-appointed prophet. There was no arguing with men who were inspired. Discussion with all the countless host of heretics, dissidents and men with erroneous beliefs was possible only by a rigorous use of reason.[59]

Thomas's rationalism was at home under the authority of the post-Gregorian papacy and in a social order dependent upon the aristocracy and the urban citizenry. This was its hour. After the defeat of the omniscient 'Holy Emperor' and before the victory of the modern national state, the patrician city-state was supreme. Its time was short. The theories of the Legists, the defenders of the right of the state, and the tenor of the council of the Gallican Church in 1286 and 1289 already heralded the new era, but for a while reason and the city were dominant. *Rationis est imperare et ordinare.*[60] Reason is the power of order and self-realization in this cosmos. Thomas's cosmos had been built as a city-state by a noble God who was its *rector civitatis*, monarch and law-giver.[61] The universe, like the Kingdom of God (represented on earth by the Church) was therefore an ordered society, *ordinata civitas*. 'Since nothing exists in vain or without meaning in the works of God and of the Church,'[62] Thomas asserted, the reasoning man could feel confident in his conclusions and his observations. God, Architect, Artist and Monarch, himself guarantees the goodness, truth and beauty of the being and order of the world. Being is good, *ordo bonitatis*; all things imitate the divine Goodness which exists in simple wholeness, and strive, according to their ability, to be like him.[63] As

'King over all gods', God rules (*gubernat*) all things by means of the *regimen universale*. The order by which the cosmos is governed is reasonable because the divine Ruler himself is Reason, Mind, Intellect.* God is 'the most perfect object of understanding', *perfectissimum intelligibile*, and the noblest object of knowledge, *nobilissimum scibile*. The being and existence of God consist essentially in his thinking, understanding and contemplating himself.[64] This was the Magna Charta of European rationalism! God cannot do what would contradict logic, geometry or mathematics,[65] because reason cannot contradict itself. Thomas was a true Roman, a devotee of a linear causality founded on the rectitude of God's own knowledge and activity.[66] As a result, he rejected the dialectics of mysticism and the notion of the union of opposites: 'No one can be simultaneously wretched and happy.'[67] Thomas would have rejected modern thought, especially German philosophy, on these grounds, just as he would almost certainly have condemned Eckhart, Nicholas of Cusa, Leibniz and the Romantics.

Thomas's theology can only be understood in the light of its two-fold foundation: the Italian civic outlook and the Aristotelian conception of aristocracy. There is no end to the number of passages in which he calls God an architect, artist or physician. Thomas's God was a kind of city planner, who had constructed his world like a city or a house.[68] Thomas's careful distinctions between the rational and the supra-rational, the human and the divine, nature and super-nature, were a blueprint for a *societas humana*, a society of free men capable of the enormous self-discipline of submitting in equal measure to the authority of political reason (the state) and to that of faith (in the Church). Like a pioneer, Thomas cleared out the free open spaces in which human political society and the Church had room to develop.[69] The 'first Whig'[70] saw God as a constitutional monarch who, like a wise ruler, had given men free will so that they could develop freely, strongly, actively and politically within society. Thomas challenged the Stoic *fatum* and the misuse of astrology. God's grace was not like the grace of royal lords, which implied a loss of freedom. Man was a free co-operator, whom God asks to make a decision of conscience, even against himself. God is the friend of men; Christ's becoming Man was an act of friendship.[71] The feudal Germanic doctrine of atonement was rejected. Whereas Anselm of Canterbury believed that the insulted honour of God the King demanded the sacrifice of the Son as a just vengeance and *Wergeld*, Thomas argued that 'in order that the friendship between man and God should take a still more familiar form, it was fitting that God should become Man, since man is by nature the friend of man'. All the gifts and operations of

*The civic community produced a kind of political humanism, in which the city-state both mirrored and guaranteed the reasonableness of the universal Ruler. Whenever this Universal Ruler did not certify his good faith by the evidence of a comprehensible, well ordered society, or, put another way, whenever such balanced and integrated urban communities did not exist, God's law at once became arbitrary, and an external rule of terror (grace) imposed upon believers who were mere subjects and not citizens. One cannot understand Luther and the East without realizing this.

the Holy Spirit were attributable to the friendship of God.[72] Old ideas of divine friendship, the sources of which could be found in Stoicism and Boethius the Roman, were resurrected to support the concept of friendship of God and men. Thomas flung himself into the great Gregorian battle against the law of marriage and kinship in Germanic feudal society, which was the basis of the old racial order of things.[73] He saw human society as a natural, civilized community of friends, the *societas humana*. 'It is natural to all men to love one another; there is evidence for this in the fact that, by a natural instinct, a man will in case of necessity come to the help even of an unknown person, as for instance by telling him he is on the wrong road, helping him up after a fall, and on many similar occasions; it is as though every man were every other man's companion (*familiaris*) and friend.'[74] The experience of civic community life began to produce an Enlightenment and a first formulation of the rights of man: a rational society of reasonable, free human beings.

There was, of course, a great deal of what one might call the Homeric in Thomas's attitude to society and it would be misleading to think of him as a kind of pre-Enlightenment thinker. 'There is to be one ruler', because the peace of the world is best put in charge of *one*. In the Church Triumphant God is that One; in the Church Militant on earth it is his representative the pope.[75] Old European rationalism was, after all, the political system of an aristocratic society. It took Homer's conception of the ruler, transmitted via Aristotle, and applied it naturally to the pope. The emperor had lost the *unicum nomen*, the one and only name of saving power; the papal Church took over the task of ensuring peace, justice and order. Thomist scholasticism was the doctrine of right thinking, which was appropriate to such a political system, and the adoption of Aristotle was an intellectual reaction to a sociological reality. Aristotle's political thought allowed the aristocratic-papal system of society to find a justification in the very conception of reason itself. It established reason as the faculty by which that particular world-order achieved self realization. *Sapientis est ordinare; sapientes dicantur qui res directe ordinant et eas bene gubernant.*[76] Thomas's wise man was a thinker who put order into things and governed them; hence the professor of theology was higher in the spiritual hierarchy than the pastor.[77] The noblest mark which could be set upon a man in the spiritual order was ordination to the priesthood, which set the clergy high above all unlearned, unspiritual laymen.[78] The bishops, as *duces*, were the leaders of the army of Christ in its crusades, and the kings of the earth (who used to be the Hohenstaufen Emperor's 'under-kings') were to serve the pope as his vassals.[79]

Thomas followed Aristotle in subordinating the individual and the family to the political society, the *bonum commune*.[80] The 'natural political order of society' existed prior to the individual, because it was an earthly representation of the divine order of mind and reason. Hegel and Marx also owe a debt to Thomas.[81] This rational political order was ruthlessly committed to slavery, warfare and capital punishment because the eternity of punishment in hell was necessary to the *ordo rerum*, the universal order, and 'due order', *debitus ordo*, could be upheld only if merit and reward, sin and punishment were balanced *proportionaliter*. In secular society people might have to be sentenced to perpetual banishment for the purification and cleansing of society.[82] The 'society of the good will be made purer by the separation of such' (...*bonorum societas purior ex eorum separatione reddatur*). The common good was always set above the good of the individual, the *bonum particulare*. 'The lives of a few infected persons (*pestiferorum*) hinder the common good ... Hence these people are to be removed by death from human society.' As for the opinion that they might possibly be salvaged, Thomas dismissed it as 'frivolous'. The danger which such evil men created as long as they were alive was greater and more certain (*majus et certius*) than the good which could be expected to result from their cure.[83] Since man was one of the noblest creations of an aristocratic God, he was obliged to purify himself by asceticism and intellectual discipline. If he refused penance and purification, the official administrators of the Spirit of God and of right thinking had no choice but to purge him.

As man militant, man perfected (*vir perfectus*), the Church marched forward to meet Christ.[84] The masculine intellect achieved mastery of souls and bodies and, above all, of the mother world, matter. Thomas took over the Aristotelian interpretation of the *anima*, the spiritual soul, symbolized by the hand.[85] The hand, which can grasp all things and can be used to attack or defend itself manfully, became a symbol of the western European intellect. Thomas, with a typical aristocrat's contempt for the 'servile arts', compared manual labour and the practical sciences and arts to games.[86] 'Inventions' were 'diverting spectacles' from Thomas's time to the age of the baroque theatre and its machinery. Similarly, history was degraded to the level of rhetoric. Thomas's Church was a Church in which the clergy were administrators of the Spirit; kings and learned men (*eruditi*) were in her service. Kings ruled over secular society, learned men over the realm of mind.* Right down to the nineteenth century the clerical Church, true to the Thomist world-order, stuck to its alliance with 'Christian princes' (against emperors and kings) and with Aristotelian scholars. This tremendous victory of the masculine, Roman, Western world over matter, the feminine, irrational, popular, underground elements, naturally and inevitably aroused violent reactions throughout the mother world, but the decisive counter-blow was not struck until the ancient aristocratic world began to collapse.[87] Not until 1854 was the dogma of the Immaculate Conception entirely accepted and the corporal assumption of Mary in Heaven only in 1950.

'Our resurrection will conform to the Resurrection of Christ.' 'Man is a natural object.' (*Homo res naturalis est*.) These two related propositions of Thomas's thinking were guaranteed by God, who was Mind, Reason, Creator, universal Order and sole Ruler.[88] Such a union could continue only if the 'open rationalism' behind it was maintained by a variety of sanctions, legal

*Thomas, the aristocrat, has no place for 'the people' in his world order.

machinery and general restraints. It relied on the social order of city, aristocracy, and *Curia*. Because this magnificent 'open rationalism' had been enriched by the non-rationalist substratum of faith, it was partly protected against a violent swing to a-rationalism and anti-rationalism or mystical-romantic hostility to reason itself, but it may well be true that the peculiar historical conditions of the patrician state were uniquely conducive to it. In its perpetual struggle for analogies, encounters and accommodations between 'the world' and 'the world above', it was not unlike the interweaving of heterogeneous elements in archaic society. There was a profound affinity between the city and aristocracy and the peasants and people. When the leaders of political and social life were no longer able to bridge the gap, the unity fell apart into spiritualism and materialism.

It is reliably reported that at the end of his life Thomas thought of destroying his life's work and his systematic philosophy. Exhausted by his endless efforts, he drew nearer and nearer to Neoplatonism. The sinister Fleming who was his friend and helper throughout his career, William of Moerbeke, (*circa* 1215–*circa* 1286) was undoubtedly an influence in that direction. We know that William was a Neoplatonist because his writings on geomantics were included in the 1277 ban of Paris. He had travelled widely in Greece and had been Archbishop of Corinth. At Thomas's request, he translated a large number of Neoplatonic works, and improved existing translations of others. His translations of Proclus (the *Theological Introduction* in 1268, followed by the commentaries on the *Timaeus* and Parmenides) let loose a Neoplatonic storm over Europe.[89] In 1260 he translated Aristotle's *Politics* (again at Thomas's request) – a work unknown even to the Arabs. By an irony of fate, the work translated by Thomas's friend and companion was to become the favourite weapon of secular political thought against Thomas's curial world, while the spiritual enthusiasm of Proclus and the 'mother world', the world of matter and the masses and the people, dissolved it from within and from below.

9

THE REVOLT AGAINST THE CURIAL
UNIVERSUM (1282-1348)

AT the turn of the century, 1299, a great wave of eschatological fear and hope swept a throng of pilgrims toward Rome.[1] After some hesitation, Boniface VIII declared the year 1300 a Holy Year; the first *Anno Sancto* of the Roman Church. The papal canonists celebrated the Pope as a 'human god', *deus humanus*,[2] to whom all men are lawfully subject in all things, both secular and spiritual.[3] The Bull *Unam Sanctam* of 1302 laid claim to world dominion, a claim which was not revoked until the time of Leo XIII in the final years of the old European order. The Bull was an almost desperate effort on the part of that great jurist, Boniface VIII, to gather all the centrifugal forces of the time – nations, minds and souls – into one fold. The years 1280–1300 had been colourful and active. The range of personalities and views was immense. Roger Bacon, Henry of Ghent, Godfrey of Fontaine, Jean Quidort, Witelo, Dietrich of Freiberg; Berthold of Mosburg, Peter John Olivi, Angelo Clareno, Ubertino of Casale, Pietro d'Abano, Marsilius of Padua, John of Jandun, Arnold of Villanova, Dante and Ramon Lull; Duns Scotus, Ockham and Meister Eckhart; they were all living at this time. In Germany, the 'first German movement' was about to begin. From 1290 onwards, preaching in convents of nuns was in the German language. In 1313 Mainz went into political opposition to the papacy, followed in 1330 by Cologne and in 1355 by the league of churches in the Rhineland. Northern Spain and southern France were crawling with heretics. A Catalan theology derived from Olivi was the core of a Beguine Church (the *Begine Boneta*). Various Dominican and Franciscan opponents of Thomas Aquinas in England acted out a prologue to the struggle against the Council of Trent. In 1295 the Model Parliament combined knights and burghers in a constitutive assembly, the Commons, and by 1301 England mounted a National Front against the *Curia*. In Italy, in 1300, the University of Padua began to become Europe's foremost centre of Averroism and Atheism. Spirituals, physicians, astrologers and jurists organized to repel Dante's 'Black Beast', Boniface VIII.

The first really violent attack came from France. The national councils of 1286 and 1289 mark the real beginning of the Gallican Church.[4] Its prelates, as Gallican Fathers, gradually joined the masters of arts and the secular clergy

158

of the University against the Mendicant Orders and the absolutism of the pope. Master Henry of Ghent, the son of a tailor, assumed the championship of the metaphysical rights of matter.[5] He defended the will against the intellect and bishops and pastors against monks. His compatriot and pupil, Godfrey of Fontaines, defended love of country in debate against the Parisian Averroists, who considered it an extension of self-love. Godfrey denied their assertion: it was love of a higher good embracing and transcending ourselves. Henry's formula was clearer still: for the 'common good' one's rulers and one's native land can demand anything of the individual, even life itself. Henry arrived at a sort of Platonic communism; the community as a totality (*totum integrale*) was more important than the individual. The people were responsible for their princes. Henry and Godfrey reflected the vitality of the great Walloon and Flemish cities[6] whose independent political life moulded their thinking and affected the world of ideas.

Northern democracy met and joined Aristotelian absolutism at the University of Paris. The union of these two forces in the hands of Philip the Fair was a great source of his strength, because it extended the rights of the community. For example, a heresy obviously concerned everybody in the community, and therefore only the community could really condemn it. In a similar vein, Godfrey argued that the pope was only the agent of the Church and not its ruler. Such thinkers naturally turned to the king in order to defend the *bonum commune* against the tyranny of the *Curia*. The new King declared war on 'our Father the Pope' as 'Father of his Country', and confronted 'our Mother the Church' with his 'Fatherland'.

The quarrel between Philip the Fair and Boniface VIII ended with the Pope's imprisonment. The 'Avignon captivity' (1309–77) pushed royal and papal theories to a first climax of extremism. The second climax fell in the reign of the French jurist, Pope John XXII. Thomas and William of Moerbeke had tried to establish Aristotle's *politics* as a working system in the service of the *Curia*, and between 1270 and 1330 the curial Thomists were all enthusiasts for the divine right of the common good and society which transcended personal and private rights. Aegidius of Rome, James of Viterbo and Remigius of Girolami (the man who told the Florentines that 'unless you are a citizen – *civis* – you are not a man') proclaimed the Church as a totalitarian society: *Ipsa ecclesia ... bene ordinata ... tota secundum totum sic conjuncta et connexa ...*[7] The Church as a political society and the Church as a community of grace were one natural and supreme kingdom, whose sway must be acknowledged by all men.

Paris – the Sorbonne, the Gallican Church and the King denied this radical naturalism. John of Paris (1306) protested against such a mingling of the orders of nature and grace. Like Ockham at a later date, he distinguished between the clerical and lay societies of the Church – *congregatio fidelium* and *congregatio clericorum* – and regarded the pope simply as a delegate of the Church who could be dismissed. The princes, who held the ancient rights of

the emperor in the matter of Church reform, might, through the instru-
mentality of the cardinals or the people, excommunicate and depose the pope.
The Parisian state-intelligentsia was the instrument by which 'Most Christian
King', Philip the Fair, defeated the Roman Pope.* He forced the Pope to consent to the abolition of the rich Order of the Templars, and to the extermination of its members as heretics, perverts and traitors to God, the Church and
their country. A series of state-controlled Inquisitorial trials were held in 1307.
The *Curia* began to do penance for overextending its temporal power, but
history has a curious kind of built-in irony, which Philip's smashing victory
over the *Curia* and the Templars could not escape. In 1793, in the Lodge of the
Grand Master of the Order of the Temple in Paris, the last of the holy kings of
France, 'the healers of wounds', was profaned and beheaded by the sons of
the Spirituals, the new 'Brothers'. No restoration could restore the sacred aura
to the throne. History's accounts are inevitably settled.

The long residence of the popes at Avignon had important consequences for
Europe's intellectual history.[8] At Avignon, the *Curia* was forced to face the
variety of contemporary movements from which it had been insulated at
Rome. Secondly, a very considerable number of Europe's thinkers were held
in protective custody there and, thirdly, at Avignon, the papacy was set down
in the very heart of the world of the Three Rings in southern France. Avignon,
as late as the days of Cagliostro and Swedenborg, teemed with sorcerers,
astrologers, geomancers and alchemists and the Pope was soon involved in
such questions. John XXII summoned a congress of all available scientists (i.e.,
humanist natural philosophers) and alchemists (i.e., practitioners and specu-
lators) to discover whether alchemy had a natural basis. Like many of his successors, he himself was addicted to astrology, but opposed to alchemy, which
had become very popular in the mendicant orders. A close companion of St
Francis, for example, had been deposed from the Generalship of the Order in
1239 for his alchemical experiments. Elias was one of the first in that long line
of Franciscans who were, at the same time eschatologists, natural scientists
and political frondeurs. A typical member of the Avignon community was
John of Rupescissa,[9] a spiritual physician, chemist and prophet, and frequent
inmate of the various gaols of his age, both those of his own Order and those
of Avignon. Among his most notable feats was the discovery of the 'fifth
essence' in all things, which was rediscovered by Paracelsus. John prophesied
to the *Curia* that it would lose all its worldly goods and return to apostolic
poverty. In 1318, a papal commission condemned Olivi's view of history,[10] and
John's views were also suppressed. The *Curia* rejected the *finis medius* (as
Olivi had it) or the *tempus medium* (according to Gerard of Borgo San
Donino) and denied the idea of the preparatory stage to the new age of the
Holy Spirit, which was supposed to begin at Avignon. The papal censor
declared that to assert that the vision of God took place in time, *in via*, implied
seeing our final end as lying within history, i.e., within the temporal order.

*Philip's chancellor, Dubois, was a pupil of Siger and Thomas.

Since a vision of fulfilment in history meant that God manifests and fulfils himself in time (in the kingdoms of the Father, the Son and the Spirit), it was akin to an insight into the processes of God in nature. Thus, the *Curia* was compelled to recognize that there was a real affinity between the spiritual view of history and alchemy. We have seen the connection in Bacon and Lull, and it is even more obvious in the alchemical tracts,[11] dedicated to Boniface VIII and other princes, attributed to Arnold of Villanova. The *passio Christi* is seen as enacted in the *passio* of the elements; chemical change corresponds to transubstantiation, communion and the redemption of the world by Christ (as in the *Flos Paradisi*). Quicksilver,[12] for instance, is led like a lamb to the slaughter, and sheds its blood 'to deliver mankind from poverty and wretchedness'. After three days comes the resurrection of the quicksilver, fair, white and transfigured. This alchemical language persisted right down to the age of high baroque in the eighteenth century, and traces of it are preserved in our concept of the inertia of mass.

These monkish alchemists who lived and worked in Avignon began one of the most momentous developments in the history of man. Their vision of the reign of the Spirit and their hope of the end of things ended in the absolute opposite, a completely materialist spirit of experiment. They thought that changing the world and its transformation through Christ could be accelerated by the chemical transformation of its elements. (Marx, Leibniz and Böhme are the heirs of this idea.) Things must be changed radically, from the root, from the mother, from matter upwards; man must change himself radically as well, by renouncing the power and dominion of the ancient world and accepting total poverty. The battle over poverty reached its climax at Avignon. In 1323 John XXII's 'everlasting edict' condemned as heretical the conviction held by the Spirituals and a considerable number of Italians, that Christ and his Apostles had no possessions of their own.[13] As late as 1331 the Franciscan Order petitioned the Pope to lift the ban imposed by Gregory IX on the vow of poverty in the Rule of the Order. Meanwhile, Cesena, General of the Order, and Ockham had sought refuge at the court of the Emperor Ludwig, fleeing from a corrupt papacy abandoned to riches and world dominion. At the *Curia*, after the defeat of the Spirituals and the sanctioning of wealth, powerful groups busily transformed the Church into a genuine state complete with a bureaucracy and a hierarchy of jobs. All offices and dignities, including even papal vicariates, became saleable commodities, though it was not until 1389, in the reign of Boniface IX, that their sale actually became a matter of routine. There was a thorough commercialization of Purgatory, the ransoming of souls, and indulgences.

Elsewhere resistance to Avignon encouraged the growth of Italian political humanism. Hatred of Avignon forged an alliance between French and Italian Spirituals, astrologers, alchemists, Averroists and legists. Increased pressure from the Inquisition during the second half of the thirteenth century merely drove intellectual and religious nonconformism further underground. Occasionally, a group would be smoked out and a trial would follow, as in the case of the proceedings against the 'Sect of the Spirit of Liberty' – *Secta Spiritus Libertatis* – held between 1306 and 1311.¹⁴ The discovery of the sect took place when its members began making converts under the very eyes of St Clare of Montefalco in her own convent. The saint herself was beset by the sectaries with questions, doubts and insinuations. This was a favourite Nicodemist technique. The heretics disguised their own doctrine behind the questions of eager enquirers, and thus threw investigators off the track. It was used again in the sixteenth century. The pathetic weakness of the Church was revealed when the heretic could cite Holy Scripture while the saint was forced back onto revelations which she personally had received from God. The views of the sect consisted of a bold, free-thinking type of quietism, reminiscent sometimes of Fénelon and sometimes of Rousseau and Madame de Warens. They believed that a man in a state of grace can no longer sin; such a 'perfect man' (*homo perfectus*; cf. the Cathars) is no longer obliged to obey the Church; he can do what he wants.¹⁵ Sin and vice (in political terms, war and tyranny) are as necessary as grace and virtue. All that happens is good.* God is the Author of all things; Hell consists simply in the inability to assert one's own will, while Heaven is the freedom which makes all things possible and permissible.

The leader of the sect, Bentivenga, a man with a high reputation for sanctity, tried to win over Clare of Montefalco herself by an argument based on the texts. He told the saint: 'If I could but preach it openly, I would very shortly set the world to rights (*rectificarem*).' At that point this enlightened gnostic leaned upon the altar (the setting of the discussion was the monastery church) and said: 'God has told me that there is no "devil" excepting Himself.' For the demon is wisdom, and God is wisdom, so God is the devil. It had taken thousands of years for archaic society to distinguish between God and the devil, only to have a voice from the underground of the people openly put them together again. Bentivenga had been a member of an Apostolic Sect of Eastern and Catharist inspiration, but later became a Franciscan. His views spread rapidly through the Conservative wing of the Order which, in turn, transmitted it to wide circles among the clergy, female religious orders and educated laity in central Italy. The Inquisition was often under the control of the Spirituals, and at Avignon, Ubertino of Casale complained that he had been persecuted by the conservative Franciscans for using the Inquisition against this sect.¹⁶

The *dolce stil nuovo* was admirably suited to this type of religious anarchism. Literary Italian¹⁷ was the language of an aristocracy which had found a form of linguistic expression perfectly suited to its profound desires. Literary Italian was an assertion of the independent self-sufficiency of the 'noble heart' and high-flown Neoplatonic-gnostic wisdom against the old monasteries and

*This was the beginning of that approval of things as they are, in a mystical affirmation of the whole of reality, which was to play so large a part, in an attentuated form, in the English seventeenth and eighteenth century theologians and in the gnosis of German idealism.

the bishops and popes. Its language, poetry and secular spirituality were an inheritance from the Templars, the Catharist and Waldensian intellectuals.[18] A profound anticlericalism of ancient lineage was embedded in this society which was ready to respond to the call to resist Avignon. The Italian University was an outgrowth of the lay schools of late antiquity,[19] where the orator from the beginning had been forced to hold his own against the theologians, who were outsiders.[20] Most of the friends of Marsilius of Padua belonged to this milieu. Albertino Mussato was one of a group of judges and professors at Padua who regarded true art as something divine, a theology in itself. In his polemic against the Dominican Giovannino of Mantua, Mussato proclaimed poetry as the Godhead in activity! *Quisquis erat vates, vas erat ille Dei*!

Ancient poetry, rhetoric and politics were all enrolled in the defence of religious and political independence against the *Curia* and its clergy. The alliance was well illustrated in the life and work of Brunetto Latini (d. 1294), the Florentine ambassador in France and author of an encyclopaedia in the French language written for this type of laity, *Li Livres dou Tresor*. The *scienza politica* was the noblest of all the sciences, he wrote, and the *dolce stil nuovo* was that in which a noble Italian lord discovers himself. This is why these men flung themselves into the study of law. Cino of Pistoia, the friend of Dante and precursor of Marsilius, made a violently anti-Curialist defence of the *jus nostrum*, the Roman civil law, against the 'law of alien lords', of popes and canonists. Cino stood for a clean and absolute division between spiritual and secular power. The natural science of this group was even more aggressive. Pietro d'Abano, physician, philosopher and astrologer, who was educated in Constantinople and Paris, and who introduced Averroism to Padua, aimed at destroying the whole outlook of curial absolutism – Thomas's teleological cosmic order. There cannot be any such thing as providence, he argued, and hence the papacy cannot be its official organ. Since nature has its own unalterable laws, there can be no miracles and no superior direction of natural events.[21] Pietro worked out the horoscope of the Christian religion in order to demonstrate its purely relative position in the cosmos.

Avignon thus faced the Spirituals asserting the relativity of the pope in the order of salvation, the king of France asserting his relativity in the political order, the Averroists in philosophy and the Sorbonne in law. In 1324, two masters in the faculty of arts in Paris, John of Jandun and Marsilius of Padua, collaborated to produce the *Defensor Pacis*. Bologna's Averroism, which had reached Padua,[22] had already established relations with Paris through Aureoli, Matteo da Gubbio, Giacomo da Piacenza and others. Jandun, who wrote a commentary of Pietro d'Abano (transmitted to him by Marsilius), differentiated faith and science, (the latter alone being demonstrated by reason) which was reflected in the division between the clerical Church and the state. Philosophically speaking, there was nothing that could be said about the supernatural, but only about 'living, and living well' (*vivere autem et bene vivere*).[23]

Marsilius, 'the greatest heretic of our age' (as Clement VI called him in 1343), was a physician, Averroist and lawyer. His heresy was to dare to apply to the secular community the criteria of the Aristotelian *bonum commune*, or the common good, which the Avignon canonists claimed were exclusively applicable to the Church. Marsilius argued that the state was a work of human reason and will; it was men who made the state. No reliance was to be placed upon the laws made by religions (a discovery made in the world of the Three Rings), which mix truth and falsehood together. The state must be based upon pure reason and rationality. Thomas had ascribed the guardianship of the *ratio* to the papal Church; Marsilius now transferred this, the highest office in Western Christendom, to the state. The only true authority is that of the state. The enthusiasm for reform of the Franciscan Spirituals was the tremendous driving force within this practical Aristotelianism. Marsilius was not a cold jurist but, like Duns Scotus and many other Franciscans, a combination of intellect and passion. He desperately wanted to force the 'corrupt Church' of this 'impure' hybrid world to reform itself by differentiating between the divine and the human. In a very direct way, he secularized the ideas of Joachim and the Spirituals. The state was to serve progress by keeping its laws in a constant state of development through reason and practical experience, *sensata experiencia*. 'Truth is a daughter of time' because it is relative to the present stage in the process of salvation.* Within the state, it is the people who should rule, and among the people the more competent part – *valencior pars*.† All legislative power resides in the people, who can even depose their princes. The 'people' here is the *novus populus*, the 'new people' regarded as a (monastic) community of salvation. Joan of Arc and Rousseau are both incomprehensible without this translation of the idea of reform into political terms. 'The people' undertook to protect and carry out the task of the Spirituals and all the other Christian reforming Orders and sects repressed by the authoritarian Church at Avignon. It is the right – indeed, the duty – of man (as the son of the *homo spiritualis*) to create his own state and his own *religio*, because the message of Christ is the message of freedom.[24] Marsilius demanded freedom of conscience and religion for all men, and energetically defended heretics and unbelievers against any kind of coercion.[25] He used the various protests of Paul, Augustine, Chrysostom and Bernard of Clairvaux, made in the name of the (redeemed) individual against the world-state of Rome (or Byzantium), in order to attack the new world-state, the Avignon Church and, in doing so, revived Augustine's Church as a 'community of citizens'. The Church is the community of all who believe in Christ;[26] the people should choose their own priests and bishops and restore the papal Church to the poverty and humility of the apostolic age. Marsilius characterized the arguments of the canonists of papal supremacy as the fruits of arrogance, fantasy and credulity. The clergy should limit

---

*This phrase from Aulus Gellius became a motto for humanists and publishers in the sixteenth century.

†cf. the *sanior pars* of the monastic Rule.

themselves strictly to spiritual things (the cult and the administration of the sacraments); everything secular belongs to the state and the people.

Marisilius introduced into the political sphere what had already been achieved by Duns Scotus, the 'legist of God' as Landry called him, in theology.[27] 'God is infinitely removed from creatures' – *Deus distat in infinitum a creatura*.[28] Scotus rejected Thomas's synthesis as insufficiently reverent. Man's place in relation to God was not clearly differentiated in quality. There is, Scotus asserted, a yawning abyss between God and man, Faith and science, theology (which is a practical science) and philosophy. God is freedom: that is, He is utterly free will, bound only by the laws of logic and the first two statements of the Decalogue. He is not bound to the creation of the world, or its redemption, or the moral order. God could have left the world uncreated and man unredeemed. Theology (which, with Augustine, he dismissed as the holy science of the pagans) is entirely powerless to grasp this God who is 'wholly other'.

Scotus pushed Thomas's work of enlightenment to its furthest conclusion by showing all the things which man cannot know of God (*theoremata*). Opposite this God who is 'wholly other' stands man, surrounded by a stern and profoundly alien world: human personality is 'the extreme of solitude' (*ultima solitudo*; as in Augustine and Kierkegaard).[29] *Ordo* is not a hierarchial cosmos in which man is assured of his natural and supernatural status, but a multitude of particular laws and situations confronting the individual person and demanding either his consent or his refusal. Human life is atomized; it dissolves into a host of single moments, each with its own individual worth as an action performed in obedience to the law. A person realizes himself in a series of free acts of love of God, the world and things, because each moment fresh demands are made of him and old ones renewed.

This is really a kind of Christian existentialism with its sharp awareness of the thisness of things, *haecceitas*, and of their positive individuality. Antiquity, even Aristotle, was so locked into the magical totality of archaic society that it could understand individuality only as the negative of universality. Franciscan thought broke the magic circle and gave to individuality – and with it matter – an entirely positive value. *Materia magis est necessaria quam forma*.[30] Matter is more necessary than the intellectual principle which gives it form. Oxford's Franciscan tradition in natural science (represented by Grosseteste, Bacon, and many others) laid the foundation for materialism essentially because it took the human person and its freedom of action in relation to individual things so seriously and spiritually. Such a position made tremendous demands on humanity, even greater than those made by Thomas. The Thomist vice was turned still tighter. Man – the individual – had to do justice to four separate worlds at once, each of which in its own fashion had to be taken with equal seriousness, and which confronted him simultaneously with demands and menaces in the form of evidences of love (God), principles of thought (the metaphysical world), moral commands (the moral order) and natural laws (the natural world). Scotus, who was both a Spiritualist and an almost anarchical individualist, fled these pressures, as men of his spiritual disposition so often do, and tried to take refuge in political absolutism. A supporter of Boniface VIII, and as such driven from Paris in 1303, he saw nothing in natural law to which he could appeal against tyranny. A man must endure it in obedience to God, even as he must accept God himself. The prince has the right to extend the kingdom of God by the use of threats and violence; hence he may take the children of Jewish parents and impose baptism upon them (an idea which Thomas opposed).

Scotus had developed a theology which was intrinsically inhuman. Since the universe had been split, shattered to its very depths, nothing was left save atomized individuals confronting one another. Will (in God) confronts will (in man). Nothing but a strong hand can bind them together and only 'the Mother': matter on this earth, and the Mother who is in heaven, can ease the tension. It is easy to see how Scotus helped to prepare the way for the Marian dogmas. To Scotus himself, this order in which opposites remained unreconciled was endurable, because he was an intellectual and an ecstatic mystic. His fanaticism about purity of mind and heart made him akin to Spinoza, and the spiritual kinship appears clearly in the mathematical, architectural mysticism of his 'golden treatise' (as Longpré calls it) *De Primo Principio*. It is not only its literary form which recalls the *demonstratio geometrica* of Descartes and Spinoza, but also its *amor dei intellectualis*. God, as total unity, as unique first Being, expresses himself in the Trinity, which is 'supreme communicability, supreme lovableness, supreme integrity and totality (*totalitas*)'. This perfect Goodness imparts itself in acts of free giving, *liberalitas*, expecting no return. Scotus slew with one stroke the entire spiritual system of barter and reward at the heart of the 'old Church'. With an iron logic, he deduced the Trinity from the Unity while, at the same time, inserting a series of tempestuous prayers reminiscent of the mysticism of those Arab intellectualists to whom he owed so much. 'Thou living, Thou most noble Life of reason and will ... Thou Blessed ... Thou clear vision of thyself and most lovely love' – *Tu vivus, vita, nobilissima ... Tu visio tui clara et dilectio iocundissima ...*[31] Scotus provided the link between Abélard's hymns to the Holy Ghost, Descartes's *claire et distincte* and Spinoza's vision of God. During the latter part of his life, he lived in very great danger and died in 1308 in Cologne, the home of Meister Eckhart.

William of Ockham, like Scotus, combined an ecstatic sense of the omnipotence of God with a boundless admiration for human reason and free will.[32] Like Descartes (see his *Traité de la manière de dresser l'esprit*), his was a 'geometrical mind' which longed to teach his contemporaries to think correctly. For archaic society, from Plato down to Alcuin and on to Thomas, thinking had been an expression of being. The hierarchical structure by which things were governed seemed naturally to use the form of words. The universal was reverently represented in valid concepts as though under sacramental signs. Magical in its primitive structure, sacramental and authoritative in its development, thinking in this sense was an echo of the judgments passed by the very *ordo* of things; hence it revolved around authorities – the classics and the Fathers of the Church, those who gave valid expression to the sacral-political order of the universe. The innovator who dared to pronounce a word of his own was a devil, desiring to set up a word of contradiction against the divine rule of the Logos; an Antichrist, seeking to incarnate himself by his own power in opposition to the Word of God who had become flesh in the Son. The ancient Church expressed this divine cosmos in its liturgy, hallowings and sacraments. Similarly, the ancient law of the people acted upon it, seeking in its judgments to discover and embody justice itself – that just law according to which the cosmos itself had been fashioned. *Deus est justitia; Got selve is das recht:* to think and act in accord with God's own order of government was what the judge tried to do. He took his seat at the door of God's house and like the priest or theologian declared in his judgments the legality of the divine order. Human thought, then, was a representation of the law and order of the divine realm of the cosmos. This is the historical significance of universals. Medieval realism referred its words and concepts to universals because they were anchored and guaranteed by universals.

Ockham created a new language, new words, new thinking: language was now to be a democratic convention between free individuals, who reach understanding between themselves on the meaning of each word and concept. Thinking no longer meant echoing the sacred word, reproducing the sacred meaning of each individual thing by reference to its link with the universal. Thinking meant understanding the correct use of common concepts which were intended to stand for individual things as natural signs (not sacraments) and so to express them.[33] The universal was merely a conventional sign for plurality,[34] and natural universals were constructed from particular individuals which happened to resemble each other.[35] This nominalism was built upon the logic of Aristotle, Porphyry and Boethius. Eleventh-and-twelfth century dialects were important as preliminary stages, and Ockham used them together with the *sermoncinalis scienta*, the science of the value and rational use of language, built up since the beginning of the thirteenth century by the Paris masters of arts.[36] The great logicians, William of Shyreswood and Petrus Hispaniensis, whose *Summulae Logicales*, translated into Greek, recast the whole of Byzantine logic, were his immediate precursors.

Nominalism was more than a new logic. It was the expression of a deep transformation. The old, seamless order of the cosmos had been, at last, totally destroyed. We have followed the various steps in this process and can now, perhaps, see more clearly what they were. Gregory VII had destroyed the old Church's authority and his successors had removed the sacred character from the king-emperor. Cathars, Waldensians and reformers had attacked the sanctity of the father, whose words, as *pater-familias*, expressed the 'right order of things' in the household. The magical and sacramental guarantees of the old order had been undermined by monkish alchemists, who changed things and refused to accept the sacredness of matter. Finally, the universe had been split by the theology of right-and left-wing Spiritualism. Scotus saw God receding into the remotest distance, and, therefore, Ockham concluded that each separate individual must make words for himself, as city, fraternity and guild did in their pacts and alliances. The new citizen must assert himself by voting in councils and democratic assemblies,[37] and equally by acting for himself in thought.

Ockham was the founder of modern European democracy and the 'rights of man'. The powers and rights which formerly belonged to the king, priest, noble and father devolved upon each single individual. Every man became a 'kingdom' (like Gottfried of Strasbourg's *Tristan*), and, as such, capable of concluding pacts and alliances on his own account. He had the right to voice his opinion on all matters. Voting took the place of that *laus*, that spontaneous (i.e., magical and all-embracing) cry of joy with which the people of God used to elect their bishops and kings from ancient and holy stock.[38] Voting took the place, not only of the authoritative decision of the father (king or pope), but also of the voice of the *sanior pars* of the Benedictine Rule, the healthier elements of the community. Dante tells us that the individual had placed the crown and the mitre upon his own head. He could make new words and substitute himself for the ancient sacred order by which the cosmos was governed, because he had become the *vir spiritualis, novus ordo*, and the maker of the 'new age'.

After four years under arrest at Avignon, Ockham fled to the Emperor Ludwig at Pisa with his spiritualist fellow-Franciscans, Bonagratia of Bergamo and Michael Cesena, General of the Order. After signing Cesena's protest against John XXII's anti-poverty decree on 13 April 1328, he had no choice but to flee. Two years earlier, Jandun and Marsilius had also taken refuge with the Emperor. Ockham's philosophy and his anti-papal politics were very much in the spirit of the Emperor's court, and during the years between 1333 and 1349 he wrote a series of violent attacks on the curial Church.[39] He condemned the gluttonous, avaricious, ambitious professors of theology.[40] – *doctores propter gulam, aut honorem et divitias*, – the uneducated, grasping, enviously myopic inquisitors, perfectly incapable of distinguishing between heresy and orthodoxy, and the megalomanic Pope, heretically fighting the Emperor and the poverty movement.[41] His logic, philosophy and theology, in which he exposed all the old symbioses and syntheses as fictions, was closely related to his polemics. Since no bridge whatever existed between knowledge of the universe and knowledge of God, things could only be knowable in terms of themselves. God could not be known, but the world could be. It could be studied and investigated. This was the end of the old vision of the cosmos in which all things had their measure in God, and the denial of the teaching of the Psalmist, of Plato, of Hugh of St Victor and of Thomas.[42]

Measure (*mesure, mensura*, and the German *mâze* in the sense of virtue) had been the expression of the harmony of being. Ockham asserted that measuring a thing meant comparing it with some other thing, and that small units made better tools to measure with than large ones. 'Measure is the principle of knowing, not of being.'[43] Magical measure was replaced by a unit of reckoning.* Nature was neither a mysterious being nor a power nor a tendency, but the sum of existing things. *Omnis res est singularis*.[44] Ockham's concern was not so much with the individuality of things (often regarded as the basic nominalist idea), as with their singularity, their unrepeatableness. All things are single, he argued, sharply separated from each other, and not interchangeable. Ockham's universe consisted of individual bits, mechanically fitted to each other. It made no provision for things to be in common but only to be alongside each other.

The effect of Ockham's thinking was to place God and man very far apart and to make freedom something exclusive of all causality. There was therefore no such thing as human nature, only as many human natures as there were individuals. In Ockham's view individuals were composite beings, sharply divided into soul and body, and the soul exercised an external dominion over the body and the passions, like a legislator or a master. Each person was a radically independent free being, whose life was a series of single, non-interrelated actions. Good was obviously not a quality of being, nor the expression of the life of society nor of a universal final end; good signified simply an encounter between a free person and a decree confronting him from outside himself. The morality of an act depends on its rationality.

These ideas led inevitably to a doctrine of natural morality. The commandments of reason became categorical imperatives binding on all, even unbelievers. Morality was simply reasonable thought and deed. A moral act was whatever the practical reason demanded.[45] The political, religious and legal institutions, the ecclesiastical and social structures were never necessary in Ockham's view, but only contingent. They were simply constructions of positive law, without any inherent relationship to God, the cosmic order of morality. Ockham's judgment was based on the experience which men had acquired in Oxford, Paris, Avignon, Italy and Germany. They saw that Europe had become an innumerable multiplicity of confederations, corporations, cities and ecclesiastical and secular alliances. Ockham transferred their *jura et libertates*, their freedoms, privileges and customs, as expressed in their charters, statutes, proclamations and treaties and put them into the language of theology. In this sense, he was the forerunner of Locke and the prophet of the two essential natural rights of humanity – property and freedom.

Ockham's individualism was focused not so much on the freedom of the individual person as on the freedom of corporations, councils, nations and societies, which fashioned their own laws and elected their own authorities. His thought was a sober, factual presentation of the political and social realities

*The French Revolution's metric system was cherished as a sacred sign of the 'new world'; it replaced God who ordered all things by measure and weight.

of fourteenth century Europe. Everyone was fighting everyone else, and yet within the natural groupings, held together by a common egoism of speech and law, every individual regarded himself as bound by treaty, statute and his plighted word. At an infinite height, above all these laws and pacts of human, earthly society, stood God, in no way bound by them, wholly beyond men's good and evil. There can be no doubt that Ockham's desire was to protect God against the hands of men, grasping after salvation and seeking to enclose him in the grip of their pacts and their theological concepts. As a result, he set him at so vast a distance that in the end this terrifying transcendent Godhead of his turned into a 'deceiver God', an 'omnipotent enemy', a 'God of revolt' and the 'hereditary foe', against whom mankind must be on its guard.[46] Ockham's spiritual aim was to separate things which had become far too intimately involved with each other: God, nature and man; the clerical Church and the state. Earthly life could be secure only under the shadow of some protector, emperor or city, but salvation became entirely uncertain, because it was dependent on the grace of an omnipotent God who does what he will. Christ virtually disappeared from Ockham's cosmos. *His* mediators, the bishops, popes and priests, had been discredited and, equally as important, the natural law excluded all mediation between heaven and earth.

The strongest proof that Ockham's philosophy of group egoism was historically correct for the late medieval world was the rapid establishment of Thomists and Scotists and the groups within them as Realists of the 'old way', the *via antiqua*, in opposition to the nominalists, the Ockhamists, of the 'new way', the *via moderna*. After a few open decades the Dominican Order imposed Thomism on its members and the Franciscans did the same for Scotism. Despite Thomas's canonization in 1323 (a year of climax in the battle between Avignon and the Franciscan poverty movement), Thomism was in general retreat in the fourteenth century; it made a stronger stand in the fifteenth at Cologne, but it did not enter upon its triumphal progress until after the period of the conciliar movement and of the cities. It had to wait for the victory of the absolutist princes and the Counter-Reformation Church in the Tridentine sixteenth century. Scotism demonstrated the revolutionary forces in its religious origins in the Franciscan upheavals in the England of Wyclif and the Prague of Hus. It continued to pursue its preoccupation with 'uncontaminated distinctions' as late as the seventeenth century, wherever it had possession of a university chair – in Italy at Rome, Padua and Pavia, and in the Iberian Peninsula at Coimbra, Salamanca and Alcala. The doctrine of Ockham, who was excommunicated in 1328, went forward as nominalism – frequently, it is true, diluted to conform to an older scholasticism – to conquer the University of Paris in 1340 and from there, between 1350 and 1450, to attack the new German universities. Vienna and Erfurt became almost exclusively Ockhamist; at Prague, Leipzig, Greifswald and Cologne, the *via antiqua* managed to make headway. Generally speaking, Thomists, Scotists and nominalists worked side by side in all universities, but it was the last-named who were stronger and more active. In 1425, even Cologne had to defend itself against the Electors' accusation that realism had been imposed on the university. In 1444 the nominalists there took the offensive against Thomas and Albert the Great, and from that date, until the eve of the Reformation, nominalism dominated the intellectual climate of crucial German universities like Wittenberg and Erfurt.

10

THE FIRST GERMAN MOVEMENT IN ITS EUROPEAN SETTING

(1270–1350)

THE historical significance of the first German movement – i.e., that mysticism which embraced Mechthild of Magdeburg, Eckhart,[1] Tauler and Suso (1270–1350) – can be appreciated only if we see it in its setting in Europe of the fourteenth and fifteenth centuries. It brought about a powerful discharge of psychical and spiritual energy. After it passed, the people were exhausted and their quiescence was an important factor both in the rise of the princely states and in the maintenance of peace in Germany from the middle of the fourteenth century until the Reformation. In the same period the rest of Europe went through a series of popular revolts and it is possible to argue that Luther, the Protestant extremists and the peasant wars were later German imitations of Wyclif (1370), Wat Tyler (1381), Hus (1400), Joan of Arc (1430) and the Bogomil Sréckovič Gospel. During the late thirteenth century, Europe had been deeply shaken by the struggle for power in the cities between the bishops, the princes, the nobles and the guilds of artisans and small masters. In France, this struggle reached the point of revolt at Beauvais, Provins and Rouen in 1280–1, and at Paris in 1295 and 1307. In Germany, the guilds achieved success in Ulm, Frankfurt, Nuremberg, Mainz, Strasbourg, Basle and Cologne. Between 1297 and 1328 a thirty-years' civil war raged in Flanders between the great citizens (*majores, goden*) and the small artisans (*minores, gewaden*). An awakened self-consciousness among the lowest classes consolidated itself in these bitter conflicts. The people routed the French aristocracy at Courtrai in 1302, and Conink the Weaver defeated Philip the Fair, the most powerful prince in Christendom, to whom even the Pope was no equal. Vulgarized mysticism surged through the Low Countries. The motto was: 'Down with the rich and the priests!' There were disorders at Ypres in 1323 and Bruges in 1328.

The rising of Ghent (1338–75) and Jacob Arteveld's abortive dictatorship of the workers touched off a general movement throughout Europe. In 1382, twenty-six thousand workers fell in the battle of Roosebecque. Germany too had its revolts – at Strasbourg (1346–80), Cologne (1396), Regensburg, Würzburg, Bamberg, Aix, Halberstadt and Lübeck, but in fury, violence and bloodshed they did not compare with those in the West.[2] Throughout the fourteenth century, the rebellious French citizenry suffered frightful losses. There were revolutions in Paris in 1356, 1358, 1379–82, and 1413 (under Caboche and Capeluche), but the kings and princes were victorious. The Dukes of Burgundy repressed the risings at Bruges (1436–8), Ghent (1431–6, 1448), Liége and Dinant (1408–66). In Italy, already overflowing with migratory workers, unemployed and exiles (there were twenty-two thousand beggars in Florence alone), the repressed masses broke out in revolt at Bologna in 1376, Genoa in 1339 and Siena, 1355–70. Byzantium, in the final years before its collapse in 1453, was shaken by social and religious unrest; Salonica was governed from 1342 to 1352 by a 'red' dictatorship of sailors and artisans, wielding ritual terror as an instrument of government. During the same period, the Bogomil Churches, 'friends of God', and 'the people of God' were very influential in the Balkans. The term 'people of God' was used by the Fellowship (*Ciompi*) who, under the leadership of a worker, Michele Lando, set up a reign of terror and a revolutionary authority in Florence, and again used by the Jacquerie, the peasant rebels in France who rose in 1358. The vengeance exacted by the nobility was no less bloody than the terror practised by the people in 'God's courts of justice'. There were twenty thousand executions of *misérables*, homeless and unhallowed wretches. In 1380, two priests, John Ball and Jack Straw, with Wat Tyler as military commander, led the English Peasant Revolt in the name of Lollard ideas. For a short time, they were masters of London and of King Richard II. It was as 'the people of God' that the Hussite armies penetrated central Europe between 1418 and 1437. Joan of Arc laid the foundations in the French people of the sense of their mission to be the elect and the beloved of God. Her French opponents were drawn from the nobility and higher clergy while her English opponents were unable to match her.

The 'people of God' were a revolutionary force of considerable importance. Their ideas were inherently dynamic. They wanted to cleanse the earth of wicked men and then, like the new Adam, to build the kingdom of God upon it. Yet, their ideas were strikingly unimportant in Germany between the sixteenth and nineteenth centuries, except in certain currents of life divorced from the main stream: the Anabaptists and one branch of the pietist movement. There the revolt had run a different course, entirely within the realm of the soul, of the ego, the mind, nature and woman. Strong pressure from above diverted it from the social and political sides of life and forced it inward. The princes, the nobility and the imperial clergy were strong and as a result the 'kingdom of God' frustrated the development of the 'people of God'.

The Holy Empire had been desecrated in the Investiture dispute and the twelfth-century battles between emperor and pope. The old Carolingian nobility had been deposed by a new, administrative, *parvenu* nobility, and simultaneously a wave of deep revulsion against the imperial and papal authoritarian Church and its clergy had swept the land. The courtly poetry of the years between 1170 and 1230 represented both the expression of these changes and the awakening of the first German movement.[3] In *Minnesang*, the man, the knight, was an emperor, engaged in establishing his own interior kingdom – *riche*; he was joined indissolubly to his 'sovereign lady', his *frouwe*. The inspiration for such motifs came from certain Cistercian versions of the Song of Songs which were subsequently destroyed because they were too secular. Their inner power was the expression of distress and anxiety. In Strasbourg, for example where more than eighty persons were burned at the stake in the year 1212 alone, Godfrey began to develop a *minne*-ideology. He had nothing but contempt for the unhallowed and impotent liturgies of the old empire, the old Church, and society. He began to expose them as compounds of self-deceit, fiction and lies.

In the Communion consummated in *minne*, the new 'I' and the new 'Thou' established their own kingdom of soul and body, and were the mediators of their own salvation. Walter von der Vogelweide thought the pope and all the 'old' rulers were devoid of holiness and salvation. His hero, Longinus, was the manifestation of a new chivalry, the 'good anchorite' of a new, evangelical Christianity. Wolfram von Eschenbach, a forerunner of Eckhart, made an elaborate, precarious, almost baroque attempt to renovate the ancient sacred cosmos (of empire, nature, and race). His kingdom of the Holy Grail and his hero, the Knight Feirafiz, were exotic products of the world of the Three Rings and of Western spiritual reform. Feirefiz was half pagan, half Christian, half Negro and half white. The idea of the Grail was a mixture of Persian symbolism, the Templar *mystique* of the order of knighthood, the idea of the Church of the Holy Spirit, and the society formed by the new nobility. This curious amalgam rested on the ancient faith of the Germanic world in nature and sacrament. Grave symptoms of disintegration and decadence in the political and religious spheres were evident in this poetry. It was, as in the nineteenth and twentieth centuries, a substitute for theology and philosophy.

'The terrible time', the time without an emperor, the Interregnum of 1250–74, was only one of the many interregna during the thirteenth century. All the old powers, secular and spiritual – princes, emperor and bishops – proved unable to exercise their authority, or mutually frustrated each other's attempts to do so. Strasbourg suffered for decades under the ban of the Church. In the struggle between the Emperor Ludwig and John XXII, most German cities experienced periods of interdict: Erfurt for example, for three years, Zurich for ten years, Ulm for fourteen years, and Frankfurt (later to be the capital of German nonconformism and the home of *Theologia Germanica*) for twenty-eight years. The city authorities often had no choice but to force the resident clergy to perform their holy tasks and gradually they subjected the clergy to their control. A solid mass of political resistance to Rome took root in these cities. The papal policy of taxation was bitterly resented and there were protests in Mainz in 1313, Cologne in 1330, and the league of Rhineland Churches in 1355. The climax was the anti-curial manifesto of the Cologne League in 1372.[4]

These cities were the political home of sectarians and of the members of the various right-wing and left-wing religious movements. Since the twelfth century, there had been Cathars and Waldensians in all the cities of the Rhineland.* During the thirteenth century there were innumerable small groups representing new types of piety – Beguines and Beghards, Lollards, Brethren of the Holy Ghost, Brethren of the Common Life, Adamites, Luciferians, Picards, Flagellants. Their resentments began to form an *anticléricalisme des bigots*,[5] an 'ill-informed piety of a devout laity harassed into anticlericalism.'[6] Partly as a result of this the German mystics never succeeded in freeing themselves from the taint of heresy, persecution and ecclesiastical condemnation. They never achieved a legitimate, official place in the Church because their associations with the fractious cities were too intimate to be ignored by the authorities. Hildegard of Bingen and her convent suffered under the condemnation of the city of Mainz. Mechthild of Magdeburg was persecuted as a heretic and had to flee in 1270 to Helffta. In the same way, Eckhart, Tauler and Suso always worked against a background of persecution. They spoke only to a small circle of 'brothers and sisters', who were all members of an interior resistance movement to the power of the imperial Church.

The message of these great mystics became the secret treasure of a small group of initiates. The first grand movement of the German spirit received, as a result, the character of an inner emigration. There never arose in Germany the sort of humanism and spiritual democracy which inspired the West largely because the ideas of the German spiritual reformers were confined to the limits of conventicles and convents. There, in little communities of brethren, they could exercise their enlightening, instructive and formative influences. As these groups were made up largely of women and selected members of the nobility, their influence was both restricted and distorted. The ruling classes became imbued with the concept of the inner nobility of the soul, but its symbol was the woman. The soul's relation to God was that of the noble lady in the *minne*-ideology. Whatever influence such enlightened groups may have had was soon diluted and vulgarized, occasionally even perverted into heresy, as it spread through groups and circles of petty bourgeoisie.

The first German movement, the very structure of its thought and its religious experience (though not necessarily the conscious intention of its leaders) was directed at the Carolingian-papal authoritarian Church and at the theology of power which it had built up. It was cool and mistrustful of the 'unhallowed Empire'. The ancient idea of God the King became God the Spirit. The rational-political *ordo* of the *Curia* was replaced by nature as guardian of the underground and all that belonged to it. Thomist-Aristotelian logic was overthrown by the dialectics of the Spirit of God and the heart of man. Logical distinctions and separations were blurred in the warmth of the spirit. The offices of pope, emperor, king, natural father and great congregation were denied any real efficacy in salvation. The figure of God the Father was pushed back into the depths of the unnameable Godhead, and Christ the Mediator was succeeded by God the Spirit. Christ's office of mediation had been

*cf. Ekbert of Schönau and Hildegard.

dishonoured and desecrated by the clergy as had the office of father by pope and king.

The spirit and nature, which displaced the church and the political *ordo*, were the products of the Neoplatonic tradition. Elements of this fundamental transposition were inherent in the ideas of Albert the Great, and were further elaborated by Dietrich of Freiberg and Berthold of Mosburg.[7] Dietrich, the Dominican provincial for Germany, from 1293 to 1296, was a violent opponent of Thomas Aquinas. With the help of Proclus, Albert and the Arab Neoplatonists, he constructed a typically German view of things: all living and unliving creatures flow out of the divine unity and return into it again. The abyss of the soul is divine in form (*abditum mentis*); man is deeply rooted in God; in that 'ocean of all intellectuality' he beholds God and all that is created.[8] His disciples, Berthold of Mosburg (whose commentary on Proclus influenced Nicholas of Cusa) and Nicholas of Strasbourg, were the transition to Meister Eckhart (d. 1327).[9]

The Eckhart of the Latin tracts displays a limitless capacity to absorb concepts as if a barbarian had filled himself to the brim with ideas from Plato, Aristotle, Plotinus, Proclus, Dionysius the Areopagite, Eriugena, the Arab and Jewish Neoplatonists, Augustine, Albert, Bonaventure, Thomas and Scotus. Although Eckhart was a disciple of Thomas whom he defended against Scotus, he was strongly influenced by the Franciscans. In any case, Eckhart's Thomism was a strange creation. It had none of the safeguards to thought and faith provided by political humanism and the social background of the Italian cities, nor the inner discipline of papal authority. Under these conditions Thomist thought dissolved into a Neoplatonic pantheist monism. It was natural that Eckhart turned to those writings of Thomas in which the Neoplatonic elements were strongest, and it was from them that he arrived at his conviction that God is pure being.

In defending Thomas, Eckhart confronted Scotus's rigid division of the cosmos, and his spiritualism which rejected the notion of the Sacraments as physical instruments containing a supernatural power (*virtus supernaturalis*). This inevitably pushed Eckhart to question the relation between God and man and to think about the Sacraments of the Church. According to Scotus, God was not committed to the mediation of the Sacraments because his personal will acts directly upon each human person.[10] Hence the Sacrament could only be an outward sign; God can bring any predestined soul directly to blessedness, without the Incarnation of Christ, or the Redemption without grace, the Church or the Sacraments.[11] The historical Christ was thrust into the realms of the purely spiritual, a mere symbol of cosmic ordinances.[12] Since Eckhart was essentially an eclectic, he happily borrowed ideas from both Scotus and Thomas to support his theme. Armed with these two central propositions, he began to preach on God and the soul. This was always Eckhart's main preoccupation, as it had been Augustine's, but there was a crucial difference. Augustine actually lived in the community of the *civitas Dei*, the Church, and within the political humanism of the Roman Empire. Eckhart was a product of the intellectual resistance movements of Stoicism, Origen and the Hellenic East.

Eckhart's doctrine of the soul as a 'spark' went back to the Stoic theory of the nature of fire, which Seneca had metaphorically applied to the conscience. Origen christianized Seneca's metaphor and Proclus had refined it to refer only to the very core or 'fine point of the soul'. Dionysius and William of Moerbeke, who translated Proclus, introduced the idea of scholasticism where it became part of the concept of the *synteresis*, the ground of consciousness; the later concept of the *scintilla animae* was unknown to scholasticism.[13] Thomas built the indestructibility of the *synteresis* into the permanent foundation of Western humanism. Not even in Hell could this core of our nature, as established by God, be destroyed. Eckhart transformed it into an anarchial mystical solipsism, in which the divinely established soul-ego engulfed both God and the world. This imperialism of the heart burst out in his German preaching.

The very idea of expressing scholastic terms in German was revolutionary. It anticipated the way in which the second German movement (from Hegel to Nietzsche) was to borrow from gnosticism and secularized Protestantism. The whole systematic intellectual achievement of Western political *humanitas* had been based upon clear-cut distinctions and static proportions. The language Eckhart spoke – and it became the language of German thought – took no account of the *polis*, the *civitas* (*Dei et hominum*), the *ecclesia*, the *imperium*, nor of those fruitful dualities and oppositions within which independence and freedom were assured to God and man. 'The new context of all speech was the soul seeking God and straining towards God.'[14] 'Flow', 'pour into', 'unite', 'transform', 'mould', 'animate', 'activate' and, again and again, 'make God-like' and 'annihilate' were the Orphic mainsprings of this vocabulary. Man was no longer separate from God, because the soul itself brought forth and commanded him. This terrifying process within the will unleashed cosmic storms of hatred and love in the Godhead and in the soul. The old doctrine of the indwelling of God in the soul was the basis of Eckhart's thought. The soul had a dwelling, which he called a 'ground'; 'something'; 'spark'; 'spirit'; 'reason'; 'fortress'; 'light'; 'fire'; 'torch'; 'power'; the 'essence'; 'highest part'; 'husband in the soul'; 'tabernacle'; or, in Latin, *aliquid, essentia animae, apex mentis, scintilla, synteresis*. There are whole catalogues of these names.[15] Out of this divine depth the 'reason' (the soul's own reason) rises 'above the distinctions of the three Divine Persons and out into the undifferentiated abyss of the Godhead, into that still, silent desert where nothing stirs.'[16]

The elaborate scholastic definition of the Trinity had been swept away. Nothing was left but a scheme of relationships between God and the soul.[17] Eckhart wiped out divine transcendence, and tore down the barricades between East and West which a thousand years of thought had erected. The tremendous struggle to think of God as both three-fold and one, was dismissed. Eckhart's Trinity was no more than the way God comes to self-knowledge. The primeval, nameless one slumbers eternally beyond the Trinity.[18] God is not spirit nor person nor image. Like Dionysius, Eckhart rejected the concepts and the notions of proportion which Roman *religio* had devoted to the consideration of God. 'God is measureless in giving, and the soul measureless in taking and receiving.'[19] At the centre of his conception of things, political, intellectual and religious aspirations were one. In political terms, neither the empire, nor the old Church, but the soul was the Kingdom of God:[20] 'There is no difference between the only-begotten Son and the soul.[21] The soul was in its essence like the Son; it joined in the play of the vital process within the Godhead. In intellectual terms, both God and the soul were intelligible light. The noble intellect of man could force its way into the very depth of the Godhead and immerse itself in the Father himself, origin; kernel; marrow; root; blood-stream; of the Godhead. Man's blessedness was his intellect.[22]

There was in this lofty intellectualism an echo of Thomas, especially in the emphasis which Eckhart laid on friendship between God and man.[23] The friendship of antiquity[24] led to the noblest of Eckhart's preoccupations: the care of souls. He pitied the poor dumb layfolk, whom pastors neglected in his time as they always had. Nothing had improved since the prelates of the Rhineland had begged Hildegard to make her missionary journeys among them, because they themselves had nothing to say to the people. Like his spiritual descendant, Luther,[25] Eckhart wanted to tell the people that God was near. Friendship meant kinship which bound the soul to God.[26] The Sacraments and other aids to salvation offered by the authoritative high Church were good and ought to be diligently used; but they were not the last word. Beyond all Sacraments, beyond grace itself, the divine soul could immerse itself in the immeasurable Godhead, who is all and nothing. Eckhart spoke to a 'poor folk' of nuns and groups of earnestly religious people, many of whom were in great distress. Some had been excluded from the Sacraments because they had no money.* Others had been denounced as heretics. Some lived in cities which had been under an ecclesiastical ban for so many years that the Church had plainly ceased to function. Some had no idea to which bishop (as in the capitular quarrel at Hildesheim in 1363) or emperor or king or pope they were supposed to be loyal in time of civil war or schism.

Eckhart's unsystematic way of thought rebelled against systems which he saw as threats of domination by alien powers (powers, that is, which were alien to the soul).The dynamic and alarming character of his ideas was an expression of the almost desperate situation in Germany, so desperately in need of his message of consolation. Every representative of the old order had failed; not one had been able to find the word which would reach the soul of the German people. Even Bernard of Clairvaux, to whom Eckhart owed so much, failed to find it when he came to Cologne.[27] Eckhart found the word. In his attempts to resolve the antinomies and intellectual difficulties of the

*cf. the account in the *Vita Heriberti* in the twelfth century.

Thomist and the Scotist systems, he plumbed the depths of the soul of his people. He became the very expression of its yearning to penetrate the ultimate depths of God and to proceed outwards from God to comprehend the whole world of things. It was he who moulded the language of German thought and its mystical, dialectical logic. Henceforth, spirit was to stand higher than God in the framework of German thought, and Godhead higher than God the Father. All the mediators – Christ, the priesthood, political society – withdrew into the background. Within the soul God created the entire world. The German soul was king, pope, priest and prince – everything, in fact, which further west became the political rights first of the prince and then his heirs, the 'elect people'. The universe was not a cosmic state under the rule of reason but an immensity of sheer strength and power. The world was 'being' and 'becoming' and the presence of God. 'All creatures are pure nothingness' – *Omnes creaturae sunt unum purum nichil*. The Ego says this 'no', because it contemplates and achieves itself in the all.[28]

Eckhart replaced the dualities of the Western Roman Christian world (nature-mind, logos-nature, thing-concept) with the old monism of archaic society. The soul was the crown of the new system. It hovered in sovereign majesty together with God. The next step was taken by a disciple, Johannes of Star Alley, who asked if the word of the soul was not as mighty as the word of the Heavenly Father. In fact, that word of power was pronounced in each of the great systems of German philosophy. Eckhart had established within the very heart of German thought that divine Trinity which was invoked as witness and as ultimate refuge in every imperial edict from Charlemagne to Frederick II. It was in the ground of the soul that the Holy Trinity dwelt, doing its noble work and playing its endless play.[29] Every good man was God's Heaven.[30] God had all power in Heaven and on earth, except in one respect: man has been unworthy.[31]

Johannes Tauler was Eckhart's disciple, and defended his master even though he was persecuted for it. For the guidance of convents of nuns and groups of friends of God, Tauler transformed Eckhart's lofty intellectualist and mystical philosophy into a doctrine of God, the world and life which became the basis of European quietism and sentimentalism. Wherever there was a sense that the ecclesiastical order had grown still and unhallowed, and people were trying to re-animate it from within, to permeate it or to overthrow it, Tauler's spirit took root. Both Rousseau and Kant owed a great deal to this man. In Germany, he became the secret Emperor of all the 'silent in the land' who were engaged in building up their own 'secret empire'[32] within their own souls. If, at first, his outlook seems less radical and less cataclysmic than Eckhart's it must be remembered that he was a member of a persecuted underground.[33] The enormous pressure upon him and his hearers can be felt in almost every sermon: be content to be despised and condemned, to be persecuted or killed; cast yourselves upon God! This political situation was the seed-bed of quietism, of a quiet, yet firm spirit of resistance. It produced a

Nicodemism which surrounded all delicate questions with careful circumlocutions, but it also created a new formulation of the rights of man which first
came into being on the fringe of orthodoxy and amongst small groups of nonconformists.[34] Tauler did not reject civil or ecclesiastical authority; he preached
a pietistic abandonment to their rule – 'though pope, bishops and prelates
should be as wolves around me, I would yet endure them.'[35] He showed, however, that they had become thoroughly unholy and impotent to save, doomed
to destruction by their lust for power, wealth and honours.[36]*

Since the pious soul which abandons itself entirely to God is made God-like
by grace, the inner man can build his Church and his empire within himself.[37]
Besides the Church's sacramental priesthood, there is a spiritual priesthood.[38]
Within Christendom[39] every inward spirit, hence women as well as men may
belong to it.† The Church, the true bark of Peter, is 'that inner depth in man
wherein Christ rests'.[40] It was easy to see Rome as a synonym for vain pomp.[41]
Tauler's sermon at the dedication of the Cologne Cathedral, on 26 September
1357, was on that church which is within the inner man: all your external
holiness, your saints and your relics cannot help you. The three holy Kings
and the eleven thousand virgins, the fair cathedrals and the golden spires are
without saving power. 'It is not the churches that make the people holy but the
people who make the churches holy.'[42]

Since the inner man was the true Church, simony took on an entirely new
significance. For Humbert and Gregory VII, simony had been the battle-cry for
the overthrow of the old world and its replacement by their spirit Church.
After Tauler, simony became the slogan with which the new spirituality
attacked the Church itself. According to Tauler, a man practised simony if he
performed good spiritual works with selfish intentions or with a thought of
reward.[43] He and his disciples were excommunicated because they taught that
good works, the Sacraments and spiritual practices had grown impotent, that
monasticism was not a way to salvation, and that serious and aspiring souls
were led astray by a false spiritual discipline whose end was self-seeking.[44] The
greater part of the members of religious orders lived in false holiness, mere
'Jews', relying on cults, ceremonies and good works.[45] This was the beginning
of the violent attack on monasticism,[46] which Erasmus summed up when he
said flatly, *Monachatus non est pietas*.‡ What good are these outer things,
Tauler asked? Can they help us to become new men within ourselves? The

---

*There was also a certain amount of petty-bourgeois resentment against the great lords.
The *Imitation of Christ* and the whole *devotio moderna* movement which shared a common
foundation with Tauler became one of the most momentous forces during the succeeding
centuries, partly because of this class resentment.

†cf. Abélard and Fénelon.

‡One of the most important motifs in European intellectual history from late medieval
times until the nineteenth century was the attack on monasticism: Franciscan and stoic
humanist, religious condemnation of monastic failure and corruption. Hundreds of councils,
chapters, papal Bulls, imperial and royal edicts were devoted to reform of the orders, but the
disillusionment of the people and the intelligentsia remained.

New Testament is within us. Tauler criticized the Old Testament's 'insupport-able burdens' and cruel judgments.

Despite his radical position, he was not unaware of the perils and pitfalls of mysticism. He foresaw that many would fall prey to the temptation to take short cuts in the spiritual life. Tauler's fears were soon confirmed by the degradation of spiritual discipline which occurred in religious life in Europe from the fifteenth to the nineteenth centuries. He easily saw through the 'free spirits',* those mystics of human reason who take their own lesser light for the light of God himself, and suppose that their unruly natural desire is God at work in them because they 'know' they are capable of attaining God.[47] The others were harder to catch. Some might have received great things from God – secret things, revelations and gifts. Some might even have religious genius or have spent much time training themselves spiritually. Yet, Tauler pointed out, they had not really abandoned their own 'I''s. At bottom they clung to their identities.[48] Others believed that they had become, through their services in religion, their own Jerusalem and the Kingdom of God on earth;[49] they let themselves be seduced by the 'sweetness of the spirit'. Although such people had travelled only half way along the road of self-negation, they foolishly claimed to have God. In fact, they were only tasting the fullness of their own earthly nature.[50] Such spiritual practices and endeavours merely imprisoned them in self-love.[51] Tauler was well aware of the dangerous effect which Eckhart's preaching had on many minds. His sermons poisoned them;[52] they were misled by them and thought that by short cuts, easily and at little cost, they could attain the furthest reaches of wisdom and truth.

Tauler saw this world of the late middle ages with singular clarity. He observed its pursuit of God and the spirit and its yearning for riches and well-being. It was impossible for him to know that he was witnessing the birth-pangs of a new age. He could only see how lust for spiritual and temporal power and dominion was present in all classes, high and low alike. His answer was to declare that man must abandon all things – 'leave them to God'. When he has become perfectly resigned (*gelassen*), he must press and strain toward God, careless of Heaven, Hell or the devil. Neither love nor sorrow, nor a 'god of his own thinking or making'[53] ought to hold him back. Such was the new age! As with the Fraticelli, Tauler's conviction of its coming had an eschato-logical basis. The Church was as torn by sects as in the days of Dominic, when God had been ready to destroy the world for its evil deeds; yet there was hope because man could see far more of Christ than ever his disciples saw.[54] God called his chosen friends and brothers, to whom he gave himself utterly, here, today and in eternity: 'Is this not a wondrous thing and a festive, joyous and blessed life,† we in God and God in us, here in time and there in eternity and unspeakable bliss?'[55]

*cf. the free spirits of German theology.
†cf. Fichte.

The new religiosity was a product of the exaltation of mind of a brother-hood bound together in God – friends of God, daily receiving the Holy Spirit in inwardness (*innechait*) and unity (*eynicheit*). Each day was the feast of Pentecost.[56] This was the beginning of the vulgarization and profanation of the paschal and pentecostal world. The joy of Easter Day had been turned into a source of everyday energy. There had been a foreshadowing of this in the world of the courtly epics, the world of Arthur's court, where all was splen-dour and feasting,[57] but now the 'people of God', with its exaltation of spirit and joy, had been released from the Church's paschal and pentecostal liturgy. In a real sense, this was the beginning of the people of the Western world, with all their revolutionary propensities. Tauler's revolution of the heart did not issue in any transformation of political society. He knew its nature too well to expect that.[58] The 'third kingdom', the 'secret kingdom', was to be built within that depth of the soul which was the image of the Trinity.[59] The high politics of this inner kingdom consisted of prayer, offered up for Christendom in its need.[60] The world depended upon the inner nobility of heart of the spiritual man as 'many masters' had declared, from Plato, Aristotle and Proclus[61] to Albert, Dietrich and Eckhart. The spiritual man could find the word of God through reading the Bible with his understanding illuminated by the divine light. Perfect surrender to the love of God was the key to such wisdom.[62] This *amour pur* sustained the piety and industrial ethos of Beguines and Beghards in their spinning-sheds and workshops.* Tauler's life and work was a kind of introduction to spiritual and practical living in the emerging world of the petty-bourgeoisie whose work and prayer he knew so well.

Henry Suso had what used to be called a warm social sense. He saw very clearly that every inward man ought to give up whatever his neighbour might need.[63] He had an affinity with the primitive communism of the Fathers and urged men to take from things only what necessity demands. In him the broad streams of traditional mysticism turned grey, muddy and turgid with emo-tionalism, individualism and solipsism. Within the narrow, cramped compass of small convents and groups, morbid tendencies began to develop. There was a desire to attain mystical experience by force, a yearning for encounters with God, for ecstasies, for visions. Those corruptions which Tauler feared began to eat like a cancer into the great movement.[64] Biographies of female mystics were written by their sisters in religion. Spiritual experience was perverted to bodily sensation as in Elsbet Stagel's *Lives of the Sisters of Töss*. Throughout the subsequent history of pietism, until it emptied into Romanticism in the nineteenth century, ecstatic women and feminine mysticizing were to be domi-nant aspects of the movement. Bettina von Bretano, Günderode and the Lady poetesses of the nineteenth century are directly descended from their Sisters of Töss.

The first German movement was, despite its deep penetration at the popular

*European industry had its roots in the *devotio moderna* and the poorhouses, houses of correction and workhouses of Calvinism.

level, unable to achieve an agreement with the governing forces of the land, or to co-operate in re-shaping political, social and national affairs.[65] Even the Emperor, Ludwig of Bavaria, the 'Saviour', 'Redeemer' and 'Prince of Peace'[66] as the Italians called him, won no real support in Germany. Western spiritual Franciscans, lawyers and humanists gathered at his court. It was they who cited Otto I to justify the deposition of John XXII, they who revived the old imperial literature and who supported the Emperor's stewardship of the Church. There were potential points of contact between political affairs and the first German movement, but they were not taken up. Only in combating the Flagellant* movement did the German mystics play any active role in affairs. Tauler and Suso defended themselves against this perversion of their ideas, but they would go no further. The way of salvation of the inward men must never be an external one. It can never save a society or reform a people. In effect, the first great German movement washed its hands of politics and society. By this abdication it handed over all possible aspirations for religious and political renewal to the princes and *their* Church. The fate of the Reformation and the counter-Reformation was decided in advance. The princes would have to assume the task of renewing the world. They would construct their own ecclesiastical domains, as executive agents of the Holy Spirit. There was no other way. The decision had been taken already by the first German movement, when it refused to see the task of renewal in the political and social sphere as a valid spiritual objective.

*The Flagellant movement, which poured out of Italy, overran Germany and Bohemia in two successive waves in 1260 and 1349. The movement was a kind of inner crusade against a decadent Church. The Flagellists wanted a *geswinden kêr*, a sudden and total conversion, which was to be done by directly imitating the Passion of Christ: God desired to renew himself in each penitent. This explosive movement was exterminated according to the directive of Clement VI of 20 October 1349, but in reality it had gone underground to re-emerge in the Hussites of Bohemia, the *devotio moderna* of the Low Countries and the raving enthusiasts of Luther's day. For the content of their ideas, see A. Hübner, *Die Deutsch Geisslerlieder*, Berlin-Leipzig, 1931.

THE NEW AGE OF SALVATION

(Fifteenth Century)

THE popular outburst of religious enthusiasm that occurred during the years after 1380, dealt a blow to the European spirit from which it never entirely recovered. The shock waves caused by the movements associated with Wyclif, Hus and Joan of Arc were felt during and after the Reformation and were certainly to blame for a good deal of the bitterness of the century which began with Luther's thesis. At the same time, the failure of the conciliar movement to reform the Church and the fall of Constantinople in 1453 produced a momentous shift in the entire political and religious environment. The events of those years produced a powerful and resolute will in the rulers to break the resistance of opponents to the prevailing order of society. The kings and the high secular and spiritual lords were terrified by the idea of 'salvation from the people'. The *Curia* anxiously faced the democracy of the Council of Basle, while Christendom at large nervously watched the Turkish advance. At the same time, the disillusionment of the 'little ones', the 'devout souls', at the anti-reformism of the 'great world' began to develop into the *devotio moderna*. These were the forces which, in conflict or in co-operation with each other, fashioned the political and ecclesiastical absolutism of the modern world and the fanatical underground resistance which accompanied it. The radical violence of the commissar who is determined to impose conformity was born in this age of crisis. The only hope seemed to lie in emergency laws, which over the years hardened and became permanent.

Wyclif and Hus were the first to demonstrate to Europe the possibility of an alliance between the university and the people's yearning for salvation. It was the freedom of Oxford that sustained Wyclif. Oxford was not a bishop's See; the Bishop of Lincoln (its overlord after 1214) was a hundred and twenty miles away. Since the Chancellor of the University was arrayed with privileges which were the envy of the popes and kings, he attained increasing power.[1] In 1274, after a series of bitter struggles the two nations, French and English, which had corporately constituted the University, were dissolved. Henceforth, there was only one nation, the English, which controlled the city. During the thirteenth century, there were battles among the mendicant orders with and about the university. Robert Grosseteste (1175–1253), a Franciscan sympathizer who was Oxford's first Chancellor and Bishop of Lincoln, successfully defended her liberties, and as a result the university became the centre of a Franciscan-humanist spirit. Its illustrious representatives – Bacon, Duns Scotus and Ockham – were products of the anti-Thomist teaching of John Peckham, William de la Mare and Roger of Marston.

As a mercantile city, Oxford must have helped to mould the intellectual attitudes of its professors. The town had close relations with the world of the Three Rings, and in 1260 the Chancellor of Oxford was given jurisdiction over the considerable Jewish colony. Bacon, Scotus and Ockham owed the breadth of their thought to their contacts with the Mediterranean intelligentsia. Around 1260 Balliol College, where Wyclif took the degree of Master in 1358, was founded for poor young men by John de Balliol as an act of penitential reparation. Between 1260 and 1274 Walter de Merton, former Chancellor of England, founded Merton, the most important of the colleges for twenty poor students and a number of priests. In 1379, New College, richly endowed, brought to a close this first series of foundations which made Oxford's colleges the home both of the children of the nobility and of talented poor men.[2] In Oxford, the faculty of arts dominated all the others which, as in the case of Siger of Brabant, produced a situation potentially charged with revolutionary significance.

The high nobility who sent their sons to Oxford and the university itself protected Wyclif. In this climate of opinion, he began to attack the alien, money grubbing, French Pope of Rome and to champion a pure gospel. Like the Cathars and Waldensians, he denied the value of the Sacraments, the cult and services of the official Church. Wyclif was a son of the Gregorian reform's left wing. The friends of Gregory VII had declared simoniac Sacraments invalid; Wyclif merely pushed the argument one step further. All Roman priests were simoniacs. He charged them with polluting the Spirit of God. The pope did indeed derive his power from Caesar – but not from Christ. In 1381, the great peasants' revolt, under the leadership of the communist priest John Ball and of Wat Tyler, took its stand upon Wyclif's doctrines; in 1382 Nicholas Hereford defended Wyclif before the whole University. Not till 1411 did Oxford submit to the overwhelming alliance of pope, archbishop and king and surrender her liberties. Seventy years later it rose again as the leader of a humanist-religious movement of reform (William Latimer, More, Grocyn, Colet, Linacre, Erasmus). In the meantime, the Lollards, as a religious-political underground movement, continued to teach and transmit the heritage of Wyclif.

From the fourteenth century to the days of Thomas Garrigue Masaryk, the dilemma of the Western slavic peoples has been the same. The forces of political and religious independence in the Slavonic and Magyar borderlands of Europe between Poland's Baltic coast and Transylvania have always sought the help of the dynamic nonconformism of the West against Catholic Vienna and Orthodox Moscow. What Calvin was to be to the Polish and Hungarian nobility, Wyclif was to his Bohèmian disciples Hus and Jerome of Prague. There had been a fairly large community of Bohemian students at

Oxford* during the course of the fourteenth century, who brought back Wyclif's ideas and spread them.[3] The founder of Prague University was the Emperor Charles IV, a man of French, Czech and German blood. He made Prague a golden city, to rival golden Rome and golden Kiev. Its St Vitus's Cathedral, the Hradčany, and the Karlstein sanctuary, the Escorial of Bohemia, attracted artists and humanists from Germany, France, Italy and Hungary. They came together in Prague's painters' guild, in the four nations of the University, and in the humanist life of the Emperor's court. The Emperor who spoke German, Latin, French and Italian preferred above all to be a Czech and to speak Czech. The Czech masters of arts at the University, with all the welter of European movements to choose from, selected two with sure instinct: the idea of religious reform, and the idea of the nation. They fused these together to make the first Czech movement, so totally different from the first German one, though the initial impulses were very closely allied. In both a nation began to discover itself for the first time.

Hus was more than 'the representative in Bohemia of an academically watered-down version of Wyclif's doctrine'.[4] He was a timid but ambitious man, presumably of poor peasant stock. The Prague in which he lived was an exciting and vivid place. The German professors tended to be nominalists. They had close ties with both the higher clergy of the country and with intellectuals abroad. The Czechs were realists and reformers who wanted to raise the moral level of their people and their clergy by giving them both a spiritual and national education. Jan Milič (d. 1374) opposed the simony and moral laxity of the German higher clergy. Matej of Janov (d. 1394), a Doctor of Paris, rejected the veneration of relics and images and declared: 'The Bible alone suffices.' Thomas of Stitny (d. 1401) discussed theological questions in the vernacular, i.e., in Czech. These men had already prepared the ground when Jerome of Prague, in 1401, transplanted the writings of Wyclif. Jerome had studied in Prague and England, and travelled as lecturer, student or missionary to Palestine, Paris (where he lectured in 1405), Heidelberg, Cologne, and later in Poland and Lithuania. There he made contact with Russian Orthodoxy, and prepared the way for religious and nationalist panslavism. Everywhere Jerome was a representative of the 'new learning', and everywhere he was violently opposed by professors, bishops, kings, and popes. He was the first Czech humanist to win international fame.

John Hus, Master of Arts, ordained priest in 1400, began preaching in 1402 at the Bethlehem Chapel in Prague, which since its foundation in 1391 had been a centre of the religious and nationalist spirit of reform. The pompous rhetorical court humanism around Charles IV concealed a massive anxiety about death and dissolution. Hus saw through the façade and was deeply moved. Augustine, Ambrose, Anselm, Gregory the Great, Chrysostom and Wyclif formed his thought and gave him words with which to express the latent feelings of the young Czechs in the nobility, the clergy and the people.

*In the same way the 'Little Entente' was later to bring people to Paris for their studies.

Reform of the clergy was to prepare the way for a reform of the people. The heavy authority of the German prelates and their worldly way of living was to be destroyed. Popular preaching nourished the popular movement, which, in turn, spurred on Hus. After the year 1405, Hus began to write in Czech. He composed Czech hymns for the mass, and, probably during the year 1406, began to reform the Czech spelling, in some ways, his greatest work. His letters and tracts (especially his work, in exile, on the moral improvement of the lower clergy and the people), reproduced the spoken word of his preaching and shaped the Czech language.

Like all the other mother tongues of the people in Europe, Czech was the outcome of a religious resistance to the father-régime of the Roman pope and his Latin authority. Dante's Italian was minted by Francis, the Spirituals, and the heretical culture-ideal of the *dolce stil nuovo*. Wyclif and Chaucer made literary English a national language. Luther's German was the language of the first German movement. The French revolutionary generals of 1792 returned to the language of Joan of Arc. It was concise, direct and free of circumlocutions, a language which, by its very simplicity, rejected the grand manner of Latin rhetoric and hierarchical authority. Europe's secular literature was in its essence anti-Roman. The Latin clergy and Latin scholarship fought it because it offered the public an alternative to the religious life. These vernacular literatures were secular sermons on the good sense of the laymen's way of life. But the worldliness of the vernacular was, in essence, rooted in religion. It grew out of the nonconformism of the thirteenth and fourteenth centuries. The Spanish Inquisition quite rightly saw its chief enemy in the Alumbrados, Erasmians, 'Lutherans', and recognized the essence of their challenge by forbidding *all* religious literature in the vernacular.

Between 1378 and 1417, the Roman Church, whose predominant characteristic ought to have been its unity, was split into two. There were two popes, Benedict XIII and Gregory XII, and bishops took sides. Under these conditions, Hus was forced to take increasingly extreme positions. The Archbishop of Prague, Zybnek Zajic of Hasenburg, the higher Czech clergy and the German prelates and professors supported Gregory XII, while the Czech professors and nobility refused to accept either pope. Understandably, Hus could no longer ask for the Archbishop's protection which he had enjoyed till then, and by 1409 Hus had joined his public, nobles, professors and people, who gathered at the side of the King, Wenceslas IV. This was the period during which the Hussite doctrine of the nation and its Church evolved. Hus began to define his doctrine in his preaching:

'The Church is the *universitas* (the same as university) of the elect, and as such is called the mystical body of Christ (cf. below, Joan's appeal to the Church in Heaven) . . . Our Holy Mother the Church consists of three parts . . . the people, the secular lords and the clergy.' (*Ecclesia est praedestinatorum universitas et illa vocatur corpus Christi mysticum . . . Integratur autem sancta mater ecclesia ex tribus partibus . . . vulgus . . . seculares domini . . . clerus.*)[5] By making the people the instrument of reform, Hus created the national holy people as the answer to the divisions within the Church. He cited Chrysostom and refused obedience to the Pope. Is the Pope not just one among many rivals aiming at power over sacred things? Despite his excommunication, he continued to preach in the woods and the fields, and to call to his listeners in their own 'holy' language that he had 'good news' for them. Rome commanded that Prague's Bethlehem be razed to the ground, but the people preserved it as the crib of the nation's rebirth. In 1413 Hus preached once more in Bethlehem. 'I will glady die for the gospel which I have proclaimed and taught.' These, his authentic last words on the scaffold, were in perfect harmony with numerous Catholic testimonies to the joyous deaths of sectarians.

The cheerful, confident assurance of these national martyrs suggests that the liberation of the national language had unleashed profound inner forces within the depths of the human psyche. Deeply felt needs began to strain for expression in these men. The fresh witness of their blood testified to the power of their feelings and their heroic and cheerful deaths were hallowed in popular songs, prayers and folk-literature. At last through the thinking of theologians and philosophers, an individualism was born, which denied the old cosmos of Latin rhetoric in which thought and speech were not means of self-expression but subordinate pieces of the fabric of tradition and systematic rhetoric. The existentialist thought of Kierkegaard and Nietzsche, both sons of pietist parents, which called on the Spirit as witness, is no more than the modern manifestation of this development. Five hundred years of folk and national literature had prepared a language for them; a language distilled from the manifold reactions of the people to the first martyrs of popular salvation.

There is considerable evidence of Hussite influence in France during the first decade of the fifteenth century. We know that Joan of Arc had the Hussites constantly in her thoughts,[6] and that she wanted to crown her life's labours by pacifying Bohemia. Her accusers and judges felt that the Hussites and her followers were, in reality, one single dangerous movement of the submerged people. The parallels were striking. Both Joan of Arc and Hus were hailed as the saviours of their peoples. 'The Kingdom of God in Bohemia' was the aim of the Hussite armies. In the last days before the Judgment of the World, they wanted to cleanse the earth of all evil and impure men. It was from the Czech people that redemption and salvation were to come in the dissolution of the world which was felt to be at hand. The needs and sufferings of the poor sustained and intensified their expectation of salvation and their faith in themselves as a chosen holy people.

The Franciscan movement was as important as the Hussite in forming the substance of Joan of Arc's uprising. St Francis may be seen from this point of view as the first of the nationalist saints. Joan of Domrémy's mother tongue was at once Franciscan and royal.[7] The lady of Bourlemont, who owned the castle of refuge where Joan and her people used to leave their goods and cattle for safe-keeping during the numerous inroads of the Burgundians and Armagnacs was a distant relative of St Francis's mother. She also owned the May Tree, the ancient magic tree with its holy well – the sacred place where Joan awoke to her mission as a Holy Maid. The Lady of Bourlemont was, in addition, married to a Joinville, a man of a renowned crusading family. Joan was to turn the outward thrust of the crusades inwards, accomplishing the salvation of her people in battle with the English, that unholy people whom she herself unhallowed. There were other close historical links between Francis and Joan; popular legends used the same imagery for both saints. The Fioretti of St Francis and the contemporary history legends of the French people are remarkably similar.[8] Both Francis and Joan were able to use the archaic idea of salvation with all its ancient powers and the specifically Christian calling which they represented. This fusion was the origin of the awareness of salvation in the European nations.

The main difference between Joan and the Franciscans was that she narrowed their universal mission and crusade to convert the entire human race into a campaign for the salvation of one particular country, France. The history legends told of her by the French people represent her as the redeemer of 'God's holy kingdom', France.[9] In the same way the Spirituals' prophetic version of history represented Francis, and after him Olivi, as redeemers of the world. If Francis was the new Christ, Joan was the new Mary, bringing the 'poor folk of France' to birth as a holy people.[10] Poverty and weakness were the signs of election. The Dauphin Charles was born in a poverty like that of the Child Jesus. Joan made this wretched weakling into the holy, wonder-working King of France. She, who was neither pope nor bishop, gave him the holy kingdom of France and imposed upon him a three-fold mystical negation of himself. If he were to go as Emperor on a crusading mission to Jerusalem, he must first be converted, be reborn, and rise up as 'France's son'.[11]

Joan was a firm adherent of the ancient 'religion royale'. She called upon the names of the holy Kings Charlemagne and Louis, and thus renewed the old alliance between the ancient people, cities and kings against the infidel nobility and higher clergy. She had compassion, like Christ, for the wretched peasantry, which the alien German nobility hunted like animals. 'Peasants exist to be flayed and hanged.'[12] The villains would have preferred the ferocity of the Turks to a life of slavery under such Christian lords.[13] Joan belonged to the class which was bringing a new world to birth. The pope, the emperor and the king were to be her three sons.[14] Joan was fighting God's war; her army was a crusading army, waging a holy war against the English.[15] Her saints fought with her army and, since they were on her side, they obviously spoke French. The angels too fought in the air on her side.

She was 'Franciscan', 'très simple', holy as only Francis's nearest brothers and companions were holy.[16] Like him she heard her voices in the woods, exulted in the joy of nature and, though surrounded by learned men, remained quite poor and simple, the angel of the Lord. She brought God himself into Orleans, and gave her people that eschatological *froide* which is the joy of the eternal Pentecost.[17] She longed to make all peoples into one nation of peace. Continence, penance and lay-monasticism were to purify the poor, disintegrated people of Christendom and make them into a 'People of God upon earth'. Joan saw France as the Hussites saw Bohemia: it was 'the garden of the Gospel', a paradise and a cathedral. The King's Chancellor, the Archbishop of Rheims, and the whole body of high nobility and clergy refused to believe that *God was in France*, refused to believe in this girl, who had been thrown up by the great wave of the people's distress and yearning for redemption.[18] At Paris, Richard the Franciscan preached penance, the approach of Antichrist, and the expulsion of the English; the evangelist Catherine of La Rochelle wanted to supply equipment for her troops.[19]

Joan succeeded to a certain extent in holding aloof from these and other 'false prophets' (always a great matter of anxiety to 'true' reformers); but she was unable to escape from the charmed circle of archaic folk-religion. The history legend of the people reports that she refrained from spells and enchantments but that, like Francis, she possessed ancient magical powers over animals, men, plants and fruits.[20] With all the scrupulous attention to detail of an ancient saga, the legend tells how she lost her holiness. In the splendour of its power she had swung her miraculous sword and butterflies had fluttered about her banner, those primeval heralds of rebirth and the forces of the soul.[21] Suddenly, her sword broke, her standard-bearer fell, her speech became weak and merely human; she turned into a poor, God-forsaken maid, and died.[22] The blend of archaic folk myth with Christianity is apparent. Like Francis, Olivi and the Spirituals, she died as a Folk-Christ for the rebirth of her people. Her tragic death recalled the Passion of Christ.*

The historical Joan, cheerful and confident, died on 30 May 1431. Her pyre was built 'like a kind of sanctuary',[23] and on her head she wore a paper mitre bearing the words 'Heretic, Witch, Apostate, Renegade'. The mitre which recalls Dante's new man crowning himself with the crowns of pope and empire, stood for her heresy. She had consecrated herself and the people, and had made them bearers of salvation. Joan was the May Queen and the Holy Maid of archaic society. Even her condemnation took place in May. The accusations against her had been meticulously prepared in advance. Between forty and seventy theologians, jurists and canonists took part. Although her judges correctly determined the facts, they failed to understand the spirit.

*Joan's folk mysticism was tied to the land, to nature and to the saving power of individuals. The mysticism of the Low Countries was entirely different in spirit. The abyss which separated the folk movements from the intellectual mysticism of Gerson or Nicholas of Cusa was never bridged. The result was that the city and the council, which ought to have found a potential ally in the folk movements for reform, were actually the main enemies of Joan's ideas. The judges of Joan of Arc scarcely waited for the pyre to be kindled, because they had pressing commitments at the Council of Basle, where they played prominent roles in the conciliar reform.

How could a group of post-Gregorian rationalists grasp the nature of this fusion of the archaic pagan myth and Christianity? To them, the whole business was a diabolical *confusio*. The significance of this trial was not the pettiness of the place-seeking clergy, nor even the justifiable anxiety of the English who felt keenly the attack on their holiness. What gave this trial its enormous importance was the direct confrontation of the authority of the late scholastic order and the 'Underground'. For the first time in European history, these submerged inchoate, mute and primitive forces found a spokesman and, even more important, a language. The drive toward salvation of the French peasantry presented Europe with the reality of this 'Underground' and for the next 500 years literature and popular thinking were obsessed by the collision between the yearning for salvation of the simple folk and the philosophy of the authorities.

Her accusers were not blind to the significance of this revolt from below. The sixty-second article of the official indictment charged Joan with 'seducing princes and people' and 'stirring up war'. Authority could not tolerate an initiative from the people and, in the words of the text, the consequent confusion of the Christian peoples. The indictment continued in these words: 'Men and women will be setting themselves up on all sides, and giving out that they have had revelations from God and the saints ... as has already been seen in many cases, since this woman brought herself forward and began to give scandal to the Christian people and to extend her devices.'[24] A new alliance began to develop between orthodox princes, the *Curia* and the universities against the superstitions of the people. It was invoked again in the letter of the English King to the Emperor and all Christian princes and in that of the University of Paris to the Pope. Enlightenment and suppression were fused. State inquisitors were 'to sit in judgment of heresies, witchcraft... superstitution and similar crimes ... to destroy them and to tear them out by the roots'.[25] In the years around 1400, the first major battle against the 'superstitions' of the people – Wyclif and John Ball, Hus and Joan of Arc – took place and the winners were the holders of power. The victory over the people and the simultaneous failure of the movement to reform the Church left a residue of bitter disappointment and cynicism in Central and Western Europe, from which Italy alone escaped.

Avignon, the 'Babylonian captivity of the Church', had ended in a forty-year schism (1378–1417). One group of powers – French-Spanish-Habsburg – had their Pope, while a north-and-east alliance, German, English, Norse, Slavonic, had their Pope. The Council of Constance (1414–18) deposed three popes, but neither it nor the Council of Basle (1431–49) succeeded in reforming the Church. At the latter, the new political and social forces – cities, lawyers, professors, and even some of the lower clergy – were more strongly in evidence than ever before, but it was too little and too late. The collapse of the Conciliar reform movement had many causes. The various rivalries – between the *Curia* and the emperor, and between the kings and the estates – made it impossible to achieve a preliminary political agreement as a foundation for ecclesiastical reform. But equally as important was the absence among the leading thinkers of the Conciliar movement of a coherent, forceful and comprehensive plan. The supporters of the conciliar theory were victims of an incomplete, almost primitive view of the world.

A perfect example of this shallow approach was the work of Dietrich of Neim, a German official of the papal Chancery.[26] This 'herald of the imperial splendours of the high middle ages' belonged to the school of Ludwig of Bavaria. He appealed to Frutolf, Otto of Freising, Hildegard of Bingen, Peter de Vinea's compilation, Alexander of Roes and Marsilius as sacred witnesses to the divinely willed *ratio* of the Carolingian-Ottonian-Hohenstaufen Empire. Since history is reason and the proof of God's spirit and order in this world, Dietrich argued, man needed only to return to the Ottonians and Christendom would undergo a rebirth. This monstrous simplification plainly ignored everything that was going on within Europe. Peter d'Ailly and Gerson were less naïve and more representative of the new forces within Christendom, but both were caught by their dogged desire to make a careful separation between faith and knowledge, to recognize in each its own laws of being, and to maintain them both accordingly.

Peter d'Ailly was a pupil of John de Mirecourt. When both Nicholas and John were condemned he remarked bitterly, 'they condemn, out of envy, many things which are afterwards publicly taught in the Church'.[27] D'Ailly made word-for-word transcriptions of Mirecourt, Roger Bacon and Ockham. For him the cosmos was not sacred. It was simply split into an order of natural law, which man may investigate, and the order of God's grace, which he must accept unconditionally. Although Peter d'Ailly began his career with a remarkably open mind, he despaired as he grew older and his thinking became alternatively legalistic and mystical. His temper hardened after he had achieved a lofty intellectualism. He recoiled from the excesses of the popular movements of his day, was suspicious of Hus, and was unsympathetic to the possibility of 'salvation from the people'.

D'Ailly's successor as Chancellor of the University of Paris was Gerson, a strict nominalist positivist. The object of Gerson's theology was to achieve 'a few assured concepts', *pauci et certi termini*, and he eventually reduced the number of acceptable terms to the point at which nothing could be said about God.[28] God the Father remained an unknown, and all attempts to attach names to him were vain. This hidden God was totally removed from the cosmos of anointed kings and bishops with their sacramental *ratio*. God dwelt in an ice-cold remoteness. No man could comprehend why God elects and why he damns. It was God's will that angels and men be tormented with the pains of Hell.[29] The frightful vacuum stretching between such a God and man had to be filled with feeling, affect, *desiderium*. Ironically, Gerson's pre-Protestant nominalism gave birth to sentimentality, although he hated the sentimentality he thought he detected in Flemish mysticism. What he wanted was a hard kind of feeling, an iron will, identical with reason; Gerson used *ratio* and *voluntas* as synonyms (as did Nietzsche and Marx). Men were to direct their wills to carry out the laws of God. By means of strict training they were to discipline themselves and to learn self-control.

Starting from reason, and from a heart frozen with anxiety, Gerson arrived at the dialectics of sin and grace, the interplay of opposites – *antiperistasis spiritualis*. He realized that man must, in suffering and temptation, in humility and poverty, bow his head under the law of contradiction. He longed for a great union of the old Victorine mysticism and of Bonaventure, but he remained a man of learning and intellect. He was extremely suspicious of love, whether heavenly or earthly, and mistrusted spiritual friendship between men and women as he found it among the Beguines and Beghards of Bruges. The great mystic Ruysbroek seemed to him a mere pantheist. All the old symbiotic unions of God, the world and man were so much humbug. He saw in world history the will alone and believed that nothing but will and the anxious effort of the ego could make things better. Like Nicholas of Cusa and Erasmus, Gerson was surrounded by the religious movement in the Low Countries, but his answer to all the people's extravagances of spirit and feeling was the Church as an authoritative law. The clericalism of the modern Church owes a good deal to Gerson's fear of the spirit at large and popular emotional religion. His fears and his nominalist attitudes led him to advocate a rigorous, professional clergy. Gerson was opposed to translating the Bible, and he demanded that inquisitors strenuously supervise the entire civil life of the laity. They were to listen to the guests at banquets, for instance, to ensure that nothing improper be said against the Faith. Penance, contrition and self-discipline seemed to him to provide the one and only way out of a fundamentally desperate situation.

The most important men of the conciliar reform movement between 1390 and 1440 were all prisoners of their theology. Man was, in their thinking, condemned to an eternally bad conscience from which he could find no relief. They were unsure of themselves, both as to knowledge and as to Faith, and their faculties were paralysed by this uncertainty. One bold attempt to break out was made by Nicholas of Cusa (1401–64). His mystical philosophy was an effort to reunite and reconcile the antagonisms of the age. He wanted to harmonize the old Empire and the old Church, the conciliar idea, the first German movement, the movement in the Low Countries, the Hussites, the Mohammedans, the Eastern Orthodox and the Western Nonconformists. He was the great enlightener, the preacher of tolerance and the unity of all religions. He could make such an attempt because he was a part of one of the greatest of the new movements, the Brethren of Common Life at Deventer.

Attempts have been made to represent the Flemish-Low German movement stretching from the brotherhoods in Zwolle and Deventer to Erasmus and Sebastian Franck, as something ambiguous and decadent, as mere refined sensibility and enervated melancholy. Certain scholars point to its mood of scepticism and resignation, emancipation and pessimism, and regard it as the swan-song of a tired middle ages.[30] Although there were certainly decadent elements in the movement, there was also a tremendous historical vitality. Later English and French deism, enlightenment, religious and political tolerance were all in certain respects the results of ideas originally conceived in the *devotio moderna*.[31] Around 1387, in the house of the Brethren of the Common Life at Zwolle, a movement of reform began which spread to monasteries and lay-groups. It was a typical movement of the middle ages in that it aimed to restore what it thought of as ancient purity, but its environment was unusual. The Low Countries in the late fourteenth century were soaked in heresy and ancient nonconformism. A wealthy high clergy, well-endowed monasteries, rich cities and social classes were at odds with each other but united in opposing the kings of France and dukes of Burgundy. New and vigorous forms of existence, throbbing with life were springing up everywhere. Rumours of war, energetic daily politics and an apparently boundless lust for profit dominated the cities. Civil war was latent in every city and district and borough. A struggle between the great citizens, the guilds, the fraternities and the manual labourers was always about to break out. Despite the ferocity of these internal conflicts, the Low Countries developed a strength which later enabled them to assert themselves against the French, Spaniards and English.

The brotherhoods, the reformed monasteries and the religious movements amongst the laity sought to escape the problems of the day by turning inwards. 'Our salvation is not grounded in any alien work; our kingdom is in ourselves alone.'[32] 'The kingdom of God is within you; so you can reign, if only you will. For there is a fertile memory within you, if it be tended. There is an illustrious understanding with you, if it be properly trained. And there is also a holy will within you, if it be preserved.'[33] In the first stage an inner kingdom was developed where, according to Nicholas of Cusa, 'our royal and imperial spirit' is required to act as judge between true and false. Initially it was conceived only as a relationship between the ego and the divine thou, Christ.* All the secular realms, the economics and politics of cities and citizens, prelates and princes, were rejected from the outset. The universal success of the *Imitation of Christ*,† like the earlier success of stoicism, was a result of this fundamental attitude of personal resistance. At first, men retreated to the fortress of the Christian conscience; later they were seeking security in divinely enlightened reason. The individual recognized his duty to build his inner kingdom in defiance of all the great powers of this world, which eventually included all Christian confessions and religious parties. Augustine and the Fathers were summoned to the aid of the work of Christian enlightenment which now began. The monasteries and brotherhoods of the *devotio moderna*

*cf. Bernard of Clairvaux and Tauler.

†Geert Groote and Thomas à Kempis are both candidates for the authorship of the *Imitation of Christ* (*ca.* 1415), the most widely-read book, after the Bible, of all world literature. Van Ginneken, F. Kern and others favour the authorship of Groote.

took to copying books. Geert Groote, a bourgeois intellectual, 'a chattering, covetous, good-for-nothing, ever greedy for books' (as he described himself in a letter to Ruysbroek) made translations of the liturgy into the vernacular for the benefit of *devotio moderna* groups.[34] The holy writings of the Church Fathers, and even of pre-Christian authors, provided valid witness to the inner kingdom.

This was the heritage of Nicholas Krebs of Cusa. His wisdom came from the 'God-tasting' wisdom of the German mystics and the *devotio moderna*.[35] His preaching was directed, as a kind of spiritual collation, to the lay communities formed by Eckhart and Ruysbroek. For their benefit he provided a spiritual interpretation of Holy Scripture, basing himself on Hildegard of Bingen and Joachim of Flora. He transcribed Thierry of Chartres, and made his own works into an anthology of the whole anti-Thomist heritage of Christendom.[36] As a friend and pupil of the anti-Thomist Heimerich of Campo, he had a strong affinity to the pantheistic Albert the Great.[37] As a disciple of the movement in the Low Countries, he demonstratively acknowledged his debt to its great progenitor, Eckhart. The great collection of Eckhart's writings in the famous Codex of 1444 can be traced to his initiative. His 'Four Sermons in the Spirit of Eckhart'[38] defended Eckhart's doctrine of the eternity of the world (which John XXII had condemned in 1329), and envisaged the world as a manifestation of God. 'The world is the invisible making itself visible ... Eternity can realize itself only in the mode of time.'[39] 'What is the world but the manifestation of the invisible God; what is God but the invisibility of visible things?'[40] God creates himself in the world; the world is 'God created', 'God caused' (*deus creatus, deus occasionatus*) the universe is 'God made sensible' (*deus sensibilis*) and man is God made human.[41] God is the simplicity and the unfolding of all that is. God is, in all things, that which they themselves are; they are, in him, himself.[42]

Nicholas of Cusa, like Plato, St Thomas, Kant and Hegel, was an eminently political thinker. He was deeply concerned to overcome and synthesize the antinomies and contradictions of his age. His experience of his own times told him that the intellectual positions of Thomism could not prevent the disintegration of salvation. Thomism was, in addition, unable to reconcile mortal enemies – Catholics, Orthodox, Hussites, Individualists, Deists and Mohammedans. It could not lead to discussions which might help to arrive at common faith and action. Nicholas tried to reach into the ground of being and God, which is common to all, a dimension deeper and a dimension higher than the Thomist-curial level.[43] He was driving toward that point where all finite things are hidden in the super-reason of God (symbolized by the globe that is limitless and the centre that is everywhere). As in the case of Leibniz, each of Cusa's philosophical and religious ideas can be translated into a political answer to some burning question affecting the empire, the Church, Europe, or the individual conscience. This is what differentiated him from the 'stay–at–home' men and women of the Flemish-German movement; he had come out into the world, and as a humanist at the councils and as a prince of the Church he attacked the problems of the day at that profound level where real decisions are taken.[44]

Nicholas of Cusa became the hero of a Catholic enlightenment which reached out to embrace all the potentialities of old Europe.[45] Like Anselm of Havelberg and Joachim of Flora to whom he had ties, he was profoundly affected by his personal experience of different religions, *varietas rituum*.[46] In 1437–8, returning from Constantinople where he had been negotiating a union with the Greek Orthodox, he conceived the idea of his work *On Learned Ignorance*, in which he delivered mystical thought from the insular world of the Low German movement and used it to overcome conflicts in the world of politics. With divine self-confidence, he asserted that the various confessions possess a relative truth within world history, in which God's universal work, the gradual improvement of mankind, takes place. Greeks, pagans, Jews, Mohammedans, Hussites,[47] and Western Christians have been called by God to serve him according to the particular character of their own country, people and confessional outlook. In the year following the fall of Constantinople, he wrote a discussion of religion between all the religions of the world (*De Pace seu Concordantia Fidei*), in which the Logos (intellectual reason) announced that: 'Religion and the worship of God, in all men endowed with the spirit, are fundamentally, in all the diversity of rites, one and the same.'

The world of the Three Rings had come to life in his enlightened spirit.[48] He looked toward a future state of Catholicism in which the full historical individuality of all the different conceptions of God and of all religious confessions, and the full political rights of all classes and callings would be preserved and cherished in a *coincidentia oppositorum*, a harmony of opposites which does not destroy tensions but maintains them.* This universal Church of the future, which Cusa identified with the 'Third Kingdom of the Holy Spirit',[49] presupposed the overthrow of that kind of authoritarian thinking which acknowledged only one doctrine and way of salvation. He intended to overthrow it by using Eckhart's mysticism and an equally mystical mathematics. These two weapons against the clergy were to be a theological science of the laity. Mathematics was the science which transcended the limits between reason and the infinite.[50] The infinite when grasped by reason, became finite. In precisely the same way the infinite God, when manifest in history, has expressed himself in the variety of confessions and his Spirit in the world has produced the individual soul. The human 'I' was thus divinely assured. Since man's heart and mind could judge the world and the Church, it followed that the layman could declare that the clergy and their Church had no saving

---

*It is understandable enough that the eighteenth-century Enlightenment should seize upon this (in 1787, J.S. Semler translated the dialogue); but it is cheap and inaccurate in this connection to speak, as Stadelmann does (pp. 155 and 162) of 'attempts to smooth over' and of 'Masonic' ideas, simply because Cusa, like the Fathers of the Eastern Church, attributed the possession of a 'reasonable religion' to all enlightened minds in all ages.

power. The layman, through his own science and his own State-Church, assumed control of grace and salvation. 'Our royal and imperial spirit' could distinguish between holiness and unholiness.[51] The next step was to be the priesthood of every believer and the emergence of Martin Luther.

DANTE TO MACHIAVELLI

Italy's Political Humanism (1300-1527)

Non aspettar mio dir più, ne mio cenno:
Libero, dritto e sano è tuo arbitrio.
E fallo fora non fare a suo cenno:
Per ch'io te sopra te corona e mitrio.

(PURG. *Conto 27, 139–42*).

WITH these words Virgil (the personification of the state and natural reason) took leave of the spiritual ego in the earthly paradise. Together they had traversed world history (which to Dante, as to Poggio and Machiavelli meant barbarism, criminality and Hell on earth), and at last the ego had reached interior freedom. These words are a clue to an understanding of Italian political humanism in the age of Dante and the Italian city-states.[1] The human will, *libero, dritto e sano* was the new palladin. Its promptings were to be obeyed. Man had placed the crown and mitre on his head and proclaimed himself the new emperor.[2]

The new emperor was the intellectually and politically self-reliant individual, the man who wrested his own sacred language, Ciceronian Latin, from the scholastic and barbarous clergy. He challenged their corrupt theology with his own sacred poetry, and constructed his own theories of salvation, humanity, nature and society in defiance of the power ideologies of the barbarians, the German emperors, the Italian tyrants and popes.[3] Although they were anti-imperial, anticlerical and anti-medieval, the Italian humanists were closely connected with everything they so stridently opposed. Many ended as secretaries of princes or as members of the high clergy. Their opposition was a plea rather than an act of defiance. They wanted the unpleasant reality of politics to be understood spiritually, and they tried to convince their rulers of the need to accept their responsibility for a way of salvation for the people. Italian humanists were at once moralists, preachers (successors and rivals of the mendicant friars), educators, lay monks and pope-emperors. Dante, Cola di Rienzo, Savonarola and Machiavelli fought openly while the lesser ones made hidden contributions in philological and critical notes and observations.

All the tendencies to be found within this world of political humanism were already present in Dante. He was a disciple of Siger and of Thomas, and a descendant of the Catharist-Albigensian aristocracy of the *dolce stil nuovo*, and of the Fraticelli and of the Spanish-Arab intelligentsia of the world of the Three Rings. He was at once a Hebrew prophet, an Etruscan priest and a Roman imperialist.[4] He was a 'magnanimous sinner' – *magnanimus peccator* – like his counterpart, Boniface VIII, and was torn asunder by lust, anger and pride – *lussuris, ira, superbia*. Dante was the first of the 'bad' heroes.[5] The figure of his forefather Farinata degli Uberti, tragic, noble and undismayed, was a self-portrait. The Averroist Farinata who, with Siger, denied the immortality of the soul, stands erect in Hell, in the city of heresiarchs, defying both Hell and the Godhead who makes him suffer. Dante's hymns of hate against the Black Beast, Boniface VIII, against all his foes, against the corrupt Church and the debauched Empire, were outgrowths of Franciscan spiritualism. His haughtiness was much like Roger Bacon's. His invective against the Council of Vienna,[6] the tone of prophecy and invocation in his work, and his intention to change the world were the most obvious expressions of his inheritance from the Franciscan prophets of history.[7] Dante was never entirely certain about his attitude to the paternal world in which he lived. On the one hand he was the leader (*dux* and saviour-leader) of the inner emigration of all of Italy's humanists and reformers. They were all to an extent *fuorusciti, émigrés*, although not always literally, because they were seeking pure and uncontaminated names to give to God and man, to the state, the Church and society. Thus they were more or less compelled to adopt a new father: 'The Renaissance was born in the *émigré* mentality.'[8] Dante chose Virgil as his father. *Romanum imperium de fonte nascitur pietatis*.[9]

The Roman Empire sprang from the source of divine compassion and providence, which, with its aid, drew man on to *civilitas* – 'civilized' culture.[10] Augustine and the fourth-century legends of Silvester and Constantine were the channels by which these maxims of ancient Roman faith reached Dante. On the other hand Dante chose the most paternal of all the old fathers, the Emperor, to be the saviour-guardian of the civilized world.[11] The Emperor was to impose an ascetic virtue on society,[12] and 'to receive the control of the world government which the Church, once it had been purified, would no longer possess.'[13] As in the ninth heaven of the *Paradiso*, he was to lead mankind upwards into that spiritual kingdom of humanity where the good pagan, the heretic and the Christian are united in spirit, in culture, in politics and in love.[14] In the new communion of saints and spiritual minds, all elect good men were at once Romans, Christians, Franciscans and Italians – members of the glorified Empire and the glorified Church.

Shimmering with apocalyptic hues, the New Jerusalem, the spiritual individual's kingdom of civilization and culture came floating down to earth. Because of a complexity of premonitions and backward glances characteristic of the fourteenth century, it was still adorned with the theatrical masks of the emperor of the last age and the angelic pope. Dante's blessing upon the living

Emperor Henry VII and his curse upon dead popes must not be allowed to obscure his real preoccupation with the new, spiritually developed individual. The new man had a Roman and classical education. He was the new priest and prophet, mediator and sage in the realm of salvation, and was Pope and Emperor in one. He cherished *his* sacred lore and *his* sacred song and carefully preserved the word as received from antiquity.

Italian humanism was an extraordinary and peculiar combination of Utopian fantasy and cool, matter-of-fact realism. The same person often combined an interest in party-politics in the narrowest and pettiest sense with sweeping schemes for world-wide reform. This was partly because of Italy's typical Nicodemism, the necessity of concealing what is primary and ultimate. The grand ideas were often only half expressed and muffled in symbol and allegory. Bold and sweeping ideas, however, were very much a part of the prevailing atmosphere. Wide-ranging discussion took place among the nobility and bourgeoisie in Florence's palazzi and country houses, to an extent in imitation of the discussions which used to take place in the court of Frederick II[15] and which later gave birth to Italy's academies. Dante himself participated in these discussions among the *filosofanti*. As the leader of a new aristocracy of personalist morality, and spokesman of that circle among the laity which had long been yearning for its own culture and its own status in sacred matters, he was able to show them that redemption began here on earth. A just and virtuous life within the *humana civilitas* did not depend upon the emperor, the pope, or a monastic renunciation. Stoicism, epicureanism and classical rhetoric were considered useful aids and grew in importance after Dante's time. The old powers of salvation (the emperor and the papal Church) were first redecorated and transfigured by this new spirituality, but later, when subjected to criticism, were found to be wanting in sanctity and thus reduced to mere secular history.

Cola di Rienzo, tribune of the Roman people, presented himself as a second Francis, come to sustain the collapsing *imperium*.[16] He was a 'knight of the Holy Ghost' and appropriated the inscription on the seal of Otto III, whose cult and concept of Rome he revived.[17] His first aim was to be procurator of the imperial papacy and the empire.[18] In place of 'one holy Church', Boniface VII and the Bull *Unam Sanctum*, Rienzo set up the 'holy unity of the Roman people', *Sancta unitas populi Romani*.[19] To construct his Italian empire, Rienzo began the most colossal propaganda display ever conceived until the advent of the revolutionary liturgies of modern times. He allied himself with the communes, with the humanist hopes for a way of salvation and with the faith of the people in the redemptive power of the city of Rome.[20] He drew also on the current of historical prophecy among the anti-papal spiritualist monks. Although he was a humanist and man of learning, he had much in common with Joan of Arc. Like her, he wanted to bring about salvation through the awakened people. He too tapped an underground source of power: the popular reverence for the ancient Christian and ancestral saving power of Rome. His magnificent liturgies for the days between Pentecost and the feast of St Peter's

Chains in 1347 awakened forces which had long been dormant. He first seized power in Rome by occupying the Parliament in the Capital. Next he laid down a basic programme of reform for imperial Italy:[21] 'The creation of an army, reorganization of finance and legal administration, speed in the administration of penal law, laws to provide against the return of the deposed aristocracy, relief for trade and commerce, the introduction of social welfare, and a tightening up of the moral standards of the clergy.'[22] The climax came at the Synod of Italian liberty, beginning on 1 August, when the Italian nation was proclaimed as a holy and redeeming nation, because of the saving power it possessed in antiquity and in Christian times.

After he had been imprisoned by the Emperor at Raudnitz on the Elbe and by the Pope at Avignon, Rienzo made one more attempt. This time when he regained power in Rome, like a ruthless *condottiere* of the type of Cesare Borgia, he carried out a judicial ritual of blood and sought to cast a spell of terror over men's minds. A parliament was convened in the Franciscan monastery on the Capital, strikingly reminiscent of the Jacobin Club in Paris, which also met in a Franciscan house. Like Robespierre, he suffered no one to say a word against him. His death was, if possible, more grisly than those of the French Revolution. He was burned to death on a pyre made of thistles in front of the mausoleum of Augustus; Jews, the unholy ones, were the only people allowed to approach his ashes and even they, only to collect them and fling them into the Tiber.

Rienzo's fate was a warning to all Italian humanists. From him, they learned that the direct road was not open to political humanism. They would have to proceed by series of detours. The 'man of the spirit' (the humanist revision of Franciscan spirituality) could not build the new kingdom through political revolution. He could only use the magic of words, poetry and the beauty of the liberal arts. Petrarch's famous letter to Clement VI was evidence of the degree to which Rienzo's synthesis remained a model for fourteenth-century Italian humanism.[23] Petrarch had followed Rienzo's career with close attention and was obviously deeply moved by the ideas for which Rienzo had fought. In the letter, he joined them all together: religious devotion, the cult of relics, the pathos of national feeling in the idea of rebirth and the cult of Rome, and reverence for the classical past and its sacred monuments and ruins. Another humanist, Boccaccio, wrote to Giacopo Pizzinghe that the Roman *imperium* had been ruined because their Italian forefathers had neglected their responsibilities and had permitted aliens and barbarians to gain control of Rome.[24] The old *imperium* had been lost forever, but a new one could be built through art and poetry. Virgil's *Fourth Eclogue*, that ancient song of Rome's rebirth, would be heard anew and he himself would join the chorus.

Enmity towards the barbarians and a persistent hope in the popes as guardians of Italy's liberty and the rebirth of humanity were characteristic of the humanism of the fourteenth century. Innocent III, in his struggle with Frederick II, had imparted a specifically anti-German and nationalist colour to the ancient sacral-political term of abuse – barbarian. At the same time he directed Italian hopes for salvation to the 'true emperor', i.e., the Pope.[25] Petrarch had a somewhat less national interpretation of the word barbarian, especially when he wrote to German contemporaries.[26] A barbarian was someone who deliberately excluded himself from the one holy Roman-Christian culture of soul and spirit. With extraordinary shrewdness, he observed that there was a humanist Germany which was the nucleus of the West and a barbarian eastern Germany beyond the Elbe and the Danube. He accepted the teaching of the Franciscan Spirituals about the stages in world history, but went on to work out a specifically Italian concept of the middle ages. The entire period from Constantine to his present day, he regarded as an unbroken era of barbarism.[27] He felt that Constantine, more than anyone else, was to blame for it, and he argued that since the age of Constantine the pure Church had been thoroughly corrupted. In his *Book Without a Name*, he called the French *Curia* of Avignon Hell itself and the whore of Babylon.[28] The Pope was Antichrist, a reincarnation of Nero, Julian and Nimrod. 'The first age of Christianity, an ideal image of the primitive Church, and the moral ideal of ancient Roman virtue' were regarded as one single sacred inheritance.[29] A reform of the Empire, the Church and learning were the means by which that sacred antiquity could be restored.

It is not always easy to be fair to Petrarch, because he had so many of the most irritating characteristics of the typical intellectual. The son of an exiled Florentine, he grew up in the papal territory at Avignon, and lived off the popes and tyrants against whom he wrote. He began by citing Augustine (*De Contemptu Mundi*) to show how worthless was his own quest for love and fame, but went on to transform Augustine's God-centred 'ego' into the sheer solipsism of the *Canzioniere* and Laura-lauro symbolism.[30] His emphasis on the ego, beloved and crowned with laurel, degenerated into a Rilke-like narcissism where the only remaining object of consciousness was a single reality, the ego admiring and praising itself. The ego aspired to be a monastic, ascetical sage (*De Vita Solitaria*) and to follow in the footsteps of Jerome. The new self would then inherit the powers of salvation which had belonged to the sages of the ancient world. It is easy to understand why his 'perpetual pathological preoccupation with himself'[31] got on people's nerves. His secular hermitages, at Vaucluse, Selvapiana and Arquà, were exclusively dedicated to the contemplation of the ego, and this a-social egocentric sat comfortably inside them, freely criticizing the rulers of his day. He remained disdainful of the 'uneducated people' who were, after all, quite incapable of mastering the holy Latin language. Nothing would do but the creation of a new class of educated men.[32]

A brand new type of man had emerged, the intellectual, and he seemed to have a good many rather disagreeable features. He called everything in the world into question except his own ego, which he interrogated incessantly for the answers to his problems. He was the self-proclaimed heir both of prophet and priest and had as a result to work out in his own life all the antinomies embodied in both. The weaknesses of this novel figure are today only too well known, but there were (and are) many strengths as well. It would be hard to find a man who made greater contributions to the development of western Europe than Petrarch, the first of the intellectuals. He hated Averroists, doctors, astrologers and all determinists. He disliked scholastics, 'vain and empty' lawyers and theologians. These aversions were, however, only the negative aspect of his fundamental wish to liberate the individual.

Personality needed a certain separateness in which to find itself. The powerful organizations of Petrarch's day refused to permit such personal withdrawal. In the Aristotelian system and scholasticism. Petrarch discerned an alienation of man from God and from himself. The triumph of the natural sciences, i.e., of immanentism and fatalism, was dangerous to freedom and humanity, and these ideas were the substance of his complaint against Averroist Paris and Avignon, where astrology and magic were in control. The intellectual as a phenomenon was the product of two religious streams. One was the mystical religiosity of Francis of Assisi, the Joachimites, Bernard of Clairvaux and Augustine. This was the current which was to be continued in the schools of the Florentine Platonists, the French humanist circle of Faber d'Etaples, the English humanists around Colet, the Germans of Mutian's circle and Erasmus. The other current, the craving for purity, with its strong philological and scientific bent ran from the Verona group of discoverers to Poggio, Valla, Pomponazzi and Descartes, and on to Port Royal and Pascal.[33] In his efforts to achieve a critical, self-sufficient status for the individual, Petrarch endeavoured to fashion a new ethic for the laity (*De Viris Illustribus*). The examples provided by the Bible and the lives of the Fathers, he believed, were no longer effective guides for the art of living.[34] Instead men ought to cultivate the civic virtues, 'probity' (*probitas*, from Livy) and 'honourableness' (*honestas*, cf. Joan of Arc's *prud'homme*). Faith was no longer a religious, political or feudal concept but a synthesis of loyalty and reciprocal trust. It became the quintessence of political humanity. In his 'Africa' he presented a kind of Roman Christian–spiritual complex as a new patriotism which began to become the inner homeland of the intellectuals of the Western world: *Plenus sum Italicarum rerum*.[35] 'To hurt nobody': to give each his own, to live honourably, were his maxims. He was pessimistic about the state of the world and saw it hopelessly sunk in corruption, lust for power, fatalism, pseudo-science, superstition and anxiety.

'It's enough for me to be a poet.'[36] Although Petrarch said the words, his friend Boccaccio lived them. Boccaccio was born in Paris, the illegitimate son of a Florentine commercial agent. As a law student he lived amid the lascivious court life of Naples and had a good opportunity to observe this Italian society with a disenchanted eye. The wealthy bourgeois were bigoted, conservative and opportunistic; the nobility was sceptical, frivolous and equally bigoted. These two classes, bourgeois and nobility, had joined forces with the mendicant orders for mutual advantage and together they formed an unholy trinity which Boccaccio ridiculed in the *Decameron*. In a way, the *Decameron* was the other half of the Divine Comedy. Like all bourgeois polemics since Gottfried's *Tristan*, it was a declaration of the bankruptcy of the old sacred world and of the impotence of its morality. It pointed out that a healthier, more natural and youthful world was growing up in the midst of decay. His ideas were anti-curial and anticlerical,[37] and his famous defence of poets was a defence of lay thought against theology. The true theologians were the poets and those who proclaimed the pure word of God and of holy Latin.

Language emerged as the reform of life itself. It offered a new vision of God and a total criticism of the great political and ecclesiastical powers. If left to follow their natural bent, the Italian successors of Petrarch and Boccaccio would probably have turned to biblical study and textual criticism. Their precarious political position and the wider political situation of Italy made tinkering with the Bible too dangerous. As a result, their preoccupation with language was stunted and deformed. In the work of Lorenzo Valla, who died as a papal canonist in 1457, it was turned into a cult in which language became a 'great sacrament' and a sign of salvation (*magnum sacramentum, magnum numen: Elegentiarum libri* ...). These ideas had certain similarities to the approach to language of the Arab savants of the World of the Three Rings, and eventually led Valla to begin a work on biblical criticism which Erasmus published in 1516. But Valla was always very careful to cover himself in such works and to conceal his real views. In his *De Voluptate* (1431) where he presented nature as an ancient but always youthful goddess, he cunningly divided one speech among several characters in the work, as if he was actively attempting to conceal serious, and indeed heretical ideas, behind the trappings of a masquerade.[38] The work had immense influence on later writers.

The practical failure of late medieval monasticism and the political anti-clericalism of the Italian laity determined Valla's way of thinking. Monasticism had degenerated into hypocrisy and immorality. The whole existence of the clergy and of the monks consisted of a refined egotism. A new healthy Christian life of the laity would be possible only if nature were fully incorporated into life and recognized as a fundamental moral force. 'What nature had created ... can be naught else but holy and praiseworthy ...'[39] In his defence of the holiness of nature Valla based himself on Lactantius, the Church Father. The whole, complete man of the first and second paradise could experience the full power of earthly and heavenly pleasure, because voluptuousness was the heavenly and earthly bliss which Aristotle had already perceived in Divinity itself.[40] Valla recognized this pleasure as the foundation of all human effort in poetry, philosophy, science and life. Pleasure (*delectatio*) was the aim of all things, and the only true virtue whatever the name given to it. *Charitas*, Christian and natural love, became pleasure, love, fulfilment. The essential feature of this doctrine was a kind of monism, which may at first appear to be entirely bound to the natural world, but was in reality the gradual expression of an inner, far more important, spiritual monism. In essence, what Valla was saying about pleasure was merely another way of saying that no difference existed between God and man.[41]

Valla bitterly attacked the three clerical maxims of poverty, chastity and obedience and condemned them all.[42] He went to great lengths to prove that virginity was not only unendurable but also unhealthy. His object in both cases was to show that the old, sinful, clerical man had lost the power to save and that the new Christian man, who harmoniously united God and nature in his life, had assumed it. Even his irreconcilable opponent, Poggio Bracciolini, was very close to him in this respect. Although Poggio had been an official of the *Curia* for nearly fifty years, he was well aware that the majority of the clergy and monks were 'fat and lazy hypocrites', of no use whatever to the people or the Faith.[43] In Mateo Palmieri's *Della Vita Civile*, the peasant who gets up early to plough and sow was compared to the monk who gets up in the middle of the night to pray, to the disadvantage of the monk.[44] In another and more devastating work, the *Facetiae*, Palmieri turned the world upside down and described it with laughter, obscenities and drolleries of all kinds. Like Boccaccio, he exposed the hypocrisy of the ruling classes, of the clergy, the savants and nobles.

There was more than enlightened social criticism in these lampoons. Its power had a different source: the archaic world. The reappearance of attitudes of the ancient underworld can be seen clearly in the May pictures of Botticelli, Ghirlandaio, Giorgione, etc. We have seen how Joan of Arc embodied these elements, and most observers would accept that they were there. Not so many scholars have been willing to see Italian humanism in this way, but its ribaldry, phallic jokes, carnivals and sexual grotesqueries were certainly the expression of precisely the same archaic drives. Italian humanism was open to influences from below. Aspects of this archaic society were very much a part of life in fifteenth-century Florence with its fertility rites, May Queens, and magic of all kinds. It impressed itself on the thinking both of the rulers (the Medici) and of the ideologies of *la gente nuova*. The controversial new worldliness and the paganism of many humanists were an expression of this submersion in archaic elemental kinships and connections. The peasant and the peasant-citizen of this seamless, sexually-connected world danced and sang in honour of 'holy Spring', *Primavera*. Most fourteenth-and fifteenth-century humanists started out as 'little people', as peasants from the countryside.[45] What was new was not their worldliness but their spirituality. Their attempt to educate themselves independently through the Church Fathers and the Stoics, the Epicureans, nature and Plato was new. Their sincere desire to create a Christian life justified by activity in the world and in ethical conduct was new. They observed the world so sharply because they had to master it intellectually and spiritually, and because they considered the models of scholasticism and the old asceticism inadequate and beside the point.

Poggio perceptively observed that the vice of avarice and covetousness had important social and economic functions. It financed the construction of public buildings and the whole economy.[46] This spiritual-humanistic criticism was the first comparative sociology. In *De Nobilitate*, Poggio analysed the role of princes and popes in the evolution of true culture and observed with penetrating accuracy the characteristics of the old European nobility, of the inherited city-state traditions, and of the alien German, French and English aristocracies. Systematic observation of society would lead to a true inner nobility of disposition. Poggio used his analyses to develop the idea that men are guilty of the many misfortunes of life because they do not follow 'right reason'. He pleaded that the man of his day who lived a life based on the mind and the true Faith and who died for it was nobler than the Stoics. He would be so upright that a Socrates and a Scaevola would turn pale. Poggio saw with his own eyes the heretic Jerome of Prague burned at the stake in Constance.[47] The experience overwhelmed him and his fellow humanists. The thought of Italian humanism was driven more deeply into concealment. Its religious concern sought expression in discussion about true nobility, in its passion for education and in its Platonism. Education could take place through conversation in society.[48] There must be a concordance of the right speech with the right life.[49]

Guarino Veronese, who opened his Greek school for all western Europe, and Vittorino da Feltre, whose Christian humanism aimed to train body and mind harmoniously and who called for a Christian experience of the world, love of God and neighbour, were animated by a deep faith in the power of right education. Education for the good and blessed life (*bene etiam beateque vivere*) of this Christian Stoa was to be accomplished through praise and encouragement, not through terror and enslavement.[50] The education of the new man was directed against the old God of terror and of the sacral-political rulers. It was nourished by a Franciscan disposition and classical education. No external power could limit the freedom of the man who educated himself. Bernardino of Siena, who celebrated the inner kingdom of man, preached against Guelphs and Ghibellines, against the political sectarian spirit and against tyranny. He surveyed the world with its vices and virtues, but remained serene. Prophetically he foresaw the power and greatness of science and the tremendous capacity of man: 'The will is the emperor of the universe' (*La volontà è imperatrice di tutto l'universo*). This overweening spiritualism with its faith in progress and its ontological optimism was the prelude to the humanism of the French mystics of the seventeenth century, which in its turn laid the religious foundations for the 'high Enlightenment' of the eighteenth century.

At the height of the fifteenth century the city-states and republics were delicately balanced as a counterweight against the pope and foreign kings. Each had a distinct intellectual atmosphere and acted as a focus for the collection of certain forces. Padua, which after 1404 became part of Venice, was strongly anti-Thomist and a centre of natural science and Averroism. Rome was the papal city and seat of an anticlerical intelligentsia bordering on atheism, which gathered in the Roman Academy (*Quiranalis*) around Platina. Naples was anti-Roman, anti-papal, aggressively enlightened and materialistic. In between and in opposition to all the rest stood Florence and its academies. Between the founding of the Florentine Academy in 1459 and the death of Ficino in 1499, there was a tremendous surge of intellectual activity. It was partly caused by the influx of Greek theologians who had come for the unity negotiations with the Roman church to the councils of Florence and Ferrara in 1438.

In the years after the fall of Constantinople (1453), a flood of émigrés descended on the city. 'The world renaissance was invented in Italy by a Byzantine clique ...'[51] Byzantine humanists like Nicephorus Choronos (d. 1328) rejuvenated the old sacral-political ideology of the 'renewal of classical studies'.[52] Simultaneously, the dispute over Plato or Aristotle as the guiding stars of philosophy was revived among the émigrés. (Gennadios and George of Trapezunt argued against the 'Platonic pagans' Plethon and Bessarion). These émigrés owed their warm reception in Florence, in noblemen's palaces and great bourgeois houses, to the fact that their spirit-religion corresponded exactly to certain political, religious and spiritual needs. These nobles and laymen were arrivés socially and economically, and the new Platonism became a kind of secular religion.[53] This universal theism allowed a spiritual and religious justification of practical life with its thirst for pleasure and beauty. It helped to support the political policy of these Italian cities which from the twelfth to the fifteenth centuries had permitted Turks, unbelievers, heretics and pagans to live peacefully within the city's protection. Florence had also contracted treaties and commercial pacts with powers of the non-Christian world. The ultimate development of this Platonism was to reconcile God and nature and to assure the individual of this religious and political state of grace.

Marsilio Ficino, the philosophist, as Vives rightly called him, admired the Areopagite, Scotus Eriugena, Avicenna and Algazali.[54] He revered Plato as a theologian and in contrast to the 'learned ignorance' of Nicholas of Cusa he developed his 'learned religion' (docta religio). He believed that he had to save the piety of his day, which had sunk to a low level, through his religious philosophy.[55] His thought was entirely entangled in mysticism, occultism and astrology against which he made occasional attacks without being able to break out of its bonds.[56] Although he wrote his attack on astrology ten years before Pico, by the time Pico began Ficino was once again zealously paying homage to astrological practices.[57] He believed that love was the fundamental force of creation and that everything was dissolved and absorbed in it. This ecstatic apotheosis of love spread through Italy like a sweet poison.* It evoked a vague, sensual and intellectual pan-eroticism which transformed Roland the Carolingian hero of God into a servant of the new love.[58] Ficino was a deeply medieval anti-intellectualist, but he did reveal some of the genuine concerns of those circles which tried to fashion an ideology for themselves in Platonism.[59] His thinking led to a new vision of man as the artist who had the capacity to become everything: animal, plant, God, or devil. The hero, not Christ and his

*cf. Rousseau and Wagner in Italy.

priests, was the special mediator between God and man. Man, as the God of this earth, could do everything that he really wanted. Science, wisdom, and magic were the roads to salvation and the attainment of divinity.

The man to fulfil this dream was the child prodigy Giovanni Pico della Mirandola.[60] He was the son of an imperial count – which may account for his Ghibelline anti-papal tradition – and the heir to a great fortune which made him independent. From the age of fourteen on, he absorbed the knowledge of the World of the Three Rings at the universities of Bologna, Ferrara and Padua. At Padua his teacher Elia del Medigo strongly influenced him in an Averroistic direction. Later he studied at the university of Paris. There is not one of his 'thoughts' that cannot already be found in his teachers and models. Thirty years before him Manetti and Alberti had developed a complete theory of the self-conscious, creative man, and he owed the best of his thought to Nicholas of Cusa.[61] Pico wanted to visit Germany just to examine Nicholas's library. In his famous treatise *On the Dignity of Man*, he revived the old Pelagian position that sin is the necessary correlation to human greatness. Man needs sin in order to shape himself: *sui ipsius quasi arbitrarius honorariusque plastes et fictor.* This treatise was the introduction to his 900 theses (*Conclusiones*) which he published in Rome in December 1486.[62] He invited all the scholars of the world to come to Rome at his expense in order to attend a disputation on them. This baroque desire to grasp all in all aimed at nothing less than a synthesis of Aquinas and Averroes, Scotus, Avicenna, Plato and Aristotle. The whole philosophical knowledge of world history was to be compiled by a world alliance of free spirits. A *pax philosophica* would take the place of the *pax romana* of the old empire and of the *pax Christi*, of the old Church. Pico rejected the veneration of the cross as idolatry; he argued against the whole 'external cult' of the Church, entertained critical views about transubstantiation and defended Origen.

Old Cathar and Waldensian heretical ideas and resentments, loyally carried on by the Italian nobility as a tradition, reappeared strangely and wondrously transformed by the extreme rationalism which Pico owed to his Paris studies. There was also an addition of Neoplatonic pantheism according to which God was 'all in all'. Nature, philosophy, religion and the Gospel formed an inner unity. Pathetically Pico declared: 'There is no science that transmits to us a more certain knowledge about the divinity of Christ than magic and the Cabbala.' Pico sought the divine in all things, and naturally emphasized cosmology, ontology and theodicy. Unfortunately he failed to realize that God, nature and man lost their status in this brilliant spectacle of philosophical thought, because it destroyed all the objective distinctions on which theology, anthropology and natural science must depend. Pico was a brilliant young man entangled in the web of magic and occultism. He sought fame desperately and even resorted to attacks on astrology in order to get it. Although he solemnly proclaimed the freedom of man, he was himself ensnared in world-immanence and fatalism. Stripped of the magical glitter of his language, all that remained of his philosophy was a narrow, sterile rationalism. He tried to hide this from himself through stylistic sophistry and plays of thought, while his despairing soul thirsted for divine grace.[63] In the end, he sought refuge with Savonarola. Florentine Platonism led nowhere. The decline of the freedom of the Florentine Republic after the French invasion, merely sealed the fate which it had already prepared for itself.

It is unfair to judge these fantasies spun around Florentine fireplaces without considering the environment. This idealism was a despairing reaction of humanist rhetoricians, poets and lay thinkers against the front of physicians, politicians, naturalists, technicians and materialists, who were becoming ever stronger. In Florence itself Galeotto Marzio da Narni declared this Platonic-magic-alchemist religion to be a pseudo-science. He proclaimed himself a pupil of Aristotle and of Padua and a scientific materialist. 'Where there is no body, there is also no human life', he asserted. Marzio criticized all metaphysical philosophies of the time from top to bottom.[64] He ridiculed the idea of the immortality of the soul and the stupidity of the conceited masses. In his view ignorance was the only sin. The Christian Faith was nothing but superstition and credulity. There were prodigies and miracles in all religions. Man could become blessed in any of them if he were good. But his goodness was a matter affecting only man, his knowledge and reason. The enjoyment of God through love was possible only through knowledge and conscience. This enlightener based himself on Augustine, only with a different emphasis than Pico's. Ironically, both Marzio and Pico drew their ideas from the World of the Three Rings and differed in a sense only in the importance given to one set or another.

Naples also had an academy, which had been founded by Beccadelli. There Giovanni Pontano (d. 1503) made his great contribution and the Academy was rightly named in his honour (academia Pontaniana). He was a true servant of his King against the Pope and the barons, a strong, self-enclosed personality as his statues and works testify. His political ethos was derived from Aristotle Cicero and Seneca. He was deeply conscious of his role as poet and minister and unshakeable under the blows of fate.* He was the embodiment of the overweening man, who was a law unto himself and the heir of the old kings and priests.[65] This cultivator of freedom was an earthly god, but he was not a solitary one. Pontano hated all monastic and egocentric, insular lives. His was the credo of political humanism: 'I proclaim myself to be a man living in a civil community, in the society of men, occupied with many things ...'[66] By many things Pontano meant the state and the prince, the family, nature (which determines the formation and temperament of man), virtues and proficiencies.[67] He denied the immortality of the soul and fought the superstitions of the people and the clergy which he considered politically and humanly dangerous.

This Neapolitan circle stood very close to a certain Roman intelligentsia which was centred in the Roman Academy. Filippo Buonaccorsi, called

*Pontano lost every one of his children and in 1495 his position as well, when Charles VIII conquered Naples.

Callimaco, its greatest mind, expressed its anti-Platonic, anti-papal, anti-authoritarian tendencies. Later as the vice-chancellor of the King, he advised him to make the Church into a national Church and the prelates into state officials (*Consilium Callimachi*). The most important members of the Academy were arrested in 1486 by order of Paul II and accused of infidelity, immorality and conspiracy against the Pope. Among them were Pompanio Leto and Platina (Barolomeo Sacchi, d. 1481). Platina, a favourite of Pope Pius II and of the Gonzagas, dedicated his work, *Concerning the Vices of Popes*, to Sixtus IV under whom he rose to the position of official papal historian and in 1475 to the post of director of the Vatican Library. Like Bernard of Clairvaux and Petrarch, he condemned the clergy for its avarice, sensuality, arrogance and idleness, its ignorance of itself and the teachings of the Faith. He summoned philosophy – as a lay theology – to the task of purging life (*emendatio vitae*). True nobility was to be achieved only through Stoic-Christian virtue (*de vera nobilitate*). In his book on the prince (*De principe*) there was much that foreshadowed Machiavelli especially the demand that the prince assert himself ruthlessly.

Between political humanism and Macchiavelli, there were three men, who represented major aspects of the development of Italian thought: Frulovisi, Piccolomini and Savonarola. Tito Livio de Frulovisi, a man wise in the ways of the world, had lived an adventurous life in Italy, England and the Orient by the time his great work *De republica* appeared.[68] It was published some time before 1434, and was strongly reminiscent of Marsilius and the French legists. The state represented Spirit in its concrete universality; its unique properties were the highest power and the supreme educational force over the men entrusted to it. The state ordered, ruled, and directed all. Frulovisi recommended that the duty to work be applied to all classes. Like the great utopians who came later (Bruno, Campanella, etc.), Frulovisi glorified work as the new *opus dei* and sang the praises of agriculture in particular. He wanted to break the power of the Church through his own strong state. 'I want the prince to be the teacher of religion.' The prince was to appoint bishops and priests and exercise a strong control over his state and national church. State absolutism was combined with a (Franciscan) spiritualism in Frulovisi. Justice could be saved only by the state because the Church of Rome had hopelessly corrupted it. The Church had degraded all other political relations as well, and he illustrated this in his comedies which were called *Oratoria*. The yearning for peace was the ultimate theme in Frulovisi, but he saw only one hope for it: the state would have to force men to be good.

Enea Silvio Piccolomini had all the instability and awareness of the humanist intellectual. He was a politician, journalist, and a man of letters who fed on contradictions but never overcame them.[69] Fascinated, he portrayed the hectic, restless and vice-ridden life at the courts of kings and popes.[70] He was tormented by a drive to be active and shifted his allegiance nervously from the conciliar movement to the Emperor, and, at the last, deserted both to serve the

Pope. His political thinking ended up in an unconditional caesarism: the ruler stands above every law. 'We are convinced that states can only be maintained through weapons, not through laws.'[71] The magic of power and the magic of the mind dazzled him. When he became Pope Pius II, he called upon the founder of Rome, the pious Aeneas of Virgil, as his religious and political father. 'Will you fight once more, old grey priest?' he asked himself almost accusingly, as he began to arm for a war against the Turks. 'Yes,' he replied, 'I will fight not only with prayers but with weapons!' Among the weapons he was prepared to use in the service of his powerful state were the sciences and poetry. Princes, therefore, should promote scholarship so that the religious-political rebirth of Christianity and classical culture could be carried further.[72]

Pius II was the herald of Julius II who rode into battle as *papa terribile* but who at the same time, with the help of his artists, Raphael and Michelangelo, wanted to build Rome from within into a palace of the reborn cosmos. Julius II died in 1513, in the year when Machiavelli wrote his book *The Prince*. Leonardo, the dark antagonist of this papal world-renaissance, died in 1519, Raphael died in 1520, and Machiavelli died in 1527, the year of the imperial sack of Rome. An epoch came to an end. During that era, Franciscan thinking had slowly come to dominate Rome. Franciscan generals became popes. Bonaventure was canonized in 1482. Raphael followed Franciscan and cusanist teachings in his 'School of Athens'.[73] Julius II who called Julius Caesar his father and lord, at the same time fostered Franciscan philosophy for personal reasons. Monastic, ascetic, spiritual and political reform, war and crusade, total renewal of the world, of the Church and the political community were completely alien to these papal rulers. Their *possesso* was a would-be ancient triumphal procession to the Lateran, a symbol of power and an imitation of Cola di Rienzo's victory parade of 31 July 1347.[74] The mental attitudes of the reform thinkers, Savonarola and Machiavelli, were naturally equally foreign to such papal absolutists.

Both Savonarola and Machiavelli were political humanists who painfully recalled the lost golden age of political purity, freedom and civic virtue. Both wanted to preach this anew to a degenerate race. One important influence on Savonarola was the Augustinian monk Luigi Marsili, who was the adviser of Chancellor Salutati.[75] In his 'Letter Against the Vices of the Papal Court,'[76] Marsili had demanded a broad democratization of the use of the Bible and of theology. Neither, he argued, ought to remain reserved as a ruler's ideology and a 'secret knowledge' of the hierarchy, but should be made available to the whole people who needed it for its civic and political salvation. Michael Savonarola (d. 1464), Girolamo's grandfather, had been Professor in Padua and the personal physician to the d'Este family. In his scientific works he had shown himself to be a sober observer of nature, of the physiognomy of men, of the healing power of baths and mineral springs, as well as a critic of authorities.[77] His grandson wanted to secure salvation for the 'people of Florence'. He filled himself with the angry rebellious ideas of his friend

Giovanni Pico della Mirandola, of Giovanni Nesi and of those Florentine intellectuals who, like the *filosofanti* around Dante, gathered for discussion in the cloister of San Marco and in Ficino's Academy.[78] Savonarola's writings suggest that like earlier humanists he wanted to promote the true cultivation of the *studia humanitatis*, but to keep such studies spiritually pure the political community had to be purged of all corruption.

Savonarola's severity in matters of reform was an inheritance from the political humanists of the early fifteenth century, the state chancellors and monks who fought for the freedom of the Florentine people against the Visconti depotism. It was also derived from the resistance of the Fraticelli and kindred spirits to Rome-Babel. Savonarola's attitude was supported both by Aristotle and Aquinas, who had given absolute ascendance to communal as against private interest.[79] Although his great undertaking failed, his ideas exerted a great influence on many of his contemporaries and successors. His effect was by no means confined to a lunatic fringe. Guicciardin (d. 1540) who, along with Machiavelli, was one of Italy's most acute and tough-minded political thinkers made careful excerpts from Savonarola's sermons and applied the apocalyptic themes of Savonarola in the furious polemic of the *Ricordi* against the Roman Church.[80]

Historical analysis often involves correcting imbalance. In Savonarola's case, it is always important to remember the realistic, political and humanistic elements in his make-up. In examining Machiavelli and Guicciardini, the two famous prototypes of political realism, it is equally as important to recall the irrational, prophetic, fanciful and supernatural elements in their ideas. In 1498 Savonarola was burned at the stake and in that same year Machiavelli became secretary of the State Chancellery. The rapid spread of Machiavellianism in the chancelleries of Europe has been, doubtless correctly, associated with the anxiety caused by the fall of Constantinople and the subsequent fear of an invasion from Asia.[81] The shock waves of a great change, wars and the fear of civil disturbances certainly hastened the development of an absolutist philosophy. Men were anxiously looking for one saving name, leader, sword or system. Machiavelli and Guicciardini had been appalled by the apparently hopeless condition of political and religious life in Italy. Machiavelli bitterly sought to unmask Christianity as a political ideology of the *Curia* and the clerical Church. Guicciardini wanted to see the world freed from the 'tyranny of rascally priests'.[82]

The newly awakened conscience of the layman and the anxious monastic awareness of the Spirituals were fused in both men and produced in them an alert tension. Machiavelli, who sought the true power of salvation, thought that he had found it in the ancient idea of salvation in the pure Roman Republic or of a Swiss democracy.[83] He contrasted the unholy figure of the tyrant, based on a man like Castruccio Castracane, with his prince, who was a holy version of the *uomo virtuoso*.[84] Neither Heaven nor earth would be able to resist his prince, who would be both fox and lion, and whose power would be fearful and yet fruitful. Burckhardt pointed out the doctrinaire and fantastic element in Machiavelli in his *Study of the Renaissance in Italy*. The fox and the lion were medieval symbols in popular political sermonizing. Machiavelli's use of them suggests how lonely and disillusioned he was, the solitary preacher who could see in the evil world no more than a brutal struggle for power between two malevolent great beasts. Like Joan of Arc, Machiavelli proclaimed that he loved his country more than his soul.[85] The religion of nationalism was beginning to grow out of the despairing loneliness of the individual.

Machiavelli also had wider allegiances. He wanted to free nations from world history in which everything turns into evil. Since world history could be predicted – (a view which he shared with the Spirituals), political science became the inheritor of the Joachamite historical prophecy. World history was a scientific testing ground for the validation of theories and doctrines. It could be mastered by the saving cleverness of the truly educated man. By means of religion, legislation and an army he would rescue men from chaos and lead them to the commonweal. Machiavelli and Guicciardini valued every religion (Christian as well as pagan) only as an ethical and political force. They saw them as powerful pillars of order, and as sources of good laws and morals. They did not believe in divine intervention in human affairs and considered true and false miracles as practically equivalent.[86] All this has perhaps been overemphasized. Enlightened Christian humanism of John of Salisbury, Ramon Lull, Cosimo and Lorenzo Medici, of Manetti, Ficino and Salutati, taught very much the same things. Machiavelli and Guicciardini were much more in harmony with their predecessors than is usually suggested.

Ragione di stato meant the salvation of society by the good sense of the laity. Machiavelli's position historically is about half-way between the utopians of the *Libro delle Figure* and Campanella. He also belonged to the host of renowned and anonymous political and moralist preachers. He remained without influence in Italy, where he was just one among many. In France and England, on the other hand, he became enormously influential because he transmitted the experience of the political humanism of fourteenth and fifteenth century Italy, its pessimism, its disappointments, and its hopes for the salvation of men in society. Machiavelli and Guicciardini wrote in the people's language because they wanted to influence laymen. Although they tried to work out the reality of the state, politics and history, they could not escape the ideology and the spiritual language of Latin, Roman and Christian humanism.

While Machiavelli and Guicciardini continued to look to traditional sources for the energy to reform society, new forces arose, which had very different aims. The humanists began to degenerate during the sixteenth century into rhetoricians, birthday orators, and phrase makers. Understanding of nature and man began among the opponents of this humanism: the physicians, the craftsmen (mathematicians, opticians, mechanics, gunsmiths, engineers) and artisans (the workshops of Brunelleschi, Luca della Robbia, Masaccio and

Donatello) and finally the impromptu poets, pamphleteers, comic writers and journalists of the people.

Paris of the thirteenth century and Oxford of the fourteenth had prepared the way for the union of Aristotelian natural science and medicine in fifteenth-century Padua. The economic and political independence of the northern Italian cities gave the development further impetus.[87] Under the protection of Venice, the leading anticlerical and anti-papal state in Italy, ideological thinking began to give way to the investigation of nature, causal proof to the experimental method. Latin humanism and the investigation of nature with its strong, popular bias were growing further apart, but there was one group uncommitted to either extreme, the men around Alberti, Luca Paccioli and Leonardo da Vinci. *Santa cosa la masserizia* – household goods are holy. The old simple utensils in the family (*della famiglia*) were also holy. The practical living man could only realize himself through these things.

Alberti recognized relatively early that Latin was not the vehicle to express such thoughts.[88] He was the son of a rich Florentine merchant family which had made a great deal of money in the French trade. The family may originally have come from Genoa. Alberti was a good Aristotelian when he emphasized man as a citizen of the community (*cittadino primario*) and not as a private person (*uomo privato*), but he broke new ground by suggesting that man can attain self-realization through manual labour. Mastery of nature was to expose the fictions of the politicians and theologians and lead to a true natural life. Man must teach himself through work how to achieve fulfilment. Suffering and the inevitable intractability of things taught objectively, and toughened man. This view of suffering was radically different from the suffering passion of the Christian ego immersed in the contemplation of its sins. Man became a worker.* The artist shaped the world with his hand and spirit, and in so doing presented the Platonism of old, patrician Europe with one last triumph: painting. In the crown of all arts, man became 'equal to God'.[89] Beauty was no longer identical with a passive, contemplative view of God, but with graciousness, *leggiadria*. Closely related to the wit of the enlightenment, and intimately linked with reason and spirit, *leggiadria* conceived and moulded things into the beautiful form of the work of art. Beauty was also work, sweat and spiritual experiment.

Leonardo da Vinci was the greatest representative of this movement. He was the illegitimate son of a notary and of a peasant girl. At the age of thirteen, he entered Verrocchio's workshop and became an artisan and fine mechanic. In these Florentine workshops, physicians and artisans would congregate and pursue their scientific experiments. Nearly two hundred years later in the Paris of Mersenne and Descartes, the artisan's workshop would play a similar role. Art and skilled craftsmanship had formed a political-social unity in Florence since 1293, when artists were granted the same constitutional rights as physicians, apothecaries and scholars. From the time of the popular vote on

*Sombart thought he saw in Alberti the founder of the bourgeois ideology of work.

the construction of the Cathedral in 1294, the people of Florence had taken an active interest in all the controversies about the design and decoration of the three great monuments of the city, the Cathedral, the Campanile and the Baptistry. It was a kind of broad, popular education in the arts. The popular awareness of the role of the arts was a crucial aspect of Leonardo's consciousness. When he tried to grasp things with his hands and mind, he was, to an extent, expressing the independent attitude of the people of Florence and its confident craftsmen.

Leonardo's teacher had been the greatest Italian mathematician in the fifteenth century, Luca Paccioli.[90] Paccioli was a Franciscan from a lower middle class family of Borgo San Sepolcro, the old Spiritualist centre. He had already been strongly interested in commercial mathematics as a private tutor in Venice where the only state professorial chair for commercial arithmetic was located. In a wandering life which took him to all the courts and universities of Italy, he had propagandized for his science through mathematical lectures. Paccioli regretted that only technicians and artists, not scholars (humanists and theologians) were concerned with mathematics. In his *Summa de Arithmetica Geometria, Proportioni et Proportionalità*, published in Venice, 1494, he treated every number according to natural history, cosmography, dogma and sacrament. This was the old Franciscan number mysticism with its combination of eschatology, apocalyptical and magical elements.[91] He inserted whole verses from Dante and Petrarch into his scientific prose, and developed his doctrine of mathematical proportions as a means of measuring the natural and supernatural world.[92] For Paccioli the pre-eminent organ of perception was the eye, the portal *per la quale lo intelletto intende e gusta*. The eye was nobler and more important for knowledge than the ear.* Leonardo's eye was neither the utopian-spiritualistic, Platonic-Augustinian eye of the old world, nor the new wholly scientific one. Like Paccioli, Leonardo thought of the eye as an organ of knowledge, a demiurge, a world-creator, world-thinker and a delicate instrument for grasping all things.

Leonardo was an intellectual who wanted to understand, grasp and create everything,[93] and any attempt to render his universal drive innocuous distorts the peculiar position of this many-sided genius in the history of the European spirit. The French intellectuals understood this aspect of Leonardo very well, and have written brilliant essays on him. Leonardo, the fatherless child, was deeply committed to the maternal world of magic and of the countryside. He was at home in archaic society with its promiscuities among man, beast and thing. Leonardo always saw man and beast (horse) as equals; for example, in *Leda and the Swan*.[94] He was a kind of bisexual and was twice accused of sodomy. Like Paracelsus, he compared the movement of the heart with that of

---

*Luther was to reverse Paccioli's conclusion and to reduce the eye and exalt the ear which hears the word of God, as the organ of salvation. The nonconformist, sectarian and Calvinist Dutch and Western Europeans were to equip the 'desanctified eye' with telescopes and microscopes for viewing the smallest and greatest secrets of nature.

the earth and the circulation of the blood in man with the circulation of the waters. He was always prepared to sell his sorcery to the *condottieri*, Sforza and Cesare Borgia, and once boasted *Io servo chi mi paga* ('I serve anyone who pays me'). Leonardo, a *condottiere* of art and the technical skills, was very much like the political *condottiere* in spirit and he knew it. His 'Titanism' ('I know' ... 'I can' ... 'I will' ...) was related to theirs, and ultimately he hoped to outwit them. Hence the obscene mystification which speaks from his pictures. His Mona Lisa, his Jerome and his John the Baptist, indeed all his pictures, disclose either 'an extremely profane, rebellious, perhaps blasphemous spirit',[95] or at least the magical-technical experiment of a coldly glowing, greedy mind. 'From the theory of shadows he derived the Virgin of the Rocks; from an analysis of light, the chiaroscuro of the Mona Lisa; from the treatise on movement, the frenzy of the cavalry battle of Anghiari; from the casuistry of the passions, the drama of the Last Supper.'[96]

Leonardo experimented with men, animals, fruit trees and clouds. He recognized no difference between animate and inanimate things. In his days as an apprentice in Verrocchio's workshop, he had once seen Pollaiuolo dissect a corpse just to be able to sketch the sinews, points and muscles, and it had impressed him. According to his own words, Leonardo filled 120 volumes with anatomical studies. He saw no difference between the eyesight needed to design a new cannon, paint the head of a Madonna, sketch an ink drawing, prepare the casting for a mould of a horse, construct a whirlpool of flowing water and lay out the city plan of Imola.[97] He sought to make the mechanics of man into a useful science.[98] From the very beginning, his painting was a 'machine to produce fear'.[99] All his pictures remained just that. His artistic techniques were based on shrewdly calculated methods of construction which would disappear or could be removed after the completion of the painting, like the mould of a cannon and the gigantic triumphal horse for Sforza. They were designed to produce shuddering astonishment and fascinated enjoyment. Leonardo practised painting and technique as magic. In the end, a deceived deceiver, he let himself be fascinated by his own works and thoughts, absorbed by his own objects to whose magic he himself succumbed. He became their prisoner and helplessly surrendered to every new image, sight and operation of power.

Leonardo was the first of a series of European intellectuals to contaminate himself by his own works and monomania. He was purely an artificer and instrument builder. In all his bulky notebooks he never once mentioned the political ruin of his country, which agitated Michelangelo day and night. After the defeat of his great patron, Ludovico Sforza, he immediately went over to the victor, Francis I. Although he heaped derision on *le bugiarde scienze mentali*, the Thomist and Platonic metaphysics, he was himself saturated in folk-cosmologies and myths, apocalyptic utopias, magical phantasies and dreams. The moon was suspended in its elements as an egg yolk in the white. The terrestrial body was 'of the fish species'. Like a shark or a whale, it breathes water instead of air; grass and trees, animals and men grow as hair and beard from its skin, the stones are its bones. Leonardo defined energy as 'a supra-sensuous capacity, an invisible force ... which is brought about through a random external power of motion and is poured into bodies which (then) are diverted and drawn away from their natural condition. Since it gives an energetic life of wondrous activity to them, it forces all created things towards changes of form and state.[100] Energy was an infused grace of nature. In an orgiastic, demonic way, he described how energy consumes itself and how it kills. Leonardo also knew anxiety and the occasionally apocalyptic tone of his prophecies is reminiscent of Bacon, the Franciscan Spirituals, Campanella, and Dürer's *Dream Vision*.[101] He sought to master anxiety by description or by miraculous, technical structures, utopian constructions, fantastic temples, city plans, fortresses, churches, mausoleums and again and again by machines.

To exorcise and appease death, primitive men had once built their first dwellings; the building and construction mania of tyrants, dictators, absolute rulers and thinkers of modern Europe, their Atlantic walls and world-systems, were prefigured in the restless activity of Leonardo. Exhausted, on his death-bed he confessed 'how he had sinned against God and man, because he had not properly cultivated art'. In the first edition of his *Lives* Vasari described Leonardo's death-bed conversion to Christianity and with utter fascination celebrated the 'wondrous and divine Leonardo', and 'his kingly and noble character'.[102] He depicted him as a wonder of the world, just as Frederick II had been in his day. In the second edition, Vasari had him die in the arms of the French King, Francis I. Leonardo, the man without a father or fatherland, the court painter, engineer and arranger of festivities, died on 2 May 1519, in the royal castle at Amboise. The conqueror of Italy, Charles VIII, had been born there and in the midst of the lascivious, dissolute and ostentatious Renaissance world of the French court, a young man, confused and deeply moved, broke away from this libidinous mingling of God and the world: John Calvin.

13

THE SECOND GERMAN MOVEMENT
BETWEEN EAST AND WEST

Luther and Maximos the Greek

(Sixteenth Century)

LUTHER'S relation to the German people was very similar to that between St Francis and his people or Joan of Arc and hers. He too drew salvation from the people and for them, but with one vital difference. Luther was a product of that peculiar German *Angst*, the hatred and suspicion of the official Western Carolingian Church. The Church had failed miserably in its attempt to transform the *Angst* into absolute trust and to gain the 'whole man's' devotion* to God, the Father, who had said, 'I am thy God.'[1] Faith for Luther meant 'throwing oneself and one's entire existence upon Jesus Christ'.[2] He exploded on his country like a 'theological atom bomb'.[3] He was well aware of his powers and their strong likeness to a cataclysm of nature. He once said that the grace of God is like a sudden shower: 'it falls on a piece of land and when the land has dried up it goes away again ...'[4]

This religious genius had submerged destructive forces within himself of which he was quite aware. He knew, for example, that he could have brought about a great and bloody revolution, one so great 'that the Emperor would not have felt secure on his throne'.[5] 'It gets harder and harder for us to grasp the real Luther ...'[6] His writings can easily be split up into a collection of contradictory aphorisms. Almost every word he wrote can be disproved by something else he wrote. The chaos which followed him, and indeed surrounded him while he lived, is not surprising. The Lutheran princes and universities and established churches with their scholasticism and discipline fought desperately to dam up a stream that threatened to burst through all its banks.[7]

In terror and anguish of conscience Luther was pursued by the alien figure of the Lord God, as the Slavs of the twelfth century had been pursued by the German God. This strange God threatened him, forcing his monkish vows from him and turning him into a bond slave.[8] In the end Luther could not bear to touch him at the celebration during Mass.† He finally broke down

*It is certainly significant that *totus homus* was a cardinal point of Luther's whole system.

†This fear of his went on quivering inside him for the rest of his life, until he 'unmasked' the Mass as the work of the Devil.

utterly in the face of that terrible figure of God the Father, as he had in front of his own father in the flesh.[9] This father crisis and the way he weathered it – the whole father experience, in fact – was of fundamental importance for Luther, as it had been for St Francis and Joan of Arc. Luther's flight from the Transformation, from the culmination of the sacramental act meant the end of the Church, of ontology and metaphysics and of all the old cosmic order.

Luther could not bring himself to look God in the face as a free man, nor to stretch out his hand.* Luther was unable to go hand in hand with him, as all the lordly, freely-born kings and emperors, bishops, priests and magnates before him had walked, ordering, building up, and organizing the world. The fearful figure of God the Father represented a law which it was utterly impossible to fulfil. His father in the flesh, Hans Luther, had furiously opposed the flight of young Master Luther to the monastery. He regarded the great storm of 1505 as the work of the Devil and did not hesitate to tell his son that his calling to be a priest was equally so. After young Luther had said his first Mass, his father repeated the charge, and in 1521 Luther was still confessing to Melanchthon that no other words had ever made such a deep impression upon him.[10] This irreconcilable spiritual and psychological situation was intensified by the insoluble intellectual and theological problems of his environment. To begin with, in the Erfurt arts faculty he had been brought up as an Ockhamist.[11] Later, he had entered the Augustinians, who were likewise Ockhamists. His 'despairing Pelagianism' was an attempt to bridge an unbridgeable gap.[12] God was the 'entirely Other', whose will and wish decided all things and forbade all things, while man had to fulfil his commands in a natural, immanent world-order. This grandiose Ockhamist emphasis on the idea of the 'entirely Other' drove Luther to despair.[13] Was he one of the damned? How could he face such a dreadful God? How could he wrest salvation from him?

Luther had a brilliant career at the university and in the monastery and was soon regarded by everybody there as a second Paul. He belonged to that generation of precocious, ambitious, angry young men who typified the age and the young University of Wittenberg. Melanchthon, for instance, left Heidelberg in a huff when he was fourteen because they had refused to make him a Master. At seventeen he was giving lectures in Tübingen, and at the age of twenty-one he was Luther's right-hand man in Wittenberg.[14] These young men had no time for spiritual discipline. In his struggles against the Flesh, Luther fled from reason, which his Ockhamist heritage had closed to him, and from spiritual training, which his lack of discipline made impossible.[15] He found his salvation in work. When he was in the monastery, as he wrote to Prior Lang of Erfurt in 1516, he needed two secretaries. He was so busy that he gave up the struggle against the flesh – explaining that sexual desire was irresistible – and surrendered himself to the stream of his native, inborn

*The hand of God for the middle ages was the symbol of the certainty of salvation: *got selve is das recht.*

religiosity. This was without any doubt an event of world-wide importance in the spiritual history of mankind. Luther, the religious genius, trusted only his own inner voice and secularized the discoveries and knowledge of the whole field of mysticism by using them for his own ends. The person called by God became an inspired individual.[16] The Holy Ghost became the voice of a genius, heard in the depths of the spirit and the heart. Instead of private revelations, there were the revelations of the private person; instead of the prophet speaking as the mouthpiece of the voice of God, often very much against his own will, we hear characteristic tones of the salvationist, who experiences his own demonic nature and all its emanations as the work and will of God.

The small 'I' of the mystic assumed the gigantic proportions of the ego of the man of genius, and before long the ego began to claim God's spiritual flights and the Gospel teaching as its own glad tidings. Luther secularized the whole concept of ecstasy and used the word *excessus* to denote a flood of passionate emotion. 'We are all saints.'[17] 'No one who refuses to accept my teaching can be saved.'[18] The ego took over the office, duties and responsi-bilities of the pope, the emperor and all the free-born Church lords. It provided certainty of salvation.

Luther's 'Pelagianism', was an expression of the self-confidence of the salvation-bearer and salvation-bringer of archaic society. He brought salva-tion for the 'beloved German people'. There were two essential constituents in his conception of salvation of the people. The first was a reflection of the fundamental attitudes, the view of God and the world, which had character-ized the first German movement,[19] and which Luther adopted. He owed an enormous debt to Meister Eckhart, Tauler and the *Theologia Germanica* which he brought out in 1516 and again in 1518.[20] The second was his im-mersion in the spiritual background of Manichaean and popular, radical beliefs. This is not a question of the observer's denominational position but of historical evidence. The pre-Christian deity, the outburst against the main forces in history, the world, Rome and reason, and its rejection of freedom of the will were certainly very much part of that Manichaean underground we have followed in this book. The elements of religious, theological and political nihilism and anarchism had been latent and partially hidden from the public eye in the first German movement. Under the social and historical pressure of the new conditions of the sixteenth century, the rise of the Princes to absolute power, the peasants' strikes, the early capitalism in the German towns, these elements were made far more intense and burst out in the frenzied longing for salvation felt by wide sections of the ordinary people among the Enthusiasts and by Luther.* Despite his desperate attempts to prevent it, Luther, the volcano, really came into his own as the salvation-bringer. No matter what

*The fateful relationship can be seen in the various connections which historians have found: Luther and the Schwärmer, Luther and the Anabaptists, Luther and Eastern Ger-many, Luther and German pietism of the sixteenth, seventeenth and eighteenth centuries.

it cost, even if he was forced to tell 'mighty lies', he was determined to be absolute master of his Gospel, his own glad tidings.[21]

After the Bible and Augustine, Luther learned more about God, man and all other things from the *Theologia Germanica* than he did from any other book.[22] In the preface to the second edition, he wrote: 'God grant that this little book may be more widely known, then we shall see that the German theologians are undoubtedly the best, Amen.' This little book, edited and thus highly commended by Luther, became a second New Testament for Karlstadt, the Anabaptists and the Spiritualists;[23] for Denk, Hatzer, Schwenckfeld, Franck and Valentin Weigel.* According to the *Theologia Germanica* nothing is real, except the will of God and the will of man. Nothing else. The new, liberated human being had no fear of Heaven or Hell, no interest in redemption or damnation. 'The new man' underwent a process of inner pulverization by which he atoned for his sins and entered the kingdom of Heaven here on earth. 'These people stay in such freedom, that they have quite forgotten the fear of punishment and Hell, as also the hope of reward or Heaven; but they live in utter subjection, obedient to the eternal Goodness in the freedom of their love ...' Profoundly conscious of his sinfulness, the sinner gave up all idea of redemption and was quite satisfied if he were 'called upon to be a miserable footstool to all the devils in hell knowing himself to be unworthy even of this. He cannot desire any other man's comfort or redemption, either from God or from creatures, but will glady remain uncomforted and unredeemed, neither damnation nor suffering disturbing him.'[24]

Luther began, where the *Theologia Germanica* left off, at the 'comfort of despair'. He debased the mystical experience to a much more primitive level and then turned it into a new doctrine of salvation for all men. 'Sin cannot separate us from God, even if we commit murder and fornication a thousand times a day,' he wrote to Melanchthon in 1521.[25] Christianity meant the continuous ability to feel free from sin though sinning, all sins being thrown upon Christ.[26] It was both awful and consoling at the same time.† Sin was not annulled; on the contrary, it never stopped growing. Man would sin for ever and ever, and Luther himself, who died physically swollen by gluttony, testified eloquently to the truth of this proposition.[27] Even though the 'wages of sin are death' man can, in the very depths of this sinful life, experience an unending joy: the 'joy', the *joie* of the people, of the heretics and martyrs of the eleventh to the fifteenth centuries. It was the joy of St Francis and the joy which Joan of Arc found in her experience of redemption. This joy enabled the Enthusiasts and the Anabaptists to face death on the gallows.

*Orthodox Lutheran theology was cautious about the *Theologia Germanica*, and Calvin completely rejected it for very much the same reasons which prompted the Catholics of the Counter-Reformation to put it on the Index in 1621. The dilemma both for Luther and the authors of the *Theologia Germanica* lay in the fact that although they opposed the free spirits and the Schwärmer, they were intimately tied to them. As a result their formulation of doctrine helped to foster tendencies which they wished to repress.

†This attitude to existence made Luther the spiritual father of Romanticism.

Such joy comes when Christ wraps our sin in the mantle of his grace. The man who is blessed by God, who has tasted God, can do what he likes. 'Sin bravely and believe more strongly.' (*Pecca fortiter, et crede firmius.*) Luther's ego discovered and experienced salvation. In the depths of his conscience he judged the world. The judgments passed by the *homo spiritualis* by Münzer, Karlstadt, Schwenckfeld, Denk and Franck, against the pope and the emperor, Rome and Wittenberg, against any and every political party and Christian denomination, grew out of this ecstatic knowledge; they were eschatological in temper. Luther sang his hymn to joy despite his increasing involvement in family and university life, in relationships with friends and princes. In the midst of the world, he retreated from the world. A year before his death, he looked back over his life of struggle: 'hard have I fought', he wrote, 'as one fearing terribly the Judgment Day and yet at the same time longing in my bones to be saved and redeemed'.[28] (*Ego serio rem agebam, ut qui diem extremum horribiliter timui, et tamen salvus fieri ex intimis medullis cupiebam.*)[29]

Luther and the Enthusiasts were 'latter day saints' who, despite persecution, watched over 'God's poor little lantern', the pure doctrine of the invisible Church, which was a lost remnant under the banner of the Word.[30] 'A sweet thing is the Church, and the saints are hidden away.' (*Abscondita est Ecclesia, latent sancti.*)[31] This was the spirit of the arresting sermon on the world by Sebastian Franck, who saw history as an unending spiritual Golgotha.[32] The Enthusiasts and the evangelical revolutionaries, the Anabaptists and Spiritualists were equally certain that the true Church is at all times composed of tiny groups of solitary individuals, the 'Saints, persecuted by the devil and the representatives of earthly power.'[33] Their conception was absolutely in line with Luther's innermost spirit. In the *Grosser Katechismus* he gave his own idea of the Church: 'I believe that there is a holy host and company of pure saints on earth, under one head, Christ, all called together by the Holy Ghost, of one faith and mind and understanding ...'[34] Who are these saints? All Christian people who have renounced outward works and trust in God alone. Luther's famous scolding, which with his growing anguish of mind increased during the latter years of his life, was a kind of sacred grumbling. He raged against the unholy saints of the old world, who had depended on the Roman whore, on the sacramental techniques of the Universal Church. 'But look, is it not accursedly brazen of the saints of perdition* to imagine that they can invent a better life and a higher state than is taught by the Ten Commandments ...'[35] Nobody can keep even one of the Commandments unless he gets help from the Father, and yet these unholy people rest their faith on religious services, sacraments and secular organization. A fundamental inner distrust of the Church, the state and the worldly regiment mark Luther, together with the Anabaptists, pietists and Spiritualists, as children of the first German movement.

*i.e. the saints of the Roman Church.

Obedient suffering is commonly cited in an attempt to conceal the spiritual anarchism and nihilism latent in Luther's vulgarization and secularization of a sublime mystical experience. In reality, Luther degraded sublime moments on the summit of human experience and cheapened them into small change for everyday use. The true mystical moment is exceedingly rare. At the pinnacle of rapture, the spiritual marriage, all earthly things and ordinances melt away to nothing, burn to ashes, in the fire of God's burning love. Luther tried to devalue this rare and dearly purchased oneness with God to the level of a daily event. He dismissed reason and worldly ordinances, which ought to be surrendered very seldom even at the summit of the spiritual marriage and cast them aside as paltry godless things, below the truly religious person's dignity. The mystic's most precious and costly experience, attained with the greatest difficulty, suffering and self-discipline, was reduced to the level of any ordinary Christian. Anyone who claimed to be full of the spirit could thus imagine himself to be superior to the laws of this world and human society. The real object of all this lay in Luther's attack on human reason. His incredible, indeed monstrous mistrust of the mind reflected a profound antipathy to reason and demonstrated his own total lack of spiritual discipline. He had never experienced the redeeming, liberating power of the spirit that stands above matter and above the flesh.[36]

Luther suspected reason as a tool of the ideology of Rome and the West. His invective against Aristotle and Thomas was incessant. He even charged Thomas with never having understood a single chapter of Aristotle or the New Testament.[37] Reason was only good for the practical things of life, in all other respects it was a devil's whore,[38] a bitter enemy to God,[39] 'the source of the sources of all evils'.[40] In his very last sermon in Wittenberg he thundered against reason as a whore who deserves to be banished to the toilet.[41] There was dread behind this condemnation. Luther was afraid that the poor ordinary human being would miss salvation by believing in reason and not in God. Devilish reason must not be allowed to dominate men.* By his attitude Luther became the spokesman of the German-Slav East. Originally a religious but later a social and political absolutism of princes and new church lords began to arise on these foundations. These men knew nothing about political and religious humanism or about sacramental and rational co-operation between God and man. The poor sinner had by nature no right in God's eyes to any voice in the state or the world. He had no free will but was entirely at the mercy of his Lord and his terrible grace.[42]

Luther's battle with the West began with *De Servo Arbitrio*,[43] in which he attacked Erasmus of Rotterdam's *De Libero Arbitrio, Diatribe sive Collatio*. Erasmus's great reply was western Europe's manifesto against Luther, the Enthusiasts and the spiritual nihilism of the East.[44] The German humanists Mutian, Zasius Pirkheimer, were strongly influenced by this defence of the

---

*Luther could only conceive of a tyranny of one sort or another. Men would be tyrannized by God or by reason, and of the two the tyranny of God was preferable.

West and began to turn away from Luther. 'Even in Melanchthon, sentiment was on the side of Erasmus.'[45] Only psychotic prejudice could deny that this work by the chief spokesman of Western Christian humanism was not a fitting close to Erasmus's life. His last words as he lay on his deathbed had been *Lieve God*.[46] His very last piece of writing, *Von der Reinheit der Kirche*, fittingly rounded off a life that was utterly dedicated to the renaissance of classical studies and Christianity. He died serenely certain that the Church would find shelter in the religious ethos and the thousand year old tradition of western Europe.

Erasmus was a product of the *devotio moderna*'s humanistic wing whereas Luther belonged to its left, fanatical wing.[47] Like Nicholas of Cusa, Erasmus took *renascentia* to mean a rebirth of all branches of learning, morals, the world and the Church.[48] This renaissance would be initiated by Christ himself.[49] Erasmus's biblical scholarship was shared by Colet, Faber, Morus, Budé, Calvin, Zwingli, Cisneros, Reuchlin and Melanchthon.[50] It was part of the radiant unity of Christian reforming humanism during the years 1500–20, before it broke up into the opposing camps of Reformation and Counter Reformation. From 1515 to 1519 Erasmus expected the dawn of a golden age.[51] The world was on the threshold of everlasting peace. There would be a blossoming of Christian living, together with a resuscitation of scholarship and science (*bonae litterae*). It seemed to him as if by a miracle all the best minds had pledged themselves to restore the highest state of culture possible. There had to be a true golden age.[52] This was no visionary dream but an expression of the brilliant flowering of humanist thought which had begun at the turn of the sixteenth century.

In the year 1506 the French humanist Bovillus Lull introduced Nicholas of Cusa to Spain. In 1512 Faber d'Etaples wrote his commentary on the Epistles of St Paul. In 1516 Erasmus's New Testament in Greek appeared, and in 1517 the Alcala polyglot Bible by Lebrixa and Erasmus's Spanish followers was published. Zwingli in Zurich, Melanchthon in Wittenberg and even Calvin had been saturated by this Christian humanism. Hopes of genuine reform were focused upon Charles v. For decades the imperial Chancellery nominated Erasmians as a third force, in an attempt to reconcile the increasingly hostile opponents of the Reformation and its protagonists. Charles was to continue to try until the end.

Erasmus had begun to develop his own programme under the influence of the Franciscan Jean Vitrier, who was always Erasmus's ideal of a monk.[53] The *Enchiridion Militis Christiani* argued that the way was 'back to Holy Scripture'. 'The restoration of theology must be preceded by a study of the good virtuous pagans of ancient times and the Church Fathers.' Erasmus was never to give up this central preoccupation with a reconciliation of the conflicting parties and with peace. Purification of morals would lead to a new order for state and society and the Church would be cleansed by the conscience and wisdom of Christian humanism.[54] Since 1519 he had been watching with deep dismay the rise of a different world, the world of salvation from below. Enthusiasts, freethinkers, religious anarchists, showed how differently the same Gospel could be read. In the hands of a narrow group of cultured people, the humanists, the Gospel had one significance, but quite another among radically-minded ordinary people. There were the anguished, embittered lower clergy, the lay priests, itinerant priests and miserably-paid Mass readers, the rural and feudal proletariat and the lower classes of the rich cities.[55] How different the non-Carolingian East was from the West became increasingly clear to Erasmus from the course of events. In 1524, the year he published *De Libero Arbitrio* the Peasants' War broke out and with it the explosion of the underground.

Luther had, Erasmus argued, rejected the whole spiritual and intellectual heritage of Greek experience from Origen onwards, and of Latin religiosity from Tertullian to the present day. In this long tradition the only people who in any sense agreed with Luther were one Manichee and Wyclif. Erasmus could claim all the martyrs, scholars, saints, all the universities, councils, popes and bishops of the past. How could the supporters of the new Gospel be compared with these? Who had granted them the right to behave as though there had been no Gospel in the world for the past 1,300 years? Was Christ supposed to have neglected his Church during all that time?[56] Was the spirit to be found in a thousand years of Christianity, or in the new, self-glorified ego of Luther and Karlstadt? In his defence of man and his freedom and dignity, Erasmus drew on the Christian humanism of England and in particular of John Fisher. He even dared to call Pelagius and the Stoics in to his side which provoked Luther's gibe that he almost seemed to regard Pelagius as one of the Evangelists.[57] Luther held free will to be nothing more than an empty phrase, fit only for sinners, but Erasmus, basing his argument on the Old and New Testaments, the Psalms and St Paul,[58] defended his basic thesis that free will may be wounded but not destroyed by sin. ... *Quamquam enim arbitrii libertas per peccatum vulnus accepit, non tamen exstincta est* ...[59] What of the whole vast company of the saints, all the good and righteous men of history? Is all that they have done supposed to be vain delusion, mere sinfulness?[60] Why does God let us strive and struggle, if all our work and activity is meaningless? Only a cruel God could determine in advance the unspeakable sufferings of those who have shed their blood for him.

Erasmus attacked the very heart of Luther's thought revealing the underlying social idea rooted in Luther's peasant cosmos. Luther's God was a king who rewards his warriors unjustly. Erasmus began to unmask this God as a demon, a devil, as Luther's own father had done before him. Luther's God was a cruel and perverse lord, who treats his serfs carelessly and flays the skin off them.[61] The innovators and the supporters of Luther had monstrously exaggerated the concept of original sin. They had been led astray by St Augustine, who in the heat of his battle with Pelagius had allowed himself to be drawn into untenable assertions.[62] They had made God out to be even crueller than Dionysius, the tyrant of Syracuse, for this God of theirs only made laws to trap men into sin. They had become utterly entangled by their assertions about God's absolute power and sovereignty, and man's absolute lack of power and grace. This ghastly game had disgraced God and man! The renaissance (*renascentia*) of the world through Christ would come about only if human beings co-operate in it and are free to make their own decisions. Free will is necessary so that the wicked man can be punished, and God can be freed from the slander of cruelty and injustice. We humans can be free from despair only if we lose all our false certainties but continue to dare to do our best.[63]

Luther's tract *De Servo Arbitrio* which ran through ten editions in a single year was the answer to Erasmus. It was his masterpiece, and he took it more seriously than the whole of his external struggle against Rome. It was the first work he wrote after his marriage and was dedicated to his father. The fearful self-destructive dialogue with the terrible, incomprehensible figure of God the Father thickened into a demonic fury. God was *Sturm und Drang*, creative tempest, absolute, inscrutable, incomprehensible Will (*voluntas inperscrutabilis et incognoscibilis*).* There was no sense or reason in this Will, which was itself the law of all things. Right is whatever it wills because it wills it. This sovereign and almighty God alone does everything that is done. (*Omnipotentiam Dei voco non illam potentiam, qua multa non facit quae potest, sed actualem illam, qua potenter omnia facit in omnibus*.) In the *De Servo Arbitrio* Luther provided a self-portrait of unique explosive power and significance. It was a portrait of the man of genius possessed by a demon, the man made in the image of his own God.[64] Only the ecstatic who lets himself be utterly taken by the divine spirit can face such a God. Again and again Luther insisted that no one can see a jot of meaning in Scriptures unless he has the Spirit of God within him.

Erasmus attacked this divine rage and its ecstatic excesses in the two volumes of his *Hyperaspistes* (1526). This anti-Lutheran tract was the foundation both of Catholic apologetics and of orthodox Lutheran dogmatism. Melanchthon, already profoundly shaken by Luther's spiritual violence, received from it the decisive impulse that finally set the tone of his own scholastic-humanistic dogmatism! Erasmus began by referring to Melanchthon's friendly reception of his tract *De Libero Arbitrio* and then went on to answer Luther directly: 'All the Church's teachers, all her authorities and Popes, are immediately dismissed as fools if you do not like what they say. Karlstadt, whom only a short while ago you regarded as a man inspired by the Holy Ghost, is now suddenly damned by you as one of the organs of Satan. First you worked up the peasants into a fury, then you betrayed them. And you call me a sceptic? Well, it is true, and I am glad to be described as such in all

*The same fundamental creative power, restrained by a latin sense of proportion, can be seen in Michelangelo's *The Last Judgment*, in his *Christ as Judge of the World*, his *Sybil* and his *Prophets*.

earthly concerns, that is to say as a man who does not easily make final pronouncements' (*qui non facile definit*). 'The Church herself,' Erasmus went on, 'has often been sceptical, has often put off giving her opinion on a matter for centuries, but you are carried away by an absolute lust for condemning people.' For the first time Erasmus contrasted the Catholic Church with Luther's own Church (*tua ecclesia* – an allusion to Luther's emphasis on his own God, *Deus tuus*): 'I and other Catholics like me cannot grant you any more authority than your own comrades-in-arms do – Zwingli, Ökolampad and so on – who differ from you over so many high and holy things.'

Erasmus pointed out the great dangers arising from Luther's teaching the people that there is no such thing as freedom of will and that everything happens by necessity (*mera necessitate*). Erasmus was a man of 'the grand form' and he realized what the destruction of such a doctrine would mean. Like Descartes after him and, later still, Voltaire, Erasmus was horrified to see how the people were seizing greedily upon Luther's teaching and setting about the work of destruction. Luther was turning ordinary people into atheists because he left them without any sort of knowledge of God, nor hope of approaching him. (*Ignorato deo deum colere et gratias agere, servire deo non possum, dum nescio quantum mihi tribuere, quantum deo debeo.*) Again and again Erasmus made the same charge against Luther, that he discussed the most difficult and involved problems of theology with and in front of the uneducated, inquisitive, irreligious masses. The questions themselves were profaned, distorted and perverted. 'I treat the Word of God humbly and respectfully, whereas you, Luther, act as though you were the lord of Holy Scriptures, not one of its preachers.' (Here Erasmus gives a brilliant description of Luther's 'wayward genius' and his habit of bending the Gospel to his own purposes.) 'You are continually forcing your own interpretation of Scripture on us as the Word of God. You exaggerate in the wildest way the desperateness of the human condition and human nonentity (*reductionem in nihilum*).

Erasmus saw clearly Luther's deep folk Manichaeism and its origins which were to be found in Augustine and Orosius. He accused Luther of making two gods fight in and around man. The first was a terrible God of the Old Covenant, the God of the Law, who spoke a different language from the other God, the crucified God, who brought kindness and glad tidings.* Erasmus also bitterly accused Luther of lacking the humanistic outlook (*civilitas*): 'I converse with you in Latin, you utter what you have to say against me in the German of peasants, mariners, artisans and blacksmiths.' Luther's allegiance was to the tradition of the mendicant orders, while Erasmus, as a humanist, was intellectually and socially against them. 'You call for revolt, and can see revolt arising everywhere because your books are written in German.'

The first volume of the *Hyperaspistes* ended with a grave and moving description of the way Luther's revolution had thrown all the previous social,

*It is interesting to recall, in this connection, that Lutherian theologians, including Harnack, have ever since the sixteenth century been particularly kind to Marcion.

political and intellectual conditions into confusion. The second volume contained Erasmus's defence of mankind and humanity. The world, history and nature together made up a divinely created cosmos, not a chaos ripped asunder by frightful tempests caused by God raging at human rebelliousness. Again Erasmus started with Luther's *hubris*.* Erasmus pointed out that Luther had dismissed everything which had been handed down from father to son for over a thousand years and all the valuable testimony of Christian thinkers and pagan sages. Luther was a terrible simplifier, determined to catch Christians on the horns of a false dilemma and the over-sharpened points of his doctrine. His thesis, 'If the will is free there can be no grace', was nonsense. Grace assists and supports the free will. Once again Erasmus presented Luther's God as a perverse and cruel tyrant who kept friend and foe alike in an unbearable grip and drove both to despair. He laid down impossible laws and demanded impossible tributes. He is a father who toys cruelly with his children.†

Against the barbarous simplifications of Luther, the mendicant monk, with his teaching about the damnation of all earthly goods and values, Erasmus appealed to the tradition of both ancient classical and Christian worlds of culture. He called to men's commonsense. Human individuals and mankind as a whole are not absolutely godless and wicked. Erasmus's splendid defence of man against Luther was based on a fundamental proposition of Christian enlightenment: 'There have been left in man signs of all that is noble and worthy; he has an inclination towards all that is right and proper, despite the fact that in most people there is a greater tendency towards the opposite.' 'Nor is there in man any evil rejection of God, as there is in the devil; there is more weakness than malice in him.'[65] Erasmus asserted that Luther ignored the differences in temperament, habits, environment, experience and temptation in his damnation of all mankind. For Luther, the whole man (*totus homo*) was simply evil, and this evil had been created by God. Erasmus showed convincingly how Luther necessarily believed in God as the source and origin of all evil.‡ Erasmus denied this flatly: God is a good artist, a good God (*bonus artifex, bonus deus*), an enlightened monarch who never forces anyone to do anything, but invites them to do it, allowing them the utmost freedom.[66] Erasmus violently rejected the Lutheran dogma that man can no more do good of his own accord than an axe can do anything without a carpenter, or clay without a potter.[67]

Erasmus's defence of man came to a climax in a defence of world history.[68] Luther had refused to acknowledge any virtue in individuals and nations of pre-Christian times and had called Erasmus an atheist because he thought

---

*Erasmus calls it *Trotz*, significantly, the only German word to be found in the entire tract.

†How deeply this passage grasped the significance of Luther's resentment against his father in the flesh – in *Eisleben* – and his spiritual father – in Rome – and the authoritarian systems of Aristotle and St Thomas!

‡This is also true of Eckhart, Nicholas of Cusa, Scotus, Ockham, Boehme and the German idealists.

that many pagans had done admirable things.[69] Had any pagan ever been so criminal as to attribute to mankind the things that Luther charged it with? Erasmus went on to show emphatically that even unregenerated human beings are good, even if only to a limited extent. They are by no means the utterly evil creatures portrayed by the Manichee Luther.[70] 'A thing is not godless simply because it is imperfect.' (*Nec statim impium est, quod est imperfectum*).[71] The Jews had had the Law, which was a good thing; the Greeks, men of genius, had had great natural gifts; even Pilate had not been evil, only weak, and Judas himself could have changed his will and acted well if he wanted to.[72] Citing many examples from ancient history, the Bible and his own day, Erasmus showed how free decisions are possible in human history and denied that history is the work of the devil, or that man, as the devil's hireling, can only play an evil role.[73]

Erasmus had been very well disposed towards the young Luther but there was an unbridgeable gap that separated Luther, the Enthusiasts, Eastern Germany and the people's yearning for salvation from the humanist world of the West.[74] Luther's grace had burst all banks and overrun the dikes like a raging torrent. The individual was alone with his God, with the spirit of God overshadowing him, summoning him to renew the face of the earth. Luther had sown his seed and reaped the whirlwind. In his ecstatic experience of God, there was no theology, no metaphysics, no ethics, no culture, no state nor church, no history, no mankind seeking salvation and meaning.

As early as 1525, Erasmus saw the essential nihilism of Luther, and Melanchthon, Zwingli, Calvin and the first Visitors of the Lutheran communities began to realize it as well. An anxious soul like Urbanus Rhegius saw it and his highly popular instructions to Lutheran preachers, 'How to Speak on the Most Eminent Articles of Christian Doctrine with Prudence and without giving Offence', reads like a dossier of evidence especially collected for Erasmus's benefit.[75] 'There are many who hardly mention penance when they are discussing Faith and the forgiveness of sins, holding that those who do not do penance can still believe in the Gospels and receive forgiveness of their sins.'* He went on to deplore the fact that certain preachers abused the Mass in the most dreadful terms, and declared that it was an abomination, which had to be avoided lest salvation be lost. Some even said that the priests crucify Christ all over again in the Mass...† Many preachers, Rhegius continued, were satisfied with destruction, instead of trying to be constructive ('do only break and not build') pouring contempt on Holy Communion 'as a thing unnecessary'.[76] Others told the lower orders (the *pöbel*) 'We have no free will at all. Whatever we do we have to do.' (In other words, the simple people think that God is the author of sin.) Many have misunderstood 'the article

---

*One can see the rapid process of secularization already at work, which led eventually to German idealism.

†This was precisely what Luther had done. In 1525, the year of *De Servo Arbitrio*, he had demanded that the Mass, like any other blasphemy, should be punished and suppressed.

about Christian freedom', with the result that a hundred thousand people were killed in Swabia, Franconia and Alsace in 1525. Peasants, artisans and the lower classes generally were turning on theologians and other educated people, saying that they had been directly enlightened by the Holy Spirit. Rhegius was afraid that these enemies of culture would win the day. If so, 'Germany will become absolutely barbarian again.' How many preachers there were who derided virginity and fasting! Some even denounced prayer, saying that 'all this praying and blabbing is a heathenish error and hypocrisy – God takes no pleasure in it'. After his comprehensive picture of this outbreak of religious nihilism Rhegius gave some very sensible instructions about the way to teach the Christian religion, instructions that are often very close to the Catholic point of view.*

People are often surprised that Luther's attacks on his enemies increased in violence as he got older. Was it not an open secret that he was the uncrowned pope and emperor of a much strengthened Germany? (Exactly what Dante and Rienzo had longed to see in their own country.) Had he not won the greatest victory ever achieved by a single human being in the internal history of Europe? Why then, on the eve of death, was he still cursing the whore 'reason' and that 'pig of a Pope'? In *Against the Papacy founded in Rome by the Devil* (1545), Luther revived the medieval horrors and bloodthirsty popular insurrections against the priesthood, as in the twelfth century murders of Arnold von Selenhofen and Thomas Becket. With ghoulish thoroughness, he demanded that the tongues of the Pope and his *Curia* be ripped out by the roots and nailed up on a gallows in order of precedence, like the seals on their bulls. They could then hold their councils either on the gallows or in Hell with all the devils. These words ought not to be dismissed as mere vulgarity. They reveal Luther's deep-seated despair at the collapse of his innermost desires. The purification of heart and mind and the direct contact with God that he had hoped for had become a reality in only a few isolated cases. Were there any more pious men than there had been before the revolution? Probably fewer. Lutheranism itself was being driven out of the Carolingian West into eastern Europe. It had been made over to the princes and infiltrated by modernizers with an alien outlook. He had watched the annihilation of his most active disciples, the Enthusiasts and Anabaptists.[77] These swarming nonconformist hordes had often been the first to seize upon the Lutheran explosive power and had taken it out into the wicked world in the hope of blasting that world out of existence. Within Luther's lifetime they had ended up at the stake and in the prisons created by Lutheranism itself.

The subjugation of this Lutheran left (particularly in the years 1522 to 1526) meant that its spirituality was pushed into the underground, where it was to nourish and distort all subsequent German intellectual movements up to the time of the Romantics. It left them with the stigma of the shifty look,

*The longest chapter, on the honour due to the saints, was omitted in the subsequent edition as being too Catholic.

bad nerves and spiritual tensions. The seal was set on this once and for all by the pact that Luther and Melanchthon made with the princes, the civic rulers and the university authorities. Orthodox scholastic theologians waged a desperate battle against ideas and personalities emerging from the underground, until the middle of the eighteenth century, when they themselves began to succumb in their turn and were mocked at and derided as godless and soulless. The tragedy of orthodox Lutheranism had begun. Spirit and spirituality, conscience and inwardness were never to attain legitimacy and authority. Yet without such authority, there can never be any genuine open rationalism. The forces of the spirit must be able to gain official sanction from the legitimate bearers of religious authority, and this was no longer possible in Germany.[78] The Lutheran state church not only had to fight off the Reformers, Zwinglians and Papists, but also the young rebellious impulses arising in its own bosom, which were often its best forces.

At Christmas 1521, the preachers Storch, Stübner and Drechsel arrived in Wittenberg from Zwickau and with them Enthusiasm took up residence in Luther's capital. His friend from his university and Reformation days, Karlstadt, at once joined the movement. Zwickau was a mainly Slavic town and after 1450 it had been filled with the Hussite tradition in its fundamental, social-revolutionary form. From nearby Bohemia, it had been infiltrated by members of the Bohemian and Moravian Brethren. The people were trying to work out their own salvation – out of the Bible, out of the 'pure Gospel', out of the spirit (of God). Sometimes an individual or a whole community would be seized by the movement, sometimes it would stir only the poor in a manner reminiscent of the enthusiastic sects in Italy during the eleventh, twelfth and thirteenth centuries.[79] Occasionally the popular search for salvation became a military uprising determined to achieve the Kingdom of God through a crusade, not unlike the army of Joan of Arc. 'Let the minds burst out against each other', Luther had declared at the beginning, when he had still been willing to engage such men in open discussion. These men had taken his appeal seriously. His clarion call against Rome and Romish statutes, against the wild and foolish powers of the world, and against the German princes had aroused them.[80]

The spiritual individualism of the Enthusiasts and the Anabaptists was a joint creation of the young Luther, the German mystics (Eckhart and Tauler) and the *devotio moderna*. Frequently, especially in the case of the 'silent in the land', they were sympathetic to humanism as taught by Nicholas of Cusa and Erasmus – i.e., an enlightened form of Christianity, which could perceive the voice of God in Turks and pagans and every kind of Christian denomination. This faith, in a region beyond all denominations and religious groupings, was combined with Luther's fundamental concern for the 'freedom of the Christian individual'. Such a man had no need of any mediator – pope, priest, prince or professor – to help him to understand the word of God as manifested in Holy Scripture. Luther, of course, hated these people for having carried out his ideas with logical consistency. They tried to live what he had taught and it enraged him. To the very end, Luther remained an other-worldly, monkish person, who never accepted the consequences of his own ideas. He was an example of an identifiable type: the man of genius without responsibility. The Enthusiasts and the Anabaptists actually achieved Luther's new kind of Christianity – no theology, no intellectual culture, no connection with any state idols or any world rulers. Each separate human individual was to listen for the Word of God by himself, to pass it on, and to live it out with the help of the Bible.

Their attempts to realize the Lutheran ideal took two distinct forms: that of the revolutionary political wing, and that of the pietist wing. Perhaps the most famous of the revolutionary politicians was the Zwickau preacher, Thomas Münzer (d. 1525) who led a band of peasants quite certain that they had been called by Luther.[81] But there were others. A group of Low Country preachers seized power in Münster in 1530, as did Jürgen Wullenweber in Lübeck. These men were determined to establish the Kingdom of God upon earth. They were going to erect 'God's most Christian city', 'the United Community and Brotherhood of Christ'. The similarity in tone between these slogans of Anabaptist Münster and the revolutionary Florence of Savonarola is striking. As in Florence, a new city of God was to be created by force. A new 'sacred' terror was to punish as sin any deviations, and opposition would be ruthlessly crushed. Once the city had been purified, it would launch propaganda campaigns on a broad scale to be followed by military undertakings worthy of Joan of Arc or Hitler. It was not a coincidence that Robert Hamerling, the Lower Austrian poet, was a man of the same stock as Hitler, someone who like Hitler came up from the peasant underground. These Lower Austrians who had been tucked away in isolated villages in the narrow stretch of woodland between Bohemia, Moravia and Inner Austria, were very much the same in 1900 as they were when Hamerling produced his epic called *Jan von Leyden*, about the Anabaptist Kingdom of Heaven in Münster. This kingdom was mobilized not only in the military sense but also in its economics and propaganda. Its religious and political fanaticism, its solidity, its conduct of war and its desperate resistance to a coalition including almost all of Europe, demonstrated what powerful forces could be released and harnessed by the lower classes. The new apostles of salvation roused these submerged groups to action.

The peasant wars, which went on in a desultory fashion in southern Germany and Austria from 1525 to 1625, are sometimes described as episodes. In fact, this entire colossal phenomenon of revolt from below is usually dismissed as unimportant. The execution, banishment, expulsion and persecution of Anabaptists and Enthusiasts in Germany and the central European countries is for a good many historians a mere interlude. It was nothing of the sort. Despite the defeat of Austrian Anabaptism in the late 1520's it continued to live on in the underground of the people, and those who dismiss it would do well to study the events of 1933 in detail.[82] The Lutheran theologian Chyträus, observed after a tour of the area: 'In Austria there is almost too much religious freedom. Everyone who is driven out of any part of Germany for any reason whatsoever seems to find his way here.'[83] Between 1529 and 1530 the imperial Diet decided that Austria should be brutally subjugated, but the Anabaptists were not wiped out. They were still strong enough in 1550 to hold an international council in Venice.[84] In the meantime, Lutheranism had decided against freedom of conscience, and had become a state church under the domination of the princes. The German princes and their Church undertook to root out those things which had initially been the innermost concerns of the Lutheran reformers. The prince was ready to defend the Reformation against its radical offspring.[85] Melanchthon, deeply disturbed, confused and apprehensive about this, looked at the Zwickau prophets and asked himself again and again whether they came from God or the devil. Luther stifled this question by the simple method of condemning the movement and calling upon the princes to deal with the hordes of Enthusiasts. They had dealt with the peasants and would now drown the Enthusiasts in their own blood. 'The peasants,' he said, 'no matter how many thousands of them there are, are all thieves and murderers.' As Lortz points out, 'his attack on the peasants was so savage because it was really directed at the Enthusiasts'.[86] Five years after the execution of Thomas Münzer Luther was still afraid that another scourge might arise like Münzer, whose spirit is still alive.

The 'silent in the land' were ultimately ineradicable – like everything that disappears into the silence and secrecy of the underground. Their leaders, men like Denck, Caspar von Schwenkfeld (d. 1561) and Sebastian Franck (d. 1542–3) were persecuted, driven from one place to another, and forced to adopt the poverty-striken, unsettled, wandering life of the German nonconformists.[87] They joined the German proletariat of preachers, scholars and poets that was to ferment in society and intellectual life from the sixteenth to the nineteenth century.

The most celebrated figure among these men who carried on the heritage of the early Luther, and of the first and second German movements, was Sebastian Franck. 'Franck's ideas flow down into the modern world by a hundred channels.'[88] 'To Luther and the Lutherans Sebastian Franck was like a red rag to a bull.'[89] Franck was born in Donauworth in 1499, the last year of the century and of a dying world order. In 1515, he was a poor student of the liberal arts in Ingolstadt, where Luther's opponent Eck and the subsequent Anabaptist leader Hubmaier were later to teach. His enthusiasm for Erasmus dated perhaps from these early days. Later, as a poor Catholic secular priest, he was profoundly shaken by eschatological anxieties. 'He was appalled more than anything else by the ordinary man's dreadful alienation from God.'[90] Where were the bearers of salvation? Where was anyone really preaching the Gospel and giving an example of real Christian living to the wretched, downtrodden ordinary people? Franck went through all the various denominations.

For a while he was attracted to the Anabaptists to whom he had much to be grateful for, but nowhere could he find the answer he was seeking. He pursued his solitary way through the age, joining and forsaking one group after another. His mind had been stamped by the religiosity of the early Luther, by Tauler and by the *Theologia Germanica* which he was later to paraphrase.[91] He was also strongly influenced by the humanist spirituality of Erasmus.[92] Despite this, 'there is no gainsaying that his later heresies which made him such a hated figure came from Luther'.[93]

Franck met Paracelsus for the first time in 1529 in the thick of the Anabaptist world of Nuremberg, and was deeply drawn to him, especially to his conviction that God was pure Spirit and the various churches mere church walls and masonry.[94] The two men were also alike in longing for peace and an end of the murderous religious divisions. While Paracelsus, like Albert the Great before him, sought God in Nature, Franck sought God in history.[95] When the devil's influence was so manifest, in an age witnessing the collapse of all order, with every man taking up the sword against his neighbour, God must be there too. God was in history; God was history. The heretics,* Franck began to believe, carry the torch of true faith and reason through time. Time only seems to have fallen victim to the world, the pope and the spirit of evil. Franck's teaching was that history had hitherto always been written by the victors, though it had been made by the vanquished: *triumphus penes victos*. Victory was nevertheless with the defeated.[96] Although Franck was a friend of the Garden Brethren and the Anabaptists, and had taken his spiritualizing wife from among them, he was not imprisoned by their resentments. Franck definitely belonged to the petty-bourgeoisie. He had learned the notoriously heretical trade of soap boiler. Despite these facts, intellectually he was an aristocrat who dared to weld his conflicting ideas into one positive whole.[97] God was in everybody; he was all things to all; he was in every genuine paradox.

Franck's experience on the fringes of the different denominations gave rise to two conclusions: One was the idea of tolerance, the leading idea of the early enlightenment and the first piece of fundamental historical thinking in Germany since the twelfth century.† The other was the idea of dialectical argument. 'All judgments contain the deepest contradictions within themselves and, if both sides are not taken together, none of them can ever be really understood, no matter how clear and obvious they may be.' Thomas Münzer had already tried in a similar way to achieve a positive solution to the difficulties raised by a one-sided interpretation of the Bible. Franck, in his turn, as a true pupil of Erasmus, aimed first to uncover the poison of self-will and of false self-assertion in all the Christian denominations, and secondly to

*Franck was the first to turn this word from a term of abuse into a word of praise.

†When Franck died, his library was found to contain not only Plotinus, Origen, Tauler and Chronicle Histories, but Rhabanus Maurus, and Rupert von Deutz's *De Victoria Verbi Dei* as well.

get rid of it. This was to be accomplished by means of dialectical argument, the only science that could reconcile intellectual opposites and bring peace. 'The fourth faith', the Church of the future, the Kingdom of the Holy Ghost, could only be built up in the hearts and minds of the inward man.

Since Franck had to defend himself against persecution by the various orthodoxies, including his chief enemy Luther, he naturally tended to dismiss the problems of dogmatic Christianity in favour of a pure religion, or rather religiosity of the spirit, nourished on the Stoic, Neoplatonic mystical sources of the first and second German movements.[98] Here he came very near to that attitude of the early enlightenment which was to spread into the Low Countries. That inner kingdom of the Anabaptists and the 'silent in the land' was quietly borne by Socinians and Arminians coming from places as remote from each other as Italy, Poland, Transylvania and Strasbourg. It is not, therefore, surprising to find that Franck's account of the rise of the nobility reminds one of Rousseau and the political humanism of fifteenth-century Florence; his Christology contains all the essential elements of the deism of England and the Low Countries.

Franck was a carrier of ideas, and perhaps his most important historical role was in propagating and carrying the ideas of the first and second German movements into the topsy-turvy social and political sphere of the sixteenth and seventeenth centuries. The two German movements were the unmistakable origins of his individualism, his ideal of the resigned man and his dissolution of the historical Christ, which is pure Eckhart. His dialectical argument that God is what every man thinks he is, 'God' to one man, 'devil' to the rest, has the same hallmark. Franck believed that God is in every pair of opposites, because he is in all things and above all things. The *Paradoxa*, his most important work, was entirely conceived in the spirit of the *Non aliud* of Nicholas of Cusa's *coincidentia oppositorum*. Although Franck never mentioned Nicholas by name, he was bound to his world and religiosity by a thousand spiritual ties. Not least of these was his incipient nationalism, i.e., his belief in salvation in and through the German people.[99] This nationalist faith tied Franck to the whole trend of German humanists (Bebel, Pirkheimer, Nauclerus, Wimpheling, Peutinger, Celtis, Irenicus) and equally closely to the joy and redemption of salvation from the people, the movements that centred around St Francis and Joan of Arc, and later about Nicholas of Cusa and his brother and mortal enemy, Luther.

Franck died in 1542, Paracelsus a year earlier, Copernicus a year later. In the year that Franck died, the works of Savonarola and Erasmus, the renewers of the one true Church, were published in one volume in Antwerp. The Spanish humanists and Erasmians had already fled to the West, especially to Italy and the Low Countries. In Italy itself, in 1540, the great emigration of religious nonconformists began which in the following twenty years was to rob the country of its élite. In 1541 Calvinism triumphed in Scotland under John Knox, and in Geneva under Calvin himself. Finally in 1541, the last echo of a whole era, the well-known disputation took place between Lutherans and Catholics in Regensburg. By that time Juan Luis Vives had died in Brussels in 1540, and Charles v's conciliation policy had failed. The humanists were dying off or being harried out of existence. The absolutism of the various religious parties and the modern state had triumphed all along the line, bringing in its train war, the terror of the established Churches, a narrowing of minds and a hardening of hearts.

There is good reason for grouping Franck with Copernicus and Paracelsus. All three dared to think thoughts for which their time was not ripe but which were to determine the thinking of later centuries. All three were deeply medieval figures. Copernicus for instance, regarded the sun neoplatonically as a ruler. He imagined that every natural object possessed a spiritual power, and had little interest in the mechanical arts and the experimental method.[100] Only his position as a Canon preserved him during his life from the persecutions to which the other two were subject. The fate of Paracelsus, who wandered over the whole of central Europe unable to find asylum, shows that a class of poor German scholars, a kind of *Gelehrtenproletariat*, had been formed organically out of the world of Enthusiasts, Anabaptists and political nonconformists.[101] Paracelsus, whose life frequently crossed with Franck's, found his audience not in the universities where he was ridiculed by theologians, physicians, Aristotelians, professors and students and driven out by their mockery and hatred, but among the humble people of the lowest class and in the Enthusiast and Anabaptist communities. Despite his struggles to escape inwardly from these people, they had a decisive influence on his view of the world. His 'social-ethical and social-political writings' have only begun to be published in our own days.[102] The spiritualist socialism and communism of Paracelsus combined the main elements of Franciscan spirituality and Anabaptism. 'The law of the Gospel transcends the law of the Empire.' 'Is there any body of people more cruel to the poor than the priesthood?' The pope is the earthly Lucifer, his walled church the incarnation of evil.* Paracelsus wanted to bring down the enemies of God, 'the Antichrist, the idol (the God-the-Father of the canonists and the dominant Church), the Emperor, the usurers, and all those who are against God'. Christ and 'the apostolic heart' would bear salvation despite Rome, Geneva and Wittenberg.

Paracelsus mistrusted the moderns as much as the ancients. He belonged to the Catholic radical and utopian line which led directly from the Fraticelli to Thomas More, Campanella and Robespierre. He called for an order of justice and goodness upon earth, and denied the fatalistic egoism of the conservatives, who were prepared to leave the world to the devil so long as they could retain their own power.

On the other side, the monastery and the palace were drawing closer in a

*The construction of the Vatican was begun in 1450 and may be seen as Rome's answer to European spiritualism. This was true of the buildings of the baroque period as well. They were bulwarks against the Spirit.

defensive alliance against radicalism. Both offered the sheltered pursuit of salvation, remote from the world as in the Escorial and later in Versailles, and their attendant monasteries and religious foundations. In 1548 the Burgundian court ceremonial was introduced in Madrid simultaneously with the final campaign against the remnant of the followers of Erasmus. Their crime had been to teach, like Paracelsus, that *monachatus non est pietas*. Since the monk assured the salvation of the rulers by making it remote and removing it from the world, the monk was a vital prop of the authoritarian state. The monasteries of the absolutist period, from the sixteenth to the nineteenth century (and in Spain and South America even later) were bulwarks against the unexpected eruptions of the spirit. They were to maintain their purity by being distant, remote and confined to a dominant élite. The Enthusiasts and Paracelsus had quite different ideas. They aimed to carry salvation and knowledge – saving knowledge – out to the people. The New Jerusalem was not to be a cathedral, nor the city of Rome, nor an empire, but a new ordering of earthly society based on freedom, equality, justice and goodness. To this end, brotherly love was to be active and effective in both the religious and the political spheres. Brotherly love demanded the equality of men and the social estates, as well as a new system of labour which would give the poor a right to work and to own property.[103] Paracelsus rejected charity, in the sense of organized benevolence, as a false solution and a self-deception. The tasks facing contemporary society were too great for charity and could only be solved by rational planning and social legislation. There must be obligations of service and enforced labour for idlers. All men must be made to work together in a spirit of brotherly love.

Paracelsus had an equally radical idea of peace. He was 'one of the first people to be fundamentally opposed to the death penalty' and he condemned war outright.[104] This religious and political Utopianism was not pacifism. Paracelsus acknowledged that it might be necessary to murder tyrants for the sake of the common good[105] and, as a physician and natural scientist, he believed in the existence of men without souls, merely animal creatures, nothing but flesh, 'to be bound and held like wood or stones'.[106] How close was he to the idea of making better use of this human material through the combined efforts of people with souls, that is, with the right spirit? Spiritually-minded political Utopians are always especially prone to such ideas. Paracelsus was busily engaged with the transmutation of natural forces and elements and presumably never considered disciplining the new man, like Faust in the crucible, under the yoke of the absolute state as the princes were soon to attempt to do. He did not succumb to the temptations held out by his own thoughts, possibly because he was in such close touch with reality. He was, after all, an itinerant physician and scientist, eager to pass his knowledge and experience on to the people. He was, Metzke aptly puts it the 'Luther of the physicians'.[107] He attacked everyone who refused to face up to reality and despised all the 'rhetorical chatter' of schoolmen, priests, humanists, writers and poets. He demanded living knowledge. Experience must be the ground to which everything else must be referred.[108]

Paracelsus was deeply moved by the state of need and anxiety in which man, the 'noblest of creatures', lived, and he was obliged to witness daily the fragility of human existence. As a result he had become convinced of the uselessness of abstract general principles in the face of the concrete individual circumstances of life. Mental health, physical health, spiritual health and hence politics, science and religious faith, were matters which were intimately united and for this reason he did all he could to reconcile man to that fearful, terrible thing, nature. 'Nature' is 'more than man', he wrote.[109] Man cannot 'be sure of any of his members for a moment',[110] and he has to admit 'that to more than three-quarters of our world we have no contact'.[111] To the political humanists of western Europe, the cosmos was a domestic affair in which human beings and all other things were rational and rationally at home, but to Paracelsus and, following him, Germany as a whole up to the present century, nature was a dark and mighty power pregnant with secrets, a power in which good and evil, God and the devil, freedom and necessity, cosmos and chaos, were all intimately united.[112] Man must submit in suffering obedience to this deadly world of fearful forces and to its intervention in his affairs.[113] This terrible thing, nature, is ultimately nothing less than the dark side of God himself, in which he is pleased to hide himself completely, ('for God letteth Himself to be uncertain').[114] Nature, and through nature God, is revealed to man in the struggle waged by all living things. The 'order of nature' is preserved only by constant stresses.[115] There is in nature 'ever one thing against another, one plant against another, one root against another'.[116]*

Paracelsus's experience had nothing in common with English and Italian empiricism. To him it meant an active penetration to the productive powers, salt, sulphur, mercury. His doctrine became a favourite form of gnostic-cabbalism during the baroque period, and there were obvious reasons for it. Despite all this irrationalism, pantheism and dangerous dynamism Paracelsus's aim was to enlighten and to assist human reason.[117] God had created the 'light of nature' for human beings, and commanded them 'to feed themselves with the work of their hands'. There was no more curious investigator into the secrets of nature than the itinerant Paracelsus. He had discovered that nature was not to be rifled of her secrets and that the human mind was bound up with nature, including the nature of a land, a region; man, climate, animals, rocks and plant life formed a unity.[118]

Paracelsus believed that the human mind can experience nature, and the human soul can experience God, only through a process of obedient service. To him, Luther's incalculable, all-controlling God was manifest in nature as a mighty force of destiny over human lives: every life has its 'predestined end',[119]

*Böhme took up this idea of Paracelsus's that 'there is no life without poison and violence' and that 'the grimmest and most violent things' are the 'unique causes of life and movement' and gave it a wide audience.

predestined in nature and history, its own law of development. Paracelsus was the link along which the *dira necessitas* of Ockham and Luther was transmitted to Calvin and to Darwin and Marx. A harsh all-powerful inevitability ruled over man as an historical being. Where the Greeks and the scholastics had considered the cosmos and nature as unchanging and endless, Paracelsus argued that nature, too, had her own time. He saw time as a positive phenomenon, in which vision he was close to Franck and to the Fraticelli. Time, with clocks, and voyages round the world and the invention of printing, began to enter into the European consciousness as a new god.* It was something that could not be dodged, or overcome, even by a saint. Everything depends on timing, the right time. *Kairos*, the moment of sacred history, as in Christ's words 'Your time is always, my hour has not yet come' became meaningful in a sense, just as the remote idea of brotherly love had been transferred from the sphere of ideals into the world of practical, political ends. If time were now so important, obviously the wrong time could ruin everything.[120]

Paracelsus was stunned by the significance of his discovery, especially by the part played by time in the make-up of reality. Time is something 'that they have never thought about so far'.[121] There are 'many kinds of years.'[122] 'Therefore all the ages should be carefully studied – the hour, time, man, the world, illness.'[123] Heaven is not some kind of spherical construction rotating in the beyond, or a magical crystal palace, but the whole temporal constellation, both cosmic and historical, without which there would be no world or nature and no historical reality. At this point, he wandered off into Neoplatonic and astrological conceptions. He was especially fascinated, for instance, by the Great World Year, a conception passed on from the World of the Three Rings to the cosmic thought of the sixteenth, seventeenth and eighteenth centuries by way of the rich Italian tradition that dates back to the time of Cecco d'Ascoli and Pietro d'Abano.

The tremendous flood and variety of his writings is deceptive, for they are in fact a monologue in which the same fundamental ideas recur again and again in different perspectives. This was not because Paracelsus was a monomaniac or a fanatical egoist but simply because there was no basis for communication between him and the dominant class of German society in his day. This class was afraid of Luther's progeny, who would, they feared, only bring chaos. They regarded the revolution as having come to an end with the creation of the national Lutheran churches and the Protestant universities. There was only one prophet, Luther, and his spiritual children were pushed into the underground. Before very long there was only one kind of knowledge, Protestant scholasticism. The whole body of Luther's writing, the first great German treasury of quotations, was restricted to the 'purely religious use' of the individual. There were indeed many passages about society and the duties of society, but they were, on the whole, ignored. It was left to the great German poetry of the eighteenth and nineteenth centuries to enter upon the full

*Hölderlin: 'For the mind of God hates what is not in time.'

Lutheran heritage. The new universities (Marburg 1527, Königsberg 1544, Jena 1558, Helmstedt 1576, Altdorf 1581) had only one function: to deliver to the princes and their underlings an ideology, a body of thought for public officials and the clergy, teachers and professors.

Melanchthon, the timid, gentle great-nephew of Reuchlin, trembled under the fiery breath of his genius friend. Although he was dwarfed publicly by the men of his generation, this quiet man accomplished an incredible historical feat. Calmly, as though nothing had happened, he constructed a new doctrine of natural law based on Aristotle and Biblical theology which in many respects is identical with that of St Thomas.[124] The similarity to Thomism was not accidental. The exterior circumstances were similar. An open rationalism was needed based on the authority of the princes and the legal thinking of the towns and communities.[125] Aristotle, Cicero and Galen, the Stoics, the 'natural light of reason' and free will[126] were the necessary elements in the construction of a new natural theology which contained in embryo the whole of English deism and the German enlightenment of the eighteenth century.[127] This rational doctrine about God, the world, and man was crystal clear, as orderly as a rich patrician's house. According to it, the world was created in 3962 BC and had been deliberately organized by Providence for the benefit of human beings.[128] The moral law bound the human citizen to obedience to God and civil society. The state had been directly instituted by God and was independent of the Church.[129]

This rational, domesticated cosmos was built on the edge of an abyss – the abyss of Luther's unknowable God. If man had been broken by sin, God had denied him any insight into the structure of being. God could only instruct man through faith and religious feeling, fear, conflict and hope. Melanchthon was, therefore, unable to develop any Christian doctrine of being or any metaphysic. In the first edition of his doctrine of faith, he explained that knowing Christ meant knowing his acts of charity, not his two natures or his incarnation. He went on to develop a philosophy comprising Aristotelian dialectic, physics and ethics. His gentle Erasmian thinking came close to dissolving the historical Christ and the Sacraments into mere guides to good behaviour, not unlike Zwingli's approach.[130]

But there was an abyss between these refined and general laws of thought and the fanatical, irrational faith of Luther. For practically the whole of the sixteenth century Lutheranism did not dare to think about the Christian God, or the Trinity, or the Incarnation, or the doctrine of salvation. Once the first excesses of religious feeling and sentiment and broken-hearted contrition were over and there were no further volcanic eruptions, no more experiences of conversion, chaos necessarily followed. There was an unbearable tension between the richness below, in the subconscious, the soul and the yearning of the heart and the rigorously enforced emptiness above; that is, in the intellect which was forbidden to think about God. In the resulting spiritual void, and in the absence of spiritual education among the people, that chaos which

Rhegius had already described during the 1530's was bound to spread. Melanchthon had renounced metaphysics. His special type of spiritualism had made metaphysics impossible for him. At the same time, his doctrine of free uninhibited education further loosened the ties of intellectual discipline. The result of these two factors was that by 1590 Lutheran teachers generally were beginning to complain that their students could no longer think or speak or write and were fast becoming uncultured barbarians.[131]

Certain humanist circles strove to reconcile the different denominations and refused to abandon systematic thought. The old Lutheran enemies of reason arose at once. All this was the work of the devil. To Daniel Hoffmann and his followers, metaphysics was 'the wisdom of the flesh' (*sapientia carnis*). Greeks, schoolmen and Jesuits were all heathens and barbarians. The irrationalists were supported by the school of Altdorf, where there were scientific Aristotelians influenced by Padua and by the Pietists and by other spiritual heirs of Luther. They also received support from the Teutonic philosophers of the Agrippa-Paracelsus-Boehme school. Nevertheless, the Spanish neo-scholastics – Fonseca, Suarez, Vasquez, Oviedo, Mendoza, Arriaga – were quoted from 1600 onward with almost canonical authority in Lutheran text-books on metaphysics. Jesuit scholastic philosophy conquered all the Dutch and German Lutheran academic institutions. At the same time the brick Gothic Protestant churches as far North as the Baltic were being filled with highly ornamented baroque pews.[132] The books of devotion produced by the Wittenberg theologians Habermann (1567) and Kegel were simply transcriptions of early Jesuit mysticism. Book One of Arndt's *True Christianity* which brought the first wave of rejuvenation into Lutheranism, was largely borrowed from Tauler and the *Imitation of Christ*; Book Two from Angela of Foligno; Book Three from Tauler, and Book Four from Raymond of Sabunde, quoted almost verbatim.[133] In all the Lutheran universities with the exception of Altdorf, i.e., in Helmstedt, Wittenberg, Jena, Leipzig, Giessen, Tübingen and Rostock, Suarez's *Disputations* became the handbook of scholastic metaphysics.

The success of this rational scholastic metaphysics was a triumph for western Europe. Luther and Lutheranism claimed a victory, however, which until recently has been more or less ignored, i.e., in the rise of modern Russia and the Russian Church under Ivan III. To appreciate this, some background material must be recalled. Ivan III had been engaged in a struggle with his brothers and the other princes, the republic of Novgorod, Lithuania and the Tartars. As part of this campaign for supremacy, he was married in Rome in 1472 to the niece of the last of the Byzantine emperors, and thus became the heir to Constantinople, and the regent of the third Rome. He could call himself the holy Czar.[134] In Moscow itself a religious struggle was going on between Greek *émigrés*, humanists and friends of the Reformation who had come under western European influences, and the bishops, monasteries and spiritualist monks of the Empire. Moscow had become the fulcrum of many political and religious forces after the fall of Constantinople. The scales eventually fell on the side of political and religious absolutism and with this the legitimacy of religious resistance and nonconformist reform was shattered.[135]

Further to the West, the Slav nobility of eastern and northern Germany were finding in Lutheranism an ideology that ensured it control over a country that in its social structure already belonged to the East. The ancient Slavic nobility of the area had encouraged German settlement during the twelfth and thirteenth centuries, but by the beginning of the sixteenth century they had destroyed whatever elements of Western freedom the settlers had brought. 'The victory of East over West was accomplished first in the social structure. Originally the German immigrants obtained better property laws than they usually possessed at home, often enjoying the so-called Flemish law, which was regarded as the best possible. By the end of the sixteenth century, on the other hand, the peasants east of the Elbe had the most wretched property laws to be found anywhere west of the Polish border. In the beginning, the newly established German towns had been given the superior status of Magdeburg and had been almost on the same level as the free cities of the Empire; but by the end of the fifteenth century most of these towns had sunk into a position of hopeless dependence on the princes and into very lamentable straits indeed. This process was completed in the sixteenth century.'[136] 'The will to religious reform, which had allied itself with the reactionary forces of the feudal upper nobility, collapsed under the pressure of the ever-increasing absolutism of the Grand Dukes of Moscow.'[137] There was no independent clergy, no intellectual élite, no town communities nor free peasant organizations, to prevent the Grand Dukes from taking absolute control of the country's spiritual life.

A similar process took place in eastern Germany, which developed 'its own particular form of Lutheranism'. 'An exaggerated Augustinianism deprived of all its anti-Manichaean elements paradoxically united with an extreme form of Pelagianism grew up.'[138] The world was seen as Satan's kingdom and the spiritual man, the man of religion, was well advised to stay at home with his Bible and his kith and kin, listening to the word of God. If he ventured forth over the threshold, he would be assaulted by the wilderness of the world, a horribly sacrilegious place utterly devoid of any signs or symbols of salvation. In the world every man was on his own, and had to fight his way through it as best he could. Man's eyes had been de-sanctified by Luther and they were unable to see any signs of mutual inter-dependence of a democratic kind between God and man, grace and the human spirit in the ways of the world. Men were devoid of grace in a world deprived of grace and at the mercy of harsh necessity and the laws of nature. Life was a struggle for existence. The only reason that men were not continually at each other's throats was that God had ordained certain compulsory powers: the state, the established Church, and all the written and unwritten taboos of the community. Anxious in his conscience and fearful in his obedience, the solitary individual kept a wary eye on this severe God and on his equally severe earthly masters.[139]

Luther had doubtless not wanted it this way. He had been the salvation-bearer of the people. He had pierced the thin skin of Western humanist rationalism as the eastern German Lords had pierced the colonisers' attitudes and the rights and freedoms of Western settlers and towns. In despair and anguish, Luther had plunged into the murky depths and had made contact at the deepest level with the people's ancient faith in the goodness of things, even the worst of conditions. This was the source of his great power of relieving anguish, and of bringing joy out of the clogged and impeded underground passages. In this process he had become the real creator of the German language. As Jacob Grimm has said, through Luther modern high German became a Protestant dialect which as late as the mid-eighteenth-century the Catholic south of Germany was quite unable to understand.[140] Only when that part of the world had become so profoundly protestantized itself, by Jansenism and subterranean protestant infiltration, could it accept the terms of the questions and problems of classical and romantic poetry and idealistic philosophy.

Nevertheless, there is one thing that should be realized. For the person who experiences the cosmos as a Catholic, the fundamental questions facing the German mind in the eighteenth and nineteenth centuries were not real but only pseudo-problems. He feels no need for any intellectual or imaginative reconstruction of a world split from top to bottom. He does not need a new sacramental system in an idealized world strongly tinged by Pantheism. Nor is he inspired by poetry, nor by a sentimental world of feeling and emotion. Luther's basic and uncompromising division of the cosmos into separate entities – an unknowable God, a self lost in sin, a natural order at enmity with God, a shaky reason and an emotional clamouring for salvation – does not exist for him. If Austria has had no philosophy to speak of, except for a few post-Protestant thinkers, and yet has had a plethora of mathematicians, natural scientists and humanists, the reason is that the Catholic south of Germany never considered certain questions worth discussing. In the light of their experience of the world, such questions were just not real. Luther, the religious genius, had preserved salvation for the desperate spiritual hinterland of the populations of the East but in doing so had cut himself off, not only from the Catholic south, but also from that part of the German west that had been reformed by Calvin and Zwingli. Calvin and Zwingli were the most dynamic heirs of the political humanism and rationalism of the Mediterranean world. Luther's fanatical irrationalism was foreign to both of them. Thus Lutheranism was driven increasingly westwards.

As early as the Leipzig disputation of 1519 with Eck, Luther had defended the Eastern Church in almost the same words as Erasmus was to use in 1525 to defend the Roman Church against Luther: 'I ask every Christian to consider carefully, in a spirit of Christian charity, whether it is not shameless injustice to throw out all those thousands of martyrs and saints of the Greek Church during the last thousand years and to try to dethrone those who are in Heaven?'[141] To prove the continuity of his Reformation with the past he returned to the Greek Fathers, Chrysostom and Basil the Great. Melanchthon also wooed the Eastern Church, in his 'Address to the Patriarch of Constantinople' in 1559. In 1573 the Tübingen theologians, especially Stephan Gerlach, tried to institute ecumenical conferences and soon Lutheran theologians had constructed the idea of the *consensus quinque secularis*: the view that the Eastern and Lutheran Churches had a common foundation in Holy Scripture, in the canons of the early Church synods, in the traditions of the Greek Fathers and in common enemies who had all been condemned by the ancient Church.[142] These common enemies were the 'Westerners'.

In 1438 and 1439 councils had been held in Florence and news of these had been carried by Greek *émigrés* to Moscow. By 1480, Moscow had taken over the Byzantine ceremonial and also the Byzantine hope of salvation. During the fifteenth century a storm of hatred arose against the Latins, against Rome, Western humanism and rationalism and this spread through the whole world of the Eastern Church. It was quite clear that the Easterners preferred to live under the yoke of Turks and Tartars than under the Roman mitre.[143] This hatred was in harmony with the resentment felt by all the irrational movements that had arisen out of Lutheranism and its underground in eastern Germany. Its objects were Rome, the West, England and France. This hatred is still felt today.

Luther's discovery of salvation through the spirit and the underground world of the people and his hatred of 'devilish' Western ideological superstructures, scholasticism, Roman law, church organization, philosophy and human reason, paradoxically brought about a new kind of receptivity to the Western classical-Christian intellectual inheritance. The peoples of the barbarian East had always regarded this tradition as an alien system thrust upon them against their will, but until Luther they were powerless to criticize or defend themselves against it. The first stage of a new and more inward attitude was the eruption of violent feelings of resistance and rejection. Lutheranism was unable to maintain the tension of a confrontation with the West, so Calvinism soon had to be called in to continue the inner struggle. In the next stage, the idealism and romanticism of the third German movement, a final effort was made to salvage Western elements and integrate them into a synthesis with the Eastern underground world.

There is abundant evidence of the nature of the East–West dialogue which began to assume ever deeper intensity in the second half of the fifteenth century. During the years 1470 to 1480, the emerging Russian state reacted violently against the West. In 1494, the Hanseatic outpost in Novgorod was forcibly closed. In 1525 the Order of Teutonic Knights became a secular state. But the most illuminating evidence of all is to be seen in the life of Luther's historical counterpart and contemporary, Maximos the Greek. In the seventeenth century Maximos the Greek achieved the status of a Church Father whose writings had been divinely inspired. Modernists and traditionalists alike cited him as one of the highest authorities and venerated him as a canonized saint. Maximos was the first philosophical thinker in Russia. His first activity was that of an orthodox reformer of the Russian Church. He came to Russia in 1518 when he was nearly fifty years old. He had been in turn a humanist in Italy under the name Michael Trivolis, then a monk in Savonarola's monastery, and later still, from 1506–16, a monk on Mount Athos, where he took the name of Maximos the Greek. His dramatic life (1470–1556) illustrated the difficulties and potentialities that existed when the barbarians of the East met the intellectual heritage of western Europe. Between 1520 and 1530 the West was engaged in an enormous process of simplification and elimination. Integration was felt to depend on the assertion of a restricted number of doctrines. Both Luther and Maximos were men of a 'few truths', as later Loyola was to be called. Out of a bewildering and burdensome abundance of intellectual and cultural goods Maximos chose 'the one thing necessary' for the barbarian world of the East. At first, as a sensitive Greek intellectual Maximos was fascinated by Russia, but the burden of civilization which he bore eventually proved too great for him. After years of penance and renunciation he ended his life in martyrdom.

Maximos was the first mediator between Russia and the West. He founded the scientific study of Russian grammar and philology. His ideas were at the root of the two great opposing movements that flourished in Russia from the seventeenth to the nineteenth century; the Raskolniki and the moderns. He was as influential and ambiguous as Augustine or Hegel.* Maximos came of a distinguished Byzantine family, which had fled from the Turks to Corfu in 1460. His father was in Rome in 1472 when Princess Zoe-Sophia was betrothed to Ivan III. The Princess's guardian, Cardinal Bessarion, hoped by this marriage to win the Slavs over to his side, and to use them to liberate his country from the Turks. As Rome had once wooed the Franks, Byzantium now wooed the Russians. In this effort the Roman Church joined gladly. Russian representatives had been invited to council meetings in Rome in 1438 and 1439 – and they had returned to Moscow hating Roman politics but full of admiration for its technical achievements, art and general culture. As late as 1519 Leo X offered the Archduke Wassili the crown and an autonomous patriarchate and supported his endeavour to win back his paternal heritage, Constantinople, if in return he would unite with the Roman Church.[144]

Maximos grew up in the over-heated atmosphere of a politically divided, highly educated Greek intelligentsia, tense with passionately held hopes,

---

*One of Maximos's disciples was Count Andreas Kurbski, who was forced to flee to Lithuania in 1564, into what he called the 'polish barbarism'. In the second decade of his exile, Kurbski developed the idea of 'Holy Russia' and its 'Holy Empire': *Svatorvskaja imperija*. (145)

disappointments and humiliations. He himself was a passionate, sensual, ambitious and greedy person, who experienced to the full the many-sided world of Italian humanism. In Florence he was the pupil and protégé of Lascaris and Florentine Platonism. In Bologna and Padua he listened to the Averroist Nifo. He lived successively in Ferrara, Milan and Venice. Later he was to attack all these humanists and their worship of heathen antiquity, their naturalism and amorality, but at this time their complicated, decadent culture had a powerful effect on him, as it had on the entire East, both attracting and repelling him. Soon the hatred of Rome that was all around flared up in him too, and he wrote violent diatribes against 'His Un-Holiness Pope Alexander'.[145] He observed with savage bewilderment the mixture of spiritual and worldly elements in the person of the Pope, but at the same time he was fascinated by the pomp of Roman ceremonial. From 1496 to 1498 he lived in Venice and was on intimate terms with the famous printer Aldus Manutius. Later, in Moscow, he was to write enthusiastically about the great cultural significance of printing.[146] His attitude reminds one of Erasmus's enthusiasm for this 'almost divine instrument'.[147] Luther too attributed the enormous spread of his writings to printing.

In the latter years of the fifteenth century political unrest and the confusions of war did a great deal to diminish the wealth and power of the great patrons who supported the humanistic movement. This was another reason why the humanists' freedom of movement and thought came to an end in the sixteenth century. Maximos became secretary to Giovanni Francesco Pico della Mirandola, who had passed on his famous uncle's inheritance to Zwingli. On his ducal estate – he was a Count of the Empire – Pico encouraged imperial hostility to the popes and the cult of Savonarola,* whose biography he wrote. In 1501, he fled for protection to Maximilian I and Maximos was left to fend for himself. It was in that same year that he had his first conversion. Under the influence of Savonarola and his study of the Greek Fathers he renounced 'pagan Italy' and its 'neo-pagan' humanists and retired into the Christian Italy of Pico, Savonarola, the Franciscans and the Carthusians.[148] It was mainly an ethical conversion, and meant giving up the twin vices of the Greek intelligentsia, sodomy and homosexuality. He had discovered to his cost that the ancient mythology dragged one down into concupiscence.[149] Between 1502 and 1504 he was a Dominican at San Marco, but he left a disappointed man.† After Savonarola was burned at the stake an unhealthy atmosphere of reaction had set in and even Savonarola's memory was persecuted. The nervousness and narrowness of mind following upon the great defeat depressed him.

---

*Maximos subscribed to Pico's veneration of Savonarola and later wrote enthusiastic tributes to Savonarola which were widely read in Russia.

†Later in Moscow he was always extremely careful to conceal this part of his life, although he described life in the Dominican Order in very great detail. In his attack on scholasticism, he ignored St Thomas, although he occasionally referred to Albert the Great and Duns Scotus. He suggested that St John Damascene should be the educator of the East.

Maximos had not yet found what he was looking for, the purity of the Gospels, and the splendour of the early Christian Church. Nor did he find it in the ten vain years he spent on Mount Athos. His sojourn there was simply an expression of the tremendous fascination that the orthodox religion had for the East, 'this religion which is such an intimate part of the Greek and Slav soul, and its national consciousness.'[150] It was no more than the return of the prodigal son.

The atmosphere of Mount Athos was anti-Latin. To the accompaniment of the most impressive penitential liturgy, Maximos said goodbye to his old name, Michael, and his worldly Latin life. He spent the next three years as a lay brother and the following ten as a simple monk. He never became a priest, and in reality remained a man from the West, with the critical outlook of the true humanist. The monks of Athos never lost their mistrust of him. After the decadence of San Marco he now experienced the decadence of Mount Athos – the loose morals, the clique-warfare, the wealth and especially the luxury of the idiorhythmic, small communities of monks living on a family basis.[151] As a follower of Savonarola at St Francis, Maximos stood for the absolute poverty of the monk. He had been in San Marco at the time when the monastery had been forced by the *Curia* and the superiors of the Order to accept property and revenues again, and the experience had embittered him. He later continued the struggle in Russia against the wealthy Russian monasteries with all their vast properties and feudal serfs.

The ten years on Mount Athos were decisive for him. The internal political struggles there helped to sharpen his diatribes against Rome, and on his arrival in Moscow he immediately published his *Discourse against the Latins*. As he grew older, he saw the issue more clearly and preached to East and West alike that the most important thing of all was inner renewal. Athos found him embarrassing and packed him off on anti-Latin missions which were no doubt also to test him. These took him to the Balkans, Corfu and Egypt. At the end of April 1517, he left Constantinople on a mission for the Patriarch. Moscow had asserted its independence seventy years before and his task was to bring it back under the Patriarch's jurisdiction.* The Greek Patriarch sent the foreigner off on his dangerous mission to Moscow with full honours. The whole of Athos presented him with a letter of introduction to the Russian ambassador, Kopyl, describing him as a 'very fit and proper person'.

Moscow needed serviceable men to bring some sort of order into the confusion of its ecclesiastical affairs. In the second half of the fifteenth century Russia's power had grown enormously and for the first time for 212 years the country had entered upon international relations and opened its borders to influences from abroad. Individual minds had begun to stir. As is always the

*The intricate counter-point in relations between the Eastern and the Western Churches is worth noticing: in the same year 1517, Maximos's former patron, Lascaris set out for Egypt on a mission for Leo x to try to win over the Sultan for an anti-Turkish policy. Both Lascaris and Maximos were Greeks, but one was Western and the other Eastern.

case where there is over-rapid development, periodic panics had occurred. The end of the world was expected in 1492,[152] but at the same time people had high hopes for immediate salvation. The two things often go together. Violent feelings of inferiority to the high level of civilization in the West were compensated for by ecstatic adoration of Russia and the person of the Czar. The new title, 'Holy Emperor', was tested politically for the first time in 1473, against the Livonian branch of the Teutonic Order.[153] In the report of an anonymous author on the journey to the Council of Florence, 1438–9, Russia was called the home of the true Faith, and the Grand Duke Wassili a second Constantine.[154] The fall of Constantinople had a prodigious effect. It was 'the first historical event in Europe that went directly into Russian literature. In that year the way was opened for a deeper Russian participation in the affairs of Europe.'[155] 'Byzantium has fallen, but Russia is still growing and the Church of Constantinople has fled to the Third Rome, that is, to the Great New Russia' claimed the writer of the *Chronograph*.[156]

The school named after St Pafnuti of Borovsk, whose grandfather had gone over to Christianity from Tartarism, assumed the role of harbinger of salvation, and became a political and religious centre for the imperial house. It played a part that was in many respects similar to that played by the Merovingians' family monasteries and by Saint Denis in the courtly life of medieval France. From about 1443 onwards the Grand Duke, the Czar, began to be regarded as a quasi-divine being, in spite of resistance to the idea amongst he nobility, the monastic orders and Western intelligentsia. During the decisive years between 1470 and 1530 the Grand Duke of Moscow succeeded in achieving absolute authority over Church and State. The Czar's supremacy was achieved, however, only after a critical period extending over half a century, when there was continual conflict between spiritual reform, Western enlightenment, popular atheism and superstition, aristocratic rebels and freethinkers. This was the background to the situation in Moscow when Maximos was ordered to go there.

The Habsburgs were represented at the Russian court by Count Herberstein, the author of the first European book on Russia. In his discussion of the quasi-divine power of the Czar Wassili III (Ivan) in his *Rerum Moscoviticarum Commentarii* (Basle 1551) he described how the Russian people almost worshipped their Czar as an incarnate god, and said, 'It is not clear whether the Prince has to be a tyrant because the people are brutish and uncultured (*immanitas*) or whether they are made as uncultured, harsh and cruel as they are because the Prince is such a tyrant.' This *immanitas*, this primitive power, was something quite outside the scope of the concepts of Western humanism. It had created a person who was both a divinity and ruler. The irrational Godruler-subject relationship also existed in the Slav and German-Lutheran colonies of the East. This was the essential common element linking the Russian and eastern German cultural worlds. The underground of the entire area was filled with submerged sectarian excitement. This was the world which Hamann, Herder and Dostoievsky all tried to bring into the light of day. The dwellers in the underground patiently endured a fearful ruler and a fearful God, and took their revenge in hatred and resentment against Western superstructures and ideologies, rationalism, scholasticism and enlightenment. Dostoievsky rejected Catholicism, Socialism and nihilism. These were all on the same level as far as he was concerned and he argued that this underground was a result of Russia's continual subjugation to foreign despots. The underground would exist as long as the Grand Inquisitor had control over the world.[157]

Moscow had been cut off from the patriarchate of Constantinople by Turkish domination and as a result of this the Russian Church had gradually sunk into an advanced state of decomposition. Central Russia, which was still semi-pagan, had been subjected to various Islamic influences and Tartar fetishes. Towards the end of the fifteenth century Joseph of Volotsk wrote that all the Church dogmas were being questioned and that the Church's authority was utterly shattered. Never before, he said, had there been such confusion in Russian Christianity, since the time when it had first been introduced into the country. 'The doctrines of the Faith are opposed in public squares and the privacy of people's homes: there are doubts everywhere.' A reform movement of an individual and spiritual kind, perhaps originating with the Hussites, began to spread from Novgorod and Pskov to the Moscow court itself. It took its name from the converted Jews in Lithuania and was known as the Judaising sect.[158] It criticized the vast compound of religion, politics, wealth and superstition that made up the monastic and ecclesiastical world in Russia. As a movement towards enlightenment it had enjoyed tacit protection under Ivan III, but toward the end of his reign (he died in 1505) the outward manifestations of this 'heresy' were brought to an end by a series of mass executions.

The Archbishop of Greater Novgorod, Gennadius Gonzov, realized that other methods were needed if the Russian Church were to be made capable of resistance to the influences streaming in from the West. He turned boldly to the West itself for help and got together a body of Latin translators, headed by a Slav Dominican called Benjamin. They were ordered, among other things, to complete the Slavonic (old Slav) translation of the Bible and to produce a handbook on the liturgy – parts of which were taken from William of Durand. The Roman Vulgate took the place of the Greek Septuagint. Gennadius also introduced Latin courses for the younger members of the nobility in Novgorod. He had at last gone too far and in the subsequent reaction in Moscow in 1504 he was deposed. Nevertheless his ideas had taken root, and his translation of the Bible was the basis for the first printed Russian Bible, which came out in 1663.

Ten years after this body of translators had been disbanded, Wassili III, the son of Ivan III and Sophie-Zoe Paleologos, formed a new group to mobilize the Greek intellectual heritage for Moscow's benefit. He collected the remaining members of the Novgorod group and at the head of this team of translators he put Maximos the Dominican. With his renunciation of the West Maximos had chosen his new name after Maximos the Confessor.[159] His own theology often followed that of his predecessor, often word for word, and was strongly Platonist.* The chief feature of his doctrine was a radical dualism. During his trial for heresy from 1525 to 1531 Daniel the Metropolitan of Moscow and Bishop Dositheus made certain charges which are interesting not only for their own sake but also with regard to Luther and the Enthusiasts. Maximos was accused of teaching an heretical Christology, according to which Christ remained with the Father only for a brief period of time. His earthly body was an evil thing which stayed behind on earth. Maximos was also accused of teaching that the incarnate Lord was little more than a fiction. Only the divine side of his nature had ascended into Heaven. Dositheus asked Maximos: what is the truth about the statement attributed to you by a number of people, that when Christ ascended into Heaven he left his body behind on earth and that it now roams over mountains and other deserted places, burned up and blackened by the sun like a piece of charred wood? Christ the Prolet, wandering through the people, was a Russian folk myth, going back perhaps to the Christolytes of the eighth century. Maximos may well have combined it with his extreme form of spiritualism, and, if so, it would provide a further example of the connection between spiritualistic ideas and religious folklore which was also characteristic of the German areas of Europe at this time.

Maximos was a master of Nicodemism, the art of concealing one's most personal convictions in matters of faith. He was indeed obliged to do so if he wished to survive the dark, fanatical and suspicious atmosphere of central Russia. The Platonizing ecclesiastics of the East, Psellos, Plethon, Michael Apostolios, John Argyropulos and even Bessarion, were often remarkably double-faced about what they said. But it is quite startling to see how Maximos, even in Moscow, still remained a humanist on the Western model, with the missionary consciousness of a Savonarola and the critical outlook of an Erasmus. He defended personal piety against the externals of religious worship and Church life, with an enthusiastic conviction of an almost Lutheran kind. He asserted with vigour that he had been inspired by the Holy Ghost and filled by God himself, and that he had been introduced into the most secret meanings of the Holy Scriptures. Daniel the Metropolitan probably accused him directly of being a Lutheran.[160] His political aspirations had something of the zealous crusading activity of a person like Calvin. His aim was to bring Moscow back to obedience to Constantinople, and to get the city's support for a crusade to restore the Byzantine Empire. In Moscow, however, the dominant feeling was one of intransigent Russian nationalism. Men would have nothing to do with war on the Turks and they were wary of the Greek *émigrés*.

The great theoretician behind the political and religious absolutism of the

---

*After the time of Photius and Xiliphin, Aristotelianism had been the dominant ideology. Platonism was looked on with suspicion and most of the Churchmen who inclined toward union with the West were Platonists.

Czars, Joseph of Volotsk, Abbot of Volokolamsk, regarded the Czar as the image of Jehovah, the fearful God who reveals himself in thunder and lightning.[161] 'God has given the Czar power and authority over the Church and everything else that concerns Christianity.' One of Joseph's pupils was Ivan IV (the Terrible). This word for terrible – *Grozny* – signifying someone at once terrible and splendid, could be applied to Luther's God as easily as to this Eastern potentate. Ivan later adopted his master's teaching as the official ideology behind Muscovite absolutism. At the Church Council of 1530 Joseph defeated the idea of a movement of Christian poverty, led by Abbot Nil Sorski, which denied the monastic right to extensive property.

Maximos, who had by now been in prison for several years, was accused of having described Ivan III as a butcher, a hangman and a tyrant like the emperors of old, and also of having told Daniel the Metropolitan that the only things Ivan was interested in were hunting, feasting, revelling, acquiring property and extravagant living. As a pupil of Savonarola and the reform humanism of western Europe, Maximos had realized as soon as he arrived in Moscow how profoundly Tartar influences had impregnated its speech, its decorative art, its strategy, its popular beliefs and its ceremonial, and how strongly this Russian world had been influenced by Islam. Its own popular beliefs were essentially identical with the archaic salvation ideas current in sixteenth-century western Europe.[162] Maximos accused orthodox believers of behaving like Mohammedans by prostrating themselves at prayer, and opposed the popular practice of simply covering drowned bodies over with earth in the fields, so that their – sacrificial! – healthy flesh might help the harvest as a kind of relic.

For the third time in his life he had to witness the triumph of political and religious totalitarianism over a Christian movement of poverty and spirituality. First he had seen it at San Marco, then at Athos, and finally in Moscow. After the great fire at Twer in 1537, he ventured once again to preach against blind external religion. People clung too anxiously to the pomp of ceremony, hymns, ikons, bells and sacred vestments. He cried out for inner piety instead of outer obedience. The Moscow council forced him to recant, to give a second sermon on the fire when the burned-out Cathedral was rebuilt, and to congratulate Bishop Akazius on restoring religious worship to its magnificent old form. The most virulent opposition, however, was aroused by his translations and emendations of the Bible. People in Moscow, as indeed in the West of former times, had a fetishistic attitude to old words and were determined to hold on to them. He tried in vain to get his inquisitors to see that Scripture had to be understood 'according to the spirit' and not 'according to the ink'.[163] The Russians regarded his Biblical work as an attack upon their saints and the authority of their Church. At the same time, eager to act as mediator between East and West, he praised Latin monasticism, especially the Franciscans and the Dominicans, and even dared to acknowledge the pre-eminence of St Peter and the dignity of the pope of Rome. All this was treason. As an accomplished

Nicodemist he did indeed manage to camouflage his praise of Western institutions by making continual attacks on 'the three Latin heresies': the *Filioque*, the belief in purgatory, and the use of unleavened bread for the Host. In his anti-Latin writings, he also attacked one of his Moscow contemporaries, the German physician and humanist Nicholas of Lübeck, who had studied in Padua, had been associated with Gennadius of Novgorod, and was now working for the union of Eastern and Western Churches. Nevertheless, Maximos was very moderate in his invective. The Muscovites generally accused the Latins of thirty-two heresies. One anonymous Russian writer, in his polemic against Nicholas declared that the Latin Church had Satan for its head and devils for its tail and that its church doors were decorated with images of the devil.*

The East looked both defensively and admiringly to the West. The Kremlin was being built in the *more italico*, and A. Fioravanti, P. A. Solari, Alevisio and many other Renaissance architects were at work in Moscow. Maximos's Russian writings were the first descriptions of the civilized West to be widely read. He wrote of the University of Paris, Venetian printing, and Christian and neo-pagan Italian humanism. The finest and greatest town in Italy was Florence. Maximos adopted the crisp, popular style and attitude of the Fraticelli in their story of the life of St Francis and described the life and death of Savonarola as a true follower of Christ, determined to free Florence from its plagues of sodomy and usury.[164] In a commentary on one of Gregory I's homilies he described the voyages being made by the Spaniards and the Portuguese, and referred to the discovery of America: 'and today a new world is to be found down there, a new human society ...'[165] Thus Maximos introduced not only the European West to the Russian East, but America too.

Maximos the Greek is an outstanding example of the way in which Western religious humanism could awaken tremendous powers in a man of the East. This religious humanism, often in a much simplified and truncated form, touched the westernmost end of the Eastern world in the Wittenberg of Melanchthon and the Centuriators of Magdeburg. Hordes of young men like Flaccius Illyricus, eager to learn and to teach what they learned, streamed out of Bohemia, Poland, Hungary, the Balkans, into Lutheran (and later the Reformed) universities.[166] Enthusiasm, spiritual intoxication, humanistic and evangelical education were mixed in their struggle for a 'right spirit'. These men went out to procure salvation for their people by producing their own Bibles and national vernacular literatures which they directed against Rome and its Latin. This was the new word of God, emanating from the personally inspired individual. Enormous powers were released by this alliance between popular spiritualism and reform humanism.

*It is fascinating to note that this was exactly what the German people had often seen in Western cathedrals. It is also interesting to compare these images with Herder's impressions of Italy and Goethe's notes on Italy. Herder came from Riga and Goethe had been influenced by Gottfried Arnold, the spiritualist.

Herder, the Antichrist, who came out of this revolutionary spiritualism of the East, kindled the second wave of religious-inspired nationalism among the peoples of the East. Maximos was a personification of this outburst and undoubtedly must be placed on a par with Luther. In the long years he spent in his Moscow prison, the Greek humanist who had once had such a lust for life was transformed through streams of tears into a man of prayer and atonement, a Slav saint. The ageing man had been refined in the fire of the East. The young Prince Andreas Kurbski, whom Maximos educated, wrote a famous letter to Ivan the Terrible. In it the young Prince rejected the totalitarianism of the Czar and defended the Western attitude of mind. Maximos so influenced his fellow translator, Nil Kurliateff, in the direction of nonconformism that he was later suspected of heresy. Later, both Raskolniki and supporters of the state claimed Maximos as a saint. The West had released colossal forces in this man.

14

THE RISE AND FALL OF THE
SPANISH SPIRIT

WHILE Luther and Maximos were still alive, Spanish humanists and Erasmians were trying to save Spain from extremism. Spain, as the centre of the World of the Three Rings, had already been opened to Europe in the twelfth and thirteenth centuries. It had played a decisive part in shaping scholasticism, Gothic architecture,[1] courtly culture (minnesang, music) and mysticism.[2] In the late fifteenth century and the early sixteenth century the work of Archbishop Raimund of Toledo[3] had ripened into the Erasmian movement around Cardinal Francisco Ximenez de Cisneros. Humanists of European stature and universality emerged from this school; Antonio de Lebrixa, the brothers Juan and Alfonso Valdes, Juan Luis Vives.

The political testament of Ferdinand the Catholic transmitted to Charles V by his Secretary of State, Pedro de Quintano, pledged Spain to a world policy in the service of Christianity. Its motto was: 'Peace among Christians and war against the infidels.'[4] Under the shield of this slogan the Erasmians at the court, in the State Chancellery around Charles V, and later around Philip II, began their heroic enterprise. They wanted to establish a third force between Rome and Wittenberg. True to the cosmopolitanism of Erasmus,[5] they hoped to bring together the nations of Europe which were destroying themselves in warfare, in a league of Christian nations. This work was supposed to be crowned by a reform council of the world Church. The opponents and disciples of these Erasmians were to elaborate these beginnings historically in four great works: in the Spanish Renaissance of scholasticism, in the Tridentine theology of free will and grace, in Spanish natural and international law, and in the ethics of colonialism, which grew out of the dispute between Las Casas and Sepulveda, and which in the end aimed to realize the old idea of good heathens.

Ferdinand the Catholic united Castile and Aragon through his marriage with Queen Isabella in 1478 and in 1492 subdued the Moors in their last stronghold in Granada. In all these enterprises the great Queen herself was deeply involved. The last words of his motto, *guerra contra infieles*, war against infidels, contained both the grandeur and misery of the Spanish people. The Spanish Church and its leaders suddenly tried to eliminate their Moorish, Islamic and Jewish heritage in one terrific exertion. They wanted to become orthodox and to defend orthodox Roman Christianity[6] in Europe and the world. They were driven by the realization that they were not united. Spain was, after all, no more than a loose association of superficially converted Moors, Jews and rebellious individuals.[7] 'The internal unrest of the Spanish character'[8] came to a ferment in the discovery of America, in the Asian mission of Francis Xavier, in the establishment of the Society of Jesus and in the mysticism of Theresa of Avila and John of the Cross. It came to a ferment in the Inquisition driven forward by the people, and the peoples' monastic order, the Franciscans, and in the expulsion of the Jews (1492) and the Moors (1609).[9] In 1492 when the expelled Jews were leaving Spain, Christopher Columbus, who probably descended from a Jewish family, put to sea. Four years later in a letter to the 'Catholic King' he mentioned the expulsion of the Jews and his first voyage as part of the same historical development.[10] His son Ferdinand, meanwhile, had become an avid collector of the forbidden writings of religious nonconformists which he incorporated into his library. Very often the leaders of anti-semitism were *conversos* from former Jewish clans.[11] Right-wing reformers, like Ignatius, and right-wing mystics, like John of the Cross, had always to defend themselves against accusations that they were *alumbrados, illuminati*, sectarian Enthusiasts and Lutherans. Nor were the charges entirely baseless. Spanish mysticism and Spanish heresy were never far apart.

All these movements saw man as the battlefield. In each Spaniard God and the devil, Moslem and Jew, heretic and orthodox entered upon a long, bitter struggle. An ancient Manichaean-Asiatic heritage, already evident in Orosius, the Spanish simplifier of Augustine, came to life again. The external world was only a stage-setting, an arena for the struggle. The world was pleasure, charm, the temptations of gold, slaves, women and land which lured men's passions. These things could be made to serve masters, power, fame, nobility or independence,[12] but at the same time they were challenges to be overcome through asceticism, cultivation of the soul and soldierly discipline. The great Spanish theatre of the Golden Age, the reform monastery, the domination of gigantic conquered lands across the seas, the Inquisition and missions were intimately related phenomena. The Spaniard did not cultivate the land. Agriculture in Spanish hands declined catastrophically.[13] Until the nineteenth century there was no such thing, strictly speaking, as an economy. In the fourteenth and fifteenth century the Spanish left this to the Germans, the Revensburg Trading Society and the Fuggers,[14] and then to the Flemish. Later they had to leave it to the French, the Dutch, the English, and the Americans. The Spaniard built cities, monasteries, and palaces, as settings in the world theatre and as suitable trappings for its world-spectacle.[15]

There was no real colonization of America.[16] At bottom it was never seriously attempted. In both hemispheres the Spaniards erected structures of government which, like the Gothic cathedrals, seemed to be built from above. Their régimes were imposed from on top and never penetrated the soil or struck roots. Spanish South America today is in the same situation as Spain in the fifteenth and sixteenth century. Shocked prelates suddenly noticed that the country and the people were neither Christianized nor civilized. While the English, French and Dutch for two hundred years sat on and settled narrow stretches of the North American coast, the Spanish itinerant shepherds, descendants of Islamic-Arabic nomads,[17] soldiers, monks, and missionaries wandered through the enormous spaces of South America, India and Japan, praying, coveting and conquering. They sought to subject men and materials to God or to their greed. What counted was the individual, personal man, the 'Son of a noble somebody' (Hidalgo means *hijo de algo*) not primarily monies and lands. Huge fortunes were lost or lands ruined in an amazingly short time. The Spanish inability to grasp the world was the greatest manifestation of the Manichaean spirit in Europe. It was strikingly linked to the magic fear of all archaic societies and cultures, of touching the beneficent and malevolent secrets of nature.

All Spaniards were noble-born, of pure blood and faith. They were nobles as were the Hungarian *Ur* and the Polish *Schlachtiz*. Isabella, who signed her proclamations, 'I, the Queen', was only the supreme comrade of these 'I's' who were all kings.[18] Calderon and Cervantes were hidalgos. All her life St Theresa set great store on her descent from one of the best families. Ignatius raised his battle flag as a noble *Caballero de Cristo*. These noblemen were horrified when they considered that Spain did not consist only of Hidalgos. These pure-blooded, orthodox Christian, noble people constituted only a small island in a sea of incestuously bred Moorish-Islamic and Jewish half-Christians, sacrilegious Lutherans, Calvinist scoffers and heretical Germans. The Spanish spirit infected all too easily the Spanish soul. Theresa rang the alarm throughout the world: 'Sleep not, sleep not, there is no peace on earth.' Spain declared a permanent crusade which has continued until our day.[19] After tremendous exertions, all these crusades collapsed; Ignatius became Don Quixote; the Hidalgos, *higos de tal*, became whoresons, Lazaro de Tormes and the picaresque-novel made feeble-minded idiots into kings, witches out of brilliant ladies, vagabonds and beggars out of the rich conquerors.[20] What had begun as a lofty work of spiritual revelation ended as a caricature.

The conversion of the Jews in the fourteenth century, accomplished under the pressure of terror and anxiety, had been wholly superficial. The waves of conversion in the fifteenth century of Jews, Moors and Islamic Spaniards, were even more so.[21] 'Today one can hardly form an idea of the extent of this dismay.'[22] The most important aides and advisers to the throne, bishops, monks, preachers, bankers were descended from converted families. The ground underfoot seemed to be giving way. People were perplexed, irritated and fearful because of the depravity and the pestilence of the Jews. The reaction of the Catholics became violent. Depravity became the word of the day, the demand for a purge the slogan. It was eagerly seized upon by the lower classes.* At the same time the 800-year struggle between Islam and the Christian kingdom came to an end. The Moslems were of the same Spanish descent as the Christians.[23] The rural masses in the eighth century were only superficially Christian. Their conversion to Islam had been both quick and painless. The number of Arabs and Syrians who came to the country as conquerors, is estimated to have been 25,000 at the most and of the 200,000 Moslems who lived in Granada in 1311, only 500 were of Arabic descent according to an Arab document.[24] 'There were two parts to this historical masquerade, first, the Hispanicization of Islam under a Mohammedan disguise, and then the subsequent Christianization of this Hispano-Moslem culture in the Christian kingdoms. The superficial mask of an allegedly Germanic tradition completed the process and conditioned the entire history of Spain and a great part of the new world as well.[25]

The Spanish-Moslem intelligentsia allowed the spirit of the World of the Three Rings to materialize. The heart of the poet al-Ramadi 'knew how to beat to the rhythm of all the three religions which Cordoba professed.'[26] The Islamic spirit and Islamic piety sank deeply into the Spanish character and Spanish Christianity.[27] Many elements drawn from Islam deeply influenced society.[28] Islamic, ascetic knightly orders, like the Almoravides transmitted their ideology of the holy war, of the *jihad* and *ribat* to their Christian successors. The mortal fear and anxiety before the Last Judgment became a characteristic trait of Spanish religious feelings.[29] The consciousness of belonging to 'the chosen people of the orthodox' determined the Islamic mentality and the Spanish character. Despite the most terrible acts of violence, Spain remained bound to its Islamic heritage and to that smouldering, Asiatic-African popular underground which the rule of Romans, Goths, Arabs, Hapsburgs and Bourbons could never subdue. The struggle between above and below, between ideologies, rulers, styles of religion, legal systems and the archaic folk underground which went on in the cultures and nations of Europe, was most concretely and remarkably illustrated by Spain's history.[30]

Spanish art can help us to understand the spiritual struggle. Lützeler said of the Cathedral of Zaragoza:[31] 'Christian religiosity hovers over the abyss of a different metaphysical feeling; the Arabic mosque ... The absence of direction leads the worshipper to lose himself in a mysterious ubiquity.' The heavy darkness of Spanish interior architecture is found again in the backgrounds of Ribera and Zurbaran, in Murillo and Valdes Leal. Even the brightnesses in Goya are set against a demonic black. Ignatius was to immure himself in this darkness as an atonement, and John of the Cross, saw it as 'dark night'.[32] Black and brown, the colours of the lower class, predominate by contrast to the Roman-liturgical colours of power, red, gold, blue.† 'The light rarely

---

*The French Revolution was likewise a people's struggle for the purity of the nation against the vices of an aristocracy and high clergy of foreign extraction.

†In a sense the brown of the Brownshirts was a perverted Franciscan heritage and folk dress.

exerts an effect. It is almost unmotivated and lost. There is something jolting about it, since it struggles for the heights, half-smothered by a misty vapour.'[33] Even the bright, constructive intellectuality and iridescent mysticism of the Moors was absorbed by the folk underground.

In Spain, architecture was essentially Moorish until well into the seventeenth century. Moorish art was 'a true kingdom which even after the political defeat of Islam lived on substantially in the conquerors'. Texts in praise of Allah were found on altar antependia. The Moorish ornamentation, however, was interlaced by the jungle-architecture of the Spanish baroque. The final section of the clock-tower of the Santiago de Compostela Cathedral, consecrated to the 'Moor-killer', resembled an over-ripe fruit. The architecture in the famous sacristy of the charter-house in Granada became a 'volcano of decoration'. Deeply mythical algae, nodes of fruit, a 'religiosity of a thousand stimulations', as if consecrated to an Asian fertility God, poured over this 'most incredible work of vitalistic architecture on European soil'.[34] In an orgy which extinguished the spiritual entity called man, sudden floods of pain and voluptuousness became manifest. The love of painting horror scenes, and dreadful presentations of the Passion burst out in the blood plastics in which the blood appears in every phase of its coagulation, smearing, and flowing. The churches were filled with the pictures and statuary of the heads of decapitated saints and sawn-off bodies. This orgiastic spirit expressed itself in the monstrous obscenity of Spanish colloquial speech[35] and in the bullfight as the only Dionysian communal ceremony which Europe still possesses.*

The folk tradition was only superficially touched through Christianization. Whoever wanted to live as a Christian went to a monastery. In 1623 there were 32,000 Franciscans and Dominicans and in 1626 there were 9,088 monasteries for men. At that time 30 per cent of the population may well have belonged to religious orders, but they had little effect on the land and its people, who still surrendered to the primal powers. Year in year out, the fields, olive groves and vineyards were destroyed by the wandering herds of the *Mesta*. Sometimes as many as six million head would be driven across the countryside and there was no recourse against the special privileges of the *Mesta*, who continued to roam at will until 1836. In 1812 the first genuine Spanish constitution, imposed by Napoleon, abolished tortures and the Inquisition. Ferdinand VII re-introduced it and in 1848 twelve Spanish Catholics wrote to a Protestant pastor that they had decided to extirpate heresy in their city: 'Do not compel us to besmirch our hands with your blood ... For even though the official Inquisition is officially abolished, it nevertheless continues to live in the national spirit.'[36]

The people, as in Russia and Byzantium, harboured a wild hatred of foreigners. After the twelfth century it was turned against the French[37] and, long before Luther, against 'the German dogs'.[38] All strangers were viewed as enemies. German printers and merchants, Moorish nobles and Jewish bankers, Italian humanists and English sailors threatened to rob Spain of everything:

*All rise to honour the bull fallen in sacral struggle, who is at once hero and demon.

the purity of her blood and faith, her rule on sea and land, her language, spirit and soul.

The first attempt to bring 'the light of Christian-humanist enlightenment' into this world was made by Francisco Ximenez de Cisneros and his circle.[39] Ximenez was a Franciscan, Isabella's confessor after 1492, Primate of Spain after 1495 and the Grand Inquisitor in 1507. He fought against the ecclesiastical nobility for twenty years in order to bring about an inner renovation in the Spanish church. He was not able to get rid of the gigantically swollen clerical proletariat, but he trained a monkish élite which sympathized with Erasmus. It was the advance guard of reform Catholicism and not far, inwardly, from Protestantism. In 1498 Cisneros founded the university of Alcala de Henares. There was no law faculty, since Cisneros detested jurisprudence, no place for canon law, because he loathed canonists. Everything was to be centred on philosophy and theology. Thomism, Scotism, and Nominalism each received a chair. This was a sensation for the awakening intellectual Spain. Salamanca, alarmed, replied competitively by establishing three nominalistic chairs for theology, philosophy and logic. The second novelty in Alcala was the direct study of the Bible with the help of the ancient languages. Chairs were to be established for Greek, Hebrew, Arabic and Syrian. Cisneros established a small Academy for biblical research in his palace, and after 1502 assembled humanists as his collaborators. The entire polyglot Bible (Latin-Greek-Hebrew) was available in print on 10 July 1517. This work was created by converted Jews and humanists trained in Italy and Paris. Their leader was Lebrixa, who with Erasmus established the right to free biblical research and criticism. The object was to convert Spain to the pure Gospel. Although Erasmus had edited the Greek Bible, the *Novum Instrumentum* in Basle, the Protestant reform had still not started. Catholic reform seemed to be moving ahead of it. When Cisneros died, his biblical research vanished, the men and women of the religious reform were slandered as 'Lutherans' (Lebrixa's teacher, Pedro de Osma was called the first Protestant) and denounced and persecuted as *Alumbrados* and *Illuminati*.

Inspired Dominican and Franciscan nuns, Jewish *conversos* and a circle of Enthusiasts, had made up the membership of the early Spanish reform movement. After 1517, the influence of Erasmus began to dominate the purely Spanish influences.[40] In his foreword to the Greek New Testament and in the *Paraclesis ad Philosophiae Christianae Studium* (1516), Erasmus had already proclaimed that the translated Bible belonged in the hands of every woman, every peasant, weaver and pilgrim. The theologians were the arch-enemies of the use of the Bible among the people. But the true theologian could be a weaver or a day-labourer who hears and follows the word of Christ in the Gospel. In 1517 Cisneros invited Erasmus to Spain. Unlike Maximos the Greek, Erasmus shrank from the tremendous task: *non placet Hispania* he confessed to Thomas More. For him Spain was a different, strange, terrible world. The secret anti-semitism of this Low German may have been a factor in his decision. Like many Europeans he considered Spain to be completely Judaized. Despite this refusal, a canonist in Seville translated his *Querela Pacis*. In it Erasmus condemned Christian kings for starting wars in order to strengthen their tottering authority over their own people. The book made no impression on Spain. Minds were not yet ripe enough for this call to peace.

In 1522 Erasmus dedicated his paraphrase of the Gospel according to Matthew to Charles v. Despite Luther and his own denunciation in Rome and Spain, he stoutly upheld his old convictions: the Gospel is wholly unknown to the broad masses, it must therefore be translated in all national languages from German to Hindustani, since many simple people do not even understand the meaning of the *Credo*. Erasmus was championed by Gattinara, Chancellor of Charles v, the Bishop of Valencia, Pedro Ruiz de la Mota, and Dr Luis Nuñez Coronel, who had been a shining light of scholasticism in Paris. Pope Adrian vi, Erasmus hoped, would make peace in the world through a reform of the Church. As a *citizen of the world* (as he proclaimed himself in his letter to Zwingli)[41] Erasmus came to the court of Charles v of Spain in 1532 with his writings. And here he became the soul and the spirit of a religious revolution which gripped the universities and all those who yearned for reform of the Church. Erasmus brought the Gospel and Paul, and exerted a vitalizing and edifying influence.[42] A volume of his selected essays appeared in Latin bearing the coat-of-arms of Archbishop Fonseca, printed by Eguia, the university printer of Alcala. The Grand Inquisitor himself approved the Spanish translation of the *Enchiridion*.

The country was intellectually and spiritually parched and famished. In 1523, as in the eighteenth and twentieth centuries, Spain had translations of the Bible so long as the three religions (Christian, Jewish, Islamic) lived peacefully alongside one another. Bibles were forbidden after the expulsion of the Jews, since it had been noticed that many who had become converts under compulsion taught their children the Mosaic law from the Bible.[43] Anyone who did not go into a monastery remained without any religious or secular teaching. The Erasmian Archbishop of Valencia, Manrique, wanted to provide preachers since the whole country thirsted for them. Sermons were held in cities only eight times a year. Six hundred localities in the diocese of Valencia had not heard a sermon since they were Christianized,[44] and Valencia was the best-ordered region. Catalonia, for example, drew its preachers from Valencia.[45]

Spanish Erasmianism was inseparably linked with the movement of the *Illuminati*, the *Alumbrados*, the *perfecti* and the surrendered. All of them were concerned with an inner-directed Christianity, a living personal experience of grace. God was sought in their own souls, in the full renunciation of the world and worldly things. Tauler and the *devotio moderna* were introduced to Spain at the same time as Erasmus. Francisco d'Osuna, in his *Tercer Abecedario*, taught that external church ceremonies were nothing without the inner emotion of the heart. Alacaraz taught: 'The love of God in man *is* God.'[46] Melchor

Cano was later to see the essence of the *Illuminati* in this statement. In 1524 Francisco Ortiz preached, before the imperial court in Burgos, that Christ is as completely present in the souls of the righteous as he is in the altar Sacrament. This statement was repeated by the future imperial preacher Gil Lopez who, like Ortiz, was a pupil of Francisca Hernandez. In this early period the right and left arms of the religious reform movement were hardly separable, although the orthodox *recogidos* (collected ones) attempted to protect themselves from the heterodox *dejados* and *perfectos* (the serene and the perfect).

The principal book read by these *Illuminati* was not Luther's (in 1525 three Venetian galleys loaded with Luther's writings were confiscated in Granada) but the *Enchiridion Militis Christiani* which appeared in Spanish in 1524.[47] Erasmus had written the *Enchiridion* because of his enthusiastic discovery of St Paul. He proclaimed the demands of the conscience. Popes, kings, prelates, all follow the masses and their inclination towards evil. Only a small flock is prepared to follow Christ in purity, poverty, simplicity and to it alone is the kingdom of God promised. He enlarged the pietist attitude of the *devotio moderna* into a criticism of the enlightened religious rationalism of the time. He linked his demand for an inner-directed Christianity with a repudiation of the bad clergy which was perverting the people through superstitious practices, and which was itself superstitious and tyrannical. This criticism caught fire in Spain. Maria Cazalla constantly cited the *Enchiridion* to prove that the entire cult of the Church was only a Jewish ceremonial complex. The strongest effect was achieved by the statement: *Monachatus non est pietas*. If monasticism no longer validated piety and embodied true spirituality, then all of Spain and her old church structure was a chimera.

It is possible that Ignatius of Loyola abolished choir, prayers, seclusion and uniforms in his Orders under the influence of *Monachatus non est pietas*. The right and left wings of the reform movement were not yet separated in these years 1523 to 1532. The young Ignatius, as a student in Alcala, had been referred to the *Enchiridion* by his confessor, Miona. Miona, who himself became a Jesuit twenty years later, was at that time a friend of Bernardino Tovar, the guiding spirit of Erasmianism in Alcala, where Ignatius himself was considered an *alumbrado*. He formed an apostolic lay group with some poor students and they distributed alms. Much of the money belonged to Diego de Eguia, whose brother Miguel de Eguia, the book printer, was a great friend of Erasmus. In 1526 and 1527 Ignatius and his friends were forbidden by the Inquisition to conduct missions. In Salamanca he was once again warned, when he claimed the Holy Ghost to be the initiator of his missionary endeavours among the people.[48]

The evidence of the influence of Erasmus and this early reform movement on Ignatius is overwhelming. His *indiferencia* (indifference), the prerequisite 'for finding God in all things' was not far from the 'giving oneself to God' of the *dejados* and the *recogidos*.[49] He was close to the spirit of Tauler when he wished to give himself to God 'as if he were a snowflake falling from heaven'. His maxim 'Thy love and grace suffice for me' accorded with the *Enchiridion*. Although Ignatius severely rejected Erasmus later as sons so often reject their spiritual fathers,[50] he included a selection from Erasmus's best writings in the colleges and schools of his Order: Cicero, Virgil, Demosthenes, Erasmus, Melanchthon and Sturm were the guides.[51] Slowly, hesitatingly, his young Order detached itself from mysticism, and the ecclesiastical and political radicalism of the Erasmian early reform. For a long time it refused to participate in the policy of persecution which had been adopted in 1533.

From 1527 to 1532 Spanish Erasmianism experienced its high point in the service of the world policy of Charles v. The Erasmians at the court seriously considered a world reform through the Emperor. Erasmus himself did not share these dreams. He aimed for peace through the balance of power among the Christian princes. The imperial policy was conducted under the slogan *un Monarca, un Imperio, y una Espada* (One Monarchy, one Empire and one Sword). The days of Ludwig of Bavaria again came to life. But the Emperor failed. His efforts to induce the rich Spanish Orders to give him money for the Turkish war were in vain. Spanish monasticism replied with a public accusation against Erasmus at a session of the Cortes at Valladolid in 1527 and demanded an investigation of all his works by a theological commission of monks. The Emperor, the archbishop, the Inquisition, the Benedictines, the Bernardines, the Cistercians and the Jeromites were for Erasmus, and only the two mendicant Orders (Dominicans and Franciscans) were against him. He was criticized for a profusion of heresies, and especially for his demand for religious tolerance. After this attack had been defeated, a general staff of Erasmians (Valdes, Vergara, Virnes) began a counter-attack.[52] Between 1527 and 1533 a broad stream of Erasmian thought deluged Spain, guided by a small élite. It was directed at women, who constituted Erasmus's main public, bourgeois merchant princes and reform-oriented humanists, but it also penetrated deeply among the lower strata of the population.

The year 1527 in which Machiavelli and Castiglione died was a crucial one in the developing struggle over Erasmianism. The Valladolid conference on Erasmus was held, but equally as important, in that same year imperial troops sacked Rome. The horror of the *Curia* led inexorably toward the anxiety and narrowness of the Counter Reformation. The Franciscan General, Quinones, told the Emperor that if he conducted himself in such an unseemly way towards the Pope, then he could no longer be called Emperor, but certainly a Captain of Luther's. This was dangerous. Alfonso Valdes wrote his *Dialogo de las Cosas Ocurridas–Roma* in defence of the Emperor and as proof that the sack of the city was an act of judgment by God.[53] It was a long accusation against the warmongering papacy and against Rome's avarice where a price was set on everything from Communion to Extreme Unction. With sober irony Valdes described the atrocities of the imperial soldiery in Rome. But what were they compared to the scandals of the whore-mongering cardinals and the atrocities of the *Curia*? Was it so bad if Rome were plundered and its relics carried off? Most of them had been hawked about all over the world. 'I myself have seen the foreskin of Christ in Rome, Burgos, Antwerp; in France alone there are more than 500 teeth of the Child Jesus. The milk of the Mother of God, the feathers of the Holy Ghost are preserved in many places.' By the sack of Rome God had opened the eyes of Christendom so that it could see how sunken in superstition it was.

Through Valdes, the Erasmus of the *Encomiom Moriae* spoke, and in Valdes's *Peregrinatio religionis ergo* Calvin found the inspiration for his treatise on relics. This total rejection of the archaic world, of its magic-sacramental cosmos, was rooted in the *devotio moderna* of the Low Countries. It now became politically virulent on a world scale through the pens of these Spanish humanists. In his great accusation against Catholic paganism Valdes sought to prove that the old pagan Gods were represented in contemporary Catholicism by saints. Thus Mars was St Jacob and St George; Neptune was St Elmar; Bacchus was St Martin, Venus was Magdalene; the dionysian bull sacrifice had become the bullfights in honour of St Bartholomew. This dialogue was circulated all over Spain, and Ferdinand Columbus had it copied in 1528 for his library in Seville. When the papal nuntius Castiglione, the famous author of *Cortigiano*, ordered it to be destroyed the Grand Inquisitor Manrique declared that he could find nothing bad in it. Indeed some of the pages were very edifying! Manrique told him that writing against the morals of the pope and the clergy was not a sufficient reason to institute a trial for heresy. This was the imperial, Erasmian Spain of 1528.

Valdes now composed his main work, the *Dialogo de Mercurio y Caron*. It was a great utopian expression of the bewildered wisdom of a Christian man of the enlightenment, not unlike More's *Utopia*. A cardinal, a bishop, a nun, and adviser of the French king, etc. are seated in Charon's boat on their journey to Hell. Only a simple married man from among the people and a Franciscan have found the way to Heaven. The hell-bound souls do not understand why they have been damned. Have they not performed a thousand services for the Church, purchased indulgences, etc.? Mercury then tells them of his journeys through Christendom which is sunk in lust for power, luxury, lies and bellicosity, and asks: Are you not ashamed to call yourself Christian, since you live worse than the Mohammedans or wild beasts? You do not know what true Christian living is. You persecute as fools and criminals every handful of simple laymen who let God enlighten them or begin a life of the practical imitation of Christ in constant inner prayer! In the final text Valdes deleted an invective against chastity (*monachatus non est pietas!*) and portrayed several noble priestly characters. Basing himself on Erasmus's princely paragon, Valdes projected a new image of the good Christian king.

Machiavelli had Spain in view when he described Cesare Borgia (Borja) and Ferdinand of Aragon as the type of the modern despots of the national state.[54] As Ortega y Gasset put it, his 'prince' was the 'intellectual adjunct of an Italian to the deeds of two Spaniards'. Historians tend to present Spanish politicians and thinkers as the opponents of Machiavellianism, but this makes sense only if one remains aware of the subtlety of the interconnection. The practice and even the ideology of Machiavellianism and of the totalitarian system of modern absolutism were presented to the world by Spain. It is no accident that nineteenth century South American dictators still embodied Machiavelli's fox and lion in a classic unalloyed form, but it was not the Aristotelian-scholastic political scientists of Spain who created the true anti-type to Machiavelli, as is so often presumed, but the Erasmians, who were the first to dare to introduce purely Christian categories into political thought. The good King Polydorus, like all the positive characters in Valdes, had gone through a purgatory of sins and atonements until grace overwhelmed him. The inner transformation of the King brought about the reformation of his state and, with the permission of the Pope, he also reformed the Church. The King was bound to the people through the social contract. When he failed to carry out his obligations, the people were also released. The King was to be educated along Christian lines and the nobility obliged to let its sons be taught a trade and the liberal arts. New, industrious cities arose, and unbelievers voluntarily converted to Christianity. Polydorus's counsels to his son contained the highly important Erasmianism ideas about peace. Under the pressure of the political relations of the time, Valdes did not dare to condemn war against unbelievers openly and completely, but limited it to defence and pointed out that a 'terrible poison hides' behind the war against unbelievers, that disintegrates one's own society and one's own state.

Erasmus's ideas of peace and tolerance brought about catastrophe for the Erasmians. The world wanted war. This became clear to them when they came to Italy in 1529 with the imperial court for the crowning of the Emperor by the Pope. When Charles v landed in Genoa, Juan Gines de Sepulveda greeted him with a speech against the Erasmians. He censured the 'sacrilegious opinion' that 'Christian tolerance' forbade fighting against unbelievers with the sword. Actually Erasmus had for a long time declared himself against all wars, even wars against unbelievers, although finally he yielded and recognized a conditional right to war against infidels in his *Consultatio de Bello Turcico.* Sepulveda, however, came from the school of the Italian Aristotelians. The state had the right to use all natural means for its aims and for the commonweal. There was no room for enthusiasts and enthusiasms like those of Erasmus about peace and about the political power of the intellectual and spiritual transformation of the individual.

The crucial figure in the struggle over the Erasmian heritage was the Emperor himself. The vast questions of colonial policy and administration, which he had to determine, have altered the subsequent history of the world, and his failure to establish a responsible authority in the colonies was part of the broader failure which his life involved.[55] Charles v, as the last Burgundian, was a product of that unique atmosphere in 'the autumn of the middle ages'.[56] At the court of the Dukes of Burgundy the very old, the ecstatic and the daringly new mixed in a remarkable way. There was an unprecedented spirit of self-confidence. The men of the court of Charles the Bold believed that the Burgundian lands were the best lands of Europe, the *terres de promision*.[57] *C'est en ce monde une paradis terrestre*, sang Molinet. This earthly Paradise was not glorified without warrant. The Celtic, Greek and Roman heritages had created the most intellectually radiant centre in this region stretching from the Low Countries to the Mediterranean Sea. Charles the Bold took after his Portuguese forbears physically. His character bore the projecting spirit of the great enlightened rulers of the World of the Three Rings, alloyed with the archaic heritage of the north. The Burgundian region was a hodgepodge of the alien elements and its pattern of rule created the model for the mastery of Spain. Charles the Bold developed a pompous, strictly formal court ceremony which aimed to overcome anxiety and worry through strictness of form. Charles v introduced it to Spain. 'Orders of the Fleece', the idea of the crusade, and the assumption of the role of saviour of Christianity, was Burgundy's programme. This was also the programme of Charles v and of Spain. Burgundian culture, overburdened by many different undergrounds and super-structures, was a melancholy one. Its melancholy was 'horrid in Hugo van der Goes, elegiac in Gerard David, sickly in Lucas van Leyden, titanic in Peter Breughel'.[58] A general gloominess hovered over its literature. But the melancholy was fruitful in the *devotio moderna*, in the *Imitation of Christ*, in Erasmus and Charles v, who were indeed fellow countrymen, and in Philip ii.[59]

If the Crown did not give up the struggle for a humanization of the *ecomienda* and for the legal establishment of the Indians, the credit for this belongs to Bartolemé de Las Casas, (1474–1566). What Erasmus, Valdes and Vives had preached, this simple layman lived. He experienced the obligation of the Gospel while living on his *ecomienda*. Transformed himself by the experience of the spirit of God, he intended to change the world. In 1515 he went back to Spain in order to represent the cause of the Indians at the court of Charles v. Cisneros appointed him procurator general of the Indians. He became a Dominican in 1523 in the hope of winning some support in his struggle. He crossed the ocean seven times to procure suitable decrees for the Indians from the Emperor and the Pope. It was he who, in order to protect the weak Indians, advocated the importation of strong Negroes as slave labour. Spain cannot forget him since his *Destruccion de las Indias* was soon translated in all languages. This ruthless portrayal of a cruel colonial régime led to the anti-Spanish historical criticisms of the Dutch, English and French.[60]

Unshaken by all his failures, Las Casas began in time to radiate a uniquely benevolent influence. The Indians were viewed by many theologians and jurists as barbarians, as morally and humanly inferior servants. Las Casas denied it and fought restlessly for the improvement of their lot. The 'Indian Council', the Spanish legislation for the Indians (culminating in the *Leyes Nuevas* of 1542),[61] the new natural and political law and the colonial ethics of Vitorio, Soto and Suarez, were results of the work of this man. Las Casas carried the Erasmian ideas of peace, freedom and tolerance to the New World, ideas which were being destroyed in the old.[62]

When Charles v returned to Spain again in 1533, there were no more Erasmians at his court. The spiritual climate of Spain had completely changed. Relentlessly Castilian Spain had eliminated the other Spain and the Europeanizing humanists. 'Castille destroyed Spain.'[63] The brief open period which had begun in 1480 with the invitation to foreign scholars and the reform movement around Cisneros, had already been limited by the expulsion of the Jews in 1492 and the supervision of printers ten years later. By the 1530's everything seemed to become narrow and hard again. The government vigorously suppressed the intellectual and folk underground.[64] Rodrigo Manrique, the son of the famous Grand Inquisitor, movingly complained of the darkening in Spain where every educated person and scholar was being terrorized, declared a heretic, persecuted as a Jew, etc. 'Our country is a country of envy, arrogance and barbarism.'[65]

Juan Luis Vives (born 1492 in Valencia, died 1540 in Bruges) was the greatest Spanish humanist. A friend of Erasmus, Budé and More, he had been a professor at Oxford from 1522 to 1528. Afterwards he lived in sickness and poverty until his death, faithful to his motto, 'Without Complaint'. He lived the heroic life of a layman who had been seized by the spirit of the Gospel. All the potential greatness of Spanish Erasmianism was embodied in Vives. He petitioned his friend Pope Adrian vi to call a reform council for the renovation of the Church and Christianity. This could only take place under peaceful conditions, and in his commentary on Augustine's *De Civitate Dei*, Vives criticized the war policy of the *Curia* (for which he was put on the Index several times). He demanded the prohibition of all wars. No European before the twentieth century gave the problem of peace a more penetrating consideration than Vives. He constructed a new doctrine of the state by synthesizing natural law, Roman law (Cicero) and Christian ethics. Peace would come only from a new education of the individual, the family, the masses and nations. Vives was the first to perceive the vital question of 'one world', the community of nations of the twentieth century. As 'the father of empirical psychology' (*De Anima et Vita*, 1538) he strove to bring into daylight the long neglected and overshadowed underground of man.

Vives was the initiator of public high schools which became the basis for Bacon, Comenius and the Encyclopediasts and modern education for women.[66] He combined the tradition of primitive Christian experience and the methods of city administration in Bruges in his welfare programme and sought to lay the spiritual and social basis for the life of a Christian as peacemaker. Peace can grow only when the individual can live morally, as a Christian, in the world.[67] The family was the basic unit in the construction of a peaceful world and in 1528 Vives formulated his doctrine of the duties of the married man. This was a bold thrust into the unexplored areas of Christian anthropology and social doctrine, a venture beyond the old linear ideologies. It was an attempt to think of the whole man in a new way amid the breakdown of the archaic society. The significance of this venture has only been realized again during the last fifty years. The movement for the 'open family', the struggle of F. Künkels, E. Rosenstock, Michels, Weizsäcker and others for a new Christian anthroplogy, in its much maligned daring could call on this pioneer. Vives's ideas quickly became fruitful in western Europe. The civic welfare programme for the poor in Venice, Lyons, Antwerp, Paris were guided by the principles of *De Subventione Pauperum* (1526). Secularized neo-Calvinism was also influenced by it, as was the *humanisme dévot* and Francis de Sales. In Spain, he shared the fate of the Erasmians, personally ostracized, persecuted and then intellectually plundered.

The Spanish reaction against Erasmianism condemned the Erasmians as *Alumbrados, Illuminati* and Lutherans. This was a reasonably correct, instinctive association. The Erasmians were indeed related to the left-wing tendency of a great reform movement. A wave of trials began. The cities and universities of Flanders and Germany began to be filled with Spanish emigrants, who had been denounced as Lutherans in their homeland. Some of those forced to emigrate actually found their way to Luther. Juan Diaz took part alongside Bucer in the religious disputations in the Parliament of Regensburg. In 1546, his brother Alfonso had him murdered by a servant to wipe out the stain on the family honour. Francisco de Enzinas, Melanchthon's friend, translated the New Testament into Spanish and dedicated it to Charles v. He was then arrested as a Lutheran, but mildly treated by the imperial authorities in Brussels. He fled to Melanchthon and became first a Protestant and later professor of history at Oxford. Until the fifties he formed a bridge between official Spain and the Spain in emigration. The Inquisition and typical Spanish historiography usually portray the situation very simply: students and educated persons contracted highly infectious, heretical ideas in the wicked north and began to declare themselves as Lutherans. The historical actuality is more complex. These Lutherans came from Spanish Erasmianism and the early reform of Cisneros. Their spirit of reform was undoubtedly strengthened by their European experiences. Carranza, later a famous Primate of Spain, is an example. Because of his experiences at the Council of Trent, in the Italy of the Waldensians and the Catholic reformers, he became a believer in justification through faith which doctrine was widely accepted in places remote from Protestant Germany. Carranza was entirely a product of Erasmus. Dr Constantino, the best preacher of Spain, died in Seville as the head of the Lutherans. His writings were no more than a heart-warming evangelism, full of trust in the grace of God, and an Erasmian mistrust of all the external trappings of the faith. Like Carranza, his only crime was to have turned to the simple man in the street and appealed to his moral conscience.

In this atmosphere the Spanish theologians and political thinkers struggled to bring about a rebirth of Thomist scholasticism and to create a new theory of the state and the new international law.[68] Characteristic of all of them was a sober view of the conditions of the time and an increasing consideration of the collaboration between man and God, grace and freedom. They were concerned to restore the balance between God and man. Francisco de Vitoria (1483 or 1486 to 1546) who fathered the renaissance of scholasticism in Salamanca, had studied in Paris for a long time. He wanted to revive the belief in reason as a gift of God. His work united ancient philosophy and its natural law with a faith that possessed the power of religious reform and the openness to comprehend the world. He was the democratic Thomas Aquinas. Soberly he established the borders between absolutism and divine grace, and in his famous *Relectio de Indis* sharply criticized the Spanish colonization of America. Vitoria did not accept universal rule of the emperor or pope.[69] No war to convert indigenous populations through violence was permissible. There was no natural law of conquest in the name of a higher civilization or a better faith. Vitoria neatly distinguished between nature and supernature, which was enormously difficult to do after Luther, Calvin and the Nominalists had dismembered their respective spheres. His 'secularization of internal law' for which he is still blamed by Spaniards today was nothing but Aristotle's and Aquinas's yes to a broad sphere of natural order.[70] The corollary of this affirmation was the right to free trade, the right to emigration, the freedom of the seas. As Suarez pointed out, 'The governments of pagans are as legitimate as those of Christians!' For the first time, from the orthodox side, the world was viewed as a lawful community of states, peoples, races and persons of different faiths and different political structures. Only a philosophy of law that based itself on a new theology could be so free in its thought.

The influence of Vitoria was particularly evident at the Council of Trent, where there were sixty theologians from Vitoria's school alone.[71] The highpoint of the Council was the justification decree of 13 January 1547. According to it sins were not only covered (as Luther asserted) but truly remitted and inwardly destroyed. Justification was not only an outer favour of God and a mere attribution of Christ's justice, but a true inner renovation and sanctification through grace and love, which is infused into the soul through the Holy Ghost.[72] This justification decree displayed an insight of extreme psychological refinement. It analysed the act of faith and constituted the man of modern times, who was aware of his powers and possibilities precisely because he was a fallen man, tainted with original sin. At any time he could decide for grace, if he would make use of his will. This was an enormous exaltation of man, and its adoption was a triumph for the Spanish theologians in Trent. The Franciscans from Cisneros's school opposed this adjustment in the relationship between sin and grace, but the Salmaticensians fought successfully for their point of view.[73]

The best mind of the Salmaticensians was Domingo de Soto (d. 1560) who elaborated the *powers of fallen men* and the *rationality of predestination* (against any arbitrariness of God and man).[74] Soto, a pupil of Vitoria, was Charles v's confessor and presided during the disputation between Las Casas and Sepulveda. He was visibly impressed by Las Casas because his theology posited the co-operation of nature and supernature, man and God. It followed that there ought also to be a new collaboration between Spaniards and Indians and between men of different faiths and cultures. This was the essence of *Catholic Enlightenment* and was, as theology, the great result of the political and religious efforts of the Spanish Erasmians in the preparatory years of the Council.

Pope Paul III had once offered Erasmus a cardinal's hat, and then appointed a series of bearers of the Erasmian 'third force' as cardinals: Contarini, Morone and Pole. In his *De Libero Arbitrio*, Erasmus had taken a stand against Luther not as a liberal humanist but as one deeply gripped by the consciousness of the almighty power of grace. Thus, there was, before it became a stumbling block at the later Trent Council, a *sola fide* theology which linked together Melanchthon, the Spanish Erasmians, the men of the Catholic Reform in Italy, France, England and the 'oratory of divine love'. All these humanists and reformers wanted a strong personal faith and an active collaboration on the part of man in God's work of salvation. At the religious disputations in Regensburg in 1541, the imperial Erasmians achieved a partial agreement with the Protestants. Granvella, Naves and J. de Weeze proposed to Charles v that he elevate the united formulas to a doctrine of the empire, without bothering about Rome. The imperial-Protestant *Interim* of 1548 in Augsburg was the result of the negotiations between the Erasmian Pflug and the Spaniards Pedro de Soto and Maluenda. The Tridentine reform decree of 1546, on the reform of the study of the arts and biblical science, betrayed a strong Erasmian influence. Erasmus had been dead ten years and his followers were declining because of persecution. Yet his greatest desire – to unite freedom and faith – was rescued by the Salmaticensians and the Jesuits. While waves of new persecutions broke over Spain after 1556, the great Jesuit Salmerón emerged as the defender of Carranza, and the Jesuits developed a theory of the right to resist good enough to suit the Scottish Calvinists.[75]

The triumphal march of the theology of freedom through the world was the work of Ignatius of Loyola. Through his spiritual self-discipline this Basque knight succeeded in stamping a new leading idea on the Spanish nobility. The nobility was at the highpoint of its historical development and also of its crisis. It was in danger of losing itself in the excess of its passions, in the measureless reaches of America, and in the excessive demands involved in the service of the emperor and of the European kings. As a 'noble knight of Christ', *noble caballero de Cristo*, Ignatius spiritualized the earthly service of the king. The longing of his contemporaries and peers for honour was tempered by Christian discipline and freedom.[76] He taught them that the divine majesty and its sovereign will was everything. Yet this supreme king was at the same time the free God over all the world, who had called man to freedom. A spiritual intoxication of freedom pulsed behind the demand for obedience in the Exercises. The Jesuit Exercises and the Calvinist ethic were the two most powerful forces in the moulding of modern European man. The Jesuit was ready to follow the call of God, because God was always greater. He was expected to seek God in all ways, and to find him in all things. By listening attentively he sought to hear God's command to man in concrete, personal situations.

A 'mysticism of deed and rejoicing in the world' arose in the circle of Ignatius's first disciples, *in actione contemplativus*. This new asceticism was supposed to accept the world serenely, receiving it and overcrowding it, as Clement of Alexandria had demanded of a Christian man; he must be *kosmios kai hyperkosmios*, completely worldly and unworldly at the same time.[77] This was the perfection of the Roman tradition in Ignatius. The man of discretion merged Benedict's Rule, part of which was literally carried over into his Constitution, and the Roman tradition of Innocent III and Francis of Assisi.[78] At a time of crisis the great Pope of the middle ages had given action precedence over contemplation and Francis had won joy in the world, in God's creation, from unconditional obedience, work and poverty. Ignatius, whom his great friend and successor Lainez called 'a man of a few truths', never became a highly learned theologian.[79] With a sure instinct he chose what he needed for his internal crusade from the patrimony of the Church Fathers, from the circles of the *devotio moderna* and from the stream of reform humanism around Erasmus and Cisneros.

The strict discipline of the Exercises succeeded in releasing positive forces from the Spanish chaos.[80] The Exercises fascinated the popular and the personal underground of the Spanish nobility and the intelligentsia of Europe. Even more strongly than Dominic, Ignatius succeeded in creating the first religious intellectual movement in Europe. Only that heterodox Neoplatonism and gnostic spiritualism, which since the late antique world flowed as a subterranean current among Enthusiasts and nonconformists of all kinds, was able to exert (and still does) an equally strong fascination on European intellectuals. The first Jesuits already possessed that boundless optimism, that daring courage of exploration and investigation, which a little later was to make the French Jesuits the pioneers of the Enlightenment of the eighteenth century. Ignatius showed the intellectual how he could become a child of God, a saint – *with* all his gifts and values of mind, grace, personality. Ignatius helped European intellectuals come to the same fruitful self-understanding, which Calvin had created for west European merchants, politicians and activists. The Jesuits showed the astonished and eager intelligentsia of Europe how the intellectual could become blessed and holy, through constant accomplishment in his calling as historian, astronomer, jurist, mathematician, nobleman, soldier or politician. Man was to sacrifice his intellectual work to God, calmly surrendering it to the glory of God and to the assistance of the suffering souls and bodies of his neighbour. It was suddenly possible to develop all one's personal forces in religious service. Ignatius released an enthusiasm which led the Jesuits on a world mission to Africa, India, China, Japan and America.

Francis Xavier, the *conquistador das animas*, the missionary of India and East Asia, probably offers the most impressive example.[81] Francis belonged to a Basque noble family which had lost its lands because of its opposition to the Spanish king. The young Francis Xavier drew the logical conclusions from this destruction of his family. He became a soldier of Christ and never hesitated when Ignatius suddenly sent him off. His famous letters show how he grew into his role as missionary, open to the world, mastering ever new difficulties and oddities. Francis Xavier broke once and for all with the traditional idea of sending inferior priests to the missions. Europe's best human patrimony was only just good enough for the pagans, barbarians and infidels.[82] The ambition of the Jesuits to take on alien, distant and difficult tasks to meet the worldly, the unbelieving, the dissenting elements, led them as explorers and missionaries, as church politicians and pastors, to what was probably the most exciting adventure of the mind that modern European intellectual history has known. Jesuits courted Lutherans and Calvinists, atheists and materialists. There was hardly a religious disputation during the seventeenth century in which they did not participate. Henry of Navarre, who as Henry IV made peace between French Huguenots and Catholics, had a Jesuit, Pierre Cotton, as aide and adviser. Cotton, was a bitter foe of the Catholic League which called for a crusade against heretics. Jesuits dared to make a radical criticism of the magic world, of the legends and saintly traditions of the Church. The highly critical *Acta Sanctorum* appeared in Antwerp in 1643. Daniel Papebroch (d. 1617) by dint of hard work established the laws of historical criticism, the methodology of the study of sources and of the historical auxiliary sciences. Bellaremin had already studied at Louvain and given a presentation of the doctrines of the Protestant reformers, which because of its objectivity became a reference work for the Protestants themselves. Trévoux's *Mémoires* successfully competed with the Calvinist periodicals in the Low Countries.

The most alarming side of the Jesuit movement was its theology. The Jesuits developed the idea of blurred conceptions in the intellect. Cognitions are the less true, the more generally they are held. In ethics Molina had already seen that moral statements were less correct if they were broadly formulated. The Jesuits arrived at this revolutionary discovery because of their activity in the world. Daily they observed the layman's need to orient himself and to make decisions among various possibilities and dangers. Such a decision could only be a choice between a greater and a lesser evil. From there, they pushed on to their famous and much criticized theology and ethics of probabilism, which can be roughly equated with modern relativism and functionalism. Men arrive at their convictions on the basis of their probability and they must act accordingly. Clearly they can only make ethical or moral judgments of a contingent kind. The considerations which make up such judgments have no more than relative validity and therefore there can be no conviction certain enough to justify a crusade or a holy war. Molina's ethical theory might be called situational. It went well beyond Platonism, Aristotelianism and the ideologies of old Europe. (It was no accident that the Jesuits were the sharpest critics of the theory of divine right and of the archaic, magic world-order). Thinking of such radical originality was not to recur for hundreds of years.

The Jesuit order originated with the group organized by Ignatius with his six friends in Montmartre in 1534. At his death it numbered twelve provinces with 101 houses and 1,000 members. Confirmed by Paul IV in 1540, in 1542 it reached out to India, in 1549 to Japan and Brazil, and in 1563 to China. With 600 colleges and academies it became the greatest scholastic order and the mightiest educational institution of Europe. Ignatius died in Rome in 1556. In the same year Charles V retreated from active life. The Erasmian generation which had tortured itself in its trials and tribulations between 1500 and 1530 was nearly exhausted. The radical change of climate within Spain began to become terrifyingly apparent. The fires of persecution raged against left and right reformers. Jesuits were persecuted as *Illuminati*, pietists and enemies of the country. The religious reform movement was almost smothered. All this was the expression of a great anxiety and insecurity. People sensed the inner failure of the explosion of overseas expansion and were deeply aware of the failure of Charles V's world mission. The violent attempt to pacify the Low Countries and to make England Catholic again (through royal marriages and missions, and finally through the Armada of 1588), was a kind of desperate, rearguard action. These were quixotic adventures, sallies into a world of enemies and opponents. The Spanish people who had painfully tried to purify itself in the century between the expulsion of the Jews (1492) and that of the Moors (1608) realized that its entire internal struggle had been in vain. Outside, the whole world was full of enemies of Spain, of the pure Faith, and of the majesty of Christ. It tried to paralyse the pain of this awakening in two ways: through the intensified persecution of the heterodox and through the formation of its great orthodox mysticism.

Oh grandes, oh riquismas conquistas, de las Indias de Dios, de aquel gran mundo, tan escondido a las humanas vistas. The author of these words, the mystic Juan de los Angeles was looking for the America of God (*las Indias de Dios*). This great new world that lay so far from human sight was to be found in the soul. The crusade was within. The great mysticism of the golden age arose from the shock which Spain received in the Reformation. The outer devastation of Europe by Protestant heretics increased the horror at the inner devastation of Spain. The Church was corrupt. A disorderly and extravagant mysticism with more than a trace of hysteria and sentimentality was corroding its internal substance. Externally the Inquisition was everywhere. No one was safe, not even the members of the religious Orders, or ecclesiastical superiors.

The great Spanish mystics faced this double threat at all times. In resisting the ecstatic rapture of the decadent, and the fanatical persecution of the Inquisition, they developed a religious consciousness which was tough and flexible. Garcia de Cisneros (not to be confused with the Cardinal) worked out exercises which greatly influenced Ignatius.[83] Bernardino de Laredo, a physician and a Franciscan, pointed to a fruitful approach in his *Ascent of Mt Zion*. Interest in medicine, natural science and Franciscanism became characteristic of the great Spanish mysticism. It aimed at authentic psychic experience, verification and experimentation in the love of God. It wanted to make an exact distinction between individual affects, deceptions and illusions, and genuine contact between God and the soul. Petrus of Alcantara (who deeply influenced Theresa), Diego de Estella (occasionally Philip II's preacher) who celebrated man as deified (*deificado, endiosado*) in his union with God, and Juan de los Angeles, lived and taught Franciscan mysticism. Juan de los Angeles investigated the psychological phenomena of true and false spirituality, of authentic and unauthentic rapture (*raptus*) in God, and spoke of introversions and extroversions. He cited many authors from the World of the Three Rings besides countless rabbinical works, and used ideas from Boethius, Origen, Dante, Luther, Zwingli and Wyclif. Like so many Spanish mystics he was strongly influenced by Tauler, Ruysbroek, Gerson and the *devotio moderna*.[84] On one occasion he also cited Leone Ebreo's *Dialoghi d'Amore*, which was a fundamental work of intellectual Platonic mysticism, influential as late as Bruno and Spinoza. In the late sixteenth century and throughout the seventeenth century Tauler and the men of the *devotio moderna* became the thematic foundation of Spanish quietism. Spanish mysticism grew in a straight line from quietism to a simplified Christian doctrine, which emphasized inner prayer, and rejected all external, pious practices. The arduous struggles of the sixteenth century necessarily ended in spiritual exhaustion. Disposition, feeling, being pious is all and sentimentality absorbed objective being.

When Paul IV, the bitter foe of Ignatius became Pope the harshest Inquisition yet seen was launched. Cardinals Morone and Pole went to prison. Burnings at the stake and expulsions were to extirpate the plague of Lutheranism in Italy. This wind from the Counter-Reformation helped the Spanish reaction after the abdication of Charles V. The ambitious Grand Inquisitor Fernando de Valdes, the Archbishop of Seville, contemptuously brushed aside the new mystical devotional literature, as a 'spirituality for joiners' wives'.[85] He found his best support in the Dominican, Melchior Cano, who fought the mysticism in his own Order as 'pietism' and who raged against all readers of Tauler, Herph, etc. He was especially violent against the Jesuits whom he simply numbered among the *Illuminati* and against the master of the new poetry, Luis de Granada. Granada was a pioneer of the people's language and of the love of nature. Even Ignatius recommended him. He was very much loved in England where his works were translated in 1598. In his mysticism the Erasmian tradition of inner prayer and a Dominican tradition of spiritual prayer that derived from Savonarola fused. His *Libro de la Oracion* owed much to Savonarola and Erasmus (who at that time were often published together).

Fernando de Valdes wrote to Paul v that the Lutherans should not be treated with the same mildness as the lower class Jewish elements and Islamic backsliders. Since they belonged to highly placed families and occupied high positions, they were obviously much more dangerous. Valdes called all the nobles of Spain Lutherans who came from the school of Cisneros and Erasmus, read Tauler and Herph and protected the mystics. In 1558 people were burned at the stake, who only a few years earlier would have escaped with a minor punishment. A visible sign of the beginning of the reign of terror was the trial and sentencing of Carranza, the Primate of Spain. Cano detected the Erasmian heritage in Carranza's *Commentaries on the Christian Catechism*. He sensed a revolution in Carranza's inward Christianity, a revolution which would subvert the entire Church and make scholasticism unnecessary. His first criticism merely declared that Carranza had discussed and presented the Bible in the language of the people. Language became the first battle-ground. The mystics were defenders of the vernacular because they were determined to bring the message of salvation to the people.[86] At the same time, they were often poets and writers themselves. Luis de Leon, one of the great masters of the Spanish language, defended it against the Inquisitors, and denied that Spanish was an improper vehicle with which to discuss noble and lofty ideas. The theologians of the old school and their allies in the Inquisition tried to protect their hierarchical social and religious system by preserving the hierarchy of words and clinging to Latin. *Vive en los campos Cristo.* 'Christ dwells in the fields', was de Leon's answer. De Leon was, perhaps, the greatest of the humanists left in Spain after the persecutions began, and he, too, spent four years in a prison of the Inquisition. Job, Plato, Horace, the Stoics and Erasmus were joined in his breast and produced the renewal of religion mirrored in his commentary on the 'Song of Songs' written for the nun Isabel Osorio.

Valdes's Spanish Index appeared in 1559. Its aim was to annihilate the mystical and humanist writings of the *devotio moderna* and the Erasmians through a strict prohibition of religious literature in the language of the people. The possession of forbidden books was punishable by death.[87] Under the pressure of persecution and suspicion, Theresa and John of the Cross created the Carmelite reform as a bulwark of inner prayer. Despite constant self-examination and self-criticism Theresa and John continued to be suspected of Illuminism, and their books were published only after they died. In 1588 Luis de Leon, the publisher of Theresa's works, still had to defend them against the charge of being dangerous, and even thirty years later his nephew, Basilio Ponce de Leon, had to write a defence of the work of John of the Cross. The *Noche Oscura*, his major work, was accused of being the source of all the *alumbrados* and heresies in Seville. As late as 1601 the Dominican Alonso Giroi demanded a complete prohibition of all religious books in the people's language.

This was the spiritual environment during the reign of Philip ii. Far more than has been generally understood, Philip ii continued to defend and protect the religious and humanistic reform movement. Melancholy, anxious, the heir of his Burgundian blood, the King gradually withdrew from Spanish life, overburdened by the demands of the country. The royal Inquisition owed its annihilating, crushing influence under his rule not least to the hesitation and indecisiveness of his anxiety-ridden conscience. The infinitely slow-grinding mechanism of the Spanish Inquisition was much softer than the brutal aggressiveness and expansiveness of the Inquisition in other countries. In Spain it had to be incited and goaded into a fury over and over again through the 'anger of the people'.[88] The noble cliques and orders feuded with one another in hate and envy.[89] Philip II had defended the work of Erasmus against Rome in Louvain and in the Low Countries, where attempts had been made to put it on the Index. Dr Arias Montano, the King's chaplain, authorized him to assume the protectorate over the polyglot Bible that Erasmus had published in Antwerp. Montano probably also obtained the librarian's post in the Escorial for Fray José Siguenza, the preacher at the court of Philip II. Nothing was more characteristic of the atmosphere around the King than the conversion of Siguenza. For a long time Siguenza had sharply attacked Erasmus, and preached in a flowery baroque style. Suddenly he proclaimed the 'naked gospel' and would no longer hear of Judaism, lawful belief, superstitions, scholasticism and rhetorical phrases! The most important work of religious literature of the era was *Los Nombres de Cristo*. It was an anthology of passages from the Bible and the Church Fathers, compiled by Luis de Leon but at the same time an introduction to the basic verities of an inner Christianity. For Luis, Jesus meant health, his teaching and work of salvation demanded the recuperation of the whole man. To the generation of Philip's time, *Los Nombres de Cristo* was what the *Enchiridion* of Erasmus had been for their grandfathers.

Theresa of Avila would almost certainly have perished if Philip II had not saved her. Her role in Spain was not unlike Luther's in eastern Germany, in that she bore salvation from out of the depths. 'In my most inner recess (*muy muy interior*), in a very great depth – I cannot say how it is, because I have no scientific training', the soul perceived the society of God, the indwelling of the Trinity in it.[90] The kinship and the chasm between Theresa and Luther is evident.[91] For Luther and Theresa man was a battlefield on which God and the devil engage in terrible battle. Theresa experienced the deepest underground, churned up in her own unconscious and in the lives of her own people.[92] The demonic element in mysticism can never be taken seriously enough. Mysticism has been one of the most explosive elements in European history and Theresa, the noblewoman, much concerned over the honour of her house and clan, was an extraordinary example of its power. Her first profound religious experience was inspired by the nobleman Frances of Salcedo, who had practised inner prayer for forty years.[93] The religious lay-movement opened the eyes of the young nun to her own depths and bottomless abysses. But how long and difficult was this way to the mastery of the depths! She herself reckoned (from 1535 on) fourteen years for inner, meditative prayer and thirty-three years (1549 to 1582) for the life of contemplation. This was further divided into two segments each containing two periods: 1549 to 1561 (the period of the quiet prayer of the provisional simple union with God), 1561 to 1582 (the period of the union with God as the perfect union in the spiritual marriage).

Theresa needed thirty-three years in order to collect her new spiritual experiences step by step from sacrifice to sacrifice. Each word corresponded to a concrete accomplishment, a building and a forming of substance in the very core of her personality. Modern artists, poets and geniuses think that they can transcend such painstaking self-discipline. The spiritual history of the last 400 years has seen countless examples of men, from Rousseau to Nietzsche, in whom a moment of inspiration created havoc and disorder because they ignored the wisdom of Theresa. The modern men of genius have been a terrible scourge because they took a moment of blinding illumination to be the direct inspiration of the Holy Ghost. Without discipline, they could neither verify nor control their experiences and they shattered what they touched. There is something terrifying about the rashness and irresponsibility of so many intellectuals, philosophers, poets and artists of recent history. Because they imagine that their momentary illuminations and inspirations are revelations, they easily fall into one or the other gnostic system. They concoct norms of politics and a world-view, whereas they themselves are completely incapable of distinguishing between their own souls and the objective irradiation of the Holy Spirit. The 'encounter with the demon' and with the chaotic underground of her own people was no momentary experience for Theresa,[94] but a consciously accepted life-long struggle, a testing. For Luther, the creator of the German heart and forefather of all German poetry of experience, the 'I' was the sphere of the heart that always rebels against the almighty God who invades it in floods of anger and grace. For Theresa, *man* was the bearer of the responsibility for salvation and for the entire human society. The whole man was an arena of the spirit.[95] Theresa was familiar with Luther's storms, which also broke out in her soul. Often enough she herself wondered suspiciously whether it might not be the devil who was hiding himself in the form of an arrow of light. Her favourite image was the irrigation of the soul through an elaborate system of gardeners' pipes. This was an illusion both to the physical tragedy of the country, that was never irrigated sufficiently and patiently enough (even in the eighteenth century the irrigated areas did not amount to a hundredth part of the country's entire surface) and to her inner devastation. Both outer and inner drought could only be overcome through endlessly patient and tenacious work by the free spirit and will.

Theresa had St Francis's primordial trust in God. She wrote her experiences and observations in books which 'earnest men' compare with 'a holy writing'. Even Luther who announced in his testament that he was a personality not unknown to Heaven and Hell, was never more arrogant. Her horror of

Luther and Lutherans was genuine. They wanted to condemn Christ again and set flames to the world.[96] To spread the Faith or to convert a few heretics, kings should be willing to lose a thousand kingdoms ... Theresa saw France devastated by the Huguenots: 'I would, as it seems to me, have sacrificed a thousand lives to save one or two of the many souls who have perished there.' Her maxim became: 'Among the many enemies of God may at least His few friends be truly good.'

She associated Luther's face with a vision of Hell in which she experienced herself transported there body and soul.[97] 'Here ... it is the soul which rends itself.' Her description of Hell recalls the concentration camp flogging cells and totalitarian torture-chambers. She was led through a long, narrow, dark and stinking passage at the end of which she was pressed into a hollow in the wall. 'In this pestilential place where no hope of any comfort was at all possible, one could neither bend down nor sit.' She saw Protestant Europe and Catholic Spain forfeited to this Hell. In her emotional matter-of-factness she made the following comment on unsecluded Spanish monasteries: 'I do not understand how we can still wonder that there is so much and so great an evil in the Church, if even those who should have served all the rest as models of virtue, have so fundamentally destroyed the work which the Spirit of salvation in past times left behind in the estates of the orders ...'[98]

Theresa began her reform of the Carmelite order at a moment in history which, according to her conviction, was no less fateful than the hour of Francis. Her converts were to be Franciscan in their poverty, 'poor and small in everything, like the stable in Bethlehem in which our King was born!' Determinedly she took cognizance of what had most deeply confused and disturbed the Spanish people: the truth that despite the greatest efforts, including the use of armed violence, it had not succeeded 'in putting out the fire of heresy that reaches out ever more around itself ...' 'Therefore it seems necessary to me, that what happens during a war when the enemy has invaded the whole country should happen here.' By a retreat to the fortresses, the monastery-fortresses, by means of prayer, work, sacrifice and denial, the world was to be wrested from evil.

'I shall say nothing of what I have not experienced through observation of myself or others.' Her writings 'sound like the documents of subjects who provide material for scientific psychology in psychological institutes'. She was always in search of scholars and theologians who were scientifically equipped to test and to explain the authenticity of her mystical experiences.[99] 'There is something great about science.' 'No genuine scholar has yet disappointed me.' This observation was made together with the remark that for seventeen long years she had to frequent the company of insufficiently educated father confessors. 'The security of conscience and the freedom of the spirit is something great.' Theresa knew that there was no absolute security in the spiritual and clerical life, not even for saints! Sobriety, indeed aridity, is all those strong souls need.

Once when she was very anxious over the salvation of certain persons, Christ said to her, 'Daughter, there is a great difference between darkness and light. I am true. No one will perish without perceiving it.' This was *the* great experience of Theresa, with which she absorbed the rapture of St Francis, the joy of Joan of Arc and Luther's experience of the depths. God allowed himself to be perceived, perceived precisely in those deep layers and inner dimensions of personal existence which up to then theologians, scientists and physicians had not touched and which they only dared approach by means of exorcisms, abjurations of demons and magic practices. Calvin tore the spirit as intellect away from the sphere of magic; Theresa raised the soul from the depths into the light of day for critical testing and observation. There was something monstrous in this which perhaps could only have happened in the unusual Spanish situation.

The theologians were horrified by this attempt to reveal the depths. Could this outbreak be from God, they asked themselves? Must it not be from the devil? The father confessors and advisers ordered her 'to show the fig' to the phenomena. (The thumb is pressed through the index and middle fingers.) The Carmelite convent in Medina del Campo still has a device to ward off evil that Theresa herself is supposed to have used against an apparition of Christ, a shell-shaped piece of horn in a metal ring. This was the end of the magic world which had at last destroyed itself. The magic (sexual) means foundered against Christ who for Theresa and modern times finally departed from the orbit of the ancient world, and its magical cosmos. Christ who appeared to Theresa as the Resurrected, comforted her for having used the magic means against him, in obedience to her father confessor. But he did not comfort her when the spiritual director forbade her the inner prayer. 'When, however, even inner prayer was forbidden to me He (Christ) seemed to be very offended. He ordered me to tell those from whom this prohibition had come that this was tyranny.'

The ancient world, including Aquinas and scholasticism, had not dared to pierce the integument of magic. It remained objective in its doctrine of souls. The virtues and burdens and the struggles of the soul were understood in terms of the ruling cosmos of ancient thought. What lay below it, those dimensions of depth, were considered demonic and inaccessible. Medieval discussions of the soul were like the stillness of the sea lit by the divine sun. This sea of the soul has been a symbolic perception since the days of the ancient Egyptians. The Greeks and Romans knew the soul as a sea and realized that it could only be navigated under very special conditions. Theresa was the first to dare to penetrate its depths. In so doing, she made a break in the continuous tradition of Western philosophy which had always chosen to see the soul from the outside. Traditional natural philosophy considered the soul as an objective reality. The new Spanish mysticism of Theresa and John of the Cross was 'directed inwards'. It was 'subjective and anthropocentric'.[100]

The papal nuntius Sega persecuted her publicly as 'a disturbed woman'.

Her most important ecclesiastical friends and collaborators in the reform of the Carmelite Order, John of the Cross and Jeronimo Gracian, were thrown in jail. The frightful persecutions that Gracian had to endure from his own Order, demonstrate emphatically that this whole phenomenon of Spanish mysticism called forth demonic forces of hatred and destruction.[101] In her letters, Theresa often used pseudonyms, so as not to endanger the persons addressed or concerned. She often called Gracian and John of the Cross 'Seneca' or also 'Senequita' (little Seneca) recalling the great Spaniard whose philosophy of resistance to temporal powers has frequently consoled the best Spaniards in times of corruption and absolutism. Theresa and John of the Cross applied Seneca's great imperturbability and the stoical force of quiet and highly concentrated balance of mind to the mastery of the inner self, and to the demonstration of perception of God. This distinguished them fundamentally from all egoistic, subjective and emotional mysticism prior to them.

The Hell which Theresa saw in her vision was prepared for John of the Cross by his own fellow-monks who defended themselves against his reform. They dragged him to Toledo in chains in 1576 and locked him up in a stinking, tiny garret where he could barely stand, sit or lie down. They beat him every evening in the refectory before the entire monastery and threatened to withdraw bread and water from him. They refused him a change of clothes and facilities for washing himself. Yet this man who experienced Hell on earth described Heaven and the way to it through asceticism. The 'prayer of quiet' was the first step of contemplation. The 'simple union' was the second step. Ecstasy and the passive purgation of the mind prepared the soul for spiritual marriage. His works (*Subida del Monte Carmelo, Ascent of Mt Carmel*; *Noche oscura del alma, The Dark Night of the Soul*), are masterpieces of the human spirit.

John of the Cross (1542–91) was the father of modern mysticism and modern metaphysics. He was the son of a Castilian nobleman and a woman of the lowest social class. The woman and her three children were left to their fate by the noble family after the early death of the father. She became a weaver and had a hard time making both ends meet. The boy, John, tried his hand as a joiner's and tailor's apprentice. In this blood-and-honour-haunted world, the young John was put to the test very early. As a hospital nurse and Jesuit pupil he learned how to be patient with others and hard on himself. Some of his most beautiful mystical love songs were written then. In the imagery in the *Dark Night of the Soul* and in his renunciation of grace for the sake of the mystic union with God, the 'Mother', the Arabic, folk religious underground, awoke again.[102] By contrast, Theresa, who was a pure Castilian, hated the south, especially Andalusia.[103] John was determined to compel the maternal south to serve this new Father-Spirit. In his doctrine of mysticism, he intended to hold only to the Bible and personal experience. With its help, however, he abstracted the ego and made it into an experiment of the God-seeking mind. In Theresa's unconscious acceptance of the Greek and early Christian conception of the playing God and man, she had conceived the struggle of the soul as a divine game,[104] and had warned her nuns not to be 'womanish' but to bear themselves like men in all things and as such 'to challenge God so that He can no longer escape us, nor ever want to escape us'.* Through this game, earth could become Heaven. 'Is it not something beautiful that a poor nun of the St Joseph's convent can eventually come to rule over the whole earth and the elements?'

This was exactly John's point of departure. One should live as if there were only God in the world. The ego must test its possibilities in this experimental field where only the relation between the (divine) 'thou' and the (human) 'I' exist. It begins by stripping itself of everything earthly in a scientifically exact, strict and sober manner. Step by step in this experiment it advances ever deeper into God, until it attains the final union. John anticipated the experimental situation of Pascal, and has rightfully been recognized as a precursor of Descartes. In France he exerted a deep influence on Francis de Sales and Pascal, on Bossuet and Fénelon.[105] Lofty intellects have always been fascinated to watch a temperament of great passion and complexity discipline itself and conceive of itself as an experiment as a psychologist or physicist would. He observed each transformation of the nucleus of his personality as if the different stages were processes in a cyclotron.

St John's ascent to the pinnacle of human aspiration was also the end. Only a few natures are capable of such heroism of objectivity. Strong inner forces are needed to maintain mental and spiritual exaltation against one's time and its ruling power. After John and Theresa the intellectual and personal forces of Spanish mysticism diminished, while the desolateness of the political, ecclesiastical and social relations remained. Indeed it became even more frightening from the late sixteenth century onwards. The defeat of the Armada and the failures sealed by the peace of Westphalia in 1648 were only outer signs. Spain had exhausted itself. A thousand-year civil war between the above and the below and between Christians, Jews and Mohammedans had bled her white. She had produced neo-scholasticism, its doctrine of natural law, its mysticism, its world-mission, and the Jesuit order, but these creations were constantly threatened by the Inquisition. Moreover, the inner resistance of the dark forces from the underground had compelled Spanish thought to assume an unassailable purity and objectivity.

Not every one could be a hero and saint like Francis Xavier, Theresa and John of the Cross. The pressure of conformity was imposed on their successors and the tension which it produced everywhere in Spanish life gave rise to certain kinds of thinking which also occurred in the other Catholic countries during the Counter-Reformation. But nowhere did they emerge so clearly as in Spain, because nowhere else was the pressure of victorious ruling powers – absolutism and feudal Church – so overwhelming. Quietism, stoicism, criticism, scepticism, disillusionment, classicism, pantheistic biologism, and in

*cf. Hildegard of Bingen's *tempus muliebre* and her contest of the *ordo virtutum*.

addition the comprehensive criticism of society in literature and art (from the picaresque novels of 1530 via Don Quixote to Goya) were reactions against this terror, and at the same time attempts to replace the lost kingdom and world position through an inviolable inner kingdom of the soul, of the mind and of creative culture.

Jeronimo Gracian, Theresa's protégé, described his eventful life that ended, far from Spain, in a very personal autobiography, *The Pilgrimage of Anastasius*, which in its intense sensibility resembled the confessions of pietism and the 'beautiful souls' of the seventeenth and eighteenth centuries. Shortly before his death, Gracian unleashed a last great attack on quietism (*Leviathan*, 1614). He had already in 1611 deplored the many Catholic quietist books in his *Diez Lamentaciones*. He was certain that such ideas would open the door to Luther.[106] These Catholic authors, reported Gracian, borrowed Tauler, Herph and Ruysbroeck, and treated the whole external cult and its pious practices as the trimmings of religious egoism. The quietists taught that to pray for one's own salvation was selfishness, and to hope for rewards in the other world was wrong. Pilgrimages, indulgences, the cult of saints and the veneration of Mary were of little use. The only thing that mattered was inner prayer, complete imperturbability and surrender to God. Gracian was so disturbed because he knew exactly how close this quietism was to the original orthodox quietism of St Theresa herself. He saw that the perversions of the original, beginning in Spain, were trickling into all western Europe and undermining and loosening Catholic objectivity.

Gracian knew perfectly well that Theresa's mysticism could easily be misunderstood. Her mystical experience of the dialectic of love (for example, in *En las manos de Dios*) had strong quietist overtones. She wanted to accept everything from God: honour or shame, darkness or light, joy or sorrow, drought or flood, foolishness or wisdom, desert or abundant earth, (*Desierto o Terra abundosa*), Heaven or Hell (*Dadme infierno o dadme cielo*). The soul was to seek God in itself, in its own depths. (*Buscando a Dios*): 'Nothing confuses you, Nothing frightens you, Everything passes, God does not change, Patience achieves everything, He who clings to God, needs naught; God alone suffices.' (*Nada te turbe, Nada te espante, Todo se pasa, Dios no se muda, La paciencia, Todo lo alcanza, Quien a Dios tiene, Nada le falta: Solo Dios basta.*) The secularization of this fundamental mystical experience produced stoicism. Resistance to the external church and world order led to quietism.

The stages in the unfolding of quietism can be followed in the life of Juan Falconi (1596-1638).[107] He was the son of a lawyer near Granada, and his works were first published in 1660. Prior to that time they had been distributed in manuscript to the circles of the inner resistance. Although he was soon placed on the Index in Italy (where, as in France, he exerted a powerful influence), he was printed in Spain throughout the eighteenth century.* Falconi

*A history of printers in the totalitarian countries of the sixteenth to the nineteenth centuries is a pressing need in the growth of a genuine intellectual history.

based his ideas on the Fathers, on Tauler, Gerson, and on the Spaniards of the Reform. He wanted to teach all men a simple, easy way to union with God through inner prayer, in a renunciation of external, mechanical practices. For him, complete withdrawal and submission to God's will was possible for the simple man who could be any man in the street. No prelates or kings were required. Falconi led directly to Miguel de Molinos, with whom he shared the phrase, 'How simple, how easy it is after all ...'

Quietism grew in the spiritual climate of the Spanish stoicism of the sixteenth and seventeenth centuries.[108] Both stoicism and quietism owed a great deal to the *devotio moderna* and to Erasmus, whose spiritual testament *The Preparation for Death* (translated many times into Spanish), was a link between quietism and stoicism. As in his *Modus Orandi Deum* (Seville 1546), Erasmus again attacked the external church apparatus. Many poor sinners entered the kingdom of God because they simply placed their whole trust in him, whereas many others, provided with all the Sacraments and ceremonies of the Church were damned. Death quickly became a major preoccupation of the intellectual Spaniard because his personality, cut off from archaic society and the sacred bonds of the old world, was lonely and alone. The poetry of loneliness, the longing for death of the ascetics, and the meditations on death of the Spanish stoics, were rooted in this situation. The passionate self had been cut off from its natural (or more correctly, unnatural, namely historical) conditions. Despairingly and courageously it sought an independent status in order to assert itself against nature and death. Thus Quevedo said that life is a deception and a comedy. Truth lay only in a contempt of life, in poverty and suffering, in death. Job and Seneca had taught the art of the right endurance of this evil, depraved world. Quevedo (d. 1645), a Christian stoic, condemned the decadent, worldly, ecclesiastical society of Philip III and Philip IV in his great political and social satires (*Suenos* and *Buscón*).

Spanish stoicism had a world-wide influence because it was joined by a Protestant stoicism, coming from the Low Countries, the homeland of Erasmus. Similar frustrations had grown out of the bitterness of the scholars over the narrow church world of the Protestant national churches, their regulation of the universities, the quarrels among the sects and finally the martial frenzy of the European parties. Justus Lipsius (1547–1606), the great Calvinist Jurist, Professor in Jena, Leiden and Louvain, became an Erasmian Catholic. He was the founder of neo-stoicism outside Spain 'because he was concerned with the problem of how the philosopher should assert himself in the world, in a world which is evil'.[109] His problem was also the main concern of Spanish intellectuals. Spain had irretrievably split into two hostile worlds. There was one Spain, in which an inflexible ruling caste, a petrified aristocracy and ineffectual king had joined forces with the common people. The understanding between them was evidently deep and genuine.[110] Any inner unrest was effectively restrained by an elaborate apparatus of asceticism, monasteries and court ceremonies. But there was also the other Spain. A handful of intellectuals, scholars and artists kept watch over the heritage of the Jewish-Moorish intelligentsia from the World of the Three Rings, the heritage of the Cisnerian and Erasmian reform.

The protest of these eternal Protestants took different forms. Emigration was the most obvious but least influential one. One of the more interesting of the *émigrés* was the monk, Fernando de Texeda, the author of *Carrascón*. He went to England, became an Anglican and undertook to refute the 'papists' with the help of the authors of the Counter-Reformation, among whom he neatly dissected the Cisnerian from the Erasmian heritage. This type emerged in every century. Jose Maria Blanco (d. 1841), the Canon of Seville, who also ended up in England as a Unitarian and a poet, was a representative of this type in the later eighteenth century. Blasco Ibanez, who wrote his invective against the Spanish Church in France (*La Cathédrale*), represented it in the nineteenth century. In the twentieth century it is impossible to forget those brilliant names who represent Spain in Paris, London, North and South America (Picasso, Madariaga, Sanchez Albornoz, Amerigo Castro etc.). Spanish intellectuals, from Ramon Menendez Pidal up to Carles Cardo and Castro, have never been able to allow the disputation between the two Spains to come to rest because their own existences reflect that historical reality.[111] What George Santayana, an American and Spaniard, confessed about his 'double life' (*doble vida*) applies to many of them. 'I have always been both a Catholic and an Atheist.' 'In natural philosophy I am a cynical materialist, and a Catholic free thinker at the same time.'

Occasionally, historical pressure and inner temptation (exactly as with the Russians), have become too much for these intellectuals and they brusquely break off the disputation between the two Spains in their own breast and become fanatical advocates of the old world. This is, it must be emphasized, the essence of the Romantic's situation, namely of the isolated intellectual in a barbaric land. He has no social or political support for his own nonconformism and the barbaric underground of his own personality constantly entices him to submerge. An extraordinarily striking example of this dilemma was the behaviour of the generation of 1898. Originally liberals and Westerners, they plunged themselves in the 'dark night' of the core of their personalities, and from unrestrained condemners overnight became the blindest enthusiasts for old Spain. Today intellectuals everywhere are tempted to succumb to this solution. They are too weak to remain small islands of resistance against the terror of the internal Inquisition of the totalitarian closed worlds. That is why the '*via crucis* of the civil spirit' in Spain is of such importance to us.

The outer emigration of the Spanish ex-Jesuits (who often became Calvinists), ex-Benedictines and ex-Catholics, always exerted an influence on the inner emigration. Those who stayed behind were always aware of the writings and artistic works of the *émigrés*. They sought their release in several varieties of what has been called the inner emigration. The most conservative form was a scientific criticism.* It discharged itself in scholarly disputes, in the debates of Spanish Thomism and Molinism especially, but also in historical works. The passion for judgment and for critical discovery of one's own intellectual existence was prevented from showing itself in the political and ecclesiastical life. These quiet scholars and scientific critics in the monasteries, archives and remote castles, became powerful when the French enlightenment borne by the Bourbon kings invaded the country. Suddenly the potentialities of independent enlightenment concealed within the Spanish intelligentsia became visible. The Benedictine Benito Jeromino Feijóo y Montenegro with his Encyclopedia (*Teatro Critico Universal*, eight vols., 1726 to 1739) battled against superstitions and backwardness. His work was in no way inferior to the great French encyclopedists who began in 1750. The Frenchified intelligentsia rejected the classical tradition of old Spain in the eighteenth and nineteenth centuries so thoroughly that the world of the great Theresa and of John of the Cross was entirely forgotten and only brought to Spain's consciousness by northern romanticism. To a great extent this rejection was the other side of their terrifying fear of being swallowed by the volcanoes from the people and by the unconquerable ancient powers.

The Spanish (and Italian) classicism of the Counter-Reformation was a unique phenomenon of the 'centre'. It mediated between the inner emigration, the conformists and those who had reverted to the old order. At the same time, it absorbed stoic and quietist influences. This classicism can only be comprehended in the light of the purgings of the intellectual life through the Inquisition between 1500 and 1570. The old clerical and secular nobility, the university clergy and the professors of the Counter-Reformation had triumphed and classicism celebrated the victory over the underground.† Things were to be portrayed according to eternally valid ideals, not as they were in the low earthly world of the manual labourers and women. The classic form was called upon as the guarantee against every heresy, deviation and rebellion. A narrow morality and nationalism was supposed to control the pietistic and illuminated feeling and heart.

After the 'open' Christian humanism had been overpowered, Dominicans and Jesuits brought forward a new humanism of repose, of classicism, of poetry and rhetoric. Ultimately it was a rebirth of the ancient ornamental culture of old, Platonic, noble Europe. It was an escape for the awakened intelligence which found a haven in the school, monastery and theatre. The frequent degeneration into mannerism showed how insecure the consciousness of this classicism was. There are early signs of this degeneration in the

---

*Someday, a thorough investigation of this phenomenon will be made, and we shall see with amazement how many varieties of European conservatism have arisen because of and through it.

†That this underground was far from dead must be obvious to anyone who takes a sober, unbiased look at the orgiastic eruption and of the colossal vitalism of Baroque architecture. Purely spiritual interpretations of this phenomenon are lamentably incomplete.

style of Guevara (d. 1545) who was Charles v's court preacher. Its nervous irritability, its smoothness and technique, aimed to feign and simulate the authentic victory of form over matter.* A high formal culture was created once again in this Spanish-baroque Europe, but it was hollow. It was corroded by an inner cancer: hypocrisy. The split between being and appearance ate away at the conscience of the very best men of the seventeenth century. For them classicism, even scientific classicism, did not prove to be a viable path.

State, Church, and society defended themselves against all reforms, and therefore also rejected any form of open rationalism for which valid themes and historical relevance were absolutely essential. The thinkers in despair fell into scepticism, which occasionally propelled them towards stoicism or a Christian asceticism, but more often plunged them into a pitiless naturalism. Naked, cynical thought-structures thrived on the soil of Spain, both in the mother country and in its off-shoot at the court of Naples. Extreme naturalists whose ideas the Marquis de Sade expressed in his novels, were thoroughly at home in the court society of Naples. The atmosphere in late baroque Naples must have been quite incredible. An atheistic naturalism and nihilism developed before which Nietzsche's Superman looks like a stolid, home-cooked dream of German pietistic spirituality.

'To play with open cards is neither useful nor pleasant.' 'The best thing is to play Providence by holding people in a state of unrest through uncertainty.' 'Evil lies in waiting, and a great cunning is necessary to deceive it. The player never plays the cards which the opponent expects, even less those which he wishes.' The author of these words, Balthasar Gracian became a Jesuit at the beginning of the Thirty Years War. In his *Oraculo Manual y Arte de Prudencia* (1647),[112] he had practically written a manual of the tactics of lying. Through it one can defend oneself against society, while speaking its language for the sake of appearances. His aim was rather different. Gracian worked out these urbane techniques to help the layman assert himself in a world in which only lies, deceit and crime existed. Just as Theresa and John of the Cross had taught that disillusion could be consciously used to free the mind and soul for the struggle for God, so Gracian wanted to free the mind of man so that he could assert himself in the day-to-day struggle for existence. 'The whole of life must be a continuous thinking, so that one does not lose the right way. Repeated reflection and prudence make it possible to determine the course of our life in advance', he wrote. To succeed in this, one must see through society and its ideologies, which only veil the real power relations. Under a pseudonym Gracian wrote his three-volume novel *El Criticon*, which was a radical exposure of the world of the Spanish-baroque ruling classes. Gracian was no cynic. It was not his fault if divine order and human chaos were so manifestly separated in Christian Spain. Gracian wanted to help the layman and ended in a dungeon because of his courage. His world success began when the

*Late Dutch Calvinism, Cartesianism and Counter-Reformation classicism all moved in this direction.

internal political opposition in Louis xiv's France propagated his work. For Spain he proved only that great disillusion could no longer be expressed.

Art and literature were the only vehicles left through which to protest in Spain. The picaresque novels began to appear between 1540 and 1550 and they took up the call for reform in Church, state and society in their Nicodemian sermons. Whores and beggars, through their lives, preached what men ought not to do. The picaresque novel was 'the product of an irregular asceticism, which made an instrument for improvement out of the autobiographical confessions of hardened sinners.'[113] In a thousand masks – of thieves, pimps, cowards, fools – the Nicodemism of a people's opposition, as in the animal epics of the late middle ages, in the buffoonery, and in the Viennese *Wurstl*, subtly proclaimed its rejection of the shallowness, the lust for power and money, the intolerance and the hypocrisy of the ruling classes.

'Each man sees things in his own way', said Don Quixote.[114] Cervantes was a pupil of the Erasmian Lopez de Hoyos. In his *Don Quixote* he announced 'a personal doctrine of freedom and humanity'. This epic was a great enlightenment throughout.[115] It shed a light on the nation's madness and its confused arrogance which was fond of hiding its anxiety behind a strong code of honour, and cult practices of the Church and society. The Spanish Inquisition had seen this at once and deleted many sentences, for example, the sentence that good works without the proper inner disposition are of no worth and the raillery over the useless prayer of a 'million Ave Marias'. Cervantes took over the criticism from the *devotio moderna* and the Erasmians of 'Catholic paganism'. He knew that in the Pantheon in Rome the cult of All-Saints had taken the place of the cult of all Gods, that *la Monda* in Talavera was a pre-Christian feast and that Mary took the place of Venus.[116] He had alluded in the splendid foreword to his aversion against the scholastics and to his devotion to freedom (with the verse from Horace: *Non bene pro toto libertas venditur auro*) and to the commandment to love one's enemy (with the verse from the Gospel). His concept of the nature of Christian charity as well as his most important ethical and religious ideas were symbolized by the *Knight in the Green Mantle*.[117] Green was the colour of salvation in Islam, of the Templars and other sects. The Green Knight led an honest, simple, worldly life without sitting in judgment on others. This Diego de Miranda lived according to a plain, upright lay piety in the spirit of the Evangelists and St Paul. In *Don Quixote*, Cervantes had said everything that still could be said in words at the end of the sixteenth century and the beginning of the seventeenth.

Cervantes died in 1616 and Lope de Vega in 1635. The great Calderón (1600–81) belonged to a later generation and the contrast between the two periods is extremely vivid. Calderon was a contemporary of Rembrandt (d. 1669), of Spinoza and of Angelius Silesius (both d. 1677), of Comenius (d. 1670), Milton (d. 1674), Hobbes (d. 1679), of the Cartesians, Jansenists and pietists. By this time, Spain had already moved away from Europe, even though it once again achieved a great triumph in the south German–Austrian high baroque and in the reign of Louis XIV. The colourfulness and the contra-puntal tonalities of the world of Cervantes and Lope were now reduced to a few hieratic themes. *La vida es sueno*: life is a dream. Only if a man lets himself be controlled and held in check every moment through the fear of death and the Last Judgment, can he avoid arrogance, rebellion, and inner and outer chaos.[118]

Calderon's art, in effect hung great sacred masks over the smouldering fire of the underground. To see how the people really lived, one must turn to the folk-art. There life was painted as a jungle of passions, hatred, lust for pleasure, cruelty and ecstasies. It had burst every control, and erupted into the painted and draped wooden statuary of the baroque processions and Passion plays, and also into architecture. There anti-rationalistic, subjective, pantheistic vitalism was dominant. Even intellectuals of the twentieth century, Unamuno and Ortega y Gasset, are still under its spell. Their assertion *razon versus vida* (reason is against life) quite naturally made them incline towards German romanticism.[119] The art of a Federico Garcia Lorca sought to purify and trans-figure this orgiastic, extravagant barbarism.[120] Lorca was a man of the Spanish lower classes who went from village to village in order to bring the treasures of classical high culture to the people through his presentations of classical plays. At the same time he expressed the dark, archaic underground of the people in his own folk-plays (*The House of Bernarda* and *Blood-Wedding*).

The words, the gestures and the people are brought home by 'Mother Death', the primordial mother-earth-folk-country, who could have stepped out of the early cult symbols of the pre-Roman age. His *Lament for Ignacio Sanchez Mejias* (the bull-fighter and former lawyer who was gored by a bull in Seville), his Andalusian Ghazal and his *King of Harlem* poured into the art of today, where ice-cold intellects and glowing hearts have begun to erect gorgeous mosaics made of pieces from the barbaric, folk-underground. This hour of barbarism and intellectual technique is the hour of Picasso and Salvador Dali and political ideologues. An archaic Afro-European under-ground has been connected to a superficially Europeanized superstructure. Just as in Nazi Germany, the humanistic, democratic, European elements in Spain are merely a façade which can be shaken off at any time. The Spanish thinkers and literati of the nineteenth and twentieth century heralded the coming of this age. Its beginnings were visible as early as Ignatius's time.[121]

The modern Spanish intellectuals were both logicians and scholastics. They knew how to play the instrument of pure, deductive, juridical thought. The surface was always clear whereas their underground was deeply clouded by an archaic mentality, by primordial friend-foe complexes, and by a strong blood and-honour-bound monism. This exclusive thought tolerated no gods outside its own class, and its eternal principle was 'one god, one faith, one race, one absolute state'. Yet the entire elaborate structure was no more than a mask behind which the desperate, presocial ego lurked. The phenomenon of *Krausismo*, which swept over Spain in the nineteenth century, can probably be explained this way. A third-class German idealist philosopher, Krause, a pantheizing romantic with a Kantian superstructure, suddenly became Spain's official thinker. As critics of the age, these intellectuals were often peculiarly acute and had a special feeling for the decaying and the emerging. Their prototype was Donoso Cortés, the master of the false alternatives which have fascinated the semi-civilized middle strata of Europe ever since the Romantic age: the dictatorship of the masses or of the élite, the rule of the knife or the rule of the sabre. These two choices are still with us, perhaps more than ever.[122]

The unfortunate situation of Spain was partly a consequence of the suppression of the internal disputes among the Christians, Jews and Moors and among the humanistic and nonconformist elements in the sixteenth century. An élite of reformers, humanists, mystics, Jesuits, scholastics, legal thinkers and missionaries exhausted itself between 1480 and 1620 and bled to death in an attempt to initiate this necessary dialogue of opposites and to continue it after it had been driven from public life. If one may speak of a heroism of the mind then this was it. After her decline Spain became a colonial country. Alien rulers, the Bourbon kings, and a Castilian ecclesiastical and secular high nobility ruled over the arid country.[123] The enlightenment which now streamed in from abroad, and which in the eighteenth and nineteenth centuries reached a small intelligentsia, was an artificial structure, like the Spanish hymn that Frederick II of Prussia composed for Charles III. It was as artificial as the reform programme of Prime Minister Pombal, the son-in-law of the Austrian General Daun. In such a country, earthquakes (Lisbon 1755), cabinet upheavals (Pombal 1777), pronunciamientos (generals' revolts) and *Putsches* determined intellectual history which sank into a series of unconnected episodes. Things of the mind were saved in the seclusion of a monastery, in a few noble families, in prayer and in some historical works. Only an artist gave outer expression to his responsibility: Goya (1746–1828).

Ever since the sixteenth century, Spain has excited a peculiarly fruitful ambivalence. From that time on, Germans have hated 'Spanish arrogance', Spanish soldiers, generals, politicians and the 'Spanish boot' of Jesuit scholasticism, while, at the same time, receiving the flow of Catholicism in the Counter-Reformation. The saints of Spain, Ignatius and Francis Xavier, Theresa and John of the Cross, the peasant saint Isidor and many 'pious folk practices' wandered through the underground via the Low Countries into Germany.[124] The German enlightenment's sharp criticism of Spain was answered by the Spanish myth of German romanticism. Spain's influence on England and France was equally contradictory.[125] It has always been both Spains that fascinate Europe. Only in Italy, a country which she helped to mould, was Spanish influence decisively and totally rejected.

15

ITALY OF THE COUNTER REFORMATION
(1527-1870)

IN the sixteenth century the Spanish pincers across Italy included Milan and Naples. Through the Jesuits, the Counter-Reformation, the Inquisition, baroque art and state power, it began to place the country under an absolutist post-Tridentine Catholicism. Spanish Erasmians were still fleeing to Italy, although the atmosphere there after the expulsion of most of the religious individualists was hardly a happy one. Between the sack of Rome in 1527 and 1633, the intellectual riches of the country were exhausted so that Italy in the seventeenth and eighteenth centuries was in many respects like Spain. Classicism, mannerism, rhetoric, historical erudition and academic school culture flourished under the hegemony of absolutist courts, the schools of the religious orders and occupation troops. In Italy folk comedy, satire and stories became the expression of the lower classes. The ability to live in two worlds, in the world of the mind, of truth and inner conviction, and in the other world of society, its culture and political usages was the double foundation of the Italian intelligentsia from the late seventeenth century on.[1] The art of the façade, politeness, the mastery of diplomacy (three different but related phenomena) grew deep roots while a melancholy scepticism and bitter-sharp realism about universal relations arose as well.

Unlike Spain, however, there was no decline in the liveliness and variety of its intellectual life. The Italian states and city-states, political humanism, the world-immanent rationalism of the Averroists and the beginnings of experimental investigation of nature led to long, continuing battles which left their mark on the entire sixteenth-century.[2] Venice and its University of Padua continued to fight against the Spaniards and the popes, and new, religious, reformist or natural, philosophical resistance cells were constantly being formed in Spanish Naples. Even sixteenth-century Rome, despite the Counter-Reformation, remained a shelter where daring thought could find refuge in the palaces of rival cardinals or the protection of anti-Spanish popes. The enlightened pantheistic humanists of the fifteenth century, who had found a covering shield in the Roman Academy were still at home. Their great iridescent erudition and ambiguous knowledge was still present in the whole sixteenth century but the shock of 1527 and the influence of Trent forced them to retreat and to modify their thinking. They still managed to preserve and accept many pagan and nonconformist, extra and anti-Christian elements, but only by transforming them into aesthetic elements of art and form. Never since the days of Constantine and his basilica were more extra-Christian elements changed into Christian form. The Jesuits conquered Italy and built the first high baroque church in Rome, Al Gesu (1568 to 1575). Their motto 'To the greater glory of God' implied that all pagan, humanistic, rationalistic, and irrationalistic, pantheistic and archaic elements could be 'saved', if art and beauty could bend them to the service of propagation of the Faith and the Roman Church. This was a very great gamble. If the tension of this Faith were to slacken even slightly, the artistically constructed, formal cosmos would become a mere façade, concealing a gaping void. The dread of this baroque nihilism in which the disenchanted eye would see through the curtains to the emptiness behind, was one of the strongest propelling forces for Newton (*hypotheses non fingo*), as well as for Leibniz.

Rome in the sixteenth and the early seventeenth century was more than an artistic structure. It was a demonstrative answer to Luther and the Enthusiasts, to Calvin, to the Italian Averroists, atomists, pantheists, Socinians and nonconformists. A manifold shock produced this situation: Rome wanted to prove to the Protestant world that no longer believed in the redemptive power of the eye and of the earthly sacraments, that the eye of man could see God. The city was to be a heavenly Jerusalem on earth. In it God was visibly present in a thousand churches, chapels, monstrances, figures of saints, relics, paintings. This shock-reaction had not yet begun in 1520, when Luther in a letter to Leo x sought to expose Rome as 'a head and kingdom of every sin, of death and damnation'. The Romans had heard that sort of thing for centuries from their own preachers of repentance. It first began in 1527. Rome had to stand by and watch the Lutheran imperial mercenaries treating hosts, relics, women, pictures of saints, and churches 'as less than dung, as filth', 'besmirching, profaning, murdering'.

The abyss became visible and the Roman Counter-Reformation and the rebuilding of Rome of the sixteenth and seventeenth centuries were born of the dread it inspired. Anxiety and despair were reflected in the bull of Paul III inviting all Christendom to the Council of Trent (12 May 1542). 'Hungary oppressed by the Turks, Germany in danger, the whole world in fear and mourning.'[3] The fear of the Turks, which as always caused great anxiety, led to a renewal of eschatological expectations and reformation work. At the same time there was dismay over the heretics, who brusquely rejected any collaboration with the papists. In 1535 Luther declared to the Nuntius Vergerio, 'We do not need the Council for ourselves. We are certain of all things through the Holy Ghost and need no Council ...' The Protestants wanted only a lay council in which the papal party was the accused. At the disputation on religion in Regensburg, Butler declared that to embark upon the work of reform with the Pope was like providing for the security of the open road with highwaymen and for the freedom of the seas with pirates.[4] The historic formula, *cuius regio*, *eius religio*, symbolically established the line of demarcation between the two new worlds of salvation.

At first only the *urbs*, the city of Rome, remained to the Roman Church for the purpose of self-presentation and verification. It was to take a long time until the Tridentine justification decree (1547) and the Eucharist decree (1551) were assimilated by the consciousness of the rest of Europe that had remained Catholic. The doctrines of the co-operation between grace and freedom, God and man, of the effective power of the sacraments, of the Church as the exclusive sanctifier slowly evolved. All things and creatures, all good super-terrestrial and sub-terrestrial forces, all the living, the saints and the dead were to celebrate earthly life as an act of thanksgiving and a feast of the majesty of God. All this was set before the eyes of the masses by the baroque Rome of the Counter-Reformation. Lutherans and Calvinists *heard* salvation, religious nonconformists *thought* about it, the Averroists *knew* it to be immanent in nature, the pantheists *felt* it in the universe, the mystics *tasted* it in all things. But the Roman-baroque Catholic heard, thought, knew, felt, tasted and *saw*. Above all, he acted it out in the world theatre of the Roman baroque which in a remarkable way sought to unite the concerns of all enemies. Hence the fascination exerted by the Jesuit theatre on the Protestant school culture. This attempt to give visible form to the Lullian and Cusanian concordance of all opposites – in baroque Rome as the cosmic city – suited the utopianism of Leonardo, Michelangelo and Campanella.[5]

Rome was that Utopia. It was the harmonious 'Heavenly Jerusalem', 'the City' built out of 'living stones', in which 'unity totally embodied itself'.[6] In the anxieties of the twelfth and thirteenth centuries the French cathedrals had been so conceived. The great builders of the cathedrals were concerned both to restrain the lower class and to outplay the intelligentsia from the World of the Three Rings. Like the founders of the Clunian monasteries on the pilgrims' road to Spain in Moissac and Toulouse, they did not hesitate to use foreign, Islamic and folk motifs. This same anxiety created the baroque Rome of the Counter-Reformation. All enemies were to be over-trumped and outplayed. All would be made visible, even the ecstasy of St Theresa. (The arrow of divine love was shown as it penetrated her heart.) This utopia of baroque Rome lived in constant anxiety lest anything escape its perfection, its presentation, its service. Therefore all real colours, tones, themes, men, races and continents were to unite in the great world theatre of the total, united world Church. Play, work, prayer, celebration, erudition and charity were all to become part of religious service. This exclusive activity and perfection could only maintain itself through merciless persecution of dissenters, who did not believe in this visibility or who wished to look above and beyond the cupola of this round cosmos. Galileo and Copernicus were condemned because they denied the sacred roundness and uniqueness of this Platonic totalitarianism.

The titanism of this composition, of this very calculated joining of the most heterogeneous elements first became entirely open and visible in the creator of St Peter's in Rome, Michelangelo. *Il Terribile*, the Terrible One, as the Romans called him (and Julius II, his Moses), *il divino*, the one inspired by divine creative powers, as Vasari called him, had already tried to create that total work which the temple with its six orbits represented in Campanella's *City of the Sun*. In the *Last Judgment*, painted for Paul III, all mankind (presented in the pictures of the Old and New Testament, pagan antiquity and the popes) was to stand around the sublime spectacle of the Sacrament of the Mass.* God on earth appeared in the form of the Host and his representative, the pope with his court. Yet nobody can ever really see this as a total work of art. Nobody really pays any attention to the symbolic significance of the figures from world and sacred history, from the Old and New Testaments, nor to the medallions of the popes, painted uninspiringly but proficiently by the hand of a pupil. They all pale into unessential histories, because here, as in Protestant spiritualism, the history of redemption has been deprived of its power by the sheer might of the composition and the colossal genius of its creator. Everyone looks with amazement and terror at the glorification of genius, symbolized by the God of Creation. This God who calls Adam out of the clay, with the finger of the artist, is the portrait of the 'new man' – Michelangelo himself.

Man, 'the earthly god', forms the unformed earth. Michelangelo united the art-theology of the fifteenth and sixteenth century with religious nationalism. In his aim, he was not unlike Joan of Arc and Luther. With a monumental force, hardness and one-sidedness, in supreme self-confidence, 'the Terrible One' asserted that only Italian art (i.e. painting) not, for instance, the painting of the Low Countries, was close to God in its sublime works and would preserve itself until the end of days. Michelangelo had gone from the road of the Catholic early reform of Vittoria Colonna, Juan de Valdes in Naples and Occhino, Pole and Caterina Cybò, over to the Counter-Reformation and had become friends with its leaders. He embraced the total religious and political renovation of Savonarola, who had deeply influenced him as a youth. Michelangelo was acting very much in the spirit of Savonarola when he offered to undertake to build the Jesuit church in Rome at his own expense. Michelangelo's seriousness, loneliness, and titanic will drove him on in his constant struggle to redeem the chaotic world, entangled in impulses and conflict, in artistic form.

The same utopian drive can be seen in the ideas of Campanella. His total state united the ideas of the Fraticelli with primordial communistic and Anabaptist themes. He had been deeply influenced by Thomas More's *Utopia*, but perhaps even more strongly by the tales of the Incas and their Sun God.[7] This Dominican's sombre masterpiece exerted a great influence on Condorcet, Diderot, Robespierre as well as on Saint Simon and Fourier. It was far superior to the utopias of all those who followed him, except for Harrington's, and is still important in Russia, where it was published in Moscow in 1947 by

*Luther was so terrified by it that he could no longer read the Mass.

the Soviet Academy of Sciences. Campanella was a new type of political fighter who aimed to think scientifically and to act politically in order to change the face of the earth and of man.[8] He came from a family of agricultural labourers in Calabria and from the beginning he was resentful of Spanish hegemony. He organized a conspiracy to overthrow the Spaniards and Jesuits in Naples in August 1599, and won over 300 monks (Dominicans, Franciscans, Augustinians) to his cause. He sat in a dungeon for twenty-seven years, was placed on the rack seven times and was finally freed by Pope Urban VIII. He then searched all over Europe for supporters through whom he might realize his ideas. He petitioned Galileo for help, dealt with James I of England, made contact with Gassendi and the circle around Mersenne, searched vainly for Descartes in Holland, proposed to stage a totalitarian propaganda campaign for Richelieu, and died on the day he himself had foretold, with the celebration of an astrological liturgy of the dead.[9]

Campanella hated scholasticism, especially the teaching of his namesake Thomas, as hostile to science. In opposition to it he constructed his total state as a scientifically ordered, politically guided paradise on earth. In the centre of the new state was a giant temple of the sciences and arts: the altar of the new world god, of man, a masonic lodge, the Encyclopedia's and Conte's world church all in one. There ruled il Sole, a priest-prince, and at his side stood three high-ranking princes, Power, Wisdom, Love (the Abélardian trinity). The inventors of all laws and cults, Moses, Osiris, Jupiter, Mercury, Christ, Caesar, Alexander and all the Romans stood behind; the highest ruling council was constantly kept informed about all novelties, inventions and happenings by ambassadors and spies sent all over the world. This state had only one concern: the disciplining of the new man. With the ecstatic sobriety of the spiritual enthusiast, and under the mask of pure science, Campanella asked: we men discipline dogs and horses, why then do we show so little concern about disciplining man into a buona razza, a good race? The officer, Love, is responsible for the disciplining of the new man. Ceremonious religious and astrological scientific preparations at the suitable hour of conception were to assure the breeding of highly valuable human material. Women were communal property. Men and women were to be fully militarized and always to carry weapons, and they were also to be fully mechanized and equipped with all sciences and techniques.

Readiness to serve the commonweal was the key. The State would make gifts to the heroes and heroines of labour and war, and honour them by public feasts. Foreign wars were necessary for the spread of this totalitarian system. They were sacred acts, attended by the priest-officers. In addition, there were wars within the country; Campanella described Peoples Courts with scenes like those in Koestler's Darkness at Noon. The people argued at length with the criminals and the condemned until they accepted the punishment as something deserved. Anyone who had committed an offence against freedom, God, or the major officials was mercilessly put to death. In the dungeon of the

Spanish Inquisition in Naples, Campanella imagined an even harsher Inquisition for his state! Sins and crimes were identical. The task of the *Sole* and of the highest priest-officers was to purge consciences (*purgar le coscienze*). The people confessed to the officers, who learned just what sins were prevalent in the state. In a ghastly atonement rite, a frightful travesty of the sacrifice of the Mass, the 'Sun' would finally purge the state.

A spiritualistic world-man was the basic concept of this utopia. Philosophic materialism revealed itself in Campanella's system in its most elementary form. The nature of materialism, which is, after all, no more than spiritualism run wild, has never been more clearly illuminated. Pure spirit was to transform pure matter. Campanella was convinced (along with the Fraticelli, Roger Bacon, Lull) of the imminent renovation of the world. He believed that he had to prepare the way for it by his theory of the state. The *City of the Sun*, therefore, was both an utopia and, as Campanella's own commentary on it in the *Questioni sull'ottima Repubblica* suggests, a theory of the state.

As a spiritualist, Campanella defended the legitimacy of his demands for the community of property and women. In him the crudest biologism, as with certain communities of enthusiasts and sectarians (on which he based himself), went hand and hand with spiritualism.* Campanella wanted to make all men into state monks, who in total poverty and total obedience carried out the law of Christ and of nature. Christ had already instituted a perfect republic. Campanella presented his state as a work of pure thought and of pure reason in order to prove that the Gospel was in conformity with nature. Sexual communism was not in contradiction to the Gospel, because it was not contrary to nature. He often compared the sexual intercourse of horses, cattle and hens with that of man. Only mothers and sons were not to have relations with one another, because he had observed that a horse did not want to mount its mother. Sexual relations between fathers and daughters was another question. After all Solomon, the prime model of Christ had 700 wives. Campanella viewed his *City of the Sun* as an apostolic community, a brotherhood of new men, who must be educated by the pope-monarch through means of terror, asceticism, science and reason of state. Campanella was a spiritualist and positivist, and yet a true reflection of that baroque Rome which we have already observed.

Rome was by no means the only centre of Italian intellectual and spiritual activity. A massive, world-immanent Aristotelianism still held out in its bastion at Padua. The courts of Naples and Ferrara had become centres of religious unrest. The consort of Ercole II of Este, Renée de Valois, had turned Ferrara into a headquarters of Erasmians and reforming prelates. Cardinals like Pier Paolo Vergerio, Contarini, Pole, scholars like Marc Antonio Flaminio and Aonio Paleario, preachers like Occhino and Vermigli, courtiers

---

*We have noticed the same phenomenon in Frederick II of Sicily, and we shall meet it again in Frederick II of Prussia and in Nietzsche, the heir of revolutionary pietism.

like Carnesecchi and Caracciolo, poets like Vittoria Colonna and Catarina Cybò travelled to and fro between Naples and Ferrara. In 1537 nine cardinals and bishops of this circle addressed a memorandum to Paul III demanding a direct and sweeping reform of the Church. This highly important document spoke the language of Christian conscience. It appealed to this conscience and to human decency and breathed the spirit of moderation, practical wisdom and conciliation, which had always marked the best Italian political and religious humanism. Cardinal Contarini pleaded with the Pope, 'All rule is a rule of reason ... A pope must know that it is free men over whom he exercises this rule.' As in Spain, the militant course also triumphed in Rome in the anxiety-reaction against Protestantism. These Catholic friends of reform were denounced as friends of Protestants and semi-heretics. In 1540 the great persecution annihilated these men and women or forced them to join the growing stream of Waldensians, Anabaptists and free-spirited religious humanists who were fleeing northwards over the Alps. Renée de Valois, who was a highly intellectual woman, conducted mathematical and astronomical studies. After 1540 she professed her adherence to Calvin whom she sheltered for a time, and defiantly declared, 'Catholicism is an idolatrous religion'. As a king's daughter she was able to stay in Italy up to 1560, but finally she too was forced to return to France. Most of the friends of reform had already fled to Germany, England, France and Switzerland by the beginning of the fourth decade. The leaders were followed by several entirely Protestant communities (like Lucca, Modena), which emigrated with all their possessions.

After the persecution of the Protestant, the persecution of scholars, poets and historians began. They had been allowed an amazingly free creativity since they wrote in Latin and only for a small circle of selected intelligentsia. The natural philosophers, Palingenio Stellato, Aonio Paleario and Scipione Capece, were condemned and burned at the stake. Even the last independent Italian state could no longer grant protection. Paolo Sarpi, the merciless critic of the Tridentine Council whose history he saw as a story of the extensive corruption of the Church, was liquidated in 1607 by hired assassins. The period of clandestine book printing and book selling began, and a new element of moral corruption and public deceit joined the many others which already afflicted the Italian character and conscience.[10] In addition there was a strong spread of superstitious pseudo-sciences during the transition of society from inner anarchy to bigotry.

In the stream of the emigrants of the 1540's, along with the Waldensians and Lutherans, there were anti-trinitarian, free-thinking, religious humanists who were persecuted by Catholics, Lutherans, Zwinglians and Calvinists and were later to be found in Basle and Zurich, in Amsterdam, London, Cracow and Transylvania, where they developed several of the principles of western European enlightenment.[11] Italian Anabaptists were predominantly of the lower class, (weavers, tailors, shoemakers, manual workers of all kinds). During the emigration they arranged the secret Anabaptist Council in Venice in 1550. For them Christ was only a God-filled man, the Roman Church was diabolic, and there existed no legitimate ecclesiastical higher authority. Several courageous and learned intellectuals, Curione, Sozzinus, Biandrata, Acontius and Gentile, emigrated with this lower class, and a remarkable reciprocal influence arose. The lower class carried its ecstasy and expectation of salvation over into the thinking of the intelligentsia, instilling them over and over again with a mystical ardour, and for its part the lower class accepted the deistic rationalism of the intellectuals in ever stronger doses.

At first they found a welcome in Switzerland, where the intelligentsia preferred Zurich and Basle. Celio Secundo Curione, an ancestor of Jacob Burckhardt, had vainly tried to support himself as a professor in Italy under the protection of the Counts of Montserrat and the Countess Renée in Ferrara and Venice. In humanistic Basle, he came together with an international emigration of Anabaptists and *Illuminati*. Here David Joris, the great Dutch Anabaptist leaders, M. Borrhaus and Castellio, together with Curione, Socinus and Occhino, the former Capucin general vicar, formed a front of the 'silent in the land' which very soon made itself distinctly noticeable by a lively propaganda activity. To an increasing extent, it was directed against Calvin. They were disappointed by the lack of freedom of conscience in the Calvinist principalities and municipalities and embittered by Calvin's heresy trials, especially by the execution of Servetus. It was probably Lelio Sozzini who wrote Servetus's *Apologia* for him, and Curione his valuable little book *On the Extent of God's Kingdom*.

What had the Gospel to do with stakes and with worldly power? Socinus believed that the thousand-year amalgamation of religion and state power could be destroyed only by severing the Spirit from the Trinity.* The Reformation as a liberation of man from the administration of the Spirit by earthly power necessarily led to the severance of the Spirit from the Trinity. Lactius Sozzinus identified faith, conscience, divine and human spirit. There was no difference between the Holy Spirit of the Trinity and the concept Spirit of the mystics and philosophers. The Spirit had become free, and according to Socinus could no longer be appropriated by the rulers because God always calls up new spirits to reveal and to live the truth.

Curione's little book, which he dedicated to Sigismund August of Poland, looked partly like an historical commentary on, and proof of, Socinus's theses. Curione judged the middle ages (cf. again Tertullian's concept of the middle ages) as a thousand-year epoch in which Satan, through power and cunning, dazzlingly deluded man into accepting his kingdom as the kingdom of God. The 'holy tradition' so often appealed to, the agreement over many centuries in things of faith and the spirit, had proved to be a fundamental

---

*As a matter of fact, from the ninth to the nineteenth centuries state treaties, like the emperor's diplomas in the 'Holy Empire', had always been signed in the 'name of the One and Indivisible Trinity', whose dominion was administered by emperors and popes. Sozzini realized that Protestantism took the same view.

error which often contradicted reason and Holy Scripture.[12] The devil had invented the medieval ideology of the kingdom of God and thereby also limited the doctrine of justice, which limits God's goodness and mercifulness. 'To limit the kingdom of God means to limit the mercifulness of God and all its divine attributes along with it.' The true kingdom of God lives in the secret church of the persecuted, not in the violent ecclesiastical lords of Calvinism, Catholicism and Lutheranism. Curione, who died as a citizen and professor of Basle, made a great effort to veil the radicalism of his criticism. Neither he nor his friends succeeded, however.

Calvin's challenge to its orthodoxy paralysed the life-nerve of this Italian emigration, and pressed it still more into a religious rationalism, into a humanistic deism stripped of its Christian core. Calvin had vigilantly dogged the ways of these Italians to England, Poland and Transylvania. He could not prevent a Biandrata, as the court physician in Poland and Transylvania, from becoming the leader of the Unitarians, but in Switzerland he could drive their activity completely underground. With the dying out of the first emigrant generation around 1560 (twenty years after the death of the Spanish Erasmians) these Italian heretics left Switzerland (with the exception of Basle). Cracow, the seat of a famous university, a trade centre and meeting-place of different peoples and races, became their new headquarters.

As physicians and royal Polish officials, headed by Faustus Socinus, Laelius's nephew, they came into contact there with a circle of Italian manual workers, who were, as a conformist humanist complained, subject to at least 'six-hundred heresies'. The young Faustus asserted himself in this difficult area and rose to become the leader of the anti-trinitarian movement which has been called Socinianism after him. Faustus had received his introduction to nonconformism in the Siena Academy of the *Intronati*. Since Dante's time serious religious and political problems had been debated in these discussion circles. In the 1540's the princes and Inquisitors dissolved or transformed them into sterile aesthetic clubs. The abolition of the Academy of the *Intronati* appeared to Faustus as a sign of the barbarization of Italy.[13] On his wanderings through Anabaptist upper-Italy, through Lyons and Basle, and then again in the court service of the Medicis which he finally left in 1574, Faustus developed his religious rationalism step by step. His followers were to speak later of a *religio rationalis* and B. Wiszowaty (Wissovatius) wrote its basic book (Amsterdam 1685): *Religio rationalis seu de rationis indicio in controversiis etiam theologicas ac religionis adhibendo tractatus*. Reason, as the judge over the quarrels of theologians and confessions, revealed their dogmas as ideologies of the ruling church powers!

Faustus himself developed only the fundamental doctrines of Socinianism. Redemption was conceived as a moral influence on man by the exemplary educator, Christ. He asserted the natural-primitive state of Adam before the so-called 'fall of man' (and thereby the dissolution of original sin and its replacement through a natural progress of man *in* history) and the definition of religion as a method.* Faustus understood this comprehensive and ambiguous slogan of the seventeenth and eighteenth centuries (cf. Descartes's method of correct thinking, the methods of praying, living mystically, reckoning, and working correctly, in the baroque and the early Enlightenment) as a *via*, *ratio*, as a means of reaching God. *Imitatio Christi* – this basic concept of the *devotio moderna*, with whose left wing the Socinians met at every step, now meant a simple discipleship of Christ in a reasonable secular life that conscientiously held to the Ten Commandments of God and the counsels of the Gospel.

Faustus Socinus was personally of a conciliatory nature, but there was one thing about which he was adamant: the advocacy of a radical Christian idea of peace. What Paracelsus, the Anabaptist, and Erasmus had thought before him, he condensed in the experience of a thousand-year persecution of all nonconformists and the experiences of his own life between 1530 and 1580. There can be no war willed by God. The Old Testament must not be set in the place of the New. The Sermon on the Mount allows no war. Faustus in principle mistrusted secular power. The true Christian had only the choice of becoming a martyr or of emigrating. The radicalness of these ideas drove Socinus into lonely exile and he died, alone and forsaken, in 1604 in a small Polish village. Biandrata died in the same way around 1588 in Transylvania and Occhino in 1565 in Slavkov near Austerlitz. At the same time Socinus released a subterranean expansive power which in the following centuries decively helped to shape the history of both western and eastern Europe.

The effects in eastern Europe were largely attributable to Biandrata. He was a physician, theologian, and popular Enlightener.[14] Through him the 'pure man', Christ, became the Liberator-Christ for the oppressed and the poor, for the lowly, who until then had been enslaved by the God-image of the rich and mighty. In this antithesis Biandrata described the true Christ, who not as the second son of the Trinity but as the son of the only God and a mere man took the sufferings and anxiety of the weak, the insulted and the injured upon himself. The Christ of the popes, rich, strong and powerful, accompanied by countless schoolmen and philosophers, provided his followers with cities, estates and tithes. Biandrata roused into furious activity the Spiritualism of the East. The border regions of Europe, in Poland as far as the Black Sea, were stirred by the methods of thought of Italian Spiritual humanism.† In the sixteenth century spiritualism in the East had not yet gone far. Maximos the Greek could not assert himself as a political renovator, but only as a saint and

---

*Among the Italian *émigrés*, the idea of method was soon related to the study of history in a characteristic way. Curione, Bruto and Bernardino Bonifacio wrote instructions for the study of history, which were to be cited by all spiritualists, even as late as Harnack, in proof of the corruption of official churches,

†This first wave of Western spiritualism was followed in the eighteenth and early nineteenth centuries by a second, unleashed by Boehme and Baader. The third wave of Marx and Engels released the tremendous explosion of the world revolution.

a penitent. The ambiguity of Dostoievsky and the Russian writers and philosophers of the nineteenth century still stemmed from this intermediate stage. Between Maximos the Greek and Lenin, the important Eastern spiritualist was forced to be a writer and a *littérateur*, because he could contact the people only in small circles of the underground. This was also true of Hegel's situation as a frustrated politician in Prussia.

The waves also rolled towards the West. Under the pressure of the Counter-Reformation the Unitarians of Poland, Moravia and Transylvania wandered to Holland, England and America. In England this spiritualism possessed an important bridgehead in Jacobus Acontius, who was a notary and secretary of a cardinal. Disgusted by the embittered struggles at the Council of Trent, Acontius turned to the Reformation. He arrived in England, after living in Zurich and Strasbourg. In 1560 he became a fortifications engineer for Queen Elizabeth, and a few years later a commissioner for soil improvement. His writings found a wide circulation in England, Holland, Switzerland and Poland. He himself was excommunicated from the *Ecclesia Peregrinorum*, the English organization of the Protestant refugees from Europe, since he taught deism and accepted only a few articles of faith. Acontius represented a practical, dogma-free Christianity, which through tolerance (even towards Catholics!) was supposed to prove its Christian character and its superiority over all confessions which mutually excluded each other from salvation. This theory and practice met the needs of the broadest circles in Calvinistic-puritanical, dictatorial, occupied west Europe: they could no longer make any inroads in Italy.

Giordano Bruno was inwardly closely related to these *émigrés*. The poetical life-work of this former Neapolitan Dominican illumined the art and spirituality of the Roman baroque with the same sharpness as Campanella did its political structure. Bruno's *Spaccio della bestia trionfante* was a total inversion of the cosmos. Jupiter was no longer a god of worlds but an infinite man, who himself had created Heaven and earth. His portrayal of the genius, struggling with divinity like Jacob, in *Degl'eroici Furori* (1585) read like commentaries on Michelangelo. Bruno was the grandfather of European, especially German, romanticism, not because he celebrated heroic madness as a form of knowledge but certainly because he rejected all rational conceptual construction. He presumed to make the most ultimate statements on the cosmos though he was barely familiar with the concepts and problems of astronomy and mathematics. Bruno 'felt that he had received a revelation and conducted himself like a prophet'.[15] Maliciously, jeeringly, he made fun of the vain, 'mendacious' Plato, the 'envious falsifier', and the 'laughable' fancies of Aristotle, the 'fool' Archimedes, and of all his special friends, the scholars, the clerics and mathematicians (including Copernicus).

This typical romantic renunciation of the worlds of culture, reason, science and faith later animated a dozen giddy-headed geniuses between Nietzsche, Klages and Rosenberg's *Myth of the Twentieth Century*. In Bruno it grew out of his defeat in the public disputations in Paris. In London and Oxford, England's prosaic aristocracy and schoolmen could derive no palpable content from the word-play of this man, who over and over again let himself be carried away by the spell of the magic of contrasts. Out of his experience of hate and loneliness in 'hard' England, that had rebuffed him, Bruno resorted to his mother-tongue and thenceforth wrote in Italian. Bruno wanted 'to sing the mother', the orgiastic primal ground of the country, of the people, of the cosmos giving birth to itself in the whirling chaos. Classic ancient thought had consciously clung to its victory of masculine reason over the world of maternal power, of female matter, and of the (considered as female) lower class in the coining of words. Plato, Aristotle and Plotinus had overcome matter as woman.[16] In Bruno, there was a revolution of the spiritual underground.[17] Mother-matter began to overpower masculine, domineering reason, and to force it down into its service. Behind all this there was an androgynous leading idea, that of a return to archaic depths in which there is not yet any separation between above and below, man and woman, spirit and matter. Bruno's notorious obscenities and ambiguities arose out of his attempt to live in the underground, and to retrieve the all-consuming and all-animating fire from it. Bruno, who interpreted his own love poems philosophically in the *Eroici furori*, sought to fuse the rapture of the mystic with the ecstasy of sexuality and the Eros of the spirit-filled seer and seeker.

His end at the stake on the Campo dei Fiori in Rome on 17 February 1600 signified no loss for the sciences which owed him nothing, and not even for the philosophical thought of Europe to which the same ideas had been flowing from a hundred streams since the twelfth century, from the World of the Three Rings. But it certainly was a terrible blow for the conscience of the European intellectuals, for the consciousness especially of the Italian intelligentsia. Bruno had personally propagandized for his world-view all over Europe and had deliberately become a martyr to it in his seven-year imprisonment in a Roman dungeon. This world-view was, like that of most of the educated from the sixteenth to the twentieth century, a compendium of rash thoughts, deep-going resentments and psychic twists. In Bruno's case it was borne by the conviction that one must live and die for its truth. The burning of Giordano Bruno, and the other poets between 1540 and 1600, deepened the repression of philosophers and the religious need for truth, purity and divine power. The desire to return to apostolic origins retreated into the dimensions of the aesthetic.

The Counter-Reformation transferred the search for purity from religion to art, and in this sense Giorgio Vasari may be regarded as the 'Church father of modern art history'.[18] In his *Le Vite Dei Piu Eccelenti Pittori Scultori ed Architettori* he carried over the ideology of history of the Franciscan Spirituals and the new nonconformists to art history. Spiritualism became purism and classicism in the sphere of art criticism.[19] The traditional Franciscan division of history into three ages reappears in the guise of epochs in the history of artistic style. First, there was the pure greatness of the antique world. The *maniera antica* decayed after the time of Constantine and was replaced by the darkness of the middle ages, of the *infelice secolo*. Its roughness and awkwardness ruined the purity of the classic gospel. The rebirth began with Giotto and individual elect salvation bearers of true art. Progress was made in the increasing mastery of the natural and the rising freedom of the *maniera* until perfection was reached in the golden age of Leo x (this was the recuperation against Luther) through the earthly-heavenly trinity of Leonardo, Raphael and Michelangelo.

Vasari was the Sebastian Franck and Gottfried Arnold of art history. Frightened by the threat of a decline and fall into a new barbarism, he wrote his history as a guide for the few elect spirits of the future. God – and this was a very great miracle – beginning with Giotto had reawakened art, the glad tidings of the beautiful, to life. Since the renovators of art are God-called, Vasari was especially happy when he could describe artist monks, who, like Giovanni da Fiesole, Don Lorenzo degli Angeli and Giovanni Agnolo Montorsoli served Christ and pure art at the same time. Apprehensively, he noticed how individual artists sank into 'the shadows of sin'. In the introductions to the *Lives* he gladly observed the virtues and glorified the poverty that so often spurred artists to the highest achievements. The third kingdom (*terza maniera*), the modern, was ushered in by Leonardo, whose sacral marks were: *buona regola, miglior ordine, retta misura, disegno perfetto, e grazia divina*.

All these ideas can easily be translated into the leading concepts of the Calvinist, Cartesian and Jansenist thought of order, rule, method, grace, and measure. This inner spiritual unity helps incidentally to explain the dogmatic prestige of Vasari in spiritualist Europe of the seventeenth to the nineteenth centuries. Leonardo was followed by Raphael upon whom God had showered all the graces of nature. Vasari portrayed him as a new Francis; his genial nature was so full of graciousness and charity that beasts and men adoringly admired him. Anyone who worked under him was to be judged blessed, and blessed are those who follow him, for which they will also be rewarded in Heaven. Vasari concluded (as the Spirituals concluded their Lives of Francis and of Olivi) with Castiglione's farewell: Raphael has regenerated Rome. In this fullness of time God finally took pity on mankind, sunk in the darkness, and decided to send a spirit to earth who, more celestial than earthly, led pure art to the peak of perfection: the divine Michelangelo. Vasari created an ideology for the religion of art enjoyment and art criticism which was to a large extent an expression of old fashioned spiritualism. Art was saved by this process from condemnation and was permitted to satisfy hearts in the Europe of the Counter-Reformation and Calvinism.

Galileo, who was born in 1564, the year in which Michelangelo and Calvin died, consciously took the passion of the new investigators and scholars upon himself. He could have avoided this, had he renounced the language of the people. The language of the people was the language of heresies, of laymen, of the uneducated, by inheritance the enemy of the 'grand form' and of Aristotelian-Thomistic notions of authority. It was the friend of experience, of manual work, of commonsense and of the ordinary man. The most bitter reproach hurled at Galileo was that he used the language of the heretics and the 'people's enlighteners'. The old, aristocratic cosmos, thus, lost its authority. New popular concepts and the patient probing of the reality of the world along many small paths replaced it; tested hypotheses dislodged the old rationalistic arrogance.

The new natural sciences were an offspring of the people. The great technologist and metallurgist, Vannoccio Biringuccio spoke the language of the bronze caster, goldsmith and miner, and in humour, scepticism and sobriety, the language of the plain people. This applied not only to mechanics and all the unfree arts, which traditionally had been ignored by the universities and left by the theologians to manual workers, bronze casters, shipbuilders, master workmen and war technicians. It was even true of mathematics. The great mathematician of the sixteenth century, Nicolo Tartaglia, was the son of a keeper of post horses in Brescia. As a boy, in 1512, he was crippled after being beaten by French soldiers in the Brescia Cathedral. As a young man in Verona, he earned a threadbare living as a mathematics teacher for merchants, artillerists and engineers. He died poor and suffering in Venice in 1577. Tartaglia learned plain, practical occupations during his acquaintance with poverty and the sundry tasks it imposed. The language of his *Quesiti et Inventioni Diverse* preserved the tone of a Venetian workshop, of an arsenal, and of a merchant's warehouse.

In order to clear the way for the new investigation of nature, Galileo had to wreck the Roman baroque. For him Rome was no longer the cosmic city, the presence of the heavenly *polis*, in which the high priest Joshua (the pope) ordered the course of the sun and administered the motions of the Heavenly City. Such authority demanded high service, not only from the subjects but, above all, from all their representatives. The cult must be strictly practised; divine law that ruled the spherical earthly salvation-city by the stars must be obeyed. Paul IV, for example, the same Pope who re-established the Roman Inquisition, never called a consistory without first consulting his astrologers.[20] Most important of all was the universal acceptance of the heavenly philosophies of Plato and Aristotle. The curial advocates annihilated Galileo with the word of the Old Testament, of that high priest who with raised arm let the sun stand still through his prayer, while his brothers fought the battle against the infidels. Had the sun gone down, the victory would not have been total. This appeal to Joshua and Moses once again expressed the old Carolingian, curial and magic-archaic world order, as did Gregory XVI's encyclical in 1832 for the last time, two hundred years after the condemnation of Galileo. Priests and kings, king-priests, were the only true guardians of salvation in the well-sheltered sphere of the ancient, Roman *polis*.[21] Only a giant could destroy this sacred structure, encompassing heaven and earth, and its *ratio* centred in Rome.

Galileo grew to this gigantic stature in Padua and Venice. His acquaintance with the manual labourers and the lives of the common people helped to keep a spiritual Franciscan piety alive within him. He was born in enlightened Pisa where he later studied medicine and mathematics. Galileo was a member of an old Florentine family which had already played an important role in the fourteenth century. His father, Vincenzo, was a merchant and a famous music-ologist. His school years in Santa Maria di Vallumbrosa, in an old monkish-humanistic college of the reform movement, perhaps transmitted the decisive spiritual stamp to his character. We know too little about them. From the very beginning Galileo felt himself drawn to manual labour and to the people. Later he often said to his friends that he would have become a painter if he had been given a free choice of occupation. Like Albrecht Dürer Galileo said, 'I do not know what beauty is but I do know that it is to be found in the "right", the "correct", the "useful" and "naturally true".' Like Leonardo he was interested in the technique of war; he worked in Padua as an instrument maker, turner, joiner, and metal caster, gave private lessons in technical subjects (theory of fortifications, etc.). The best names of the European nobility of the world of nonconformism were to be found among his students. His own course of study was irregular and wholly free of guild limitations. It drove him to the precise and the exact (*esquisito* and *esaltessa* were his favourite words), to the simple and the natural. From 1592 to 1610 Galileo taught in Padua, which was still both anti-clerical and anti-Thomist. There Aristotle had been inter-preted scientifically by Pietro d'Abano, and as early as the fourteenth and fifteenth centuries the nature of motion had been actively investigated.[22]

Scholastic humanism still held with Ptolemy that the hypothesis of the rota-tion of the earth would have many advantages for itself, if the ridiculous of such an idea were not a hindrance. What is perfect could only be static, round, motionless. Ten generations of Paduan investigators of nature had carried out fundamental changes in European scientific thought.[23] The logical, hier-archical causative proof had begun to yield to the experimental method of investigation. Galileo taught in Padua, Venice and later in Florence before a courtly society of interested dilettantes. He gave two lectures for them on the form, position and size of Dante's *Inferno* in 1588 at the Florentine Academy. His learning was combined with manual labour and intercourse with the people, among whom he sought refuge. Galileo lived anxiously. He had to be constantly on guard not to let himself be overcome by the old thought and by the magic of the old world. For decades he struggled inwardly with Aristotle and Plato. His famous dialogues and letters were not fictitious conversations, but faithful reflections of a long, inner dialogue with himself. Naturally, he fled to the people in whose commonsense, experience, irony and humour he sought confirmation of his ideas. A simple woman of Venice, Marina Gamba, bore him four children, one of whom was the enchanting Suor Maria Celeste.

She became a nun, but always remained more than a daughter to him. She was a pupil, friend and adviser. Her letters to him while he was in prison are superb. Maria Celeste loved and honoured her father as the man who penetrated the entire heaven with his mind. She knew that the real chasm existed not between Galileo and the Church, but between Galileo and *questo mondaccio*, the corrupt, vain, power-seeking world of the Roman high baroque, which once more sought to preserve an authority that it could nevertheless no longer assert.

Galileo sought confirmation for his new ideas in the realism of the people's poetry, in Ruzzante, the Paduan humorist, in Francesco Berni, the Florentine satirist, in Ariosto's *Orlando Furioso*. He abhorred the baroque utopianism he found incarnated in Tasso's *Jerusalem Delivered*. Galileo sharply separated poetry and truth, which for the medieval humanists and theologians had been a holy and valid unity. Like theology, philosophy and science, poetry was a rhetorical self-presentation of the cosmos and of the 'grand form'. Ever since Jerome and the Greek Fathers, a thousand-year-old humanism had cited the ancient poets, philosophers and Christian theologians as authentic witnesses for its rhetorical, logical, hierarchical cosmos-structure.

Galileo declared the bankruptcy of all humanism. Its theology, philosophy and poetry could no longer claim to present a correct world-view. In the light of his natural scientific investigations the old view of the world proved to be the result of superficial observations, deceptive analogies, misleading combinations and fallacious sensory delusions. The system was held together externally by a logical formalism. In its superficiality and arbitrariness the old theory revealed the bondage of the human mind to sensory impressions, habits, passions and the conveniences of power.[24] Galileo anxiously sought to free himself from this mixture of 'poetry and truth'. Even the new natural science was still permeated by magic and rhetorical concepts. Kepler, his great contemporary and correspondent, still lived entirely in this magic-humanistic cosmos.[25] Galileo, for example, avoided the idea of gravitation, of attraction, out of an aversion to magic, to *causae occultae*.[26] He was afraid of becoming involved in magical speculations. Galileo sought the natural explanation of things and thus he found Gilbert's theory of magnetism very attractive. By the use of a natural explanation, Gilbert struck right at the heart of the natural philosophy of the baroque which explained the relations of things as the result of sympathy. At the same time, it attacked the idea of an animated world, full of anthropomorphic activity. For Galileo, the attraction of tides was not a mixture of speculative, visionary and natural-scientific moments – as so many concepts still were in Kepler – but a 'purely speculative thing' of a new order of reality.

In 1609 Galileo invented his telescope (an improvement on the Dutch instrument). Was it important if the baroque humanists and theologians refused to look into it and confirm his discovery of the planet Jupiter? In Advent, 1614, the Dominican Tommaso Caccini preached against Galileo in

Rome. Mathematics, he claimed, is a diabolic art. Mathematicians as the originators of all heresies should be driven out of all countries. In February 1615 Galileo was accused before the Holy Office for the first time. In 1616 Copernicus was placed on the Index. Galileo commented bitterly in a letter to Piero Dini: for seventy years he (Copernicus) had remained unmolested, now suddenly he was damned as a heretic. The struggle against Galileo which broke out was a struggle of despair on the part of the Roman curial baroque, which once more aimed to save the *Urbs* as the law giver and representative of the cosmos. In vain did Galileo defend Copernicus's Catholicism. Movingly he implored the teachers and leaders of the Church not to misinterpret the primacy and kingship of theology above all other sciences. He cited Augustine and attacked 'closing the road to free investigation concerning the things of the world and of nature, as though they had already been discovered and made known with certainty'. Galileo was convinced that Holy Scripture did not err, but its commentators, who wished to cling to its pure literalness, certainly did. That was the origin of the anthropomorphic image of God, a God with hands, feet, eyes, anger, remorse, hatred, forgetfulness, ignorance. Holy Scripture required, he argued, an intellectual exegesis. Scripture and nature both started out from the divine Word, from Creation, the former as a dictate of the Holy Ghost, the latter as the executor of God's commands. In its mode of expression Holy Scripture had adjusted itself to the powers of comprehension of barbaric, uncultured peoples.

In 1632 Galileo stirred Italy's public opinion by publishing his *Dialogo dei Massimi Sistemi*. Through the words of his deceased pupils and friends, Sagredo and Salviati, he defended in this work the Copernican world view that had been prohibited since 1616. In the language of the people and of lay society the worldly nobleman Sagredo, from the 'wonderful city of Venice', and the Florentine Salviati, who directly defended Copernicus, debated with Simplicio, the Aristotelian, Ptolemian simpleton, in whom Pope Urban VIII thought he recognized himself. The central question in the discussion was whether the sun or the earth is the centre of the universe. But the real question which was posed by Galileo's dispute was whether baroque Rome could assert itself as a City of the Sun. Must it surrender the rule of the cosmos? Were God's works of creation no longer to be administered only by priest-kings? Were courageous investigators to calculate the behaviour of the universe with mathematical certainty? (The Inquisition trial found particularly incriminating the assertion of the *Dialogo* that in some things the scientific knowledge of man is equal to divine knowledge.)

The participants in the dialogue agreed, of course, that the cosmos is the work of God, the almighty artist (*fattura d'artefice omnipotente*). His noblest edifice is the constitution of the universe whose greatness surpasses all others in nobility. Salviati declares: We (Copernicans) seek to ennoble the earth, to refine and to perfect it, in that we compare it to the heavenly bodies. But Simplicio insists: the sun and the moon were created to serve the earth (*al servizio della terra*). Simplicio's use of *terra* always means the *Urbs*, Rome. The noble authoritative position of the sun and moon in the cosmos rests on their motionless, changeless, perfect, restful being. To this Sagredo replied: 'With great reluctance do I hear that a changeless and unchangeable nature is attributed as a special sign of nobility and perfection to the heavenly bodies, and that in contrast to this the changeable and the moving is condemned as imperfect ... I, for my part, consider the earth to be most noble and admirable for the very many and diverse alterations, mutations and generations which occur incessantly upon it ... If it were the most beautiful crystal or the most splendid architectural structure, the earth would be worthless were it unalterable, indestructible, motionless. Those who exalt its indestructibility and inalterability do so because they want to linger here for fear of death.'[27]

Sagredo, thus, uncovered one of the genuine motives behind all baroque creativity, its ancient, almost pagan dread of death. Sagredo next declared that it was presumptuous of certain men to assert that their powers of comprehension were the only measure of what nature could accomplish. Simplicio replied in vain. Both friends were in effect releasing nature, the universe and God from the clutches of Aristotelian deductions. They spread a planetary image of the earth before him and referred to Magellan's sailing around the world. Then they compared the position of the sun in Persia, America, Moscow and Spain. Their similes were not drawn from ancient poets, but the transport of commodities, the complex structure of overseas trade. They closed their argument with lavish praise of the telescope: it has pleased God to permit its invention in our time. We can now look into the greatest of distances. And when Simplicio, horrified, objected that if one abandoned Aristotle who would then guide men in philosophy? Salviati answered: only blind men need guides in open country. The world has become knowable, calculable and useful. As open country it no longer consists of unknown and savage landscapes (like Dante's world as a forest of sins). For its control and conquest one no longer needs salvational leaders and structures.

Galileo had hoped that the *Dialogo* would please Urban VIII, who as a student had manifested considerable interest in science and technology. He may well have attended Galileo's mathematical lectures in Pisa from 1586 to 1588. The Pope's strong reaction to Galileo was more than personal pique. It was an expression of the inner failure of the Roman baroque. As the world ruler in the Thirty Years War, Urban VIII believed that he held all the threads in his hand, and he had failed terribly.[28] He was at odds with the Emperor, Spain and Venice. He had no support in France because of Richelieu's prudence and his secret alliance with Sweden was made public after the death of Gustavus Adolphus. The prestige and the power of the Roman Church was at an extremely low level at this crucial moment in the Counter-Reformation. Thus, an inner political success was needed to offset the outer political defeats. Galileo was to be suppressed by the great Barberini Pope in the way that every great lord of the noble world of old Europe punished a disobedient, rebellious servant (*servus et poeta!*). Urban VIII declared Galileo's investigation, and science in general, to be *una fantasia particolare*. A self-willed individual dared to toy with ideas which were the exclusive domain of the omnipotence and wisdom of God, expressed in Holy Scriptures, and embodied in the *polis* Rome! *Fantasia particolare* applied to all the natural science of the past from Bacon on. The Pope correctly grasped the element of arbitrariness in these Spirituals, alchemists, astrologists and pansophists, but he fully misunderstood the ethos of free research. A large proportion of the ecclesiastical and secular world rulers of our time still cannot understand it. For them there is only purposeful, scholastic knowledge in the service of a hierarchy of power. Galileo revered science as the highest obedience to God, the most intense contemplation of his revelation in nature. 'All wisdom (*filosofia*) is grasped only by One, and that is God.' To destroy the fixed authority of scholasticism, Galileo revived the *docta ignorantia*. For him, as for Nicholas of Cusa and Franck, the assertion of human ignorance against divine omniscience was a means of denying the claims of scholastic knowledge with its arrogant certainty. The modern investigator of nature strove for the whole truth. He knew that he would never completely understand the *polis*, the kingdom of God, but he would give his life for its truths and experiments. In order to describe the provisional character of human knowledge and the eternal task of the investigating mind, Galileo quoted Gellius's aphorism, *Veritas temporis filia*.

Galileo was thrown into prison and presumably subjected to torture, although the records are not explicit. He was sentenced on 22 June 1633. Seven cardinals solemnly declared that Galileo had espoused the heretical teaching that the sun was the centre of the cosmos, that the earth was movable and moved diurnally. The Inquisitors and theologians had proved that this opinion was heretical and contrary to Holy Scripture. Galileo was ordered to recant, and he recanted, in a remarkable ceremony of subjection: I, Galileo, ... at my age of seventy years, personally brought to trial, and kneeling before you, Most Eminent and Most Reverend Cardinals, general Inquisitors in the whole Christian Republic against wicked heresy ...' Before these defenders of salvation of the *Urbs* and of the Roman cosmic sphere, Galileo swore on the Gospel to recant the false opinion that the sun is the centre of the world and that it does not move and that the earth is not the centre of the world and that it moves. This recantation of a scientific conviction was carried out in exactly the same sacral-political form as the recantation of the cult of the pagan gods. From the eighth to the thirteenth century Slav tribal princes who entered the service of Christ the King would appear before an imperial bishop and solemnly pledge religious and political obedience (*fides*) to the kingdom of Christ. *Con cuor sincero e fede non finta abiuro, maledico e detesto li sudetti errori e eresi ...* 'With an unfeigned sincere heart and faith I abjure, curse and detest the above errors ...' The oath of abjuration ended with the obligation to denounce those who might be heretics ... All Galileo's writings and new editions of his works were forbidden. The condemnation of Galileo was announced (like a victory over the Turks) by the public ringing of bells, by newspapers, by papal messages to the whole Catholic world, to all universities, monasteries, and private scholars as information and a warning. A dismayed silence fell over the Catholic scholarly world. Galileo's many friends and pupils in all Europe knew that he had been forced to commit a perjury.[29] Men of our century, accustomed to the managed confession in totalitarian states, would not be as stunned as were Galileo's contemporaries. As the first of its kind, Galileo's recantation caused an immediate reaction. Descartes hurriedly destroyed his Copernican *Traité du monde* and the Catholic world passed the pre-eminence in research to the Protestant.

After Galileo's condemnation the natural sciences emigrated from Italy. Those who remained as scientists had to escape into total specialization or into intellectual play. Natural scientists, forced by the religious-political situation became indifferent to all philosophical and religious references. The exclusion of all spiritual influences in their work was to be disastrous for the intellectual development of the nation. No further attempt was made to combine the world of matter and the world of faith. The former was left to experts and dilettantes (who were appraised identically), while the latter was staked off as the domain of the religious-political ruling powers. Even the poets emigrated from the narrowness of the homeland. Metastasio, Goldoni, Alfieri, the great critic Giuseppe Baretti, and Beccaria, the heir and renovator of the brilliant legal tradition of the Italian communes, all left Italy.

History became a special preserve of Italian science. It had a splendid tradition as an ideology of political and religious resistance as in the case of the Gregorians of the eleventh and the Fraticelli and Spirituals of the thirteenth and fourteenth centuries. This tradition had been revived in the sixteenth century by Machiavelli and Guicciardini and then by Sarpi, the sharpest critic of the Council of Trent and a friend of Galileo, who was murdered in 1611. P. Giannone in his courageous *Civil History of the Kingdom of Naples* (1723) made the last attempt to hold the truth of the time and all times against the ruling powers of the day. He atoned for his temerity with excommunication, exile, the dungeon, despair and death. 'The history of the terrorization of the investigators and thinkers of Italy is yet to be written.'[30] Carpi remarked about the Italian intelligentsia, 'There was no lack in Italy of pious and learned personalities who clung to the truth and wanted to serve it, but they could neither write nor publish.' 'Every man was compelled to wear a mask because without it no one could live in Italy.'[31]

G. B. Vico (1668–1744) occupied a special position in this development. Vico, who died insane, had been deeply stirred by the fantastic Neoplatonism of the Renaissance. His countrymen Bruno and Campanella had also influenced him. The Fraticelli ideology of the Third Kingdom, which from 1300 on resisted all attacks in its Neapolitan bastion, completed his indoctrination. Vico was a bitter foe of the investigation of nature and of Cartesianism. He rejected Thomas and Aristotle and instead developed a trinitarian metaphysics. God was the infinite; man the finite capacity, cognition, will. He was, perhaps, most important as the transmitter of the Joachimite heritage to German idealism, through his theology of history. Vico's spirit was a secret fire. His passion glowed against the gloom of his restricted environment. Although in some ways he was ahead of his time, his roots were completely fixed in the Spanish-Italian courtly baroque humanism and spiritualism. Vico transferred the order and determination of the human race from Campanella's total state to history. He saw history as an elaboration of Providence. Providence was the first principle of nations. Providence, as ideal eternal history, bore within it the history of all nations, cultures, religions, poetry, legal forms, and intellectual personalities. Every culture had to pass through three stages of development: the stage of the 'gods', the stage of 'heroes', and the stage of 'men'. Although he accepted the platonic and spiritualistic concept of historical decline, he limited it to the specific historical era within each given stage. This was principally because he was more actively concerned with the *corsi e ricorsi*, with the possibility of a re-birth of nations, and cultures.

This return and renovation had to recapture the whole creative force of the middle ages. For the first time in Italian post-renaissance thinking, the middle ages were seen as something positive, the age of heroes and barbarians. Vico's historical ideas marked the birth of romanticism. They were a reaction against enlightenment, natural science, experiment and atheism. The right shapers of history were to make history because the recipe had been revealed. The Venetian Abbot, Antonio Conti, saw this in Vico's works at once, and recognized its great significance. In a letter of 3 January 1728,[32] Conti wrote to Vico that the new edition of the *Principi* ought to include an introduction in which Vico could point out at the beginning that the determination of future events was now possible according to the known laws of eternal history. Vico wanted to know all world history, so that he could mould the future and educate the young and the nations.

Vico's God-Spirit, who makes history, suited the needs of German and French neo-gnostics and idealists. At last there was an opportunity to fix the free-floating Spirit, which had been released from the Trinity. The Spirit, which thus freed, had fled to the insecure resting place of the heart and disposition, could now be set in some objective frame of reference. Spirit was not in history but above it, guiding and directing it. In Italy the Spirit was administered through the sacraments of the Spanish and curial world-order. Vico's essential idea could not, therefore, be understood. As a result, his influence was restricted to the circle of the reformers of jurisprudence; men like Genovese, Filangieri, Mario Pagano. Vico's historical theory was an anticlerical lay theology in its deepest essence of culture, of poetry and art. It was the history of God on earth, and as such could only maintain a tiny following in the Neapolitan school, whose last great master, Benedetto Croce, logically sought to fuse Vico and German idealism.

History was by no means the only way of escape. There was always music. In the early middle ages German singers and choirs had enchanted Italy. Even as late as 1500 foreign musicians (German, Flemish, French) dominated Italian musical life. It was the Counter-Reformation which really altered the role of music in the life of Italy – by permitting it to continue to be the one remaining free manifestation of the Italian spirit. Palestrina glorified the Council of Trent and the eunuch choir of the popes was formed in 1562, twenty years after the introduction of the Inquisition. It continued to function up to the end of the nineteenth century, the end of the middle ages of the Church.[33] From the sixteenth century on Italian music became a hypnotic, morbid art which produced the illusion of a mystical rapture. Soul, spirit and responsibility went under in its streams of feeling. Everything became purely artistic. Escapism dissolved itself in a dimension beyond faith and knowledge, beyond all social responsibility and freedom. The opera houses in Venice, Rome and Naples became the centres of cultural activity. This operatic industry with its chemically combined formula of dreamy sentimentality and the magic of the artistic star was the precursor of the film industry, the opium of the masses in the closed societies of the present.

Italy of the mid-seventeenth century was a bizarre mixture of singers, adventurers, *Cagliostros*, lovers, beggars, classicists, academicians and gallant abbés. The police were everywhere. Bigotry and frivolity were curiously combined. The sexual libertinism and lasciviousness in the Spanish-Italian-French sphere was a logical historical consequence of the political and religious terrorization. This situation naturally invited Jansenist purism to take possession of all those minds which yearned for cleanliness, for a purer separation of God and world, spirit and matter. Italian Jansenism was an uncommon, multi-levelled phenomenon.[34] For a time it united almost all the religious and political nonconformists who had furtively survived the persecutions from the twelfth to the seventeenth centuries.[35] Rome itself was the centre of Italian Jansenism. There from the very beginning Port Royal, Arnauld, Pascal and Quesnel found ardent defenders in the Curia. The highest prelates fought for Jansenism and the pure doctrine against the political direction of the Jesuits. Although many of these men were not Jansenists themselves, they formed a coherent group of 'groomed, cultivated minds' open to everything new. They wanted to reconcile faith and reason by applying the principles of Jansenism.

The destruction of Port Royal, the persecution of Quesnel and the condemnation of the Jansenist Church by Utrecht caused a great stir. An inner-Catholic International of culture, research, candour and ethics was formed, stretching across France and Italy, which united scholars, priests and investigators. The great front included the Benedictine historians of St Maur near Paris, the Muratori, Benedictines, Oratorians and Dominicans along with professors from Padua and Pisa.[36] The *archetto* in the Palazzo Corsini in Rome was the centre of the Jansenists and the Enlighteners. Under the protection of

Benedict XIV, an enlightened Pope, a network of resistance cells lengthened out all over Italy. Small groups of cultivated men, anti-Jesuits, anti-Thomists, Catholic Enlighteners, Augustinians and Spirituals sprang up everywhere. Naples again proved to be an opposition centre in the south against the Curia and the Jesuits. As Catholic reformers the Jansenists became the pioneers of the Enlightenment in Italy, and very often alliances were formed between Enlighteners and Jansenists. Together both fought against absolutism and the Inquisition, scholasticism and casuistry, and for reforms in Church and state, the education of the clergy and the people. They believed that the Gospel should be brought to the people, which forced them to attack the Jesuits who, even after Benedict XIV's decree of permission, were the foes of any translation of the New Testament into the language of the country. It was a bitter irony that the Jesuits, formerly the pioneers of freedom and of Catholic resistance, were now its foes. They had been worn out by the Counter-Reformation and princely absolutism, powers which they had served to the point of self-sacrifice. In the late eighteenth century they were thrown away by the master-builders as worn-out tools.

The Jansenists first sought the protection of the enlightened princes. When they did not find it in the Piedmont of the Savoyard Charles Emmanuel III and Victor Amadeus III, they tried Tuscany whose Grand Dukes had already tried to defend Galileo. The famous synod of Pistoia and Florence took place in April–May 1787 under the protection of Leopold, a Hapsburg Grand Duke. This great Jansenist *Assemblea* to reform the Church resembled the French national assembly, indeed the Revolutionary Convention itself. The sharp language of the reformers was clear. De Vecchi declared that Augustine needed no superfluous and swollen commentary by St Thomas. He could exert a much better influence in pure and unfalsified form. His revolutionary Augustinianism was directed against the '*attentate* of Gregory VII' and against the curial ideologies of world rule which made a universal despot out of the pope. The whole misery of the inner, spiritual religious life of Italy was exhibited with shocking candour in the debates. This national synod of Tuscany failed in all its religious, ecclesiastical, and educational ideas of reform because of the sudden death of Emperor Joseph II. Grand Duke Leopold had to return to Austria as his successor. The sudden outbreak of the French Revolution discredited and intimidated the reformers. The persecution and hunting down of Jansenists began immediately after Leopold's departure. In 1797 the Bull of Pius VI *Auctorem fidei* condemned the Pistoia Synod and all Italian Jansenism.

The Italian intelligentsia was once again driven back into concealment. Even in the nineteenth century it still bore the marks of the Jansenist, Calvinist spirit. Mazzini, the poet of 'young Europe' and his slogan 'For God and the People' were both directly in the tradition of Italian spiritualism. German idealism was imported to replace the native ideology, which had been virtually eradicated by the exile and persecution of its spokesman. Manzoni's romantic poetry was the purely Italian reaction. It was in many respects a new non-conformist theology. The new poetry abandoned the rhetoric and artificiality of the old world. It inquired with existential seriousness about the essence of being, the destiny of man and nature of divinity. The atheism of Giacomo Leopardi was one manifestation of the revolt of the layman's spirit and yet it had more piety and earnestness than many so-called religious writers. The atheist Leopardi and the Catholic Manzoni, who owed his evangelical radicalism and his high appreciation of the individual conscience to the Fathers of Port Royal, were agreed that the social and political renovation of their country depended on a new awakening of the moral consciousness and conscience.[37]

After the victory of the French Revolution the baroque-curial world realized with horror that all the heresies had risen again from the ashes. Every spiritual and religious doctrine which had been held by heretics from the earliest middle ages had been reborn in radical, secular and political form. The embattled orthodox theologians of nineteenth-century Rome saw the thousand-year continuity very clearly but they could only deny the validity of the heresies. They retreated into bitter reaction. Once more the Church under Gregory XVI in the encyclical *Mirari vos* called for the annihilation of all the heresies by a Carolingian alliance of the Roman cosmos-Church with the Catholic princes.[38] Rome became the last fortress of Constantine, Charlemagne and the Counter-Reformation. It saw itself surrounded by enemies on all sides. *Mirari vos* deserves close attention in our context, because it reveals from the orthodox point of view the same inner continuity of theme which so strikingly characterizes the heresies. It begins with a reference to the suppression of the Roman uprising of 1831. 'We had, therefore, punitively to tame with the rod the obstinacy of such persons whose unbridled anger was not mitigated, but heightened rather, by our long-lasting impunity and our long-suffering indulgence.' (The *virga ferrea*, 'the iron rod' of Emperor Charlemagne and the Emperor-Pope, disciplined rebels against the kingdom of God.) 'Wrong, unashamed science and unrestrained freedom celebrate insolent victories.' 'And now we see the decline of public order, the collapse of authority and the overthrow of all lawful power draw nearer and nearer. This flood of evils is to be ascribed to the conspiratorial work of those secret societies in which, as in a sewer, everything that was sacrilegious and blasphemous in the heresies and pernicious sects flows together.'

The Pope exhorted the bishops to take steps against all 'innovations'. 'For may you zealously consider that any innovation whatsoever affects the whole Church and that according to the word of the holy Pope Agatho, nothing may be diminished, altered or added to what has been properly determined, but is to be preserved inviolate according to word and meaning.' (*Roma aeterna* shelters all salvation under her eternal static dome.) Gregory XVI rightly saw the Holy See as 'a fortress wall ... a sure refuge, a peaceful haven and a treasure house of countless goods.' (Once again, the golden Rome of the fifth to the eighth centuries.) 'Hence it is completely senseless and highly offensive to her (the Roman fortress Church) to speak of a renovation and revival as necessary to assure her existence and growth, as if one believed she were exposed to decline, eclipse or other such failings.' The dangerous enemy of this *polis* of salvation was 'that foolish and erroneous opinion, or better said, that insanity, that freedom of conscience for all should be proclaimed and achieved. It was exaggerated and intemperate freedom of opinion, which prepared the way for this contagious error which has spread widely to the harm of the cause of the Church and civil society.' 'For experience proves, and from very ancient times it has been known, that governments which flourished in wealth, power and fame, pitifully collapsed through this one evil, namely, through unbridled freedom of opinion, freedom of speech, and lust for innovation. To this also belongs the freedom of book selling which cannot be condemned enough or sufficiently abhorred ... a freedom which many foster and demand with criminal zeal.' The Pope based himself on the book burnings of the Apostles, Leo x and the Tridentine Index. 'For the poison of error will never be annihilated if the corrupting germs of the evil do not go up in flames.'

This *polis*, based on Plato, Aristotle and the Roman *religio*, must be defended by Christian princes. Therefore all Christians are duty-bound to serve the princes loyally and obediently. Gregory xvi recalled the Christian soldiers who bravely and devotedly served pagan emperors. 'These magnificent examples of unshakeable loyalty to the princes, which necessarily resulted from the holy prescriptions of the Christian religion, condemn the horrible insolence and wickedness of those who foam at the mouth with contemptible lust for unbridled freedom and sink so low as to dismember all the rights of the authorities, and to bring peoples into slavery, under the guise of freedom. To this aim are sworn the criminal factions and machinations of the Waldensians, Beghards, the followers of Wyclif and other sons of Belial, who were the blemishes and the blots of the human race and therefore rightfully punished by the Apostolic See with excommunication. For these pernicious persons bend all their powers to naught else so that they may with Luther jubilantly congratulate themselves that they are free of everything. And in order to arrive at this goal more easily and more quickly they reach boldly for any criminal means.'

The Pope exhorted the bishops to see that 'every root of bitterness be uprooted from the fields entrusted to you, that every germ of trouble be annihilated so that a rich harvest of virtues may ripen.' 'May moreover the Rulers, our beloved sons in Christ, actively lend themselves to these common wishes for the weal of the Church and State, and indeed by virtue of their sovereign power which, let them consider, they have received not only for the guidance of the world but most especially for the defence of the Church. May they always realize that whatever is done for the salvation of the Church is done for their authority and peace.' Established by God as 'fathers and defenders of peoples...' they have the obligation to care for the inviolability of the Church.

For European intellectual history the conquest of the papal states by Piedmontese troops signified the beginning of the liberation of Catholicism from the ideology of the ancient and medieval cosmos of Rome.[39] Rome once more had a secular ruler. The realm of the individual began to be revived. The individual became open to Christian forces which were beyond political obedience to the old *polis*. For Italy of the late nineteenth and twentieth century this meant the first creative encounter of all the intellectual forces of the nonconformist and orthodox movements, which for a hundred years had reciprocally exhausted, warped and depleted each other. 'Neo-liberalism', 'reform Catholicism', political humanism, the deep humanity, irony and meticulousness of modern Italian poetry, rest on the fact that these very old front positions emerged after 1870. The communion decree of Pius X, who was raised in a Waldensian environment, was part of the same spirit which moved Leo XIII to welcome the progress and freedom of the twentieth century. The Christian Democracy of Don Luigi Sturzo and Papini and *La Ronda* arose. The profound ethical striving of political extremists (like Antonio Gramsci) and of liberals, like Benedetto Croce, and of Catholic scholars forced into nonconformism, like Buonaiuti, were expressions of that fruitful encounter.

16

FROM CALVIN TO DESCARTES AND PASCAL (1490-1661/2)

CALVINISTS were 'the pioneers of the modern world'. They developed the religious forces of western Europe in the sixteenth century, its international politics in the seventeenth century, and its science in the eighteenth century. They created the new Europe of work, ambition, colonialism, war-economy and natural science. Through them, Europe first became wholly Western. They completed a development which had begun with the Roman popes, the Gregorian reforms and scholasticism. The inner history of Europe after the Calvinist period, that is, from the nineteenth century on, was an attempt to overcome the attitudes fixed by the Calvinists.[1] It became vital to revive the intellectual exchanges with the East, which had been allowed to languish, but it was equally essential to revive the inner dialogue between the intellectual superstructure and the psychic and elementary underground of the individual personality. The rigorous Calvinist division of society into two warring camps had to be overcome if a healthy flow of ideas between nations and confessions was to emerge. In Geneva, in the empty, deconsecrated Cathedral, there stood, and still stands, a simple chair. It stands on the spot where once the altar and the throne of the bishop stood. Like the chair of an ancient Roman senator, its startling severity reminds us that it was the throne of the new world God. Maître Calvin sat on it.[2]

Calvin was a product of the hard intellectuality of late scholasticism. Parisian thinking was strongly Ockhamist and, despite attempts to restrict it, this theology ruled the intellectual world from 1450 to 1550. It made a rigorous distinction between the natural and supernatural. In religion it preached terror before the incomprehensible majesty of God, in morality dusty severity, and in philosophy an arid scepticism. Calvin, the son of an episcopal administrator added to it the anticlericalism and nationalism of that educated and acquisitive French bourgeoisie which had been the support of kings and the nation since the days of Jacques Coeur, the royal merchant who financed Joan of Arc.[3]

The themes of the great French Enlightenment of the eighteenth century were present in the ideas of pre-Calvinist bourgeois humanists of the fifteenth century. God and nature obliged the individual to serve the commonweal and the safety of the nation. Chartier's definition of a patriot established the binding link between Joan of Arc, Jacques Coeur, Calvin and Rousseau: *Après le lieu de foy catholique, Nature vous a devant toute chose obligez au commun salut du pays de votre nativité et à la défense de celle seigneurie, soublez laquelle Dieu vous a fait naître et avoir vie.*[4] They were strongly rationalistic and animated by a zeal for political and religious reform. These bourgeois humanists looked with mistrust upon *La Cour*, the court of salvation that Francis I had created and furnished with a gloriole of twenty-two cardinals.[5] They were suspicious of the neopaganism of the Italian humanists whose ideas had been flowing into Paris as a result of the Italian campaigns of Charles VIII and Louis XII. They were repelled by the licentious life of the ecclesiastical and secular nobility, as well as by the corruption of the mendicant monks. The *cordeliers*, the Franciscans, enjoyed an especially bad reputation.

Between 1480 and 1530, French humanism was anti-Italian (as later it was to be anti-Spanish). It arose as a reaction against frivolous Italians who questioned or even denied the existence of God, freedom and immortality.[6] When Calvin entered the debate, he reproached his French humanist comrades for not being sufficiently radical and earnest about their own ideas of reform. He accused them of cowardice and failure to proclaim their faith in his reformation. They were not serious enough about the need for reform in both Church and state and were helpless against scoffers, sceptics, liberals and atheists, like Agrippa of Nettesheim, Des Périers, Rabelais, Dolet and Servetus.[7] Calvin was not entirely fair. French humanism suffered under the choking grip of absolute rulers and its timidity was certainly understandable. Even as eminent a man as Lefèvre d'Etaples (Faber) could not have survived without the protection of Marguerite of Navarre.

Lefèvre was an admirer of Nicholas of Cusa, and defended Reuchlin in 1514. He translated the Gospels in 1523, and the entire Old Testament in 1530. His allegiance was to the *devotio moderna* and from it he derived an idea which he transmitted to Calvin and which was to become a cardinal point of the movement: self-denial as the principle of duty.[8] Like Tauler, Lefèvre, who was often persecuted, understood the practical need of self-denial in suffering, and the importance of resignation, serenity and love. Lefèvre saw life from the viewpoint of death. Calvin also meditated upon it from the viewpoint of death, but as an activist he went one decisive step further. He included the need for activity, the will to work, and the very real struggle for existence of the Western bourgeoisie within his larger religious system. Their natural tendencies and ways of thought were both consecrated and justified. His meditation (*meditatio futurae vitae*) 'endowed the present-life with a feeling of responsibility, shaped it into a process charged with divine energies and made it a battlefield in which a decision would be made for or against God and His Kingdom.'[9] World history was full of demons (Calvin got this from Budé). Every man had to take part in the struggle for order, for the kingdom of God, and for his glory. Certainty about salvation, as the Ockhamists had taught, was impossible, so one had to fight the demons of this world without thinking of oneself.[10] Men had to do good, unless they wanted to be ensnared by evil.

The only end must be the glory of God whose authority and majesty alone are sufficient rewards.

Calvin was a well trained lawyer. He knew Roman and Canon law, and he handled with ease the objections to this ethical approach which came from French humanists. It was no coincidence that Calvin's *soli deo gloria* and Loyola's *Omnia ad majorem Dei gloriam* were so similar. Calvin's community of the elect had a political direction and intent fully as evident as that of the Jesuits, and there can be little doubt that Calvin saw his church as a direct opponent of the Jesuit movement.[11] Calvin had an eye for the political realities of his age and he knew where his doctrine had favourable prospects. The very essence of the doctrine was a kind of social theory. An inescapable division of mankind into two classes had been made at the time of creation. There were two nations, the elect and the damned. An unknowable God, whose purposes were obscure, had ordained this division and man with all his works was helpless before it.[12] This unknowable God was not only obscure, but also entirely spiritual. The pure spirit of God was available only to the elect. Through its revelations alone could Scripture be interpreted or the community rightly governed.[13] Through it, the spiritually guided leadership could control the community's church-discipline, child-training, morality, culture, education, war and peace. Even communal hygiene was a matter of concern to the pure Spirit. Every individual was forced into the service of salvation. All those areas of thought and activity that do not serve salvation (theatre, beauty, sex, luxury) were forbidden. The Spirit revealed itself most fully in the Law of the Old Testament. The Gospel of Christ had become a mere commentary on the Law. Calvin realized, long before the Catholic poets of the twentieth century, that man runs terrible risks when he is exposed to the arbitrary and irrational pleasures of luxury, sex and beauty, and he had also realized that no absolutist régime can assert itself if it permits such arbitrary pursuits to exist. Pleasure, the arts and sex are snares for man but they are also enemies of the state. The rulers can never be certain that through pleasure or art men will not break out of the concrete of the closed society and enter into forbidden relations with God and the devil. Men may again erect their own inner kingdom without regard for the state, kingdoms like that of Bernard of Clairvaux, the *Minnesang* and the first German movement.

Calvin was a political thinker of the greatest stature.[14] Tawney and Rosenstock have rightly compared him with Marx.[15] Hobbes, Montesquieu and others were literati in comparison. The great revolutionary utopians like Campanella, Robespierre and Rousseau (of Geneva) were both related and yet far from him.[16] Calvin was the first to try to seize systematically the entire inner life of man. The 'City of God' confiscated everything, including the individual's subconscious drives. Geneva was to be a model cell for a total world revolution. Thus Calvin carried Plato's expulsion of the poets and Aristotle's conception of the primacy of the communal over the individual to their logical conclusions.[17]

Calvin alone saved the Reformation in Europe from outer destruction and inner absorption by the Counter-Reformation and Counter-Reform. He did so by reinterpreting the Burgundian city of the late middle ages in spiritual terms and by turning humanism into a political force. When Calvin fled from France, he naturally sought refuge in cities which most closely approximated his ideal. Strasbourg, which for centuries had been the emotional and intellectual entrepôt of all the various streams of European intellectual history, and which lay at the half-way point on the Amsterdam-Venice spiritual highway, would have been his first choice. As early as the twelfth century the cities in the old Burgundian territories, in Flanders, northern France and western Germany, in a bitter 'war of all against all' had established themselves as collective dominions.[18] They had become strong, closed commonwealths with an anti-individualistic fundamental feature.[19] These cities were very like animal collectivisms, bee and ant societies. They imposed a harsh, modern discipline and demanded subordination and collective work both in earning a living and in defence. They cherished a hatred of all foreigners and had no compassion for 'useless creatures'.[20] This was the source of Calvin's rejection of mercy which led in the long run to the Calvinist jails and poorhouses, to Calvinist factories and to the class-struggle.

Antwerp's history is a perfect example of the rise of a new urban religious spirit. From early times the old city had been characterized by its 'complete absence of consecration'.[21] Authority was felt to be entirely local and there was no sense of allegiance to anything beyond its borders. It was a naked place in a naked land, without spiritual adornment or supernatural garments.[22] The leadership had become absolutely ruthless. They used their control of the Council and their wealth in an exhausting day-to-day struggle against the lower class, bishops, princes and kings. Their consciences could no longer be appeased by the extremely rich ecclesiastical usages and customs of the corporations and foundations.[23] They needed something more satisfying and Calvin brought them just that. He turned their unhallowed communities of self-interest into instruments of salvation.[24] He taught them how this was to be done and, far more important, he demonstrated the perfect compatibility of their lives and his doctrine. They became elders of the congregation, members of the congregational court; they elected pastors. In short, these rich burghers became the custodians of their own salvation and that of the community. They built schools and universities and forced everybody to emulate their frugal, avaricious and ambitious way of life which they saw as sanctified, as blessed by success – by power, wealth and high social status. Had not God blessed Jacob and Israel with fat herds? The cult of Israel, i.e., the success of one's own chosen people, gripped Calvinist western Europe. Christian names were rarely used, and baptism became a kind of circumcision in which worldliness, sexuality and luxury were circumcized. These new names stripped off the sacred power of the old world of the fathers and the popes. The new name was the first step toward the new man.

The old world died hard. Archaic society had deep roots. The individual subconscious mind continued to resist the total claim of Calvinism. The purges grew more violent, as the raw material proved to be intractable. There is a natural tendency among scholars to gloss over this aspect of Calvin's Geneva.[25] To do so is to miss the whole point of Calvin's great undertaking. These purges and totalitarian techniques were part of the essential spirit of the movement, and the sympathy of modern Calvinists for the Eastern system of today is further evidence of it. 'Teachers were spied upon by pupils, parents by children. In four years there were fifty-eight executions and seventy-six banishments in this city of 20,000; entirely innocent persons were held responsible for the plague in terrifying witch-trials and condemned to death. Calvin punished criticism of his constitution with torture and the sword; it was sedition and Godlessness.[26]

Persecution as such is not the unusual factor in Calvin's Geneva. Dissenters have always been badly treated in religio-political systems from the dawn of time. What is unusual is the spirit in which the persecutions were carried out. This persecution was international and total. Calvin carried on a voluminous international correspondence through which he watched over the purity of his doctrine and discipline. This was an entirely new supranational Inquisition which displayed other features than those of the Catholic Inquisition of the princes, the episcopal commissars and papal emissaries. The chosen people, the Calvinist municipality, for example, worked out its own redemption by constantly uncovering immoral and godless ways of life. It saved itself by destroying political or doctrinal nonconformist thinking among others. Everyone was obliged to mind his neighbour's business. Everyone was obliged to go to Church twice on Sunday. Everyone had to work. The court, jail and poorhouse were part of the system. A man attended the needs of his salvation or he was cast into Hell as unteachable and unworthy of salvation. The filthy and abominable factories of the Calvinist seventeenth and eighteenth centuries were the very embodiment of this Hell in which the poor and the propertyless deservedly atoned for their damned existence. To this very day in the Calvinist countries of Switzerland, Holland, England and America (as in the Dutch language) 'sin is primarily linked with the loss or the squandering of money'.[27]

Capitalism certainly did not arise directly from Calvinism as Max Weber believed.[28] Economically, Calvin's thinking was much more conservative than that of many Jesuit theologians. His Geneva placed draconian restrictions on the freedom of the economy, just as much as it did on the freedom of the mind. There had been capitalists in Genoa, Pisa, Venice and Florence since the eleventh and twelfth centuries, and later a great many of them in France, Flanders and the Rhineland. The early Calvinism of the sixteenth century and the strict, purely religious, seventeenth-century Calvinism saw gold only as a means to promote its great political and religious aspirations – spread of the Calvinist kingdom of God. Calvinism's real significance for the inner history of Europe is not to be found in the development of capitalism in a narrow sense but rather in the rapid secularization of society. For a variety of reasons Calvinism's elements degenerated more quickly into worldliness than those of Lutheranism and Catholicism. The great contributions of Calvinism in the seventeenth and eighteenth centuries to natural science, jurisprudence, philology, the critical arts, medicine and mathematics were the accomplishments of a disintegrating theology.[29] The pure spirit of God was applied to critical distinctions among worldly elements. It was used in a much broader context: in the art of war, in organization, colonial rule and the control of the mind, matter and nations. This extension of the spirit to the world of matter was the real contribution which old Calvinism made to the growth of capitalism.[30]

Calvinism disenchanted the cosmos. It dissolved the conditions of archaic society, and in their place set spirit and matter. The world became a battlefield that must be conquered. Finally, and perhaps most important, it isolated the human ego. The individual human being was torn from his fellow creatures and the world of things, which was degraded to mere matter. Calvinism developed a new, matter-of-fact way of treating things, weapons, commodities and men, which was unthinkable both in the magical cosmos of archaic society and in the sacramentally linked world order of Catholicism. 'This self-estrangement from fellow creatures is part of the nature of capitalism. Capitalism does not exist in its pure form when hierarchical, neighbourly, feudal or familial considerations prevail between buyer and seller, or employer and employee.'[31] Whereas men in archaic society had always regarded animals and things as fellow creatures and equal participants in the drama of salvation, the new men of Calvinist society put aside such collaborative ideas.

Walther von der Vogelweide had talked to his staff as 'Herr' and St Francis had talked to the birds. As late as the eighteenth century, animals were still widely regarded as legally responsible for their deeds, and animal trials were not uncommon. Magical awe and sacramental reverence before things, a fear of violating the divine order and beauty anchored in nature, hindered Catholics from laying hands on the things of nature. Men could not be used as matter either, at least not with a good conscience. Even the Fuggers cited theological opinions to justify their financial operations. In Spain during the eighteenth and nineteenth centuries, men still considered canals and flood control as forbidden interferences with the divine order of nature.[32] The Calvinist had no such irrational reservations. For him, the earth and the world of matter had no sacred significance. The earth was damned and no corporeal act could change one jot of the eternal decree. The things of this world could at best be put into God's service, no more. The world became a monastery in a new, terrible sense. In it the 'elect of God' constructed a new discipline. Work, military service and personal behaviour were subjected to the laws of the terrible God, who demanded total submission and perfect obedience.[33]

The new army drill of Maurice of Orange fully reflected the spirit of Calvinism. An individualistic rabble of mercenaries was hammered into uniformity. Soldiers were to be mass produced. Each one was a mere interchangeable unit in a larger entity. Each man was to be absolutely like his neighbour. Men became material commodities.[34] As in primordial times, the commodity and the weapon once more became one. The de-consecrated thing became a commodity and weapon in the commercial and military operations of the capitalists.[35] Modern industry arose in the weapon, uniform and armaments industry of the late sixteenth century. Army drill and factory discipline simplified and debased life to a degree unknown even to a beggar. As Mumford has pointed out, killing is, after all, merely an extreme simplification of life. The evil world was to be robbed of its false beauties, charm, colours, fragrances and sensual temptations. Its real nature was revealed in mines, factories, battle-fields and counting-houses. The world was a bulwark to be conquered or a trial in which men and things were completely consumed.

In 1589 Amsterdam erected the first workhouse for vagabonds in a former convent of Poor Clares. In 1595 it built the first prison for men, and in 1603 a secret prison for the sons of honest burghers. The Calvinist saw no difference between the poorhouse and the prison.[36] *Miseris et malis* was written over the entrance to the jail-poorhouse in Dessau. Poverty meant that grace had been denied. Thus the only way to improve and better the poor was through a rigorous programme of work, and by the seventeenth century inmates of Calvinist institutions were often leased directly to capitalist entrepreneurs. The insatiable demand for factory labour and for soldiers was satisfied to some extent by this means. It is suggestive that all six Catholic poorhouses failed, while the Protestant poorhouses flourished.

There was no room in such a system for compassion. 'The conception of the punitive Lord of Judgment visibly hardened minds against poverty and suffering.' 'He who fell was kicked.'[37] Pity was an offence against divine pre-destination which intended that the poor and the workers should serve its glory. Charity corrupted morals and interfered with work. The elect piled up their money in the counting-houses. It was God's will. So was the poverty of the workers and soldiers who served in the factories and the army. The Huguenot Mandeville transformed this theological class system into a biologi-cal and sociological world-law. In his *Essay on Charity and Charity Schools* (1723) he argued against making mankind totally happy. 'It is clear that among free people where slavery is forbidden, the surest wealth exists in a great mass of hard working poor ... In order to make society happy it is necessary that a considerable part of it be ignorant as well as poor.'

The Manichaean heresy reappeared in these ideas. Calvin, who was a Picard, may well have been influenced by the heretical past of his native country. Calvinist misanthropy and hostility to nature was pure Manichaean dualism. It turned the earth into a hell, because it saw the earth as Hell. Six-to eight-year-old children were sent to the mines, dragged out of their sleep and taken off to factories. The average life expectancy fell to fifteen years. The earth was a 'vale of tears'. Even Andrew Ure, the great defender of Victorian capitalism, denied that the children needed sunlight.[38] Gaslight was enough. In this work-world of terror, air and drinking-water were poisoned. Fallen nature had been broken and then, later, replaced by an artificial, intellectually produced nature.*

Calvinism unleashed tremendous forces, precisely because it suppressed and rejected other equally powerful forces. Nature, sexuality, the sensuousness and beauty of the fine arts were violently repressed, but this repression had to be paid for. Greed, ambition, vengefulness and arrogance burst out, as it had in the days of pre-Benedictine monasticism. A new militancy, not seen since the age of the fierce Eastern monks of the fourth century, arose. Once again, as in fourth-century Constantinople, Alexandria and Antioch, spiritual fanatics defended their Spirit at councils. Far more important than the militancy, which Calvinist repression of the natural side of man evoked, was the generation of a new fear. An age of fear began in the West. Just as Ivan IV had been afraid of an independent Church, because his subjects might no longer fear him, the Calvinist began to fear his own personality. He was afraid of the outbreak of his own underground, of naturalness, of sex, of humanity. He strangled nearly all the original Christian and evangelical virtues. He denied the essential spirit of the land of the Sermon of the Mount and the lilies of the valley. Joyous poverty, peaceful resignation and selfless giving were contemptible in his eyes. He denounced them as expressions of spiritual laziness and carnal lust.

There was one more Christ-like virtue to trample under: love itself. The way had indeed been prepared by the spiritual attitudes of late medieval piety, the *devotio moderna* and Ockhamism. Calvinism finished the job. Love became an ambiguous, trembling and yet arrogant love of God alone. Compassion was debased. It became weakness unworthy of the strong and pious. The Calvinist's terror at his own violated nature drove him to flight into the world. He raped and de-consecrated the body of nature with telescopes and microscopes and the surgeon's forceps, with range-finders, measures and numbers.

The rapid secularization process of Calvinism in the seventeenth and eighteenth centuries was the unfolding of this inner dynamism. The individual fled the terrors of his own psychological underground and plunged into the battles of the stock exchanges, European wars, commercial, military and colonial operations on the world seas. The sea became a gigantic stage for Calvinist escape from the self.† Literature, too, in the areas under Calvinist influence played a similar role. In western Europe Calvinism overwhelmed the Free Churches, Lutheranism and sometimes Catholicism itself. The new

*The neon lights of the modern city continue to reflect this tradition. Man has built himself a new Jerusalem lit by electricity. Nature has been banished.

†The sea has always represented the subconscious in one modern interpretation, that of depth psychology. It is suggestive in this context to see a connection between Calvinist seamanship, exploration and travel, and the profound psychological tension which the doctrine produced in its believers.

novels, travel books, nature poems and autobiographies were the first coherent attempt to modify the rigour of Calvinist theology. Until the time of Gide and Brecht, western European literature was to be preoccupied by the attempt to restore the elements of the human personality, which had been condemned and banished by Calvinism. As time passed the belles-lettres began to abandon the attempt to correct theology and demanded its liquidation instead. Yet even the most anti-theological of modern writers has been unable to efface the mark of Calvinism in his thinking. Some good examples can be seen in the struggle between good and evil in Anglo-Saxon detective fiction, the pathos of distance and purity in T. E. Lawrence, and the pathos of debauchery in D. H. Lawrence. Epics of heroes, of pioneers of labour, science and discovery were a Calvinist heritage. Calvin's Moses, his *heroicum ingenium*, was the model for the hero of Western literature, the spiritually violent man of genius.[39]

The monstrous harshness of the Calvinist world-view shocked Lutheranism and Catholicism. It exerted a fascination upon them from which neither has completely recovered to this day. Lutheranism feared Calvinism as the devil. Lutherans burned their own preachers at the stake who were suspected of inclining towards Calvinism. The Catholicism of the Counter-Reformation evolved its methods of prayer, its spiritual book-keeping and its juridical severity in the shadow of Calvinism. Neither Jansenism nor neo-Catholic humanism would be comprehensible without Calvinism. The most remarkable aspect of Calvinism is not the effect its narrowness and asperity had on subsequent generations, but its subtle transformation into an ideology of free men. The bourgeoisie, who first spread it, soon found themselves locked in a life and death struggle for political liberty. Calvinists, especially in England and the Low Countries, needed the help and friendship of the free church movement, and this alliance, forged in necessity, freed the Calvinists to exert a creative and fruitful influence on the history of Europe.

A crucial factor in the development of Calvinism in France was its mobilization of the powerful forces of the Waldensians and Albigensians who had been suppressed and persecuted for 300 years.[40] In the last decade of the rule of Francis I, a wave of persecution rolled over the Waldensians in Provence. Only a few thousand were able to fight their way to Geneva. During centuries of persecution, the peaceful Waldensians had roamed through all western Europe. Waldensian pre-reformation manuscripts and translations of the New Testament into Provençal are still quite common.[41]

The Albigensian heritage was even stronger. No persecution had been able to break the heroism of the *perfecti*. Nothing had been able to shake their ascetic dualism. They still saw the world as an immortal struggle between the pure spirit of God and evil matter. The same landscape, the same cities, places and clans which had produced Catharism in the thirteenth century, now professed Calvinism. This continuity strengthened the fundamental Manichaeanism of the new movement. It also, paradoxically, hastened the secularization of Calvinism. The Albigensians, like all persecuted Christian sects, had been forbidden to practise any aspect of their cult. Since they could not train a clergy, support churches and chapter houses, nor appoint any public leadership, they became secularized in a very literal sense. The obvious need to conceal what they were really up to led them to adopt worldly callings and activities. The decision to go underground had inevitably a secular tendency. To maintain the purity of their Faith, they had to communicate with each other. In short, they had to be able to travel without arousing suspicion. They became bankers, physicians, merchants and weavers. This process went on for generations and whole families became subterranean agents of the invisible church. In some cases, time would erode the inner urgency of the calling, but the fundamental attitudes, secrecy, suspicion, resentment of worldly authority, would pass on from father to son.

Albigensian criticism of Catholic dogma, sacraments and philosophy, survived in this way, and passed into the Huguenot movement. Huguenot biblical science reflected the ancient Albigensian rejection of ecclesiastical and worldly authority. Albigensian resentment and hostility strongly coloured Huguenot philology and their doctrine of the right of resistance. The pure spiritual Faith of Albigensianism has always tended toward enlightenment. It wanted to destroy the Catholic superstitions of the uneducated, carnal masses through science and true wisdom. French Calvinism took over the basic mood and the religious-intellectual climate of Albigensianism. It also inherited the inclination to secular activities and habits. This transformation took place with surprising swiftness. The religious impetus changed into political resistance under persecution. When the persecution abated, French Calvinism flowed back into the world, stronger than ever. It carried the philosophy and philology, the mathematics, the natural science and jurisprudence of the seventeenth and eighteenth centuries along with it.

The early French Protestants had been laymen. The first Protestant community in Meaux des Briçonnet elected the wool-carder Pierre Leclerc as its pastor.[42] They were weavers and drapers. They were humanists and jurists like Farel, Calvin and Bèze (who characteristically was both a jurist and a classical philologist) and later autodidacts like Antoine Court and lay preachers like Rabaut. They were noblemen, great lords and generals like Gaspard de Coligny, and lawyers like Claude Brousson, the creator of the ministry for the 'Church of the Wilderness'.

New inspirations enriched Calvinism through these men's daily experience of life. Their occupations accelerated the trend toward secular organization. Catholic persecution began at once. There was an obvious need for a strict spiritual and political order. At the Academy in Geneva Calvin tirelessly trained young men for sacrificial service in France.[43] The first Synod, in Paris in 1559, was secret. It set up an established Church (*église dressée*). Its order (*police*) had been ordained by Christ, and was proclaimed holy and inviolable (*sacré et inviolable*). The Synod's structure reflected the legalistic taste of the French bourgeoisie. The model was the court structure in civil jurisprudence.

The Provinces of the Synod formed a mighty religious-political body inspired by God's Spirit and Word. It administered itself democratically and was in a real sense the model for the Revolutionary Convention.*

The modern nation, as a conspiratorial community of inspired, enlightened bearers of salvation, was born in the meetings of these Calvinist enthusiasts. They were progressives in a thoroughly modern sense. The 40,000 members of the Reformed Church found confirmation in Calvin's teaching of the rights of the estates, and of the people to resist the extravagance, cruelty and weakness of the kings. They felt themselves to be the élite of the nation. Under a prominent, gifted leader, Admiral Gaspard de Coligny, they waged a civil war in France from 1562 to 1598. Had they triumphed, power over all Europe would have fallen to them. Nothing in Europe would have been able to resist the triumphal march of this army of God and the purges of its commissars. The people under arms had been commissioned by God's wrath to purge the world of all 'lewd persons' and 'enemies of God'.

The Catholic world was stunned and appalled. They saw before them the rise of a Huguenot International, stretching from Geneva to Scotland, England, the Low Countries, the German southwest, and encompassing the whole eastern edge of Europe from Poland to Transylvania, up to the Croat Bogomilian country. They saw it as the revival of the first Manichaean International of the Albigensians in the thirteenth century. And again the anxiety of the weaker side unleashed a dreadful reaction. Franciscans and Dominicans preached a crusade against the heretics, the enemies of salvation, the profaners of the Eucharist and of holy relics and images. Their words recalled the days of Agobard of Lyons and the Albigensian and Waldensian wars. Pius v, a stern Dominican, demanded the extermination of the Huguenots in France. Catherine de' Medici, the weak and irresolute ruler, vacillated. In 1572, on St Bartholomew's night, all the Huguenot leaders and as many of their followers as could be seized on the spot were murdered. Coligny's head was brought to Rome. The extermination of the Huguenots (*Hugonotorum Strages*) was celebrated in a triumphal Mass. Splendid processions filled the streets and a special, commemorative medallion was struck. On one side, an angel raised the cross in one hand while killing Huguenots with the other. The reverse side bore the image of the Pope. This monstrous deed split France into two nations. Protestantism was forced to become a worldly, political resistance movement. 'Perhaps the most momentous consequence of St Bartholomew's night was the fact that for Protestant France any further consideration of the spiritual basis of the religious struggle had become practically impossible.'[44]

A war of annihilation broke out between the Huguenots and the 'Catholic League'. For decades, churches, monasteries, villages and entire areas were destroyed and devastated. This paroxysm of hate mercifully could not last for ever. The fury of the struggle finally burnt out. It left the nation completely

*The first president of the Convention was, appropriately enough, a Huguenot pastor, Rabaut-Saint-Etienne.

exhausted. Henry IV was thus free to begin the work of pacification and reconstruction. The Edict of Nantes (1598) assured the Huguenot nation 100 towns
(for eight years) and 800 church communities, divided into sixty-two district
synods. Although Henry of Navarre lost his life as a result of this settlement,
he had managed to serve the internal peace of France for half a century.
During this brief interlude, a genuine dialogue between Catholics and
Huguenots took place. This was the golden age, when Huguenots met the
Catholic intelligentsia in the salon of Madame Des Loges. It was the beginning of tolerance, science and intellectuality of the early Enlightenment.[45]

In the midst of the persecutions, the hatred and intolerance, a reaction
against both Calvinist and Catholic fanaticism began to emerge. In a sense, it
had always been there. Its sources lay deep in the Stoic and Franciscan
traditions. Lull, Nicholas of Cusa and Erasmus were its patron saints, but in
the late sixteenth century it began to gather new vigour, the vigour of a man
like Rabelais. Calvin hated Rabelais passionately, and Rabelais responded in
kind.[46] In Calvin's theology he saw a monstrous presumption which made a
tyrant of God and slave of man. Rabelais was an ex-Franciscan who had
transformed Franciscan love of creatures and cosmic joy into an enthusiastic
'vitalistic and dynamic triumph of corporality'.[47] Rabelais still retained much
of the openness to the world and nature of the Franciscans of the sixteenth
century.[48] His folk-epic *Gargantua and Pantagruel*, the greatest work of French
folk-literature to the present day, celebrated the joys of the natural life of
man.[49]

Rabelais set free everything that Calvin wanted to bind, to ban, to repress
and to damn. The underground of archaic society broke out in a flood of
ribaldry and sex jokes. Rabelais combined the pathos and realism of the late
medieval, folk preachers, the precision and observation of a Paracelsian
physician and the refined erudition of the baroque humanists. All of his
enormous gifts served the one, great cause, the goodness of man. Rabelais
preached man's right to be free of the suffocating dungeons of mad dogmas.
He was the prince of scoffers, the master of jesters and the lord of exuberance.
Nothing heavenly, but all things earthly, could be made holy. Despite his
claim that he preferred drunkards and syphilitics to the wise, he belonged in
spirit to the liberal tradition of Thomas More, Nicholas of Cusa and Erasmus.
He wanted to build an earthly paradise for a free, tolerant and contented
humanity. This was the essential idea behind the Abbey of Thélème. Gentlemen and ladies would be able to withdraw into a better world, where they
could really enjoy the things of this world. There would be festivals, celebrations and various studies. A six-storied polyglot library was to adorn this
cathedral of the new man. The Abbey of Thélème fused the tradition of
Gottfried of Strasbourg, the Minnesingers' grotto of love, and the Italian
tradition of court circles and select academies. It was a transitional phenomenon, leading from the world of the academy, which was fast disappearing,
to the new Benedictine foundations and the salons of the Enlightenment.[50]

There were other forces at work, which were not originally French, but which profoundly influenced the growth of the idea of tolerance in France. In the previous chapter we followed the stream of emigrants from Italy and Spain. These men – Anabaptists, freethinkers, Erasmians and Waldensians – bore the Church of the Spirit to Venice and Switzerland, and later, as we saw, to eastern Europe. In 1550 the Anabaptist council in Venice united this secret international of spiritualists, free-thinking and a-dogmatic nonconformists. Within a few years they were able to gain a footing in the Low Countries and England where they created the Deism and the tolerance of the early Enlightenment. Rabelais was a messenger from France to this open world. He conceived of the new man, capable of admitting ignorance, open to self-irony, attentive to the welfare of soul and body and adaptable in every sort of human company. The new man would be well-travelled, and learned in 'the Book of the World'. He would honour truth even when it lay with the enemy. He would be well aware of his own insignificance, and of the fact that he was no more than a tiny point in the universe. He could, therefore, be intolerant only of conceit, torpidity and violence.[51]

Jean Bodin (1520–96) portrayed this international of nonconformists in his secretly distributed work, *Heptaplomeres* (1588 to 1593).[52] In it a Catholic, a Lutheran, a Calvinist, a Jew, a Mohammedan, a representative of natural religion, and a man indifferent to religion peacefully discuss the kinship of all religions. The basic ideas in this work come from Aristotle and the World of the Three Rings. Bodin developed a science of comparative religion in which he tried to demonstrate the influence of environmental factors on the individual religions. His other positions, for example, those on the paradox of the incarnation of God, the redemption, the Eucharist and the salvation of the most miserable of men, stemmed from revolutionary spiritualism. Bodin had a strong feeling for the positive elements in the individual historical religions. He knew of no criterion for *the* true religion, hence the state had to tolerate them all. Reason and natural law and the ethics of Stoicism would suffice to achieve earthly bliss.

Bodin was by no means a mere sceptic. He was among other things a great political economist. In 1574 he started his investigations of the origin of shortages in France. At the same time, he was a political thinker of great sophistication, who worked out the idea of state sovereignty. In his *Six livres de la République* (1576) he developed the consequences of this idea in terms of enlightened absolutism. His thinking had a strong legal flavour, but his passionate espousal of freedom of conscience, justice and peace often carried him beyond the limits of jurisprudence. Bodin embodied that second French humanism which set itself against the fury of the warring confessions. He had studied in Toulouse, where as in the Albigensian days the enemies still clashed with each other.* After Toulouse, he went to live in Paris, where he came into close contact with prominent Huguenots. As a councillor of King Henry III

*The University itself had been a product of the Albigensian wars.

in Laon, and also as a deputy of the Third Estate at the Assembly of the Estates General in Blois in 1576, he acquired the experience that made him realize that all Europe was in the throes of a profound transformation. If men were to cease slaughtering one another in religious wars, then a new sense of moderation and human dignity, freedom, law and tolerance had to be constructed. Concrete reforms of the state and society, jurisprudence, economy and education were equally important.

Cautiously he began to work out some proposals for reforms, and his book on the State was the first volume of a great work on a well-ordered universe. He saw clearly that religions had been transformed into militant political ideologies.* He saw furthermore that men were using God to justify erection of earthly tyrannies. Thus he stressed that sovereignty does not come from God, but from human needs. The state was merely an association of families. In it the father was the supreme master of the fundamental, social unit. Bodin, the man of the early Enlightenment, was the author of the conservative idea of the middle way, which the Romantics later distorted. As Bodin looked about, he thought that there was visible confirmation of this theory both in geography and race. France, the country in the middle of the temperate intellectual and spiritual climate, lay between the cold, dry democratic north and hot, intelligent, lazy and theocratic south. In France the man of reason and moderation was at home.

In his *Essais* (1580 ff.) Montaigne tried to verify Bodin's leading idea. The very word *Essai* expressed the undogmatic quality of Montaigne's thinking, or, as Friedrich puts it, 'Montaigne's urge to exist in his own uncertainty.'[53] Silently, unobserved, these ideas undermined the fortresses of dogmatic certainty. Like the imperceptible impact of pietism and the 'Silent in the Land', Montaigne's thinking infiltrated the arrogant positions of absolutist doctrines, ideologies and confessions. Its apparently infinite openness for everything natural was irresistible. There were no questions which could not be asked. What is man? A very dignified and a very wretched being, 'the most miserable and fragile of all creatures'.[54] Insignificant man ought not to try to hold God and the world in the strangling grasp of his reason and Faith.[55] Man is a being of contradictions and habits and both environment and habit determine his religious attitude. Man is also open to illusion and reality. He can accept the 'truth of facts' (*vérité des faits*) sentiently, obediently, pliantly 'in their apparent concreteness'.[56] Montaigne believed that traditional ways of life, historical and social realities and psychological phenomena were such facts. He saw man as an ego who carefully observes itself, always alert, critical and open.[57] A central feature of this self-analysis in Montaigne is what Friedrich calls 'persistent self-negation', the ultimate aim of which is to experience death in the 'wisdom of obedience'.[58] This attitude toward death represents a superb secular translation of the essence of the spirituality of the *devotio moderna*. The *docta ignorantia* has become *l'ignorance doctorale*.[59] It implies

*Karl Kraus once observed that every ideologue thinks of war.

'sentient contact with the unperceived cosmic order',[60] which is to be obeyed in the limited contact with little things.

Montaigne almost never cited the Gospels. Plutarch and Seneca were the foundations of his 'philosophical pastoral care' and his praise of inwardness.[61] In Chapter Three of the first book of the *Essais* he defended primitive peoples denounced by Christians as wild and barbaric. *Chacun appelle barbarie ce qui n'est pas de son usage.*[62] For Montaigne, the barbarians were the systematic thinkers, the Aristotelian schoolmen,* and all those who nail man to the cross of their closed systems of relations and who throw him in the dungeons and on the pyres of their closed worlds. The fundamentally heroic tone of his *Essais* and their immanent Christian character was soon perceived and admired by the Catholic neo-humanists, by Jean-Pierre Camus and François de Sales.

In the midst of the bitterest battles between Huguenots and Catholics at the age of thirty-eight, Montaigne retired to his castle. He left a very promising career as judge and councillor in the parliament of Bordeaux, because he felt a compelling need to try to reconcile the bitter antagonisms in the world around by quiet contemplation. His own family had been deeply sundered by the religious warfare. 'A brother and two sisters had joined the Reformation. A niece, who had been raised as a Calvinist, had later converted – allegedly under his influence – to Catholicism and was pronounced blessed in the following century. One of his cousins was a Jesuit. His wife's family were notorious enemies of the Huguenots.'[63] Montaigne like Bodin was a foe of the Catholic League and like his friend Charron carried on his meditations in the shadows cast by St Bartholomew's night. He was distressed by the Huguenot and Catholic firebrands, who were devouring the country and its minds.

Montaigne's friend and greatest direct disciple was the priest and pastor Pierre Charron, who wrote the main ethical work of the religious Enlightenment (*Traité de la Sagesse*, 1601). It was completely independent in dogma and in its attitude to moral questions. It was not unlike the works of Bacon written between 1605 and 1620. Charron's *de la Sagesse*, Lord Edward Herbert of Cherbury's *de Veritate* of 1624 and Grotius's *International Law*, all came into being as the European centre was destroying itself in the Thirty Years War. There is another point to notice about Charron's book. In it religious humanism awoke once again on this southern French soil of the World of the Three Rings. In the midst of a civil war, it rediscovered itself in stoicism, very much in the spirit of the *devotio moderna*. 'Man is the true science and the true study of man.'[64] Charron argued that although man suffered from vanity, weakness, inconstancy, misery (*vanité, faiblesse, inconstance, misère*) he was also distinguished by a strong will. The crucial idea for Charron was the *Preud'homie*. According to Charron, the enlightened and sceptical, worldly-wise, introspective, noble man could acquire the virtues of right being, life and knowledge, through a natural and reasonable life. 'I want

*He himself came from the Franciscan and Lullian tradition of Sabunde.

men to be good without heaven or hell.' 'I want you to be a good man because nature and reason (that is God) will it. The world-order, of which you are the least small part, so requires it.'[65] This stoic-Cistercian concept of righteousness is reminiscent of Aelred of Rievaux's *Book of Friendship*. Charron, who wanted at one time to become a Cistercian, believed that through this discipline of righteousness the pious and virtuous philosopher could be raised above the quarrel of the confessions: *La religion est postérieure à la preud' homie*. Religion was obviously inferior in Charron's eyes to virtue. Religion was no more than the actual creeds of the two parties in a ghastly civil war. Voltaire, Diderot and Rousseau all copied from Montaigne, but they read Charron too. Their criticism of religion was born of the war experience of the lacerated South, in that World of the Three Rings where Albigensians, Waldensians, Calvinists and Catholics clashed with one another.

In this setting of religious scepticism, a few men tried to liberate the divine and the human from the grip of the religious parties. Francisco Sanchez (1550 to 1622) fitted easily into these circles. Sanchez, a Portugese physician, had been professor of medicine at Montpellier and Toulouse. His scientific, epistemological scepticism was directed at the grip of the Aristotelians and scholastics on the truth. In 1580 he published his book, *That nothing certain is known* (*Quod Nihil Scitur*). In that same year the first books of the *Essais* appeared and William of Orange, the liberator of the Low Countries was banished by absolutist Spain and the Roman Church.[66] Like Descartes, Sanchez employed doubt as a method. Man should not try to arrive at an absolute truth, as all ideologies claim to do. If he is modest, he can use his powers of observation, experiment and judgment to gain a conditional knowledge, in other words, a purely human knowledge. He must 'be careful to observe all the hindrances and inadequacies that are peculiar to our perception.'

The spirit of Charron and Sanchez found powerful support in the Low Countries, which had inherited the economic position of Venice and the Italian city-states.[67] They also inherited the special position of Venice in European intellectual history. They became the refuge of Huguenots, Lutheran sectarians, Polish and Hungarian Enthusiasts, Italian and Spanish humanists and natural scientists. The Low Countries transmitted the Enlightenment to England and strengthened the inner resistance in France. They became the publishing centre for France, and sent streams of enlighteners and pietists to Germany, as well as deep into Russia. In the Low Countries, Manichaean heretics, free-spirits, groups of the right and left reform movement had been active since the late eleventh century. Beguines and Beghards, the woman's movement, the first German mysticism, *devotio moderna*, Eckhart and Tauler were all at home there. Ruysbroeck, the symbolic spokesman of the region profoundly influenced Geert Groote, Thomas à Kempis, Nicholas of Cusa and Erasmus. Surprisingly, he had a very great effect on the sober, strongly dualistic Averroists and Aristotelians of the Paris scholasticism of the thirteenth and fourteenth centuries, from Siger of Brabant down to John of Mirecourt. These men were extreme rationalists, who pushed relentlessly toward immanence. Despite their rigorous rationalism, many of them professed an often neoplatonically garbed pantheism. This curious combination of doctrines must have been nourished by the smouldering underground of the people. The Parisian masters could not fail to be affected by the popular ecstatic revivals and mystical convulsions. They began to try to seize God through a passionate intellectual effort. One can follow the tradition of the passionate grasping of God from low-German versions of the Song of Songs to William of Moerbeke and to the reception of the divine-passion by Leone Ebreo, Giordano Bruno and Spinoza.

The struggle for political, social and economic freedom in the Low Countries was closely linked with the struggle of these sharply accentuated groups, parties, and estates for religious freedom. Religious freedom meant a way to self-knowledge and the right to use their own experience of the world in searching for a holy conscience.[68] As early as 1525, Luther was appalled by the ideas which some men from Antwerp discussed with him. To them the Holy Ghost was nothing else but reason and understanding. The statesman Coornhert, who was born in Amsterdam in 1522 and became Secretary-General of the States in 1572, was an example of the same development. He drew his enlightened ideas on freedom of religion, freedom of conscience and tolerance from his own political experience. These ideas led him to the threshold of a natural religion, free of dogma, and paved the way for the early Enlightenment and Deism of seventeenth-century England. Coornhert asked: What has been the use of the violent efforts of Charles v and Philip ii to subject Europe or the Low Countries to one creed?[69] The rich and politically experienced patricians in Amsterdam and the countless groups of 'Silent in the land' wanted to read their Bible and interpret it by themselves. They wanted freedom of economic enterprise (against all Lutheran, French and Calvinist state economic systems and regulations), freedom of the seas (with Hugo Grotius and Graswinckel) and also the freedom to conclude political alliances. Boxhornius, Jean de Witt, Noodt, Huber and especially Pieter de la Court were the representatives of this statesman-like, upper bourgeoisie.

The freedom of their economic activity did not seem assured to them without a liberal state constitution and religious self-determination. In a very characteristic way, Court attacked the corporations of professors, who monopolized science, as much as the guilds monopolized the crafts.[70] These patrician, liberal tendencies centred around the Republican party and its seat, Amsterdam. The militant Calvinism of the broad, lower strata of the people was always hostile to it. These Calvinists were convinced that the struggle for the freedom of the Low Countries against Spanish, French and Roman absolutism could be won only when the people had been united in the strictest Calvinist discipline under God. They rallied around the House of Orange and the gubernatorial party which held the military direction of the great struggle in its hands. The Huguenot refugees became far more extreme under the influence of the religious and politically militant thought of these circles.

The leader, William of Orange, the 'Liberator', had been born a Lutheran, and raised as a Catholic. He became a Calvinist at the decisive moment of the great struggle against Spain and Rome, and died with these words on his lips, *Mon Dieu, ayez pitié de mon âme et de ce pauvre peuple*. As leaders of 'this poor people' the House of Orange assumed a very great power. They threatened to become the founders of a militant Calvinist absolutism. There were terrible potentialities in these great popular leaders. Maurice of Nassau showed what these potentialities were when he became Governor of the West Indies Company's holdings in Brazil. His aim was evidently to create a colonial totalitarian state, and he used military and political techniques on an almost modern scale. At the same time, the Jesuits were trying to do the same thing in Paraguay. These colonial experiments are an important clue to the thinking of the early baroque era. They demonstrate beyond any shadow of a doubt that the totalitarian ideas of Campanella, Bacon or Hobbes were not empty fantasies. Whenever these men of the baroque got the chance, they put them into practice. The men of the baroque seriously intended to subject everything in human life to the service of the one divine and governmental majesty. These colonial experiments and the totalitarian thinking of the age were important contributors to revolutionary Jacobinism.

In the midst of the conflict between patrician liberality and the absolutism of the House of Orange, Oldenbarneveldt, Arminius and Grotius began to develop their remarkable ideas. All three failed to achieve what they had set out to do, but their defeat made them more fruitful for the later ages than success at the time could ever have done. Johann of Oldenbarneveldt was a *Ratz Pensionar*, a secretary of the States General, and a kind of permanent advocate of Holland. He has been called 'the most gifted of the Netherlanders' and 'the second founder of the Dutch State'.[71] He was a great legal scholar, profoundly imbued with Calvin's work-ethos, but despite the strong Calvinist strain in his make-up he remained passionately committed to patrician tolerance and freedom. His motto, which he drew from Nicholas of Cusa and Erasmus, expressed his position: 'To know nothing completely is the surest faith.' He was a clever and often daring statesman. He had to be in order to guide Holland through such dangerous years. In the end, he was defeated in the struggle against Maurice of Orange and radical Calvinism, and the 'Father of the State' was executed in 1619.

Oldenbarneveldt had taken Arminius, the Leyden theology professor under his protection.[72] Like his protector, Arminius attempted to fight back against the increasing bitterness of the confessional conflict. He was a victim of the inexorable dialectic of spiritual history. The historian can see in his tragic career a perfect example of the interplay of the forces between a social and political substructure on one side and a religious superstructure on the other. The Calvinist consistory of Amsterdam had requested his theological help to put down internal opposition. Resistance to the merciless, damning Calvinist God was growing steadily in Calvinist communities. Arminius began an intensive study of the Bible and patristic texts. The results were unexpected. He became fascinated by the idea of freedom. To the horror of his Calvinist brethren, he came forward with a new doctrine which ascribed to man the freedom to accept or to refuse God's grace out of his own free will (not as a consequence of an absolutist divine decree). This doctrine reflected the struggle for existence and the self-consciousness of a patrician class striving for freedom and free trade. Immediately a considerable following gathered around him. They were called the Arminians or Remonstrants. The Calvinist synod of Dortrecht, of course, condemned this doctrine of the Remonstrants, and these revisionists were persecuted everywhere with Calvinistic consistency. Oldenbarneveldt paid the death penalty for his advocacy of the atheistic Arminius.

A few years later a reconciliation between Calvinism and Arminianism was attempted at the Theological College in Namur. This school founded by Duplessis-Mornay and by Moses Amyraut, the theorist of hypothetical universalism, remained a special case. Most of the other Huguenots became more, rather than less, dogmatic. The ferocity of Catholic persecution drove them to hold the extreme tenets of the doctrine of predestination more tightly. Persecution and suppression were, as always, unable to stop Arminianism from spreading from Holland into other Protestant countries, especially to England. Persecution only succeeded in forcing Arminianism into a secular and rational form. Calvinism became responsible for the creation of its own deadliest foe. Secularized Arminianism undermined the closed state, church, and theological doctrine of Calvinism. Together with Socinianism, which arose out of Catholic reform-humanism, it became the element of secularization, enlightenment, democracy, of tolerance, of the movement for peace and freedom in Protestant Europe.[73]

Oldenbarneveldt's fall sealed the fate of the Arminian, Hugo de Groot (Grotius).[74] Oldenbarneveldt was executed in 1619, and Grotius condemned to lifelong imprisonment. Grotius was a descendant of an old family of burgomasters and regents. He was a child prodigy, and was sent about the country at official expense to display his learning. At the age of twelve he converted his Catholic mother to Calvinism. He won his literary spurs with a defence of the theft of a richly laden Portuguese ship by the East India Company (1604, *De iure praedae commentarius*). This work was commissioned by the East India Company. Naturally it dealt with the freedom of the seas (*Mare liberum, seu de iure quod Batavis compedit ad Indica commercia*) and hence the right of the Dutch to their Asian trade. Grotius was the new Paul of international law. In 1621, after he had spent two years in prison, he managed to escape by hiding in a chest of books which his resourceful wife had smuggled in to him. They moved to Paris and in 1625 he wrote the standard work of European international law, *Concerning the Right of War and Peace* (*De iure belli ac pacis*).

Grotius, who had been strongly influenced by Arminius, believed that men were naturally free. Since neither Church nor state could curtail this freedom, civil society could only exist by the acceptance of a rule of law. As he looked out at the world, he saw what seemed to be international anarchy. If men could only grasp the mechanism of human society, they might hope to control it. That mechanism was the natural law. Reason and equity should provide the basis on which men and nations of goodwill could reach an understanding.

Like most successful intellectuals, Grotius went from failure to failure in his personal life. He could stay neither in Holland nor in Hamburg, to which he fled in 1632. His diplomatic missions were unsuccessful. His mission to Paris in 1634 as Swedish ambassador ended in failure. In the centuries after his death, his reputation has grown. The Grotius Society was founded in London in 1915. The League of Nations and the U.N. are based on his ideas. In the Atlantic community he is considered to be the greatest teacher of international law and political science. Today we can see how much he owed to his precursors, the Italian Gentile, and the Spaniards, de Vitoria, Soto, Vasques, Covarrubias, Suarez and Ayala. Some of these men went far beyond Grotius in the sharpness of their juridical definitions and precision of the questions they formulated.

From the point of view of this study, it is less important to trace the lineage of Grotius's ideas than to see him in terms of the spiritual tradition to which he belonged. Grotius was the late flowering of the *devotio moderna*. In his work its religious rationalism ripened. Its civic commonsense, its egocentric conscientiousness and its strict division between God and the world, were elevated to universal validity. The *devotio moderna* had become the sober simplicity of a legal philosophy which all those who believe in God and (or) reason, in divine (or) human law were duty-bound to accept. Even if there were no God, the statements of natural law would still be universally valid and binding in their effect. Grotius's little book *Concerning the Truth of the Christian Religion* went through 110 editions. It was translated into dozens of languages, even Arabic. This success may well be compared with *The Imitation of Christ*. Grotius's motto *Ruit Hora* meant more than merely making the most of one's time. It was a secular expression of the profound sense of the transiency of existence, which had been so deeply rooted in the *devotio moderna*. It meant that men had so little time on earth. Thus Grotius, like his kinsman, Gerrit Groote, was ultimately a teacher of righteousness and the right way to live. He was the precursor of John Locke.

The Holland of the Calvinists and Arminians was locked in a life and death struggle with the political and sacerdotal powers of France and Spain. The open, pragmatic peoples of the Low Countries were repelled by the gloomy and ostentatious court ceremonial of Madrid and Paris. They turned away from the closed and windowless little worlds of salvation in Spain and France. At the same time they dismantled the sacred conception of nature. Dutch painting portrayed landscapes, interiors, animals, food, hams, plants, fish and hens, instead of glorifying the sacred altar. Art left the presence and the divine service of the earthly kings. Men looked at nature objectively, that is, they divided spirit and matter. They were free to concentrate on the technical mastery of nature. Amsterdam, which had assumed so many of Venice's functions, took on the function of engineering centre.

Holland's engineers were the leaders of their profession in Europe in the sixteenth and seventeenth centuries. Only in Italy did they have rivals in water control and land-reclamation. The Dutch built dikes and canals which saved time and served as the first railroads of the Continent.[75] Like Venice, Holland developed a glass industry. Glass lengthened the day inside the house and spectacles increased the working age of man. The Hollander Cippersheim invented the telescope in 1605. As early as 1590 the Dutchman Zacharias Jansen had invented the compound microscope. With its help fifty years later, the merchant Leeuwenhoek became the first bacteriologist. The eye, which for a thousand years had been the sacred instrument for the Platonic-Augustinian contemplation of God, had finally been profaned. In the mirror, the eye examined the self, critically and admiringly.[76] The eye looked at the shape of man. Visual observation became part of a secular and introspective Calvinist era which led directly from Rembrandt to Rousseau.[77] The ground lens made possible the scientific separation of the ego from nature and matter, which became the characteristic mark of science and thought in the seventeenth century. Glass made life and thought objective. It placed yet another barrier between man and the organic cosmos of old Europe. The eye was no longer sacred. Man and nature had been torn apart, God and the world were far apart. Only a politics of power could restore the unity of the state, and a theology of the pure spirit, the unity of religion. At the base of all this lay a deep despair over the insurmountable abyss between God and the world.

When in 1642 Richelieu defeated the last conspiracy, Pope Urban VIII said about him, 'If there is a God, he will certainly have to atone. If there is none, he is an excellent man.'[78] In these words the whole horror and tension of the baroque which appeared so monstrous to its successors is hidden.[79] Here are the two orders of Pascal and Jansenius, and Descartes's knowledge of the evil spirit (*spiritus malignus*) of matter and the divine Spirit who cannot err. Both premises were valid. Both were believed and maintained: 'God is' and 'Richelieu is an excellent man'. Mazarin was another example of the tension between the two orders of existence. When he died in 1661, he confessed that he could feel no remorse for his sins.[80] He had merely stolen vast treasures and piled them up in his palace at Vincennes. As he lay dying he had the meaning of the Mass recited to him. Perhaps he had never bothered to learn it in his previous career.

Richelieu's three-headed portrait by Ph. de Campaigne strikes us as being more open, despite a certain vulpine quality, than does that of Descartes or the mask-like face of Leibniz, whose shadowy ambiguity horrified his contemporaries. The character and work of these great destroyers revealed the same duality.[81] It was as if Calvin's God had become flesh in these men. 'We must break down many more walls before we arrive at our goal', wrote Richelieu to his king after the fall of La Rochelle.[82] During the siege of this city he sent a message to Madrid that this struggle was the beginning of the extirpation of heresy in all Europe while at the same time he was vigorously supporting the German, Dutch and Scandinavian Protestants. This Cardinal of the holy Roman Church no longer believed in Christendom, no longer believed in Europe, no longer believed in a free (Erasmian) interplay of the grace of God and the deeds of man. Like Descartes and Pascal he bore the turbulence of all these forces and passions in his soul. This emerges clearly from his early polemical writings against Protestants. He condemned them for wanting to surrender society to anarchy and chaos by their demand for freedom of con-science.[83] Hierarchy and authority are necessary in order to avoid the worst evil: anarchy. Protestantism delivered the state to the will of the people, but the people was a hydra-headed beast who does not know its own passions. It was a deaf and dumb mass.

Richelieu was so terrified of anarchy because he had lost faith in the silent and gentle force of grace. He had lost the healthy sense of respect for what has grown organically in history. This anxiety and despair united him with the great revolutionary ideologists of the French Revolution, who were his spiritual children. He prepared the way for them by 'making' the absolute state. Desperate activity and a desire to do everything by himself expressed his personal fears and those of the entire baroque age, of falling into his own abyss. In their innermost recesses the men of the baroque could no longer believe in a natural encounter, to say nothing of co-operation between the separated worlds of God and man, spirit and matter. A titanic system was constructed to enforce discipline on men. They waged war on the mothers, everything feminine or changing, especially the Church and the people, both of which they saw as feminine. Descartes and Pascal sought to subject female matter to male mathematics. Richelieu, who in so many ways was spiritually close to Calvin and John Knox, fought against 'the impure, self-seeking, maternal régime of Maria de' Medici with its soft female compromises'.[84] The victory would be obtained through his male reason.

At the high point of the crisis, Louis III said to his mother, Maria de' Medici; 'I honour you as my mother, but I serve the state more truly than I serve you.'[85] It was Richelieu who wrote the sacral promises of Maria's other son, Gaston of Orléans, which Gaston swore to Louis XIII. Not only would Gaston love Louis but revere him as his father, and swear before him as before the altar.[86] Richelieu founded a new father cult for his king and for the state. Richelieu was a secular Gregory VII. Like Gregory he revoked the ancient, sacred blood-rights of the hereditary nobility of the land.* He tore

*They continued to retain and exercise their traditional right to have incense offered to them three times during the Mass.

them away from their castles and their fiefs and enslaved them in the service of the court. Later this nobility was to react with cynicism and profligacy against the compulsory and celibate service of the new God Father. But for the moment the absolute King and his all powerful reason were triumphant. Through a terrible new court ceremony, the absolute King developed an inexorable technique by which he observed and regulated every least movement of the soul, the mind and the body.

In the age of Calvin the strongest tendencies were in favour of Richelieu. Richelieu would have never been able to subject the Roman Catholic court party, the old nobility and the colourful variety of the provinces to his omniscient state if he had not had French neo-Calvinism as his unconscious but most trusty ally. The period of peace under Henry IV had produced a schism in the ranks of the Calvinists, while hurrying on the already rapid progress of secularization among them. Only a small part (mostly bourgeois and manual workers of the low class) stuck to the spirit of the old resistance. The high nobility, the military and the engineers were fascinated by the ascetic demands of the new state. The state was God on earth. It took everything and offered in exchange the honour to be allowed to live and die in ceaseless and highly strenuous work. Young neo-Calvinists, thirsting for action and ready for sacrifice, served under Richelieu at La Rochelle in 1628, in the struggle against the last great fortress of old Calvinism.[87] It was for them and with their help that he made ascetic service to the national state into a new religion. Richelieu had no room for opposition in his system. Marillac, the keeper of the great seal and the last champion of Mother Church and medieval universality, had to be jailed, and the remarkable Bassompierre imprisoned.

'Bassompierre stood for all that was most deeply opposed to the hard schematizing spirit that had emerged: unspoiled freedom in happiness and danger and complete independence ... His castles were razed ... All over the country began the great breaking down of walls which since time immemorial had enclosed proud individuals and the uniqueness of their clans. The great dam builder, the Cardinal of the Roman Church, began to tear them down...'[88] Upon these ruins the new national state was built with the help of the neo-Calvinists, that is, the third and fourth generation after Calvin. An apostate Huguenot pastor formulated the doctrine of absolutism at the end of the century: *Un roi, une loi, une foi dans le royaume*.[89] A woman of a famous Huguenot family, the d'Aubignés, became the king's mistress, Madame de Maintenon. By persuading Louis XIV to revoke the Edict of Nantes, she completed the annihilation of her own people and the triumph of the neo-Calvinist doctrine of the one law and one faith under one king. The ascetic and disciplined Huguenot nobles who entered the political service of the Cardinal, enabled him to purge his state of all self-willed persons, individualists and anarchists (old Catholics, old Calvinists and feudalists).

The Calvinist intelligentsia also joined him. It was they who carried out the orders of their absolutist masters in the cultural life of France. The magnificent people's language of old France, of Villon and Rabelais, was purged. This purge destroyed at least as many castles and kingdoms as the crushing of the nobles. Richelieu created the Académie Française to destroy the old and lovely language of the people. The man who became permanent secretary of the Academy was Valentin Conrat, an elder of the Temple de Charenton, the Huguenot Church of Paris. Conrat regularly visited the salon of the Catholic intelligentsia at the Hôtel de Rambouillet, which had been so completely saturated in Jansenism that it was virtually Calvinist, and he also took part in the Protestant salon of Madame des Loges. The same elements later gathered in the Académie de Caen, which was also devoted to the purging and cleansing of the speech and intellectual life of the nation.[90]

Richelieu has the dubious distinction of being the father both of modern absolutism and the cultural politics of the 'cold war'. He began a planned campaign, employing an army of preachers, literati and poets, to support his own domestic and foreign policies. A circle of lawyers, archivists and writers was collected and placed under the leadership of Chapelain. In 1635 his pensioner, the terrible monk Campanella, began to preach his ferocious doctrine of the *guerra spirituale, la guerra literale.*[91] Centuries before, Pierre Dubois, the pupil of Siger of Brabant, had once recommended a similar employment of intellectual workers in the service of the state. The same abysmal dualism, the same terrible separation of matter and spirit, had moved Dubois as drove Richelieu and his commissars to wage war against the opponents of the regio-political system. Neither Dubois nor Richelieu were able to believe in a natural and historical co-operation of the two separate worlds of body and soul.

Of all Richelieu's lieutenants, none was more important than the Capuchin Père Joseph, the 'grey eminence' and the Master of the Terror.[92] Joseph, whose full name was Joseph François Leclerc du Tremblay, was born in Paris in 1577 as Baron de Maffliers.[93] His father was Jean Leclerc, the French ambassador to Venice, and his mother Marie de Lafayette, a born Calvinist. His parents gave the precocious child a brilliant education. He learned Greek, Latin, Italian, English, Hebrew and Spanish, that is, the languages of the World of the Three Rings (not German!). He studied law, philosophy, mathematics, and the building of fortifications. Journeys through Italy (with a long sojourn in Averroistic Padua), Germany and England completed the humanist education of this highly intellectual, highly active and very suspicious mind.[94] He experienced his conversion in the circle around Bérulle and Madame Acarie and became a Capuchin in 1599. His spiritual mentors were Francis of Assisi, the 'quietist', convert Scot, Benedict of Canfeld, and above all the fathers and the men of the *devotio moderna*, especially Tauler and Ruysbroeck. To these men Père Joseph owed his imperturbable inner spirit. He began to devote himself to the methodical propagation and systematic application of the doctrine of inwardness. Père Joseph's *Introduction à la vie spirituelle par une facile méthode d'oraison* has many striking similarities with a contemporary work, Descartes *Discours de la Méthode*.

Père Joseph entered Richelieu's service around 1613, and became fascinated by this man of power. He gradually changed from a man of prayer into a man of action. Père Joseph believed that the slothful and vicious human stuff of the people, Protestants, pagans, etc. (the *res extensa* of Descartes), could be subjected to the creative spirit (the *res cogitans* in Descartes) and that he could prize the key to the heavenly Jerusalem on earth from the evil spirit of the world (*spiritus malignus*). Joseph failed in this venture as did the whole baroque age. The Père Joseph of the *Introduction* who had written more than 1,100 letters of spiritual direction to his spiritual daughter Antoinette d'Orléans, a multitude of tracts, and 400 exhortations, became a bitter, sharp dyspeptic old man. He attacked the quietists and spiritualists and turned on his own spiritual children. In his introspective meditation of 1635 (*Dix jours*), written three years before his death, he portrayed himself as worn out, diffused and emptied of substance. 'I have poured myself out in all too many alien matters, I have misused my time and I know from my own experience what an evil it is not to be united with God ...' *Je sais par moi, qui, en punition de mes fautes et pour avoir abusé du temps que j'ai eu, n'ayant tant de loisir maintenant de penser à mon intérieur, et qui suis toujours distrait en diverses occupations, le mal que c'est de n'être pas uni à Dieu ... et combien il est nécessaire pour cela d'être en bonne compagnie ou l'on puisse se fortifier et entr'aider les uns les autres.*[95] His early spiritual intoxication had been replaced by disappointment.

Père Joseph and other arrogant baroque thinkers consumed themselves and ended their lives like the scorched shells of wartime tanks, destroyed along a road. 'When I look out on the world now, how it and I live, we have lost all judgment and no longer differ from the pagans and Turks, except in a few externals.' 'The Church is still pure in a few souls – if that were not so, God would either destroy the world by fire, hasten the last judgment or create a new world.'[96] In desperation, Père Joseph hoped that the world might end now. His whole life had been dedicated to a crusade against the Crescent, and in his old age he had to confess that there was really no difference between Turks and Christians. This was the end of a man who had been raised in humanist and Franciscan optimism to conquer the world for God.

Marin Mersenne died in Paris on 1 September 1648, in the fateful year of the Treaty of Westphalia.[97] The life work of this friar was no less bold and daring than that of Père Joseph. As a pupil of the Jesuit College of La Flèche, Mersenne had absorbed that optimism which made the French Jesuits of the seventeenth century into the pioneers and bearers of the Enlightenment. Mersenne thought the time had come to explain the world mechanically and in the terms of natural science. He was firmly convinced that progress in the sciences would lead to a religious understanding of the cosmos. *Harmonie Universelle*, his major work written in 1636–7, was devoted to this proposition. He was so certain that science could only lead to religious truth that he busily assembled a collection of exceedingly unlikely workers in God's vineyard. There were atheists like Hobbes, non-Aquinists and sceptics like Gassendi, men on the Index like Galileo, and Calvinist heretics like Huyghens. Mersenne corresponded, he translated, he urged others on, he travelled and visited. He was the Leibniz of his day. His ceaseless activity was directed toward the formation of a kind of spiritual academy uniting the learned 'if not of all Europe, then indeed of all France', in which the great thinkers of the time would dispute and discuss problems with one another. He revived the ideas of Nicholas of Cusa, which he introduced to Descartes, and kept Descartes in contact with the world for nearly twenty years. Mersenne acquainted Descartes with the work of Hobbes and Galileo, Pascal and Jansen. He was the greatest propagator of Cartesianism in France.

Descartes, like Richelieu to whom he dedicated books, accomplished something eminently important for France.[98] He united Thomist scholasticism and the thinking of the bourgeois, ruling class which was rising to power.[99] At first he intended to renew Thomism, but he came under the influence of Calvinism, and its Catholic counterpart, Jansenism, which was beginning to develop. The result was that peculiar rationalism which expressed the self-consciousness of the new bourgeoisie, while fascinating them at the same time. Its fascination lay in the fundamental structure of his thought. By a supreme exercise of will, he had gained control of himself and had mastered the anxiety of drowning in a chaos of passions. He subordinated time, the temporal-historical, the natural, the creaturely and the individual, and severed these things from the sacred sphere of reason. During the Thirty Years War Germany, Holland, Switzerland, Italy and Hungary had been drenched by waves of irrationalism. The underground of the people had discharged mighty streams of revolutionary spiritualism. Descartes had seen these things and was terrified by them.[100] In the famous dream at Ulm on 10 November 1619, Descartes felt himself 'hard pressed and frightened' (as he himself says) by ghosts, and nearly overcome by a whirlwind. He sought refuge in the chapel of a school building, but only got as far as the courtyard, when he noticed that he alone was struck by the storm of the time.[101] 'Other people stood together and chatted. I was astounded and shaken to see that they, untouched by the wind, stood firmly on their legs, while I could move only bending forward against it ...' This dream revealed his mission to Descartes. He would work out a method of thinking that would grant mankind absolute security against illusions, deceptions, and evil temptations. Like Luther, Descartes started out from an experience of shock and fear, but he overcame it by the power of thought. He developed a mental technique very much in the spirit of the Exercises of Ignatius and the 'methods of prayer' of *humanisme dévot*. He demonstrated that rightly cultivated reason could grasp the mathematical order of the natural world, the mechanism of man and the automatism of animals. The door to mechanical and mathematical explanation of the cosmos was opened.

When Luther had faced the reality of the incomprehensible God, he had sought salvation in 'pure faith', in 'faith alone'. Man could only achieve his independence by losing himself in God as a sinner and yet be redeemed. Descartes sought salvation in reason but this reason still had much of the primal trust that Luther had created out of the psychic substance of the people. That confidence in the goodness of things could not be annihilated by suffering despotism, or enslavement. Luther's *Credo, ergo sum* and Descartes's *cogito, ergo sum*, are ultimately related.[102] Descartes wrested his faith in reason from the constant possibility of a confrontation with a demonic God, an omnipotent and deceitful spirit who deceives and seduces men into falsehood. The rationalism of Descartes rested on the simple assertion that God could not be a liar and a deceiver.[103] Granted this assumption, Descartes could relatively quickly deduce the existence of God and a true science of the mind. God has, as the Psalm says, ordered the world as cosmos in measure, number and weight and called upon man to reflect upon this ordering of the cosmos and to realize himself in it.

The *spiritus malignus* of the almighty God of lies was a reappearance of the devil-God of the enthusiasts of the East.[104] Luther and Calvin had both conceived of a super-God. Descartes overcame him by concentrating his superiority in one dimension, that of truth and falsehood. Descartes achieved this by means of Thomist scholasticism and of neo-Calvinist-Arminian thought. He offered consolation against despair by restoring faith in reason. With God's reason man could measure, count and think all earthly things. Right thinking was universal science. Descartes was the heir of Lull and Nicholas of Cusa, and he knew their works.

His rationalism was a negative theology. In great awe and reverence before the authority of God, it shrouded his essence in silence. Descartes rejected the Aristotelian-scholastic concepts of God on grounds advanced by Tauler, the *devotio moderna*, Erasmus and all religious reform humanism from Petrarch on.[105] On the other hand, he fought for order more passionately than any thinker from Aquinas to the present. *Et je ne saurais, sans pervertir l'ordre, prouver seulement que l'âme est distincte du corps avant l'Existence de Dieu.*[106] His oft-cited and frequently misinterpreted *Cogito, ergo sum* means: I am 'a spiritual substance, which has nothing corporeal in it (*une substance immatérielle et qui n'a rien de corporel*) and I think and exist, because the never-lying majesty of God has created me as a spiritual being. God has destined me to investigate and to control the world of matter'.[107] Descartes was convinced that no philosophy was as compatible with Faith as was his own.[108] Descartes, the self-conscious nobleman, formed his ethos from Seneca, Montaigne and Charron.[109] He saw his rationalism as a spiritual order of being created by the divine majesty. As early as 1630 he wrote triumphantly to Mersenne: 'All men to whom God has given the use of reason are obliged to know the latter and themselves. It was in this sense that I began my studies and I believe that one can prove metaphysical truth in a way which is even more enlightening than the proofs of geometry. Be not afraid, I beg you, to assure and to proclaim publicly everywhere that God has established these laws of nature just as a king establishes laws in his realm.[110] Descartes compared the greatness of God with a king, whose majesty is the higher in proportion to his distance from his subjects. It would be rash to think that our imagination is as great as his power!

The catastrophe of 1648 wiped out Spain's position as a world power, and Westphalia burned itself into the Spanish consciousness forever. The France of Louis XIV inherited the court-ceremony of Madrid and the Spanish rationalism of post-Tridentine Catholicism. According to the Spanish tradition, mastery could only reveal itself in the remoteness of the monarch from his subject. The Spanish court ceremony protected the majesty of the king and at the same time was a protection against the king. It was the expression of a world dominated by anxiety.[111] The king celebrated his life as a *Mathesis universalis*. Every act and gesture (dining, walking, even giving birth) was a public state action which maintained and confirmed the magical machinery of the cosmos. Descartes's concept of reason was a king of this type. The king wills that truths should be true, and therefore they are true. The divine King has become reason itself.[112] God's existence is the foundation of all things. Most men do not keep their distance when they revere God. They do not honour him as 'an infinite and incomprehensible being'. Instead they cling to a narrow name and its syllables. They become atheists because they do not understand that the laws of nature are lesser realities than his incomprehensible power.[113] Descartes was always more or less consciously concerned by the Calvinist doctrine of predestination. His letters to Mersenne raise the question whether it could possibly befit God to damn men eternally.[114] Descartes constructed his rationalist philosophy 'against those who assert that God constantly and always deceives the damned and he can likewise deceive us all'. 'The foundation of our faith and our whole creation is the conviction, shared by Augustine and Aquinas, that God cannot lie (*Deus mentiri non potest*) so that I wonder how so many theologians can still contradict this fundamental proposition.'[115]

Since God in his majesty can never lie, he guarantees to man the certain use of his mathematical reason. In the political terminology of baroque humanism this assured man the right to be 'a part of the public whole' and the ability to serve his fellow-citizens with the correct moderation and discretion.[116]

Like Lull and Nicholas of Cusa, Descartes was convinced that his *Méthode* could solve all the problems of the 'exact sciences'. He himself defined it as *methodum ad quaslibet difficultates in scientiis resolvendas*.[117] But only logic, mathematics, and deductions from general principles counted as exact sciences.[118] Descartes built his kingdom of reason with few architectural ideas. He paid a tremendous price to the 'incomprehensible divinity' in order to win this (slim) security and certainty. He had to sacrifice history, empirical nature and individualism to it.[119] Although Descartes, the new monk, observed the stars and planets, had a garden wherever he lived and practised vivisection on rabbits, dogs and fishes, he had nothing to do with modern natural science. He rejected Galileo's investigations and reproached the new natural science for not being concerned with the substance, the essence and the first causes of things. Descartes refused to see that modern science had to ignore such things in order to be able to conduct the experiment at all. He was an Augustinian humanist and utopian, in the tradition of Roger Bacon. He dreamt, like Francis Bacon, of technical progress, while speaking without any precision at all of countless experiments that were still to be made.[120]

Descartes passionately denied that he had anything in common with the great utopians like Campanella and Bruno, whom he condemned as innovators,[121] and with absolutists like Hobbes.[122] He could not conceal elements of the utopianism and the will to power of the baroque age, which had infiltrated his thinking and which so shocked modern students like the Lutheran existentialist Jaspers and the Thomist Maritain.[123] There was a dictator hidden in Descartes, who imposed his laws on things and dictated to them how they were to be. Ultimately Descartes wanted to be an earthly angel. He wanted to see everything at once, to behold causes and consequences together, and to see deep within them. He imagined he had angelic knowledge, unsullied by matter and he wanted to present this in the purest geometric forms. He intended to reduce all reality to a few mathematical statements and geometric figures.[124] In his theory of the nature of man, he argued that body and soul were completely heterogeneous elements. His theory was rigorously dualist. The soul touched the body only at one point in the brain (in the pineal gland). Ironically, Descartes closed the circle, which had taken the original stoic idea of the vital spark in the soul and turned it into the mystical *apex mentis*, by returning it to its naturalistic origins. God was the factor which regulated the relation between body and soul. The moment that men no longer believed in God's power to regulate the mechanism of the order of nature, the little wheels of the human being and the automatism of the beasts would tick over on their own.

Descartes had received Pascal's youthful writings through Mersenne, and the two men exerted considerable influence on each other's development.[125] In his *Pensées* Pascal often played on the favourite themes of Descartes which obviously fascinated him. It is unfortunately not possible within the scope of this work to do justice to the tragedy of Pascal. His influence has been very great, especially among intellectuals, who have become hypnotized by their own, real or imgained, despair about faith and reason. Some of these people regard Pascal as the greatest religious spirit in French history. Pascal was certainly a great personality, but his greatness was essentially destructive. He had an enormous capacity for hatred and over-simplification.[126] He knew only two realities; the world of mathematics, geometry and of strict natural law (*esprit géométrique*) and that of the eternally rebellious heart, fighting against God (*esprit de finesse*). Man is torn between faith and knowledge. In sheer desperation, he must take the risk of asserting the existence of God and plunging into the divine abyss, which may be mere nothingness. This was Pascal's famous wager: He who wagers that God exists wins infinitely, if he wins, and loses almost nothing if he loses. A thinking man has no choice but to wager that God exists. We can do nothing but live as if we believed.

Behind the typically baroque playfulness of the conception there is a religious nihilism of terrifying aspect.[127] The wager is, to begin with, true and valid only in the innermost recesses of the heart, in the spiritual dimension. Only there is God a blissful 'all' and the 'I', man, a blissful 'nothing'. The two can and do play with one another, and delude one another in the way which German mysticism also taught. Drawn out into the dimension of day, of creation, of the history and the total reality of the cosmos, these mystical experiences become terrible, murderous simplifications. The spiritual sights of the *simplificateurs terribles*, once they have burst out of the spiritual dimension, transform earthly life into a hell. Take as an example the deserted Port Royal which still retains its concentration camp character. The spiritual simplifiers want to subject the world to their false alternatives and conclusions. If Pascal is looked at from this point of view, one sees that he belongs to this group. His whole wager-situation and its alternatives is false. It is false as the dualistic dismembering of the cosmos into an *esprit géométrique* and an *esprit de finesse*. In history man cannot wager with himself as to whether God exists or not. If he bets that God does not exist, he wins a great deal, not a little, as Pascal argued. According to the Gospel, he wins the whole world and all its kingdoms.

One can see the truth of this proposition in the worldly success of both the right and left totalitarians. These people are all immanentists who have accepted one alternative of Pascal's wager, whether they call themselves bourgeois, religious, materialistic or idealistic. It is equally false that one loses nothing by betting that God exists. If God exists, man may certainly lose everything, on earth, in history and in the world of spirit in which he struggles for the primal trust in the living God. As Job said 'Though He slay me, yet will I trust in Him' (13.15). Pascal's wager is not theology, it is literature. He asks a question which may not be asked, even by those willing to play for ultimate stakes.[128] Pascal began that dangerous modern religious literature which so often completely loses God in its intellectual and imaginative experiments. Its literary aspect is by no means the most dangerous consequence of his thinking. Pascal's wager is essentially an expression of a destructive religious nihilism. Because it was so profoundly negative, Pascal was driven to construct a complete, world-encompassing system of theodicy. It was to be a steel structure which would serve as the ultimate bulwark and rationale of Christianity. The famous *Pensées* were the fragments of this great work which was never written. In the *Pensées* one confronts the same elements which characterized so much of the religious writing of the baroque age – the pessimism, the desire to build gigantic systems, the nihilism and the despair. Catholicism was reduced to a

Calvinist-Cartesian dualism. The universe was split into pure spirit and evil matter. No room was left for human joy or the delights of existence. There was no understanding or sympathy for creation, for creatures, individuality or history. What was left was the iron necessity of the dualistic world view. This was the intellectual core of the Jansenist movement.

In Jansenism, the strict morality, the hard dualism and the arrogance of Calvin and Descartes entered Catholic life in western Europe. It permeated the monasteries and seminaries, and conquered the pulpits of theologians and bishops' thrones. Despite the Index and an embittered counter-attack, it rapidly won over a great part of educated Catholic France, and made converts among highly placed Roman cardinals. By 1750 it had spread to Germany and central Europe, 100 years after its initial condemnation. As late as 1781 Emperor Joseph II declared that the Bull *Unigenitus*, issued in 1713 against a hundred and one of Quesnel's theses was invalid in the dominions of the Austrian Empire. Jansenism was extremely useful to the absolutist monarchs of the eighteenth century. It was subservient to the state. It believed in scientific progress and a reform of the Church by the state, and, as a result, soon played the same role at Catholic courts which Lutheranism filled in Protestant countries. It was no accident that German Protestants in the eighteenth century sought a union with Jansenism.

Like all Christian reform movements and most of the secular intellectual movements as well, the beginning and rise of Jansenism was linked to a clan, a kindred group of 'inspired ones', and to the *genius loci* of a place. Port Royal, the monastic centre of Jansenism, just outside the gates of Paris, was founded by the Arnaulds. The Huguenot, Antoine Arnauld, the lord of La Mothe and Villeneuve, came to Paris in 1547. He became Attorney General under Maria de' Medici and after the massacre on St Bartholomew's Night he, together with his entire family except for Isaak Arnauld, became Catholics. His son Antoine (1560–1619) represented the University of Paris against the Jesuits in Parliament in 1594. He was a typical Huguenot patriarch and reared his twenty children in the strictest fear of God. All were highly gifted and serious with a hard, rather legalistic, temper. These children formed the generation which created Jansenism as a movement. Jacqueline, Mère Angélique Arnauld, was a coadjutrix to an abbess at the age of eleven. She later became an abbess herself and reformed the charitable organization for gentlewomen known as Port-Royal. Over the years she built it into a place of refuge and resistance for the *solitaires*, the men hermits of this Augustinian Manichaeanism. Bishop Jansen (Jansenius) and his Louvain theologians had originally wanted to work out a weapon against the Protestant doctrine of predestination and grace, but while doing so they became hopelessly entangled in the Augustinian doctrines of the great theologian's last years. We have already noticed how Augustine reverted to the Manichaean positions of his youth during the final struggle against Pelagianism, and the Jansenists fell into the same theological difficulties. Their revived Manichaean dualism put them into contact with the ancient Albigensian heritage which was still very far from dead in France, and was a great source of strength. At the same time, they moved very close to Calvinism with which they shared the determination to defend the glory of God against any libidinous approach on the part of man.[129]

Angélique's brother Antoine, the great Arnauld, became the leader of Jansenism after the death of Jansen the Saint-Cyran. He demanded a return to the penitential practice of the primitive Church. Men, who were essentially sinful, ought to receive the unapproachable God in the Sacrament of the altar very rarely. Only a small number of blessed and elect were worthy of receiving him (how close here is Luther's anxiety and Calvin's awe). In *De la fréquente communion* (1643) the sombre gospel of the Jansenist practice of salvation was proclaimed. It found the approval of fifteen bishops – and was not ecclesiastically condemned. Antoine defended Jansenius's *Augustinus* (1640), which was placed on the Index in 1642 (but which was printed in 1643 and again in 1652 in Rome itself). The resolute spirit of old Calvinism and of Catholic reform humanism reappeared in Antoine. He fought against royal absolutism and took the side of the episcopate in the controversy over the royal right to appoint bishops. He was also against the absolutism of the *Curia*. This spirit of resistance led Jansenism from Port-Royal into the great struggle against Louis XIV, who ordered the monastery to be destroyed in 1710. Next Antoine attacked the Jesuits whom he accused of an indecent union of the things of this world and those of the next, and finally he led the Jansenists against Rome itself. As a result of the enemies he made in this war on several fronts Antoine Arnauld had to withdraw to the Spanish Low Countries, and he died in Brussels in 1694. His brother Henry, as the Jansenist bishop of Angers, took a middle position between Port-Royal and Rome. Another brother, Robert, was a jurist and, like his grandfather, a financial official at the Paris court. Robert was the father of fifteen children, but later lived as a widower and hermit in Port-Royal. There he translated the Fathers, Augustine, Theresa of Avila and the writings of reform humanism.

Port-Royal came to be a kind of secular monastery, strikingly similar to Augustine's priestly communities. Its inhabitants were men and women with clear minds and glowing hearts. They were filled with the zeal of the awakened and the ardour of the prophets. Slowly the battered remains of the once flourishing reform movement of the time of Erasmus began to gather around them. More had survived the persecution of Counter-Reformation absolutism than is generally accepted. Jansenism took over this humanism's classical education, its study of history, its philosophy and criticism of the humanities. It needed these 'historical auxiliary sciences' to be able to defend itself against Rome and the Jesuits. Nothing was to show this more clearly than the Jansenist weekly, *Nouvelles Ecclésiastiques*, which was published in Paris and Utrecht.

Together with the political weeklies (of Bayle, Leclerc, Basnage) and the learned periodical of the Jesuits, the *Journal de Trévoux*, it created an invaluable journalistic preparation for the Enlightenment. The *Nouvelles Ecclésiastiques* was founded as the organ of the Jansenist Church party which had been formed after the Bull *Unigenitus* of 1713 had condemned Jansenism. Twelve bishops belonged to this party. From 1716 to 1728 even the Archbishop of Paris, Noailles, belonged and the party had strong supporters at the Sorbonne, in the universities of Rheims and Nantes and in the Parliaments. This party hoped to convene a general council against the verdict of Rome. The fact that the royal court, under the influence of the Jesuits, did not ally itself with these radical, active and historically powerful forces of French Catholicism contributed substantially to the fall of the monarchy in the French Revolution. The resentment of the persecuted Jansenists fused with the hatred of the Calvinists and the bitterness of the nobility which had been stripped of its power. A deadly enmity grew up against the redemptive power of the wonder-working king and his guarantor, the Roman pope. The long period of truce, the 'Clementine Peace' under Pope Clement IX, which lasted from 1669 to the beginning of the eighteenth century had given the Jansenists under Quesnel the opportunity to spread and to saturate France with its doctrines.

One of the most important of these doctrines, historically, was the idea that man was no more than an automaton driven by the conflicting wills to good or evil. Actions were determined by whichever of the two was the stronger. Jansenism taught that the will to do good must be imposed on an unruly human spirit. Asceticism and strict discipline could switch the will in the direction of faith. The spirits of men must be controlled and the evil world of matter must be co-ordinated and organized to serve the divine spirit. The Jansenists were organizers, censors and controllers. They extended their discipline to the churches, corporations, administrative bodies and local governments. It does not require much historical imagination to see what sort of historical function such a movement might perform, once it had been secularized. The Jansenists replaced faith in the hierarchy with faith in the apparatus.[130] They made the clergy into managers. The priest became an official of the apparatus. This 'Catholic Calvinism' was politically more dangerous than the original old Calvinism, because it had faith in the clergy which old Calvinism had rejected. Jansenism transformed the faith in the priesthood into faith in the just administration of the bureaucratic political apparatus of the absolutist state that guides progress and the mind.[131] Nothing is more merciless toward itself and toward others than the pure spirit. This spirit had chosen to administer the 'greatness and misery of man' (the *grandeur et misère de l'homme* was Pascal's basic theme) through compulsory education, compulsory military service and progress.[132]

17

ENGLAND:
THE COUNTERWEIGHT TO EUROPE

ENGLAND does not belong to Europe. Since the eighth century England has considered itself another world, *alter orbis*,[1] circling the Continent like the comet on the Bayeux tapestry which was regarded as an omen of the Norman conquest in 1066. It was the same comet that Newton's friend, Halley, calculated in 1692.[2] According to popular belief comets appear in times of crisis. Thus England has always intervened in the history of Europe when a religious, spiritual or political balance was disturbed. The influence of Roger Bacon, Duns Scotus, William of Ockham and Wyclif in the thirteenth and fourteenth centuries was as significant as that of Locke, Newton, Bolingbroke, Hume and Darwin, or the wars of England against Philip II, Louis XIV, Napoleon, Wilhelm II, and Hitler. This reaching out to Europe has usually ended with lightning retreats. After England's attempt to assert herself in France was wrecked in the hundred-year civil war between the houses of York and Lancaster, by the 'witch' Joan of Arc, and by the terrible loss of blood, England pulled back from the Continent. The shock of the defeat in France awakened the realization that the Continent was invincible when its depths were stirred.

In the same period a truce was concluded in the war between the nobility, the bourgeois classes, and the cities which had rallied around Lancaster or York.[3] The extensive destruction of the old nobility was also a factor in England's future policy and intellectual life.[4] England's expeditions to Europe, her wars, which after 1660 became 'grand cavalier tours', and the various diplomatic offensives and propaganda campaigns from Wyclif's Bohemian schools and Tyndale's *Studium* in Wittenberg to William Penn's pietistic missionary journeys to Germany and the spread of Newton's thought in Europe, were all 'adventures'. They had much the same character as the overseas expeditions of the age of colonization which slowly began to develop under Henry VII. The Englishman went abroad to try his luck, and to see how life was constituted in other world-systems.[5] He went to Europe as a vigilant spy in order to appropriate superior skills, techniques and sciences, but he went overseas and to the colonies in order to see himself confirmed by the spread of his way of life in India, in the Sudan, in Arabia and America. The Englishman was afraid of Europe and he expressed this fear in the settlement and development of the Empire.

348

One possible source of the English anxiety about Europe may have arisen from the fact that Britain was a little Europe of its own. Scots, Welsh, Irish and English lived split up into an Anglo-Saxon-Celtic lower stratum and a Norman-French aristocracy, bitterly opposed to one another. As late as the end of the fifteenth century this poor and backward country consisted of a mixture of Celtic, Latin and Germanic elements. The Church, which as early as 673 had called a Synod at Hertford for all England, was the great unifying factor.[6] The religious union prepared the political unity. Bede in his Church history, Boniface and the churchmen of the eighth century, were the first to conceive of England as a unity.[7] They were followed by King Alfred and his circle of reformers and translators in the ninth century and the clerical political theorists in the eleventh and twelfth centuries.[8] The Church with its organization and Faith bridged the serious conflicts hidden in these peoples and races. In a sense England's nationalism has been religious from the beginning.

The Roman Church was never very strong in England. Morgan, 'the man of the sea',[*] developed a theology of the free man as early as Augustine's time. We have already noticed how Morgan's ideas had forced Augustine to a dangerous, semi-Manichaean over-emphasis of the doctrine of grace. Much more remarkable is that Pelagian doctrines contained in essence the doctrines of English Deism from the seventeenth century on. This extraordinary continuity is partly explained by the fact that Pelagianism did not die out during the middle ages in England. Bradwardine (d. 1349) was one of its best known exponents. Besides Pelagianism (and deeply linked to it) there was a strong Manichaeanism, a cruel, naked splitting of the cosmos into a kingdom of grace and faith and an earthly kingdom of strife, of natural necessity, of human knowledge. Robert Holkot, an Ockhamist, who died in the same year as Bradwardine, demanded that strict separation of theology and philosophy for which Wyclif, the conscience of his generation, the protégé of Oxford and of the Duke of Lancaster, found the suitable political formulation for the state and the people.[9] From Wyclif on, the three movements against Rome and Europe ran parallel: the political action of the kings and their bishops, the scientific movement of the theologians and professors and the political movement of the people of the lower class and their priests. Wyclif's sermons stirred up the peasant revolt under Fox and Wat Tyler in 1381. The heirs of these inspired men and of their folkish enthusiasm and evangelism were the Lollards. Their descendants in turn made up the hard core of the Puritans in the sixteenth century, of the radical religious nonconformists in the seventeenth, and of the political revolutionaries in the eighteenth century.[10]

During the years between the Act of Supremacy of 1534 and the Glorious Revolution of 1688, England often threatened to break up into the folk and religious elements which stood in constant opposition to one another. The most characteristic and remarkable creations of the English spirit were developed in the process of overcoming this danger and the anxieties surrounding

*Latinized – Pelagius.

it: the House of Commons, the Church of England, the theology of free-trade and the English philosophy of tolerance and individual freedom. The struggle for unity is reflected in the thinking of the period as well as in its social institutions. Philosophical ideas in England, more so than anywhere else, are expressions of the age. This is true despite the impressive, formal and logical tradition of the English Universities. Thus English philosophical ideas are never mere assertions of a system of thought, but means of registering the political, religious and economic experience of society, of the nation. Every English philosophy is a memorial to the political conditions of the time, as much as the great English poetry is a memorial to the religious state of the nation. The especially sharp contrast in English between the written form of the language and its pronunciation reflects the beginning of a trend to turn away from Europe. The fact that the Englishman still spells words as he pronounced them in 1500 can be used as evidence in the study of this development.[11] This isolation was part of a larger European trend as well, and in the same decades, between 1490 and 1540, Russia, eastern Germany, France and Spain closed themselves off into autonomous bodies.

Thomas More stood out as a great opponent of the withdrawal from Europe and, as Chambers argues, offered an alternative to the nation as a vehicle for reform.[12] As an Erasmian, a judge and state chancellor, More had tried to prevent Henry VIII from leading England away from Europe, and in his *Utopia* which first appeared in 1516 he tried to work out the philosophical details of his alternative programme. More pursued conservative goals. He protested against the new princely absolutism and against the predatory activity of the nobility, who seized the land from the peasants in order to turn it into vast sheep-breeding grounds. Here, as in his policy against Henry VIII and Thomas Cromwell, More offered a moderate defence of monasticism. 'Parts of the Utopia read like a commentary on parts of the *Principe.*'[13] Nevertheless the content of the *Utopia* is far more revolutionary than that of Machiavelli's *Principe*. More was considered by Oncken as the father of English imperialism,[14] and used as a model by socialists and communists from the eighteenth to twentieth centuries. The Utopia is a pagan, perfect ideal state. Its origin may be traced to Plato, Epicurus, Erasmus and the monastic state of Franciscan spiritualism. More's utopianism set up a colonial, agrarian-communistic régime, which in its total planning and sacral terror has not been surpassed by any later political ideology. On the other hand, More's Utopia contained essential features of English Deism, and of the English Enlightenment.[15] Pleasure was the highest good, and to live virtuously meant to live according to nature. (More stood midway between Valla's *De Volupta* and Gassendi's *Renewal of Epicurus*). Religion was essentially morality.[16] More reduced religion to a few simple propositions (the immortality of the soul, reward and punishment in the beyond). Above the individual positive religions there stood a universal rational religion of the state, in whose religious services all had to take part.

More wrote this invective as a citizen of London, *urbis Londini et cives et vicecomes*. He condemned Christianity for its corruption and wars and cried out the warning: England will be ruined through the ruthless greed for gain. The luxury of the nobles and the propertied classes and the military power of the 'Christian princes' was a terrible contrast to the misery of the masses, the disabled war veterans, the parasitically exploited tenant-farmers and the expropriated peasantry. The treatises on statecraft of scholasticism (*haec philosophia scholastica*) spoke glibly of the 'duties' of a 'Christian king'. In the place of this ineffectual chatter, More demanded a realistic civic philosophy which fitted the concrete situation (*alia philosophia civilior, quae suam novit scaenam eique sit accomodans*). This was to become the leitmotif of English thought via Locke to Bentham. The raging class struggle of all against all could only be ended by abolishing private property under a new state-structure. His Utopia was a working model of such a state. There, men lived in planned cities each containing six thousand families. A six-hour work day was required of everyone whereas in England an immense lazy mass of priests, monks, rich men, noblemen and women did nothing. (Like the puritans and capitalists who were to come, More denounced idleness as laziness.) Society was a pact established among all citizens so that they can help each other to obtain honest pleasures. The rational enjoyment of an 'agreeable life' (*vita iucunda*) was the aim of existence. More anticipated one of the fundamental propositions of the classic economic theology of the eighteenth century.

Utopia was a modern military state. The Utopians had no use for treaties, since all the world could see how the Christian princes broke treaties and profaned the Faith and loyalty of their peoples. The Utopians waged war only in defence of their country, of their friends, or on behalf of humanity, for example, to free an oppressed people from a tyrant (*humanitatis gratia*). They also defended their trade and monetary interests with arms (here More foresaw the colonialism and imperialism of the Elizabethan and Cromwellian age). Wars were waged by the whole people, including the women. Wars were prepared in advance by bribing and corrupting the enemy, and were waged with the support of mercenary troops. They could be brought to an end by acts of terror which he regarded as useful means to intimidate a future enemy.

Next, More turned to religion, which was directly associated with the art of war. Most of the population worshipped a supreme 'unknown, an eternal, infinite, inexplicable, divine being that is above all human understanding and is spread throughout the universe by a divine force.' Christians lived in Utopia too. They seem to have been permitted to choose their own priests. Prudently More left this ticklish point open, but in any case intolerant neo-Christians who fanatically opposed other religions were cast out of the state. The Utopians had evidently learned the lesson of the bloody religious wars, and as a result, they guaranteed complete tolerance and religious freedom, allowed every creed to conduct a moderate amount of propaganda. Nevertheless they forbade and condemned any forcible conversion. Like Erasmus,

More was convinced that even the best religion could be destroyed by wars and superstition. Only belief in the immortality of the soul, in Providence and reward and punishment in a future life was binding upon all. The pious contemplation of nature was an equivalent of divine service. Work and accomplishment promoted the eternal salvation. For this reason the Utopians conducted social work on a great scale. They worked on soil improvement, building roads and bridges, gladly taking hard and dirty labour upon themselves.

In his portrayal of this labour morality and asceticism More established the link between the Utopianism of the old Franciscans in the *Liber de figuris* and the newly emerging utopianism of the Puritans and the sects. Public games and military exercises took place in the stadium after the state religious service. Domestic policy was administered by a kind of holy terror and political discussions were permitted only at definite times and places. The connection between this and Jacobinism and the other forms of revolutionary spiritualism of the nineteenth and twentieth centuries is evident. The agrarian-communistic and evangelical programme, which was preached by the chiliasts, communists, and Anabaptists in the year after 1650 by men like Hartlib, Everard and Winstanley, was not unlike that of Utopia. More foreshadowed the various possibilities in English history up to the twentieth century and portrayed them with the irony of Erasmus. Nevertheless his joking, his fiction – as with all English thinkers – served as a cloak for a terrible earnestness. 'All present states appear to me as a conspiracy of the rich, who under the claim of the good of the state represent their own interests' (*quaedam conspiratio divitum de suis commodis rei publicae nomine tituloque tractantium.*) The rich and powerful think up all kinds of tricks for appropriating the labour of the poor and for depriving them of its fruits, and they declare this exploitation to be law. All the crimes in the world come from greed for money. Thousands die in years of famine, but the storehouses of the rich are full of grain. More concluded his Utopia with a curse on money which men see as the font of all blessing. Marx and Engels relied upon this critique of society.[17]

The reformation of Henry VIII, his countermanding of the Pope and the Supremacy Act of 1534, had enabled the English King to set himself up as the head of the English Church. Henry's reformation signified the victory of a secular clique of the nobility over a clerical clique.[18] The worldly nobility and the wealthy bourgeoisie acquired the rich English Church property of the abandoned monasteries, abbeys, foundations, etc., at a laughable price, or as downright gifts, but they paid for them with a bad conscience, which was one of the main reasons why so many of them were sympathetic to the revolution, Puritans and nonconformists. Until 1688 they were never entirely free of the fear of being forced to return these properties. Another effect of Henry VIII's act of violence was that it killed off the great humanism of the 'grand form', espoused by Catholics like John Colet, More, Thomas L. Elyot and John Fisher. This humanism reached as far back as the stamping of the English style by the reform circle around King Alfred in the ninth century. It continued to the early seventeenth century. 'Intelligibility and effect were everything, it sought a practical way to think.'[19] The morality of this medieval tradition was already very bourgeois. Its strong ethos of commonsense was united by the Catholic humanists with the whole cultural knowledge that Europe possessed around 1500. It was very much in the spirit of the *devotio moderna*.

This high world of culture died out gradually.[20] After about 1540, new religious movements began to stir. The pressure from Europe played a decisive role in this change. In 1538 Pope Paul III called for a crusade against apostate England. All Englishmen who supported Henry VIII were to be treated as slaves. The Council of Trent isolated England, which found itself surrounded by hostile Catholic powers. From 1568 on seminaries for English priests were established on the Continent for the purpose of the eventual re-Catholicization of the country: in Douai in 1568, in Valladolid in 1589, in Seville and St Omer in 1592, and in the years 1598 to 1604 in Madrid, San Lucar and Lisbon. Douai was perhaps the first seminary of world-Catholicism created according to the dictates of Trent.[21] The English people reacted vigorously to the threat. They had already been given a strong dose of anti-clericalism and anti-popism by the Lollards and the emerging Puritans. The thirty-nine articles of Faith of the Church of England, of the years 1562 and 1571, were aimed directly at Trent. They condemned the sacrifice of the Mass as a 'blasphemous fiction' (*blasphema figmenta*). In 1559 the strongly anti-Catholic Act of Uniformity was passed and an anti-Catholic legal system was to prevail for 250 years.

The Test Act of 1673 established anew that every public official must receive communion according to the rites of the Church of England, swear allegiance to the English king, abjure the doctrine of transubstantiation and declare that the substance of bread and wine is preserved in the Sacrament after the Consecration. These facts have played a tremendous role in later English intellectual history. The magical and sacramental elements had been removed from the English mind. All ontological connections between the world and the super-world were destroyed. England became a country of extreme sobriety and bizarre fantasy. Religion and the Church were administered, cared for and determined by state and society. Mystical needs and the legitimate desire for a union in visible form of the natural and supernatural, the divine and the earthly, were discharged through the English belief in ghosts. A predilection for ghostly, fantastic, uncommon events and deeds became a substitute for the forbidden belief in miracles. Eccentricity, enthusiasm, neuroticism and sexuality, the aversion to call things by their right names, anxiety before the 'sensuous incarnation' of beauty and of art (visible beauty is vice) were grounded here.[22] Visual beauty represented moral danger ... English prose style and English poetry sought to compensate the spirit for an irreplaceable loss.

The official Church of the bishop and prelates had submitted quickly enough to the King. Under Henry VIII the bishops had to send even their sermons to the court for censorship. Royal commissioners supervised every religious service and carried out the royal orders. 'Many methods of the modern police state were employed at that time, 400 years ago, to spy on and intimidate a Church of dubious loyalty.'[23] Queen Elizabeth treated her bishops like domestic servants. From then on the English rectory became an administrative cell of the state. The Church announced the state's regulatory decrees and measures to an illiterate population. The English Church was ruled as a department of the state. The bishops had to attend the sessions of the Upper House very regularly if they wished to receive better and more richly endowed dioceses. As a result they were often away from their dioceses for the greater part of the year. The Crown named all bishops and deans. Today this means that a prime minister, who need no longer be a Christian, can create his bishops. The obeisance of the bishop, the oath of loyalty to the Crown, today still begins drastically enough with a solemn acknowledgement of the throne's total ecclesiastical authority: 'I do hereby declare that Your Majesty is the only supreme Governor of this Your realm in spiritual and ecclesiastical things as well as in temporal ...' It concludes with the assurance that the bishopric has been received from the throne alone. '... and I acknowledge that I hold the said Bishopric as well as the spiritualities and the temporalities thereof, only of Your Majesty.' The abject position of this state Church became visible in 1927–8 when the House of Commons, a thoroughly non-religious body, after a brief debate, declined a revision of the prayer book which the Church had worked on for fourteen years, and which had been completely approved by the Church Assembly (a Synod of laity and clergy). Thus non-Christians forbade the English State Church to reform itself.[24]

The *Book of Common Prayer* was created by Thomas Cranmer in 1549 and revised in 1552. This prayer book of the 'common people' and the 'congregation' of the chosen people is a masterpiece of English genius. It contains all the brilliance of this Church. Clear and beautiful in sound, extraordinarily wide in scope, it offers something for everyone. Both the Puritan and the Catholic can draw something from it for his home use.[25] The Authorized Version of the English Bible which appeared in 1611 was a summary of the English biblical translations of the sixteenth century. It was based on Tyndale, who had worked under Luther in Wittenberg. The prayer book and the Bible not only constituted the inner foundation of the Church of England but also the most important vessel of the English language, culture and spirituality until the beginning of the nineteenth century. Through these books the English people learned to understand themselves as a chosen people, like Israel.[26] It read the Bible as its own history, as a report of its defeats, battles and victories.

England's inner intellectual and psychic development, in spite of all the earthquakes and shakings, has something of the long tempo of geological processes.[27] Besides the thousand-year continuous development of English law, this is reflected most strongly in the inner constitution of the state Church. Its theory was created by Richard Hooker (1554–1600), at the height of the Elizabethan age, in *The Laws of Ecclesiastical Polity* (1594–7). Hooker was the Thomas Aquinas of this new-old Church and like Aquinas he subjected it to the overlordship of reason and authority. This patriarch of Anglicanism showed the English genius for compromise most impressively.[28] Hooker fought Rome with the Bible, and Geneva with scholastic reason and old church tradition. This war on two fronts eventually exhausted the Anglican Church but in Hooker the struggle had a monumental stamp. He still saw the universe as a hierarchy, well-ordered in structure from worm to angel. 'The laws of well doing are the dictates of Right Reason.' Morality was the self-presentation of reason. The specifically English, university humanism came to the assistance of Hooker's urgent desire for a religious and political settlement. The universities were concerned to make an adjustment but they were slowly losing their influence on the minds of the nation. Hooker's compromise also mirrored the intellectual climate of the Elizabethan age. The Elizabethan court with its cabals and love-intrigues was a kind of autumn of the middle ages, like Burgundy in the fifteenth century. It dreamed England's past and future together; it felt that a new age was beginning, a feeling peculiarly reserved for ages torn by great conflicts.

It was the hour of Shakespeare, who in the dream-image of his stage presented old England's archaic greatness, her Danish, Celtic, Saxon origins, her romantic Catholic Mediterranean connections, the bubbling gaiety of the people, and the mockery of the nobility.[29] His technique employed both the old and the new. It contained all the faustian ambiguity of the baroque age and yet it drew life from the wonderfully rich cosmos of old England seen (and broken) through the prismatic lens of his highly self-willed individuality. In his work he sang and asserted the old song, i.e., the magic patrimony of the people. Even at the height of the sixteenth century some hundreds of magical songs and sayings were still practised in England which went back to Celtic, pre-Roman and Anglo-Saxon times. Shakespeare knew them, but he also knew the broader traditions of the archaic society which had incorporated a considerable treasure of knowledge and tales from Mediterranean antiquity. He was also familiar with the humanism, the rhetoric and the antique cultural patrimony which was part of the social grace of any civilized man from the time of King Alfred to that of King James I. With the nonchalance of a man of the pre-critical and pre-Reformation age, Shakespeare joined the most disparate elements and in the magic of his plots and his verse he linked pagan and Christian elements, fate and providence, the hard realism and sharp look of the common people with the platonic heaven of ideas. He played to the ordinary people and to the great lords of old England, and openly defied the envy and hate of the Puritans and the jealousy of the rising middle classes. This was the 'merry old England' of fairies and magicians, of poets and show-men, buffoons and drink-loving sages, which shortly after Shakespeare's death went under in the storm of sermons unleashed by puritan and nonconformist ministers, and disappeared forever in the revolution.

Shakespeare wanted to amuse, to entertain those who commissioned him, these noble lords living between yesterday and tomorrow. And he did this by dragging before their eyes all that the sagas and history, the folk-wit, the customs and the brilliant exploitation of a rich narrative heritage was able to give. An unmistakeably hard line runs through Shakespeare's whole work: Shakespeare worked for lords. Their morality and immorality, their outlook, determined the personages, distributed the roles in this, their world. The people were degraded to the status of a lower class which was only allowed to display its maxims, rough-house tactics, forms of play, dances and spectacles for the amusement of these lords. This was the pitiless harshness of the governing class which monopolized all *serious* matters. It was in the comedies that the natural cruelty and exclusiveness of this courtly world became drastically visible. If citizens play the main roles then they are patricians, noble citizens of the ancient *polis* and of the Mediterranean city-states of the new Europe. The lower class man, excluded from taking an active part in the celebrations, feasts and political culture of society, is a symbol bearer of the gluttony of the lower passions and of the demonic underground. Spirits and demons in Shakespeare always had plebeian features.

'Not all the water in the rough rude sea can wash the balm from an anointed king' (Richard II, Act III, Scene 2). This is the key to all the historical dramas. Behind it, there lay a genuine theory of kingship, which Shakespeare indirectly imparted to his noble paymasters. Nothing at all, neither crime nor misfortune could erase the anointed signs of salvation of a true, consecrated king. The new rise of the English monarchy after the storms of the revolutionary century (1550–1680) can be completely understood only if we keep in view this unshakeable belief of Shakespeare in royalty. Shakespeare dared to pass sentence on England's kings as murderers, traitors, perjurors, precisely because strict standards made the inviolable power of the king even more brightly visible.* Doubled and sunk in a terrible abyss, *King Lear* shows the tragedy of king and father. How different is the treatment of this theme in Dostoievsky's *Brothers Karamazov*. The fall of the Czar-Father and the rise of English royalty can be seen in the former and the latter. Shakespeare's king-plays delineate the process of purgation: namely the strong, even if often unconscious will of the English high nobility, of its best part and of the royalty attached to it to cleanse itself, to rise from the carnage and murder of the recent past.

In a thousand forms, Shakespeare unveiled the first, comprehensive pre-

---

*Compare this concept of kingship with the treatment of King Mark in the *Tristan* of the German citizen Gottfried of Strasbourg. Its illustration of the difference between the English and the German belief in royalty, is interesting: the German Emperor was broken in the dispute over investiture, just as the naked man of sin, Mark, became the king without salvation. Kingship was forced into the eschatological sphere (the 'third Frederick' and the last Emperors of the thirteenth to the sixteenth centuries). With the King fell the father. The inability to believe in the Father in heaven and in the father on earth became the most powerful spur of the German Reformation, of the German irrational and idealistic movements of recent centuries.

sentation of modern man. A new anthropology was outlined for the first time. Man was a being of many contradictions, which are reciprocally awakened and nourished. In these fields of tension, the whole man comes to self-realization. In order to appreciate this deepened dialectic, the Shakespearian man need only be confronted with the comparatively simple virtues and vices and codes of honour among characters in plays by Corneille, Racine, Calderon, or even Schiller. In Shakespeare's figures, Heaven and Hell, submerged and revealed, clash within the individual spirit. Vices and talents, gifts and lusts, temptations from below and above interplay in such a manner that a vice (pride, ambition, love of power, envy) can turn dialectically into a virtue, say the lofty aspiration of a noble spirit, if the conditions are right. At other times when an ill wind blows, virtues and talents change colour and become vices and weaknesses. Man as the world riddle, as cosmos and chaos, was for the first time seen as a world of inner dimensions in Shakespeare. He transferred the journeys to Hell of Ulysses and Dante into the inner dimensions of man. This renunciation of objectivity showed the absence of the antique motif in him, and at the same time the Protestant and spiritualistic motives of the sixteenth century.

When we turn to Francis Bacon, we confront an equally ambiguous personality. Bacon dreamed of an alchemistic universal science that could explain all natural things according to a simple alphabet of nature consisting of a few formulas and numbers. His famous demand *dissecare naturam*, let us dissect nature, was meant to be the motto of the *regnum hominis*, the kingdom of man. Bacon himself never got beyond the dilettantish activities of the great lords of his day. His experiments were playful and inquisitive, very much in the spirit of the baroque age. While stuffing a hen with snow because he wanted to observe the delay in putrefaction Bacon caught a cold and died. Although he gave his life to it, he was really a scientific charlatan. As a disciple of Thomas More, he was a genuine critic of ideas. His theory of the way in which ideas are conditioned by society, milieu, feeling, language and environment was a valuable addition to More's work, and his consideration of colonialism was entirely in More's spirit. Bacon was possessed by the hunger for power, possession, honour and influence. He wanted to hold the world in the palm of his hand. His drive to power made him the natural advocate of the inductive method and of an oppressive colonial and scientific policy.[30]

The inductive thought of Bacon was England's answer to Spain. The Spaniards were determined to master the evil world from above through monasteries, castles and fortresses. They thought deductively in the Aristotelian-Platonic tradition of old Europe. Bacon's inductive thinking exploited the naked world from below. This induction represented the transference of discovery, of mercantile exploitation and the opening up of colonial, unknown lands (and things) to philosophy and science.[31] The earth was a colony of English lords. Bacon certainly saw it that way in his *New Atlantis* (1620). In the centre of a new England which he imagined to be on the Solomon Islands, stood the 'fellowship of the House of Solomon' as 'the eyes of this realm'. The fathers of this House were carried in sedan-chairs like Roman cardinals or like popes. They blessed the people while croziers and shepherds' staffs were borne before them. They were popes of a new world-empire whose goal was knowledge of the laws of nature and the extension of human mastery of the world. Clinics, laboratories, paper-making factories, power looms, orchards, stock farms, blast furnaces, engine houses, flying machines, submarines would be built. The most modest people of the earth who could not sufficiently deplore the excesses of Europe, would convert the whole world to its ideas.[32] Every twelve years the New Atlantis sent out twelve spies called 'merchants of light'. Disguised as nationals of other states, they spied upon the world and carefully evaluated foreign books and research.[33] This was no mere Royal Society or Academy. The citizen of New Atlantis was a sketch of the ideal explorer and colonialist. Cecil Rhodes was perhaps its most perfect fulfilment and T. E. Lawrence its end. By Lawrence's day it was no longer possible to unite in one man the will to power, the play of the intellect and the satisfaction of the understanding.

Lord Bacon possessed the absolute nonchalance of a lord of the old world, as his excellent essays show. Bacon wrote them for young noble lords who were anxious to carve out careers for themselves. He chatted to them about death ('It is as natural to die as to be born')[34] about envy as a driving force of society, about price regulations and about atheism.[35] Atheism, he argued, leads man to philosophy and law, to reflection and to a natural piety. Times which incline to atheism are peaceful civil times. Superstition, however, rests on the lower class and its terror. Superstition continues to thrive because of men's great dependence on tradition and external rites. Cunning prelates, filled with ambition, constantly strive for gain, and above all barbarous times, especially times of social unrest, foster the growth of superstition. Bacon saw clearly that one superstition could fight another. The aroused people were not afraid to use the most terrifying purges to scourge the opponents of their superstitions, even if the opponents were also believers in superstition. Bacon knew perfectly well that power was not confined to the Elizabethan court circle. In his chapter 'On Seditions and Troubles' he admitted that the lower classes were in ferment and fighting to break out.

The object of the essays was to provide guidance for young noblemen. He recommended that on their educational tours abroad they should visit the places where people gathered; these were as instructive as discussions with ambassadors and social events in good society. 'Studies serve for delight, for ornaments and for ability.'[36] Bacon's ideas were a splendid expression of old Europe's aristocratic humanism. He was very much in his element when he chatted about the construction of manor houses. Sarcastically he observed that in the strange, tremendous edifices of the Vatican and the Escorial there was hardly one agreeable living room to be found. He talked about the laying out of gardens and of colonial plantations.[37] Here he offered a manual for

English lords who wanted to equip a colonizing party in a manner both prudent and wise. The political background was as follows: whoever rules the sea has freedom of trade, whoever rules land alone will find himself in distress, despite his victories. England owed her greatness to her dominion of the seas.[38] Finally, he let his imagination conjure up a vision of things to come, the rise of new social strata and religions. Bacon predicted that the changes would cause great revolutions, not merely local rebellions and dissensions of political cliques, and he warned men to proceed very cautiously in combating new sects. They could not be fought successfully by bloody persecutions.

Lord Edward Herbert of Cherbury's *De Veritate* (1624) was another expression of the self-assurance of this old nobility and its urbane good sense. Hooker had helped to create Herbert's faith in the reasonable and discerning powers of man's natural instinct, but the serene self-confidence of his class was perhaps a more important source. Herbert belonged to a social group who were on top and felt very confident that they would remain there. They were convinced that they could restrain the people and keep the king in check, and were not afraid of the pope, Spanish tyranny, the Stuarts or the enthusiasm of the sects. Their high spirits could find no better expression than the lofty rationalism of Herbert, who took what suited him from the spiritual and religious treasures of the past. The enlightened European nobility was to cling to Herbert's ideology until 1789.

For the monarchy and that part of the nobility linked to it, the Reformation had come to an end with the assumption of power over the Church. The people, the City of London, and the lesser nobility had been the losers. The petty gentry in particular refused to acquiesce in this state of things. They had borne the weight of the permanent wars against Europe, and borne the burden of what they regarded as an anarchic social order in which each great Lord did what he pleased. All this made too many demands on their consciences and knowledge. What had actually been changed? Were the new bishops of the Church of England any less occupied with pomp, rites and superstition than the old papal ones? What use was the literature of the court? How could such superficial literary knowledge of the oceans contribute to real knowledge of the wild sea (also of the wild sea of the inner passions)? Toward the end of the sixteenth century the bourgeoisie and the people began to look to the new English natural science for answers. They began to use it as a weapon in the hard struggle for existence.

Investigation of the sea was one area in which the new drive for understanding of nature attained full expression. It was done essentially without royal support. Queen Elizabeth I possessed no genuine understanding of the navy, and the Stuarts were not much better. The old kings had been fearful of the sea as the element of revolutionary Protestantism and of the people. Under Elizabeth, however, a layman and amateur, Richard Hakluyt, the first great maritime writer, wrote his *Principal Navigations of the English Nation* (1589, then three volumes 1598 and 1600). It was the Bible and the Homeric epic of

24

English navigation. Heroism at sea, trade, politics, sea-power and building the empire were one and the same thing.

In 1600, six years before Galileo's first publication, Gilbert, Elizabeth's private physician, brought out his *De Magnete*. It was the first printed book concerned exclusively with an object of natural science discussed on a purely experimental basis.[39] His thought still belonged to the great tradition of natural philosophy of Telesio, Patrizzi, Bruno and Campanella, but his instruments were nautical. His experiments were inspired by the labour of English miners and his tests often utilized the processes of the contemporary ironworks. Gilbert was proud of his acquaintance with Cavendish and Drake, the victors over Spain, and he frequented the company of mariners, seamen and pilots. He was greatly influenced by the works of the ordinary seaman Robert Norman, who upon retirement had applied himself to the problem of compass production and recorded his observations. The mathematical foundations of Gilbert's work went back to the efforts of London business men, who had set up a special two-year chair of mathematics in 1588 as their contribution to the war effort against Spain. The object of the study was to improve navigational techniques and the training of sea officers of the navy. Mathematics, astronomy, maritime matters, investigations of nature, war and trade were all bound together in the lives of these Londoners.

Another striking example of the union of commerce, the navy and science was the foundation of Gresham College in 1598.[40] Elizabeth's great financial adviser, Sir Thomas Gresham, who also founded the London Stock Exchange, provided in his will for the establishment of the College and endowed seven professional chairs. The mathematicians, astronomers and natural scientists of the College maintained very close connections with shipbuilders, captains, navigators and naval officials. Thus scientific enthusiasm and desire for progress joined forces with the radical spirit of Puritanism in supporting the navy and foreign trade. To the men of the City of London at the beginning of the seventeenth century, religious enlightenment and scientific progress, the rise of the middle classes and English freedom were all part of the same programme. Gresham College was the forerunner of the Royal Society which was founded in 1662.[41]

Men like Robert Boyle brought to the Royal Society the same attitudes and interest which had so marked Gresham College. Boyle was a deeply religious man and a theologian. He believed that he had discovered God's pattern in creation and was firmly convinced that he could succeed in transforming the elements.[42] His friend Newton was beside himself with joy over Boyle's alchemistic experiments. Much of Boyle's work was more pragmatic, and the other members were even closer to the mining and mercantile interests. The Society was stimulated by social and religious reformers like Hartlib, Bury, Petty and Evelyn. John Dury (*The Purpose and Platform of my Journey into Germany*, 1631) cast light on the reasons for its beginnings. On his journey for information through Europe, Dury sought a basis for a union of all Protestants. His religious plans began with a reform of the schools based on the ideas of Bacon and Comenius but he was by no means averse to conducting industrial espionage on the side. While talking religion he was also interested in pharmaceutical remedies and technical progress 'either in Peace or Warre'.[43]

While the scientists and naturalists were striking out in all directions and undermining the belief in superstition, the Stuart monarchs made an extraordinary and daring attempt to maintain at least one sacrament as a valid bond between Heaven and earth, the sacramental kingship. The English nation had officially abjured all the sacraments of the old world in the oath of the state Church against transubstantiation. Its sea-faring, scientific, commercial élite, and its awakened masses regarded it as their right to destroy the remnants of magic in their surroundings. Many of them saw the meaning of their lives in the struggle to erect an earthly, rather than heavenly, system of authority. James I was entirely at home in the old cosmos. He wrote defences of his divine right which were perfect expressions of Platonic-Aristotelian medieval humanism of the grand form. He wrote a book in defence of the belief in witches and refuted Reginald Sest's *Discovery of Witchcraft* (1584). The old cosmos was one. It was a seamless fabric of magical belief and practice. Coronations, court ceremonies, the prerogatives of the holy, inviolable king who healed the sick, were deeply rooted in it, and they survived only as long as the belief in that cosmos. Charles I read the Bible, Tasso, Shakespeare and Jacob Böhme in order to strengthen his belief in salvation from the royal blood, but his belief in it was no longer shared by the majority of his subjects. His arrogance and deceit infuriated them and strengthened their resolution. For a hundred years they had been duped by the king's church and by the royal bishops. The time had come to make 'salvation through the people' a reality.

The English Revolution was the prototype of the three great European revolutions: the French Revolution, the 'German movement' (of Fichte, Hegel, Schelling, the Romantics, up to Marx and Nietzsche) and the Russian Revolution (from the Raskolniki and Dostoievsky to Lenin).[44] Like the Russian Revolution, it was the attempt of spiritualistic sects to build the kingdom of God on earth. The dark underground of the folk-soul erupted in anxiety and hope of salvation. Failure was inevitable. No social order can be built on the rim of a volcano. Only when it had run its terrible course could something permanent be built on the ashes. It was driven by fear. The English revolution was 'the desperate reaction of western Protestantism backed against a wall ... Charles I always considered Richelieu the real author of the English Revolution.'[45] The outer enemy was only one cause of the tremendous anxiety which drove the uprising. The people feared the Stuarts with their God-king ideology and they hated and distrusted Archbishop Laud.[46] His adoration of 'the beauty of the saints' was alien to them. Perhaps they suspected that Laud was an agent of the Counter-Reformation and Catholic absolutism.

The revolution began when the Archbishop tried to introduce the Anglo-

Catholic liturgy into Scotland. The proletarian Scottish people had long ago concluded a covenant with God and it rose in opposition. The Scots were filled with a gloomy religious fervour. Their political preachers began to pour over the land south of the border and their armies were a constant threat to the throne.[47] England began to split into a small king's party of bishops, nobility and officers, and the people, at first represented by a 'parliament of millionaires'. 'Its leaders were members of the middle class which had risen as a result of the plundering of the churches in the Reformation, its backbone a network of capitalistic colonial societies, its most important confederate the money-power of the City.'[48] 'King Pym', as the people called the leader of the revolutionary parliament was the business manager of a colonial company.[49] He was 'a genius of mediocrity', a great hater, who promised to treat the Catholics 'like mad dogs'. In his speech at the opening of Parliament in 1640 he declared: 'We now have an opportunity to make the country happy, by removing all hardships and pulling up the causes of evil by the roots.'[50] This was the totalitarianism of Utopia, which always aims to create a new Heaven and a new earth.

In the following year, a revolt broke out in Ireland. At last, the Utopians had their chance. A conquered territory and a subject people offered the ideal field for experiment.[51] The revolt in Ireland was 'at one and the same time a Sicilian Vespers, an eve of St Bartholomew and a peasant war'.[52] Four-fifths of the population was Catholic, but the entire populace was subject to English religious laws. A priest who read Mass was drawn and quartered alive. When the Irish finally revolted, they gave the English utopians the perfect opportunity. The English parliament looked at Ireland as booty of the Revolution. It organized the war against Ireland in the manner of a gigantic commercial enterprise 'giving out shares in it as the French Revolution was to issue its assignats',[53] an interesting gloss to Utopia and New Atlantis.

The Revolution really got rolling after the Irish revolt. Pym and his group discovered the great secret of seizing and holding power in people's revolutions by dispelling the people's anxiety and by organizing the terror. The people feared the king and the Church of the bishops. They were afraid of France, Spain, the pope, the Irish and Catholics, but most of all, of themselves. They hated the 'Arminian plague' and cried that 'the bishops are to blame for everything'. They were furious that these papists dared to assert that God bestows his grace on all men. The Calvinist, puritanical 'people' insisted upon having a tyrannical God. Baxter preached that 'God delights in the torments of the damned.'[54] During the next twenty years new conspiracies were discovered daily. Whereas Parliament was essentially concerned to secure its rule, the people sought to purify themselves as the chosen people of God. 'God is creating a new world here' preached Baillie. The sermon became the main form of revolutionary speech-making. Communities and sects represented the Party sections and Jacobin clubs of later times. It was a court of the Last Judgment in permanent session.

Oliver Cromwell was a country squire. He and a good many of his kinsmen, of whom twenty-two had seats in Parliament, owed their lands and wealth to the seizure of church lands in the sixteenth century. His allegiance was naturally to the Enthusiastic sects. After the revolution broke out, he became active in the parliamentary investigations and purges. Scandals were being ferreted out all over the country. The purging of the Church was the most important purge of all.[55] A special committee for scandalous ministers was set up in order to remove and replace them. By this time the English people had been extensively proletarianized. The country was full of dispossessed peasants, vagrant manual workers, demobilized soldiers and petty bourgeois in dire straits. The old Manichaeanism, dualism, Enthusiasm of the Cathars and of the spiritualistic sects of the middle ages had broken out again with extreme virulence. Cromwell and his followers realized that purges were the way to destroy the humanist world of culture and the sacramental order of the Church. That world was exposed as idolatrous and the servant of foreign powers.* The semi-educated leaders of the lower classes preached hatred of the incomprehensible and alien philosophies of the ruling class.

Charles I had gathered a small band of humanist poets, writers and liberal Anglican theologians at Court. Many of these men had been strongly influenced by the Socinians; others were Arminians or Unitarians or Deists. Their work produced some noble declarations on behalf of the free spirit, tolerance and the creative power of reason and history. Thomas Fuller (*Sermon on Reformation*), Jeremy Taylor (*Liberty of Prophesying*) and Chillingworth (*Religion of Protestants*) were the most distinguished of them. The people of the streets, the petty bourgeoisie and the Puritan fanatics were suspicious of such ideas. How could they understand declarations about freedom when they were completely enslaved by their own Enthusiasm? The circle which Lucius Cary, Viscount of Falkland, gathered together in Great Tew must have seemed to them as godless and blasphemous as the worldly pleasure and the courtly pomp of Charles I. The great hour of these Enlighteners was to strike only after the revolution had been crushed.

In the first shock of the revolution, aristocratic humanism was thrown back on its ultimate weapon, the art of dying nobly. Like Boethius and Thomas More, royalist lords died in the grand manner, 'an example for God and man.' This spectacle was offered to the people by Strafford, the last great political champion of the old monarchy. For eighteen days he held the eyes and ears of England as he fought for his life. His speeches belong among the greatest documents of old Europe's political humanism. In his most important one he declared: 'Let us, my Lords, not become practised in the art of murder as our forefathers were.' This struck at the heart of the new régime. To establish and settle a renovated people on a new earth the leaders of the revolution had

---

*The same resentments burst onto the surface in both the Russian and the Nazi Revolutions. Rosenberg's *Myth of the Twentieth Century*, for example, was a characteristic expression of revolutionary pietism and its hatred of Western humanism.

accepted the necessity of practising that very art. Both Strafford and his formidable opponent, Pym, exalted the law and preached against violence, terror, arbitrariness, but Strafford understood the law to come from above as an assertion of the hierarchic cosmos and of royal and humanist values. Arbitrariness from 'below' was an assertion of the anarchic underground of the people. When Pym declared, *Lex rex*, the law is king, he clearly meant the exact opposite, the strong self-assertion of salvation from the people. By 'arbitrariness' he understood the 'lawless' dispositions of the property and the lives of people indulged in by the great lords, like Strafford. In his speech on behalf of Strafford, Charles I declared: 'Consider what a tender thing is conscience.' A few days later the Earl of Essex replied, 'Parliament is the conscience of the King.' In the first German movement around Eckhart there had been flickerings of the idea of the conscience of the God filled heart. In the English Revolution, it was realized by the political community of the religiously inspired whose conscience condemned the old lords and kings to death. The English people could not forgive the king for signing Strafford's death sentence nor the twenty-two bishops who were too frightened to vote at the trial in the House of Lords. The king and the king's church had shown that they could no longer possess a conscience and a God filled heart.

On the scaffold Strafford turned for the last time to the people: 'I ask everyone who hears me to reflect earnestly, with his hand upon his heart, whether the beginning of a new life must be written in blood.[56] This appeal to the heart of the people was the surrender of the old world. He ought to have called upon all the powers of Heaven and earth, except that one. From that time on the heart began its rise to world power, the heart of a new England and the English people. The inner light and the stirrings of the heart were henceforth the commands of God. Richelieu, who may well have helped to get rid of Strafford, remarked upon hearing the news of his death, 'The English have killed their greatest man.'

What were the sources of this Puritanism of the heart? Much of it came from Scotland, where the foundations of a broad republicanism had been laid in the fifteenth and sixteenth centuries. Through a close connection with the French Huguenots, Calvinism had become a folk religion of raging, political power. Christopher Goodman, the friend of Knox in Frankfurt and Geneva, had written reflections on the duty of opposition to a 'Godless king'. (*How superior powers should be obeyed and how therein they may be lawfully and by God's word resisted*). Buchanan's work *De Jure Regni* of 1579 had terrified all of old England and was burned at Oxford University as late as 1683. Buchanan was the theoretician of the Puritan right of resistance. Like many Puritans he owed a debt to the Jesuits and especially to Mariana's *De Rege*, which he studied as a refugee in Bordeaux, Paris and Coimbra. By the beginning of the seventeenth century James I saw all England undermined by the Puritan preachers, who declared all kings to be natural enemies of the true Church and sons of the devil.[57] The Scots were organized in communities where they chose their own priests and elders and they were called Presbyterians. This was the Anglo-Saxon form of 'inspired democracy', one of the most powerful forces in the history of England and North America. The Scottish people, as a chosen people, had concluded a Biblical covenant of the brotherhood of the nation in itself and with God. Baillie called God its first Covenanter. Warriston, another preacher of this time, understood the covenant as a glorious marriage of the nation with God, as the establishment of the kingdom of Christ on earth. After the middle of the sixteenth century Scottish Puritans travelled about England, where the High Church persecuted them with deadly hatred. The two foes confronted each other in the time of Laud as had the Cathars and Innocent III at the beginning of the thirteenth century. The Puritans believed themselves called by their stern God to build his kingdom on earth. Since they could not do this in an England polluted by idolatry, they often emigrated.

The tragedy of Oliver Cromwell, his isolation as dictator (1653 to 1658), the necessity of subjugating Ireland, Scotland and England by force, was also the tragedy of English Puritanism. The longer the revolution and its purges continued, the less freedom of action it had. The leadership were caught between the fanaticism of the sects and the slowly strengthening reaction of the Royalists and Anglicans. Cromwell had raised the banners of 'freedom of conscience', of 'the true freedom of the Christian man', of a 'free Church' and a 'free state'.[58] He had identified England with Israel, the chosen people, and proclaimed his army as the 'army of God'. Carlyle, who edited Cromwell's letters and speeches in 1845, and who was a disciple of the German movement, saw him rightly as an armed prophet. Cromwell's prophecies were soon denied by the realities of his world. The spiritual worth of his appeals was reduced by each new calamity. His appeals to the Irish people proclaimed that the English Army brought freedom. The poor Irish people had, he stated, been oppressed by wicked priests for all too long. Immediately after this a bloodbath began. Instead of inspiring religious zeal, Cromwell's treatment of all the Irish gave Sir William Petty the material for his new science of statistics and political arithmetic. His main work, entitled *Political Anatomy of Ireland* dealt with the scientific and political problem of hanging 500 leaders in Ireland, of selling some 10,000 people as slaves and of confiscating two and a half million acres of land. Next he discussed rooting out the names, the language and the customs of the Irish.[59] Here was a scientifically garbed utopianism with a vengeance. An entire land and people was to be transformed to conform to the ideas of one man. Cromwell had begun his career soberly, slowly and undogmatically as only a great Englishman could begin. Increasing pressure from the sects forced him into ever more radical expressions in speech, slogans and total action.

Chiliasm had become popular during the 1620's at first as a belief held by intellectuals and professors like John Mede. A chiliasm of the lower classes was added during the great crises of 1639 and 1640. Enthusiasts and Anabaptists spread swiftly. The Brownists, also called Independents, who had been despised as a group of uncultivated lower class people, began to make converts among learned and highly-placed personalities. After 1643, antinomian influences became apparent in the chiliastic Enthusiasm.[60] The opponents of these 'enemies of the law' accused them of being the children of the Anabaptists of Münster, but in reality the Antinomians were originally non-political and quietistic. Inspired by the divine light, they felt themselves free of all authority. In the excitement of the twenty-year civil war, many moderate Enthusiasts joined the radical left wing. On the extreme left there were the Levellers, inspired radical democrats, whose leader John Lilburne cried that kings were monsters who had usurped the law and offices of God. The battle-cry of these militant groups had a strong effect on the peaceful Antinomians and on the ordinary soldiers and the lower class. The Levellers demanded freedom of religion and equality of all before the law. Emissaries of the Levellers went to Bordeaux and kindled a republican movement in the Huguenots' civil war. In England they formed the opposition to Cromwell as a party of the people, of the little man, who wanted to co-determine his political fate.

The Diggers were another sect who responded to the increasingly radical demands of the people with an unusual programme. They dug up uncultivated crown lands and planted fertile fields for the poor. Under the guidance of Everard and Winstanley, the Diggers formulated their world-view in the manifesto 'True Levellers' Standard Advanced, or the State of the Community opened and presented to the sons of men.' 'In the beginning the great creator Reason made the earth a common treasury for beasts and men.' The Creator, God and reason were identical. All land-owning lords denied the commandment, 'Thou shalt not steal' because they had acquired wealth and property through extortion of the people. The Diggers felt themselves summoned by the Holy Ghost to fight against these Pharaohs. They proclaimed the judgment, 'Let my people go' and the people would redeem the country. The Diggers said that they were cultivating Crown lands only but they argued that all the land owned by the successors of William the Conqueror had right-fully reverted to the people. In 1649, the Commonwealth decided to stamp out the Diggers. Their homes were destroyed, their crops laid waste. Winstanley turned to the Parliament and the army: 'The poor should own the land.' Holy Scripture must be really and materially fulfilled, for Christ was the Head-Leveller. Winstanley's earlier writings had been purely theological, chiliastic essays (*The Mystery of God, The Breaking of the Day of God*). Under the pressure of political persecution, he arose as the acknowledged leader of religious communism. His main work was finished in 1652, *The Law of Freedom*, dedicated to all the nations of the earth.* Winstanley showed Cromwell that social conditions had not changed despite the revolution.

*Like the Russian chiliasts of 1917, the Diggers regarded the earth as a kind, mystical matriarchal power.

Anarchy still ruled from above. The clergy and land owners tyrannized the people. Winstanley's ideas were a mixture of prophetic-utopian and realistic elements soberly thought out. He was concerned about a new social order, where there would be no buying and selling. Land was to be common property, and all authorities would be chosen yearly. Everyone would deliver the products of his labour to communal warehouses, and compulsory labour service was required from all up to the age of forty.

The opposition of the radical sects to the dictator and Lord Protector, Oliver Cromwell, had become irreconcilable. Here were men who had drawn the logical consequences from Puritanism's 'inspired democracy'. Cromwell's and Baxter's commonwealth was a Church and a chosen people, whose members sat in deliberation around the one and only sacred 'Table of the House' in Parliament.* They had no room for such radical opposition. A Communion of discourse and counsel had taken the place of the sacrificial Mass of the old world. It was the exclusive right of this community to deal with spiritual affairs and through its holy deliberations it was granted the power to dispense the 'public spirit' as the bread of life. This public spirit was the source of the eighteenth-century idea of a secular public opinion. Public spirit was obligatory for all, and especially for thinkers, philosophers and jurists.[61] It was the Holy Ghost, which expressed itself in the talk exchanged among the members of the community. Like St Peter's in the Roman baroque or like Campanella's Temple of the Sun, Parliament enclosed within its walls the salvation of the lawful earthly globe. All those whom Cromwell's commonwealth excluded did not choose to believe this, and they grew narrower and more exclusive.

The solution to the problem of defending the new city of God appeared quite simple to the Puritan Samuel Gott. His New Jerusalem, printed in 1648, was the only great bourgeois Utopia of the times. Gott thought that the fascination of the Puritan theocracy was so great that Christians would let themselves be cleansed by it and Jews converted without protest. They would establish a new life based on the Bible, science, domestic economy, education and sport, in a 'new covenant' of God with men. James Harrington was much less naïve. He recognized how incredibly difficult things really were. After twenty years of preparation, he wrote Oceana and placed it at Cromwell's disposal as the pattern of a new political order. Harrington had visited western Europe and studied the government of Venice which had aroused keen interest in the Protestant world because of its independence and its battle with the popes. In his Oceana Harrington extolled this bulwark of European nonconformism which he called 'Adriana'. Oceana strongly influenced Locke and Hume, who hailed it as the only valuable model of a commonwealth. John Adams compared the significance of its discovery of the inner connection between power, government and property with Harvey's discovery of the

*The table of Cromwell's parliament played the same role as Calvin's chair in Geneva.

circulation of the blood. This Utopia determined essential features in the constitution of several American states (that of Carolina as early as 1669).[62]
Later it shaped the ideas of Sieyès and through him the constitution of the
great French Revolution and thus the French constitution to this day.
Harrington was the only one among his contemporaries to perceive the social
and economic change underlying political and social revolutions.

Harrington began by arguing that the monarchy in England rested on 300
great landholdings belonging to the nobility. If the inspired democracy of the
Puritans were to stay in power, it had to distribute the land among at least
5,000 proprietors. This was its fundamental insight: the distribution of
political power in the long run follows the distribution of landed property.[63]
Harrington knew what the men of the Weimar republic recognized too late,
and German democrats after 1945 have often chosen not to see: that a balance
of power as security against absolutism must be based on an economic
balance. Accordingly Harrington wanted to base the republic on a new
agrarian constitution. Large estates should be broken up. The nobility as a
natural aristocracy (Harrington himself came from an old family) should assert
its position in the state through education and public service. As a senate it
had the right of nomination, but the people of the 'Commons' decided, and
the officials could serve as executives. Religious life was to be developed under
the control of a national council of religion which guaranteed religious freedom. Education to develop a civil and moral discipline had very great significance for Harrington. Every politician should be first of all an historian and
world-traveller; he must get to know as many countries and constitutions as
possible.

If Harrington's *Oceana* implied a critique of Cromwell's commonwealth, of
its insularity and totalitarian exclusiveness, then Milton's *Paradise Lost* may
be regarded as its obituary.[64] Milton had seen a vision of a new age arising in
the Revolution. England offered the world the spectacle of a nation awakening to freedom. This spreading of the blessings of freedom and civilization
among the kingdoms of the world concerned all peoples. He thought a great
deal about 'The ready and easy Way to establish a free Commonwealth' (1659
to 1660). Depressed by the excesses of the Revolution and by Cromwell's
failure, isolated during the Stuart restoration, Milton declared that the 'mass'
(the chosen people incapable of salvation) was not yet mature enough to make
a reality of human rights: freedom of thought and trade, freedom of the press.
Bitterly he sang a requiem for the commonwealth. Paradise on earth had been
lost through men's own fault. This world belongs to the earthly rulers, proud,
highly-gifted men. In Milton's poem Lucifer had Strafford's features.

The Republic collapsed in 1660. The Stuarts and their gay and flippant
court society returned. From 1660 on, the Puritans and Free Church sects
were officially excluded from public life as nonconformists and dissenters.
The vengeance of the victorious episcopal Church of the monarchy drove
them out into trade, science and the underground. For the next 200 years they

corroded the foundations of the High Church and enriched England's inner development with ever new political and religious impulses.

Thomas Hobbes (1588–1679) was born in the year of the great victory over Spain, and he died in the year of Parliament's decisive victory over the aristocratic monarchy, the Habeas Corpus Act of 1679. The French materialism of D'Alembert, Lagrange, Turgot and Condorcet was based on Hobbes, who was a most un-English thinker. He had lived in France for almost twenty years as a student and emigrant and met bitter opposition in England. Hobbes was educated along Puritan lines at Magdalen College in Oxford. His extremism was strengthened by Descartes, Galileo, and the atmosphere of enlightened Calvinism around Mersenne. His materialism and absolutism were the expression of his boundless despair at the horrors of the English Revolution. Hobbes was a model of the two-faced character of modern European conservatism. His romantic pessimism and fear of the 'barbarism' of the people took refuge in intellectual and political systems which in their revolutionary implications went well beyond anything imagined by his enemies. The key to Hobbes's philosophy and theory of state (*Elementa Philosophiae*: Leviathan, 1651) is found in his *Behemoth or the Long Parliament*.[65] This was published for the first time by a German in 1889 – 100 years after the French Revolution. The England of the Stuarts had forbidden the publication of this work. If England really was in the state that Hobbes described in four brief dialogues dealing with the years from 1640 to 1660, then the only choice for the future was between a 'dictatorship of the dagger' and one of 'the sword', that is, from 'above' or 'below'.

Hobbes was essentially a spiritualist and the horror which he felt as he looked at the world expressed itself in his political theory. Men in a state of nature live in a war of all against all, he argued. They are always likely to fall back again into barbarism and chaos if a total state, a Leviathan, were not able to maintain the rule of reason, peace, wealth and sociability through its laws. The Leviathan was the Puritan commonwealth revived, a secularized city of God. Since the priests have proved to be unfit and unworthy, theology will be replaced by the law (which Hobbes declared to be 'the conscience of the citizen') and by mathematical natural science. Like Descartes and the later Calvinists, Hobbes regarded geometry as the pure science which would rescue man from barbarism, darkness and passions, by throwing a bridge over the chaos of the instinctual drives.

Hobbes must be called the last excess of the revolutionary years. His was an immediate, on the spot reaction. John Locke's was the mature late reaction. He liquidated the Revolution, by absorbing it into a philosophy which retained the contradictions, rather than overcoming them. Locke was a spectator of the 'glorious Revolution' that brought the House of Hanover to sovereignty instead of mastery in England. In 1689 his first *Letter on Tolerance* was published, the same year in which the Declaration of Rights confirmed the rule of parliament. Locke can be described as English democracy expressed in philosophy. In him the great transformation, which had been in preparation since the Revolution, received philosophical expressions. From then on England's thinkers renounced the war of principles 'to the bitter end' because they knew that the nation might break up and crumble into its original elements and peoples. That is why English thinkers and theologians have been so eminently considerate, prudent, politically and socially aware, so intent upon adaptation and compromise. Radicalism was left to the poets. There was validity in the assertion that the thinker 'was only the gifted interpreter and mediator of what at bottom everyone somehow possessed and knew'.[66] 'It was as if the mind of the Englishman was a small democracy in which the rights of a minority were jealously preserved, and opposing impulses and ideas could live in mutual tolerance with one another.'[67]

As 'the father of the English Enlightenment' Locke developed his philosophy of commonsense and of natural religion (as he understood Christianity) on the basis of a great renunciation. For him there was no longer a metaphysics, cosmology, ontology and theology in the old sense of the cosmos-structure. Locke did not recognize the structed patterns of authority of the old world and of the 'grand form', which the baroque age sought to restore. He suspected that they were oppressive castles (Temple and Bastille) which imprisoned men. He argued that there are no innate ideas, and thus destroyed the dominating heavens of Platonism. The mind of man, the citizen, is at the beginning a blank white paper void of all characters. Men learn to think by dealing with their surroundings and knowing them inwardly and outwardly in 'sensation' and 'reflection'. Thought is a social, psychological and political process. Self-interest, or the assertion of oneself in the community of well-educated citizens, determines virtue. 'Good and evil are nothing but pleasure and pain, or that which occasions or procures pleasure or pain to us.'[68]

Locke defined the Church as a free community of men, which reflected his interpretation of the social contract.[69] The members of a church agreed to worship God publicly in a way which they chose. The Church had no reason to use violence and 'like a club for claret', had no power of decree over the civic duties of men.[70] The state is no more obliged to defend a religion than, for example, the East India Company. Locke did not mean this cynically; he only wanted to bring to an end the 150 years of church struggle, religious discord and civil war in England. He also wanted to preserve England from the fate of France, where the revocation of the Edict of Nantes had again inflamed religious conflict. Hence the restriction of the Church to a civil society. The understanding accepts no commands of a cosmic religious-political order of authority, and conscience understands the Bible as a message of reason and a purified morality of self-enjoyment.

Locke's thought reflected the new earthly cosmos of the 'gentleman', who from 1688 to 1945 ruled England as nobleman and citizen. Locke's ideas were not meant to apply to everyone. For example, he had no tolerance for atheists and Catholics and was a shareholder in colonial societies which carried on the slave trade.[71] The laws of his philosophy were as valid as a gentleman's agreement and were meant to apply to well brought up ladies and gentlemen, who were cultivated in a Christian humanist way. Its laws were designed for the cosmos of their castles, estates, salons and learned societies.[72]

Isaac Newton was rightly honoured by the English as a national hero. He was a king of the new age. His burial in 1727 was marked by the pomp and circumstance formerly accorded to the princes and monarchs.[73] Newton created a cosmic machinery in a way which was entirely characteristic of the post-revolutionary time. This cosmic mechanism was described in the classical work of mathematical natural-science: *Philosophiae naturalis principia mathematica* (1687). Copernicus, Kepler and Galileo had laid the foundations of a mechanics of the heavenly bodies. The universe had become a calculable machine in which the heavenly bodies obeyed earthly laws of gravity. There were no longer any transcendental orders (as in Aristotle, Plato, Dante). Newton's mathematical approach was related to Descartes, although he was very critical of Cartesian hypotheses.[74]

In one sense Newton's theory of the cosmos as a balance of forces was a transference of the political theory of 1688 to the universe as a whole. Newton's law of gravity for example, which determined and made known the orbits of celestial and terrestrial bodies corresponded exactly, as did Locke's idea of tolerance, to the religious and political situation of England at the time. It further loosened the grip of magic on the cosmos in order to establish a mathematical calculation of celestial mechanics. Confidence in the political stability of the earthly balance in the state and in society was the necessary prerequisite for such a conception. Given such confidence, it became desirable to examine that balance in the whole universe. Lastly, it required a deep trust in a benevolent, omniscient constitutional monarch of the world, who preserved the universe in its well-weighted equilibrium. Newton's God intervened from time to time, regulating and adjusting the planets in their courses but only in order to overcome disturbances. God embodied absolute time and absolute motion in himself. The universe was God's edifice and casing.[75]

Newton's view of the universe was strongly influenced by English Platonism. It was this Platonism which enabled Newton and English philosophy to maintain an optimism about things and a sense of the beauty of holiness.[76] Something of the old world view was saved, despite the puritan rejection of Roman sacramentality and the baroque idea of kingship. Its cosmic vision was semi-magical, semi-sacramental. It enabled the English lords to enthuse over the beauty of the universe without being subservient to the state Church or to Rome. They could worship the order of nature without having to accept a nearby Monarch as its controller. This Platonism became a substitute for the Roman Mass and the cult of the Anglican Episcopal Church. It dissolved magic and sacramentality into an optimistic faith in the harmonious interplay of all impulses, weights, men and stars in nature. It was very suitable to a gentleman.

The life-work of Anthony Ashley Cooper, Earl of Shaftesbury (1671–1713), whose education had been greatly influenced by Locke and More, was a commentary on Newton's optimism and religion. He was a forerunner of the French and German nature-enthusiasts, sentimentalists and pantheists. (Rousseau, Diderot, Herder, Goethe, Schlegel and Schleiermacher were influenced by him). He came from one of the country's great Whig families, in which the liberality of the gentleman implied hatred of the High Church, of Rome and of the plebeian Puritans and sects. In order to escape the church of the priests Shaftesbury deified nature as the great temple in which God and his harmonies were embodied. He hated Jehovah as the God of persecution, barbarism and sacrifice and as the God of the Puritans, and accused the Christian clergy of blasphemously abusing God, the universe and man. The devil and Hell represented the dungeon and the gallows in the absolutist states of the earth. 'A devil or a hell may prevail where a gaol and a gallows are thought insufficient.'[77] In his struggle against the High Church, Puritans and sects, Shaftesbury secularized Augustine's ontological optimism ('all that is, is good and right') and stood Thomas Aquinas on his head, 'All beauty is truth.'* He created an inner-worldly liturgy and ritual service of 'the good, true and beautiful', which well-bred lords could celebrate in nature and social life. His favourite concept was 'harmony', and he was forced to deny evil and sin, because they were the certainties of the enthusiasts and clerics. The place of the priest was taken by the virtuous cultivated man, who viewed beauty disinterestedly and perceived in it the world soul. The place of the enthusiast was taken by the creator and a vessel of God. Sympathy and friendship (instead of political subjugation), the beautiful (instead of the holy), the naturally sublime (instead of the supernatural), virtue (instead of sin). Thus Shaftesbury tried to work out a middle way, which freed the liberal gentleman from the dilemma of being bound either to the conservative High Church or to salvation through the people.

Deism was the religion of a society of noblemen and great bourgeois lords. Between 1690 and 1740, it emancipated itself from God the Lord, just as it had emancipated itself from the king in two revolutions. From now on it accepted God and king only as constitutional monarchs, as shields of honour for its own interests and plans, as symbols of its power. Freedom of thought, Lord Bolingbroke maintained, ought to apply only to the upper classes; the people were to be kept in check by the traditional religion. In his *Idea of a Patriot King* (1738), Bolingbroke sketched just such an enlightened king, who reforms his country in a moderate way, promotes trade and shipping and fights corruption. He also sketched the ideal of an enlightened God as a constitutional monarch. Dogmas, he argued, are absurd and shocking even to the common-sense of a Hottentot or a Samoyed. A king is a man with a crown on his head and a sceptre in his hand, a bishop is a man with a crozier and mitre.

The era of Walpole meant political stagnation for half a century. His motto

*Aquinas had said: 'Beauty is the reflection of the true, that is, of the order of being.'

was: *quieta non movere*. England became wealthy and satisfied and recorded enormous successes. The English–Dutch fleet in 1692 was victorious over France at La Hogue. As a result, France was crippled as a naval power just as Spain had been 100 years earlier. The censorship was lifted in 1694, in 1714 the personal union of England with Hanover created a solid bulwark in Europe for the insular state. From 1757 to 1784 English lords conquered the East Indies, in 1763 the Peace of Paris confirmed England as the foremost colonial power in the world. Canada, Louisiana, Florida and Senegambia were added to the already enormous Empire. This was the golden age of English deism.

'Whatever is, is right.' Everything is good in the order of the cosmos and in its laws.[78] Alexander Pope set the gospel of this optimistic world-view in rhyme in his *Essay on Man* (1733). Pope was a friend of Bolingbroke and the editor of his invectives against history, in which these lords saw only superstition, greed, self-interest and tyranny. The *Essay on Man*, long before Voltaire and Rousseau, had an enormous effect on the cultivated public of Europe. Pope was an ugly, deformed, touchy man, who had grown up in an atmosphere of evasiveness and secrecy. His parents were crypto-Catholics and lived in fear of the hatred of the people. He was insulting to his friends, full of hatreds for his enemies, and ended up as a disillusioned, lonely pessimist. He reminds one of Watteau, the cripple who painted the earthly paradise of love and tender friendship for the closed society of lords and ladies.

The most important English thinker of the eighteenth century was David Hume (1711–76). 'I was of a good family, both by father and mother: my father's family is a branch of the earl of Home's or Hume's and my ancestors had been proprietors of the estate which my brother possesses, for several generations ...'[79] Thus Hume began his autobiography. Hume wrote for a 'good company', and philosophized for the cultivated noble and bourgeois society of western Europe. At the age of fifty he went to Paris as a secretary to the British embassy there. He loved Paris, 'the great number of sensible, knowing and polite companions with which that city abounds above all places in the universe'. Hume was certain that man was a reasonable being. 'Man is a sociable, no less than a reasonable being' was the beginning of his famous *Enquiry Concerning Human Understanding*. Man is first of all man in society; 'be a philosopher, but amidst all your philosophy, be still a man'. 'Let your science be human, and such as may have a direct reference to action and society.' In his *Dialogues Concerning Natural Religion* he accused the atheists of publicly confessing their disbelief in God. They were 'thereby guilty of multiplied indiscretion and imprudence.'[80] Hume wanted to make society secure, by showing every metaphysics to be impossible, 'a mere juggle', by reducing reason to experience and custom, and by referring causality to instincts, impulses and feelings. Certain knowledge was contained only in quantities and numbers. In essence he concluded his enquiry with the suggestion that when we visit libraries we should ask: do these books contain something on quantities or numbers, experimental reasoning from facts? If not, then into the fire with them!

Hume knew that the rationalist theologies of his time were patchworks, in which no honest thinker could believe. He knew that the great systems of Cartesian rationalism were vessels, hammered together out of heterogeneous elements. 'Our most holy religion is formed on faith, not on reason ... Whoever is moved by faith to assert to it, to agree to the Christian religion, is conscious of a continued miracle in his own person, which subverts all the principles of his understanding, and gives him a determination to believe what is most contrary to custom and experience.'[81] Hume was very close to Augustine and Pascal here. His scepticism left the gates open for an existentialist faith: 'theology has a foundation in reason so far as it is supported by experience, its best and most firm foundations are, however, faith and revelation'.[82]

Kant was fascinated by Hume's abolition of causality and by his qualification of reason as a social agreement between cultivated men. Both Hume and Kant were fearful that the good human society of their time had already begun to be swallowed up by 'salvation from the depths'. Everywhere they saw orgiastic, irrational movements of religious, semi-religious and political enthusiasts. Hume rejected the Puritan Faith as enthusiastic and the Catholic as superstitious. He found certainty only in the 'regular mechanism', in the 'inner machine' of man, which is psychologically calculable, and in the social mechanism. Hume himself valued his moral writings most highly. He wanted to transform morality into a sort of psychology and social science, because the conscience of the individual could not be permitted to exist outside of society. The unexpressed fear which moved Hume was caused by the awareness that conscience was a last refuge of the absolute God and of the irrational. It had to be drawn into the life of society and transformed into a visible and open dialogue of individuals aiming to assert themselves.

Hume did not publish his most radical writings (concerning the fictions of historical Christianity and his defence of suicide) during his lifetime. What concerned him most was the defence of his English society. He wrote his neo-conservative *History of England* for both Tory and Whig at once.[83] He now appealed to the authorities whom he had demolished before. Although Hume had destroyed the idea of divine grace as well as the theory of the social contract as contradictions and follies he invoked them to secure peace and order. A cynical neo-conservatism was latent in Hume's scepticism, but there was an even greater threat in his thought. Freed from the English society which sustained it, whose inner balance of power he wanted to secure, it could become a powerful incitement for the irrationalism of the Romantics for their political nationalism (in his essay on 'National Characters') and even for Feuerbach and the Young Hegelians.[84] According to Hume man created God in his image.[85] Whereupon, as a member of the good society, he drew the conclusions that whatever is present in the idea of God must therefore be a reflection of the human spirit which created it. Thus there must be good altruistic motives which man has projected from his own nature to God.

The foundation had been laid of that paradisic theology, founded by Hume's pupil, friend and editor, Adam Smith, which attained a world-wide reputation under the title *Classic National Economy*. Its historico-political foundation was formed by the consciousness of victory of the English nobility and wealthy bourgeoisie, the governing class which had gone from strength to strength.[86] Now it began to reach its hands toward trade and industry. It is also necessary to an understanding of Smith to recall the harshness of the old Calvinist view of Hell, which had so profoundly saturated the thinking of the English bourgeoisie. The industrial revolution had already begun to turn England into a very real Puritan hell. The ontological optimism of the eighteenth century was coloured by the Calvinist pessimism, and both factors contributed to the magnitude and fantastic character of the classic political economy.[87] Historically, perhaps the only counterpart to its liturgical prizing of money, wealth and extension of the kingdom of God through expansion of the economy was the German imperial theology of the high middle ages, which also spoke of a harmony of the universe and of the 'holy empire', which had long since been broken up. The classic political economy of Smith, Ricardo, James Mill and McCulloch did not recognize the existence of a working-class or employer class. Wages were determined by the ratio between population and capital. It was entirely foreign to actuality with its assertion of the eternal laws of economics, and its view of man in an airless space. Where it did discuss social realities it presented the beautification and transfiguration of an evil actuality as an economically necessary state of salvation.

This optimism inspired Adam Smith to celebrate 'the realm of free economy' as a paradise on earth in that Bible of unrestricted capitalism, his *Inquiry into the Nature and Causes of the Wealth of Nations*. Economic freedom was the meaning and ultimate aim of social life and of the divine world order. Nature instead of providence, he argued, takes care of the pre-established harmony: 'Nature is wisdom without reflection.' The brilliant interplay of the self-interests of all individuals in the 'natural order' of society would necessarily produce the happiness of mankind. The free economy and its 'natural social order' could not be changed without unleashing the forces of evil. It hardly requires very much imagination to recognize in this doctrine the Pelagian spiritual church of freedom. This Neopalagianism feared and hated the wicked state whose princes were 'cunning and crafty animals'. It despised them as spendthrifts and violators who had for centuries disrupted the natural order of free enterprise. 'There are no things less compatible with one another than the character of a merchant and that of a prince.'[88] The Catholic Church was 'the most fearful union that ever was formed both against the authority and security of the worldly powers and against human freedom and welfare'. As a pupil of Hume, Smith cautiously observed the disruptive factors which religion introduced and which could upset the balance of power. He recommended rich donations in order to keep the clergy of the state Church quiet, and it would be best of all to have small rival sects everywhere, without privileges and support. Smith was unshakeably convinced that 'the deception of nature' (comparable to Hegel's deception of reason, of the world-spirit) would turn the egoism of the individual into the fair play of society for the benefit of all. Supply and demand, as a sacred communion and eternally valid law, was the highest reality. It bound the economy, politics, society and faith in harmony towards a life of freedom and progress.

Smith's successors identified his 'natural order of society' with their contemporary industrial structure. They understood its anarchy as a development of freedom. Deism, the will for concordance of satiated theologians and bishops of the state Church, the long rule of the Whigs as the main representatives of industry and trade, a utilitarian humanism at the universities which chose to see the beauty of the cosmos and society as fair play and balance of power, determined the success of this economic theology. Had it not succeeded in keeping God, evil, poverty, external enemies, the sects and the working-class within narrow and fixed limits? The great crises began after the 1760's. America, France and Russia proved to be important opponents. The Industrial Revolution showed openly what only the poets seemed to have known for 150 years: that there is a radical evil, that terrible powers of destruction and grace actually exist, that England consisted of two nations and that even the ruling class lived in anarchy, corruption and crime.

Literature became the only area in which such truths were openly discussed. Writers probed more deeply than theologians into the problems of sin, human misery and guilt. The radical dissenter Daniel Defoe was the heir of the utopianism of More and Milton. His Robinson Crusoe was the new man who builds his life by his own power. In the book he criticized himself, and his greed, so that Robinson Crusoe became, as so many great works of English literature were, a public confession. English satires and novels were all sermons on reform. Jonathan Swift's works were thunderous protests against the order of his day. His pessimism was further refined in the conservative Samuel Johnson, 'England's Dr Johnson'. In *Rasselas* Johnson uncovered the corruption of the world, like Voltaire's *Candide*. This great moralist rejected the arguments of Mandeville and Jenyns that those who have been born to poverty should not be robbed of the 'opiate of ignorance' through an education unsuited to them (cf. Marx's 'religion is the opiate of the masses'). Johnson was opposed to all speculation, he knew that evil lies deeper than politicians and operators can reach: 'How small of all that human hearts endure. That part which laws of kings can cause or cure.' He knew also that every faith decays and dies out completely if it proves itself unable to satisfy the intellectual and spiritual needs of new classes and of all levels of the population.[89]

The great religious uprising led by Wilson, Watts, Doddridge, Law and Wesley was the answer to the questions which Dr Johnson had posed.

William Law (d. 1761) was directly influenced by Jakob Böhme,[90] and he introduced to England Böhme's peculiar pantheism. God was, Law learned from Böhme, a 'spirit of love ... a will to goodness'.[91] There is no heaven or Hell.[92] The usual doctrine of justification, the philosophy of debtor and creditor, of Christ's compensation for God's anger, is an empty fancy of human reason. God influences the soul as magnetism does the needle. Christ unfolds in us as an inner force, like the light of the sun in a growing plant. Law's religious activism is reminiscent of Fichte.

John Wesley (1703–91) was the founder of Methodism. His revival meetings and struggles for repentance grasped the suppressed or long dormant religious powers of the lower classes in England's critical hour. 'The forces of feeling and at the same time those of the masses came to expression.'[93] Wesley was a tireless organizer, the very prototype of the manager, the industrial boss, and the political salvation-leader. He travelled 225,000 miles, preached over 40,000 sermons (sometimes before 20,000 persons) and enjoyed an indestructible health until his eighty-sixth year. Wesley was for the people and against Calvinism, mysticism, Catholicism and Anglicanism. He needed no external proofs for Christianity. He had his daily experience: 'One thing I know: I was blind and now I see.'[94] Christ had awakened him from sin, and he in turn wanted to free his countrymen, the simple people, from the clutch of the devil and the tyranny of vice and selfishness. He experienced daily the intervention of God and the devil in the course of the world, and believed in magic and witchcraft, but not in Cook's world voyages or Newton's investigations. Wesley was concerned about the divine, direct guidance of man. He had become aware that all the higher authorities of church and society had lost their power to impress the lower class. In the second part of his *Further Appeal to Men of Reason and Religion* there are remarkable descriptions of English life, of the general collapse of religion in the nation, of political corruption, the drunkenness of the people, the luxury of the upper classes, fraud in business, the servility and indifference of the clergy and the disrespect for truth. In his despair, Wesley cried out, 'O who will convert the English into honest pagans?'[95]

Wesley wanted to preach salvation to the people in 'plain sound English'. The fact that his movement spread like a fire is understandable only as a reaction of the masses to their neglect from those above. 'Wesleyanism ... was heat without light, a blind protest of the masses',[96] an ecstatic seizure of the people. Next to the *Book of Common Prayer*, Wesley's hymns were probably the most powerful teacher of piety in English history. They began that slow adjustment between above and below which has spared England from social revolutions. Methodism converted the energies and constantly changed them into a permanent, quiet revolution. Wesley's influence extended far beyond Methodism. His religious earnestness gripped other sects, indeed even the High Church and fostered that spirit of political, social and scientific reform which is still unextinguished in our day. It was the Quakers who took up and led the struggle against the slave trade. The Dissenters, who were excluded from the universities and state posts until 1859 and from some jobs until 1871 were the first to fight for religious tolerance and political equality for the broad masses.

Methodism, although it was originally free of sentimentality, was responsible for the transmission of a tradition of feeling and the heart which accelerated the development of secular romanticism. This was the heritage of feeling which arose from mysticism, from the *devotio moderna,* from quietism and pietism. The sentimental heart is simply the last degeneration of the Augustinian heart, which coveted nothing else but to preserve God in itself. James Hervey (d. 1758), whose *Meditations* was one of the most popular books of the century, was an inspired pupil of Wesley. He combined the religious enthusiasm of the Methodists with the enthusiasm for nature of Macpherson and Rousseau. Henry Brooke's *Fool of Quality* (1760) was a half-way house between Böhme and Rousseau, and a potent mixture of religious mysticism and political sentimentality. It was this mixture which was to poison the future for the romantic Enthusiasts of Germany and the eastern border states. English romanticism was forced to purify itself to a certain extent because it could not really hold its ground in constant confrontation with the very different English environment. Even Coleridge (1772–1834) who later became the leader of the Germanic-Christian-Platonic romanticism in England, was never able to escape his Englishness. His education had been typical of his time and he had been successively exposed to materialism, Priestley's unitarianism, and Hartley and Bodwin with their so-called necessitarianism. It was difficult to be a pure romantic with such a background.

Romanticism found one ally in an unexpected quarter, the Toryism of a certain group of men, who were beginning to think of themselves as ideological conservatives. Although the political engagements and concerns of these new Tories certainly contributed to a more realistic appraisal, the alliance led to a hardening of the romantic patrimony of ideas. New conservatism's great thinkers were Edmund Burke (1729–97), as outspoken a personage as the German Justus Möser, and Edward Gibbon who was a model of the conservative sceptic and cynic. After a temporary conversion to Catholicism, described in his highly interesting autobiography, Gibbon launched a massive attack upon Christianity. The first two books of the *Decline and Fall of the Roman Empire* appeared in 1776 and he was astonished when he was attacked because of it. He had not expected that the majority of his English readers 'felt themselves so bound to the name and shadow of Christianity'.[97]

Like Gibbon and Möser, Burke also viewed religion from the outside and valued it as a stabilizing and preservative factor in social and political life. He pleaded for the recognition of all European religions because they were prescriptive and useful in controlling chaos (from below). Religion was the basis of civil society and the source of all goods and satisfactions.[98] Burke was a political man and though he would never have admitted it he was opposed to the outbreak of faith more than to any other aspect of the French Revolution. Burke rejected flatly the belief 'that the people can be made happy, that laws, customs, words, men, can be changed'. Although he knew perfectly well that this credo of Rabaut de Saint-Etienne's was the essence of the French Revolution, he tried very hard to make himself and the reactionary world of Europe, which lights candles to his image to this day, believe that the causes of the Revolution were to be sought in a conspiracy of atheists and politicians who desired the aggrandisement of France.

The same Burke who dismissed the French Revolution as a conspiracy of criminals, murderers and swindlers, in other places compared it to the Reformation.[99] It was because he recognized its religious-political character that he preached a crusade against it.[100] Burke also knew that it was an armed doctrine, and that the crusade would necessarily be of long duration.[101] But he was unable to take the next step and to free himself from the great heresy of all European reactionaries: that ideas can be fought against with arms. In his call for the organic (against the manufactured), for instinct (against reason), for the concrete, historical and traditional (against the new, arbitrary, abstract), for the unconscious (against the conscious), Burke was the father of German political romanticism. Noisily he rang the alarm: 'The age of chivalry is gone; that of the sophists, economists and calculators has succeeded it.'[102] This statement was perfectly true. The aristocratic structure of old Europe from Homer to the beginning of the eighteenth century had broken up. At the same time the call for a restoration was an expression of the typical hypocrisy towards life of those theorizing, neo-conservatives. They wanted to renew the old established ways with the means and ideas of the new age, and of the Revolution itself.

Like Justus Möser and many German romantics, Burke was an involuntary enlightener. He betrayed himself when he designated the people as an artificial idea,[103] and when he attacked Hastings on English mismanagement in India and defended the American Revolution. He believed in the cleverness and sense of responsibility of the English ruling classes and he was certain that they would be able to overcome England's great internal and external crises. In the long run Burke was right, but only because this upper class was increasingly pounded and leavened by dissenters and nonconformists.

Burke's great opponent was Thomas Paine, whose *Common Sense* appeared in 1776 and his *Rights of Man* in 1791 to 1792. Paine was the most important English representative of the ideas of the French Revolution. He identified Deism and democracy. The earlier Deists had turned to the cultivated, but the uncultivated Paine turned to the common people. He regarded humanist studies as a ruse by which the clergy turned its slaves away from the natural sciences. Bitterly he remarked that the Supreme Being cannot be identical with the brutal God of the Old Testament. The Bible was a history of scoundrels; it has served to brutalize and corrupt mankind. The underground broke out in Paine. His was a popular rage, a proletarian pathos, which announced: 'for us, for the masses condemned by our masters, the old God is dead. Your Lord God is a bloody tyrant, a lover of Jewish religious-political wars of belief and massacres, the ideal of a small clique of priests and privileged Enthusiasts. We no longer acknowledge Him.' Richard Price joined Paine in the attack and in *Observations on Civil Liberty* (1776) fulminated against the imperialistic forms of prayer in the Anglican Church.[104]

Joseph Priestley, the great chemist, was an equally important opponent of the Church. Priestley was a product of enlightened Calvinism and was an Arian and then a Socinian. His strong theological and historical interest was rooted in his belief in progress. Mankind is on the way to a glorious status. He was sceptical of the English system of government in which 5,723 voters chose half of the House of Commons and 364 voters chose a ninth part of the House of Lords. He was both a Christian and a materialist in that he considered it possible to achieve the reform of all conditions through science and theology. Like Roger Bacon and many spiritualist world-reformers, he vacillated between gross superstition and enlightened thought. He saw Nelson's victories, for example, prophesied in Isaiah. His *History of the Depravities of Christianity* (1782) expounded the typical spiritualist doctrine of corruption. Priestley was pastor of the Presbyterian congregation in Birmingham and with Watt, Boulton and other pioneers in natural science he was a member of the Lunar Society, over which the physician, philosopher and writer, Erasmus Darwin, the grandfather of Charles Darwin, presided. A mob stormed Priestley's house shouting 'Church and King' and burned it to the ground. Priestley and Paine had received honorary French citizenship and had been elected members of the Convention. Driven out of England they emigrated to America. At the same time in the Philosophical Literary Society, a sister of the Lunar Society, in Birmingham, the younger Watt, Walker and Jackson maintained close connections with the Jacobin Club in Paris, 1792. In Birmingham John Dalton developed his modern atom theory.[105] In the industrial cities, benumbed by filth and misery which William Blake, the heir of Milton and the revolutionary folk sectarianism, saw as 'dark satanic mills', these dissenting theologians, manual workers, small merchants, physicians and school teachers worked grimly, enthusiastically and selflessly for progress. They were the spiritual sons of Roger Bacon and Thomas More.

England's great natural scientists were often amateurs (like Robert Boyle, Henry Cavendish, Joseph Banks, Charles Darwin, the third and fourth Lords Rayleigh and the eighth Earl of Berkeley). But they were amateurs who were also interested in politics, society, science and faith. They were England's boldest politicians and writers during the nineteenth and twentieth centuries. England owes its existence to their conscience which reacted vigorously, spontaneously and voluntarily to conditions. The result was to present Europe with an extraordinary spectacle. England could affirm itself as a conservative country, because its political and spiritual superstructure was constantly nourished through a thousand channels from below. The sectarians and nonconformists kept it in a state of change through their ceaseless questioning and self-examination. The insular position and the freedom from foreign invasion meant that neither a large standing army nor powerful bureaucracy was necessary. The fleet needed a very limited contingent of troops and was the symbol of freedom. These factors powerfully fostered the climate of balance which is so characteristic of England's mind, religion and thought. Perhaps the most important factor in this stability was the English attitude toward the spirit. Spirit was an adventure, not a poisonous gas to be bottled up. Spirit could be realized by activity and its workings could be seen openly in the society of men. Novels, satires, humour, sermons, debate in the Commons, handbills, pamphlets, scientific experiment and electoral reform were all part of this spontaneous adventure of the Spirit which roared across deserts, seas and foreign lands in order to find and renew itself. English understatement is to an extent a reflection of this active conception of the Spirit, for it urges men to *be* more and talk less, to enact their ideas in deeds rather than clothe them in words.

18

FRANCE (1650-1794)

The Potentialities of Europe

DURING the seventeenth and eighteenth centuries, France was the intellectual and spiritual leader of Europe. Despite the open and frequent outbreaks of civil war, despite the struggle with the Huguenots and despite the corruption and mismanagement of public affairs, which ate away at the substance of the country, it maintained and consolidated its position of dominance over the European mind. At the same time, a massive transformation of Christianity into secular forms took place. From the late 1580's on, a new kind of religious humanism had grown up, the creation of Catholic gentlemen and noble ladies, pastors and refined mystics. In a struggle to assert themselves against Calvinism, Jansenism and Jesuit asceticism, these people had cultivated their own God-filled personalities, or, as the Abbé Vincent said of Francis de Sales, their own egos. By the beginning of the seventeenth century, their humanism had absorbed considerable amounts of mysticism of the *devotio moderna* variety, and their ideas began to show traces of a worldly, immanent religion of the spirit. *J'aime les âmes indépendantes* ... Francis de Sales cried.[1] He wanted to spread the 'sweet scent of Jesus' in the souls of men, and to cultivate *amour pur*, a fateful idea for the following century. Through men like Jean-Pierre Camus and Etienne Binet, these ideas were widely circulated by the middle of the seventeenth century.

The optimism of the Catholic early Enlightenment fused with the optimism of modern mysticism. Cheerfully, men spoke of *felix culpa* and dreamed of the sweetness of grace. They believed that a great many would be saved, not a few, and they praised this world and the natural virtues. Almost unnoticed, the world and Heaven merged, and men began to talk of enjoying the goods of this life in the certain hope of a still better world to come. The Capuchins, Laurent de Paris and Yves de Paris (d. 1679) guided the broad stream of this God and world-blessed mysticism into ever more humane regions. In his *Palais de l'Aurore divine* (1602), Laurent sang hymns to the greatness and goodness of man which anticipated Rousseau and Voltaire. Laurent's *l'homme contemplé honorable en sa nature*, was an early form of the Gospel of the natural, good, reasonable, social, virtuous man, the pearl of creation. He praised man as *le modèle de concorde, de tous les animaux le plus accostable, le plus sociable ... Le compas et mesure de toutes chose ... Amas et assemblage de toutes perfections ...*

Yves de Paris, the greatest Capuchin of his generation, was a Parisian of the nobility of the robe, and before he joined the Order he had practised the law. He knew the world and its ways.[2] His natural theology was filled with rapture at the beauty and fullness of the world.[3] Mere contemplation of it was pure joy. He admired nature, art and science, especially physics. 'Physics is the highest among the natural sciences because it is the most curious. It possesses such beauties that he who does not love it is without a mind (*esprit*)', he proclaimed.[4] According to Yves it befits a 'nobleman' 'to visit, to investigate, and to take possession of the entire world as the domain of man'. Rapt (in a half mystical, half worldly ecstasy) Yves experienced the magic of the beautiful and good world. This world is the best of all worlds. *Il n'y a point de mal en toute l'étendue de la nature.*[5] All human talents have rich possibilities of development in this wholly good nature. Yves saw man as the child of light, and polemicized against any undervaluation and suspicion of him. He would not hear of the misery and inadequacy of man, for every human being was an eternity in himself.

Enthused as he was by the genius of his century, Yves did not overlook its social misery: the defective education of children, the decline of the French nobility, the predatory and blood-sucking exploitation of the simple people. Manual workers, peasants and petty bourgeoisie, he knew, through no fault of their own, were often in dire circumstances without any financial help, having toiled all their lives. Yves proposed public relief funds for the people. This was highly characteristic of a spiritual optimism and humanism which, earlier than Shaftesbury (1671-1713) and more deeply, had developed a philosophy of sympathy. According to it, God was a *Dieu des rencontres*, who brings together man and nature, freedom and grace, world and supernature. Spiritual humanism, as in the French Enlightenment, had become political. When Yves spoke of beauty and love, and perceived God in hearts and in reason, *sans maître et sans autre théologie*, when he raised his eyes to Heaven, to nature and to all things of art and science (he was one of the first admirers of the Gothic) he never forgot his concern over the *polis*. Just a slight turn of his enthusiasm to the right and one more turn to the left and Rousseau and Voltaire, respectively, stand before us.

In 1679, the year of Yves's death, Richard Simon's epoch-making book, *Histoire critique du Vieux Testament*, appeared.[6] This was the first great work of biblical criticism and it expressed the free and open humanism of the Oratorians. It was an entirely different sort of humanism from the mystical inspired traditions of Francis de Sales and Yves de Paris. The Oratorians were secular priests, who formed a new, non-monastic community of educated men. Bèrulle, the founder, had been an opponent of the Jesuits; his aim had been to restore the dignity of the secular priest in the Church.[7] His spirit was critical and his activity in the world strongly tinged with the political wisdom of the early Enlightenment. Condren, the second General of the Order, had been a great scholar and an acerbic critic of the Church. By the time Simon, the son of a blacksmith, entered the Order in 1662, a new popular spirit had arisen, reflecting the class origins of the younger men. Simon was a great advocate of Enlightenment. He preached tolerance for the Jews, whom he defended in 1670 against charges of ritual murder and cited St Jerome to justify investigation of the Old Testament. He believed that scientific criticism must take on the role which formerly fell to (poetic!) theology. Criticism was to be the new theology. From the time of the Young Hegelians to the present, Protestant theology has clung to this leading idea of Simon. After the appearance of his *Critical History of the Old Testament* Simon was expelled from the Oratory, but he considered himself a Catholic priest up to the hour of his death.

1661 was a crucial year in the development of France. Louis xiv began his reign as absolute monarch. The following years until his death in 1715 were ones of unusual intellectual activity and change. The heritage of Richelieu and Père Joseph had to be overcome and the inner conflicts resolved, if the absolute claims of the sun-king were to be realized. The anxiety of the baroque age can be seen in one of its strangest representatives, Jean Desmarets de Saint-Sorlin.[8] In his early years, Desmarets was sunk in a completely absorbing mysticism and from 1645 to 1660 devoted himself entirely to the contemplation of God. Suddenly in 1661 he was seized by a fanatical crusading zeal and rushed to join one of the Catholic secret societies of the time which were busily ferreting out secret heretics and handing them over to the police. Desmarets soon regarded himself as the political agent of the Holy Ghost, and in time rose to become the leader of the secret police. In his *Avis de Saint-Esprit au Roi*, he demanded that Louis xiv establish a powerful army of 144,000 soldiers to exterminate all the Godless and heretics. If this were not done, Christendom would be lost. After the annihilation of the heretics, the king should unite with Spain and the Pope and wage war against the Turks. Desmarets urged the King to use spiritual weapons as well in the campaign against unbelief. 'Pray without intermission and endure all things so that it may please God to convert the false Christians' he wrote. Penitential exercises, suffering and self-sacrifice were the ways to appease God's wrath and renew the world.

The great anxiety of the baroque (Louis xiv's court ceremony and the Versailles paradise were also expressions of it) surged up in Desmarets. A Faith, which suffered from uncertainty, tried to escape its internal tension by a desperate attack on its external enemies. Anxiety produced radicalism. Louis xiv's later attack on the Huguenots was an equally anxiety ridden response to an opposition which refused to capitulate. Desmarets's favourite trick was to send his opponents to their deaths, only after he had won their confidence through 'playing along' and talking about his own mystical experiences. This was to happen often in the following centuries. Judges of bourgeois and other societies condemned their own better or worse selves when they condemned the accused. The great dialectical game of the new Inquisition began: the Inquisitors discharged their own guilty consciences, subconscious distress and disloyalties, on the condemned who were brought before them. Desmarets descended into the underground of France, which he knew well from his own experience, and ferreted out priests who practised magic, witches, heretics, Jansenists, and quite often good Catholics. He was the embodiment of the persecution-mania of intellectuals in totalitarian states!

In his *Délices de l'Esprit*, Desmarets has given us a perfect statement of this baroque view of the world. Man's inner life was, Desmarets wrote, a palace and the great house of the Duc de Richelieu would seem to have been his model.* In it, the hero, Philédon was received in the apartment of faith, visited the loge of humility and the prison of nothingness (*cachet du Néant*). Here too Desmarets perfectly expressed the spirit of the age. The high baroque believed that it could catch, imprison, grasp nothingness in its mansions of authority, as it did wicked heretics and nonconformists. Next Philédon saw the balcony of hope, the thirty-three caverns of obedience, the grotto of patience, the halls of prayer, of mediation and of union with God. The similarity to Versailles where the celestial King celebrated the sacrament of the union of Heaven and earth in place of Christ is of course apparent. There was even a marine museum in Desmaret's heavenly palace in which various vehicles for missionary journeys were displayed. The staff of the palace consisted of Mary, the patriarchs, prophets and the Christian virtues who received and guided visitors. It is worth noting that, at this point, saints and allegories were part of the same reality. In a few years both were dismissed, together with theology, as mere fictions. An exceedingly ingenious system of mechanical staircases, on which Philédon descended when he wanted to rise led the way to the different floors. The great architect, master mechanic, magician, and mystic ruler of the palace was Christ himself. From the 'great salon of God's love', the walls glittering with marble, gold and precious stones, Philédon passed through several arcades into the 'chamber of love of the extension of the faith' (*chambre de l'amour de l'extension de la Foi*). The pathos, the fiction, the exaggerations and delusions of the baroque could find no more eloquent symbol than this fantastic palace. Desmarets published the book in 1654, and went on to realize these 'delights' as the leader of the secret police of state and Church.

'Love of the extension of the faith' was the one common element among the Jansenists, Jesuits, Pascal, Bossuet and Fénelon and Louis xiv. The difficulty lay in finding the way to carry it out. Although they tried different directions and techniques they all ended up by making a contribution to a movement which in essence they opposed and despised, the worldly religion of the Enlightenment. The Jesuits believed in order, freedom and science, but their intellectual curiosity and their optimistic trust in the progress of the kingdom of God ended by creating the secular faith of the Enlightenment in nature, mankind and progress. The Jansenists opposed the authoritarian Church, Thomist

*Another of the characteristic baroque structures, like Campanella's Temple of the Sun and the Roman baroque churches.

metaphysics and the 'natural interplay' of grace and freedom. Their polemical attacks and their rejection of mysticism robbed French Catholicism of the most solid of its old foundations, and delivered up knowledge and matter to atheist investigators of nature and to the critical philosophers of history. Faith was left to the rigorists and dreamers. Pascal's deep egocentricity, though it could fascinate minds for a moment, in the long run left nothing but brilliant aphorisms and daring comparisons. It evoked a great and authentic anxiety, because ordinary mortals could hardly be expected to gamble on Heaven and Hell or being and non-being in formulas of high literary distinction. Bossuet's defence of the ecclesiastical régime of Louis XIV and his *Freedoms of the Gallican Church* (1682) helped to create the national totalitarianism of the time of the Revolution. Louis XIV helped to bring about the downfall of the monarchy by persecuting Jansenists and Huguenots whose unconquerable inner resistance was to cost old France its life. At the same time he alienated his potential allies, the nobility, by stripping them of their power. His iron determination to finish Richelieu's programme of centralization was a disaster. Either they came to Versailles to a life of meaningless frivolity or they languished in provincial exile. In either case they hated him and got their revenge by joining the Parisian bourgeoisie to laugh at Versailles and to scoff at the sacerdotal kingship.

The Monarchy was extremely fragile despite its brilliance. Lieselotte of the Palatinate reported in her letters on the hunger of the people in Paris and on the intrigues of the 'old shrew', Madame de Maintenon. Its inner weakness can be seen more deeply in Louis's applause for Molière. In the *Ecole des Femmes*, in *Tartuffe* and *Don Juan*, Molière ridiculed the *vie dévote* of Francis de Sales, the entire programme of the Catholic Counter-Reformation and especially the re-establishment of the Christian family and marriage.[9] Yet Louis XIV laughed and applauded. This laughter was far more significant than the much cited applause of the court society for Beaumarchais's *Marriage of Figaro* on the eve of the Revolution. It shows how insubstantial were the last religious and social foundations of the age of the baroque. Molière believed himself to be a Christian, but *de facto* he was an enlightened Deist, a man for whom the holiness and the sacraments of the old world no longer had a (good) meaning.

The case of the Jesuits was simple. Since the days of Coton, an adviser of Henry IV, the French Jesuits had been closely linked with the monarchy. Their suppression in 1773 was the most decisive prelude of the revolution, but it was not their loyalty to the monarchy which caused them to fail. It was their loyalty to the world. The battle-organ of Jansenism, the *Nouvelles Ecclésiastiques*, put it this way: the Jesuits had dethroned God and set man on his throne. 'Molinism and Deism are twin brothers.'[10] The actual tragedy of the French Jesuits was that in order to win the world they became part of it. They spoke all its languages fluently, but remained lacking in their own spiritual substance. Although their asceticism sharpened and trained their understanding and will, their repudiation of mysticism and emotional clerical culture robbed them of the living sources of religious energy. The tragedy of the French Jesuits was much greater than the narrow, gloomy Pascal and his Jansenist brethren wanted to admit. The Jesuits went under in both the great intellectual battles of the West in the eighteenth century: in the attempt to Christianize China and the East,[11] and in the attempt to restore the Christian spirit to the Enlightenment.

The Jesuits developed the fundamental principles for a 'right mission'. The ideas were entirely Erasmian in spirit: empathy with the culture and literature of a pagan people, an exact study of their language, a return to the sacred sources of early times. A broad and deep humanity is perceptible here. Couplet, the procurator of the Jesuits for the China Mission, concluded his foreword to a biography of Confucius with the wish that all Europe might consider the christianization of China as its major concern.[12] The biography treated Confucius as a great philosopher and holy man whose piety was comparable only to the great Christian saints. Despite an auspicious start, the China Mission failed. The envy of its competitors led to its prohibition by the *Curia* and in this prohibition, as in the abolition of the Jesuit State in Paraguay (1609–1767) the intrinsic weakness of the Roman baroque was exposed. Vainly it sought to hide its incapacity for truly great enterprises under a giant display of ceremonies, festivals, official acts and prohibitions. The consequences of this failure have become only too obvious in our own day. Because the Church has been too weak to engage in open dialogue with the East, Christianity has lost Asia and may well lose South America. The Roman baroque churchmen could put up a grandiose front but behind it they were frightened and unable to face the demands of new areas and new challenges.

While the failure of the China Mission marked the end of the chance for the Jesuits overseas, the opposition of the Jansenists at home raised the question of the Jesuits' relation to the spirit of the age. The old intellectuality and spirit were destroyed in the struggle. The Jansenists declared themselves to be 'the party of God', and asserted that they were fighting only for the 'interests of God'. Man was only a rebel. The Jesuits intended, they charged, to replace the God of our Fathers by a weak humanized God of their own. The God of the Jesuits was nothing but a shrewd politician who made shameful concessions to the weaknesses of man. The Jesuits declared the God of the Jansenists to be a barbaric tyrant, who deserved our hatred. The Jansenist God was an absolute monarch, the Jesuit God ruled in a constitutional monarchy. The 'Hexaples', the battle-organ of the Jansenists, condemned the Jesuits for having erected a duarchy in which God and man shared world rule between them, and they were very near to the mark. In a sense the Jesuits represented the new eighteenth-century consciousness of freedom and independence. The new men would not stand disenfranchised before an earthly or a Heavenly sovereign. Against this concept the 'Hexaples' preached, 'God owes man nothing. This is the great principle and the solution of all.'[13]

Both these great enemies were doomed. The tragedy of Jansenism was no less dramatic than that of the Jesuits. As we have already seen in Chapter 16, the battle on two fronts proved too much for Jansenism. As the Jesuits failed through their willingness to compromise, the Jansenists failed through their unwillingness. The nobility and lofty spirit of the Huguenot movement ended by converting the faith in the spirit into a belief in the machinery of power. They sought to make the human will obedient to God, but it obeyed the total state instead. They tried to re-enact the Reformation within the confines of Catholicism, but the methods of the age were too frail.

One can literally see this process at work in the life and writings of Pierre Nicole (d. 1695), the great rationalist and moralist. In Nicole, the concept of pure, lofty, civic morality swallowed up religion. He led the great Jansenist offensive against mysticism and miracles which he began by an attack on the remnants of mystic enthusiasm in Port-Royal itself.* He argued that mystical experiences are but presumptions about the extraordinary, and this 'extra-ordinary way' of dealing with men had been abandoned by God after the death of St Bernard. In any case the morally well-brought-up man did not need them. Nicole carried on the Pascalian experiment and investigated the soul as if it were a cathode ray tube. To what extent are the natural or super-natural rays which enlighten the soul visible? If, he reasoned, all natural lights were yellow, and all supernatural ones green, one could easily distinguish between them, but this is, alas, not the case. Man cannot distinguish between natural and supernatural light. Together with Arnauld, Nicole developed a simple, rough psychology which became a model for two hundred years. Timidly they began to expose all extraordinary and supernatural events as self-deceptions and illusions, the products of the egoism and concupiscence of undisciplined souls. The same applied to most prayers, the value of which they were also inclined to doubt. Mystical, supernatural and spiritual events were gradually eliminated until there was nothing left but the mentality of a purified, introspective, sober and anxious bourgeois man. In order to train this man, Nicole introduced the Jesuit Exercises to Port-Royal. From 1679 to 1789 the Jansenists and their bitterest foes, the Jesuits, trained their wills and minds according to the same method.

Jansenism had presumed to defend the rights of the 'wholly other' God against concupiscent humanity. By the end of the seventeenth century it had prepared a type of man who trusted only his reason, and who assumed an extremely suspicious attitude toward everything ecclesiastical, sacramental, mystical and supernatural. When the papal Bull, *Unigenitus*, condemned Jansenism in 1713, they were still sufficiently strong, despite the persecutions of Louis xiv, to form a powerful political party. A dozen bishops belonged to it, and from 1716 to 1728 the Archbishop of Paris, Noailles, was a member.

*In this respect also the anti-Christian enlighteners were the heirs of Jansenism. Catholic France was so completely saturated with Jansenist rationalism that mysticism was felt to be faintly indecent even as late as the end of the nineteenth century.

The Sorbonne, the university of Rheims and the Parliaments took the Jansenists' side. This party united the national, rationalistic and educated Catholic bourgeoisie of France against Rome and sometimes also against the monarchy. Their weekly *Nouvelles Ecclésiastiques* was the central organ of the Catholic Enlightenment and of its struggle against superstitions, papal and clerical tyranny.

Bossuet, the Court preacher of Louis XIV was the great theorist of the divine right of kings. It has been common to see him merely as the last gasp of the old order, especially when he is compared to Fénelon, the innovator and mighty spokesman of pure love. But Bossuet was more than that. He was a great conservative, who stood in the midst of the play of new forces. He was a pupil of Bèrulle and Condren and was, as a result, strongly influenced by Jansenism. His transformation of preaching into political propaganda and rhetoric clearly showed how insecure the foundations of the 'great old order' had become. Bossuet saw in Protestantism only an unbridled subjectivism, which was bound to end either in atheistic Enlightenment or in Enthusiasm.[14] Nevertheless, his own thought was an openly subjective pan-hedonism: God creates our happiness, the enjoyment of God satisfies and gladdens man, and the senses find their true gratification in him. His lust for enjoyment and lust for power were elevated into metaphysical categories.*

Bossuet was a bishop and the creator of the national French Church. In this respect he was very like Adalbert of Bremen and the other great imperial bishops of the Salic Empire. His attitude toward the French monarchy was wholly in the spirit of the *Sacrum Imperium*. He proclaimed to the French Protestants that their reform was not Christian, because it was not *fidèle* to the kings and to the fatherland. In Bossuet's sense, as in Adalbert's, a Protestant (a heretic) could not be loyal by definition because he was a rebel against the heavenly majesty, and thus equally a sinner against the earthly majesty.[15] Bossuet loved to talk of God, who like a shrewd king patiently waits for the right time to destroy the sinner-rebels with the full weight of his wrath.[16] He was fascinated by the concept of the Last Judgment. In the presence of Louis XIV he described this *assemblée générale du genre humain* and their *grandes assises* in the very words used a hundred years later by the great revolutionaries. His images of divine judgment were literally enacted in the Court scenes and speeches of the Convention.[17] In his vision the 'divine revenge', God's *esprit de terreur* hovered over the damned and annihilated sin, disorder and rebellion (*péché, désordre, rébellion*).[18] God, Christ, 'our Monarch', has established all the legitimate authority of princes, rulers and powers and has made it our duty to obey them. Christ has built a throne for the rulers in the conscience (of the subjects) and placed their authority under his protection.[19]

Twenty-three years before the revocation of the Edict of Nantes, Bossuet

---

*Bossuet used to read Exodus, verses 19 and 20, on his knees before preaching, so that his mind would be filled with the 'majestic terrors' of the divine majesty and his sermon reflect the glory of divine and human kingship.

set Louis XIV the task of wiping out heresy in France.[20] The Church, the only legitimate authority on earth had made the kings into rulers over the consciences of men, and thus made an article of faith of the sanctified person of the king. It had raised the obedience owed them to a religious duty. The Church wipes out the first thoughts of rebellion, and discovers the hidden movements of sedition in the very depths of the heart. It controls complaints and grumbling. In return for these services, Bossuet expected the Christian King to help Christ 'to rule over the peoples who are subject to them, to extirpate the free spirits and the defamers of the Church, to promote virtue, and to pave the way to heaven'.[21]

The alliance between the Church and the throne was established. Both paid dearly for it in the next century, but temporarily they were secure. Louis XIV revoked the Edict of Nates and persecuted the Huguenots, and in return Bossuet, the imperial Bishop, celebrated the King as the 'new Constantine', the 'new Theodosius' and the 'new Charlemagne'. Bossuet put the final touches on his vision of this high baroque world, closed in horror, mystery and timelessness ('time is nothingness') when he preached, 'The Christian has nothing to investigate because he finds everything in faith. The Christian has nothing to prove because the faith decides everything for him.'[22]

The palaces of the great King and the ideas of baroque theologians were façades behind which the abyss yawned. It was characteristic of Bossuet that although he celebrated the new empire in fulsome terms and called it timeless, he was perfectly clear about the new social developments and their 'frightening diversity'. 'All the activities which I see, seem to me to be servile or vain, insane or criminal. Everywhere I see movements and actions exciting the soul. Nowhere do I see a rule or order to master it.'[23] There was no law, no order, no repose, and no moderation. He also knew perfectly well that the divine King lived in an atmosphere of lust for pleasure, dissipation and selfishness. He saw the oppression of the poor, the helpless and the innocent; everyone sinned against the spirit of fraternity. Sickness, a high mortality rate and hunger raged among the people, especially in Paris. 'So many people die of hunger before our eyes ... What I say is the truth: the permanent, public truth established through investigations.'[24] Bossuet, perhaps unconsciously, admitted defeat with these words, because he conceded that the new publicly observed, statistically established truth had at last dislodged the 'platonic, philosophically viewed' truth. The entire concept of the sacred kingship was destroyed. If truth were a matter of investigation and not of Platonic ideas, the monarchy was no longer the earthly expression of the divine order of things. Bossuet was a perfect man of the baroque, preserving what he knew was false because he was afraid of what might replace it.

On 18 March 1699 Fénelon was condemned as a quietist by Rome. His *Telemachus* appeared one month later. Fénelon's public subjection under the sentence of Rome and his banishment from the court of Louis XIV won him the admiration of that far-reaching other Europe which consisted of Quietists,

Enthusiasts, the 'Silent in the land', and nonconformists of all kinds. He knew that Louis xiv's court and ceremonial were false and that they covered up the tremendous fear of old Europe in the face of the new realities. On 6 December 1693, Fénelon wrote an anonymous letter to Louis xiv: 'For thirty years your ministers have destroyed all the old principles of the state in order to raise your authority to a pinnacle. They have raised you up as far as heaven upon the ruins of all your subjects. In reality it is your ministers who rule, hard, arrogant, intolerant and cruel beings, who in domestic and foreign policy know but one means – to threaten, annihilate and destroy everything that opposes them ...'[25]

The Adventures of Young Telemachus for a hundred years was the French manual and reader used by all Europe. In it Fénelon transmitted his aversion to and horror of Louis xiv to the world of the Enlightenment. In the tenth book he expressed his complete contempt for this monster, this beast who sucked the blood of his people, and who had no more power than a hollow idol. The book was illustrated with engravings which pictured the fate that awaited the tormented wicked King in Hell. The influence of this book and Fénelon's other writings on the subsequent course of French history was very great. Through Fénelon, the latent spiritual energies of the quietists and the *devotio moderna* flowed into the Enlightenment and thence into the revolution itself. The 'free spirit' which Fénelon preached suggested to Rome all the dangers of all the spiritual movements of the past. It implied the removal of the power of salvation from the old Church and the old monarchy and its transference to the conscience of the individual. The pious soul could not be subdued by the administration of sacred kings and imperial bishops. It was free.

The court was not blind to the danger. Madame de Maintenon, Louis xiv's mistress, realized that Fénelon, whom she had admired at first, was really an extremely dangerous enemy. What good was it if Louis xiv and his elect circle built holy kingdoms and realms of salvation in Versailles and their castles of pleasure, if this quiet Bishop with his soft voice and gentle manner built kingdoms of pure love in men's hearts? How long would awakened souls refrain from laying hands on the curtains and columns of the kingdom of this world? Nor was the threat far away from the court itself. Louis xiv and Madame de Maintenon had foolishly permitted Fénelon to draw up the Rule for the Daughters of St Louis, the charitable institution for women which they founded at St Cyr. They had unwittingly made him the spiritual director of all those who were forced to lead a double life in the world and within themselves. Fénelon told them how they could enter into relations with their God and lead a devout life without recourse to nosy priests. He undermined not only the many organizations of the hierarchy and the monarchy itself, but also the justification of all monasticism. *Monachatus non est pietas*: monkery was not an authentic piety suited to the time. What Erasmus and Luther had begun, Fénelon completed by preaching that a Christian life in the world and in time was much more difficult and of greater service than life in the monasteries of the France of the day which abounded in wealth, vanity, lust for fame, false security and worldliness.[26] Christianity had become a fiction, a total fraud: *on ne veut rien posséder, mais on veut tout avoir*. The Monastic clergy was very far from poverty, chastity and obedience. How many hundreds of families could live decently on what a monastery or a community of priests who have sworn poverty actually consumed? The importance of Fénelon was that he was the crucial mediator of such ideas to a wider public. Out of the spiritual attitude, there grew a social and political criticism which linked the German pietists and Quakers with the movement for social reform. His influence spread quickly because the united underground of nonconformism was there to broadcast it.

The rapidity of the circulation of such ideas had been increased by the decision to crush the Huguenots. The revocation of the Edict of Nantes essentially completed the transition from the age of the Counter-Reform to the age of revolution.[27] A Huguenot pastor of Nimes formulated for the King the sacral formula of the seamless totalitarianism of the world of salvation of Louis XIV: *Un Roi, une loi, une foi dans le royaume*. One king, one law, one faith in the kingdom. The stage was set for the decisive struggle. St Simon, the Catholic, in his *Cour de Louis XIV* (ch. 47), drew the balance sheet of the year 1685: the French nation ruined, its industries moved abroad. He characterized the Edict of Fontainebleau as a 'conspiracy which in order to make the horror complete filled all the provinces of the kingdom with perjuries and profanation of holy places so that the air was thick with the wails of pain and distress of the unhappy victims of error. Others for the sake of their possessions or repose surrendered, and purchased these things through hypocritical recantations. They were dragged in endless processions to churches, in which they did not believe, and received the divine Body of the most saintly of the Saints, although they were convinced that they were eating but bread. This must have been disgusting to them.'

This profanation of the last and highest Sacrament, together with the deconsecration of the name of king and priest, was to be a decisive factor in the storming of churches during the Revolution. The community-chests for making conversions which were administered by the writer Pellisson, an ex-Huguenot, worked side by side with the regiments of conversion-makers. Their administration lay in the hands of the local bishop. The bishop of Grenoble reported, for example, that he had bought eight hundred persons for Catholicism with 2,000 thalers. Attendance at an Evangelical religious service was punished by death. Persons apprehended at such services were shot or hanged, and the rest sent to serve in the galleys. The Huguenot Church fled to the South, to the old country of the Cathars and the Waldensians, to the *maquis*. It became an *Eglise du désert*. The underground burst out again. There were prophetic individuals, who proclaimed judgment on France and her Godless King, and ecstatic masses, who, like those in Orthez in the Béarn, heard heavenly voices (and had them recorded). The political and religious leaders of this inspired people of God seized the opportunity and mobilized the prophetic elements for their own political ends.* The revolutionary generals of 1790 to 1793 were modelled on men like Cavalier and Court.

From 1702 to 1704 the Cévennes War raged, fought for the sake of evangelical freedom of conscience by the great-grandchildren of the Albigensians and Waldensians. Their families, land and property were threatened along with their Faith. Peasants, farm-workers, and small artisans were called *Esprit* (the Holy Ghost of the inspired people!) by the wool-carder Pierre Séguier and summoned to the struggle. The young Jean Cavalier, a peasant boy, led the war against the experienced army leaders of Louis XIV with all the genius of the young generals of the French Revolution. By 1704 the south was crushed militarily and began to turn into the red south of political Protestantism, of the revolution and the republic, characterized by its strong moralism, its prophetism, its inspired democracy and its unconquerable will to resist.[28]

On 21 August 1715, eleven days before the death of the King, the ninety-year-old Antoine Court opened the first Synod of preachers of the resurrected Evangelical Church of France in a stone quarry at Languedoc. This 'Church under the Cross' chose the old cross of a knightly order together with the dove of the Holy Ghost as its sign of salvation. The new Templars and knights of the Holy Grail entered upon the stage of world history. The royal edicts and instructions against the Protestant revolt, which were supposed to hold the people to the cult of the 'old and royal Catholic religion' had been in vain. The hanging, jailing and sentencing of the Evangelicals to forced labour in the galleys did not cease until the sixties of the eighteenth century. As late as 1740 and 1750 many trials were held of 'new converts' (Evangelical pseudo-Catholics). The following occupations of the arrested were specified: lawyer, silk dealer, merchant, preacher. No trade, however, produced so many martyrs as the wool-carders, who, ever since the eleventh century had been the religious and political nonconformist trade *par excellence*. Paul Rabaut, the leader of the 'Church of the Desert', was the son of a poor wool-carder. His *assemblées* were community gatherings of the elect and the blessed. A total of 30,000 persons took part on one occasion in these religious services of the inspired democrats, God's chosen people in the desert. These mass meetings set the example for the grandiose feasts of the Revolution. A royal decree of toleration appeared in 1787; too late. The Protestantism of the South rushed to the Revolution with an ardent heart, hailing it as the redemption of the persecuted people of God. Rabaut de Saint-Etienne, the son and colleague of

*The way in which the Huguenot Church turned into a political resistance movement is enormously instructive to those who want to understand the spiritual development in Germany between 1830 and 1933. The rise of radical pietism and the outbreak of religious enthusiasm in the nineteenth century in Southern and Eastern Germany heralded the rise of Hitler. The inner development of Russia between 1800 and 1917 has very similar features. It would appear that when oppression robs a popular Church of its pastors, the deepest resentments are aroused and preaching of the Word becomes a kind of emergency office.

Paul Rabaut, became president of the National Assembly on 15 March 1790.[29] To the emancipated, political and liberal Protestantism of the south, the Gospel became the foundation of the Rights of Man, of the Republic, and of inspired democracy. The Protestantism of the north, which had earlier become soft and conformist, made its way in Coppet, via Rousseau, Mme de Staël and the German romantic influence toward a humanist Deism.

When he took up the Calas case, Voltaire ceased to be merely a successful man of letters and became the conscience of the nation, the 'defender of the oppressed' and the 'avenger of innocence'. The parliament of Toulouse, the old centre of nonconformism, frequently sentenced Protestants to death because of their Faith. Nobles were beheaded, the bourgeoisie sent to the galleys. Calas had been broken on the wheel under the false accusation of having murdered his son because he wanted to convert to Catholicism. Voltaire conducted a new trial in Paris which rehabilitated the dead man, and in his *Treatise on Tolerance* (1763) he portrayed the activities of fanatical, Catholic militant groups in Toulouse. He took up the defence of French Protestants saying that political, social and intellectual progress made possible a tolerance which could not have been worked out in past times. He appealed to Christ and his gospel of non-violence, cited the Church Fathers in detail against violence and the persecution of those of different belief, and men of the Church from Bernard to Fénelon. In his famous 'Prayer to God' (Prière à Dieu), he prayed to God that he might reconcile the brothers who killed each other and quarrelled in his name. 'Help us so that we help each other mutually to bear the burden of this woeful and fleeting life. May we not bear the small differences of dress or ridiculous custom as signs of hatred and of persecution. May all men recall that they are brothers. May we deplore tyranny over souls as much as they do highway robbery. May we praise God and love each other in a thousand different languages from Siam to California.'

Voltaire was a participant in four to five cases of injustice. Whole families of persecuted Protestants fled to him (as in the Sirven case). These cases (Martin, Montbailli, Lally-Tollendal) revealed the arbitrary nature of the justice of the old world. Voltaire interested Frederick the Great, Catherine II, and the Kings of Poland and Denmark in the plight of the persecuted. In 1760 he adopted a girl belonging to the impoverished family of Corneille. In order to support her, he published an edition of Corneille's work with his own commentary and introduction. His interest in Corneille was part of a great work of restoration, the publication of the complete works of all the great authors of the age of Louis XIV, through which Voltaire intended to save the French language from corruption.

Voltaire was not, as is so often said, destructive. What he laid his hand upon had been destroyed or questioned long before him. On the contrary, he wanted to restore the humanistic world and its fundamental concepts of God, man, nature. Voltaire knew that the society of enlightened and cultured persons was threatened on all sides, and he hoped to save it and the ideas of enlightened

Catholicism which he had been taught. From the Jesuits he received his deep trust in the goodness of nature and man. Despite his Catholic education he was never a very devout man. Although he clung diffidently to the Church's Sacraments he really believed only in the sacrament of speech. He also lost his faith in an early victory of the Enlightenment and in the humanization of the masses. He doubted the success of the Encyclopedia. In the end, provoked by much opposition, as a seventy-year-old Deist he began his struggle against Christianity. He could see it only as the resistance of decadent ruling powers to man's progress towards freedom, fraternity and humanity. His faith in the Enlightenment collapsed at the same time as his Christianity, or, more correctly, both took on new forms: the old man of Ferney looked towards Germany and Russia. In 1771 he wrote to Catherine ii: 'Today the light comes to us from the North', and he blessed Benjamin Franklin's grandson, who visited him, by laying his hands on the boy's head and saying: 'God and liberty.'

Voltaire was the son of a notary of Poitou and grew up in the lascivious society of the Regency after the death of Louis xiv. He hated his father so much that he would not bear the family name of Arouet and chose a new name of his own, 'Voltaire'. His other experiences of the fathers of the old world were not very conducive to the growth of love. One of the lords of Rohan – Chabot – had him whipped by six lackeys in front of the Hotel de Sully and then thrown into the Bastille, from which he was forcibly shipped to England (1726). Helpless in his disgrace – the Rohans were almighty in France – his resentment grew. In England he was taken into the company of Bolingbroke through whom he met Pope, Swift and Gay. During his English period, he wrote his *Henriade*, the epic of holy King Henry iv, the victor over the religious wars, which was a lofty hymn to old France. His *Brutus* (1729) and his sentimental *Zaïre* (1732) breathed the pathos and rhetoric of the baroque. His English experience first came to mature expression in the *Philosophical Letters on the English Nation* (1734) which, like so many of his writings, was forbidden in France, publicly burned and yet read by all. In this work, Voltaire attacked the *Ancien Régime* and its indivisible unity of feudal clergy, high nobility and absolutism. England as a land of democracy (Letter 8), of political and economic freedom (Letter 10), as the land of Lord Bacon (Letter 12), of Locke (Letter 13), of Newton (whom he compared with the metaphysical dreamer Descartes, Letter 14), was held up as a mirror before a wasted, backward France. Voltaire scoffed at Christian Europe's horror of the English vaccination and called France 'fetishistic'. He struck blow after blow at the whole archaic world and the residue of magic which still survived in the eighteenth century. France was a country where it was customary to bury Huguenot bells, to flog them and then to consecrate them as Catholic.

Voltaire attacked Descartes's philosophy which he called a *roman ingénieux* and Pascal (Letter 25), whose inner kinship with Descartes he clearly perceived. He wanted to represent 'the party of philanthropy against this sublime misanthrope'. Voltaire set great store by his *Notes on Pascal*. He often turned back to them, especially towards the end of his life. Although he admired the genius of Pascal, he could not, as a pupil of the Jesuits and one committed to his own cause, accept Pascal's damnation and contempt for all human nature: 'He wrote against human nature in much the same way as he wrote against the Jesuits', observed Voltaire. Voltaire realized that Pascal was a solipsist incapable of a real defence of Christianity. His ideas, and especially the brilliant ones, were the products of an enormous arrogance which destroyed the Christian substance. 'Christianity teaches simplicity, humanity and love of one's neighbour. To reduce it to metaphysics means to make a source of errors of it.' Voltaire sharply rejected Pascal's wager: interest should have nothing to do with thinking about God. Pascal's doctrine of predestination made men atheists and his assertion that man is wholly miserable and unhappy and the world only a dungeon simply does not fit the facts. According to Voltaire, men live active, hopeful and free lives. He had a genuine awe of Pascal (self-critically he asked himself whether it were not better to write a good work than to prove Pascal wrong). Ultimately, Voltaire was right. Pascal was of no real value to the men of the eighteenth century. His colossal egotism could not help men to find the techniques for living a more dignified life, and it was this, after all, which the Enlightenment tried to do.

After the publication of the *Letters on the English Nation* and the *Notes on Pascal*, Voltaire had to flee France. He went to Lorraine* and stayed for a whole year on the estates of independent nobles, mostly in Cirey, with the Marquis du Châtelet. Voltaire soon became the unchallenged leader of the European Enlightenment. His concerns in many ways were those of Erasmus and of Thomas More: peace among the nations and a simple faith which would preserve the freedom and worth of each man. Voltaire wanted a gentler god-king, *un roi plus doux*, to take the place of the cruel judges and soldier-kings of the old world. He wanted to teach men a faith in reason, which would be reflected in the virtues of justice and compassion. The Enlightenment was the last great flowering of the Christian political humanism of western Europe.

Voltaire was aware of his own historical position. The millennium of the 'grand form' was coming to a close, and another world was rising, that of the Enthusiasts (Rousseau!) and the masses, the nationalists, the mechanists, and the technicians of power. He composed his major work, *The Age of Louis XIV* (1751) as a picture of France in 'the most enlightened age of world history'. Voltaire hoped to impart a lesson through his celebration of the dead King, Louis xv, and his ministers. But it was not his only purpose. He spoke of politics, internal administration, trade, police, legislation, society, art and science, and of religious movements, and in doing so became the father of European cultural history, a status unattained by anyone else until Jacob Burckhardt. He found high praise for the majestic power of the baroque

*The lands and kingdoms on both banks of the Rhine offered havens to European non-conformists from the time of the Reformation until the nineteenth century.

rhetoric of a Bossuet and Bourdaloue. He recognized the case of Fénelon, the dispute over rites in China, and the decline of the Jesuit mission, to which he dedicated the last (39th) chapter, as signs of the times.

Voltaire's own courtly humanism came to an end during the years after 1751. New problems forced him to face the coming age and overcome it. In 1745 he still dared to dedicate his *Mahomet* (of 1741) to Pope Benedict XIV (1740–58). The work was a tragedy, in which he presented Mohammed as the original model of the religious fanaticism of the older Christendom. The cultivated and enlightened Lambertini Pope exchanged a courtly humanist correspondence with Voltaire. Voltaire had written *Mahomet* against murders committed out of religious conviction, against the Châtels, Cléments, Ravaillacs of his time. He wanted to separate faith and superstition: 'in a hundred different ways will I repeat that one never does God any good when one does evil to man'. In his inaugural address to the Academy on the world prestige of the French language (9 May 1746) he publicly warned of the danger of decadence and corruption of the language, of taste, of morals. Such observations were entirely within the tradition of European humanism. Civilized men had been worrying about the decline of morals as manifested by the corruption of the language from the days of the late Roman Empire. By 1753, he had begun to worry about quite different things. In a letter from Potsdam to his niece he expressed his horror at Lamettrie, *L'homme machine*, who represented the destruction of all values and humanity. At the same time he recognized in Lamettrie the spiritualistic Enthusiast: 'There are a thousand features of crazy insanity in his work and not a half portion of reason.'

Voltaire realized how much was going to be lost in the new Europe that was being born and he tried to point out what these values were in the *Essai sur les Moeurs et l'Esprit des Nations* (a fusion of two older writings, 1756, Geneva). He saw world history as a history of the stupidities of man, an old Spiritual and Erasmian motif, but also of great deeds and accomplishments in culture, economy, mind and society. Old Europe, he pointed out, had at least been free of the modern absolute rulers. Even the emperors and popes could not be considered as such. France had, from the time of Louis XI, developed more and more into an absolute monarchy. In another work of the same period, *La Loi Naturelle*, Voltaire defended the role of reason by showing that God reveals himself through reason.

By the 1760's Voltaire had hardened. He became involved in squabbles and arguments, but, more important than anything else, he began to see the coming of the revolution.[30] For the first time he became an enemy of the baroque which he had defended for so long. Voltaire confronted the monstrousness of a cruel god-king who was the protector of the baroque pseudocosmos and of its organized chaos, who did not care whether 100,000 people perished in horrifying persecutions and sufferings, inflicted upon them by nature and by each other. In the years 1760 to 1768 he lived at Ferney, the decayed estate of an old Huguenot. There he set up a small republic and made himself the enlightened sovereign. He founded industries (among others a watch-makers' colony), built roads, tilled fields, bred silkworms, cared for many of the needy and in the evenings played chess with his house chaplain, a Jesuit. Voltaire had finally fulfilled the aspirations of the secular laity. After 1,000 years of preaching and moralizing by the kings and theologians of old Europe, the bourgeoisie had turned the tables. Voltaire preached morality to the kings.

Voltaire's ambiguity, a last heritage of the baroque, came out again in his final acts. Just before his death he made a declaration to his secretary: 'I die worshipping God, loving my friends, not hating my enemies, but abhorring superstition.' Then he made his confession, took communion and signed a declaration that he wished to live and die as a Catholic and begged the Church for forgiveness if he had caused her any offence. There can be no doubt about the sincerity of both declarations. Voltaire's atheism and Deism were expressive phases of the Catholic late Enlightenment of France which had reached its hour of crisis.

Rousseau's importance was, perhaps, greater than Voltaire's. Virtually all the various streams of mystical and sectarian stamp came to expression in his capacious ego. There is hardly a false tone of feeling, joy in nature, self-intoxication, intuition, gush or enthusiasm in the nineteenth century which cannot be found somewhere in Rousseau. His fame dominated his century. He was revered as a prophet and a saint. Even Kant saw him as the authentic voice of conscience. For much of educated Europe, he stood for a new hope of leading a life pleasing to God. He was a tremendous influence, for good and ill.

Rousseau was one of those sensitive children (*enfants humiliés* as Bernanos calls them) of recent times, who have been profoundly stamped by certain first impressions. His inner culture was shaped in Geneva, Turin, Venice and on the estate of Madame de Warens. In this way he was influenced by several of the famous old abodes of European nonconformism. He was born in Geneva, 'the fifth continent' as Talleyrand put it. In the eighteenth century it was the centre of a humanitarian and liberal neo-Calvinism. Rousseau's father, a watchmaker, kept the works of Grotius beside his tools. After reading the sentimental novels of his mother, the boy reached out for his father's books. In them he found the cultural world of the artisans which united the ideas of the Enlightenment and the Enthusiasts. Rousseau tried his hand as a court clerk apprentice, as an engraver and as a watchmaker. All his life he was convinced of the religious mission of manual workers. Had not twelve poor manual workers converted the world after Christ's death?[31] Geneva was a city of justice and freedom. It became his model of a community of God-fearing and enthusiastic spirits who, as *citoyens*, shared in its authority and formed the new people's community.[32]

During the time he spent in Turin, he came into contact with all the manifold movements which could be found in that refuge of heretics. The young wanderer turned up at the Holy Ghost Hospital, where two Catholic priests, themselves probably crypto-Protestants, converted him. In thanksgiving, he erected a monument to them in *The Profession of Faith of a Savoyard Country Pastor*. He got to know Venice as the secretary of the French Ambassador and he admired it enormously. He compared it with Geneva, its Senate with that of the Romans and was inspired by it to draw up his 'Social Contract'.

He received the decisive stamp on his character as the pupil and lover of Madame de Warens. Later, in the *Confessions*, he composed a devastating portrait of her, and her home-made religion. She could not conceive of an avenging God. In her everything had to be resolved in compassion, feeling and sentiment. Cruelly he scoffed at her libido, her sexual, erotic and religious promiscuity in which earthly and heavenly love flowed along together. Actually, he himself remained imprisoned by this attitude all his life, but it was just that which fascinated his age: the seamless joining of eros and ethos, egocentricity and theocentricity, man and nature. Rousseau was an omnivorous reader of the moderns from Plutarch up to Pascal, Fénelon, Voltaire. He swallowed everything that fell into his hands. In his prophetic proclamation of nature and the naturally good man he melted it all down. There was something of Francis de Sales's *humanisme dévot*, something of the notion of grace becoming nature in the school of Fénelon, a bit of secularized Protestantism and Jansenism, and not least, the apologetic ideology of the missionaries of the eighteenth century in Rousseau's social philosophy. The noble savage was, of course, a direct reflection of the Jesuit adventures in the East.

Rousseau's great importance lay in two aspects of his work: the proclamation of an immanent religion of the ego and the formulation of the 'people's democracy'. The new gospel of the ego was in essence a self-denunciation by an intellectual. The ego could only win salvation and security from the conviction that it would only be able to continue 'to enjoy that pure delight, which arises from self-satisfaction' in Heaven.[33] The only certainty was *la sincerité de mon coeur*. Where was salvation to be found? 1. Not with the priests – of this, all these lay theologians were quite certain. The priests had been the first to ruin the cause of God through their way of reasoning about providence.[34] In a letter to the Archbishop of Paris, Beaumont, who considered the Savoyard country pastor a chimera, Rousseau declared: 'There are today few priests who still believe in God, nevertheless this does not prove that there are none.' 2. Not in the sacraments and cults of the revealed religions. All revelation is already contained in the 'Book of Nature'.[35] Rousseau no longer believed in the supernatural: 'Supernatural? What does this word mean? I do not understand it!'[36] True religion and enlightenment were only possible in an active life on earth, in which the principles of philosophic tolerance would be united with the morality of the Gospels.

Since God had given Rousseau the assurance of 'conscience' and 'the heart', he could turn to the construction of a *religion civile* without hesitation. The effect was explosive. Rousseau secularized the mystical ego and built it into his system of civil life. His community was necessarily inspired because it was made up of awakened souls. In its structure it was a heterogeneous mixture of the discipline of the Anabaptists, the traditions of the conventicles and the communities of brethren of the *devotio moderna*, the practices of the Genevan citizen-state and the maxims of the Venetian ruling clique. This structure and its ideology became the model for the Jacobins in the Great Revolution and of all state structures of the Chiliasts and Enthusiasts of the nineteenth and twentieth centuries. The *religion civile* (the religion directed by the inspired democracy as a community of brethren and a divine community incarnate on earth) was to be the religion of all citizens and fellow-countrymen and, at the same time, the religion of the fatherland.

Rousseau preached that the mind of the citizen should constantly be concerned with the fatherland, from the cradle to the grave.[37] In order to understand Rousseau's development and the Great Revolution one must remember that before 1750 'nation' was an innocuous concept. By 1755, the Abbé Coyer could write that soldiers must learn to die for the commonweal, priests must learn that they belonged primarily to their country, mothers that they bore their children for the fatherland, parents should be happy to see their sons die for it. Society should establish the cult of the fatherland through crowns, statues, mausoleums, liturgical and patriotic celebrations.[38] Coyer found a gigantic response in France. The wars with England had produced a new national feeling, which testified to the rising tide of the enthusiatic spirit. The nation had taken over the task of harnessing the anxiety of the masses who were slipping away from the securities and conditions of archaic society. *Patrie* had always been the clan, village or city. It meant an organic, highly complex community of the living and the dead, ruled by the old people, the virgins and the midwives. The industrial revolution and social changes had shaken and partially destroyed that archaic society. From the time of Rousseau to Hitler nationalism became the vehicle of the Enthusiast movement and of the decadent post-Enlightenment. New leaders tried to shelter the anxiety-ridden, uncertain masses in the nation and in the fatherland, as new communions of the living and dead on earth.

Rousseau's *Offrande aux Autels de la Patrie* appeared in 1764. The people were to be educated to the idea of a 'nation in arms'. They would be reborn on the battlefields. In 1781 the old encyclopedist Joseph Servan wrote his *Soldat citoyen*. He was later the minister of war who in 1792 declared war on Austria, the leading power of the old fathers (emperor and pope). The technical and spiritual preparation for the change in attitude toward war had begun more than 100 years before with Richelieu's and Campanella's war propaganda. A new type of unit had been created in 1671, the engineer corps. These military engineers took the place of the old priests, magicians and prophets. Rousseau's exhortation to the Polish people to awaken and cultivate the national passions, and to train children and youth in national demonstrations and war games occurred in the middle of this period of development. Through the Abbé Sieyès, Rousseau's ideas exerted considerable influence on the Jacobins. In 1788 the Abbé Sieyès wrote: 'The nation exists before all, it is the origin of all (note: *tout*, all, means the sacred whole, total). Its will is always lawful; it is the law itself.'[39]

The will of the nation is an expression of the entire community. Rousseau's *citoyen* votes, not in any mere pragmatic way, but in a sacred manner; the vote is a sacrifice. Since parties and groups are not permitted in such a state lest they form sectarian churches or cells of opposition, the citizen must accept as an act of sacrifice that the will of the people may be realized against his vote. By the terms of the 'Social Contract', the citizens have agreed to give themselves up entirely to the 'all' and to live of it, for it, and from it. This communion of all bodies and minds applies to life and death and manifests itself in the 'general will' (*volonté générale*). The general will is the soul of the *Brüdergemeine* (to use the Moravian name) of inspired democrats. 'The general will is indestructible. Since it unites many men who consider themselves as a single body (*un seul corps*, the new *corpus mysticum*), they have only one will which refers to the common preservation and to the commonweal ...' Inasmuch as they regard themselves as one body, Rousseau continued, they may properly be regarded as parts of a kind of communal ego. Rousseau wrote *La volonté générale est la volonté propre du Moi commun, engendré par le sacrifice que chacun a fait de lui-même et de tous ses droits sur l'autel de la cité.*[40] *La cité*, the 'people's community' of the nation, is the new *civitas dei*, the city of God on earth.

Rousseau was aware of the difficulties of welding the masses into a chosen people. Since the people often have no idea how to realize the general will, there must be a law-giver or salvation-leader, who interprets it and lets his will become deed.[41] 'He who dares to co-ordinate, to institute a people (*instituer un peuple*) must know himself to be capable of changing human nature, of remoulding each individual ...'[42] Each individual must become a part of the whole. The point is 'to change the constitution of men in order to strengthen them'. The native powers and faculties must be taken from the individual and he must be given alien ones: *Plus ces forces naturelles sont mortes et anéanties, plus les acquises sont grandes et durables, plus aussi l'institution est solide et parfaite.* The old dreams of the spirituals and the aspirations of Roger Bacon, Frederick II, Leonardo and Campanella, had been fulfilled. The great age of experimentation on human beings had begun.

The cruel dialectic of the *Monachatus non est pietas* continued to grind forward. As the middle ages ended, monasticism was declared a hindrance to salvation; by Rousseau's time, everyone was forced to become a new inner-worldly monk. For this was, in essence, what Rousseau demanded. As he put it, when writing of the Poles, the nation must become *un peuple des Capucins*. The transition from the old to the new order was pregnant with dangers and in the end Rousseau was frightened. Discussing the ideas of Saint Pierre, Rousseau wrote: 'What man with any understanding would dare to destroy the old customs, to change the old foundations and to give the state a form other than that which has developed continuously over a period of 1,300 years ?'[43] He was afraid of the power he had unleashed. Ironically one of the greatest leaders of mass enthusiasm of all times wanted only to put his ideas into practice in the protected surroundings of genteel houses of polite upper bourgeoisie. Voltaire and Rousseau died on the eve of the Revolution. Their remains and their works were borne in 'choral processions of the people' to the new shrines of the fatherland, just as once Rainald of Dassel had carried the relics of the Magi in triumphal procession to Cologne.

The secularization of the religious ideas of the seventeenth century, which we have been following in this chapter, took two of its potential forms in Voltaire and Rousseau. A third possibility was the so-called 'low Enlightenment', which in its destructive, vulgarized, rationalism was an important determinant in the outbreak of the Revolution. The late Enlightenment of Voltaire and the Encyclopedia had still preserved the open rationalism of scholasticism, the political expression of a noble and great bourgeois society. It was open. It was defined and left to each his own. The king, society, the faith, and the nation had secure places in it, and as a result, its thinking had great latitude. It could move freeely between heaven and earth because it was very conscious of its limitations. Rational thought was the play of intellect. It was a game carried on by men of cultivation. Because of its long tradition they knew what they could do and what they could not. It was possible to approach theistic and atheistic ideas in a matter-of-fact way, because they had the serene confidence of their place.

The low Enlightenment was something quite different. It took over the playful theses of the high Enlightenment as formulas for salvation, as eschatological judgments, as statements on the first and last things of the world, as laws. The semi-educated man of the people had been deprived of his archaic society, his old liturgies, sacraments and contents of faith. He saw in the ideas of the Enlightenment the call to a new ascetic life in the service of science, by which he meant natural science, medicine, technology and the study of popular society. The low Enlightenment was the expression of an appalling anxiety. Its rationalism was closed. Its ideas were exaggerated, desperate attempts to grasp and transmit everything in a few, firm formulas of salvation. Horkheimer and Adorno have summed it up in these words:

'Enlightenment is totalitarian ... its ideal is a system in which everything follows ... It is a mythical anxiety which has become radical ... It clings to a positivistic immanence ... Nothing can exist outside its system because the mere idea of something outside summons up all the anxiety which it is designed to quell.'[44] One could scarcely find a more accurate description of the domestic and foreign policies of the modern totalitarian states. At the same time, the ideas themselves generate anxiety and in the late eighteenth century the various panaceas and formulas of salvation pressed on people's nerves like the badly fitting cap of a tooth and caused the psychic underground to break out in Enthusiast and irrationalist movements. There was a wave of occultism and magic which met and mingled with the doctrines of the vulgar Enlighteners and produced in the secret societies a noxious brew.

The early history and initial objectives of the low Enlightenment had been lofty and heroic. Its ideals were a combination of the missionary zeal of the Cathar and Huguenot preachers, of Erasmian humanists and of nonconformists. Education was expected to produce the idea of the *honnête homme*, the Stoic-Christian educated man who was the opposite of all the *doctes*, *savants*, *érudites*. The writer of the eighteenth century became the embodiment of that ideal. He spoke to a public who had deserted the Church, the royal palace and the university for the salons, cafés, and the houses of the nobles and bourgeoisie.[45] Despised by the old nobility, persecuted by the orthodox churchmen, excluded from the universities of the seventeenth and eighteenth centuries, the writer rose to a consciousness of his own estate and mission and achieved high esteem and influence. Independent of the court, the nobility, the Church and the university, these *gens de lettres* carried out a great mission: to teach the nation.

Diderot and d'Alembert, the founders of the Encyclopedia,[46] were supreme examples of the men of letters. They were accustomed to poverty and had been severely disciplined by self-criticism. Their aim was to set up the French language as a universal sacrament, indeed the only valid sacrament. Language would overcome the opposition among the different estates, spread reason, humanity and benevolence. It would give knowledge of reality and humane education to the people. The individual sciences would surrender their splendid isolation, and the natural sciences, arts and manual trades unite for the benefit of humanity. Corruption of language and corruption of politics and society were symptoms of the same evil. The Encyclopedia, as Diderot saw it, was to be the perfect instrument to save the masses who no longer believed in the old cultural values. It would give them facts.

Almost at once, the Encyclopedia turned into the Bible of the low Enlightenment. Diderot was horrified at the way materialistic and mechanistic sectarians had vulgarized and degraded his great work. He saw that Lamettrie, Holbach and Helvétius were reducing the variegated fullness and differentiation of the world to formulas of salvation. Lamettrie preached that 'man is a machine, but also a plant'. Holbach asserted 'there are only atoms, gravity, the attraction and repulsion of things. In morality it is called self-criticism, hate, love!' Helvétius asserted, 'Everything is legitimate and permissible for the public weal.' In his increasingly violent attacks on his opponents, Diderot helped to foster what he wished to avoid. He became an Enthusiast himself. His ideas were increasingly saturated by pantheism. He spread out in all directions and ended in deep despair.[47]

In the decade after 1770 an abundance of sects and secret societies came to life. It was striking that in the thousand years between the eighth and the eighteenth centuries every one of the sects had preserved its spiritual and creedal patrimony, but a common ground had developed among them, a distillation of the Protestant and Catholic mysticism of the sixteenth and seventeenth centuries. In this common, nonconformist heritage pietistic women visionaries of the seventeenth century and Catherine of Siena were adored without reference to their creedal differences. The Vaudois country and southwest Germany were gathering points. The Grand Duchess of Württemberg harboured all sorts of Enthusiasts and provided a meeting place for the German and French Spiritualists. There was a wave of interest in oriental studies, eastern theosophy and mysticisms and comparative history of religion which poured out of these groups and entered the turbulence of French life.

The men of low Enlightenment, the scoffers, savants and scientists were soon gripped by the same wave of occultism as the people. They had done their work too well. The people, awakened by the Encyclopedia and its agents, now wanted to know everything, especially supernatural things. In Paris they turned in masses to séances, sciences, bizarre studies and experiments. At the same time the German princely courts were gripped by a similar agitation, especially the court of Friedrich Wilhelm II, where Prince Henry and the ministers Haugwitz, Waechter and Woellner, the enemy of Kant, took part in séances. Later Berlin romanticism had its roots there. Occultism was more than a mere fad. It was an expression of revolutionary optimism. It was to be a new religion: 'it alone can make an assembly of brothers out of Europe (*une Assemblée des Frères*) and make an integrated whole out of the universe, united by the same rights, maintained by the same duties', wrote Count de Gébelin in his *Monde primitif*.[48]

The hour belonged to the Enthusiasts, who had been awaiting it for centuries, and to all those who were allied with them.[49] There were the revolutionary Abbés and ex-monks, and also the representatives of that lower clergy around Jean Meslier, Abbé Grégoire and Abbé Goutte. The storming of the churches, the iconoclasm, the thousands of decapitations of statues of saints and kings of the old world in the cathedrals and the abbeys were supposed to make it visible to all that the sacraments of these priests and kings had lost their power.[50] The procession of revolutionary inspired souls was opened by Mathilde d'Orléans, Grand Duchess of Bourbon. She was the sister of Philip-Egalité and the mother of the Grand Duke of Enghien. She went over to the Revolution directly from quietism. Madame Guyon had filled her with vehement emotion against the visible Church, and its arrogance and drive for power. She demanded that men destroy themselves in 'pure love' before God. Let them accept the great judgment in humility, love, sacrifice. The young Jacobins were surrounded by female prophets. Suzette Labrousse celebrated the Constitution as the work of God. Catherine Théot, Robespierre's sister-in-law, strengthened her faith through the reading of Saint Theresa and Saint Catherine. She is supposed to have ordered Robespierre to help her with the work of salvation and to separate the good from the evil. As the Bride of

Christ she would then give birth to the new Messiah, whose precursor was Robespierre.

Robespierre himself often visited these circles of Enthusiasts.[51] He was a typical *enfant humilié*. His childhood had been wretched and unhappy. He had been the poorest student at the college of Louis-le-Grand. He was proud and sensitive, and filled with glowing resentment at the humiliations he had suffered. He came from Arras, one of the oldest heretical areas in France, and Condorcet recognized this at once by calling him *chef de secte*. As a young deputy in 1789, he had been overwhelmed by the splendour of the monarchy and rejected it: *Toute la pompe d'une cour idôlatrée*. During the session of 6 June, a high prelate showed the illustrious gathering a piece of black bread in order to arouse the pity of the Third Estate for the poor. He was interrupted by an unknown – Robespierre – with the words, 'If your colleagues are so impatient to help the poor, then object to luxury, horses, carriages ... and sell perhaps a fourth of the clerical estates ...'[52] From that day on he became the driving force in the crusade to purify the nation by purging it of all the libidinous, the rich and the corrupt.

The Jacobins chose Robespierre as their leader and he embodied the will to become the incarnation of the new people of God on earth. They were certain that they had been charged with the task of purifying the nation and of transforming it into a new spiritual community. 'The one and indivisible Republic' celebrated the sacrament of the 'holy trinity': *Liberté, Egalité, Fraternité*. This trinity was supposed to supersede the old Trinity of the Father, Son and Holy Ghost. The thousand-year struggle of the old gnostics against the Trinity reached a new high point.[53] Swedenborg's Church of the New Jerusalem was certainly one of the sources of Jacobin anti-trinitarianism, but there may well have been Italian influences as well. Buonarotti, a member of Michelangelo's family, was true to Robespierre all his life, and he certainly came from that Italian underground of nonconformism. Another of Robespierre's companions, Nicholas de Mirecourt, was another representative of the famous family which had already produced a great scholastic radical.

Robespierre and Saint-Just believed that the new republic must be based on strict moral laws. Only regular purification of the nation could accomplish this and thus the republic required a public cult.[54] This cult was practised through liturgical devotion to the 'Goddess of Reason,' and the 'Supreme Being', and in the romantic pageantry of people's meetings and processions.* But the essence of the cult was not in these ceremonies but in the great assemblies of revolutionary tribunals. There the Last Judgment was proclaimed in permanent session, and the nation prepared to become worthy of carrying out its mission of salvation for all the earth. The machine of terror purified the people and turned them into a holy nation.[55]

The Jacobins were inspired by the visions of Hell and Heaven of the

*The Munich masquerades and Wagnerian liturgies, which excited the Enthusiast leader Hitler in his Nuremberg pageants, were inspired by these revolutionary festivals.

Enthusiasts and driven by the ancient anxieties and hope of salvation of the lower class. Paris swarmed with seers and prophets. The ex-Carthusian Dom Gerle became the dedicated servant of the female prophet Labrousse, who journeyed to Rome dressed as a beggar in order to convert the Pope. The clairvoyante Marquise de Lacroix, who belonged to the *dévotes de Robespierre*, mixed together the ideas of Saint-Martin and Swedenborg. 'Ancestor Raphael' and the 'prophet Elias' walked through the streets of Paris, Amar, the ruler of the committee of public safety was a Swedenborgian. His colleague Voulland participated in the severe measures against Catholic priests, and then piously took part in secret Masses held in the cellars and barns by priests who had not sworn loyalty to the 'Constitution'. Catherine Théot, the 'Mother of God', held religious services, and dispensed the 'seven gifts of the Holy Ghost' to the 'brothers and sisters' who felt themselves redeemed and purified.*

The Enthusiasts had many enemies. Robespierre had been too 'deeply stamped by Catholicism' to satisfy the anticlericals.[56] Until 1789 he had taken communion every week, and even after that he had argued: *Attaquer le culte, c'est attenter à la moralité du peuple.* He had maintained the payment of salaries to pastors and curates and defended the lower clergy against the bishops. He opposed the expulsion of the priests from the Jacobin clubs. In a speech to the Jacobin Club on 26 March 1792 he spoke constantly about God and Providence.[57] Attacked on that account, he declared: 'to speak thus is my inner need. How would I have been able to bear all the humiliations and burdens of my childhood and of my life if I had not lifted my soul up to God?' On that evening, Bishop Gobel happened to be chairman of the meeting. Eighteen months later Robespierre again renewed his profession of faith, at which time Anarcharsis Clootz, the Prussian banker and apostle of international atheism, was in the chair. Robespierre attacked the fanaticism of renegade priests and declared that atheism was aristocratic (Diderot had said it was peculiar to kings), but belief in God belonged to the people. The Jacobins deplored his Capuchin sermons (*Capucinades*) but they listened to them.

In order to counter the growing conspiracy of atheists and materialists under Vadier's leadership, Robespierre delivered his great speech on God, immortality and the nation on 7 May 1794. Next he introduced a decree, according to which the French people recognized the existence of the Supreme Being and the immortality of the soul and ordered the feast of the *Être Suprême* to be celebrated on Pentecost Sunday (8 June). Now that the people had atoned, Robespierre apparently felt that the time had come to found a new alliance of the people with God, a Covenant, related to those of the Scottish and English puritans and dissenters of the English Revolution. Even the famous *Declaration of the Rights of Man* in the National Assembly in 1789 had been a religious document. It had been the expression of the experience

*The entire community was arrested during one of its prayer meetings and condemned to death. They endured martyrdom with the serenity of the early Christians.

of persecuted nonconformists for a thousand years joined to the theory of natural rights and freedom of conscience developed in Catholic, Calvinist and nonconformist legal philosophy.[58] In very much the same way Robespierre assembled his divine service out of several traditions. There were giant statues symbolizing atheism, discord, stupidity, envy, egoism and other enemies of 'general happiness'. Robespierre conducted the ceremony in front of the assembled people. Alone, holding a torch, he moved towards the statue of atheism, and lit it. It went up in smoke and collapsed. The new Moses and Boniface had converted his people to the true faith, pledged it to moral purity, political discipline and the firm will to purge itself.

Robespierre had gone too far this time. Neither the people nor the atheist Jacobins were willing to follow him. His last great speeches to the people were the pleas of a penitent preacher who despaired of the world. He cried that the world was full of impurity, crime and treachery. Virtue was threatened everywhere, crime, corruption and misuse of power prevailed. Vadier's triumph was complete when he showed the Convention a letter in which the 'Mother of God', Catherine Théot, proclaimed that Robespierre's mission had already been foretold by Ezekiel. He was executed as a tyrant. 'The day of the death of a tyrant is a feast for fraternity', Tallien declared. The brotherhood had condemned its salvation-leader.[59]

Saint-Just, not yet twenty-seven years old, fell with Robespierre on the tenth of Thermidor, *sa tête comme un Saint-Sacrement*, said the onlookers. He had demanded the King's head in November 1792, the heads of the Girondists on 8 July 1793, the annihilation of the nobility and all suspects on 26 February 1794, the heads of the Herbertists on 13 March and finally the head of Danton on 31 March. He was the most consistent representative of the Jacobin revolution and the first genius of romanticism. Like Pascal and Nietzsche, he longed for a heroic and dangerous life 'between mortal danger and immortality'. 'Great men do not die in their beds.' 'Conditions are only difficult for those who draw back in horror from the grave.' 'Those who make revolutions in the world, those who want to do good, only sleep in the grave.' Death-wish and hope for the future were one. 'Man, committed to withdraw from the world and himself, casts his anchor into the future and draws to his heart the posterity that is innocent of the evils of the present.' 'I despise the dust from which I have been put together and which (through me) speaks to you. You may persecute this dust and let it die. But I shall endure, even if this independent life be torn from me, since I have given myself to the centuries and to the heavens.' Saint-Just's unrestrained, proud, sensitive and neurotic soul yearned for the triumph of the pure heart. He was saturated with the spirit of Fénelon and Rousseau and in his youthful poem *Organt* he sang: 'I will go my way without arms, without defence, followed by hearts and not by hangmen.' The heart became a revolutionary force in Saint-Just. 'Citizens of Strasbourg', he cried, 'give up your German ways. Your hearts are French.'[60]

The uprising of the 'pure', the Jacobins, was over. The anxiety and hatred of the lower classes which in a thousand civil wars, uprisings and heretical movements from the tenth to the eighteenth centuries had exploded into the light of day, was once more pressed back into the underground. Robespierre had embodied the anxieties and resentments of the people. His conqueror was the sarcastic sceptic, the great atheist and mocker of religion, Vadier. The Enthusiasts were not permanently defeated. Such movements never are. Indeed, the public concerns and drives of the Revolution led to romanticism and restoration, to nationalism and liberalism. The Revolution contained in itself all the potentialities of Europe in the nineteenth century, enthusiastic glorification of the self and of the people, anarchic individualism, the spirit and structure of a people's democracy, faith in technology, science and progress. It marked the first timid step toward the beginning of a renaissance of Christian movements and endeavours. Its idea of world freedom and a league of nations, its idea of mankind, reveal 'how much the revolution was at the same time a religion'.[61]

19

THE INNER KINGDOM
Germany (1601–1800)

FROM the Regensburg disputation of 1601 to the beginning of the nineteenth century, Germany went through a period of tremendous spiritual struggle. In these 200 years, the Church of the Spirit slowly ate away at the foundation of the Lutheran State Church and undermined its powers of resistance. The inner kingdom rose from beneath, and from within, the external kingdoms, principalities and bishoprics, and transformed the traditions of western humanism into something quite different. The mighty surge of pietism in the seventeenth and eighteenth centuries reflected the pent up yearning for salvation in the underground and at the same time forced Protestant Germany further eastward.

Since Luther surrendered to the state the supervision of worldly activity, he made it the guardian of the external manifestations of spiritual activity as well. Lutheran Germany became a *terra obedientiae*; as Herder called it, a genuine expression of Luther's ethical pessimism.[1] Within such a historical situation, there were four possible courses for Lutheranism itself to pursue:[2]

1. Spiritual and secular service to the state.

2. Rationalist humanism and cultural work, as in Melancthon and his school.

3. The cultivation of inwardness and the realms of emotion.

4. The revolutionary explosiveness of the inheritance of the early Luther.

The choice of the first course, which had been Luther's preference, was confirmed in the Augsburg Confession (1555). The peace of Westphalia (1648), which extended the religious peace to the Calvinists, merely confirmed the right of the Lutheran, Catholic and Calvinist princes to reform their subjects according to their own Faith. The third violent conversion of Germany followed in the wake of the two earlier ones. The forced conversion of Carolingian Germany in the eighth century and the Germanizing of the eastern marches in the twelfth, thirteenth and fourteenth centuries had left wounds, which had only begun to heal when they were ripped open by this third unnatural conversion in the seventeenth century. Protestant peasants in Austria were dragged in fetters to the communion rail. Protestant communities had to change their confession to Lutheranism or to Calvinism four to five times a year, and nonconformists and sectarians were persecuted everywhere. Violence was done to the German conscience from which it has not yet recovered. Nicodemism, caution in making statements about the first and last things, became widespread and a hatred of all state Churches, all salvation and knowledge from above and outside, developed.

The brutal oppression of German Spiritualists, sects and dissenters and the impossibility of forming tolerated Protestant free churches poisoned the knowledge and conscience of the orthodoxies.[3] The narrow, pressure-ridden and overheated atmosphere of persecution fostered the development of the typical German overstatement. The free word was rebellious and its expression very often an ecstatic outburst. It was this which led to the overassertion and exaggeration which has been the characteristic feature of modern German intellectual history. Such lack of balance can be seen in the *Sturm und Drang*, in the young Goethe and Schiller, in Fichte, Nietzsche, in the German Youth Movement and the men of 1933.

A victory for Lutheranism would have drawn Germany prematurely into the Eastern whirlpool. A victory for Catholicism would have turned Germany into a replica of Italy and Spain. In the event neither was victorious, mainly because no state or clerical apparatus was sufficiently powerful to enforce a total solution on all of Germany. Most of the large number of German states were fairly weak and they could only preserve themselves in a balance of opposition. Ironically it was just this deadlock which saved Germany's inner life. The extraordinary flowering of culture in the eighteenth and nineteenth centuries would not have been possible if the variety of German life and its social potencies had been destroyed in 1648. For Germany the gains of the Thirty Years War were incomparably greater than the losses, although the foundations of the German cultural development in the eighteenth century were never entirely secure. While the feebleness of the German states fostered variety and preserved a kind of freedom, they were much too weak to achieve a genuine resolution of the latent conflicts within society.[4]

During the first decades of the seventeenth century the Lutheran universities (Helmstedt, Wittenberg, Jena, Leipzig, Giessen, Rostock and Tübingen) began to adopt Aristotelian-Thomistic school metaphysics as taught by the Spanish Jesuits. They needed an established store of philosophical concepts to defend Lutheran-orthodoxy against Calvinists, Enthusiasts, and pietists. The total acceptance of Suarez occurred first in Giessen, which was an outpost of Lutheranism in a Calvinist area. The theologians at Giessen had to make an effort to establish an ontological foundation for the Lutheran ubiquity and doctrine of two natures. Christoph Scheibler's *Opus metaphysicum* (1617) adhered closely to Suarez. This school metaphysics exerted considerable influence on Leibniz. It was renewed in the work of Wolff during the German Enlightenment.[5] Although Kant dismissed it as dogmatic, he did incorporate its concerns into his own programme. In general, this type of Lutheran scholasticism was compulsorily taught at the Lutheran universities for 200 years, although it was mocked, despised and attacked on a very wide front as the 'Spanish theory of reason' and 'Romish devil's work', by the old Lutheran irrationalists, by the teutonic natural philosophers, by pietists, nobles, sceptics and polyhistorians. Despite its dominance of the Lutheran universities, this Western scholasticism was never accepted in the depth and breadth of Protestant Germany. Protestant Germany was never able to adopt a theory of being uniting God and the world, and thus it was never able to accept the Western humanism linked to it, nor the ecclesiastical and governmental orders of authority of the scholastic cosmos.*

The university of Altdorf, founded in 1581 by the imperial city of Nuremberg, became the German Padua. It thoroughly rejected this Spanish ontology and declared that Aristotle had nothing to do with a theory of being, that there was no such thing as philosophical ontology, and no 'thing-in-itself'. It espoused a purely philological and natural-scientific interpretation of Aristotle. Jacob Thomasius, the very influential critic of Lutheran metaphysics, was on the side of the Altdorfians, and with him were the polyhistorians like Christian Gryphius and Pufendorf. In 1694 the university of Halle was founded and it soon became the centre of pietistic rejection of metaphysics. The fate of metaphysics in Protestant Germany was sealed when the Göttingen University was founded in 1734. It was the gateway for English Deistic influences, and at the same time the seminary of historical theology, history of the empire and statistics. The Berlin Academy, founded in 1746, joined the same front.

Swabia became a place of refuge and a gathering point of that 'old German' thought uniting God and world, man and nature, that led from Albert the Great via Paracelsus to Böhme. This tradition was carried on by the 'Swabian fathers' (around Ötinger) and the Tübingen theological schools which produced Hölderlin, Hegel and Schelling. As early as 1750 this Swabian philosophy was decried as teutonic by its opponents.[6] In a sense the criticism was fair. This philosophy tried to comprehend God in nature and man in the universe. Alchemy, magic, archaic oneness, folkish underground and strong Eastern influences were its constituent parts. This was the world of Jacob Böhme, which Ötinger and Baader transmitted to Hegel and Schelling, and the romantics to Russia.[7] Böhme saw the world as the self-revelation of God and the corporeality of the spiritual. Good and evil coincide in God, Böhme believed, and the process of the Trinity is the norm for every process of nature. When Adam was created he was like God and could articulate the essence and name of every thing as one. Through Adam's Fall, man lost this primal language.[8] Böhme's conception of the primal language was part of the rejection of the flowery language of the scholastics and the West, which was a strong characteristic of German popular religion. The various secret societies of the seventeenth century, the Rosicrucians and language clubs wanted to renew the language because the purification of language was a precondition for the renewal of the world. Human speech embodied the spoken creation of God, and the corruption of language was the consequence of the Fall. History

*cf. Karl Jasper's attack on the diabolical 'and' of Catholicism.

was thus the self-realization of God. Hegel was a direct disciple of the tradition of Böhme's historical metaphysics.[9]

Angelus Silesius's *Cherubinischer Wandersmann* revealed the same over-flowing emotion, rationalist speculation and passion.[10] The glow and the hubris of the mystic often broke through: 'I am like God/and God like I, I am as great as God/He is as small as I: He cannot be over me/I cannot be under Him.'[11] 'Man is eternity, I myself am eternity, when I leave time/and gather myself in God/and God in myself.'[12] Whereas teutonic natural philosophy honoured the sacramental character of universal nature instead of the sacraments of Lutheran orthodoxy, this mystical poetry of the Protestant baroque chose a second path of escape from the hand of orthodoxy. If reason could no longer create metaphysics worthy of belief, the heart and the emotions could master the dilemma of the joy of living and the sinfulness of the world only by a passionate and exaggerated hymn to the wonders of God's creation.

The first great wave of pietism in Germany broke out at this time. It swelled into a religious mass movement by the end of the century and was the source of the cult of sensitivity, the Enlightenment, *Sturm und Drang* and romanticism. German pietism was the most powerful movement of modern German intellectual history. Without pietism there would have been no Hamann, Herder, Goethe and Kant, nor the romanticism and idealism which followed them. Pietism expressed one consequence of Luther's conception of the human heart, which was able to reach God directly. It was a descendant of the small community which had vainly opposed the solidification of Lutheranism in the national churches, orthodoxies and scholasticism. As Antoni shrewdly observed, any vital religious movement in Germany has always been a protest. This was the result of the original introduction of Christianity as an authoritarian Church. Antoni argues that 'the religious folk life developed on its own in the semi-heretical mysticism of "contemplation", outside every hierarchy ... It sought nourishment in the sects and in the conventicles, until it found a homogeneous movement in pietism.'[13]

The first theologian of pietism, Johann Arnd (1555–1621), in his *Four Books of the True Christianity*, demonstrated the continuity of religious protest by returning to Tauler, the *devotio moderna* and the young Luther.[14] In his vices man is an arrogant, angry lion, Arnd wrote, an envious dog, a rapacious wolf, a poisonous worm, a fox, a pig. Through faith, he can become 'god with God' in whom 'the whole kingdom of God' is reborn. In these ideas, the pietistic communities were the successors of the mystical communities of the late middle ages and of the *devotio moderna*. Their revivals and conversions sought to bring the kingdom to all the world. The pietistic soul was alert. Tensely, it awaited the eruption of the kingdom of God and its growth in its own breast. Pietists recorded this history of the kingdom in their diaries, autobiographies and confessions. They saw the world subjectively through a haze of emotion. They observed the persecution of the kingdom of God in the world and predicted its fall in their visions and prophecies. Introversion and Chiliasm joined hands.[15]

At first these powerful chiliastic, magical and natural undercurrents were of no importance in Germany's public life, but gradually one wing of pietism began to turn into a movement to renew ecclesiastical and civic life. Philip Jacob Spener (1635-1705) and August Hermann Francke, the founder of the Halle Orphans' Home, tried to achieve a Christianization of daily life.[16] They formed a *collegia pietas* and concentrated on individual pastoral care and bible study-hours for the edification of adults. Spener's *Pia desideria* stimulated reform of the Church and both he and Francke were devoted to the idea of education. Spener and Francke released important energies in German pietism for a worldly activity because of their receptivity to the community ethos, the rationalism and the Enlightenment of western Europe. The pietist reformers had a new basis, the enlightened heart, from which they could attack the evils of the world. The first step was accordingly to bring about the reform of the individual, then, after the awakening and conversion of the personal life, to reform the communities, schools, universities of the Church and state, on the basis of the believing conscience and rational knowledge.

Lutheran orthodoxy tried to protect itself against this missionary aggressiveness through anti-pietist laws: 1690 Saxony, 1692 Braunschweig and Luneburg, 1700 Brandenburg, 1703 Hessen-Kassel, 1703 Hanover, 1705 Bremen, 1706 Denmark, 1707 Nuremberg, 1709 Anhalt-Zerbst. The refugees fled to the cities which were not subject to compulsory religion, especially to Hamburg, Leipzig and Frankfurt-am-Main. These were the cities of the Enlightenment and of the new German literature in the eighteenth century.[17] As is so often the case, such laws against spiritual and religious movements must be seen as evidence of their progress. Halle University became the centre of pietism. It re-educated Lutheran Germany, founded schools, and transformed the courts of nobles and princes and the homes of the bourgeoisie into stern schools of prayer, conversion and work. Pietism was able to do this because of its affinity with enlightened Calvinism. An example of the effect of the movement was the soldier-King, Friedrich Wilhelm I, 'the father', who wanted to make a new man out of himself and his state of Prussia.[18] 'If I build up and improve the country and make no Christians, it will not help me.' Friedrich Wilhelm I wanted to 'make' Christians by means of method, work, sacrifice and schooling. This could only be done by someone who was really serious about it.* The old spirit of the Enthusiasts, opposed to every 'Romish' form and fortress, was revived.

The King had the magnificent romanesque Marienkirche in front of the city of Brandenburg razed in order to build an army orphanage in Potsdam from its stones. He schooled his soldiers according to Francke's *True-hearted*

*Pietism of this variety prepared the way for the spread of Jansenism in Catholic Germany, where it evoked similar drives.

Instruction for Christian Warriors. This was the beginning of militarism as a violent co-ordination of the inner and outer man in order to make him ready for God's plans. Later he was to be made ready for the plans of the princes and the state.

Inherent in pietism, as in all spiritualist movements, was a powerful element of destruction. The pietist wanted to break 'evil' nature. This became especially clear in eastern Germany. Johann Semler, the leader of the theological enlightenment in Halle, who was a pietist by birth, has left us an interesting picture of just such a pietistic princely court in Silesian Saalfeld.[19] A strict régime prevailed there with pilgrimages at appointed times, prayer-hours and conversions. Each man scrupulously observed himself and his environment, and they all kept calendars and diaries on their spiritual life. They were always desperate about their sins and willingly over-exerted themselves in the hope of overcoming them. This perpetual contemplation of their sins drove many to a gloomy hopelessness, as was the case with one of Semler's brothers. In this overheated atmosphere, nobles, tradesmen, manual workers and peasant women fused to form the 'new people' who were firmly determined to wrest salvation from Heaven and later from the earth. Moritz's famous autobiographical novel *Anton Reiser* describes another house of such a nobleman as 'a small (pietistic) republic', entirely devoted to prayer and missionary zeal.[20] His own home was a house of anger and hatred. He describes his terror of his pietistic father, and the way he zealously tormented himself in order to convert and educate himself. The reaction to this pietism was enormous. It determined the features of the German Enlightenment. 'The first German disciple of Spinoza, Edelmann, the first theologian of the Enlightenment, Semler, and the first German psychologist, Moritz, all stemmed from the atmosphere of pietism. They developed their ideas in a struggle with pietism and incorporated it into their personalities.'[21]

Despite the reaction against it, Protestant Germany remained tied to pietism. Orthodoxy was forced to make peace with it as the Moslem orthodoxy of the eighth to the eleventh centuries had been forced to do in its struggle with Sufiism. The difference was that Lutheran orthodoxy was confronting a movement which its own founder had undeniably fostered. The Lutheran simply could not reject every element of emotion and feeling.[22] As a result pietism openly invaded the rectories and began its great work of education there, in particular with women. The pietists brought Germany into line with western Europe on this question. In France and Spain religious humanism and quietism had opened up enormous opportunities for women in the kingdom of the mind and of the soul. The intellectual enlightened salon in France of the eighteenth and nineteenth centuries carried on the 600-year-old courtly humanist tradition of conversations between clericals and noble nuns. Pietism performed the same function in Germany. It brought the women of the nobility into contact with the bourgeoisie and the lower classes and prepared the way for the growth of Sentimentalism.[23]

During the last two decades of the seventeenth century the writings of Molina, Madame Guyon and Fénelon were popular in Germany. Through Peter Poiret, a transition was made to the sentimentality of early eighteenth-century Enlightenment. Poiret combined the older German mysticism with the new French emotional mysticism and produced a powerful mixture, the effect of which could be seen in Gottfried Arnold.[24] As a young man, Arnold was a revolutionary (the other face of pietism), and took part in the communist unrest in Quedlinburg. He wanted to carry out what the Enthusiasts saw in their visions, but he thought that fire and sword could accomplish it. On the other hand, he was a neurotic personality, always going through new puberties. He proudly proclaimed himself a disciple of women (like Guyon and Jane Lead) although he had a pathological hatred of sexuality.* His power of empathy, which so fascinated Herder and Goethe, grew out of the cleavage and disruption in his own soul. He was a man of the German East and knew something about the underground. He perceived, as few before him, the demonic element in Luther. Arnold sought the true religion in a 'pure heart' and 'good conscience'. He was a voracious reader, and studied with the nervous haste of a hunter for intellectual and spiritual enjoyments. He swallowed the whole mysticism of Europe that was available to him, especially the English, French and German contemporaries (Bromley, Pordage, Lead; Böhme, Spener, Francke; Guyon, Fénelon, etc.).

Under the impact of the persecution of pietists and nonconformists in the German Lutheran provinces, and stirred by Catholic attacks on Fénelon and the quietists, he wrote his *Unpartheyische Kirchen und Ketzerhistorie* (*Non-Partisan History of the church and heresy*). In this book he sought to prove that Christians who had been persecuted as heretics since the time of Constantine were the real saints, who had carried and still carry the light of the true Faith and of reason through the darkness of the world ages. Arnold wanted to reveal the true history of Christianity in order to reform the present. 'Adam's state of innocence' can and should be renewed in a reborn society in which Christ and Belial are friends. The nuptials of God with the devil would lead to the abolition of good and evil, which he saw as the two sides of God, two components of a divine power. This was the secret dream of Spiritualism, which united Böhme, Baader, Hegel and Marx. He envisaged the new society as a collection of communities of brethren, a fraternity of the saints of this world in a new Kingdom of God.

The world of the 'heart' and that of the 'grand form', met in the unusual atmosphere of the court of Hanover. All culture centred around the electress Sophie, the ancestress of the ruling houses of Prussia, England and Hanover. She was the daughter of the 'Winter King', who in the battle of White Mountain in 1620 had lost Bohemia to the Hapsburgs and with it the Empire for Protestantism, and of Elizabeth Stuart, of Calvinist lineage who fled back

*His autobiographic *Offenherziges Bekenntnis* should be compared with the works of Kierkegaard. There are many fascinating parallels and similarities between the two men.

to the West after the defeat in the East. Descartes dedicated his *Principia Philosophica* to her sister, Elizabeth of the Palatinate, who was the Abbess of Herford and protectress of many sectarians. Sophie's brother, Karl Ludwig, was a friend of Spinoza. Leibniz's theodicy arose out of his conversations with Sophie and her daughter, Sophie Charlotte,[25] Queen of Prussia (to whom Toland wrote his 'Letters to Serena'). The muses were called to witness the literary and philosophical gatherings in the salons and ornamental gardens of these princely houses. The electress Sophie's court became the model for the others and her influence was particularly evident in the Charlottenburg of Sophie Charlotte, and in the Weimar of Anna Amalien. It was the swan song of imperial culture. All that remained were a few insular structures, which gradually crumbled into tiny foreign territories.

Leibniz knew this society well, but he also knew the German, Slavic East from which he came. As early as 1670, he recognized that Germany was the centre of Europe which he saw moving towards a terrible revolution and falling into anarchy and atheism.[26] To prevent this, he aimed to renew the Holy Empire, to refute Hobbes, Locke, Newton, Gassendi and Descartes; to arrange with Peter the Great a world council for the unification of all Christian confessions, to make the mysticism of the German Enthusiasts serviceable to a cosmic theology and to bring together all sciences into a great universal science through the *restauratio magna scientarium*.[27] He saw himself as the highest adviser of God (on earth), of the World Emperor, of the Pope, the Czar and the French king. His 'terrifying virtuosity' extended to several hundred technical, political, scientific and religious projects, to new religious Orders, insurance societies, factories, stores, automobiles, promotion of agriculture and biblical criticism.[28] He worked out plans for an invincible army, steeled through the most rigorous physical training, for a new mechanics and a theory of combinations. He was interested in windmills in the Harz and the Jesuit China Mission. He wrote at least 300 letters a year (15,000 have been preserved). He interested himself in Quirnus Kuhlmann, Poiret, St Theresa and in all Catholics, Protestant and nonconformist theologians, philosophers, mathematicians, experimenters and project makers. Like Roger Bacon and Ramon Lull, he hoped to take the whole world into his universal philosophy. He was the embodiment of both the fantastic and the tragic aspects of the baroque era.[29]

Leibniz's ideas are not easy to understand, because his rationalism played so confusingly about the phenomena he studied. Almost every sentence could have been phrased differently, and often they seem to express several ideas at once. He may well have been Europe's greatest genius. New projects and proposals always sprang from his inexhaustible impulse to play. He wanted to know and to undertake everything, to be familiar with everything. It is difficult to decide whether he believed in anything at all. In the profoundest sense, Leibniz's thinking was a kind of game. It was the lofty game of the baroque which sought to recreate the play of God, the play of man, the play of the

Church as the late antique world and the Church Fathers had seen it.[30] 'God is universal harmony' he wrote, and the task of philosophy was to write the new Gospel of the *Theos geometres*.[31] God, the geometrician and mathematician, created the cosmos, as the Psalm says, according to measure, number and weight, and therefore the universe plays God's game on earth out of its own force and wisdom.* His theodicy written for the queens and princesses of baroque Germany was an account of this cosmic game.[32] The divine universal harmony was an edifying justification of man's liberated 'spirit of inventions and dominion'.

Leibniz's basic ideas came from the geometric mysticism of the middle ages, from Chartres in the twelfth century up to Nicholas of Cusa. God as an infinite sphere whose centre is everywhere and circumference nowhere, had first been conceived in the *Liber XXIV philosophorum* at the end of the twelfth century.[33] Leibniz rationalized divine providence and turned it into the exact concept of *Mathesis divina* by which the absolute maximum of perfection could be reckoned. Since man can both understand and employ this divine calculation, he can anticipate future things from his insight into the perpetual interconnections. Man can and must 'plan salvation'. Leibniz was one of the great baroque fathers of the idea of planning. His universal academies were places where politics, society, economy and religion were to be planned. His *Monodologie* of 1714 was the constitution of the modern age, in which man has assumed the planning and the direction of the earthly cosmos. It was no accident that all his life Leibniz was a point of attraction for all those world-reformers, constructors and calculators of new worlds who were encamped in every princely court. He attracted them because he was one of them. In Leipzig and Nuremberg (in the heart and centre of south German sectarianism) he had been the secretary of an alchemist society and had immersed himself in Plato, More, Bacon and Campanella.[34]

The planning, calculation and execution of salvation cannot take place without compulsion. Soberly Leibniz asserted: *Communitatibus et infantibus benefaciendum est etiam invitus*.[35] Children – and all men are children of the enlightened total state and its philosophical leader – and communities must be forced to do good. What form does the interplay of God and man, nature and super-nature, body and soul take in Leibniz's world harmony and in the popular philosophy of the eighteenth century? Wolff, for example, was quite happy to renounce Leibniz's *systema harmoniae praestabilitae* and to replace it by 'the common system of *influxus physici*'. Wolff removed what was an essential piece in the system by dismissing the harmony of God and world as a secondary hypothesis. The result was the abolition of freedom of the will as Leibniz understood it. All that remained was natural mechanism.[36] Leibniz tried to avoid this consequence of his system which was a perfectly obvious conclusion to draw: if man can think, calculate and plan the cosmos because

*Leibniz rejected the views of both Hobbes and Pascal and asserted that will was entirely free.

he is full of the spirit of God, and if he can investigate the laws of nature, does he still need a God? Leibniz had decided that to assert the superior power of God would brand him as an eternal tyrant and despot, indistinguishable from the devil. The superiority of God makes man, in his powerlessness, into an eternal rebel.[37] This was as far as Leibniz went. He was not prepared to assert that world-mechanics alone suffice. It is clear that the purely mechanical view of the universe would appeal to the thinking of Lutheranism, which could look at nature without grace in its naked causality and without regarding the distant and wholly other God.

Behind all this stood the old spiritualism, of which this kind of materialism is only one of its many sides. It was the same spiritualism which we have seen in so many guises and which is always trying to grasp the universe in its entirety. The difference was that, by the end of the seventeenth century, natural science had been finally liberated from the grip of magic. In 1648 'spirit' was replaced by 'gas', in the works of Johann of Helmont, the chemist and physician in Brussels. Until the seventeenth century it had been assumed that the combustion processes of medicine and metallurgy would occur according to a plan similar to the resurrection described in Cor. I. 40. 52. Gases were considered to be spirits, conjured up and pressed into service under certain constellations. In 1690 Bekker's *Betoverde Weereld* (*Enchanted World*) appeared, which was a great attack on the magical world, and it was translated into high German by Semler the following year.[38] Bekker's theological foes defended the actuality of magic, witches and alliances with the devil, as well as the other critical points in the Bible and dogma. Leibniz was very much aware of the extremely precarious situation. He was, after all, a mathematician himself. The confrontation with the new naturalism strengthened his determination to secure the integrity of the great game of the cosmos, as a game of pure, free spirits. Each monad was a little divinity within its sphere. His 'pre-established harmony' was a great baroque dream, a doctrinal game for the nations torn in war and civil war. Leibniz sought to fuse the kingdom of blissful individualism (referring to Theresa of Avila, Poiret, Spener and Francke), Böhme's kingdom of divine nature, and the will to reform of the Enthusiasts and world-renewers (Val. Weigel, Comenius, Henry More)[39] and a restoration of the Holy Roman Empire of the German nation.

Despite the quixotic aspects of this attempt, one cannot but admire the extraordinary sharpness of Leibniz's analysis of the German and European situation. Leibniz needed a foundation on which to support his system of harmony between God and the world. The decision to recreate the Holy Roman Empire was a perfectly rational idea, if we remember what Leibniz had in mind. In his struggle with Descartes it became clear to him that the sacraments, especially the Eucharist and the doctrine of Transubstantiation had become untenable if he employed the techniques of modern Western thought, but he needed them as authentic connections between God and the world.[40] His thinking became an apologia for the Eucharist through which he tried to restore the whole salvation-cosmos of old Europe: Church, pope, emperor, the sacraments of the religious and political orders including the persecution of unbelievers. The theodicy, the monadology and the philosophical corpus were such attempts. Leibniz's 'representation' was his favourite expression for an over-reaching totality of relations, and it had a juristic, political, mathematical, theological or metaphysical meaning, according to its context. In the *Monadologie* (1714) it shimmered as a mathematical presentation, a psychological conception or image. Leibniz used it to describe the sacramental nature of all things and connections just as the imperial theologians of the twelfth century had used *symbolice* and *mystice*. It was literally the last fundamental word of the baroque, of the 'grand form', but by the time Leibniz tried to use it in this way it had already lost its meaning. That was the tragedy of Leibniz's philosophy. He sought a great world-renewing monarch who was not to be found and he hailed his return in words which had lost their meaning.

In the eighteenth century an enlightened bourgeois and professional culture arose in the strategic rectangle Hamburg-Leipzig-Frankfurt-Göttingen. Frederick the Great's Berlin was at that time at least as much of a Western island in the East as it is today, but there was no place in Germany where the Western Enlightenment took root which was not an island. The waves of German irrationalism crashed against their sea walls, and only a few very powerful personalities managed to maintain an independent rational way of life. Goethe and Kant could, because they harnessed the energies of irrationalism without becoming its victims. The widely held view that Enlightenment, rationalism and humanism were dominant in the eighteenth century in Germany is false. It is an optical illusion. Small élites, which were only annihilated in the industrial revolution and the wars of the twentieth century, ruled the surface of Germany. The noble societies, bourgeois booksellers, humanist schools and orthodox church officials were their instruments. The superficiality of this society can be seen in Lessing's life and Goethe's observations on the stifling loneliness around every German poet and thinker. At the high point of German culture the theatre of Mannheim, from 1781 to 1808, performed *The Robbers* fifteen times, *Cabala and Love* seven times, the *Fiesco* and *Don Carlos* three times. From 1789 to 1813 Dresden granted Lessing, Goethe and Schiller together only fifty-eight performances.[41] This was the true fate of the German classics before they became a fetish on the bourgeois bookshelf, and a treasure-trove of quotations in patriotic festivities during the nineteenth century.

The bourgeois Enlightenment had a difficult time in the eighteenth century because its struggle for reason was constantly discredited by enlightened princely absolutism.[42] As it previously had used its faith for centuries, absolutism used its reason on the citizens through schools, sermons, the army, legislation, the police and a controlled economy. 'The struggle against reason in the eighteenth century was a struggle against the absolutist and cosmopolitan state.'[43] Between this governing authority and the underground of the Enthusiasts, bourgeois Enlightenment was severely cramped. It tried desperately to unite the two and to teach men to live morally and industriously. Education was to lead to civic virtue and bliss, liberation from superstitions and obscurantist, misanthropic religious and political systems. Its goal was the promotion of humanity. As a religious lay movement, the German bourgeois Enlightenment fed on the piety peculiar to the area: the Calvinist harshness and separation of 'virtue and vice', Lutheran state piety and Catholic scholasticism, and finally the strivings for freedom of the pietist 'heart' and nonconformist 'disposition'.[44]

Hamburg was the gateway to Germany for English and Dutch thinkers and nonconformists. During the first two decades of the eighteenth century the merchant and philosopher J. A. Hoffmann wrote his *Zwei Bücher von der Zufriedenheit* and *Politische Anmerkungen Über die wahre und falsche Staatskunst* which were very popular and went into many editions. Hoffmann believed that man was destined to be of use to his fellow men. An industrious life could dislodge the passions and vices. Hoffmann, who was familiar with English and Dutch conditions, demanded a 'free path for the virtues'. Like the English and Dutch Calvinists, Hoffmann thought that necessity and poverty were useful: 'They have been the mothers of a thousandfold inventions for earning one's bread honestly.' The early weeklies which Hoffmann helped to found like the *Patriot* and the *Chronik* were modelled on the *Tatler* and *Spectator*. They were to educate the burgher class under the motto 'Pray and Work' which was the slogan of the *Patriot*.

Poets, who had slowly fought their way out of the pessimism of Lutheranism or old pietism to the optimistic Faith of Deism, emerged as missionaries of the early Enlightenment. Canitz wanted to expose the 'madness of the silly world', lust for power, greed, and idleness, and his didactic poem *Die Alpen* enchanted Germany's educated bourgeoisie. In it a Calvinist Berne patrician, Albrecht of Haller, advocated a modest, simple, virtuous life of which the Alpine folk seemed to him to be happy models. Brocke's *Irdisches Vergnügen in Gott* undermined the inherent Lutheran distrust of nature by calling all natural things divine miracles. His 'sensuous worship' and enthusiasm for the beauty and innocence of nature reflected the vigour and force of the rejection of nature which Brocke was trying to overcome.* Christian Wolff (1679–1754) was one of the fathers of the German Enlightenment. Wolff went gradually from East to West (Breslau-Leipzig-Halle-Marburg). Through his study of St Thomas and Scotus, he had acquired his trust in reason. He believed that the world was created as a comprehensible machine by the watchmaker God. In it the free man has a duty to practise reason and virtue. Wolff, like almost all bourgeois Enlighteners, lived in constant horror of a reversion to the slavery of passions and superstition, and with good reason was suspicious of feeling

*This sort of hesitant, guilt-ridden affirmation of the world and reality could never have occurred in an old Catholic environment, where such problems have never existed.

as a source of the irrational. Wolff was undoubtedly responsible for the tendency in the Enlightenment to examine feeling and pleasure for their possible usefulness in the education and the culture of the inner man. Ch. A. Crusius, the pietistic teacher of Kant, decided that they were of no use, and taught that pleasure, happiness and virtue are in conflict.

In his poems and *Moralischen Vorlesungen* (Moral Lectures), Christian Fürchtegott Gellert became the educator of the sentimental man. The confession of sins turned into analysis of one's own feelings which must be examined for the sake of their purity. Friedrich von Hagedorn was the first to pronounce the timid 'yes' to life with a sharper accent. Man is good, he believed; the true and the beautiful are justified; both bring joy to man. Hagedorn anticipated the major activity of German poetry from 1770 to 1830, which was deeply involved in the same attempt to justify beauty. Poetry was a lay theology, which dared to glorify the world and its joys which the pietistic, Calvinist and Lutheran fathers could see joyfully only on Easter morning. Hagedorn's character was stamped in England: 'How noble is the inclination of genuine Britishers. Their abundance enriches the understanding. The fruit of action and the rewards of their courage are turned towards service. Favour crowns industry which power and freedom protect. The wealthiest persons are supporters of the sciences.'[45]

Hamburg looked toward England for its inspiration, and soon the other Low German ports were busily imitating its rationalism and irrationalism, its Deists, enlighteners and nonconformists. Justus Möser called London 'the capital of Europe' and in 1823 he confessed that he owed the greater part of his political education to forty years of studying English parliamentary proceedings. In London Hamann was exposed to English scepticism and enthusiasm. There he awakened to his role as a foe of the Enlightenment. Kant discussed the English Constitution 'with admiration and joy' in his lectures. In 1809 Jean Paul called Hamburg 'a London suburb'.[46] In this 'English' Hamburg the German bourgeois Enlightenment pushed forward into the political sphere. The Hamburg Patriotic Society developed from a group of freethinkers who used to gather for tea in the house of the fragmentist Hermann Samuel Reimarus (d. 1768). The shape of the new political parties of the nineteenth century began to emerge in the house of his son, the physician J. A. H. Reimarus (d. 1814). They were endowed with the ideology of the Enlightenment and an active interest in social reform. These parties actually developed from the pietistic conventicles and secret (religious) societies of the eighteenth century. In bourgeois society they stepped into the place of the old official forms of communication in church, council room, guild hall, fair and market place. They retained a good deal of the over-heated excitement of the pietist conventicle and differed only in their aims. With religious fervour they awaited the political and scientific age of progress and of the nation.

The elder Reimarus became a posthumous sensation in Germany when Lessing edited part of his writings, the *Fragmenten eines Ungenannten* (1774 to 1778). In these fragments Reimarus dealt with themes such as 'On the Tolerance of Deists', 'On the Decrying of Reason in the Pulpits', 'Concerning the Story of the Resurrection'. In the essay 'On the Aim of Jesus and His disciples' Reimarus observed that millions of men were stamped like wax from aphorisms acquired from the Bible, the Koran and the Talmud. Of Jesus, Reimarus wrote: 'He cultivated nothing else but moral duties, true love of God and of one's neighbour.' Reimarus took the decisive step and joined the English Deists: Christianity as a revealed religion became a world-immanent bourgeois theory and practice of morals.

The greatest exponent of these ideas was G. E. Lessing (1729–81). In a New Year ceremonial speech in 1743 the fourteen-year-old Lessing attacked the widely-held view that man was living in an iron age: 'in our time we obviously perceive more features of the Golden Age than the older ages have had. Indisputably this is a golden or blissful time'. We have the means 'to promote the perfect bliss of all according to our wishes'. Young Lessing concluded this written speech with the promise to serve God in the coming year to the best of his ability. 'Thus we will experience in deed that we live in the Golden Age.'[47] Lessing drew the vigour for such optimism from the pietist, enthusiastic underground. He based himself on Augustine, Tertullian and the Spirituals of the thirteenth century for his faith in the coming Third Kingdom of Enlightenment. In a conversation with Jakobi, Lessing let slip the confession that perhaps he himself might be the Supreme Being in a state of the highest contraction. History appeared to Lessing as the continuing education of mankind to the perfect identity of reason and revelation.[48] It was this chiliastic Lessing[49] who felt himself called to show the Protestant theology and the Church in his writings – not least through his edition of Reimarus – how both had to change in order to promote 'the time of a new eternal Gospel'. Lessing was an Enthusiast who could not come to terms with the Berlin Enlightenment around Frederick II.

Lessing's *Gedanken über die Herrnhuter* (1750) was an attack on the mixture of theology and philosophy of the time: 'A true Christian has become rarer than in the dark ages. According to knowledge we are angels and according to life we are devils.' Men wanted to reason subtly, he argued, but never act in a Christian way. He warmly espoused the practical missionary Christianity of the Moravian brethren against the guild theologians, because he genuinely believed that 'the man with the most pity is the best man'. This perception fundamentally separated Lessing from the German Enthusiasts of the ego and of romanticism. Because of it Lessing was prepared to sacrifice himself in the cause of literary responsibility. Lessing believed that a writer had a duty to his public, and he acted accordingly. In a sense, he created the German public. For the first time since Luther there was a real audience. The boldness of *Nathan the Wise*, of *Emilia Galotti*, of *Miss Sarah Sampson*, and of *Minna von Barnhelm* can perhaps be better understood today, now that tolerance, civil liberty and human rights have ceased to be mere phrases and have again become ideals to fight for. Lessing ended his days in embittered loneliness. In his *Erziehung des Menschengeschlechts*, he wrote: 'Go thy imperceptible way, eternal Providence! Only let me not despair in Thee because of this imperceptibility.* Let me not despair in Thee, even when Thy steps seem to go backwards! It is not true that the shortest line is always the straight one.'

Frederick II of Prussia proclaimed himself a 'pagan Calvinist'.[50] He had been called to subject and to civilize a barbaric Eastern country of Slavs and enthusiasts by the power of his will.[51] Western and Eastern Spiritualism were joined in his person with extraordinary results. Frederick was directly responsible for the Prussian political faith in 'the materialistic conception of history, not only of an economic but of a political stamp'.[52] His state enjoyed the success of the machine, and he created the state apparatus, as Ernst Moritz Arndt realized in 1806. For Europe, Frederick's career signalled the end of the old European state systems. His partition of Poland was an unprecedented event in European history: the fragmentization and partition of a great state by its neighbours after prior agreement and without a war against the victim.[53] Up to the very end of her life Maria Theresa was ashamed of her consent to the partition. Her father-confessor, the prior of Saint Dorothea, comforted her while she wrestled with her conscience.† He instructed her that in order to save the lives of her subjects, she had to accept a small injustice, the peaceful partition of a foreign state. It was preferable to a bloody war. This was good scholastic doctrine, but Maria Theresa instinctively felt that something new had happened. She sensed something which was to deprive her states of their existence too: the extinguishing of historical rights and traditions. In place of tradition, Frederick put the revolutionary deed, which changed the face of the earth, of nations and of men.

Frederick's family, the Berlin Hohenzollerns, had inherited the throne from their Königsberg cousins. They also inherited the pride in Polish royal blood, and learned Polish from generation to generation. Up to the time of Frederick II, the Prussian court aimed at a fusion of its hereditary land with the *Rzeczpospolita*, the Polish commonwealth. The decision fell to Frederick II, and he chose to crush Poland. This meant the 'expulsion of the Polish element' from his own character. The King hated the Polish little people, peasants and petty nobility. German rulers ought to rule over these half-beasts. This hatred corresponded to his contempt for German literature whose dark, ponderous sentimentality he condemned. He also hated pietism and Enthusiasm. Frederick the Great was a perfect example of the way in which neurotic aggressions and activities arise from the experiences of violence in one's past. His father forced him to become a soldier, to marry a woman he did not love and even to order the execution of his best friend. He moulded the character of his son by constantly terrorizing him. Never was the son to lose the memory of this ordeal which instilled in him a tremendous resentment of his own father and

*'Imperceptible' is the *paulatim* and *pedetemptim* of Augustine.

†A receipt acknowledging Prussian bribes made to him has been preserved.

of God the Father.* Frederick's education was the desperate attempt of a fanatical Spiritualist to form a 'new man' by a fundamental alteration of the 'old' one. Although he knew in his heart that it was unhealthy, Frederick did to his realm what his father had done to him.

Frederick's lands had suffered under harsh masters for centuries. Their histories had been stories of uninterrupted violence. The original conquest by the Teutonic Knights had left deep wounds as Treitschke has written: 'the triple pride and arrogance of the Christian, knight and German' in fifty years broke the external resistance of the shepherds, peasants, and Slavs. The clergy was fully subjected to the (secular) Order. It was forbidden to use the Prussian language, and as late as the sixteenth century German was not understood in the villages. The Grand Master of the Order, Luther von Brunschweig, presented the war of the Maccabees to his knights as an example of fearless struggle. During the fourteenth century the court of the Grand Master used to carry out expeditions in the country of the Lithuanians, burning, robbing and hunting the unbelievers 'like a fox on a rabbit-hunt', as a contemporary chronicler reported. The suffering serfs and petty burghers, the proletarian stewards and savants, who could not rise above the position of the clergy, were attracted into sects and revival movements in the eighteenth century. A super-god, a lord of the manor, a salvation-spirit broke the resistance of the wicked and demanded absolute obedience. Frederick's father, the old Dessauer, devised 'the demonic psychology of the Prussian drill': 'The soldier must fear his officer more than death and long for war.'[54] The old Dessauer in effect transferred the prevailing religious and political notion of authority to the army. By this method, the old relationship of an alien ruling class and a subject people was preserved in the Prussian military hierarchy until 1945.[55]

Physical space in the East for Frederick the Great was an area in which to exert rule. It was a field cultivated by military expeditions and a new economics and guarded by fortresses. It was also space for hunting and war, as the natural form of travel in these lands.† The land-hunger of the King was an expression of the metaphysical failure to absorb this space, which was conquered only in gulps. This concept of space was the very opposite of the ancient Western feeling for areas of salvation, places with fixed, traditional borders, marked by holy places, graves and ancient towns. Frederick's concept of education was equally abstract: 'Schools are organizations of the state', as one of his Prussian general state laws read. Frederick educated his nobility, his officials and soldiers to serve the state. The many inner reforms, often applied on a great scale, were 'means to win the war on foreign soil

*Wherever such a father-figure rules, there can no longer be a free relationship between equals nor a chance of love. Frederick's father fulfilled the same function as did Rilke's *Himmelspapa* and *Himmelsmama*, i.e., to destroy any meaningful human relationship.

†The Middle German word *Reise* (travel in High German) meant war in an *Ellend*, an alien land.

through the most intensive promotion of all the material and spiritual forces of the state'.[56]

What was the state? For old Europe from Homer to the age of the baroque it had been the *urbs diis hominibusqua communis*, a co-habitation of gods and men.[57] For Frederick II it was whatever the ego chose to make of all the self-interests of the subjects. Frederick's state could support itself on self-interests alone.[58] This conception of the state as a universal power was one of the greatest events in European history, probably comparable only to the French Revolution and the rise of Marxism. This had nothing, or only very little, to do with Machiavelli, nor was it identical with the enlightened absolutism of the West. The power of the Prussian state had no limits, except those which the royal ego set. The tragedy, the greatness and loneliness of Frederick the Great was a consequence of this. At every hour he knew that the state rested on his reason alone. He tried to keep it from falling into the dark underground, by constantly seeking the company of Cicero, Seneca, Marcus Aurelius, Virgil, and Horace.[59] He welcomed the men of the Englightenment to his court, provided that they were not metaphysicians like Leibniz or Wolff.

Frederick's state refused to recognize metaphysics and history. 'We do not have the capacity' he wrote, 'to go to the core of things.'[60] At the 'core' of things the people, the ontology of old Europe and its history lay in wait to overcome him. He feared the underground and turned away from it. Despite his historical studies, he had no understanding for the essence of history.[61] As a Spiritualist and the King of Prussia, he was compelled to reject the idea of historical obligations. Louis XIV and many politicians of the baroque period loved to confirm their historical rights to foreign lands and territories by documents and historical evidence, but in Frederick's case there was an entirely different spirit. He grabbed at history in proclaiming his rights to Austrian Silesia as he grabbed at space. To him, history was mere matter, just a means for him to gain his ends. Frederick was moved to conquer not for the reasons he chose to admit, not out of love of country nor desire for fame, but out of anxiety. He was anxious about his small, 'unnatural' Prussia, which he feared would be crushed between the old Great Powers; he was anxious about his ability to assert himself. He trusted nothing. He had no confidence in the world around him. His father had beaten him into an artificial man in whom only the restless ego had any reality. His was the ego of the king of alien space, who ruled alien nations and strange men, the *canaille*.

Under the pressure of loneliness he looked for solace and found it for hours in stoicism, in music and in the beloved French intellectual world of the age of Louis XIV. His famous saying to D'Alembert that he would have rather made *Athalie*, Racine's masterpiece, than the Seven Years War, was not a joke. The King sought immortality, but he could no longer believe in the Christian conception of it. Art in the eighteenth century sense was the way to achieve it. Although Frederick knew that war was generally accepted as an art as in Clausewitz's 'theatres of war', he could not ignore how superior the art of poetry was to the art of war. No field marshal, no colonizer, no factory owner could ever shape 'dirty' and reluctant human material like the poets could fashion words, and mould the soul.* Frederick envied the poets, the masters of language.

Frederick's cultivation of the classic French poetry and mastery of language was a reflection of his spiritualism, not a mere expression of taste. Only French poetry could give the awakened spirit the solace of total mastery of matter. The King knew only too well that German was the language of a people who were constantly giving in to matter, while trying to cover up their defeat by sentimental outbursts. It was the language of Luther and pietism. The choice of French and *realpolitik* were parts of the same pattern. The King knew no considerations or qualifications. His was a materialism which knew only power, countries, numbers, army, egoistic drives; and there is great significance in the fact that his first enemy was the old empire itself, Austria.

The authentic dialectic of spiritualism and materialism has rarely been so classically exemplified as it was in the life of Frederick the Great. His desperate spiritualism drove him to force a solution on the impure and recalcitrant world. But at least it was still a royal solution. The King knew that the old order was crumbling. The subject peoples were soon to destroy the royal ego as the directing force and to replace it with popular salvation from below. German idealism strove to prevent this by saving the royal ego and claiming that every genuine spirit was the expression of the royal ego. The German idealists enlisted the help of pietism and the spiritual piety related to it, and in the end succeeded in holding back the energies driving towards a new world structure for all of three generations.

The Enlightenment took a very different form in Johann Christoph Edelmann. The kings of Prussia feared this man who was notorious as the leader of German Deists, freethinkers and followers of Spinoza. In his auto-biography, written in 1752, Edelmann has given us an invaluable portrait of inner Germany during the psychological and intellectual crisis around 1750.[62] Edelmann came from the East (Oberlausitz). Living in wretched circumstances, he studied Lutheran theology, read Arnold, Bayle and Hobbes, and for six years was a steward with a Lutheran noble family in lower Austria. On his journey to Austria he came to a Catholic province, Bamberg, for the first time. A completely alien country was opened to him and he portrayed it as eighteenth-century Englishmen portrayed Indo-China: beggars, gallows, the wealth of Benedictine foundations, a pietist enclave in Vienna, Franciscans, Carthusians, all the pomp and circumstance of the age of the baroque.[63] 'Seeing, tasting and feeling are the three major senses of the Austrian.' To keep himself from being carried away he read Brocke's *Irdisches Vergnügen in Gott*. His own behaviour left a good deal to be desired but Edelmann lacked the courage to admit it. He behaved very badly to a pastor who had lost his position as a Socinian, and concluded as a result that 'in practice there is no

*Stalin called poets 'the engineers of the soul'.

more hateful and hostile religion than Christianity, which talks so much about love'.[63a] In 1735, he became a Moravian and Zinzendorf intended to send him as an emissary to America. By this time, Edelmann, who was still two-thirds a Lutheran, had begun to drift into the world of the sects and pietism. He began to collect eccentric books and soon had a fine library of heretical texts.

After many real and imaginary persecutions Edelmann suddenly had a conversion. As he describes it on page 110 of his *Selbstbiographie*, 'by the grace of God I have finally succeeded ... in trampling Satan completely under-foot as an empty goblin manufactured by papists, and in letting God, my creator, be everything in me'. Edelmann's conversion to Deism had a strong, revivalist tone. It was an entirely different kind of Deism from the enlightened, aristocratic Faith of the English or Dutch. Edelmann knew that he was right because of his 'own feeling'. As a result, Edelmann's Deism drove him more deeply into the underground of the eccentrics, cranks and pietists. He began to wander from place to place, always mixing with the most extreme groups of Enthusiasts, but at the end of five years with these people he was suddenly seized by 'a fear of hell'. He was tortured by uncertainty. Was it God or the devil, who was working in him? His anxiety mounted, until in a blinding flash he had an experience of rebirth: *Theosen ho logos*, the beginning of the Gospel of John, the old gnostic formula, revealed itself to him in a new way: 'God is reason.' Joyfully, he celebrated that night as his birthday. He began to imitate Christ in dress, beard and bearing, but abjured the Bible, 'this terrible idol'. The radical anti-semitism of the lower classes was spread by his attacks on the Bible. He railed against 'Moses with uncovered countenance', 'this infamous Jewish leader', but at the same time he became increasingly anti-Christian. In 1741 he wrote *Christ and Belial* against Zinzendorf: the first Christians were already shabby frauds just as their successors are today. Becoming increasingly radical, he wandered through the underground, this 'other Germany'.[64] He lived with Bohemian sectarians in Hamburg, with starving peasants who looked for grass and wild herbs to eat; he fled from court to court, from pastor's son to pastor's son (these sons of respected pastors often eagerly welcomed him) until he found a haven, in the Berlin of Frederick II. Edelmann was a product of proletarian Germany. Just how twisted and deranged this underground had become could be seen in his atheist faith in salvation and his hatred of parsons and orthodoxies.

No two men could be more different at first glance than Edelmann and Johann Joachim Winckelmann, the man who revealed the 'noble simplicity and quiet greatness' of the antique world to the German bourgeois classicism of the high eighteenth century. But appearances are deceiving. Winckelmann, a cobbler's son from Brandenburg, was every bit as spiritualistic as Edelmann. His attack on the baroque style was the aesthetic counterpart of Edelmann's fulminations against Christianity. Like Edelmann, Winckelmann was a spiritual monist: to him 'noble simplicity and quiet greatness' was identical with the one, the unmoved God, the 'One and All' of Spinoza's vision. But the one was very different from the experience of Edelmann. The 'beauty' of classical bodies was Winckelmann's delight. After 200 years of Lutheran rejection of the eye, Winckelmann re-established it as a sacred organ. His devotion to the antique, like the contemporary exaltation of nature, was the struggle of the spirit to break out of the grip of orthodox repression. Winckelmann sought a new myth and a new sacrament. Feverishly he studied Shaftesbury, Clarendon, Montaigne, Montesquieu, St Evremond and especially the Italian art historiography.*

As a spiritualist Winckelmann hated the baroque. The antique, free virtuous republic was the model he held up to the absolutism of the eighteenth century. His cult of the antique was fired by sexual excitement. In a frenzy of enthusiasm he described in detail the 'ideally beautiful' noses, hands and sexual parts of the Greek statues and admired the union of the loveliest male and female organs in the statues of eunuchs and hermaphrodites. He was aroused by the insertion of 'beautiful' animal parts in the human form, but was absolutely blind to colour and to architecture. Winckelmann was really only interested in the bodies of boys or boyish girls, but he turned his homo-sexuality into a spiritual joy in the 'ideally beautiful'. He believed that he saw a reflection of the divine perfection shining through these naked bodies. He was an orgiastic enthusiast, in flight from the chaos in his breast.

The Jansenist and enlightened Rome of Lambertini and of the *archetto* offered him its protection. His warped, furtive soul became even more twisted and warped in Rome. He became a Catholic against his convictions just to be able to get into the places where he could be near his beloved bodies, and in time became papal curator of Roman antiquities.[65] Winckelmann's passion for antiquity was a flight into a new vision of salvation and new incarnations. The eyes of the Spirit made use of the sexual, fleshly and still sinful eyes in order to see their fantasies. Winckelmann's classicism was an extraordinary combination of neuroses, of serious psychic disturbances and escapist phenomena. It was the first stage of the 'romantic sickness'.[66] This was why it was so fascinating for the generation of the young Goethe. Winckelmann died, a rouged, spectral old man, at the hands of a boy paramour. The aim of his cult of 'classical beauty' was betrayed by his intention to write a book which should show that a Frenchman 'would be incapable of becoming a great artist, an earnest scholar or an honourable man'. Like Hamann and Herder he wanted to escape from the demands of Western reason. The beautiful Greek body was a mask for enthusiastic irrationalism, just as irra-tional as Hamann's primal language and Herder's folk song and folk spirit.[67]

Johann Sebastian Bach also came from the Enthusiasts and noncon-formists. Although his ancestor, Veit Bach, had fled from Hungary as a Lutheran, his maternal ancestors in Erfurt were related by marriage to the Chiliast, Esajas Stiefel. In Bach's library, beside collected editions of Luther,

*The Italian art historians, as we have seen, had turned their works into concealed treasuries of spiritualism. This was particularly true of Vasari.

stood Tauler, Arnd, Francke, Spener and the whole pietistic edification literature, as well as many polemical writings against Catholics, Jews and Calvinists.[68] The course of his life had taken him to old-Lutheran Arnstadt and Weimar, pietist Mühlhausen, Calvinist Köthen and finally to Leipzig where the enlightened Lutheran University opposed him. Bach's great feat was to unite pietism and the mathematical rationalism of the high baroque in his *The Art of the Fugue*, but after 1745 he began to abandon the composition of cantatas and religious works. 'The retreat from the composition of cantatas into the subtle combinations of his contrapuntal meditations was a retreat from the conversations of a believer with God to the monologue of the spirit. In the last five years of Bach's life he expressed his full resignation with respect to his final aim.'[69] Bach went half way towards Frederick II and the Enlightenment when he presented the King with his *Musical Offering*. Bach's religion had become silent, but he continued to compose counterpoint. He was clearly determined not to go the way of the Enthusiasts, nor to dissolve all objectivity in feelings and phantasies. After his death, he was quickly forgotten.

At the end of his life Johann Georg Hamann made the following confession to Jacobi: 'My hatred of Babylon is the true key to my literary activity, my history and the history of my fatherland.' (Babylon, of course, was the rationalistic West.) 'Descartes never found the truth, never loved it nor perceived it …' 'Reason suppresses or destroys everything which really exalts and strengthens us in God.' 'Only the hellish journey of self-exploration can make us divine.' Socrates became Hamann's guide because 'he lured his fellow-citizens out of the labyrinths of their learned sophism to a wisdom which lies in the hidden recesses, to a secret wisdom, to the service of the unknown God.'[70] Socrates, the genius of existence, was Hamann's idol, but it was not the Socrates of the textbooks, but rather a gnostic Socrates of the mysteries. Hamann was hailed as 'Pan' by Jacobi, as 'Faun' by Goethe and called demonic by Herder. He was voraciously and enthusiastically read by Kierkegaard.

Hamann came from Riga. As a young man he became friendly with the merchant Berens who sent him from Riga to London to negotiate trade routes between England and Russia via Riga. He did little for commerce between East and West, but he started other and more dangerous relations between the underground of the West and that of the East. In London, he fell into bad company and, in the period of remorse later, the underground burst out in a genuine revivalist experience. In great detail he compared his impenitent sinful life with the history of Israel, the chosen people. He had a sudden revelation that the God who speaks in the Bible and in all the mysteries, poetry and world literature, was in himself, and wished to assert himself in him. 'All my Christianity is no more than a taste for signs.'* This experience

---

*Hamann's disciples and successors from Herder to Nietzsche imitated this preoccupation with signs. Hamann had in essence created new sacraments after the old ontology and its sacraments had been abandoned.

of revival by itself was not unusual. Its explosiveness lay in the extraordinary amalgam of traditions which Hamann combined. From the underworld of London, he had picked up a good many elements of gnosticism and Cabalism, which he grafted onto the traditional emotional outbursts of pietism and German Enthusiasm.

The historical ego and the revealed God were one, Hamann believed. God realizes himself only in history, which Hamann saw as the succession of individual personalities in time. From the identity of God and the human ego, there were two historical emanations. First, the genius as the God-illuminated individual who creatively speaks the Word of God. Hamann called such a man a *Magus* and regarded him as the poet who sees into the order of things. The second emanation of God in history was the man of action, whose mighty works are the poetry of deeds. As he wrote to Herder in 1781, 'Life is *actio*'. Passion, it followed, was divine, and he saw his own talents as a dark force out of God's depths, beyond good and evil, beyond ethics and reason which he disdainfully called 'a weather-vane'.* Hamann dismissed the 'trading spirit', Western tolerance, which was no more than a fashionable virtue, and Western despotism.

Hamann was the first priest of the night. He began the great sanctification of force and of the chaotic and demonic in man. He deliberately consecrated the darker regions in man and attributed to them the powers both of the poetic seer and the man of action. In reality, it was a self-portrait. Vainly he tried to hide his self-deification in a thousand masquerades: language, poetry, the mysteries of Hellas and the Bible. But none of those things could hide the terrifying reality that Hamann, the ecstatic, had swallowed the transcendent God. Since reason, Western Enlightenment, trade (as toil), tolerance (as consideration for others), and the Jew (as a symbol of intellectual integrity) stood in his way, he shoved them aside. His spirit in its greed for God intoxicated itself and accepted its 'sins' as evidences of salvation. Hamann was infinitely more aggressive than the King of Prussia who at least set certain limits to his land-hunger. Hamann stole more than a hundred Silesians when he snatched at the transcendence of God.

The great lords, the kings, the priests of the old world, were over-trumped by the voice of God from the heart. Hamann proclaimed the end of Western Enlightenment and its reason.†

Herder's *Die Schöpfung* contains the following instructive passage:

> *Die Schöpfung, itzt am Ziel,*
> *Harret, schweiget noch . . .*
> *Sieh den suchet, jetzt am Ziel*

*Luther called reason a 'whore'.

†The effect of the Enlightenment in the East was to produce romanticism and nationalism. This was true not only of Hamann, Herder and German idealism's eastern wing, but also of Catherine the Great, whose political and cultural policies were anti-Roman and strongly hellenist.

Gottes Schöpfung, wirft Gefühl
In sich dess, was sie vermisst,
Und der Mensch – der Gott – er ist!

Ich wie Gott! Da tritt in mich
Plan der Schöpfung, weitet sich,
Drängt zusammen und wird Macht!
Endet froh und jauchzt: vollbracht!
Ich wie Gott! Da tritt in sich
Meine seele und denket mich!
Schafft sich um und handeltfrei,
Fühlt, wie frei Jehovah sei, –
Ich wie Gott! Da schlägt mein Herz
Königsmut und Bruderschmerz!

These lines sum up the entire pathos and grandeur of the poet Herder. If we analyse the ideas in the passage, it is immediately clear that the core is simply a vulgar and barbarized version of Meister Eckhardt's mystical vision with a pietistic and biological fillip. Herder was obviously a disciple of Hamann. As Karl Barth put it: 'Herder had gone through an evolution, from Kant to Hamann, from Leibniz to Spinoza, and in his old age, a clear symptom of the fact that the path he travelled before was a hasty one, a kind of weary involution in the vicinity of the Enlightenment.'[71]

Herder raised the individual experience of self to the decisive organ for understanding life.[72] Now only one thing was at stake: 'life', 'my life', the 'life of my people'. Herder's *Volk* was victoriously preparing to shake off the superstructures of Western forms of authority, reason and humanity. It would forget the 'divine phantom' Christ, as Pufendorf had rejected the Holy Empire as an *immane monstrum*. Herder biologized the God-experience of the Enthusiasts, and worshipped the 'force in individuality'. Even the spirit was for him force, energy, nature. Herder was entirely a man of the East and he belonged to the world of matriarchy and the power of the mothers. Nature and matter took the place of (patriarchal) logic. Logic, ethics, aesthetics, law and moral sciences were now reduced to biologies. Herder turned mankind into an organism and used words like roots, bloom, plants to describe human conditions. The origin of a thing was its being and essence and the seed contained its entire being. Herder debased freedom of mind to a natural necessity. He set the collective in the place of the universal. Mankind was only a biological race or species and society only a group. The state was an abstraction, while the people, living, growing, becoming from below, was real. The moral law was nothing but the natural law, and the positive law was merely violence established by historical tradition.

Herder's political ideas reflected all these attitudes. He hated Frederick the Great, like Hamann, and celebrated the Czars. Peter the Great was a 'true patriot'. Herder's innermost aspiration was to become an awakener of the peoples of the East, a Zwingli, Luther, the Calvin of Livonia. The Ukraine was to become a new Hellas. In conceiving these aims he was forced to transform his entire heritage of Western culture, to which he owed everything. In this sense he was the first transvaluer of all values and Nietzsche only his later follower. What the Enlightenment saw as ignorance, superstition and fanaticism, Herder called 'living drive, moral and healthy nature'.

As Hamann consecrated the dark side of the individual, Herder sanctified the underground of the people. He gave intellectual expression to the forces and aspirations of the subject masses. He proclaimed their hatred of the West and used the heritage of Western ideas to express it. He justified the customs, traditions and language of the people and defended them against rule from above. In doing so, he laid the foundations for an entirely new approach to history and theology, and at the same time turned the individual eruptions of the underground of a Joan of Arc or a Luther into universal laws of intellectual activity. Until Herder the people's language had been the language of the heretic, and the individual had been subordinated to the universal. Herder changed all that and accelerated the process by which the religious enthusiasms of the people became the secular philosophies of today. His justification of the irrational and historical, and his collections of folk-songs were a liberation and an awakening, in a way a kind of romantic enlightenment. But he destroyed as much as he created. He introduced hatreds stored up over the centuries and the raging resentment of the lower class and its sectarian movements into the great debate of the nation and into the national literature.

It is nonsense to praise Herder's sense of history, as so many modern thinkers have done, without accepting what he meant by history. Herder's history, like that of Arnold and the sectarians, was the history of the underground and the few inspired spirits. 'Thus Herder became ... a ruthless tyrant, as soon as history itself seemed ... to offend his view of its nature.'[73] The link between Alfred Rosenberg's *Myth of the Twentieth Century*, the Bible of the Enthusiast movement from 1918 to 1933, was no more than a rehash of Herder's invectives against Christianity, the West and democracy. Rosenberg merely aped Herder's paroxysms of rage and hate. Herder vilified the papacy as one of the most hideous phenomena in human history and the ancient Roman Empire as a machine which had destroyed a once colourful world. He thundered against the modern art of government, free thought, cosmopolitanism, philanthropy and the system of the European balance of power. He was perfectly consistent in his polemic against Christianity and Enlightenment, Western *ratio* and its theory of being. Herder rejected all absolute values and accepted only relative historical ethics and standards of value. With such principles, there was nothing left of Western civilization.

Herder's nationalism was a myth in the same sense in which Rosenberg used the word. Only a man strongly influenced by the Enlightenment could have conceived of such an invention. The Nation was an ideology or deception, which Herder 'made' to tie together a bundle of feelings, to awaken experiences, and to set the people in motion. Herder was a plebeian Enlightener and his romanticism was a vulgar compound of the Enthusiastic tradition and the ideas of the Enlightenment twisted out of their context. By finding and discovering new myths, and glorifying folk-poetry, as 'the voice of nature', he exposed the myths of the old world: humanism and monks' Latin which poisoned the mind of the nation. 'One must read the Bible in human terms since it is a book written by men, for men.[74] The Bible was a product of the folk-spirit of the Hebrews, and theology the history of national poetry. The 'Germanists' of the nineteenth and twentieth centuries, in Herder's wake, proclaimed German literature as the history of salvation through the German 'Word and Being'. They too came mostly from the East or from the pietist and spiritualist underground. Germanistics and history became the sciences of salvation. Their enthusiasm calmed down and turned into a science when they grew older and were given state jobs. Again they followed the example of superintendent Herder in Weimar. As soon as the mentality calmed down, a flat, vulgar and materialistic, enlightened fundament emerged into the light of day. Spiritualism and materialism are only two sides of the same coin.

Kant was never taken in by Hamann or Herder. In a letter to Jacobi, he wrote about Herder: 'In general at the bottom of every syncretism there is a lack of honesty, a spiritual characteristic which is especially applicable to this great and artistic juggler.'[75] It is vital to remember that Kant came from the same background as his enemies. His family were manual workers, and his ancestors had been inn-keepers, harness-makers, saddlers of pietist leanings in the East. Kant was physically a cripple like Kierkegaard. He lived in Köningsberg, and his character was deeply stamped by pietism. All his life he lived on his island of reason and fought the enthusiasts and prophets. Although his own mentality was not lacking in ecstatic and enthusiastic features, he managed to become the great reconciler. He brought the authentic resentments of the Eastern underground into contact with the authentic interest of the West, of the Enlightenment and its political humanism.[76] He took the existential question of Luther and of old pietism with a fundamental seriousness. 'The moral self-knowledge which attempts to penetrate the impenetrable depths of the heart is the beginning of all human wisdom.'[77] Ask 'your heart whether it is good or evil ...' Man must think of himself as a twofold personality, as accused and as judge. The investigation of conscience of the old pietists – how does my soul stand with God? – became for Kant the question: how far may I trust my reason, my feeling and my faith?[78] Understanding of the spiritual capacity of man grew out of the examination of the selfish heart, inclined at all times to Enthusiasm, obscurities, extravagances.

Kant's aim was *l'amour pur*, the pure love of God, which expects no reward. His conception of it transcended the feeble ideas of Madame Guyon and the sentimentalists and returned to the monumental form of Theresa of Avila. It was pure love directed toward the moral law: 'Duty! O, sublime and mighty name! You have no charms nor flattery and yet you make us submit ourselves to you. You do not threaten. You merely set up a law which by its own power finds a way into the soul.' Kant taught that the moral law demands piety and immortality. How could man meet such demands in a world so filled with a thousand temptations, deceptions and evils? Kant preached, and Herder, Goethe and Schiller listened dumbfounded as he presented to them the actuality of evil, genuine evil, hostile to and destructive of man. They had been accustomed to see evil as a side of divinity, a trick of the world-spirit, a component of the immanent world process fostering evolution like measles, puberty or revolutions. Kant called upon man to take up the struggle against evil and to hope that they would survive the struggle against their own undergrounds.

Kant understood the lower spheres of mere sensual feelings of pleasure and aversion and the lower faculties of desire because of his familiarity with the Enthusiast underground. He knew how the lower classes resisted self-control and ennoblement and clung to superstitions and fantastic contrivances. As Karl Barth has observed, the Catholic doctrine of grace and an optimism founded in activity lie at the base of Kant's system.[79] It was the open rationalism of St Thomas which Kant revived. Like St Thomas, Kant neatly separated what belongs to reason from what belongs to faith. He shared the Thomist ontological optimism and turned against the vulgar, spiritualistic maxim that something may be right in theory but does not hold in practice. Kant wrote: 'What on the grounds of reason is valid in theory, is also valid in practice.'[80] The cosmos was accordingly a place in which man uses his practical reason to do his duty. He must confine himself to what he can conceive. He can only revere the divine and those things which he cannot grasp. It is understandable that the Benedictines should have felt drawn to Kant. He translated their striving for measure, discretion and disciplined order into the language of science. Bavarian Benedictine foundations sent their talented novices to Kant. But Kant's harmony and scholasticism were the fruits of a life-long struggle to restrain and bind the pietistic irrationalism in his own breast.

Kant dedicated his *Allgemeine Naturgeschichte und Theorie des Himmels* to Frederick II, and called his century, 'the century of Frederick'. This affirmation sprang from a sense of political realities unique in Germany in his time. Although Kant knew that the absolutist, enlightened, welfare state was 'the greatest conceivable despotism', he continued to support it because he felt that its evils could be corrected by criticism. Kant's approach to the Frederician state was positive. He resisted its attempt to make men into machines, but he offered an alternative which would enhance the dignity of men. He struggled to protect the human personality which was the secular version of the pietistic soul. Kant's definition of the Enlightenment was eminently political in a Western sense: 'Enlightenment is man's release from his self-incurred tutelage. Tutelage is man's inability to make use of his understanding without direction from others. This tutelage is self-incurred when it lies not in lack of reason but in lack of resolution and courage to use it without direction from another. *Sapere aude*! The motto of the Enlightenment is to have the courage to use your own reason!'

The victory of reason was by no means certain, and Kant saw the possibility of rejection. A man must believe in Providence and his own moral force, because otherwise he falls into despair, the abyss of perdition. Kant constantly skirted the nihilism which lurked in the East, in its endless space, and in himself. It was this attitude which united him with Frederick the Great. The entire burden of responsibility is placed on man, who can never know what is under and above him. Kant grasped the historical situation of Frederick's Enlightenment and in the *Critique of Pure Reason* wrote: 'The country of pure understanding looks like an island that lies in the ocean of illusions, dreams of power, adventures. This sea is the abyss of perdition and destruction but also the ocean of freedom and of the infinite. The soul sets out upon it although the understanding is confined on the island of the measurable.' Kant felt an enormous temptation to lose himself in that sea. As a Copernicus in reverse he had transferred all the possibilities of knowledge from the objective world to the subjective. The ego swallowed the Platonic ideas, and built its cosmos by itself in its representations. As a result, it seemingly knew nothing about the 'thing in itself'. Kant avoided this dilemma by identifying the ego with the world around it and in so doing followed the tradition of Eckhardt, Nicholas of Cusa and Leibniz. In the historical context of that epoch this was the favourite doctrine of the Enthusiasts: to give up everything in the outer world, in order to find everything in oneself.[81] Pietism and spiritualism, carried out to its logical conclusion, ended in a gigantic monism. Kant spoke of the 'God in oneself', as the authentic expounder of all revelations: 'we understand nobody else but Him, who converses with us through our own reason'. 'I, the subject make myself into the object. The subject constitutes itself as a universe.'[82] Man has a tendency to 'absolute totality', of the *totum ... unicum*, that 'grasps one and all in itself'. Repeatedly Kant referred to the tremendous idea of contemplating all things and oneself in God.[83]

There is an interesting parallel between the later interpretations of Kant's metaphysics and the development of Thomism. Both philosophies (indeed all great syntheses) can be twisted into a Neoplatonic, materialist or spiritualist total system. If the sociological premises of Kantian or Thomist thought are ignored, and if the existential tension within the personalities of both Kant and Thomas which binds the systems together is surrendered, there remain little more to these two syntheses than their claims to total validity. Kant believed in the rationality of the West. He tried desperately to establish it and to bring it into a creative and harmonious union with the irrational underground of the East. Pure reason was, he believed, the tool with which he could purify the impetuous demands for salvation of the people. He wanted to elevate such demands to the level of 'practical reason', which orders the activities of man in the society of all nations. His life-work was the only great attempt to establish peace in the German world between East and West and between a humanist, Christian upper stratum and a spiritualist, materialistic, lower stratum. Kant tried to unite the two nations which everywhere in

Europe were girding themselves for a new dispute. He could not finish his work, and suffered, he said, a 'tantalizing pain, which, however, was not hopeless ...'[84] Kant endured being a Tantalus. Those who came after him could not. They wanted to mix the fire from above with the waters from below; they wanted to be Prometheus, who stole the spirit of the Gods and Faust who drew strength from the 'Mothers' to change the face of the earth. They wanted to bear salvation to the people and to breed the new man.

Around 1750 a subterranean tremor went through Germany. A peculiar sense of impending doom gripped men's minds. The first waves of pietism had ebbed and men sensed the decay of Christianity, the emptiness of the ortho-doxies and universities and the failure of the Reformation in an especially strong way. Few succeeded in uniting pietism, Enthusiasm and Enlightenment so harmoniously as Goethe's great-uncle, Michael von Loën (1694–1776). He was a man of the world, a theologian and statesman and enormously versatile in his interests. He was an early version of Goethe. Loën who descended from Dutch burghers, combined enjoyment of the world with flight into solitude, Fénelon with Tolland and Tindal. His major work *Die einzig wahre religion* caused a furore which was not surpassed even by the public disputes over Lessing, Fichte, Ritschl, etc. In this 'true religion' there was only talk of heart, love and simplicity. The 'whole doctrine of Jesus' was nothing but 'pure love'. 'An intoxication of feeling' (Goethe's 'feeling is all') overflowed its bounds. Loën, a German Shaftesbury, identified the 'true, good and beautiful', and melted down religion, ethics and art into a nutriment of the sensitive heart. It was the philosophy of a great bourgeois gentleman.

It was not so easy for other pietists and sentimentalists. They clashed with the social and political realities, and in this conflict the heart revolted and became revolutionary. The Frankfurt pietist Johann Jakob Moser and his son Frederich Karl von Moser, opened the criticism of absolutism,[85] and went to prison for their ideal, 'the Christian as politician'. The elder Moser, the political scientist, had spoken against the enslavement of peasants in the German eastern areas, in Bohemia, Moravia, Lusatia, Pomerania, Mecklen-burg, Prussia: 'Often they are not as well off as cattle elsewhere.'[86] Pietists and other religious nonconformists, the 'educated proletariat' and a jobless lower clergy, were becoming the political spokesmen of the lower class. As early as 1685 worried people had demanded that the authorities take steps against the pamphlets of such people, 'restless doctors, professors and preachers'. From the sixteenth century on clerics had joined the many groups and fraternal societies which became highly organized by the eighteenth century.[87] Long before Schiller's *Die Räuber*, literature had described these groups and broad-cast their social protest. Their hatred of the Church was widely known. Leibniz had noticed the spread of Socinianism among the peasants, who in the eighteenth century were often condemned for their lack of faith and fondness for reading forbidden writings. In 1792 Perthes wrote from Leipzig: 'It is true that the lower classes and the savants rave against the despots and aristocrats.' Not all princes could follow Frederick II's recipe, to stick 'restless savants' in the army. Inflammable material piled up everywhere. The complaints of bad administration, the corruption of officials and the exploitation of the peasants became increasingly vehement in the second half of the eighteenth century.

The circumstances of the petty officials and the public school teachers, who received no pension but who still in the early nineteenth century had to perform socage like the peasants, were growing more desperate. The number of starving writers, dismissed preachers and professors rose during the 1770's. Karl Frederick Bahrdt, professor in Giessen, ended as a pimp. The mounting hostility of the bourgeoisie burst out in attacks on the 'aristocratic rabble' and on the 'parsons and despots'. All this began slowly to rise to the surface and to draw attention. Even in old conservative Bavaria, where the monasteries and principalities lived under the customs and law of old Europe, unrest became obvious.

The world was hard, and the pietists' reaction to it took many different forms. A significant man in this reaction was Heinrich Jung-Stilling, who died in 1817. He has given us a superb account of his childhood and pietistic upbringing. The child Heinrich was brought up on Gottfried Arnold and Reitz's *History of the Reborn*. His grandfather, a charcoal burner, enlightened the young tailor on the nobility of their forefathers who were all simple, plain people: 'In that world (in Heaven) we are of great nobility. Don't ever lose this privilege!' The child grew up in a deeply pious atmosphere. It had a solidity peculiar to old-Protestant pietism. They read Luther, Calvin, Bucer, Okolampad and the pietists in their wretched huts, but they continued to revere the magic and archaic world of the old 'folk'. Heaven and earth were united. Fairy tales and the Bible made equally strong impressions. The grandfather often saw visions in the woods, and predicted the day of his own death. The birth of German mentality, of German inwardness, from very old and new elements of an inner piety, found its magnificent expression in Jung-Stilling's autobiography.

The pietistic experience was filtered through the prism of another milieu and temperament in Karl Philipp Moritz.[88] The exaggerated pietism in his parental home overburdened the child's soul with strict pious exercises. This reaction took a worldly, anti-Christian and finally pantheistic form in Moritz. In his autobiographical *Anton Reiser, a psychological novel*, which we have already mentioned, and then in the *Hartknopf* (Hard Button) Moritz took the position of a modern psychologist and consciously affirmed the religious break in his own development. The force of the religious experience in his youth was so strong that the experience became for him the only course of legitimacy. It was a question of the authenticity of existence, to which truth was subordinated. The self had to resist the façade of conventions.* Analytic observation of

*Nietzsche, Gide and even Goethe had similar experiences.

one's own state became a kind of constant confession without absolution and developed into a substitute for the substance of faith.

For Jung-Stilling reason was the voice of the heart, for Moritz the psychological self-presentation of the ego, for Goethe the voice of nature, and for Möser the voice of history. Justus Möser was the first great European reactionary and the patriarch of Osnabrück. He was successively *syndicus* of the 'knightly order', *Advocatus patriae*, and finally Prime Minister of the ecclesiastical principality of Osnabrück. The city was ruled by a prince-bishop, who alternately was Protestant or Catholic. The old Empire was still alive there. As its representatives said, history ruled and not reason. Möser was the great advocate and thinker of historical growth and organic reality. He fought for the rights of his knights and lords of the manor against the equalizing and levelling French reason and democracy. Like so many romantic defenders of the ancestral Faith, Möser was personally an unbelieving cynic but he was convinced of the utility of myths. Möser hated the Christian view of man and all doctrines with generally valid ethical principles, because he saw them as precursors of democracy. His ideal was the *condottiere*, the man of passion and action, the political genius with a demonic twist. In his view politics was the clever direction of feelings and emotions. He presented his theory of the political usefulness of the myth for the first time in his *Schreiben an dem Herrn Vicar in Savoyen*. Positive religions were useful, indeed indispensable frauds. Möser was against tolerance. The nature of every religion required that there be no salvation outside it. 'It must, to preserve its power, exclude all others.' He fought bitterly against the Enlightenment's faith in peace, reason, equality and humanity. Man was a beast, he argued, who should be left to lie tied to the chain of his power of imagination. 'These human beasts' needed superstitions. Möser was in favour of slavery, torture, stoning and smallpox. Only as many children as could be fed would be permitted to live. He glorified plagues which decimated the people. The people who did not belong to landowners and guilds were *canaille*. The harshest punishments, serfdom and slavery would hold this people in check.

The slave was a man without stock, because bourgeois society was like a corporation. Every citizen was the owner of a share of stock. Freedom should be granted to property owners but never to the 'non-entities of a nation', the 'rabble'. The ecclesiastical and secular nobility and the men of property among the bourgeoisie were the only citizens worthy of the name and Möser defended their *libertas privatorum* in the name of 'German freedom'. 'A Saxon is guided by honour and a Christian by love.' Christianity had been responsible for making all men equal.* The history of Germany was a rebellion against and a betrayal of its own traditional greatness. Since the *minnesingers*, Germany had dedicated itself to an imitation of an alien spiritual product. Möser's *Osnabrückische Geschichte* hurled violent accusations at Charlemagne, the

---

*Another cry of the Nazi mythology.

destroyer of Saxon freedom and the old German emperors who did too little to foster the growth of the cities.

Möser was ironically a disciple of the Enlightenment which he fought. He considered the style of an epoch in the terms which Italian and French rationalism and political experience had taught him. Like Herder, he used the techniques of the civilization which he despised to defend his views against it. When he conceived of the nation as an historical body, he based himself on Sarpi, Grotius, Dubos, Boulainvilliers and Montesquieu.[89] Möser was a demonic genius, and his Harlequin, or *A Defence of the Grotesque and Comic*, was a hymn to fantasy, to dance, laughter and joy, which reminds us of Nietzsche. There were chaotic depths in the patriarch.

Möser defended a declining world, the cosmos of old Europe with its manifold estates, societies, customs, wisdoms and passions, which he saw levelled and annihilated by France. A new age of the machine, democracy and condemnation had begun. In the humanity of the Enlightenment he saw only a fashion, which it often was in the German circles which paid it homage. He set his 'historical logic' against the reason of the Enlightenment, and for him history became an ethical sanction. The despair of the great reactionaries lurked behind his thinking. Möser believed in only one possibility in view of the oncoming chaos. The rule of a small group of nobles, landed gentry and propertied city men must be maintained at all costs. To him culture was conditioned by the political rule of this group and reflected the manifestations of its freedoms and rights.

Goethe's political position was very close to Möser's.[90] As a citizen of old Europe's noble and bourgeois world order, he found nothing good in the people's movements and risings of the late eighteenth and early nineteenth century.* This fact was an expression of a congenital egoism. This was how Ch. F. L. Schultz remembered him after a visit. 'Goethe's standpoint was entirely one-sided. He played the part of the peaceful proprietor who hated to be disturbed in the cosy enjoyment of his possessions and of the existing peace and order.' But there was more to his conservatism than comfort. All his life Goethe realized that he was encircled by Enthusiasts, by men who wanted to raise salvation up from the people and the underground. He was the friend of many of them, and the early romantics based themselves on him. He was always strongly attracted to romanticism, and his greatest poems reflected this. This extraordinary brilliance was itself a kind of fulfilment of romantic ideals. The magnificent church hymn *Veni creator spiritus* was wholly and peculiarly a call to genius. For this reason it also appealed powerfully to men of brilliant intellect. The genius created a divine service of the age from the liturgy of old Europe. Goethe's concept of genius stemmed from Diderot.[91] He summoned

---

*It is entirely impossible within the confines of such a broad study to do more than hint at certain themes in treating a personality of such elusive complexity. Like Kant, Goethe was both creative and destructive. Slowly, a re-evaluation of Goethe's heritage in modern Germany has begun to evolve, but only the beginnings are visible. See Note 90 for the literature.

the *ratio* of the Enlightened French, the classic form of ancient Rome and the objectivity of the natural law to oppose the German, Enthusiast underground.

The imperial city of Frankfurt-am-Main had always been a centre of pietists, enthusiasts and spiritualists of all kinds and Goethe was imbued with pietism and enthusiasm all his life. 'I surrendered myself fully to the Halle conversion system.' His *Bekenntnisse einer schönen Seele* in *Wilhelm Meister's Apprenticeship* reflect the strength of these early influences. Gottfried Arnold was Goethe's great teacher: 'The whole of church history is a mish-mash of error and violence.' The external kingdoms belonged to the devil, or at best were masquerades. Strength lies only in nature and in the inner kingdom, the spiritual Church of the educated in heart and mind, in art and science. 'Prophets to the right, prophets to the left, the world-child in the middle', was the way he described his journey with Lavater and Jacobi, but it could well stand as a summary of his whole situation. The prophets influenced this 'world-child' deeply and were ultimately responsible for his decisive rejection of the 'external' empire.

At the coronation of the Holy Roman Emperor in 1764, Goethe met Lavater, the head of southwestern German spiritualism, who had come to Frankfurt for the occasion, 'although such worldly formalities did not have the least value for him'. Nevertheless, the procession of the Mainz electors made such an impression on Lavater that several years later, in a 'poetic paraphrase', he imitated it in the procession of the Antichrist in the Johannine Revelation, 'in such a way that even the tassels on the heads of the cream-coloured horses were not missing'. Along with the young Goethe, he attentively observed the coronation on 3 April 1764: 'how the Emperor, (Francis I) in romantic garments', 'his son in Spanish dress' (Joseph II) marched in parade. The Emperor walked 'quite comfortably' in his heavy suit of clothes. 'The young king, however, dragged himself in the enormous garments with the royal insignia of Charlemagne as in a masquerade so that, upon watching his father from time to time, he could not help smiling.'[92] In his account of this day in *Dichtung und Wahrheit*, Goethe tells us that he was reminded of an incident in the previous coronation of Francis I, watched by his wife Maria Theresa. 'When her consort returned from the cathedral in his unusual dress he showed himself to her, so to speak, as the ghost of Charlemagne. Gaily, he raised both hands and displayed to her the imperial orb, the sceptre and the miraculous glove. This made her break into endless laughter ...' Emperor, Empress and poet no longer believed in the Sacraments of the old Carolingian cosmos, from which, according to their estate, they drew different conclusions.

Goethe saw how the confessions and sacraments of old Europe lay in the dust in Germany, deprived of power. 'At the time when there were still kings, there were also still Gods.' This time was over and Goethe avoided glossing over the situation. He saw through the contemporary masquerade in which homage was paid to values and virtues which were neither believed in nor lived. 'If one wants to know the dishonesty of the Germans in all its magnitude, one must make oneself familiar with German literature', he wrote to Schopenhauer in 1814. He was equally against the creation of new Gods from the underground of the people. His position could only be one of voluntary solitude. There, he anxiously strove to keep open a few themes for conversations which the fanatics and Enthusiasts of the coming epoch would surely cut off. Goethe had spent his life in conversation. 'What would have become of me then, had I not always been compelled to have respect for others.'[93] He glorified Kant as *un principe d'humanité et de tolérance*, and praised him for the 'immortal service' of 'having brought us back from that softness into which we were sunk' and for having renewed morality. He proclaimed his adherence to the three reverences of man, the heavenly, the earthly, and the human.[94] 'Man is the first conversation that nature holds with God.' Goethe knew that reverence and its three orders could be maintained only if men kept their distance. The moment they came near, reverence collapsed into fear and greed and man would destroy himself. We should not 'disturb primal phenomena through vain experiments' but instead 'give them over to reason and faith' for meditation. Goethe was, for example, opposed to measurements made on the living body of man. The body has its own inner measure in itself, and is not to be measured with alien standards. He foresaw that this reverence would be destroyed by the common vulgarity in the age that was drawing near.

Goethe saw this demonic commonness in the lower classes and recognized that it would lead to the seizure of power from below. Since he could not believe in education for the people, he rejected Pestalozzi. These modern educators, he wrote, 'with their lunacy and mania for reducing everything to the single individual, for making themselves into little gods of independence, want to educate the people and expect to be able to resist the raving horde once it has mastered the elementary techniques of knowledge, which mastery now has been made infinitely easier through Pestalozzi.' On 30 March 1819 in a state of deep pessimism over the murder of Kotzebue, he said to von Müller, 'One must now live from day to day. No one can handle the affairs of the world any more.' After a serious illness he wrote to Müller on 24 February 1823: 'Such masses of contagious matter have been plaguing me for three thousand years.' Goethe knew that he embodied all of old Europe in himself – and thus its sicknesses, problems, its fractures, and unresolved contradictions. As reported by Dorothea Schlegel, he once said to a traveller that 'he was an atheist in natural science and philosophy, a pagan in art and emotionally a Christian'. In old Europe's noble society these connections could coexist, and in his *Faust* he tried once more to unite them. In the play, Europe, its metaphysics, philosophy, magic and natural science were resurrected and combined for the last time, but it was merely a stage-setting, a masquerade. The great sacraments of old Europe, its ecclesiastical and imperial liturgy, were now only playthings. Night, the underground of the people and the demonic also appeared in *Faust*, but their roles were different. This was not because Goethe took these forces lightly, but because he took them so seriously that he only dared to conjure them up in a play.

In the end, poetry too failed. The great consoler of his life was unable to comfort him. Only nature and natural science remained. In its service man achieved alienation, objectivity in the conscious surrender of all self-will, arbitrariness, selfishness.[95] 'Only rational empiricism can penetrate to the pure phenomenon which in my judgment is one with the objective law of nature.' In nature even the common is meaningful, because it is linked to and resolved in a dialectical process. 'Since all things in nature, especially the commoner forces and elements, are in an eternal action and counter-action, one can therefore say of every phenomenon that it is in connection with count-less others, just as we say of a free-floating point of light that it emits its rays on all sides.'[96] Goethe was unable to believe in a dialectical development in the history of man and especially of his time. It was no accident that he turned to the power which appeared as the last guarantor of Europe, Austria. He loved the company of Austrian aristocrats. He loved Austrian Karlsbad. His son died in Rome and a part of his family later went to Vienna. Enchanted he related of the Empress: 'She spoke about Montesquieu and other writers as though she had read them yesterday.' With deep concern, he saw Austria's future endangered. Hungarians were ruining the monarchy by their backward-ness and obstinacy, but he hoped 'that times may come nevertheless, when, as under Emperor Joseph, what is useful for the country will be forced upon it.'

This chapter would not be complete without a discussion of Austria, the counterweight to Germany. The difference between the two areas is, perhaps, better illustrated for the purposes of intellectual history in the problem of Protestantism than in the political struggles. The problem of Protestantism first became acute in Austria in the nineteenth century, after Jansenism and ecclesiastical Enlightenment had made Austrian Catholics as Protestant as the educated Catholics in Germany. Before that time it scarcely affected the fabric of life and this was the origin of the startling difference between Austria and Germany in the eighteenth century. Official Austria, as the bearer and heir of the medieval empire, flatly refused to accept the first and most important consequence of the great struggle over the empire and the Church: the cleavage of the cosmos between God and the world; between a heavenly and an earthly power, between the two realms: nature as a terrible *dira necessitas* and grace. Austria clung to the old theology, ontology and imperial philosophy during the great struggle. Therefore in Catholic Austria there was no area which had been suppressed or excluded from the possibilities of ex-pression. The kingdom of nature was not an object of romantic enthusiasm because it had never been damned and desanctified. There was no indepen-dent realm of an *ecclesia spiritualis* and therefore no Austrian philosophy. There was no empire of art and hence no aesthetic criteria as cosmic legislation. There was no realm of feeling and hence no elegant sentimentality. Austria remained far from the struggles of idealistic philosophy, as well as of romanticism.

Emperor, Empire and Church somehow still remained natural data, against which one rebelled and muttered in good medieval fashion. On Maundy-Thursday the Emperor, as an *Imitatio Christi* washed the feet of twelve poor men, and the Church preserved its prayer for the Emperor in its Good Friday services until the late nineteenth century. The sky was always blue and the weather beautiful on the Emperor's birthday. The old Cosmocrator was the mirror and bearer of cosmic harmony, as it had been in Carolingian times. The preservation of the magical sphere was part of the unity of the sacramental world and the mystique of the state. The Merseburg magical formulas in their ninth century form were used in southern Austria up to the 1930's. Pagan cults and customs lived alongside rich ecclesiastical Benedictine institutions. The great unification of the ontological, sacramental, and magical elements (which were not identical, but related) sheltered the country against the tense dualisms of Germany. A patriarchal social order went along with them. The noble lords, as fathers of their house (the biggest house was the *Erzhaus*, the *Casa d'Austria, la Maison d'Autriche*) were 'gracious lords' and 'gracious ladies'. They lived as masters with their underlings, but their relationship to their subjects was a link which bound the masters as much as the servants.[97]

During those years which had seen the establishment of the English and Dutch East India Companies (1600 or 1602), the Bank of Amsterdam and the Hamburg Girobank (1609 or 1619), the empire hoarded coins and buried its treasure as in the eighth and ninth centuries.[98] Primitive peasant and artisan handicraft economies prevailed at the turn of the eighteenth century. The country was bled white by the Turkish wars, but it had not only been the fault of the Turks. In the sixteenth and seventeenth centuries the Counter-Reformation and the principalities had expelled, annihilated or driven the Protestants underground, from which they emerged only in the late eighteenth century to form a religious and later a political resistance into the middle of the twentieth century. Austria had been a centre of Anabaptists. Enthusiasts and nonconformists had left their traces behind while passing through Austria from the south to the east (from Italy to Poland) and from the west to the southeast (from the Rhineland and Swabia to Transylvania and Russia). Austria had its own underground. It had its religious and political structure, its suffering masses, spiritual misery and oppression of the people just as Germany had. At the same time the old nobility had been decimated by the Thirty Years War and many aristocrats who became Protestants had been forced to flee. The Hapsburg court and the new nobility came from Italy and from the West, from all the countries of old Catholic Europe. The victory of the Counter-Reformation and of the *Erzhaus* over the underground gave rise to a fourfold reaction, which clearly contrasted with the phenomena of Germany's intellectual history: Austrian historiography, baroque architecture, the Viennese popular theatre and Austrian music.[99]

The historiography of the baroque (1620 to 1740) clung to the old theory of the four world empire.[100] The Hapsburg Emperor was the sun in the historical cosmos (*Sol Austriacus*, 1698 by Amadé of Amaden) and the head of the *republica litteraria*, He was also the heir and successor of Charlemagne and was glorified in numerous works with all those titles and attributes with which the medieval model princes from Eusebius to Erasmus had been carefully anointed.

The victory arches which embraced Heaven and earth, temporal history and eternity stretched uninterruptedly from Adam via Alexander the Great, Caesar, Charlemagne, to the present Emperor and thence to the Last Judgment. The anonymous author of the *Leben und Thatem Caroli des Sechsten* (1712) wished a happy life to the imperial house 'until the complete dissolution of this great world-structure'. Under the sacramental administration of the Emperor, the Empire flowered into that unity of spirit, power and knowledge, he wrote, which had been the goal of the savants of the Roman-Greek antique world. 'Time has placed that very praiseworthy desire on our revered, dear German fatherland, together with the highest honour of the imperial dignity, which is that Germany should not only radiate with the flame of so great a dignity, but also with the light of many sciences and understanding and become the centre in which all the lives of the arts, skills and knowledge from other countries be drawn together. Therefore let dignity and wisdom dwell peacefully and prosperously together in one kingdom, and help to distinguish a legal and not tyrannical power from its opposite. In the former, science is a citizen, whereas in the latter it is considered a bandit and outlaw.'

Leibniz came to Vienna in the hope of a fulfilment of these promises. 'In the imperial city of Vienna, Leibniz saw the ideal centre of his efforts to unite the churches, sciences and nations.'[101] He lived there from 1712 to 1714, but all his plans failed, among others one for an Academy of the Sciences. In Austria things were constructed differently, because the historical development was different. Vienna was not a spiritual empire, but an earthly, Heavenly 'world structure'. Klosterneuberg was built to surpass the Escorial and Schönbrunn Versailles. The Karlskirche in Vienna was meant to represent eternal Rome in its union of the ancient temple, the Roman triumphal pillars and the house of God.[102] Only men who believed in space as the vessel of the divine and who possessed a closed ontology could build in this fashion. The Austrian baroque was an attempt at a restoration of the Holy Empire. It was the union of different peoples under the protection of the one emperor, and the union of the arts and sciences under the programmatic leadership of the imperial reason. Finally, the Austrian baroque celebrated the victory of the one Faith over unbelief and heresy. All three themes were startlingly interwoven. There was an effervescence and outburst of passion, and even today one can still sense them rising in a hymn of deification of the Emperor, of the Empire, of culture, of the arts and sciences, and of the Faith. This was a dangerous venture: 'Spiritual' was equated to worldly, art to science, reason to Faith, Church to empire and Europe to Christianity. All together they made up Austria.

This unprecedented marriage of the earthly and Heavenly empire, of religion and politics, of Church and state, of spirit and flesh, of reason and Faith, was rooted in a unique historical situation. The victory over the Turks (1683 to 1699) was at the same time a victory over the French and Protestants. It signalled the triumph of the Jesuit programme and the Benedictine union of God and the world, of the Spanish world theatre and of Italian opera. The new great Austrian architecture had overcome France and Italy, and the imperial ideology had renounced the spiritualist communities in Germany. The baroque renovation of the Benedictine monasteries St Florian, Göttweig, Kremsmünster and Melk, aimed to restore the old Carolingian-Ottonian unity of empire and the Kingdom of God. As centres for the education and disciplining of the nobility and work-shops of the arts, they united 'classical' education, science and clerical, religious culture. The baroque Austrian foundations strove for unity. Church, monastery, imperial hall, library, art-collections and natural history collections constituted an indivisible unity. The majestic halls and sumptuous staircases were visible coats-of-arms. In a fresco in Göttweig the emperor is enthroned in heaven as a sun-god, surrounded by the allegories of the arts and sciences. These monasteries were at the same time imperial palaces. The foundation was a castle. In the original architectural plans for Klosterneuberg, the imperial throne was set up on the middle pavilion, the Spanish crown and the hat of the Austrian archduke on the side pavilion. On the central fresco of the Vienna palace library, Charles II is enthroned as a ruler over Heaven and earth, as a Roman emperor, as Hercules, and as arbiter of war and peace. The choir of the virtues, the arts and sciences, stand around him in hymnal chorus. They represent the 'School of Athens', the symbolic glorification of Vienna as the world centre of culture. At the outer edges of the luminous sphere, the 'vices' – Turks and Protestant preachers – plunge wildly into the depths. The insignia of the Greek empire float beside those of the imperial house. A Greek burgomaster's costume records the title to Constantinople. The two-headed eagle of the Hapsburgs fuses with the two-headed eagle of Byzantium, and includes the eagle of Rome, and of Dante's Church in Paradise.

Schönbrunn was designed to celebrate the victory over the greatest European foe. Not Louis XIV, but the Hapsburg emperor is the real sun-king around whose couch of splendour nature (park), art (theatre), society (tournaments) execute a courtly dance. The court historians and genealogical mystics sought to document these enormous claims. Their assertions were meant to be statements about the nature of existence, but the world of European spiritualism soon regarded them as an evil façade. The staggering ostentatiousness of their historical writing was a serious attempt to give the emperor the capacity to effect human salvation, The doubtful quality of such an undertaking was apparent even to the writers themselves. Hans Jakob

Wagner of Wagenfels, Joseph II's historian, in his *Ehrenruff Teutschlands, der Deutschen und ihres Reiches* (Vienna 1691) permitted himself the awkward question 'What makes a real emperor, the title or the country?' His answer was blunt: 'Only the power of the country. He who calls himself emperor on the stage must also be one in reality.'[103] But if he surpasses others in power among men 'he can be all that he wants to be, and can attribute to himself all the titles that he pleases'. At this point the baroque cancelled itself out. The influence of the inherent dualism of Jansenism was becoming more visible.

The great Austrian baroque monasteries were centres of clerical Enlightenment. Here began that interest in natural science on the part of monks and superiors, of monasteries which in the nineteenth century reached its high point with Gregor Mendel's discovery of the laws of heredity. But history always came before the concern with nature: it was an Erasmian, humanist concern. The challenge of Protestantism was to be met by a return to the Church Fathers and by the historical publications of the brothers Bernhard and Hieronymus Pez, Gottfried Bessel and their pupils. This great affirmation of the historical past of old Europe was the exact opposite of the denial of history by Arnold and German Spiritualism.

The hierarchy of the imperial cosmos displayed itself in the Vienna baroque world-theatre and the opera of the Emperor's court. In the theatre the sacramental and magic cosmos of old Europe was represented for the last time through allegories, spirits, machines, histories.[104] The stage was itself an allegorical device, and in the seventeenth century allegory and emblematics were generally recognized sciences. The air, water, and earth spirits, Pan, satyrs, woodsmen, and nymphs, the dancing furies, the judges of the dens with long beards, the dancing machines, animals, centaurs, demons who all played and acted along with man, showed how powerfully the archaic cult practices and customs of the people flowed into and united with the emblems of the high culture. The Austrian baroque, the Viennese theatre from the seventeenth to the nineteenth century, and Austrian music, were strikingly successful unions of the ornamental culture of the ruling class and the passionate and chaotic underground of the people. The high baroque of the worldly and clerical rulers fanned out in home and property, drawer and bed, utensils and dress from the emperor's palace and monastery down to the last village church, to the village fountain with its statue of Moses, and to the cradle of the peasant child. The baroque world-theatre with Hanswurst's merrymakings led to the Harlequinade and the *Magic Flute*. There was an intimate connection between the opera of the emperor's court and the old Viennese folk-comedy.[105]

The old Vienna Folk Theatre equalled in virtually every respect the theatre of Elizabethan London. In content and historical importance it was far superior to the Venetian and French theatres of the seventeenth or eighteenth centuries. It maintained a living dialogue between the archaic, magic folk-culture (in the magicians, magic, talking animals, spirits etc.) and the 'grand form' of the noble cosmos (in the consecrated figures of the emperor, the martyrs, missionaries and heroes). The rationalism of the Enlightenment flowed into the social satire of the nineteenth century. This was possible only because the mental attitudes of the nobles and of the overwhelming majority of the clergy were of the same type as those of the social strata still linked to the earth and the soil. The economy was almost archaic, and the legal system in Austria and the south German territories was still a part of a thousand-year old tradition. A union of the divine and the worldly was the central strand which bound the aristocrat and the peasant, the Bohemian and the Magyar into one hierarchical empire. The union of Spirit and matter also created Austrian music which was both an enunciation and a unification of opposites. Austrian baroque culture and southwest German Catholicism formed 'another Germany' until the late nineteenth century. It looked with mistrust, astonishment and bewilderment at the phenomena of dissolution and distortion in Protestant Germany. It was mystified by this culture of the pure spirit and of feeling by the philosophical, spiritual church and the new liturgies of the genius, of the poets and prophets of the people and the individual.[106]

20

THE NINETEENTH CENTURY
(1789-1945)

THE nineteenth century came to an end amid the rubble of European cities at the end of the Second World War. It was, says Heidegger, 'the darkest of all the centuries of modern times'.[1] Everything in it was ambiguous, bearing the past and the future within itself. There was hardly a thinker who did not reveal anti-humanist and anti-Christian features. On the other hand there was hardly a single great opponent of Christianity who did not suggest new possibilities for Christianity. It is possible either to extract a new Christianity from Novalis, Hölderlin, Feuerbach, Marx and Nietzsche or to construct its very anti-thesis.[2] The problem of understanding the nineteenth century lies partly in this extraordinary ambiguity and partly in the difficulty of finding a proper perspective from which to look at it. As a result, I have tried to develop a kind of shorthand, by which I mean a collection of signs and indicators which may help us to sort out some of the most significant phenomena. Our anxieties and expectations prevent us from doing justice to this century in all its greatness and fruitfulness.* We ourselves still belong to it, at least those of us do who were born around the time of the First World War. Our revolutions, reactions and conservatisms, the way we talk, write and see, are still linked to this century in which Europe ceased to be an island and during which an archaic society many thousands of years old and an aristocratic view of the cosmos of almost equal antiquity collapsed together.

During the nineteenth century, the underground of peoples, individuals and levels of consciousness became a new arena of salvation and the nations became the new Saviours. It was a period of patricide. Men slew the old fathers, emancipated themselves from God and king and began to hope for a new era of salvation, which bore Heaven and Hell in itself. The German thinkers between 1770 and 1830 were well aware of this. They were the first to try to bring the long suppressed forces of the popular underground into an open dialogue with the political and religious superstructure of the rulers. They saw the need to unite the religious nonconformism of the East with the humanism, rationalism and Christianity of the West.[3] Their efforts produced

*I hope to be able to expand this shorthand into a fuller treatment in a volume on the modern era, which I am trying to complete at present.

448

unforeseen and terrible results, because they made the mistake of believing that they themselves were the new salvation-bearers who were to establish the 'Kingdom of God'.*

In the *Bestimmung des Menschen* (1800) Fichte outlined his programme for the new century. He resolutely transferred the attributes of God to the service of men, and called upon his fellow men to begin a life of activity. Fichte's faith in the redemptive power of work was a necessary attribute and sign of the man-god. But there were others. The new man, he wrote in *Die Anweisung zum seeligen Leben*, was 'immortal and imperishable': 'All our life is His (God's) life. We are in His hand, and remain in it, no one can tear us away from it. We are eternal, because He is ... We ourselves are God's immediate life.' Fichte had merely taken over the doctrine of the *amour pur*, the pure, disinterested dedication to God, which we saw in Fénelon, pietism and Eckhart. 'As long as man desires to be his own self, God does not come to him, since no man can become God. As soon, however, as he has annihilated himself to the roots, God alone remains and is all in all. Man cannot beget a God, but he can annihilate himself in true negation and then he merges into God.' Fichte made one extremely important alteration in this doctrine. In Eckhart and Fénelon, it had been essentially other-worldly, a retreat from overwhelming external pressures. For Fichte, it became the inner meaning of the French revolution. 'God' he wrote, 'is ... a God of freedom'. 'Therefore Christianity is the gospel of freedom and equality: the former not only in a metaphysical but in a civic sense ...' The next step was even more daring. He joined the mystical individualism to the ancient idea of salvation from below.

The *Addresses to the German Nation* (1809) celebrated the German people as a people of salvation, speaking God's language and doing the deeds of God. Hölderlin saw the danger: *Verbotene Frucht, wie der Lorbeer, ist aber Am meisten das Vaterland. Die aber Kost' Ein jeder zuletzt.* The German movement was determined to taste this fruit. Joyfully it celebrated the holy war and the sacred hate, the holy people and state. It cried out for the salvation-bringer who was to reconcile Heaven and earth.[4] Nor was Fichte alone in his exaltation of hate. Schelling saw a holy universal law in wrath, in hate and in war. 'How', he asked, 'can there be a holy war, where the state contains nothing holy?' The answer was to find a 'truly divine man'. 'Wherever he appeared he would fill all people with adoration; with the brilliance of a messenger from heaven, he would suddenly and wondrously unite the divided.' Inspired by Herder and Fichte, the romantics wanted to claim sanctity for the nation, the state and its leader. Novalis ascribed the attributes of Christ to the national leader. Adam Müller claimed God and Christ as protectors of the German nation. He considered the state as 'the ultimate form' of whatever is human. Individuals vanish, the state is eternal, and superior to everything, even the

*The young Hegal, Schelling and Hölderlin bade each other farewell with this password as they left their school. They meant by it the kingdom of the human god who would change the face of the earth.

sciences. Müller espoused the proposition that 'Christ did not only die for man but also for the state.'[5] He celebrated war as the great school of character-building for the nation and vehemently attacked English liberalism.[6] In effect, the romantics had made the chiliasm of the lower classes into a secular, political faith. In a few decades Herder, Schiller, Fichte, Baader and Böhme became the teachers of the East. Their ideas penetrated Poland, Russia, Hungary and the Balkans. The underground turned them into an ideology, which burst the bonds of society in the Third Reich and has caused an uninterrupted series of explosions in Africa and Asia in the last twenty years.

The chiliasts of 1933 may have been more primitive than their predecessor the second German movement, but they were often far less dishonest. They took the words of the romantics literally, and tried to put them into practice. The Nazi propagandists could easily have written the words which Schelling used in 1811 to call for the great uprising against the enemy: 'why should science deplore the destruction of those conditions whose nothingness it has felt so intensely and so often proclaimed? Should it not rejoice that a shattering fate has brought down the structure of lies and errors, that would not yield to the soft voice ... can science succumb to the real superstition that the new can be vanquished by the old, although it is firmly convinced that only a complete renewal can bring honour and salvation. In recent times the main activity of the moribund and the inane has been to prevent just such a renewal. This whole generation of castrated libertines and effeminate dilettantes which is just as inept in its management of life as in its service to art, must perish before there can be dynamic action again.'[7]

The young Hegel, in his *On the Conditions in Württenburg* also called for a radical change: 'There is a general and deep feeling that the state structure as it now exists is untenable. There is a general anxiety that it will crumble and injure everybody in its fall ... All attempts to re-create trust in parts of a constitution from which faith has departed, and to hide the grave-diggers behind beautiful words, not only cover those who attempt such things with shame, but pave the way for a frightful explosion in which the need for improvement will be allied with revenge. The deceived and oppressed masses will punish such dealers in dishonesty ...'[8] Similarly, Fichte described the Christian belief in a hereafter as lunacy, according to which 'the whole of Christendom will assemble in a concert hall, perpetually to sing Hallelujah.'[9] Fichte's denial of Christian Heaven was equally a rejection of the old structure of Christian authority. The nation as conceived by the romantics cannot tolerate external techniques of reward or punishment.

The German Enthusiasts of the movement between 1918 and 1945 were clearly descendants of the German Enthusiasts of the years from 1770 to 1830. Romanticism's radical, revolutionary and subversive relations were often misunderstood, because they were disguised in gnostic professorial systems (Schelling, Hegel), in conservative theories (Fr. Schlegel, A. Müller), in Christian masks (Novalis), or in poetical and magical fantasy (Tieck, Jean

Paul, E. T. A. Hoffmann). German romanticism was a multi-levelled phenomenon.[10] In its deepest dimension, it was a part of a European movement which had always tried to demolish the superstructures, the political systems and religious orthodoxies of old Europe. It vulgarized the classical Enlightenment in order to unhinge reason and moderation.[11] The dynamism of this German romantic movement sprang from the union of the Eastern and Western underground. Nor is this movement entirely dead today. One of its sons is Martin Heidegger, who in 1950 could write: 'Thinking only begins when we have realized that reason, glorified for centuries, is the stubbornest foe of thought.'[12]

The movement was not confined to the Protestant north of Germany. South German Catholicism had already been eaten away by the repressed spiritualist forces within the people, and by the nineteenth century the Catholic Enlightenment, Jansenism and the civilized structures of the baroque era were no more than façades. Catholic sectarians roamed over Austria and Bavaria teaching the doctrines of the invisible Church. The Roman Church had become corrupt, they cried. Nothing but inner piety and the friendship and fraternity of the awakened could save mankind. They denied original sin and transubstantiation. There was more than a superficial resemblance to the peasant uprisings of the late middle ages. Like the medieval movements, they drew strength from peasant families and the lower clergy. Their names, Lindl, Gossner, Booss (pastors in Gallneukirchen near Linz) and Langmaier clearly suggest the traditional connections with ancient peasant families. Catholic sectarianism was important in at least four distinct ways:

1. It was in close contact with the great French irrationalist movement of theosophists, enthusiasts, world-renovators and transformers, and transmitted ideas from Lyons, Avignon, Paris and Strasbourg to Germany. There were a great many female prophets who wandered back and forth between Germany and France and carried ideas.

2. The movement influenced the most important thinker in southwestern Catholicism, Franz von Baader.

3. Baader in turn had many Russian friends and contacts. He influenced the formation of cells of Russian nonconformists and, with the help of Madame Krüdener, he fostered the migration of a good many Protestant and Catholic sectarians to Russian territory, where some of them established colonies on the Black Sea, and immensely strengthened Russian Spiritualism.

4. The eruption of south German Spiritualism in Adolf Hitler's Nazi movement in the twentieth century was another form of expression of the underground ferment in the south German states.

Franz von Baader's philosophy was a 'pantheistic ragout with a Christian sauce', as Schelling put it.[13] It was a potent mixture of the sort we have seen in Böhme, but without the other-worldliness of the earlier system. Decadent Catholic Spiritualism in Baader had a political drive compared to which the decadent pietism of Nietzsche was harmless frippery. Baader had a powerful impact on Alexander Nikolaievitch Galitzin (1773–1844) through whom his ideas poured into the Russian underground.[14] Through Madame Krüdener, Alexander I became the pupil of Baader as well, and his pseudo-liberalism was clearly an attempt to use the ideas of modern German romanticism to preserve the substance of ancient absolutism. In the semi-civilized, semi-barbarian world of Russia, the romantic movement swept forward like a tidal wave.[15]

During the nineteenth century, the intemperate, vulgar and depraved ideas of the romantics and idealists began to seep down into the broad masses. The social and intellectual classes at the top consistently failed to understand the significance of the union of the Enthusiasm of the intelligentsia and that of the masses. They thought of it as national, democratic and liberal. But it was the democracy of the 'people's democracy', not that of Basle or Amsterdam, which resulted from it. It was the liberalism of the Festival of Wartburg on 18 October 1817 called to celebrate the victory of Leipzig, and it was the nationalism of Kaiser Wilhelm II, not the liberalism of J. S. Mill or the nationalism of the West.[16]

These tendencies were strengthened by an eruption within Germany of other petty-bourgeois groups from Bohemia, Saxony and eastern Germany. Russian influences were transmitted through the many marriages of Russian princesses to German rulers and by an active programme of paid literary activity. The German masses received the message of their world mission of salvation from the popular preachers from the East. Saxon, Bohemian and Austrian lower clergy spread pan-Germanism and anti-Semitism wherever they went. These popular movements were anti-Western, anti-humanist, anti-rationalist and in time anti-Christian as well.

This was the world of Friedrich Nietzsche. A Saxon of pietist background, who wanted to be a Polish count instead, it was he who joined visions of the older pietism of the seventeenth and eighteenth centuries to the romanticism of the nineteenth century, and translated them both into the language of biological and political prophetism. He started with the old spiritualist, historical concept of the Enthusiasts: history was a meaningless activity; only 'great geniuses and saints' were important. He saw the story of history in biological terms and grasped the questions of power, of victory, leadership and subordination as the 'primitive fact of all history'. The Franck-Arnoldian concept of the élite continued to live on in him. A new age of world history had begun, Nietzsche realized, and 'to establish the rule of the best' must be the chief task.[17]

In the Enthusiastic climate, power, strife, spirit and force became theological prophetic and historical categories. They were to call forth salvation from the people and history, and to arouse Germany. The forces of the 'depths' were to be unleashed and then fettered again by the salvation-leaders of the coming world age. Whereas Swabian Enthusiasts looked for this revival in the communities of the inspired, the awakened and the strong, Nietzsche hoped for the 'superman'. The superman was an Enthusiast with a twist. He knew how to use the means at hand. He could employ technology, biology and politics to gain dominion over the world. Unfortunately the superman had a rival, Jesus Christ. Nietzsche was forced to attack Christ, and in doing so he gave high literary form to the seething resentments of the Spiritualists who have hated Christ since the days of Marcion. At last, Enthusiasm took on its ultimate form, antichristianity. This is perfectly clear in the writings of the two greatest modern prophets of Enthusiasm, Nietzsche and Rilke. 'Nietzsche was jealous of Christ, jealous to the point of madness. While working on *Zarathustra*, Nietzsche was eager to give the Gospel a drubbing. Often he took over the very form of the beatitudes just to attack them. He wrote the Antichrist, and in his last work *Ecce Homo* he behaved like a victorious competitor of Christ, whose doctrine he claimed to have vanquished. 'I am a messenger of good tidings'. He himself called his work 'the fifth gospel'.[18]

Rilke's message is no different: 'He whom they praise as the Messiah has turned the whole world into an infirmary. He calls the weak, the wretched and the sick ones his children and favourites – and the strong ones? ... How should we rise if we give our strength to the wretched, to the oppressed, to lazy scoundrels without sense and spirit? Let them fall! Let them die alone and miserable. Be hard, be terrible, be inexorable! You must go forward, forward! A few great ones, strong and divine will build a kingdom with their strong, lordly arms on the bodies of the weak and the crippled.'*[19] It hardly requires an effort of the imagination to see why Rilke was favourite reading among concentration camp commanders. Like many secularized Enthusiasts, Rilke hated and feared the 'rise of the masses'. The people were the 'damned ones', incapable of gaining salvation from the Ego, and its 'interior universal space'. Like Nietzsche, he hated all the other bringers of salvation: Christianity, Western democracy and the reason of the West. He wanted to absorb the East and the underground of the individual, and proclaim a new message of salvation.

The same underground erupted in Adolf Hitler, who was a child of the religious and political sectarians of the Valley of the Inn and the Austrian mountains. He was a clansman of Robert Hamerling, the poet of the Münster Anabaptists, and an *enfant humilié* of the lower class. As Bernanos wrote in 1939, *M. Hitler est un désespéré. Depuis six ans, l'Europe ne vit pas sous un autre signe que celui du désespoir d'un pauvre diable d'Allemand.*[20] Hitler burned with the ancient hatred of the lower classes against their oppression by Rome and the Hapsburgs, by the culture, reason and Faith of the masters. He was a talented and ambitious boy, but rebellious and angry.[21] In the school records at Linz, there is a charge against him. He swallowed the Lord's body as a practical joke for the amusement and bewilderment of his fellow students. Instinctively, the boy Hitler re-enacted one of the most ancient of the Spiritualist blasphemies. He mocked at the Host, as his ancestors in the wooded valleys

---

*The anxiety of the hungry, rejected intellectual of the petty bourgeoisie has never been more openly expressed. 'Forward' has always been the magical formula for these anxiety-ridden, terrified souls.

of Lower Austria may well have done 500 years before him. His swastika, which he first saw in the monastery of Lambach was the new sign of salvation. For in a bizarre way, Hitler was a Christian reformer.

This was the young house-painter who arrived in the hybrid, seething capital of the old Empire. He was stunned by what he saw there. To him, it was the great Babylonian harlot, as it had always been to his virtuous parents, whose ancestors had been virtual serfs for five centuries. Vienna at the turn of the century was a place of intense activity.[22] Freud was exploring the underground of the human psyche. Rilke and Trakl were trying to capture it in poetry. The city housed Franz Kafka, Martin Buber, Robert Misul, Ferdinand Ebner, Hoffmannstahl and Broch. While Hitler eked out a miserable living at the Kunstmuseum, Stalin was furiously writing his work on the national question in a little room not far from Schönbrunn and Mussolini was a labourer working on the Reichsbrücke. The streets echoed with the languages of the empire.

Hitler was fascinated by Vienna and the decadent splendour of the late baroque in Austria. When he came to power he planned a German council patterned after the College of Cardinals and wanted to establish a neo-Burgundian state. His architectural plans for Berlin, Munich and Linz and his Nuremberg festivals in the 'cathedral of lights', his artistic taste and space hunger were expressions of this fascination. His ideal was a new super-baroque kingdom of spirit and power. The inner kingdom of the Germans was to be fused with the external space of technology, machine, motion and organization. Hitler revived the bizarre machinery of the philosophers, scientists and political utopians of the baroque era, but their ideas were fantastically distorted by him. He never understood the upper world of baroque culture, just as he never understood the Vienna of his youth. He saw it all from below and squinted at it with the dazzled gaze of a man emerging from an underground vault. His palace and his *Reich* were caricatures of a twisted mind, but the forces which drove him to power were real and Hitler knew it. His career was the mirror of the weakness and strength of the German people.

Hitler's view of history was equally a distorted version of the spiritualist tradition: 'Had we never come to know this oriental nonsense, had Homer remained our Bible, how different the form that man would have assumed thereby.' To think of history, as Hitler did, from the point of view of how things might have been implied that he wanted to change it. This was of course a mark of all enthusiastic prophets of history. The bulk of German political historiography of the nineteenth century was nothing but a more or less disguised spiritualist, prophetic vision, the aim of which was to suggest to the 'kingdom', how it should have carried out a better policy and history of salvation. This was Hitler's vision of history. It was also the innermost conviction of the poets, writers and professors within Germany. No wonder they fell over like straw men before the Nazi god. They had been saturated with the spiritualism of the ruling classes, and were powerless before the eruption of a similar spiritualism from below.* They were accustomed to obey a spiritual leader implicitly. The various leaders of the aristocratic movements had always demanded 'immeasurable veneration' from their followers.

There were little churches around Feuerbach, Strauss, the young Hegelians, Wagner, the romantic materialists, Büchner and Moleschott, around Ernst Haeckel, Stefan George, Houston Stewart Chamberlain, Nietzsche, Rilke and Günther. They were prepared for totalitarianism in the sociological ferment and the spiritual, psychological milieu of these little secular congregations. They had always begun by finding their special political salvation leader either in the underground or among their own number, and next they found the necessary political and financial connections. In exactly the same way Hitler made his debut in the salons of Bruckmann and Hanfstaengel in Munich. The often ostentatious rejection of the political and the common in these little churches, their conservatism and aestheticism, were fraudulent. They favoured an affected air of disdain for the things of the world, but in reality they were tortured by their lust for power and their yearning for the 'historical hour', which they did not want to miss.

The growth of the surrogate churches in the nineteenth century was partly a reflection of the miserable condition of orthodox theology and ritual. The church proper was replaced by the opera, the concert hall and the theatre. In the theatre the dialectic of being and appearance was played out, and in the concert hall, especially after Mendelssohn rediscovered Bach, oratorios and Masses were included in concert performances. These religions were opiates not only for the people, but also for the upper classes, the educated and the middle class.[23] After 1848 natural science, technology, economics and the struggle for power among nations pushed themselves into the foreground as additional narcotics. They offered to release men from the pressure of not knowing about first and last things. Salvation was attainable by means of work and struggle. The two languages began to draw sharply away from each other. The language of the inner life separated from the language of science, which moved closer to mathematics.[24] The language of the inner life was refined and differentiated by the poets. It helped to articulate the psychic underground and to heal it.

The poets of the nineteenth century had a lofty and precarious position between the priest and the physician. Very often they saw more deeply than either because they suffered and felt more. They were on the whole supported by a type of physician who had literary sympathies. Ringseis, Carus, Freud, Adler and Jung were all physicians with a strong admixture of poet and spiritual preacher. They combined the languages of art and science in the

*The reader is urged to study Gottfried Benn's letter to Alexander Lernet-Holenia in the *Neue Zeitung* of 18 October 1952. Not one element in the romantic attack on the West is missing in Benn's letter. It is a depressing comment on the contemporary German intelligentsia.

jargon of psychologists, psychoanalysts and depth psychologists. The great romantic physicians (Carus's *Psyche* is their classic standard work) and their disciples, the historical physicians, who investigated the psychic underground of primordial peoples (Bachofen's studies of matriarchs, Rhode's history of Greek religion), developed a peculiar combination of historical research, gnosis and therapy. Freud and Jung are the last great representatives of the romantic school.[25] Their psychological explanations of the Oedipus-complex and of the class-struggle between the superstructure and the underground in the individual ran parallel to the efforts of the poets to describe the conflicts between fathers and sons and to the analyses of the class struggle by the sociologists. All three groups were in contact with the concrete historical situation.

From this point of view, we can see Freud historically as a brilliant but one-sided inventory of Vienna and of the dilapidated late baroque cosmos of the sacred monarchy. The same appraisal applies to Schnitzler, Kafka and Hitler in their respective dimensions. What was common to all of the romantic physicians* was the total immanence of the world, the identity of God and devil, god and evil. After about 1880 all romantic disguises of Christian and humanist origin were cast aside. The techniques for the treatment of the psyche were scientifically developed and partially severed from the old magical practices, although the drive to control the soul remained. It was still gnostic wisdom despite the trappings of science and technology and in time the magic began to seep back into the psycho-analytical approach, which led C. G. Jung to a deepened understanding of the crumbling archaic foundation of peoples and religion. He began to admire exotic, Far Eastern psychic techniques (like Zen-Buddhism) and to an identification of God and the devil.[26] The romantic magic circle had closed.

The central European in the second half of the nineteenth century tried to counteract this long and conscious alienation of man from his underground by an increasing emphasis on work. Work was the one remaining way of establishing contact with things. Magic and sacramental contact with them was no longer possible after the collapse of the archaic society. The workday abolished Sunday. Work destroyed cult and leisure and it took their place. From the eighth to the eighteenth centuries, at least in Catholic countries, people had the ability, the joy and the strength to observe up to 150 holidays a year. That ability now disappeared. The new worker of the nineteenth century was the scientist or the manufacturer who continued working after his employees went home. Sundays or holidays were no more. Work was contact with things. The preparation of a new economic campaign against competition made possible a new communication of man with reality, matter and things. But this communication was closed to the masses. They were

---

*And to Novalis, who had seen the green eyes of nothingness shimmer through the underground. Novalis dissolved God into a mathematical formula: God is sometimes 1.00, sometimes $\frac{1}{00}$ and sometimes 0.

unable to make such contact. They were wretched and hopeless and there was no one to help them.

Friedrich Engels was the man who made Marx aware of this misery, and brought him the perturbing message of the English underground. He was the son of a merchant from Barman and grew up in a pietistic environment. Like K. Ph. Moritz and Nietzsche he sought to break the bonds of the religious environment of his childhood. He joined the Left Hegelians in Berlin and after bitter disputes with his father (the typical father-son tragedy of the nineteenth century), he left for England as a merchant. How different and how similar to Hamann's was Engels's experience of the English underground! Engels's *The Condition of the Working Class in England* was entirely within the pietist tradition.[27] He believed that he had been emancipated from his 'philosophical pride' and his German solipsism by looking at the earthly Hell in England. At the same time the purgation released his historical prophetic powers. Engels described this Hell because he envisaged the Last Judgment and the social revolution as immediately imminent.[28] Paradoxically, the fantastic quality of Engels's spiritualism sharpened his capacity to see the material conditions. In this sense both Engels and Marx met Berdyaev's challenge to Christian thinkers nearly 100 years later: that they should at long last consider material affairs as intellectual, even as spiritual problems.

Engels's description of Manchester, the greatest industrial city of the world in his day, excels Dante's descriptions of Hell. This new Hell destroyed the validity of the old Hell and thus the entire hierarchical cosmos of old Europe. He described rivers of dirt and dung and the bodies of dead children. The workers were forced to eat rotten meat and maggoty groceries, for which they paid usurous prices. Engels collected reports from ministers, doctors, Tories and Whigs, and illustrated them by drawings from the *Times*. The workers were used 'as mere material, as objects ... a society dissolved into atoms no longer cares what happens to them'.[29] The workers destroyed each other in their fierce competition. There were great crises every five years. According to a report of the Poor Law Commissioners there were one and a half million 'superfluous' persons in England and Wales.

Engels presented the world with a picture of the underground in a literal sense. He described how 'women and children have to carry coal crawling on their hands and knees ... chains go through their legs which tie them to the coal cars'.[30] Engels saw something else on his descent into Hell. 'The workers speak other dialects, have other ideas and images, other customs and moral principles than the bourgeoisie. They are two nations, more truly separate than race could ever have made them.[31] The authentic shock of this experience made Engels a materialist. Salvation for the masses in such terrible suffering could only be accomplished through a union of theory and practice, will and action. His materialism was the product of his lofty spiritualism.

Marx's initial concept of materialism differed from Engels. Originally it had no economic connotation. It referred to the objective reality of men and things. 'The first formulation of historical materialism as a "naturalistic humanism" was determined by a critique which took anthropological nature as its point of departure instead of the absolute spirit.'[32] Marx was a deeper spiritualist than the compromising Hegel, who was a kind of neo-Carolingian court theologian. Hegel's attempt to know and to justify all things seemed to Marx to be the grossest sort of materialism. Marx said: 'Hegel takes his point of departure from the state and makes man into the objectified state; democracy takes man as its point of departure and turns the state into the objectified man.' To Marx democracy was the new socialist society, the community of brethren, in which the economy would be administered in humane terms. The fraternal members of the society are no longer estranged from their labour and all share in the holy communion of free work.[33]

Within the new society, the worker is no longer alienated from his nature as a man. A proper relationship among men and between men and objects has been achieved. Marx saw that the bourgeoisie did not suffer through alienation because they imagined that they controlled it. He defined the concept first in his report of 1842 on the debates over the Prussian law concerning the theft of wood.[34] He saw that wood (as a fetish, as a 'thing in itself') had become the judge over man whose human, social and political relation to it was neglected. 'If therefore the wood and the wood-owner as such were to legislate, the laws would not differ except for the geographical point from which and the language in which they were given. This abominable materialism, this sin against the Holy Ghost of nations and mankind, is an immediate consequence of that doctrine which the Prussian *Staats-Zeitung* is always preaching to the legislator, namely to think of the wood and the forest, and never to see a particular concrete problem politically, that is, in the context of the whole reason and morality of the state ...'[35]

Marx was concerned with the 'transparency', as he put it, of the social relations of man. In a proper social order men would be related to objects humanly and they would make them for use and not for gain. Before such an attitude is possible, man, who has been made into an object and estranged from himself, must be transformed into the natural man, whom we see primarily as a fellow human being. The social order of proletarian socialism was a remarkable *unio mystica* of the Aristotelian *polis* and the community of brethren of the Enthusiasts. Marx wanted to change objects into sacraments of man. Sacrament, that is *sacrae rei signum*, meant signs leading to the salvation of man. It was for this reason that Marx wanted to expose the 'fetish-character' of commodities in modern society as a false sacramentality. He wrote: 'A commodity is therefore a mysterious thing, simply because in it the social character of men's labour appears to them as an objective character stamped upon the product of that labour; because the relation of the producers to the sum total of their own labour is presented to them as a social relation, existing not between themselves, but between the products of their labour. This is the reason why the products of labour become commodities, social things whose qualities are at the same time perceptible and imperceptible by the senses ... There (in the world of commodities), there is a definite social relation between men that assumes in their eyes the fantastic form of a relation between things.'[36]

Within the confines of such a study as this, it is obviously impossible to go into detail in the treatment of a personality of such incredible complexity as that of Karl Marx. In the successor to this volume, which will be exclusively devoted to the nineteenth century, I hope to try to do justice to Marx. Under these circumstances I have confined myself to pointing out several themes which must be pursued if a comprehensive intellectual history of Europe in the nineteenth century is ever to be written. The first task is clearly to follow the process by which Marx's ideas became the dogmas of the new Marxist world church. The historian must study the relations between the Marxist mass parties of old Europe and the small Enthusiast communities of genuine Marxists. These relations are of a great complexity and interest especially for a history of ideas. Among their ramifications was the appearance of Marx-scholars, devotees of Marxist literature, Marxist physicians and historical scholars. The big Marxist parties, like their contemporary liberal and national antagonists, were a strange mixture of class interests, ancient anticlerical and clerical resentments. They were filled with emotions which had not been digested and equally with the apprehensions and aspirations of different non-conformist groups. The awkward mixture of heterogeneous elements in all these parties explains their impotence when they actually gained power. It also explains why the strongest and most active groups and persons within them were the most susceptible to dictatorships from the left or the right. Dictatorships appealed to their geniune dynamic element, the Enthusiast underground. It follows that the experience of salvation which drove the mass party was intimately tied to the question of leadership. It was logical that similar forces in the non-socialist parties would show similar tendencies. German history provides numerous and striking examples: the enthusiasm for Bismarck, the *entente* between the German Social-Democratic party and Kaiser Wilhelm II, and the patriotism of all parties in 1914. Is it surprising that the grandsons of all these parties of the nineteenth century sincerely received the 'Fuehrer' as the fulfiller of their aspirations?

Another fascinating area is the relationship between Marx and the Enthusiasts of the far left. Marx had to fight his own progeny as Luther had been forced to do, and for similar reasons. Marx hated utopian socialism, which perverted the marriage of riches and their owner into a universal prostitution of the community; it changed avarice into envy. In this communism, he believed the degradation of man became manifest in the degradation of woman. 'The immediate, natural and necessary relationship among human beings is the relationship of man to woman ... The whole culture of man may be evaluated in terms of this relationship.'[37] It is not entirely irrelevant to point out that Marx was happily married while most romantics and idealistic philosophers between Friedrich Schlegel and Max Scheler were on the whole extremely ambivalent about women and sex.

Marx distinguished his brand of communism from the communism of the Enthusiasts as 'genuine appropriation of the human essence by and for man ... This communism as perfect naturalism is equal to humanism, as perfect humanism equal to naturalism; it is the true dissolution of the conflict among men and between nature and man, the true dissolution of the conflict between existence and essence, between objectivity and self-activity, between freedom and necessity, between individual and species. Man is the solved riddle of history and knows himself as this solution.'[38] The sources of the new communion between man and society and between man and objects can be found in the Anabaptist ideology of the community of brethren. This is clear in the following passage: 'Material, immediately tangible private property, is the material tangible expression of alienated human life. Its movement – production and consumption – is the tangible revelation of the movement of all previous production, that is the actualization of the reality of man. Religion, family, state, law, morality, art, science, etc. are but specific manners of production and partake of its general law.'[39] What Marx and modern communism after him really wanted was to restore the relationship of things in the archaic society by a consciously elaborated production of these relations. The 'plan' took the place of the increasingly declining functional system of archaic society. The positive abolition of private property, as a form of appropriation of human life, was therefore the positive abolition of all alienation.

This human society is the new church of man who redeems himself. Before the Eucharist, the priest prays: 'Through Him (Christ) create Thou, O Lord, perpetually those gifts, sanctify, quicken, bless and grant them to us.' Correspondingly in Marx's society, the new man, the worker, creates himself in his works and in his history. He calls himself back from a state of surrender and estrangement to the communion with all men and things of the world. 'I beseech you, therefore, brethren, by the mercy of God, that ye present your bodies a living sacrifice, wholly acceptable unto God which is your reasonable service. And be not conformed to this world: but be ye transformed by the renewing of your mind ...' (Rom. I. 1–2). Renewing the world demands sacrifices. The new man of Marxian Society makes such sacrifices by rejecting the old world of sin. The worker emancipates himself from his estranged ego and 'puts on a new man' in work for the Party, as a cell of the new society. The transformation of the world and the transformation of man is seen as a unity. It is no mere accident that the only sentence that the Soviet Constitution has in common with the old Gospel is the passage from Paul: 'that if any would not work, neither should he eat'. (II. 3. 10).

Inspired democracy, as Marx saw it, was the offspring of the French Revolution. The Jacobin communities of Enthusiasts were conscious parricides. They founded the community of brethren and of fraternity and liquidated the thousand-year-old superiority of the king-father, of the priest-father and the pope-father. The father was the symbol of transcendence, the image of God on earth. Providence, dominion, order, transcendence, legitimacy and personal relation to God, were rooted in recognition of the father. The concept of the sovereign people was born of parricide. It was based on the execution of the king, who stood both for God the Father and for the paternal society of old Europe. *Fraternité* was the communion of the 'equal' which replaced the participation in something higher mediated by the Father.[40] 'True fraternity exists only among innocents.' The killing of the father was an attempt to achieve total innocence and to deny any kind of original sin which after all is transmitted through sonship: 'sociologically original sin was felt as the guilt of sonship. The eternal Father was replaced by the mother, *la Mère-Patrie*.'[41]

The revolutionary brethren wanted to gain their innocence through the new mother. This was an event of tremendous significance. A matriarchy was set up in which might replaced dominion. Dominion had existed from the time of Homer to the early nineteenth century. Lords had always marked it out by their borders, intermediate spaces and distinctions and their distances. In this sense the magical attempts of Burgundy and Spain in the fifteenth and sixteenth centuries to create distance through their court ceremonial were signs of the decadence of the old idea of dominion. The Spanish court propped up its crumbling dominion by exhibiting itself as a spectacle before the mass of the unhallowed people. Dominion was based on the old reasoning, i.e. male reason. The 'thing in itself' was an expression of magic and anxiety.

In Russia, the struggle over dominion took an unusual form. The Russians have always believed in the powers of 'Mother Earth' and by comparison with the West have never taken the bad 'little Father', the Czar, very seriously. During the nineteenth century, Russian Enthusiasm became political rather than religious, and it soon transformed the ancient Faith in the land into a motherland, the holy Russia. The people became in its eyes a holy people, oppressed and downtrodden by the little fathers. The total degradation of the father was celebrated in Dostoevsky's *Brothers Karamazov*. Stalin often spoke of the masses as the 'mother' of the Bolshevik party, from which it draws its strength.

The revolt of the brethren was equally as important as the exaltation of the mother. The brother-man who became independent took over the task of fulfilling the petitions of the *Lord's Prayer*. 'Our Father who art in heaven' became 'Our power which is on earth'; 'hallowed be Thy name' became the aspiration of the citizen to exalt his own name in society. 'Thy kingdom come' became 'our duty' 'to build the kingdom'; 'Thy will be done on earth as it is in heaven' became the demand to spur on the will to the highest possible accomplishments. 'Give us this day our daily bread' committed the politicians to guarantee freedom and bread (the motto of the Nazi *Völkischen Beobachter*.) 'Forgive us our trespasses, as we forgive them that trespass against us' became *laissez-faire, laissez passer*, and it meant that the brethren were prepared to accept the terrifying burden of absolving themselves from sin. Poets and writers played a key role as the mediators in this self-absolution. Remission of sin was never enough, because the brethren could not be certain that their absolution worked. They had to have certainty, if only to quiet their own anxieties, so they set up an inner inquisition. Each member of society was called upon to take over functions formerly reserved to absolute governments and to condemn everything which deviated from their canons of acceptable behaviour or thought.*

In their militant organization, the 'Party', the brethren established themselves in tribunals and declared that the Last Judgment was seated in permanent session. 'Deliver us from evil' was the plea that crowned this secular arrogance. The brother-man demanded security. The state was to be the total insurance company against illness, accident, unemployment, etc. Next he demanded salvation and deliverance from evil from the physician, politician, artisan and beautician as brethren of the democratic salvational community singled out to perform their particular jobs. He set up his new icons and saints in the earthly paradise: movie stars and beauty queens with their angelic faces. The angelic child-woman or ideally handsome man of the movies guaranteed at least a vicarious participation in the fulfilment of all the wishes of the brothers in the new Heaven on earth. The high festivals of God the Father and of his Son began to be transformed into the festivals of the brothers, which had to be celebrated daily lest salvation on earth be lost. The joy of Easter Day was present every day and men celebrated it in the cathedrals of light of the movie industry.

The citizen of the fatherland established himself as the Easter-man who reconciles (God and man) himself as in the gospel according to St Matthew, 'All power is given unto me in heaven and in earth. Go ye therefore, and teach all nations, baptizing them in the name of the Father, and of the Son, and of the Holy Ghost.' (xxviii. 18–19). The new trinity of the brethren under the name of 'Liberty, Equality, Fraternity' took over the duty to spread the Gospel given by the old Father-Trinity. And with armies, trade and UNESCO, it has undertaken missionary work among the infidels, i.e., peoples not yet democratized. The Easter-man has risen to the cries of triumph of inspired democrats everywhere. With his flaming sword, he has gone forth to do battle on every continent with the old powers of dominion. Nations of Easter-men have arisen and have thrown off the shackles of imperialism, colonialism and foreign domination. The communities of inspired brothers have risen from the slumber of death and become nations.†

*American communities have a long tradition of social inquisition, which is not surprising in view of the importance in American history of congregations and committees of inspired democrats.

†The national mythology of the Slavs and North Italians – an ancient fertile soil of sectarianism – about the 'prison of nations' that was old Austria, this last refuge of the old sacred dominion, reflected this new Easter myth. English and American Enthusiasts, from Seton-Watson to Gullick, with a correct historical sense were from the outset emotionally involved with this 'democracy' and supported it energetically. On the sentimentality of

The perfect citizen of our times is supposed to co-operate in a hundred societies, functions, committees, assignments and associations. Participation has been strongly cultivated in the USA and the USSR – both unions of inspired communities of brethren of Western or Eastern stamp. In both countries, the individual must co-operate because his physical and spiritual presence is needed to complete the ritual activity. His speech and action with that of all the other members establish salvation in all the communions. The modern man tries to solve the paradox of simultaneously being an all-giving father and an all-demanding, perpetually rebellious son. He attacks his lusts and concupiscence, over-stimulates his imagination and is deeply perturbed because he cannot give himself everything that he has promised. The schizophrenia of the modern scholar, educated man or politician arises from this Faustian daring. Klaus Fuchs, the atom spy, is a classic example of modern schizophrenia. These men are torn by the existence of barbaric drives and highly civilized controls, and by the impossibility of being 'God the Father' and 'Son of Man' at once.

When the tension becomes unbearable, the brothers cry out for a super-father and he hears them. Terrible dictators arise who degrade them to a servile, guilt-ridden sonship of slavery and they surrender to be sacrificed in ghastly ways by a new father Abraham. The dictator restores order. He rights the cosmos from which dominion again emerges. He divides the heavens from the earth and tears apart the forces from above and below which have mingled so disastrously. Thousands suffer and die, until he completes his work. Europe's reactionaries saw this possibility long ago. Baron Seillière worked out the problem in the 1920's and showed exactly what symptoms the poison of Enthusiasm was producing in the democracies of Europe.[42]

Within the new societies of Europe, there was the problem of converting the theory of the community of brethren into practice. What would replace the archaic society, which through centuries, millennia even, had sheltered the masses? In its strict, sacral commitments, it had regulated the society of men. Its clans, villages, noble-feudal societies and political cities were communities of the living and the dead, of those who were strong in bringing salvation (maidens, priests, wise women) and of those deficient in saving strength. It housed the things and tools of its world, and settled the places where men worked and worshipped. The cow and the wheel, the house and the sword, cradle, loom and grave of the fathers, spade and ploughshare and bodily ornaments, were all co-ordinated and mutually adjusted in a rhythm which contained the whole of life from the song of the reapers and the melody of the fishermen to the high canticle, dedicated to God, the departed and the ancestors.

Archaic society, strictly speaking, knew neither masses nor matter. It had no such concepts as modern working hours or leisure time, which together

A.J.P.Taylor, one of England's leading historians see Hans Kohn's article in *Der Monat*, June 1952.

atomize our lives. There was no mass-man, because there were no individuals or single members of society. The archaic world consisted instead of persons, who belonged to clans and confederacies, and who spoke a language which was bound to traditional norms. They were intimately related to their living and dead, saints and sinners and to their work, duties, things and homes. When others made demands on them or when they faced changes in their surroundings, they reacted in ways which were many thousands of years old. They were secure in an inheritance of countless experiences of suffering, sacrifice, misfortune, failure and success. Archaic society was tough and durable, because it had an infinite capacity to accept things as they came. It took its joys and sorrows and never doubted that they were meaningful. As a sign of acceptance they gave in return. Ritual and tradition fixed the amounts to be given in return for favours, but they also gave freely because ancient wisdom taught that it was better to give superiors and powers their due than to wait until they took what they wanted.

Although men were bound in archaic society to certain types of norms, they were not slaves. The faithful and confidential relationship which they enjoyed in relation to the persons and objects in their environment allowed them considerable latitude in behaviour. The ancient community had a certain arbitrary, almost anarchic freedom, which gave it great power to resist natural and man-made calamities. It was organic and could bend as reeds do in a high wind.* Nothing was prescribed by laws or fixed by codes; everything was sheltered in 'custom' and 'old rights'. In their respective spheres the customs allowed a much greater latitude than modern legal society can begin to comprehend. Modern society is constructed out of prohibitions and compulsory demands, which are all more or less abstract and which offer far less freedom for good cheer and happiness than the customs of the old world did. It was easier to laugh and sing and dance in the old society, because people were tied to each other by flexible, tangible bands. Men could be cheerful in the fields, because they trusted nature. They knew that everything in the world and the world above was animated. As Walther von der Vogelweide called his walking stick *Herr Stock*, so they gave names to cows, trees and objects. A few names for houses and the names of boats are all that remain of the old world. Everything else has been stripped of its living dignity and reduced to mere matter.

Two characteristics marked the ancient community's healthy relationship to its environment: a strong natural sense of colour and form and a highly developed communal memory. When the industrial revolution invaded the village, the people very soon lost their sense of colours and forms. The local handicrafts began to disappear and the fine regard for design which had been part of their houses and tools died out. The marvellously firm colour composi-

---

*This is not the organic society of European conservatism. I do not regard it as an ideal but merely as a statement of fact. The organic society of European reactionary thinking is actually far more radical and totalitarian than the ideas of true revolutionaries, who usually reflect real organic attitudes of archaic society.

tions of the local folk costumes (Pyrenees, Alps, Balkan and Tartar) were also conspicuous manifestations of the communion of man in his community with nature and things. Inorganic and unsuitable houses were placed in the midst of the village. Girls lost the firm taste for what is beautiful in the forms and colours of their wardrobes. At the same time the people lost their memory. With the decay of archaic society the power of memory waned in a few years. The fading of the songs, epics, fairytales, and magic words from memory was accompanied by the extinction of political and religious responsibility. This has been going on all over the world during the last thirty years. The African miner who returns to his tribe in the bush feels himself as remote from the ancient tribal society and its collective spirit as the European peasant lad returning from war or from work in the big city. The art and literature of modern Europe in the nineteenth and twentieth centuries have been little more than hopeful attempts to replace the waning sense of colours and forms of archaic society. Advertising and propaganda have been sent to fill the void in village and town life. Their false fashions and artificial colours are supposed to replace the real colours of the people, just as party programmes and totalitarian ideologies are supposed to restore the fascination and power of the ancient cults.

In an era when all the myths and intellectual systems of the previous millennium were being denied by those who had been their defenders, and when the archaic unity of the people was also rapidly decaying, the masses appeared.[43] But there was no one left to care for them except the sects, a few nonconformist individuals in higher society and the Left. The Left as a party was constituted at the very moment when the Left, the unconscious, the mark of woman, burst the ancient taboos and took new forms in the first psychological writings (Stendhal, Leopardi) and in romanticism. The colour of the underground was red, the colour of blood; its other shade was brown, the colour of the peasants in the middle ages. As a reaction to the Left, a new Right appeared which was the decadent form of the baroque. Arrogantly it claimed to put all things in right order, to know what was right, and to do it. By this very claim (of which its individual representatives were not always fully conscious) it succumbed to the same false magic as the Left. Its colour was black. It shoved aside the old clerical hierarchy and set up a much more terrible one of its own. It was a new clergy of lay-prelates who wanted to conquer the world. (*Gerarchia* was the name of the leading organ of Fascism).

Once the archaic idea of the tool was destroyed, men turned to a new god who is able to do anything: the machine. With its help, men could easily and quickly take hold of matter. The machine-gun was invented in 1861 (Gatling); the film in 1864 (Ducos); in 1866 the Siemens Dynamo; in 1867 dynamite (Nobel). And in 1870 Charcot employed hypnosis in psychopathology. These inventions have to be seen in the same context. The underground of man and of the universe could be put to work by means of these inventions. New and refined techniques of killing were developed. Film, especially in its perfection as sound film, has killed more people than the machine-gun. It penetrates into those dimensions which resist the outside world and opens the unconscious. It lets out all the deepest lusts and together with radio makes man into a primitive natural being. His loutish eye and his loutish ear have become one sense organ. The mouth and anus have merged as in the unicellular organisms. The comprehension of values has been radically destroyed, but the desecrated eye and ear are taking bitter vengeance. A rapid dehumanization has been pushed into motion: tele-killing, tele-acting (through the machines of great organizations, apparatus of industry and of the state) tele-vision, tele-travelling. All these things destroy vital measurements, that nearness and distance in which men realize their own identities. Long-distance travelling at great speeds dehumanizes the travellers. Look at the faces and read the speeches and scribblings of world reporters and eternal attenders of congresses who career around the shrunken orb – the old Mother Earth – in planes. They live in standardized hotels and talk, write, report and make politics about Korea, Berlin, South American Indians, central European intellectuals, etc.

The inability to handle matter rightly had been vaguely sensed by the scientists in the nineteenth century, but by no man more acutely than Carl von Clausewitz. Both Engels and Lenin saw that Clausewitz's book, *On War*, was an attempt to arrive at a new idea of matter. Clausewitz saw war as a human activity, which he compared to trade, 'which is also a conflict of human interests' and politics, which he saw as a form of trade.[44] It is ironic that one must turn to Marx, the theorist of the class struggle, and Clausewitz, the theorist of war, to find a genuine humanity and concern for the real problems of the age.* The idealist philosophers and liberal apostles of humanity were totally unaware of the nature of the great changes which the industrial revolution had made in European society. Similarly, atheist poets and thinkers often knew more about God than the theologians, and some creative artists knew more about matter and how it could be mastered than many technicians. Time was not mastered by those who ran with it, by the successful ones and the moderns, but by a few solitary thinkers, artists and saints. Space was not mastered by the economists, the military and political leaders. They merely ruled or brutally subdued it. But toward the end of the age, a few inspired architects rediscovered it. They remembered that being, building and decorating are intimately connected. 'The continuous space' of Wright, the 'flowing space of Mies van der Rohe', the endeavour of Gropius 'to keep the connection between interior space and universal space',[45] all these tendencies show not only enthusiastic or romantic residual elements, but also something

---

*It was absolutely characteristic of the nineteenth century that Clausewitz, the philosopher of political war, should have been twisted by Moltke and Ludendorff into the apostle of total war. Clausewitz wanted to understand war, which was a reality of human existence, in human terms. The Enthusiast Ludendorff wrote: 'War is the highest expression of a people's will to live. Politics must always be subordinate to the conduct of war.' Erich Ludendorff, *Vom totalen Krieg*, Berlin, 1935, p. 20.

new and different. To the modern architect, matter is no longer a dark, red, brown underground which has to be overcome and overpowered. The new builders are not trying to conquer it by constructing shimmering castles on the heights, baroque monasteries, and baroque intellectual systems. They feel no need to wrestle with the material world and to force it down like a primeval giant, as the romantics did in their crypts and graves. They see matter instead as bright, transparent space, unfolding and confirming man's spiritual powers.

While the artists and solitary thinkers struggled to grasp the new reality, the Churches tried to pretend that nothing had happened. They failed to care for the masses and for matter, and lost any formative influence upon them. As they lost their influence, they succumbed to the times and lost their language as well. The language of the Christian lost its credibility and ultimately degenerated into a kind of festive decoration for weddings, funerals, cremations and patriotic affairs. It was programme music, and nothing more. Christian preaching fell on deaf ears, and when people listened it did infinitely more damage to the spirit than all the anti-Christian and anti-Church tracts, lectures and laws. This applied particularly to the 'Christian' preachers, poets and writers important in their times. They had only a poetical, an imaginary relation to Faith, 'as did Kierkegaard himself perhaps.'[46] For many, as for Friedrich Schlegel, religion was less a means of salvation and redemption than a means of knowledge. Schlegel 'was not satisfied with its truths, but studied God and the effects of God in himself.'[47] Protestantism failed because it trusted the times too much. It mixed up eschatological time and modernity, holy spirit and egotistic spirit, holiness and genius. Catholicism failed because it mistrusted the times too much. It suppressed even its best thinkers, if they dared to approach this unexplored territory.

Protestantism may truly claim many of the cultural and scientific accomplishments of the nineteenth century. It poured itself out into these achievements in a truly magnanimous and lavish manner. As in every form of secularization, it ran a great risk in confronting the world directly. Its failure lay not in its attitude as such but in its inability to prevent the steady dilution of its Christian message. The old Lutherans, Calvinists, and pietists sheltered themselves in tight ecclesiastical castles, from which they angrily looked out on the land which had become pagan. They trusted in God's wrath to right the wrongs of their day. The sons of these superintendents, generals and pastors left the fortresses. They wanted to marry the spirit of the time to the Bible, to release 'the historical Christ' from the letters of falsified gospels and to link the heritage of the Enthusiasts, their own traditions and the human rights of the French Revolution with science and the critical historiography of the nineteenth century.

The ambiguous relationship of Protestant theology to the age can be seen in the work of Schleiermacher (1768–1834). His basic view was that 'dogmatic theology is the study of the relationship of an age to a given doctrine prevailing in a Christian church'.[48] The hunt for the spirit of the times began in earnest. Protestant thinkers rushed to find the concordance of theology and the spirit of the age. They synchronized their watches by the hour, and followed every report from the front in the newspapers. Schleiermacher's doctrinal teaching was a very subtle attempt to combine pantheism with Christianity, and his personality was a blend of professor, patriot, writer and citizen.* He fascinated the whole nineteenth century. 'His name has been established forever, perhaps his like will never be born again' declared Leopold von Ranke after Schleiermacher's death in 1834. But Schleiermacher was reborn. His spirit was reborn a thousand times with just the same special blend of characteristics. He was the model for countless writers, professors and theologians of the nineteenth century. As late as 1907 he was called 'Schleiermacher, the Church Father of the nineteenth century' and it was in 1924 before a serious attack on him by Brunner was made. As late as 1946 Karl Barth confessed: 'No one can say today whether we have really overcome him, or whether in spite of the loud and radical protest against him we are still children of his century.'

Sentimental religiosity and patrotic piety were strongly influenced by Schleiermacher, as was cultural humanism. He began the movement of radical Hegelian theologians, who exposed God as a pseudomorphosis of man. He was the first of the Bible critics to dissolve the Gospel into a mixture of different texts, interpolations and falsifications. He and his disciples wanted to show that the elements of Christianity were already there before Christ, and that the early myths of the Orient were philosophically clearer and religiously more eloquent than the accounts of creation and the end of the world in either the Old or the New Testaments. From Schleiermacher's time to the present in theological studies, Protestant ministers have carefully separated their scientific consciences from the religious faith on which they had been brought up. In many of them, the feelings against the minister-father caused them to change from preachers of the word of God to writers, instructors, or scientists.

The honour and distress, grace and historical destiny of Protestantism are committed to the continuation of this debate and of this kind of research. To these tasks belongs the awareness of the historical place of the biblical documents within the cosmos of the spiritual continents and world religions. Such an awareness is especially significant at this moment when European Christendom is moving forward into the One World. Its experiences, talents and gifts must be tested, proven, changed and purified. The work of textual criticism in the edition of the Bible must be carried on. The investigation of the age in which primitive Christianity was born is vital to an understanding of the Church, as is the compilation of a history of dogma, free of the resentments of the Enthusiasts and the orthodox, and of ideologies of the religious underground.

*He once compared the redemptive activity of Christ with the establishment of bourgeois society, in which the individual goes under in order that 'new persons, namely citizens' may issue forth. This was a good account of the process in the development of inspired democracy.

This problem has been extensively discussed by Harnack, Dilthey, Troeltsch and M. Werner. We need more preliminary studies leading to an *Histoire Spirituelle* of Christianity, a true 'intellectual history of Europe', in which the interplay of the Christian denominations and confessions will be described.

A true spiritual history of Europe presupposes collaboration with Catholics, and members of the Eastern churches.* It requires men with spiritual discipline and experience of the Church. It would involve a new critical reconsideration of the basic intentions of the Reformation and how this Reformation can be continued. From the first post-Lutheran generation onward through Leibniz, Goethe, Schleiermacher, D. F. Strauss, Feuerbach, Nietzsche up to the present, thinkers have considered themselves consciously or unconsciously as reformers. The Reformation in that sense never ended nor does it give any indication that it is about to end.

The fate of nineteenth-century Protestantism is important from a different point of view. We have suggested that the search for the spirit of the age and the anxious attempt to correspond to it led Protestantism to turn into secular science, culture and civilization. It also turned Christianity into talk. After the death of the grand rhetoric, the grand-form and the world of the archaic society and the old sacraments, Christianity became a free-floating loquaciousness. There are two fundamental sources for genuine words. They may reflect the cosmic world order (as in Homer, the Romans and in Catholicism) combining valid essence with valid appearance as earthly sacraments, or they can be thrust out of the depths of the God-inspired self (as with the prophets, saviours of the people, Luther and the Enthusiasts). In the second instance they are valid as the testimonies of a single individual. They express his awakening, his experience and his life. Once this inspiration falls from its heights the Sunday sermon, sheer religious garrulousness, emerges. The *Zeitgeist* can take over and produce strange hybrid versions of the religion of the individual spirit. Under the Nazis, German Protestantism often succumbed to this temptation. Luther, Rosenberg, the Fuehrer and Protestantism were mixed together, as in the early nineteenth century culture, the nation and education had become entangled with religion. In an essay written during the Nazi era one Protestant theologian wrote that 'honest scientific endeavour, real work and a true National Socialist community of fighters for law and performance mean more than complete agreement in theological questions. Life is prior to the intellect, faith prior to ideology. *Vita magistra theologiae*; *Christus dominus vitae*.'[49] Nothing was left of Protestant theology. As the writer himself admits, his Faith had become an ideology: 'Who can deny that our interests are closely connected with politics and technology? It is impossible to avoid this connection. Anybody who owns an automobile knows how much his intellectual life is determined by his property.'[50] The Christian Word had become part of the small-change of daily life. It was stamped on both faces

*The purpose of this book has been to supply some marginal comments to the great history of the spirit, which is yet to be written.

with the symbols of its age and jingled with superficial hopes and aspirations. It had no power to impress its own character on the age nor to bear witness to it.

The Roman Catholic Church had its own problems in dealing with the spirit of the age. It was seized by the terrible fear that all the heresies, which it had managed to control for over a thousand years, were suddenly free again. This inner fear was compounded by the serious blows which the temporal position of the papacy suffered between 1798 and 1870. The French Revolution, the rising tide of Italian nationalism, the growth of Enthusiastic ideologies and the intractability of the old Catholic countries combined to create a critical situation for the papacy, from which it has only recently begun to emerge.

'Time' and the 'spirit of the time' were the great shocks for Catholicism in the nineteenth century. Just as for Dostoevsky the 'spirit of the time' appeared as Antichrist,[51] the Roman Catholic Church could only see the evil time of revolutionaries and sectarians. Ever since Augustine the Church had regarded time with suspicion. Augustine's 'unchanging God' was enthroned beyond the pernicious and destructive times of man. This view had been established over the centuries by Thomas, by the monastic rejection of time and by the contempt for time of natural philosophers and pantheists. During the nineteenth century, scholasticism was revived to defend the papacy and with it the Thomist attitudes to time. Time is bad temporality, Thomas taught. It must be overcome by eternity which is always present in the dominion of the Church: *esse corruptibilium non mensuratur aeternitate, sed tempore.*[52] The 'bad' time endangers the Church, and deprives it of its positions in the world.[53]

Catholicism has offered many sacrifices to its deep but unmastered fear of time, among them a good part of the intellectual élite between 1830–1950. Lamennais, Döllinger, Newman and Lord Acton were either excommunicated or silenced.[54] Yet these men had begun to answer some of the most important questions of our times, and their answers were among the most exciting developments in religious thinking. A few of their problems were taken up again by their successors after they had been condemned, and in a few cases even by those who had condemned them. Just as the Catholic integralists, who occupied the leading positions in the Church, attacked the spirit of the time, Catholic progressives unfortunately began to chase after it. There were numerous attempts to refurbish Catholicism or even to adapt it to Kant, German idealism and other philosophical and political tendencies in fashion. There were three crucial consequences: the modernists were often condemned by Rome; they suffered an inner collapse and often lost their own fundamental positions; finally, the great problems, which had brought about their downfall, were excluded from further discussion within the Church. On its flight from the spirit of the times, European Catholicism of the nineteenth century lost the élite of the educated, the masses of the bourgeoisie and of the workers, and not least its most precious possession: the dominion over the religious language. It had already lost its control over education and science. Theologians began to cultivate a literary style which was alien to the world and to the spirit. Aridity and sentimentality, juridical jargon and scraps culled from the writings of the enemy were strangely blended. Even the language of great theologians like Scheeben and Möhler is unpalatable, and although Newman's prose often has a quality of touching beauty, it easily passes into a fear-ridden and spasmodic rhetoric.

Although the Catholic Church lost ground in many ways, politically, socially, intellectually and religiously, it made progress in other fields which revealed entirely new perspectives on the potentialities of the West. The opportunities inherent in the Marian dogmas for a new science of the whole, sanctified man are inexhaustible. In the period between Pius IX and Pius XII, the Roman Church began to emerge from its own millennial restrictions and proceed to a fresh consideration of its universality and commitment to the whole world. Leo XIII turned to the Eastern Church, the Slavonic and Protestant groups (*Praeclara Gratulationis*, 1894). He addressed himself to the Protestants as 'most beloved brethren', praised the progress of the time, and the solidarity of contemporary men who want to know and to help one another. He welcomed the twentieth century with a mixture of apprehension and hope. Pius XII, in his *Mystici corporis* of 29 June 1943, developed a theology and doctrine of the Church which transcends all ideologies of the *Curia* and its endeavours to secure its positions. He approved Western socialism and showed an understanding of the basic intentions of Protestants (cf. his message to German Catholics, 20 August 1952). He proclaimed his solidarity with all men of good will and the autonomy of natural sciences. Galileo and many other famous and forgotten advocates of science, freedom of inquiry and non-Constantinian Catholicism were rehabilitated.

The great sacrifices of saints, investigators, writers, poets and artists in the early and later nineteenth century had begun to produce results. There has been a renewal of the Orders. The liturgical movement and the spirituality of the *renouveau catholique* in France (Hello, Bloy, Péguy, Psichari and Bernanos), are the fruits of the sufferings of Manzoni and Fogazzaro and their contemporaries. Catholic thinkers like Maritain, Marcel, and von Balthasar have participated in the inner European dialogue and have worked for the encounter of Catholicism with the science and conscience of the times.[55] The ambiguity and fruitfulness of Catholicism in the nineteenth century also became visible in the phenomenon of neo-Thomism. The last great neo-Thomist movement in sixteenth century Spain had been a powerful spiritual movement against the Protestant Reformation and against the emergence of Enthusiast forces within Catholicism itself. The neo-Thomism of the nineteenth century began as a study of the Thomistic patrimony. It was awakened and supported by Leo XIII, Pius X, Pius XI and Pius XII. This Thomist patrimony was summoned as an auxiliary power against the modernisms of the time: liberalism, the free thinkers, pantheism, gnosticism and statism.

31

Neo-Thomism has, as a result, a slightly artificial and stilted quality. It faces a constant temptation to misunderstand itself and to become an ideology.

Hasty syntheses have often been made to defend neo-conservative and authoritarian power systems. Whenever men need a bulwark against what they regard as dangerous theories or insights, they turn to neo-Thomism. This accounts for the importance of neo-Thomism in South and North America and in southern Europe (Spain, Portugal, Italy). In spite of these limitations, the results of the renewed study of Thomas's works have been enormously fruitful. Thomism is still a philosophy which is open to the influences of time, and from it thinkers can follow lines of argument and authentic impulses which may yet lead to a philosophy capable of dealing with the problems of our day. New perspectives for the development of a philosophy out of faith have emerged already. The characteristics of this new philosophy are: a genuine open rationalism, the renewed faith in the laws of nature and a strong interest in social, scientific and existential problems considered in relation to the personality of man. This neo-Thomism with its scientific sobriety has acquired a particular significance in view of the extraordinary confusion which afflicted European thought in the nineteenth century. Not infrequently its own inner tensions pushed European philosophy into mythical, gnostic and orgiastic positions, where it easily succumbed to the temptations of the underground, impulsive, mechanistic or egotistic tendencies.

One of the greatest virtues in the original philosophy of Thomas was its willingness to deal with men as they really are. Thomas's system excluded neither the natural tendencies nor the spiritual obligations of men, who actually live in this world. Neo-Thomism, if it remains true to its origins, may create a new Christian anthropology (cf. the works of Josef Pieper and others). Albert Mitterer has begun to open up all the fruitful questions inherent in the natural philosophy of the Thomist view of the world, and it is also apparent that the earlier tendency among neo-Thomist thinkers to concentrate on social and political problems has given place to a determination to concentrate on the idea of man. The consequences of the renaissance of natural law are unforeseeable, but the revival of the political humanism of Thomas has already begun to stimulate a new kind of Christian thought, committed to relieving the afflictions of the masses. The concern with Christian democracy (Jacques Maritain), the ideas of English religious socialism (Stafford Cripps) and the American federalist theology of the neo-presbyterians, have stimulated the social thinking of the younger American Jesuits and Dominicans. Neo-Thomism stands for an inner Catholic Enlightenment which is searching for a eode of human rights and political liberties, and which seeks to free Catholic thought from the fetters of anxiety and narrowness. It opposes the parochial egocentricity of those who dodge their responsibilities and who will not face the psychic, intellectual and social needs of other groups with different philosophies. This type of thought is the voice of the authentic Thomas. It knows that every man has a responsibility for the whole of mankind. Its spirit can be seen in the compromise between French Catholicism and the Third Republic. Leo XIII's great encyclicals breathed it. The philosophy of a Christian democracy, the Catholic concern for persecuted Protestants, Jews and Negroes, and for political nonconformists are all promising beginnings of a universal Catholicism. They would be unthinkable without the work of neo-Thomism, its Enlightenment, its doctrine of natural law, its concept of the commonwealth in state and society and of the inalienable liberty, dignity and rationality of all men.

There are dangers for the Church today, which cannot be ignored. The great potentialities mean inevitably that there are great temptations as well. Some of these, which I list below, could be decisive for Europe's spiritual destiny:

1. A certain Catholic conformism which understands all the phenomena of our time in a Catholic manner. The conformists are prone to admire Rilke's 'Franciscan' soul, Heidegger's Catholic ontology and Hitler's *Reich*. These sort of thinkers can confuse European thinking. Some of them succumbed to the lure of the Third *Reich* in exactly the same way as the Protestant brethren. There was one outstanding Catholic teacher of dogmatics who saw 'in the movement of the National Socialists the sharpest and most important protest against the mentality of the nineteenth and twentieth centuries' and who wrote, 'The tablets of the National Socialist "ought" and of the Catholic imperatives stand, it is true, on different ontological levels, the former on the natural, the latter on the supernatural level. But they point in the same direction.' Such conformism leads to a perilous adjustment to the political facts and literary modernities of the times. Cultural Catholicism gradually takes up the same positions as nineteenth-century Protestantism. The same people are extremely reluctant to get involved in the burning questions of the day.

2. The attempts to exploit Catholicism as a more or less disguised ideology for the defence of privileged classes, political claims and economic concepts.

3. The effort to build a new Catholic nationalism, technically organized in totalitarian systems. Movements as diverse as the *Action Française* of Charles Maurras and the *Hispanidad* belong together.[56] Constantine, Charlemagne and Donoso Cortes are the patrons of these movements and their battle cry is: one Faith, one people, one leader, one culture. It is no more than a modern version of the old Spanish *Catolicismo de cimitarra*.

4. The temptation to set up Rome as a super-Moscow. Karl Rahner, S.J., warns the Church to avoid the appearances of the totalitarian state and Gustav A. Wetter, S.J., has pointed to a whole series of parallels between Soviet thought and practice and Catholicism. He admits that 'these analogies between Bolshevism and Christianity, above all in its Catholic form, are much deeper than mere external similarities.'[57]

5. Alluring modern systems of thought of fundamentally non-Catholic origin are often paraded as a new Catholicism. A good many brilliant Catholic writers and poets have adopted ideas which are really disguised versions of gnostic, Manichaean or Calvinist attitudes. Such influences have led to a

dilution of the specifically Christian attitude toward nature or have led to an exaltation of 'grace' in a one-sided manner, either optimistically or pessimistically.

Characteristic of all these attempts and temptations, whether they want to escape from time or whether they hunt after it, whether they disguise themselves as traditionalist or progressive, is a dangerous shortness of breath. Their advocates have lost their trust in the positive forces from below and from above, and no longer really believe in truly Christian works (prayer, suffering, sacrifice, charity, and spiritual discipline of thought). The glitter of ideas is a mask hiding a lack of faith in the divine spirit, freedom and love. The Catholics join the Protestants in the misery of Christianity. Few Christian writings, when they do not treat tertiary questions, can be taken seriously. Most of them are just hodgepodges of ill-digested and heterogeneous elements, without a genuine comprehension of their historical origins.

All intellectual discussions in our time are struggles for language. Victors in world history always loot the vocabulary of the vanquished. This applies to the Christianity of late antiquity, which turned the pagan thinkers and poets into Christian witnesses, and it also applies to the present. A world victory of the East would make the words democracy, freedom, humanism and the entire scientific and religious vocabulary of the West something entirely different. The new lords have already succeeded in taking classical Russian literature into their domain and they would soon put the language of the West to use. The inner European struggle reached its first crisis in the fifteenth and sixteenth centuries, when the national languages superseded Latin and with it the ancient, Catholic metaphysics and grand form. The Roman Catholic linguistic cosmos was preserved in French, the language of 'good Europeans', up to the end of the nineteenth century. This language had universal validity. Its innermost structure was forged by the Enlightenment and classicism, which enabled it to continue to represent Catholic Rome. In the nineteenth century poets and thinkers made a colossal attempt to forge their own languages into an independent divine kingdom, to realize the age-old dream of Spiritualist reformers of establishing a universal language. They produced several artificial languages (e.g. Esperanto, Volapük) and in a far more practical form, basic English, the English vocabulary of, say, a Chinese coolie, elevated to a universal language.

The vocabulary of the masses in Europe comprises some thousand words, a few hundred fixed sentences and two dozen favourite phrases and technical formulae. Men are able to express all available sentiments, actions and reactions in the sexual, political, social and economic spheres. The culture-industry has recognized this fact, as have the speakers at international congresses who have worked out a few hundred bits of jargon to enunciate everything to be said about God, the atom, the cell, the transmission of grace, the construction of a bridge, philosophical questions and the building of an electronic tube. The summaries of theological congresses are no different. The apparatus is dominant everywhere, and the plans and the taboos of the group are the determinants.

The expert writer and speaker is not supposed to talk about certain themes which society, the party or the religious confession does not wish to be discussed.[58] Fear, resentment and apprehension squeeze the scope of free speech. In the late nineteenth century it was improper to speak of God in good society. Today it is improper to speak of anything important. The press, the film industry, the managerial class and most publishers go out of their way to avoid most of the serious questions of politics, society and philosophy. Our anxieties have created forbidden zones. In such zones of fear an internal inquisition functions noiselessly and an apparatus of defamation grinds forward to co-ordinate all Europe behind a few slogans.

The expansion of technical abbreviations and compound words is part of this trend. The abbreviations look innocuous on the surface. Like all simplifications, they contain a real danger, the danger that the little letters will become magic. It is not an accident that abbreviations are the products of the monster organizations of our age. In a more refined form the word-creations of a number of poets and writers serve the same purpose. Rilke and his disciples are really intellectual ad men. Their language is a drug. It is meant to anaesthetize the author and the reader alike. 'Its intoxication is a rejection of *ratio* and reality. It is a flight from reality.'[59] Language is a tool to force the union of wonder and reality. It offers a drug which is supposed to solve the world riddles. The seductive art of Rilke and Jünger turns language, the first sacrament of God and man, into a hidden code behind which lurks the voluptuousness of sterile self-satisfaction.[60] Language becomes a spider which sucks the blood of everything it touches. It rejects authentic sacraments and destroys all communion. The magic world, in the service of a pleasure-seeking ego, is supposed to steal and carry off the powers of the 'other'. The historical basis for this was built by the magic societies of the language mystics of the eighteenth century and the romantic period. T. S. Eliot, James Joyce and Ezra Pound are modern language mystics, wizards who find new words and make magic mosaics out of Asiatic and African patois and other forms of language.[61]

The dissolution of the archaic society and the old, noble *polis* and the bankruptcy of the Enthusiast prophets and inspired egos killed the roots of language and wiped out its reliability. Once language had been cut loose, it lost its ability to convince and the writers of the nineteenth century began to see that they could speak in all sorts of different ways. As a result the serious thinkers of Europe at the end of the century had their doubts about language. Atheistic positivists, logicians and mathematicians of the English school of Wittgenstein, as well as men like Paul Valéry, Karl Kraus, Franz Kafka, Ferdinand Ebner,[62] Martin Buber, André Gide, T. E. Lawrence,* and Eugene Rosenstock-Huessy,[63] have devoted much of their energies to the

*Lawrence sought his release in the desert, where men kept their word precisely because he was no longer able to keep his.

struggle for a new language. Kraus once said: 'word and essence is the only union that I have ever sought in life.' He left the Catholic Church because it allowed Salzburg Cathedral to be used as a setting for Hofmannsthal's *Jedermann*. Kraus made the mistake of identifying the Church with a given cultural position, but at least he showed that he was serious about preserving the sacrament of language in all its purity.

Language is being reborn in the work and suffering of a few silent individuals. Out of their struggle, a handful of words will emerge, which will be Europe's contribution to the One World which has begun to take shape on all the continents of the earth. A few words will be a great gift. In them a thousand years of experience will be condensed. They will bear the knowledge and conscience of European man to all mankind. They will be the harvest of a millennium in which men have listened to the WORD, tried to understand it and to answer when it has spoken.

NOTES

CHAPTER 1

1. cf. A. Calderini; *Humanitas*, Brescia; 1952, VII, pp. 153 ff.
2. Justin, *Apol. II*, ch. VIII; Clement of Alexandria, *Strom.*, I, III–VII.
3. Minitius Felix, *Octavius*, ch. XX.
4. Origen, quoted by Eusebius, *Hist. Eccl.*, VI, XIX.
5. H. Lemaitre, on the new French edition of the *Stromata* of Clement, Paris; 1951, in *Terre Humaine*, Feb. 1952, pp. 109 ff.
6. G. Stadtmüller in *Saeclum*, 1951, vol. II, pp. 315 ff.; also Oscar Cullmann, *Christ and Time*, London; 1953.
7. K. Gries, 'The Roman Poets and Government', in *The Classical Weekly*, New York; 1951 vol. XLIV, No. 14, pp. 209 ff.
8. O. Cassel, discussing O. Cullmann's *Urchristentum und Gottesdienst* in *A.L.*, Zurich; 1950, 1, pp. 38 ff.; and H. Kornhardt, *Exemplum*, 1936.
9. O. Cassel, 'Zur Kultsprache des hl. Paulus', *A.L.*, 1950, 1, pp. 1 ff.
10. E. Peterson, *Theologische Traktate*, Munich; 1951, pp. 155 ff.
11. See the descriptions in Jerome and Augustine; cf. Schüller-Piroli, *2000 Jahre Sankt Peter*, Olten, 1950, pp. 77 ff., and p. 113; or The Shepherd of Hermas in the second half of the second century.
12. C. Schneider, 'Bemerkungen zur Bukslil', *Luther, Kant, Schleiermacher, Wobbermin-Festschrift*, Berlin; 1939, pp. 565 ff.
13. For an appreciation of the situation of the early Christians, see G. Kittel, *Christus und der Imperator*, Stuttgart; 1930; H. Asmussen, *Der Brief des Paulus an die Epheser. Eine Herausforderung an die Macht*, Breklum, 1949; and studies of the Apocalypse, too numerous to mention. See also F. Heilsberg, 'Zur Frage der Stellung des Christentums in der Spätantike', *MIOG*, supplementary vol. XI, 1929.
14. Martin Werner, *Die Entstehung des christlichen Dogmas problemgeschichtlich dargestellt*, Berne-Leipzig; 1941. This massive revision of Harnack undertaken from the neo-orthodox standpoint (thirty years after Karl Barth) suffers from the restrictions of its dogmatic position: 'This Great Church is the most successful of the heresies' (p. 138). She plunders her defeated enemies of their noblest ideas and finest teachers, and smites down primitive Christian eschatology, and the rest of her opponents, in the course of a sordid defamatory struggle for power. Werner is unmistakably a victim of his own resentment. His fundamental position is an instructive example of the law of spiritual history: The resentment

of the dissenter and the nonconformist is as liable to lead to a blockade of mental vision as the fears of the orthodox, the *beati possidentes*, who defend a 'pure' doctrine against 'novelties', although these 'novelties' are often, historically speaking, much older than the so-called 'pure' doctrines.

15 Buonaiuti, *op. cit.*, 1, pp. 124 ff.
16 *Eph.*, VI, II. M. Werner, *op. cit.*, pp. 126 ff.
17 *1 Cor.*, XI, 19. cf. Yves M. J. Congar, *Vrai et Fausse Réforme dans l'Eglise*, Paris; 1950, p. 233.
18 Jerome, *PL*, XXV, 902.
19 Augustine, *PL*, XXXVII, 1642.
20 Numerous examples in Werner, *op. cit.*, pp. 82 ff., 126 ff., 389 ff., 468 ff.
21 A significant view of the matter is given by Hans-Joachim Schoeps in *Theologie und Geschichte des Judenrchristentums*, Tübingen; 1949, and *Aus frühchristliche Zeit; Religionsgeschichtliche Untersuchungen*, Tübingen; 1950: the process of development and repression by which the Jewish-Christian *emigrés*, the members of the primitive community at Jerusalem, became Ebionite 'heretics'.
22 cf. K. Prümm, in *Zeitschrift für Aszese und Mystik*, 1937, No. XII, pp. 91 ff., and M. Werner, *op. cit.*, pp. 514 ff.
23 Buonaiuti, *op. cit.*, 1, p. 102.
24 On Stoicism and Christianity, see H. Roudet, *Gratia Christi, Essai d'Histoire du Dogme de Théologie dogmatique*, Paris; 1948, pp. 112 ff.; J. Stelzenberger, *Die Beziehungen der Frühchristlichen Sittenlehre zur Ethik der Stoa*, Breslau; 1933.
25 On Seneca as the spokesman of the aristocratic Roman opposition, cf. W. Kamlah, *Christentum und Selbstbehauptung*, Berlin; 1940, pp. 440 ff.
26 cf. M. Werner, *op. cit.*, pp. 261 ff.
27 cf. Heer, *MIOG*, 1949, 57, pp. 24 ff. A valuable comparison might be made of the early Christian doctrine of the four ages of the world with the American Indian interpretation of the four ages of the world in the 'Popol-Vuh'; cf. R. Girard, *El Popol Vuh como fundamento de la historia maya-Quiché*, Guatemala; 1952, vol. I.
28 *Apol.*, XLVI.
29 *De Anima*, III.
30 cf. Justin, *Apol. I*, ch. II, IV, XII.
31 *Apol.*, ch. XXIV; cf. H. Berkhof, *Kirche und Kaiser*, Zollinko-Zurich; 1947, pp. 105 ff.
32 For a correct evaluation of this, see W. Nestle, 'Die Haupteinwände des antiken Denkens gegen das Christentum', *Archiv. für Religionswissenschaft*, 1941, XXXVII, pp. 51 ff. On the alliance of Plotinus and Clement, cf. H. Rüssel, 'Die providentielle Bedeutung der greichischen Philosophie im Lichte des Christentums', *Aufsätze zur Geschichte der Antike und des Christentums*, Berlin; 1937, p. 57.
33 Clement, *Stromata*, VII, XVI.
34 On Origen, cf. H. Berkhof, *op. cit.*, pp. 43 and 192 ff.; M. Werner, *op. cit.*, pp. 270, 295 ff., 537 ff., 580 ff.; Buonaiuti, *op. cit.*, pp. 158 ff.
35 He pressed the subordination of Christ to God the Father so far that he rejected the practice of praying to Christ: *De Orat.*, XV, 1; cf. M. Werner, *op. cit.*, p. 581.
36 *De Princ.*, I, I, VI.

37 *Ibid.*, III, VI, III.

38 *Hom. in Jer.*, VIII, VII, vol. III, pp. 174 ff., in Delarne's edition; cf. vol. IV, p. 545.

39 *De Princ.*, IV, 1 ff.

40 cf. his famous letter to the Patriarch Minas in 543.

41 H. Berkhof, *op. cit.*, p. 200; *cf.* M. Werner, *op. cit.*, pp. 270 ff., 371 ff.

42 cf. J. A. Straub, *Vom Herrscherideal in der Spätantike*, 1939, p. 105; K. M. Selton, *The Christian Attitude Towards the Emperor in the Fourth Century*, New York; 1941.

43 *AL*, 1950, 1, p. 311.

44 cf. Straub, *op. cit.*, pp. 131 ff.; Berkhof, *op. cit.*, pp. 54 ff.

45 Schüller-Piroli, *op. cit.*, p. 103: *Quad Duce te mundus surrexit in astra triumphans. Hanc Constantinus Victor tibi conditit aulam.*

46 cf. E. Peterson, *op. cit.*, pp. 88 ff.; Straub, *op. cit.*, pp. 113 ff.; Berkhof, *op. cit.*, pp. 100 ff.

47 Eusebius, *Triak.*, 1, 196, 16.

48 cf. E. Benz, *Ecclesia Spiritualis*, Stuttgart; 1934, pp. 61 ff. (Marius Victorinus).

49 cf. E. Peterson, *op. cit.*

50 After singing the praises of Constantine as the new Cyrus and the new Alexander (*PG*, VIII, 12 f.) Eusebius closes his life of him by proclaiming the rebirth of the Emperor in his sons, which he assimilates to the rebirth of the Phoenix and of Christ! (*ibid.*, 92-2).

51 Straub, *op. cit.*, p. 123.

52 Buonaiuti, *op. cit.*, p. 231.

53 Buonaiuti, *op. cit.*, p. 256.

54 cf. J. Gagé, 'Le *templum urbis* et les origines de l'idée de *Renovatio*', in *Mélanges F. Cumont*, Brussels; 1936, pp. 151 ff.

55 cf. Berkhof, *op. cit.*, pp. 174 ff.

56 'De Officiis Ministrorum', cf. A. O. Lovejoy, *J.H.I.*, 1942, III.

57 *Ibid.*

58 *PL*, XVI, 67; XIV, 767 ff.; cf. 220; *Ep.*, XL and XLI; *Ep.*, LI.

59 cf. H. Hommel, 'Domina Roma', *Die Antike*, 1942, No. XVIII, pp. 127 ff.

60 cf. *Ep.*, XVIII, and the funeral oration for Theodosius, *PL*, XVI, 1389 ff.

61 cf. G. Ladner, *MIOG*, 1952, LX, pp. 32 ff.; F. Heer, *MIOG*, 1949, LVII, pp. 23 ff.

62 cf. G. Toffanin, *Geschichte des Humanismus*, Holland; 1941, pp. 3 ff.; E. Peterson, *op. cit.*, p. 97; Kamlah, *op. cit.*, pp. 103 ff. (for the foundations of this Christian humanism).

63 See his famous 'Vision', *Ep.*, XXII, XXX.

64 Schüller-Piroli, *op. cit.*, pp. 77 f.

65 Jerome is Augustine's great opponent. cf. also A. Humbert, *Les origines de la Théologie moderne*, Paris; 1911, pp. 224 ff.

66 *De Civ. Dei, III*, ch. XIV.

67 *Soliloqu. I*, II and VII.

68 *De Civ. Dei, II*, ch. XLV.

69 *PL*, XLII, 819. Written between 398 and 416.

70 *De Naturak Boni, PL*, XLII, 551; *De Praesentia De Liber; Ep.*, CLXXXVII, *PL*, XXXIII, 832.

71	*De Haeresibus, PL,* XLII, 21.
72	For the Church as the divine State, City and *Autobasileia* in the writings of Clement and Origen, cf. Werner, *op. cit.,* p. 643; as paradise on earth in those of Irenaeus and Tertullian, *ibid.,* p. 644. On the famous phrase, *salus extra ecclesiam non est,* in Ignatius, Cyprian, and Lactantius, cf. *ibid.,* p. 649.
73	*Contra Ep. Manichei,* V, VI.
74	cf. his indictment of Greek *sapientia* (*De Civ. Dei,* XVIII).
75	cf. Buonaiuti, *op. cit.,* p. 284.
76	*De Baptismo,* IV, XVII, XXIV.
77	*Libera civitas Dei: De Civ. Dei,* XVII, XVIII, XIX–XXII.
78	cf. Kamlah, *op. cit.,* especially pp. 167 ff., 226 ff.; Straub, *op. cit.,* pp. 113 ff.; Berkhof, *op. cit.,* pp. 83 ff.
79	*Civitas Hoc est societas:* XVI, XIV, XII; cf. Kamlah, *op. cit.*
80	*De Ordine,* II, IX, XXVI.
81	cf. Ladner, *MIOG,* 1952, LX.
82	*Ibid.,* pp. 48 ff.
83	CSEL 57, pp. 356 ff.
84	On the Augustinian foundation of the Enlightenment, cf. Kamlah, *op. cit.,* pp. 108 ff., 247 ff., 353 ff.; Kamlah, *Der Mensch in der Profanität,* Berlin; 1949, pp. 15 ff. It would be valuable to compare Augustine's political enlightenment with the individualist view of humanity to be found in pagan antiquity, e.g., in the cynic Theopompus; cf. J. Lana, 'L'Utopia di Teopompo', in *Paideia,* 1952, VI, 1, pp. 3 ff.

CHAPTER 2

1	For an abundance of literary material for research into these centuries, see P. E. Hübinger, 'Spätantike und frühes Mittelalter' in *DVJ,* 1952, pp. 1 ff.
2	cf. L. Olschki, *The Genius of Italy,* New York; 1949, p. 27.
3	cf. Heer, *MIOG,* 1949, pp. 32 ff.
4	But a Christ envisaged according to a Virgilian formula: cf. Claudian *PL* AA, X, 330.
5	Aen. 111, pp. 570 ff.
6	cf. M. Werner, *Entstehung,* etc., p. 683.
7	cf. Apollinaris Sidonius ca. 477 to Arbogast at Trier.
8	cf. Heer, *MIOG,* 1949, pp. 34 ff.
9	cf. P. Boissonnade, *Le travail dans l'Europe chrétienne au moyen âge,* Paris; 1921, p. 36.
10	Boethius, *Consolation of Philosophy,* German ed. by Karl Büchner., ch. XXXIX.
11	cf. Heer, *MIOG,* pp. 37 ff.
11a	For what follows, cf. O. G. von Simson, *Sacred Fortress. Byzantine Art and Statecraft in Ravenna,* Chicago; 1958.
12	cf. Berkhof, *Kirche und Kaiser,* pp. 204 f.
13	*Ibid.*
14	*PL* Epist., II, 365.
15	So Justinian of himself; see especially *Corpus Juris Civilis, De Conceptione Digestorum,* ed. Krueger and Mommsen, Berlin; 1893, p. XIII.

16 Compare Charlemagne's cathedral-octagon at Aix and the German imperial bishops of the ninth to the nineteenth century.

17 cf. José Arias Ramos, 'Un curioso cargo en la Burocracia bizantina: el "quaesitor" ', *Revista de Estudios politicos*, Madrid; 1952, No. 62, pp. 107 ff.

18 cf. his earlier picture in mosaic in San Vitale, and Maximinian's throne in the same church.

19 cf. M. Werner, *op. cit.*, p. 604 (the gnostic *ogdoas* as an extended trias).

20 The great octagon of Hagia Sophia served as the throne room, the heart of the emperor's palace; the throne stood in the place occupied in San Vitale by the altar.

21 cf. O. Schmidt, *Die Beurteilung und Auffassung der Völkerwanderung in der mittelalterlichen Historiographie*, Berlin; 1936, p. 32.

22 *Variae*, VII, 17, p. 213.

23 cf. his *De Anima*, an appendix to the *Variae*.

24 Out of the boundless sea of literature on Benedict and Benedictinism, I mention here only the works of U. Berlière and C. Butler; Philibert Schmitz's history of the Benedictine Order and, in addition, J. S. Chapman's *St. Benedict and the Sixth Century*, London; 1929.

25 cf. L. Mumford, *Technics and Civilisation*, New York; 1934, pp. 12 ff.

26 For a contemporary light on this sentence, cf. M. Bense, *Plakatwelt*, Stuttgart; 1952, pp. 60 f.

27 cf. the Prologue and ch. LXXIII; and against this background, chs. II, III, XXVII, LXIV.

28 Gregory I to the Emperor Mauritius; *PL* Epist., I, 322.

29 cf. the earlier *Vita Severini, PL* A.A., I.

30 cf. O. Schmidt, *op. cit.*, pp. 48 f.

31 *PL* Epist. II, 263.

32 *PL* Epist. II, 397, to the Emperor Phocas.

33 cf. numerous studies by A. Viscardi, of which some are collected in *Questioni di Storia medievale, a cura di E. Rota*, Milan; 1951, pp. 529 ff.

34 The *ecclesia romana* thought of as God's *polis* is an idea appearing as far back as Clement's *Stromata*, IV, 172, 2, and Origen's *Hom.* IX, II in *Jerem.*

35 cf. J. von Schlosser, *Die Kunstliteratur*, Vienna; 1924, p. 34.

36 *Liber Pontificalis*, ed. Duchesne, I, p. 239.

37 Schüller-Piroli, *2000 Jahre Sankt Peter*, p. 50.

38 *Ibid.*, p. 112.

39 *Ibid.*, p. 67: a mark of tolerance practised in this aristocratic world.

40 *Ibid.*, p. 104.

41 *Ibid.*, p. 243.

42 cf. the decrees of Eugene II, 826 (*PG* Leg. II, 17) and Leo IV, 853.

43 cf. Giesebrecht, *De litterarum studiis apud Italos*, 1846, pp. 11 ff.

44 cf. Heer, *MIOG*, 1949, LVII, pp. 60 ff.

45 cf. *PL* poet. Lat. IV, 416.

46 Gregory the Great ordered Bishop Desiderius of Vienna to give his School of Grammar a more religious cast, purifying it of the spirit of worldly letters.

47 *PL* 30, 15 ff.

48 As he says in the *Commonitorium*; cf. his later writings against Augustine, ed. A. Jülicher, 1925.

49 cf. G. Ladner, *MIOG*, 1952, LX, and the works there listed, pp. 52 ff.

50 cf. K. Vossler, *Spanien und Europa*, Munich; 1952, pp. 15 ff.

51 *Ibid.*, p. 47 ff.; cf. Pérez Urbel's biography, *Isidoro de Sevilla*, Barcelona; 1940; Heer, *MIOG*, 1949, pp. 36 f.

52 cf. W. Preisinger, *Die Weltanschauung des Bonifacius*, Stuttgart; 1939.

53 cf. Vossler, *op. cit.*, p. 54.

54 Boniface to the Abbess Eadburga, *BRG*, III, 212.

55 cf. Rosenstock and Wittig, *Das Alter der Kirche*, Berlin; 1927, pp. 513 ff., and H. Gollwitzer, *Saeculum*, 1951, II, pp. 164 f.

56 cf. the works of M. Cappuyns and F. Masai, quoted by Ladner, *MIOG*, 1952, p. 54.

57 cf. C. Dawson, *The Making of Europe*, London; 1932, pp. 156 ff.

58 cf. H. Fichtenau, *Das karolingische Imperium*, Zurich; 1949, pp. 89 ff., Heer, *MIOG*, 1949, LVII, pp. 40 ff.

59 *MG* poet. Lat. I, 89, cf. Fichtenau, *op. cit.*, p. 99.

60 On Byzantine as at once the model and the opponent of the Carolingian Holy Empire, cf. H. Fichtenau, 'Byzanz und die Pfalz zu Aachen', *MIOG*, 1951, pp. 1 ff. For the sources: C. Porphyrogenitus, *De Administrando Imperio*, and *De Caeremoniis Aulae Byzantinae*, in Bonner, *Corpus Script. Hist. Byz*, I and II; in general: G. Ostrogorski, *Geschichte des Byzantinischen Staates*, Munich; 1940.

61 cf. Fichtenau, *Das karolingische Imperium*, p. 208.

62 *PG* Libri Carolini, 2. 21, p. 80.

63 For illustrations of the ancient foundations of these cults, cf. A. C. Veit, 'Antik-sakrales Brauchtum im merowingischen Gallien', in G. Schreiber, *Volk und Volkstum*, pp. 121 ff.

64 cf. Fichtenau, 'Byzanz und die Pfalz zu Aachen' *MIOG*, 1951, pp. 1 ff.

65 Foreword to the *Libri Carolini*, and cf. III 19, 142; IV 5, 180, V 20, 211; cf. Fichtenau, *Das Karolingische Imperium*, p. 311.

66 cf. the symposium of research into the German missions, *Das Schwert der Kirche und der germanischen Widerstand*, edited by G. Neckel, Leipzig, 1934. It is marked with the political tendencies of its time, but the material it contains merits attention.

67 A valuable study might be made of Carolingian Manichaeism, the most powerful Christian underground movement in the early European spiritual scene. cf. the Priscillianist-Manichaean influences shown in the Sacramentary produced before 794 for the monastery of Ysen near Regensburg, *Das Prager Sakramentar*, ed. A. Dold and L. Eizenhöfer, text and commentary; published by the Abbey of Beuron; see Part 1, Nos. 38–42.

68 Fichtenau, *Das karolingische Imperium*, p. 181.

69 *Ibid.*, p. 171.

70 *Ibid.*, p. 102.

71 Uberweg-Geyer, *Grundriss der Geschichte der Philosophie*, II, pp. 162 f.

72 cf. Uberweg-Geyer, *op. cit.*, pp. 162 f.

73 *PL* poet. Lat. 3.429.

74 cf. P. Stollenmayer, *Der Tassilo-kelch*, Kremsmünster-Wels; 1949, p. 93.

75 *De Civitate Dei*, II.

76 G. Sarton, *Introduction to the History of Science*, Washington; 1931, II, 1. T., pp. 44 f.
77 cf. Heer, *MIOG*, 1949, pp. 55 ff.

CHAPTER 3

1 For the basic material, in history and cultural geography, see: Vidal de La Blache, *Principes de Géographie humaine*, Paris; 1922; Lucien Febvre, *La Terre et l'Evolution humaine*, Paris; 1922; H. Hassinger, *Geographische Grundlagen der Geschichte*, Freiburg; 1931, rev. ed. 1952.
2 For a basic introduction, see O. Hintze, 'Typologie der standischen Verfassungen des Abendlandes', *HZ* 1929, vols. CXLI and CXLIII.
3 cf. H. E. Feine, 'Ursprung, Wesen und Bedeutung des Eigenkirchentums', *MIOG*, 1950, LVIII, pp. 195 ff.
4 cf. O. Brunner, *Adeliges Landleben und europäischer Geist*, Salzburg; 1949, pp. 61 ff. and 240 ff.; 'Die alteuropäische "Okonomik"', *Zeitschrift für National-ökonomie*, 1950, XIII, pp. 116 ff.
5 An underlying idea in Europe's spiritual pattern. cf. Sidney Hartland, *Primitive Paternity*, London; 1909; on the 'father-crisis', F. Heer, 'Die Wiedergeburt des Vaters', *Stimmen der Zeit*, August 1951.
6 E. Rosenstock-Huessy, *The Driving Power of Western Civilization*, Boston; 1950, p. 4.
7 cf. Lujo Brentano, 'Mensch und Gemeinschaft in christlicher Schau', in *Dokumente*, ed. E. Marmy, Fribourg (Switzerland); 1945, pp. 351 ff., and especially the texts there quoted.
8 cf. F. M. Feldhaus, *Die Technik der Antike und des Mittelalters*, Potsdam; 1930: ancient and medieval technics form one continuous unity.
9 Mumford, *Technics and Civilization*, New York; 1934, pp. 107 ff.
10 cf. A. Lervi-Gourhan. *L'Homme et la Matière*, Paris, vol. I, 1943, vol. II, 1945, *Milieu et techniques*.
11 O. Brunner, *Europäisches Bauerntum*, The Hague, H.6/1951, pp. 25 ff.
12 A. Varagnac, *Civilisation traditionnelle et genres de vie*, Paris, 1948.
13 cf. the references given by E. L. Lodge, *Cambridge Medieval History*, vol. V, 1926, pp. 903 ff.; F. Rörig, 'Die europäische Stadt' in *Propyläen-Weltgeschichte*, Berlin; 1932, vol. VI; 'Magdeburg', *Miscell. Acad. Berolinensia*, 1950, II; H. Pirenne, *Les Villes au Moyen âge*, Brussels; 1927; on the Italian towns, N. Ottokar, 'Il problema della formazione communale', *Questioni di Storia medievale*, ed. E. Rota, Milan; 1951, pp. 355 ff.
14 Brunner, *op. cit.*
15 cf. H. Waddell, *The Wandering Scholars*, London; 1927; M. Bechthum, *Beweggründe und Bedeutung des Vagantentums in der lateinischen Kirche des Mittelalters*, Jena; 1941; for literature on the sixteenth to nineteenth century equivalent see ch. XVIII.
16 For further discussion of these questions and their consequences, cf. E. von Ivanka, 'Der Zerfall der Antiken Welt als geistesgeschichtlicher Vorgang' *Saeculum*, 1952, III, pp. 237 ff.

17   cf. Heer, 'Die Wiedergeburt des Vaters', *Stimmen der Zeit*, August 1951; H. Schelsky, 'Der Vater und Seine Autorität', *Wort und Wahrheit*, September 1953, pp. 663 ff.

18   Brunner, *Andeliges Landleben* etc., p. 77.

19   E. R. Curtius, *Europäische Literatur und Lateinisches Mittelalter*, Bern; 1948.

20   cf. Heer, *Das Experiment Europa*, Einsiedeln, Cologne; 1952.

21   cf. H. Kämpf, 'Reich und Mission zur Zeit Karls des Grossen', in *Geschichte in Wissenschaft und Unterricht*, 1950, 7, p. 415.

22   cf. Heer, *Die Tragödie des Heiligen Reiches* (commentary), pp. 78 ff.

23   cf. Ricci in China in 1610.

24   In 1938, I assembled two (unpublished) volumes of utterances expressing this fear of decadence, barbarism and a rebirth of barbarity.

25   cf. Adolf E. Jensen, *Mythos und Kult bei Naturvölkern*, Wiesbaden; 1951. He argues that modern man is essentially no different from the earliest primitive man.

26   Salvador de Madariaga, *Portrait of Europe*, London; 1952.

27   Schlüter-Hermkes and W. Schubart have thrown much light on this relationship in *Europa und die Seele des Ostens*, Lucerne; 1938, pp. 263 ff.

28   Schüller-Priroli, *2000 Jahre Sankt Peter*, p. 95.

29   C. H. Haskins, 'The Spread of Ideas in the Middle Ages' *Saeculum*, 1926, I, pp. 19 ff.

30   G. Schreiber, *Gemeinschaft des Mittelalters*, Münster; 1948, p. 416; *Deutschland und Spanien*, 1936.

31   *Ibid.*, p. 120; see p. 135 for the process of popular canonization. On earlier wanderings and journeys in old Europe, cf. the account of the pilgrimage and journey of the Bohemian Lord Leo of Rozmital in 1465–7, *Bibliothek des literarischen Vereines in Stuttgart*, 7, Stuttgart; 1844.

32   cf. Frazer's *The Golden Bough*, London; 1915. On what follows, cf. Varagnac, *Civilisation traditionnelle*. For an example of German romantic folk-lore see V. von Geramb, *Um Osterreichs Volkskultur*, Salzburg; 1946. On the fundamental problem, cf. A. von Martin, *Geist und Gesellschaft*, Frankfurt am Main; 1948, pp. 15 ff.

33   For an interesting instance of continuity down to the present day, see F. Seebohm, *The English Village Community*, London; 1938.

34   cf. André Siegfried.

35   cf. E. Spranger, 'Uruschichten des Wirklichkeitsbewusstseins', *S.B. der Preussischen Akademie der Wissenschaft*, 1934, pp. 610 ff.; the references given by O. Brunner, *Adeliges Landleben*, p. 347.

36   See Varagnac, *op. cit.*, There is abundant material in the three volumes of *Folklore préhistorique*, ed. P. Saintyves, Paris; 1934–6, and in the *Handwörterbuch des deutschen Aberglaubens*.

37   Varagnac, *op. cit.*, pp. 201 ff.

38   cf. Gesemann's researches into Balkan epic (E. Eesemann, *Das Deutschtum in Südslavien*, Munich; 1922.

39   cf., e.g., L. Veit, *Volksfrommes Brauchtum und Kirche im deutschen Mittelalter*, Freiburg; 1936; H. Rost, *Die Bibel im Mittelalter*, Augsburg; 1939; J. Hoeffer, *Bauer und Kirche im deutschen Mittelalter*, Freiburg; 1939; on the mediaeval

peasantry, see Lenient, *La Satire en France au Moyen âge*, Paris; 1859; A. Dopsch, *Herrschaft und Bauer in der Deutschen Kaiserzeit*, Jena; 1939.

40 cf. Varagnac, *op. cit.*, p. 254.
41 cf. H. de Lubac, *Surnaturel. Etudes historiques*, Paris; 1946, pp. 325 ff and 369 ff.
42 See Varagnac, *op. cit.* On the enlargement and deformation represented by the French Revolutionary calendar, see Rosenstock, *Die Europäische Revolutionen.* rev. ed., Stuttgart; 1951.
43 Varagnac, *op. cit.*, pp. 354 and 365 ff.
44 cf. Lubac, *loc. cit.*
45 cf. M. Mauss, *Conceptions qui ont précédé la notion de matière*, XIe. Semaine Internationale de Synthèse, Paris; 1945.
46 See P. Ringger, 'Tiere vor Gericht', *Die Tat*, Zürich; 1 December 1951.
47 'Even today, in the middle of the twentieth century, every town in Germany contains several witches, and almost every village has its Devil's Woman' (Johann Kruse, founder and director of the bureau for research into modern belief in witchcraft in Hamburg-Altona).
48 cf. Varagnac, *op. cit.*, pp. 292 ff.
49 *Ibid.* pp. 345 ff.
50 cf. Heer, *Aufgang Europas*, Vienna/Zürich; 1949, Commentary, pp. 208 f.
51 cf. O. von Mitis, *Sippen des frühen Mittelalters, Verbrüderungsbücher, Heldenlieder*, Erlangen; 1944; J. Czarnowski, *Le culte des héros et ses conditions sociales*, Paris; 1919, and Henri Hubert's preface to it.
52 Ample quantities of such evidence have appeared even in works of a literary nature, from F. Lefèvre's *Samson, Fils de Samson, histoire d'une famille de sorciers*, Paris; 1930, to Carlo Levi's *Christ Stopped at Eboli*, London; 1948.
53 Uhland, *Gesamte Schriften*, IV, 383 and 457. cf. K. Burdach, *Reinmar der Alte und Walther von der Vogelweide*, 2nd ed., Halle; 1928, p. 251.
54 cf. C. Erdmann, in *ZfdA*, 1937, 74, pp. 116 ff.
55 cf. F. Martin, *Salzburgs Fürsten in der Barockzeit*, Salzburg; 1949.
56 cf. P. Kletler, 'Nordwesteuropas Verkehr, Handel und Gewerbe im frühen Mittelalter', *Deutsche Kultur. Hist. Reihe*, 2, Vienna; 1924, pp. 52 f., 103.
57 K. Strecker, *Die Apokalypse des Golias*, Rome; 1928.
58 See, e.g., R. Valentino, *La formation de la peinture française*, Paris; 1936, pp. 185 f.
59 G. Schreiber, 'Mönchtum und Wallfahrt', *Hist. Jb.*, 1935, 55, pp. 160 ff.
60 cf. Guignebert, *Le Christianisme médiéval et moderne*, Paris; 1931, pp. 22 f., 25; R. Valentino, *op. cit.*, p. 195.
61 On trial by ordeal, cf. G. Schreiber, *Gemeinschaften des Mittelalters*, pp. 193 f.
62 cf. Emanuel von Severus, *Lupus von Ferrières*, Münster, 1940; and *Deutsches Archiv.*, 1942, 5, pp. 208 f.
63 *Temps flottant, temps dormant*: Varagnac, *op. cit.*, p. 307; cf. Lucien Febvre, *La Terre et l'Evolution humaine.*
64 C. Dawson, *The Making of Europe*, p. 211.
65 *Ibid.*, pp. 220 ff.
66 *PL* SS III, 672.
67 cf. M. Seidlmayer, *Geschichte des italienischen Volkes und Staates* (*Die Grosse Weltgeschichte*, vol. IX), Leipzig; 1940, pp. 68 ff.
68 *Collationes*, M. 133; cf. Hessel, *HZ*, 1923, p. 128.

69 According to Radulfus Glaber, III, 7, there were forty-eight famine years between 970 and 1040; cf. P. Boissonnade, *Le travail dans l'Europe chrétienne au moyen âge*, Paris; 1921, pp. 109 ff.

70 *Ibid.*

71 *Ibid.*, pp. 183 ff.

72 A. de Stefano, 'Le eresie popolari del Medio Evo', in *Questioni di Storia medievale*, p. 774.

73 K. Pfister, *Die Welt des Mittelalters*, Vienna; 1952, pp. 142 ff.

74 cf. Franz, *Die Masse im deutschen Mittelalter*, Freiburg; 1902.

75 cf. Varagnac, *op. cit.*, pp. 123 ff., and 127 f., and especially on the reasons at the popular level for the temporal success of Joan of Arc.

76 Significantly, their only emphatic introduction is in satire and parody, especially in the extremely popular animal epics; cf. Isengrim and Renard the Fox.

77 R. Hamann-MacLean, *Frühe Kunst im westfränkischen Reich*, Leipzig; 1939, pp. 14 f.

78 cf. Heer, *MIOG*, 1949, pp. 67 ff.

79 cf. Heer, *MIOG*, 1949, p. 66; F. Preissl, *Hrotsvith von Gandersheim und die Entstehung des mittelalterlichen Heldenliedes*, Erlangen; 1939.

80 In her *Gallicanus*; Lorenzo de Medici returned to the same theme, cf. E. Walser, *Lebens- und Glaubensprobleme aus dem Zeitalter der Renaissance*, Basle; 1926, p. 10.

81 In connection with Otto III, cf. P. E. Schramm, *Kaiser, Rom und Renovatio*, Berlin; 1929, vol. I, p. 128.

82 cf. J. Kirchberg, *Kaiseridee und Mission unter den Sachsenkaisern und den ersten Saliern von Otto I. bis Heinrich III.*, Berlin; 1934.

83 e.g., Leo of Vercelli, ed. H. Bloch NA 22, p. 115; *Bablionia ferrea et aurata Grecia Ottonem magnum metuunt, collis flexis serviunt.* See Heer, *MIOG*, 1949, p. 69.

84 cf. Fedor Schneider, *Rom und Romgedanke im Mittelalter*, Munich; 1926, pp. 179 ff.

85 Note the identification: *Roma caput totius mundi et aecclesia universalis ... a domno ottone Augusto imperatore ... in pristinum honorem omni reverentia redacta.* See Heer, *MIOG*, 1949, p. 71.

86 Albert Brackmann, 'Der Römische Erneuerungsgedanke und seine Bedeutung für die Reichspolitik der deutschen Kaiserzeit', *Preussische Akademie der Wissenschaften*, Berlin; 1932.

87 M. Beck and H. Büttner, *Die Bistümer Würzburg und Bamberg in ihrer politischen und wirtschaftlichen Bedeutung für die Geschichte des deutschen Ostens*, Berlin; 1937, p. 219.

88 *Ibid.*

89 cf. Heer, *MIOG*, 1949, p. 71.

90 *PL* SS 4, 467.

91 *PL* SS 14, 522.

92 *Lettres de Gerbert*, ed. J. Havet, 1889, p. 237; cf. Heer, *MIOG*, 1949, pp. 78 f.

93 cf. C. Dawson, *op. cit.*, p. 224.

CHAPTER 4

1. cf. Rosenstock-Huessy, *The Driving Power of Western Civilisation*, Boston; 1950; Mayer-Pfannholz, 'Die Wende von Canossa. Eine Studie zum Sacrum Imperium', *Hochland*, vol. 30, Part 2; G. Ladner, *Theologie und Politik vor dem Investiturstreit*, Vienna; 1936; G. Kallen, *Der Investiturstreit als Kampff zwischen germanischen und romanischen Denken*, Cologne; 1937; A. Michel, *Die Sentenzen des Kardinals Humbert, das erste Rechtsbuch der päpstlichen Reform*, Leipzig; 1943; H. de Lubac, *Corpus Mysticum. L'Euchariste et L'Eglise au Moyen Age*, Paris; 1944; G. Tellenbach, *Libertas. Kirche und Weltordnung im Zeitalter des Investiturstreits*, Stuttgart; 1936; A. Baumstark, *Vom geschicht-lichen Werden der Liturgie*, Freiburg; 1923; A. Jungmann, *Missarum Solemnia*, Vienna; 1950, vols. I and II; C. Erdmann, 'Kaiserfahne und Blutfahne', SB *Preussische Akademie der Wissenschaften*, 1932.

2 cf. E. Rosenstock, *op. cit.*, pp. 52–3.

3 *Ibid.*, and illustration, p. 41.

4 G. Ladner, *op. cit.*, pp. 60 ff.

5 *Vicarius dei: PL* Epist. sel. III, 143; *caput ecclesiae, ibid.*, 142.

6 Ladner, *op. cit.*, pp. 70 ff.

7 cf. Humbert's preface to his 'Three Books against the Simoniacs', *PL* 1 d 1, I/102.

8 cf. Ladner, *op. cit.*, pp. 51 ff.

9 *Ibid.*, p. 34.

10 The thirteenth-century spiritualist-Joachimite commentator of Jeremiah took this view of Humbert's as his starting point.

11 J. Geiselmann, *Die Eucharistielehre der Vorscholastik*, Paderborn; 1926.

12 Dawson, *The Making of Europe*, p. 224.

13 Rosenstock-Huessy, *op. cit.*, p. 80.

14 cf. A. Baumstark, *op. cit.*

15 *PL* LIV 424; cf. F. Kampers, 'Roma Aeterna und Sancta Dei Ecclesia Rei Publicae Romanorum', *His Jb*, 1924, 44, pp. 240 ff.; and *Liturgiewiss. Jahrbuch*, V, pp. 207 f.

16 Haberlein.

17 *PL*, LXXVIII, 1–40; H. A. Wilson, *The Gregorian Sacramentary under Charles the Great*, London; 1915; J. A. Jungmann, *Missarum Solemnia*, Vienna; 1950, I and II.

18 I. Herwegen in *ZRG*, 1922, 43, pp. 493 ff.

19 O. Casel, in *Liturgiewissenschaftliches Jahrbuch*, 1922, 2, pp. 107 ff.

20 cf. Bernold, *PL* 151, 986; *NA* 14, 1889, p. 620 ff.; Baumstark, *op. cit.*, p. 125.

21 A. Michel, *op. cit.*, p. 57.

22 Rosenstock, *op. cit.*, pp. 70 f.

23 *Ibid.*, pp. 83 f.

24 *PL*, CXLVIII, 45, cf. Rosenstock, *Ibid.*, p. 88.

25 *Ibid.*, p. 107.

26 *Ibid.*, p. 71.

27 *Ibid.*, p. 94; on Hostiensis (Henry of Segusio) cf. Brian Tierney, 'A Conciliar Theory of the Thirteenth Century', *The Catholic Historical Review*, Washington; 1951, XXXVI, pp. 415 ff.

28   cf. Rosenstock, *op. cit.*, p. 86, and Heer, commentary on *Aufgang Europas*, pp. 183 ff.
29   See the writings of Otto of Freising for the effect of Gregory VII in action.
30   cf. Heer, 'Gregor VII und die Revolutio Christana' and 'Der Kaiser in Kyff-häuser', *Wort und Wahrheit*, No. 12, 1947 and No. 7, 1952.

CHAPTER 5

1   Alfons Lhotsky has devoted some illuminating studies to this genre.
2   cf. H. de Lubac, *Surnaturel, Etudes Historiques*, Paris; 1946.
3   *PL*, CLXXVI, 739.
4   A glance through B. Schmeidler's study (in the collection presented to K. Strecker, 1941) suffices to give one the general outline of an uncommonly difficult problem.
5   An insight into earlier monastic conflicts can be found in K. Hallinger, *Gorze-Kluny, Studien zu den monastischen Lebensformen und Gegensätzen im Hoch-mittelalter*, Rome; 1951–2, 2 vols.; see George Schreiber on the significance of the new orders: G. Schreiber, *Gemeinschaften des Mittelalters*, Münster; 1948.
6   *PL*, CLXXXVIII, *Dialogi Libri Tres*, 1141–60.
7   *PL*, CLXXXVIII, 1201.
8   cf. H. Grundmann's brilliantly balanced presentation, *Neue Forschungen über Joachim von Flore*, Münstersche Forschungen, Marburg, 1950, 1.
9   *Ibid.*, p. 79.
10   *Concordia Lib.*, V, v, 2 and c, p. 21 5.
11   cf. Grundmann, *op. cit.*, p. 25.
12   Table XII in the *Liber Figurarum*, ed. Tondelli, vol. II; See Grundmann, *op. cit.*, pp. 85 ff.
13   Grundmann, *op. cit.*, p. 37, n. 2.

CHAPTER 6

1   Ishvan; cf. T. J. de Boer, *The History of Philosophy in Islam*, London; 1930, p. 95.
2   Lessing, in *Nathan the Wise*, Scene VII, Act 3: The Saladin sends for Nathan who has just returned from a long journey which had brought him to lands ruled by the Christian, Jewish and Moslem religions. He asks Nathan which of these religions is true. Nathan demurs from making answer and tells the Saladin the story of an old man in the Eastern lands long ago. This man had a ring that made him beloved of man and God and it was transmitted from father to son from generation to generation. Eventually it was passed on to a man with three sons whom he loved equally dearly so he had a goldsmith make two counterfeit rings – thus in private each son gets a ring and thinks it is the true one.
    Upon the death of the father the sons quarrel as to who owns the real ring. They go to court for judgment. The judge asks who among you is loved by man and God. Since nobody can answer, the judge suggests that they all live as though each one of them possessed the true ring – the one who surpassed the others then could be said to have inherited the true ring. In short Nathan (or Lessing) was urging a competitive 'co-existence' of the three Faiths.

3 Note that 1307 was the year of the death of Avicenna, while Avicebron-Gebirol was still active in 1070.

4 On the theology of Islam, see L. Gardet and M. M. Anawati, *Introduction a la Théologie musulmane. Essai de Théologie comparée*, vol. XXXVII in *Etudes de philosophie médiévale*, ed. E. Gilson, Paris.

5 On the Christian foundations, see R. Bell, *The Origin of Islam and its Christian Environment*, London; 1926.

6 On the Jewish foundations, see G. von Rad, *Der Heilige Krieg im alten Israel*, Zürich; 1951.

7 G. E. von Grunebaum, *Medieval Islam*, Chicago; 1947, p. 125.

8 Despite this attitude, ascetic fraternities only arose in the twelfth century. Mohammed's personal opposition to celibacy and asceticism probably developed under the influence of Nestorian Christianity.

9 Grunebaum, *op. cit.*, pp. 142 ff.

10 cf. Reuben Levy, *An Introduction to the Sociology of Islam*, London; 1930–3.

11 Grunebaum, *op. cit.*, pp. 9 f.

12 *Ibid.*, pp. 37 f.

13 *Ibid.*, pp. 246 f.

14 *Ibid.*, pp. 248 f.

15 cf. H. H. Schaeder, *Biologie der Person*, published by T. Brugsch and F. H. Lewy, Berlin/Vienna; 1929, vol. IV, pp. 934 ff., G. Richter, *Studien zur Geschichte der ältenen arabischen Fürstenspiegel*, Leipzig; 1932.

16 cf. Grunebaum, *op. cit.*, p. 255

17 *Ibid.*, p. 120.

18 *Ibid.*, p. 97.

19 *Ibid.*, pp. 64 ff.

20 M. Horten, in Uberweg-Geyer, *Grundriss der Geschichte der Philosophie* II, pp. 298 f. On what follows, cf. Carra de Vaux, *Les Penseurs de l'Islam*, Paris; 1921–6, 5 vols.

21 See the symposium *Environmental Factors in Christian History*, Chicago; 1939; especially A. E. Haydon, 'The Influence of Medieval Judaism on Christianity', and P. McKeon, 'Aristotelism in Western Christianity'.

22 cf. for instance the remarks on the subject in the *Encyclopedia Italiana*, XIX, p. 611; Article 'Islam', with Martin Werner's observations, *Die Entstehung des christlichen Dogmas*, 1941.

23 cf. L. Gauthier, 'Scolastique musulmane et Scolastique chrétienne', *Revue d'Histoire de la Philosophie*, 1928, 2, pp. 221 ff. and 333 ff.

24 The ideological basis of Nicodemism is to be found in gnosis and the early Christian sects. The Priscillianists defended lying in the interests of secrecy, as did Dictinius of Astorga in his *Libra*. The principle was condemned by Augustine (*Contra Mendacium*). cf. O. Stedmüller, in *Z.K. Theol.*, 1952, vol. LXXIV, p. 461.

25 cf. Grunebaum, *op. cit.*, pp. 136 ff.

26 cf. Plotinus, *Enneads*, I; VI, 6; Al-Kushairi; cf. R. Hartmann, *Al-Kuschairis Darstellung des Sufitismus*, Berlin; 1914.

27 cf. Grunebaum, *op. cit.*, pp. 167 f.

28 cf. D. de Santillana, *The Legacy of Islam*, ed. W. Arnold and A. Guillaume Oxford; 1931, p. 302.

29   K. Holl, *Gesamte Aufsätze zur Kirchengeschichte*, Tübingen; 1928, vol. III, p. 194.
30   cf. J. W. Parkes, *The Jew in the Medieval Community*, London; 1938; R. Rörig, *Mittelalterliche Weltwirtschaft*, Kiel Lectures, No. 40, 1933.
31   cf. G. Sarton, *Introduction to the History of Science*, Washington; 1931, II, Part 1, pp. 187 f.
32   *Ibid.*, pp. 109 f.
33   *Ibid.*, pp. 163 f.; the eye-witness account of Ephraim of Bonn.
34   *Ibid.*, pp. 289 f.
35   On Salerno's doctors, see Sarton, *op. cit.*, pp. 237 ff.
36   cf. J. de Ghellinck, *L'Essor de la littérature latine au XIIe siècle*, Brussels/Paris; 1946, vol. II, pp. 15 ff.
37   G. Toffanin, *Geschichte des Humanismus*, Holland; 1941, pp. 31 ff.; 137 ff.; 341 ff.; 509 ff.
38   G. Sarton, *op. cit.*, pp. 369 ff.
39   J. de Ghellinck, *op. cit.*, pp. 98, 158 ff.; 162 ff.
40   cf. also P. Brouwe, *Die Judenmission im Mittelalter und die Päpste*, Rome; 1942.
41   For the later middle ages, see E. van Cauwenbergh, *Les pèlerinages expiatoires et judiciaires dans le droit communal de la Belgique au moyen âge*, Louvain; 1922. An impressive picture of old Europe as a land of journeying with its cult-localities and pilgrim routes can be found in Louis de Sivry and J. B. J. Champagnac, *Dictionaire des pèlerinages anciens et modernes et des lieux de dévotion les plus célèbres de l'univers*, 2 vols., Migne, Paris; 1859.
42   cf. G. Sarton, *op. cit.*, p. 34.
43   J. de Ghellinck, *op. cit.*, I, p. 85.
44   G. Sarton, *op. cit.*, II, Part 1, p. 116.
45   J. de Ghellinck, *op. cit.*, II, p. 29.
46   *Ibid.*
47   cf. Angel Gonzalez Palencia, *Los Mozarabes de Toledo en los siglos XII y XIII*, 4 vols., Madrid; 1926–30; *Isis*, ed. G. Sarton, Bruges; 1936, pp. 15, 183 ff.
48   Carles Cardo, *Histoire spirituelle des deux Espagnes*, Paris; 1947; Americo Castro, *Espana en su historia. Cristianos, moros y judios*, Buenos Aires; 1948.
49   cf. Sarton, *op. cit.*, II, Part 1, p. 13.
50   cf. Heer, *Der Aufgang Europas* and *Die Tragödie des heiligen Reiches*.
51   cf. Emile Mâle, *L'art religieux du XIIe siècle en France*, Paris; 1922.
52   cf. Heer, *Der Augfang Europas*, pp. 299 ff.
53   P. Duhèm, *Le système du monde*, Paris; 1954, vol. III, p. 186; cf. Sarton, *op. cit.*, pp. 195 ff.
54   Alanus ab Insulis; *PL*, 218 f., 781 B.
55   *De Arte Catholicae Fide*. The title contains the first mention in the middle ages of the Catholic Faith, as an assertion against the Manichaean, gnostic, Islamic East.
56   Sedlmayr, *Das Entstehen der Kathedrale*, Zürich; 1950.
57   cf. Dumoutet —
58   P. Duhèm, *op. cit.*, III, pp. 184 ff.

CHAPTER 7

1 Mansi, Concil. 31; col. 968 ff. cf. J. Guiraud, *Histoire de l'Inquisition au Moyen Age*, Paris; 1938, vol. II, pp. 418 f.

2 cf. Heer, *Die Tragödie des Heiligen Reiches*, commentary, pp. 39 f.

3 Compare Henry of Albano's sharp rebuke to the German prelates in 1188, and the strictures of Peter Cantor in R. L. John, *Dante*, Vienna; 1946. Also H. C. Lea, *A History of the Inquisition in the Middle Ages*, 3 vols., I, New York; 1906.

4 Manitius, *Geschichte der Lateinischen Literatur des Mittelalters*, Munich; 1931, vol. III, p. 910 ff.

5 Flemish laymen under clerical attack sought Gregory's protection in 1077 (Canossa!) against the Bishop of Cambrai, who wanted to brand them as heretics. *PL* 6 Ep. sel. II. 328. In 1162 Flemings again fled to Alexander III at Tours because the Archbishop of Rheims had attacked them as heretics on account of their wandering apostolic life. cf. H. Grundmann, *Religiöse Bewegungen im Mittelalter*, Berlin; 1935, p. 14. There is, of course, the famous story of the same Pope's meeting in Rome, in 1179, with Peter Waldo, and the latter's appeal for help against the Archbishop of Lyons.

6 L. Olschki, *The Genius of Italy*, New York; 1949, p. 72.

7 A. de Stefano in *Questioni di Storia medioevale*, ed. E. Rota, Milan; 1951, p. 766, attempts to draw a distinction between the heresies before AD 1000 which were the products of theological and monastic schools of thought, and the heresies after AD 1000 which were the products of 'uneducated' people, *illiterati* – a throng of layfolk, craftsmen and workers, whose desire was to live 'according to the Gospel'. The historical reality is somewhat more complex.

8 cf. P. Lestringant, M. Goguel, André Siegfried.

9 cf. D. Roché, *Le Catharisme*, Institut d'Etudes Occitanes, Toulouse; 2nd ed. 1947; S. Pétrement, *Le Dualisme chez Platon, les Gnostiques et des Manichéens*, Paris; 1947; A. Borst, 'Neue Funde und Forschungen zur Geschichte der Katharer', *HZ*. 1952, pp. 17 ff., and the references therein to Runciman, Scheidweiler, Obolensky, Söderberg, Soloviev, etc.

10 cf. R. Grousset and P. Rousset, and since them, most especially S. Runciman, F. Chalandon, P. Boissonnade, R. Bonnaud-Delamare.

11 Werner Sombart has designated the year 1204, the conquest of Constantinople and its treasures by the Latins in the Fourth Crusade as 'the turning point in world history' and 'the birth of capitalism'. Lujo Brentano's attack on Sombart, Weber's and Troeltsch's criticisms in the light of the later work in economic history, O. von Zwiedineck-Südenhorst's debate with A. Müller-Armack, and Otto Brunner's researches have thoroughly demonstrated the clumsiness of such simplifications in terms of economic history. Nevertheless, the events of that fourth crusade deserve particular attention: to them was due the rise of Venice, the patron of Padua and Padua's Averroism, publishing centre for all Europe's spiritualists, sectarians, and nonconformists from the fifteenth century to the eighteenth. Since the end of the tenth century Venice had maintained lavish connections with Mohammedan princes (despite the protests of the popes) as a result of this crusade – which she regarded as a large-scale commercial enterprise – she received from them (as a reward for

diverting the crusaders) such privileges and treaties of commerce as to assure her political and economical supremacy in the Eastern Mediterranean for centuries to come. Thereby they provided the basis for her intellectual and cultural eminence. Thus it was for Venice that the crusaders conquered Zara and Constantinople, and the Greeks viewed these 'uncultured' intolerant arrogant barbarians with horror and hatred as they plundered the 'second Rome'. cf. L. Brentano, *Der wirtschaftende Mensch in der Geschichte*, Leipzig; 1923, pp. 249 and 282 ff.

12 cf. P. Bernard Leib, in his introduction to the French edition of Anna Comnena's *Alexiade*, Paris; 1952.

13 cf. A. Schmaus, 'Der Neumanichäismus auf dem Balkan', *Saeculum*, 1951, II, vol. II, pp. 271 ff.

14 Artists and painters appeared in the late twelfth century, first as heretics and then as atheists in the lower Rhineland; cf. the trial for atheism of Denk, Penz and others at Nuremberg; Leonardo's circle; and the Basle painter Hans Herbster in the early sixteenth century; cf. Paul Burckhardt, *Geschichte der Stadt Basel*, 1942, p. 25.

15 cf. A. Dondaine, H. Söderberg, J. Guiraud, *Histoire de l'Inquisition au Moyen âge*, Paris; 1935; G. Gonnet, *Il valdismo medievale. Prolegomeni*, Turin; 1942; A. Schmaus, *loc. cit.* One important source is Cardinal Torquemada's attack on the Patarists, written in 1461, *Croatia Sacra*, 1932, III, pp. 27 ff.; cf. A. Soloviev, 'La doctrine de l'Eglise de Bosnie', *Bull. de L'Académie Royale de Belgique, C. des lettres*, 1948, 5th series, vol. XXXIV, pp. 481 ff.

16 Guiraud, *op. cit.*, I, pp. 35 ff.

17 *Ibid.*, pp. 66 ff.

18 *Ibid.*, p. 76.

19 cf. Alan of Lille, *PL*, CCV, *De Fide Cath. Contra Haereticos*, II, chs. XX–XXIII, and *Disputationes*, ch. XII.

20 Schmaus, *op. cit.*, pp. 292 ff.

21 Guiraud, *op. cit.*, I, pp. 107 ff., 142.

22 *Ibid.*, p. 162.

23 *La Somme des autorités* à *l'usage des predicateurs meridionaux*, ed. Mgr. Douais, p. 132.

24 W. Weisbach, *Religiöse Reform und Mittelalterliche Kunst*, Zurich; 1945.

25 cf. Heer, *Der Aufgang Europas*.

26 E. L. Lodge, 'The Communal Movement, Especially in France', *Cambridge, Medieval History*, V, Cambridge, 1926, pp. 624 ff. and 903 ff.

27 Potthast, *Reg. Pont. Rom.*, No. 2552.

28 Guiraud, *op. cit.*, I, pp. 285, ff.

29 R. Expilly, *Dictionnaire Geographique, Historique et Politique des Gaules et de la France*, Paris, n.d.

30 Guiraud, *op. cit.*, I, pp. 403 ff.

31 *Ibid.*, p. 302.

32 *Ibid.*, p. 348.

33 *Ibid.*, p. 393.

34 Potthast, *Reg. Pont. Rom.*, No. 32391; Guiraud, *op. cit.*, I, p. 382.

35 K. Kerenyi, *Die Antike Religion*, Düsseldorf-Cologne; 1952.

36 Cicero, *Die Nat. Deorum*, II.

37 A. Zwaneepoel, 'L'inspiration religieuse de l'impérialisme romain', *L'Antiquité Classique*, Brussels; 1949, XVII, pp. 5 ff.

38 'Templorum omnium conditor ac restitutor'; Livy, IV, 20, 7.

39 'Populo id sacerdotium deferente mihi, quod pater meus habuerat' (*Res Gestae*).

40 P. Lambrechts, 'Auguste et la religion romaine', *Latomus*, Brussels; 1947, VI, pp. 177 ff.

41 J. Gagé, *Revue Historique*, 1936.

42 G. Soranzo, 'Gregorio VII e gli stati vasalli della chiesa' *Aevum*, Milan; 1949, XXIII, pp. 131 ff.; cf. *Ibid.*, 1948, XXII, pp. 309 ff.: 'Aspetti del pensiero e dell' opera di Gregorio VII e lo spirito dei tempi.'

43 In 1022 against the Manicheans in Orleans; *Radaulfus Glaber*, III, ch. 8.

44 cf. *Lexikon für Theologie und Kirche*, Ereiberg; 1931, vol. II, pp. 290 f. 'The idea of the necessity of Bible reading for all has always been consistently rejected by the Church, having regard to the Catholic rule of faith and the protection of Bible reading from subjectivism, out of reverence for the Word of God, and for other reasons and safeguards arising out of the Church's unique and divinely ordained teaching office'. (Bulls *Unigenitus* of 8 September 1713 and *Auctorem Fidei* of 28 August 1794). 1713 was an important year in the battle with Jansenism; 1794, a high point of the battle with the French Revolution.

45 M. Fournier, *Les status et privilèges des Universités françaises avant 1789*, Paris; 1890–4, vol. I, p. 442.

46 cf. Carles Cardo, *Histoire Spirituelle des Deux Espagnes*; Amerigo Castro, *Espana en su historia*, etc.

47 cf. Guiraud, *op. cit.*, II, pp. 151 ff.; J. Pou y Marti, *Visionarios, Beguinos y Fraticelos Catalanes*, Vich, 1930.

48 Guiraud, *op. cit.*, II, pp. 267 ff.

49 *Ibid.*, pp. 245 ff.

50 *Ibid.*, pp. 379 ff.

51 *Ibid.*, pp. 515 ff.

52 Gregory IX in his Bull against Frederick II, *PL ep. saec.* XIII, I, p. 653.

53 Guiraud, *op. cit.*, II, pp. 483 ff.

54 *Ibid.*, pp. 567 ff.

55 Muratori, *Ant. Italiae*, 60; ch. 121, 130 f.

56 cf. for instance the references given by A. Gemelli in *Das Franziskanertum*, Leipzig; 1936, pp. 489 ff.

57 L. Olschki, *The Genius of Italy*, New York; 1949, p. 76.

58 C. W. Previté Orton, 'The Italian Cities Till c. 1200', *The Cambridge Medieval History*, V, 1926, pp. 208 ff and 860 ff.

59 P. Boissonnade, *op. cit.*

60 A. de Stefano in *Questioni di Storia medeivale*, 1951, p. 777.

61 G. Gonnet, *Il valdismo medievale. Prolegomeni*, Turin; 1942, pp. 27 ff.

62 P. Boissonnade, *op. cit.*, p. 191.

63 'Of the Desires and Sufferings of St Francis Among the Brethren' – a fragment of Brother Leo's, banned in the Order.

64 cf. L. Olschki, *op. cit.*, pp. 83 ff.

65 cf. A. Gemelli, *op. cit.*

66 M. Lot-Borodine, 'De l'absence des stigmates dans la Chrétienté antique', *Dieu Vivant*, Paris; 1946, vol. III.

67 *De Fide Orth.*, I, IV, 13.

68 On the Stigmatization of St Francis, cf. E. Benz, *Ecclesia Spiritualis*, Stuttgart; 1934, pp. 97 ff.

69 Gemelli, *op. cit.*, p. 26.

70 The Testament of 1226. See O. Karrer, *Francis of Assisi: the Legends and Lauds*, London; 1947, pp. 274 ff.

71 *Ibid.*, p. 273.

72 Gemelli, *op. cit.*, pp. 106 ff.

73 *Ibid.*, pp. 126 ff.

74 cf. E. Benz, *op. cit.*, pp. 61 ff.

75 *Ibid.*, pp. 174 ff.

76 E. Kantorowicz, *Friedrich der Zweite*, 2 vols., Berlin, 1929–30.

77 Gemelli, *op. cit.*

78 A. de Serent, *The life of the soul in the liturgy*, London, 1934.

79 cf. J. Huizinga, *Parerga*, Basle; 1945.

80 St Thomas Aquinas's, *De Regno*.

81 E. Benz., *op. cit.*, pp. 244 ff.

82 *Ibid.*, pp. 265 ff.

83 *Ibid.*, pp. 287 ff.

84 *Ibid.*, pp. 366 ff.

85 cf. K. S. Latourette, *A History of the Expansion of Christianity*, 7 vols., New York; 1937–45; and O. van der Vat, *Die Anfänge der Franziskanermisionen*, Werl., 1934.

86 Gemelli, *op. cit.*, pp. 82 ff.

87 John of Monte Corvino, 1247–1328, the founder of the first Catholic mission in India, and who afterwards in China stood in high favour with the Great Khan at Peiping, converted many Nestorians, i.e. 'Eastern Christians', and wrote to Rome for help. The arrival of a 'godless' Lombard physician – around 1301! – badly hindered his missionary work. cf. Sarton, *op. cit.*, II, 2. T., pp. 1054 ff.

88 *Ibid.*, II, 2. T., p. 958.

89 cf. R. L. John, *op. cit.*, pp. 56 f.

90 Janssen, *Philosophisches Jahrbuch der Görresgesellschaft*, 1929, 33, pp. 137 ff.; Sarton, *op. cit.*, II, pp. 1032 ff.

91 The quotations unless otherwise indicated are from J. S. Brewers's edition of Roger Bacon, *Opera Quaedam Hactenus Inedita*, London; 1859, vol. I.

92 *Opus Tertium*, Brewer, I, p. 86.

93 e.g., *Opus Majus*, pp. 17 ff.

94 Brewer, *op. cit.*, p. 395.

95 *Beatus Franciscus*, Brewer, I, p. 298.

96 *Ibid.*, pp. 398 ff.

97 *Ibid.*, p. 400.

98 *Ibid.*, p. 402.

99 *Opus Minus*, pp. 323 ff.

100 'De cursu totius ecclesiae, secundum omnes status a principio usque ad finem', *Opus Tertium*, pp. 95 f.

101 *Ibid.*, p. 100; p. 272.
102 Letter to Clement IV in 1266; *Ibid.*, pp. 11 ff.
103 *Opus Tertium*, p. 113.
104 *Ibid.*, pp. 525 ff.
105 Sarton, *op. cit.*, II, 3, p. 953.
106 L. Thorndike, *A History of Magic and Experimental Science*, New York; 1934, p. 11.
107 *Ibid.*, pp. 359 f.
108 Benz, *op. cit.*, pp. 368 ff.
109 Anti-curial Venice republished his works along with those of the Joachimites and Spirituals. The Magdeburg Centuries honoured him, together with Francis, as one who bore the light through the dark age.
110 K. Vossler, *Spanien und Europa*, Munich; 1952, pp. 97 ff.
111 H. J. Hüffer, 'Las Relationes Hispano-germanas durante mil discientos años', *Revista de Estudios Politicos*, 1951, 36, gives the references for Lull's influence in Germany.
112 Vossler, *op. cit.*, p. 99.
113 Calvente y Vidal, 'La paz y el arbitraje internacional en R. Lulio', *Revista Verdad y Vida*, Madrid; 1943, I, pp. 456 ff.; quoted by Vossler, *op. cit.*, p. 100.

CHAPTER 8

1 On Naples, see *Storia dell'Università di Napoli*, Naples; 1924, by F. Torraca and others; on what follows, A. de Stefano, *I Tedeschi e l'eresia medievale in Italia*, Blychnis, June, 1916, (tendentious and polemical in spirit but valuable); E. Aegerter, *Les hérésies du moyen âge*, Paris, 1939.
2 cf. G. Sarton, *Introduction to the History of Science*, II, 2, pp. 834 ff.
3 *Ibid.*, pp. 844 f.
4 Pipini Chron., Muratori IX, pp. 66 f.
5 cf. A. de Stefano, *La Cultura a la Corte di Federico II Imperatore*, Palmero; 1938, pp. 33 ff.
6 *Divina provisone* and *ipsa necessitate cogente*; preface to the *Liber Augustalis* of 1231; De Stefano, *ibid.*, p. 149.
7 'Ego quidem mundi dominus', *Const.*, 1, 5, XIV, 3.
8 cf. the dedication of the *Liber Phisionomias*.
9 In *De Arte Venandi cum Avibus*.
10 cf. Bacon and Campanella on eugenics as applied both to horses and to men.
11 De Stefano, *La Cultura*, etc., p. 87.
12 cf. E. Winkelmann, and on the other side, Denifle, *Die Universtäten des Mittelalters bis 1400*, Berlin; 1885; de Stefano, *La Cultura*, etc., pp. 279 ff.
13 *Hist. Diplom.*, II, pp. 453 f.
14 F. van Steenberghen, *Siger de Brabant d'apres ses oeuvres inédites*, Louvain; 1942, vol. II, p. 410.
15 cf. J. Th. Eschmann's introduction to the *De Regno, ad Regem Cypri*, previously known as *De Regimine Principum*, translated by B. Phelans with the title *On Kingship, to the King of Cyprus*, Toronto; 1949.
16 For a bibliography on the medieval universities, see N. Shachner, *The Medieval Universities*, London, 1938; pp. 377 ff.

17   H. Slesser, *The Middle Ages in the West. A Study of European Unity*, London/
      New York n.d., pp. 98 ff.
18   Schachner, *op. cit.*, p. 275.
19   *Ibid.*, pp. 266 ff.
20   Denifle and Chatelain, *Chartularium Universitatis Parisiensis*, 4 vols., Paris;
      1889–92, I, 31; cf. P. Mandonnet, *Siger de Brabant et l'Averroisme latin au
      XIII siècle*, Louvain; 1911, vol. I, p. 18.
21   See Denifle and Chatelain, *op. cit.*, and *Auctarium Chart. Univ. Paris*, 2 vols.,
      Paris; 1894–7; M. Fournier, *Les statuts et privilèges des universités françaises
      depuis leur fondation jusqu'en 1789*, 4 vols., Paris; 1890–4; C. Cross, 'The
      Political Influences of the University of Paris in the Middle Ages', *American
      Historical Review*, 1901, vol. VI, pp. 440 ff.; C. Rashdall, *Rise of the Universi-
      ties*, London; 1895, 2 Parts in 3 vols.; P. Perdrizet, *Le Calendrier de la Nation
      d'Allemagne de l'Ancienne Université de Paris*, Paris; 1937; G. C. Boyce, *The
      English–German Nation in the University of Paris during the Middle Ages*,
      London; 1927; S. d'Irsay, *Histoire des Universités en Europe*, Paris; 1933 ff.
22   Mandonnet, *op. cit.*, I, pp. 32 f.
23   Van Steenberghen calls the intellectual movement which, since Renan and
      Mandonnet, has been known as 'Averroism' 'heretical Aristotelianism', see
      van Steenberghen's timetable, *op. cit.*, vol. II, pp. 746 ff.
24   cf. Manitius, *Geschicte der lateinischen Literatur des Mittelalters*, Munich;
      1931, III, pp. 805 ff.
25   cf. G. Fagniez, *L'Industrie et les classes industriel.es à Paris au XIIIe siècle*,
      Paris; 1877.
26   cf. Sarton, *op. cit.*, II, 2, pp., 932 ff.; G. de Lagarde, *La Naissance de l'esprit
      laique au declin du moyen âge*, 8 vols., Paris; 1932, ff., vol. III, pp. 38 ff.
27   E. R. Curtius, *Europäische Literatur und lateinisches Mittelalter*, Berne; 1948,
      pp. 132 ff.
28   cf. the bibliography supplied by Curtius; *Ibid.*, p. 133, Lagarde, *op. cit.*, III,
      pp. 38 ff.; Van Steenberghen on the *Roman de la Rose*, in the context of its
      own age (M. M. Gorce, G. Paré, etc.).
29   B. Nardi, *Sighieri di Brabante nel pensiero del Rinascimento Italiano*, Rome;
      1945, p. 34.
30   See van Steenberghen, *op. cit.*, II, pp. 439 ff.
31   Mandonnet, *op. cit.*, I, pp. 36 ff.
32   cf. his Prologue, *Phys.*, I, I, bk. I, ch. 1.
33   Van Steenberghen, *op. cit.*, II, p. 715.
34   Van Steenberghen tones down the violence of these attacks (*ibid.*, II, p. 723)
      and strongly attacks the Franciscan Jules d'Albi (note that he comes from the
      great Cathar centre) who made the gulf between Thomas and Bonaventure
      extremely clear. *Saint Bonaventure et les luttes doctrinales de 1267–1277*, Paris;
      1923.
35   cf. van Steenberghen, *op. cit.*, II, p. 729.
36   cf. E. Benz's studies of Joachim, No. 3, 'Thomas von Aquin und Joachim von
      Fiore', *ZKG*, 1934, 53, pp. 52 ff.; H. Grundmann, *Neue Forschungen über
      Joachim von Fiore*, 1950, p. 68.
37   Van Steenberghen, *op. cit.*, II, p. 707.
38   On Aristotle himself, see Werner Jaeger; also J. Zürcher, *Aristoteles, Werk*

und Geist, Paderborn; 1952; on Aristotle in the middle ages, M. Grabmann, *Methoden und Hilfsmittel des Aristotelesstudiums im Mittelalter*, Munich, 1939.

39 *Sed nihil ad nos nauc Dei miraculis, cum de naturalibus naturaliter disseramus*; cf. Mandonnet, *op. cit.*, I, p. 150.

40 *Ibid.*, p. 185.

41 *Ibid.*, p. 193.

42 *Ibid.*, p. 141.

43 *Ibid.*, II, pp. 73 ff.

44 *Ibid.*, I, pp. 180 and 103.

45 *Ib'd.*, pp. 190 ff.

46 *Ibid.*, pp. 93 f.

47 *Chart. Univ. Paris*, I, pp. 540 f.

48 M. Grabmann 'Das Werk De Amore Andreas Capellanus und das Verurteilungsdekret des Bischofs Stephan Tempier von Paris vom 7. März 1277', *Saeculum*, 1932, vol. VII, pp. 75 ff.

49 cf. L. Olschki, *The Genius of Italy*; R. John, *Dante*.

50 From Mandonnet's edition (II), pp. 174 ff.

51 Van Steenberghen, *op. cit.*, II, p. 714.

52 cf. P. Glorieux, *La litterature quodlibetique de 1260 à 1320* (Bibl. Thom. V, Le Saulcheoir Kain, 1925).

53 *Quodl.*, VI, 6; cf. e.g. *Gent.*, IV, chs. 7, 30, 40, 55; where he examines twenty-six objections against and defences of the doctrine of the Incarnation. *Quodl.* VII, 16; *Quodl.*, IX, 16.

54 *Gent.*, IV, chs. 41, 56, 62, 79, 80.

55 *Quodl.*, VI, X, 14; *Gent.* III chs. 131 ff.; *Ibid.*, chs. 123–6 and 136.

56 *Gent.* III ch. 118; *Ibid.* ch. 83, III, chs. 74, 112, IV, chs. 70, 80, 154; *Ibid.*, III, chs. 147, 152, 155, 157; *Ibid.*, III, 140, IV, ch. 6, II, chs. 44, 83, I, ch. 20.

57 A. Koller, *Essai dur l'Esprit du Berbère Marocain*, Fribourg; 1946, p. 216; P. Pottier, *Saint Augustin, le Berbère* (to which Koller refers).

58 G. von Hertling, *Augustinus-Zitate bei Thomas von Aquino*, Proceedings of the Bavarian Academy of Sciences, No. 4, pp. 535 ff.

59 *Quodl.*, IV, ch. 16.

60 cf. G. de Lagarde, *op. cit.*, III, p. 95.

61 *Gent.*, I, ch. 28, III, chs. 111 and 115.

62 *Ibid.*, IV, ch. 50.

63 *Ibid.*, III, chs. 19–21.

64 *Gent.*, III, ch. 25, I, ch. 45 ff.

65 *Ibid.*, ch. 25 f.

66 *Summa Theol.*, 1g, 2a, 3c, and elsewhere.

67 *Gent.*, III, ch. 39.

68 On Thomas's mechanistic, technomorphic picture of the world as a piece of craftsmanship, cf. A. Mitterer, *Die Zeugung der Organismen, insbesondere des Menschen nach dem Weltbild des hl. Thomas von Aquin und dem der Gegenwart*, Vienna; 1947, especially pp. 48 and 58 ff.; O. Lottin 'Pour un commentaire historique de la moral de saint Thomas d'Aquin', *Recherches de Théologie Ancienne et Mediévale*, 1939, vol. XI, pp. 270 ff.

69 See *De Regno, ad Regem Cypri*.

70 H. Slesser, *The Middle Ages in the West*, London, n.d., p. 173; cf. C. Journet, 'Note sur l'origine et la transmission du pouvoir politique', *Nova et Vetera*, Fribourg; 1952, No. 3, pp. 233 ff.; A. Krempel, *La doctrine de la révélation chez Saint Thomas*, Paris; 1952, especially pp. 610 ff. and 617, on Thomas's war against the hypostatization of society and the state, which he sees not as beings in their own right ('Holy Empires') with a necessary tendency towards self-deification, but simply as *relations* (cf. *1 Sent.*, d. 24, q. 2a, 2 and 3). cf. L. Lachance, *L'Humanisme politique de saint Thomas*, 2 vols.; Paris-Montreal; 1941.

71 *Gent.*, III, ch. 93, III, ch. 84, 73, 150, ch. 21 (based on St Paul I Cor. 3.9), 95, 54.

72 *Gent.*, IV, chs. 21 and 22.

73 cf. *Gent.*, III, chs. 123–5.

74 *Gent.*, III, ch. 117.

75 *Gent.*, IV, ch. 76.

76 *Gent.*, I, ch. 1.

77 *Quodl.*, I, art. 14.

78 *Gent.*, IV, ch. 74.

79 *Gent.*, IV, ch. 60; *Quodl.*, XII, art. 19.

80 cf. G. Groppo, 'Orientamenti negli studi dell' origine naturale della società in S. Tommaso d'Aquino', *Salesianum*, XI, No. 4, Turin; 1949, pp. 575 ff.; Lagarde, *op. cit.*, III, pp. 99 f.

81 cf. M. Reding's Graz inaugural lecture, *Thomas von Aquin und Karl Marx*, Graz; 1953. On *stasis* in Aristotle, cf. M. Wheeler, 'Aristotle's Analysis of the Nature of Political Struggle', *American Journal of Philosophy*, April; 1951, LXXII, pp. 145 ff.

82 *Gent.*, III, ch. 144.

83 *Gent.*, III, ch. 146.

84 *Gent.*, IV, ch. 88.

85 Commentary on Aristotle's *De Anima*, III, 8; 431b, 21 ff., lectio 13b.

86 *Gent.*, III, ch. 25.

87 *Quodl.*, II, art. 19.

88 *Gent.*, IV, ch. 84.

89 M. Grabmann, 'Die Proklos-Ubersetzungen des Wilhelm von Moerbeke und ihre Verwertung in der lateinischen Literatur des Mittelalters', in the special Heisenberg issue of the *Byzantinische Zeitschrift*, 1930, 30, pp. 78 ff.

CHAPTER 9

1 cf. A. Coville and R. Fawtier, 'L'Europe occidentale de 1270 à 1380', G. Glotz, *Histoire generale*, VI, Paris 1940–1; H. Pirenne, G. Cohen and H. Focillon, 'La Civilisation occidentale au Moyen Age du XIe au milieu du XVe siècle', *ibid.*, VIII, 1933; H. Pirenne, *Histoire Economique de l'Occident Médiéval*, Bruges; 1951.

2 cf. Lagarde, *De l'Esprit Laique aux Moyen Ages*, III, p. 203.

3 cf. W. Ullmann, *Medieval Papalism. The Political Theories of the Medieval Canonists*, London, 1949, pp. 76 ff. and 114 ff.

4 cf. V. Martin, *Les Origines du Gallicanisme*, 2 vols., Paris; 1949. K. Schleyer, *Die Anfänge des Gallikanismus*, Berlin; 1937.

5 cf. J. Paulus, *Henri de Gand, Essai sur les tendances de sa metaphsique*, Paris; 1938, and *Quodl.* I. qu. 10, I, p. 13, col. 3 in the Venetian edition of 1608.

6 cf. Lagarde, *op. cit.*, III, pp. 268 ff.

7 *Aegidius. De Eccl. Potestate*, l., ch. 5, p. 16.

8 cf. G. Mollat, *Les Papes d'Avignon*, 8th ed., Paris; 1950.

9 See F. Kampers, *Hist. Jb.*, 1894, XV, p. 799; Menendez y Pelayo, *Historia de los Heterodoxos Esp.*, 1917, vol. III, pp. 24 f.

10 cf. E. Benz, *ZKG*, 1934, 53, pp. 84 ff.; on the Protocol of Anagni in 1255: H. Denifle, *ALKM*, 1885, I, pp. 49 ff.; 99 ff.; (for the texts) F. Ehrle, *Ibid.*, pp. 509 ff.

11 Thorndike, *A History of Magic and Experimental Science*, III, pp. 51 ff., and II, ch. 8.

12 *Ibid.*, III, p. 77.

13 Olschki, *The Genius of Italy*, p. 176.

14 L. Oliger, *De Secta Spiritus Libertatis in Umbria Saec. XIV Disauisitio et Documenta*, Rome; 1943.

15 *Ibid.*, pp. 52 ff.

16 F. Ehrle, *ALKM*, III, pp. 142 ff.

17 K. von Ettmayer 'Die historischen Grundlagen der Entstehung der italienischen Sprache', *MIOG*, 1934, 48, pp. 1 ff.

18 cf. R. John, *Dante*.

19 A. Solmi, 'Le scuole del medio evo e l'origine delle Università', *Rivista di storia del Diritto Italiano*, 1941, 14, pp. 5 ff.

20 cf. in the life of Augustine, the feud between Ambrose and Symmachus.

21 G. Saitta, *Il Pensiero italiano nel l'Umanesimo e nel Rinascimento. I. L'Umanesimo*, Bologna; 1949, pp. 13 ff.

22 A. Maier, *Ein Beitrag zur Geschichte des italienischen Averroismus*, Rome; 1944; cf. also her *An der Grenze von Scholastik und Naturwissenschaft*, Essen; 1943; C. Calcaterra, *L'Università di Bologna*, Bologna; 1948.

23 *Def. Pacis*, dist., I, ch. 4. cf. R. Scholz, 'Marsilius von Padua und die Genesis des modernen Staatsbewusstseins', *HZ*, 1937, 156, and O. Bornak, *Staatskirchliche Anschauungen und Handlungen am Hofe Kaiser Ludwigs des Bayern*, Munich; 1933. F. Bock, *Reichsidee und Nationalstaaten vom Untergang des alten Reiches bis zür Kündigung des deutsch-englischen Bündnisses im Jahre 1341* 1943.

24 Saitta, *op. cit.*, I, p. 54.

25 *Def. Pacis*, dist., II, ch. 10, p. 247.

26 'Universitas fidelium credencium et invocancium nomen Christi': *Def. Pacis*, dist., II, ch. 2, p. 144.

27 cf. Johannes Duns Scotus, *Tractatus de Primo Principio*, critical edition by M. Müller, Freiburg; 1941, p. 116; E. Longpré, *La Philosophie du B. Duns Scot*, Paris; 1924; E. Gilson's Scotus studies in the Gifford Lectures of 1950; and an interesting study by A. M. Knoll, 'Thomismus und Skotismus als Standestheologien', *Festschrift für Karl Adam*, Düsseldorf; 1952, pp. 225 ff.

28 *De primo principio*, ed. M. Müller, p. 116.

29 cf. Lagarde, *op. cit.*, III, pp. 307 ff.

30   *De Primo Principio*, ed. M. Müller, p. 124.

31   *Ibid.*, pp. 126 ff.

32   See the following recent studies: P. Böhner, *The Tractatus de Successivis attributed to William of Ockham, edited with a Study on the Life and Works of Ockham*, St Bonaventure, New York; 1944; *The Tractatus de Praedestinatione et de Praescientia Dei et de tuturis contigentibus of William of Ockham edited with a Study on the Medieval Problem of a free-valued Logic*, New York; 1945; V. Heynck, 'Wilhelm Ockham 1349–1949', *Franziskanische Studien*, 1950, 32; Lagarde, *op. cit.*, VI, ('Ockham, La Morale et le Droit', Paris; 1946), p. 91.

33   *In Sent.*, I, d. 2q, 4n.

34   *Summ. Tot. Log.*, I, 14, in the Venetian edition of 1522, fol. 6v. B., cf. Uberweg-Geyer, *Grundriss der Geschichte*, etc., p. 578.

35   *In Sent.*, I, d. 2, q. 8 f.

36   L. F. Paetow, *The Battle of the Severn Arts*, Berkeley, California; 1914.

37   The rights of man and democracy are unthinkable without the system of pacts and the bitter competitive struggles which arose amongst the cities and between them and the princes. For an illustrative example, see E. Coornaert, 'L'Etat et les villes à la fin du Moyen Age. La politique d'Anvers', *Revue Historique*, 1952, CCVII, pp. 185, ff. cf. H. Pirenne, *Les démocraties urbaines aux Pays-Bas*, 1912. On the city: F. Rörig, 'Die europäische Stadt', *Propyläen-Weltgeschichte*, 1932, VI; Jecht, 'Studien zur gesellschaftlichen Struktur der mittelalterlichen Städte', *Vjschr. fur Sozial – und Wirtschaftsgeschichte*, XIX; H. Pirenne, *Les villes aux Moyen Age*, Brussels; 1927; R. Pernoud, *Les Villes marchandes au 14e siècle Impérialisme et capitalisme au moyen âge*, 3rd ed., Paris; 1948.

38   The German words *künne*, proclaim, *konig*, king and *küren*, elect, are all from the same root.

39   F. Ehrle, in *ALKM*, 3 pp. 540 ff.; also, S. V. Zuidema, *De Philosophie van Occam in zijn Commentar op de Sententien*, 2 vols., Hilversum; 1936.

40   cf. Lagarde, *op. cit.*, vol. on 'Ockham et son temps', Paris; 1942, pp. 23 f., 33 ff. and 44.

41   cf. *Opus Nonaginta Dierum* and *Compendium Errorum Papae*.

42   cf. R. Kassner, his Essay Volumes, Insel-Verlag, 1925–61.

43   *In Sent.*, II, q. 11 g, II, q. 11 Q7. Lagarde, *op. cit.*, V, Paris; 1946, pp. 121 ff.

44   *Ibid.*, 164 ff.

45   Lagarde, *op. cit.*, VI, pp. 74 ff.

46   cf. Zuidema, *op. cit.*, and E. Hochstetter, in *Blätter für Deutsche Philosophie*, 1939–40, 13, pp. 199 ff., who opposes Zuidema, basing himself on R. Seeberg's *Duns Scotus*.

CHAPTER 10

1   Considerable light on the psychical and spiritual state of Eckhart's circle can be gained from the texts given by F. Jostes, *Meister Eckhart und seine Junger, ungedruckte Texte zur Geschichte der deutschen Mystik*, Freiburg, Switzerland, 1895.

2   cf., Uberweg-Geyer, *Grundiss der Geschichte der Philosophie*, pp. 558.

3   Heer, *Die Tragödie des Heiligen Reiches*.

4 Hauck, *Kirchengeschichte Deutschlands*, V, pp. 639 ff.
5 Lagarde, *de l'esptir laique en moyen âge*, IV, pp. 156, ff.
6 Madonnet, *Siger de Brabant*, etc.
7 cf. Uberweg-Geyer, *op. cit.*, p. 558.
8 *De Trin.*, XIV, 7 and 9; *De Visione Beata*, ed. Krebs, p. 77.
9 On Eckhart, see E. Benz, 'Neuere Forschungen über Meister Eckhart', *Blätter für deutsche Philosophie*, 1939/40, 13, pp. 379 ff.; H. Ebeling, *Meister Eckharts Mystik. Studien zu den Geisteskämpfen um die Wende des 13. Jahrhunderts*, Stuttgart; 1941; H. Peisch, *Meister Eckhart*, Vienna; 1946.
10 Ebeling, *op. cit.*, p. 116.
11 P. Minges, *Die Gnadenlehre des Duns Scotus*, Münster; 1906, p. 67; cf. Ebeling, *op. cit.*, p. 120.
12 Benz, *op. cit.*, p. 387.
13 Ebeling, *op. cit.*, p. 288 (as against Grabmann).
14 K. Berger, *Die Ausdrücke der unio mystica im Mittelhochdeutschen*, Berlin; 1935.
15 e.g. F. Pfeiffer, *Meister Eckharts Reden und Predigiten*, Leipzig; 1857, pp. 237, 21; 89, 16 ff.; 46, 3 ff.; Serm. 55 and 547; MEW I, 39, 1 ff. cf. Ebeling, *op. cit.*, p. 210.
16 B. Geyer.
17 B. Peters, *Der Gottesbegriff Meister Eckharts*, Hamburg; 1936.
18 e.g. Pfeiffer, *op. cit.*, 194, 2 f.; 163, 19 f.; 507, 32 f.; 242, 2 f.
19 Ebeling, *op. cit.*, p. 126.
20 Jostes, *op. cit.*, p. 89.
21 Pfeiffer, *op. cit.*, 266, 4.
22 *Ibid.*, 270, 40 f.
23 B. Heim, *Die Freundschaft nach Thomas von Aquin*, pp. 123 ff.
24 R. Löhrer, *Freundschaft in der Antike*, Lucerne; 1949, p. 11.
25 On Eckhart and Luther, see the references given by Benz, *op. cit.*, pp. 400 ff.
26 Pfeiffer, *op. cit.*, 263, 6 f.; 311, 4 ff.
27 J. Greven.
28 cf. Mario Pensa, *Il Pensiero Tedesco. Saggio di Psicologia della filosofia tedesca*, Bologna; 1938, pp. 19 ff.
29 *Sermons de J. Tauler, et autres écrit mystiques*, ed. A. C. Corin, Paris-Liège; 1924, I; 1929 II. cf. I, pp. 104 ff.
30 *Ibid.*, I, p. 162.
31 *Ibid.*, II, pp. 33 ff.; cf. Franz von Baader – God and the devil would have been reconciled long since, had it not been for man.
32 cf. e.g., Corin, *op. cit.*, II, p. 83 and II, p. 142.
33 *Ibid.*, II, p. 111; II, p. 305.
34 cf. the sermon on the love of enemies attributed to Tauler, *Ibid.*, II, pp. 352 ff.
35 *Ibid.*, II, pp. 8 f.
36 *Ibid.*, II, pp. 256 ff.
37 *Ibid.*, I, p. 35.
38 *Ibid.*, I, pp. 61 ff.
39 Eckhart, too, is one with the early German middle ages in regarding holy Christendom as the union of laymen and clergy in one Church.
40 Corin, *op. cit.*, I, pp. 240 ff.

41   *Ibid.*, I, p. 98.
42   *Ibid.*, II, p. 334.
43   *Ibid.*, I, p. 249.
44   *Ibid.*, II, p. 265; I, p. 315, II, p. 93.
45   *Ibid.*, II, p. 93, p. 111, against learned theologians; II, p. 166, on valueless confessions; I, p. 161.
46   cf. G. G. Coulton, *Five Centuries of Religion*, esp. vol. IV, 'The last days of medieval monachism', Cambridge; 1950, pp. 18 ff., 121 ff., 471 ff. (On the relations between cities and monasteries), 560 ff. (On penal immunity), 731 ff. (On the situation from the end of the Reformation to the middle of the eighteenth century). On Germany and Central Europe, see the numerous works by Karl Eders on the Reformation period, and J. Lortz, *Die Reformation in Deutschland*, 2nd ed. Freiburg im Breisgau; 1941, I, pp. 87 ff., II, pp. 109 ff.
47   Corin, *op. cit.*, I, p. 75.
48   *Ibid.*, I, pp. 183 f.
49   *Ibid.*, II, p. 34.
50   *Ibid.*, II, p. 112.
51   *Ibid.*, II, p. 126.
52   *Ibid.*, II, pp. 100 ff., on the Kingdom of God, Hermann Büttner, *Meister Eckharts Schriften und Predigten.*
53   Corin, *op. cit.*, II, pp. 275 ff.
54   *Ibid.*, I, pp. 206, 112, and 88 f.
55   *Ibid.*, II, p. 84.
56   *Ibid.*, II, pp. 117 ff.
57   E. Scheunemann, *Artushof und Abenteur. Zeichnung höfischen Daseins in Hartmanns Erec*, Breslau; 1932.
58   cf. Corin, *op. cit.*, II, pp. 174 f., 196 f., 202 f., 256 f.
59   *Ibid.*, II, p. 120; p. 142, quoting Augustine.
60   *Ibid.*, II, pp. 143–4.
61   *Ibid.*, II, pp. 146 f.
62   *Ibid.*, I, pp. 240 ff.; 259 f.
63   *Ibid.*, II, pp. 409.
64   cf. F. W. Wentzlaff-Eggebert, *Deutsche Mystik zwischen Mittelalter und Neuzeit*, Berlin; 1944, pp. 59 ff.; and the references he gives, pp. 251–339.
65   See the important studies of late medieval Germany by H. Heimpels: 'Das deutsche Spätmittelalter', *HZ*, 158, 1938, and 'Deutschland im späteren Mittelalter', *Handbuch der deutschen Geschichte*, ed. Brandt, A. O. Meyer and others, I, 1939: cf. also *AKG*, 27, 1935, on Alexander Roes.
66   O. Bornhak, *Staatskirchliche Anschauugen und Handlungen am Hote des Kaiser Ludwigs des Bayern*, Weimar; 1933, pp. 16 ff. and pp. 30 ff.

CHAPTER 11

1   N. Schachner, *The Medieval Universities*, London; 1938, pp. 186 ff.
2   *Ibid.*, pp. 221 ff.
3   cf. R. F. Young, 'Bohemian Scholars and Students at the English Universities from 1347 to 1750' *English Historical Review*, January 1923.

4   V. Valentin, Weltgeschichte. *Völker Männer Ideen*, Cologne-Berlin; 1952, p. 265.

5   Op. II, 28.

6   Out of the superabundance of literature on Joan of Arc, cf. B. Hilliger, *Jeanne d'Arc*, 4th ed. Paris; 1950; E. Perroy, *La Guerre de Cent ans*, Paris; 1945.

7   J. J. Brousson, *Les Fioretti de Jeanne d'Arc*, Paris; 1932, pp. 28 ff.

8   *I Fioretti di San Francesco e Il Cantico del Sole*, ed. P. Pechiai, Milan; 1939.

9   J. Bütler, *Jeanne d'Arc, die Akten der Verurteilung*, Einsiedeln Cologne; 1943.

10 Brousson, *op. cit.*, pp. 25, 35, 53, 61 and 151.

11 *Ibid.*, pp. 43, 176, 135, 77, 151, 42.

12 *Ibid.*, pp. 97, 115 f., 167 and 46 f.

13 *Ibid.*, p. 44. This attitude, and the misery that went with it, persisted in German districts, too, into the eighteenth century.

14 *Ibid.*, p. 64; Bütler, *op. cit.*, p. 165.

15 Brousson, *op. cit.*, pp. 83, 94 f., 112.

16 *Ibid.*, pp. 211 f.; 120, 122 f., 91, 127, 168 and Bütler, *op. cit.*, p. 180.

17 Brousson, *op. cit.*, pp. 24, 38, 55, 58, 76, 82, 85, 98–9, 104.

18 *Ibid.*, pp. 261, 50, 115, 125, 131, 153, 161, 193.

19 *Ibid.*, pp. 155, 159, 46.

20 *Ibid.*, pp. 118, 169, 175 ff., 187.

21 *Ibid.*, pp. 89, 165.

22 *Ibid.*, pp. 178 f., 180, 201, 216.

23 As was asserted once more in the Bull of Canonisation in 1920; cf. Bütler, *op. cit.*, p. 320.

24 *Ibid.*, pp. 291, 298, 206, 190.

25 *Ibid.*, p. 160.

26 On Dietrich von Niem, see A. Lhotsky (S. B. der österr. Ak. d. Wiss. phil. hist. Kl. 226, 1949), 93 ff.; K. Pivec, *MIOG*, LVIII, 1950, pp. 386, ff.; K. Pivec and H. Heimpel, 'Neue Forschungen zu Dietrich von Niem', *Akademie der Wissenschaften*, Göttingen; 1951, No. 4, pp. 104–11.

27 Uberweg-Geyer, *Grundiss der Geschichte etc.*, p. 591.

28 cf. W. Dress, *Die Theologie Gersons. Eine Untersuchung zur Verbindung von Nominalismus und Mystik im Spätmittelalter*, Gütersloh, 1931, pp. 54 ff.

29 Gerson, *De Consolatione Theologiae*, ed. Du Pin. Antwerp; 1706: I, 147 d ff.

30 R. Stadelmann, *Vom Geist des augehenden Mittelalters*, Halle; 1929, 9 ff.

31 See Stadelmann for the sources, *op. cit.*, p. 110, and A. Hinna, *The Christian Renaissance. A History of the Devotio Moderna*, New York, 1924.

32 Wessel Gansfoort, *De Comm. Sanct., Opera*, Groningen; 1614, p. 814.

33 *Ibid., Sc. Med.*, p. 229, cf. Stadelmann, *op. cit.*, p. 140.

34 For a vivid picture of this bourgeois world of the Low Countries, with its reform movement, see Jan Romein and Annie Romein-Verschoor, *Ahnherrn der holländischen Kultur*, Berne; 1946, pp. 7 ff. on Groote as the last representative of the middle ages. The son of the Burgomaster of Deventer, Groote studied theology, law and medicine at Cologne, Aix and Paris, spent some time at Prague and Avignon, and for fourteen years led the life of a wealthy, ambitious scholar, until he was converted and became a preacher of penance and reform. An opponent of heretics, he was suspected of heresy himself, and

may have written the nucleus of the *Imitation of Christ* (Books 2 and 3) in prison.

35 cf. J. Ritter, 'Die Stellung des Nikolaus von Cues in der Philosophieges-chichte', *Blätter für Deutsche Phil.* 13, 1939/40, pp. 111 ff.; the references there given, pp. 148 ff., to recent work on Cusanus.

36 This is a significant point. Even his contemporaries were struck by his interest in the world of the middle ages and its history; cf. John Andreas writing to Pope Paul II in 1469: *Vir ipse* (i.e., Cusanus) ... *historias idem omnes non priscas modo, sed mediae tempestatis tum veteres tam recentiores usque ad nostra tempora memoria retinebat; ... quasi Christianus Cato ...*' (ed. G. Ubinger, *Die Gottleslehre des Nikolaus Cusanus*, 146). cf. e.g. Nicholas's own appeal to 'our (German) Hugh of St. Victor', in the course of his violent debate with the clerical Church (*Opera*, Basle; 1565, 812–17).

37 M. Grabmann, *Mittelalterliches Geistesleben*, Munich; 1936, II, pp. 325 ff.

38 Edited and translated by J. Koch (S.B. der Heidelberger Akad. d. Wiss phil.-hist. Kl. 1936/7, 2 Abh.).

39 Nicholas of Cusa, *Verbum Caro*, 1 January 1454.

40 Nicholas of Cusa, *De Possest*; De Ign. II, ch. 2.

41 Nicholas of Cusa, *De Dato Patris*, ch. 2.

42 Stadelmann, *op. cit.*, pp. 62 f., J. Ritter, *op. cit.*, p. 120. B. Jansen, in *Gregorianum* XI, 1930, pp. 380 ff., and in 'Philosophia Perennis', *Festgabe für J. Geyser*, Regensburg; 1930, I, pp. 286 ff. E. Hoffmann, *Das Universum des Nikolaus von Cues*, pp. 10 ff. Nicholas, like his contemporaries, was unable to distinguish between Plato and the later Neoplatonists; nor did he have more than an elementary knowledge of Greek (M. Honecker, *Nikolaus von Cues und die griechische Sprache*, S. B. d. Heidelberger Akad. d. Wiss. phil.-hist. Kl. 1937/8, Casanus-Studien II).

43 cf. R. Odebrecht, *Nikolaus von Cues und der deutsche Geist*, pp. 5 ff.; and pp. 24 ff. for the contrast between Cusan doubt and Cartesian, and its difference from Thomist logic. cf. also M. Pensa, *Il Pensiero Tedesco*, pp. 35 ff.

44 The significance of the Conciliar Movement as a challenge to thought cannot be sufficiently emphasised where Nicholas is concerned; cf. A. Posch, *Die Concordantia Catholica des Nikolaus von Cues*, pp. 36 ff.

45 cf. Heer, *Das Experiment Europa*. Vienna; 1952.

46 cf. E. Hoffmann, *Das Universum des Nicholas von Cues*, pp. 29 ff.

47 cf. Nicholas of Cusa's 'Epistola ad Bohemos', *Opera*, Basle; 1565, pp. 823 ff.

48 'Cribratio Alchoran' (1561), *Ibid.*, pp. 879 ff.

49 cf. his magnificent sermon on the three Kingdoms, *Ibid.*, p. 483.

50 It is precisely in the case of natural science and mathematics that Nicholas of Cusa particularly emphasised the maxim *finis philosophiae admiratio* (*Ibid.*, p. 641). This led to the sense of awe in Böhme, Paracelsus and Goethe.

51 Nicholas of Cusa, *De Ludo Globi*, I, fol. 156a and 159a.

CHAPTER 12

1 cf. J. Luchaire, *Les sociétés italiennes du* XII *au* XV*e siècle*, Paris; 1933; G. Toffanin, *Il secolo senza Roma*, Bologna; 1942 (a vulnerable consideration of the thirteenth century); C. Salvotorelli, *L'Italia communale dal secolo 11 alla*

meta del secolo 14, Milan; 1940 (for the early medieval foundations); W. Goetz, *Die Entstehung der italienischen Kommunen im frühen Mittelalter*, S. B. der Bayer. Akad. d. Wiss. 1944, p. 1.

2 cf. F. Kern, *Humana Civilitas*, Leipzig; 1913, p. 81; J. Burckhardt, *The Civilisation of the Renaissance in Italy*, XL; E. Walser, *Gesammelte Studien zur Geistesgeschichte der Renaissance*, (with an introduction by W. Kaegi), Basle; 1932 XXXVII. Both independently of each other, compare this passage (which echoes the dominant 'I am emperor' theme of German *minnesang*) with Goethe's *Prometheus* as a symbol of the liberation of the self in modern times.

3 cf. N. Valeri, *La libertà e la pace. Orientamenti politici del Rinascimento italiano*, Turin; 1941. On the connection between the sociological, religious and political fields, see also G. M. Monti, *Le confraternite medievali dell' Alta e Media Italia*, 3 vols., Venice; 1927 ff.

4 G. Papini, *Dante vivo*. Florence; 1935.

5 Walser, *op. cit.*, p. 244.

6 R. John, *Dante*.

7 cf. W. Seiferth, 'Zur Kunstlehre Dantes', *Archiv für Kulturgeschichte*, 1927, vol. XVII, pp. 194 ff.. and 1928, vol. XVIII, pp. 148 ff.

8 'Briefwechsel des Cola di Rienzo' in K. Burdach and P. Piur, *Vom Mittelalter zur Reformation*, Prussian Academy of Science, Berlin; 1912, Parts I–IV.

9 *De Monarchia*, II, V, 28; *Convivio*, IV, V.

10 cf. J. Balogh, in *Deutsches Dante-Jahrbuch*, 1928, X, pp. 202 ff., and *Speculum*, 1929, IV, pp. 323 f.; T. Siverstein, in *Speculum*, 1938, XIII, pp. 326 ff.

11 Curator orbis, *De. Mon.*, XVI, 61.

12 *Briefwechsel, Cola di Rienze*. ed. Burdach and Piur, *op. cit.*, pp. 218 f. and 335.

13 F. Kern, *op. cit.*, pp. 35 and 45.

14 *Ibid.*, pp. 103 ff.

15 *Convivio*, II, 12.

16 *Briefwechsel, Cola di Rienzo*, No. XLIX, Z. p. 54.

17 *Ibid.*, p. 203.

18 *Ibid.*, Part II, pp. 448 ff.

19 *Ibid.*, Part II, p. 592.

20 *Ibid.*, Part II, pp. 608 ff.

21 Between the eleventh and eighteenth centuries, legal administration and jurisprudence formed part of the essential basis of national and political humanism; cf. W. Engelmann, *Die Widergeburt des Rechtskultur in Italien durch die wissenschaftliche Lehre*, Leipzig; 1938.

22 P. Hiltebrand, *Rom, Geschichte und Menschen*, Berlin; 1944, p. 240.

23 *Ep. Poet.*, II, 5, ed. Rossetti, vol. III, pp. 4 ff. Also in Burdach and Piur, vol. I, Part II, pp. 66 ff. and 619 ff.

24 *Lettere ed. e ined.*, ed. F. Corazzini, pp. 195 ff. cf. Burdach and Piur, *op. cit.*, pp. 510 ff.

25 cf. K. Burdach and P. Piur, *op. cit.*, vol. I, Part I, pp. 351 f., and pp. 32, 183 ff., 221, 286, 340; and IV, 4 and V, 5.

26 Petrarch's 'Buch ohne Namen' in Burdach and Piur, *op. cit.*, vol. VII, Berlin; 1933.

27   cf. H. Baron, 'Franciscan Poverty and Civic Wealth', *Speculum*, 1938, pp. 9 ff.; see p. 35 on Platina.

28   Petrarch, in Burdach and Piur, *op. cit.*, pp. 42 ff.

29   *Ibid.*, p. 70.

30   cf. C. Calcaterra, *Nella Selva del Patrarca*, Bologna; 1942. On Laura-Lauro, cf. E. Wolf, *Petrarca*, Leipzig; 1926, pp. 15 ff.

31   A. von Martin, 'Petrarca und Augustin', *AKG*, XVIII, p. 65. Attacking H. W. Eppelsheimer 'Zur Religiosität Petrarcas', *AKG*, XII, pp. 372 ff., who there attacks E. Walser's interpretation of Petrarch.

32   E. Wolf, *op. cit.*, pp. 11 f., rightly stresses that Petrarch used Latin because he saw it as 'an irrational potency'. L. Olschki, *The Genius of Italy*, New York; 1949, p. 214.

33   W. Kaegi, in his introduction to E. Walser, *Gesammelte Studien*, vol. XLVI.

34   L. Olschki, *op. cit.*, pp. 200 ff.

35   From a letter to Nelli, 'Petrarch's correspondence with German Contemporaries', ed. Piur, *op. cit.*, p. 217. cf. G. Toffanin, *Geschichte des Humanismus*, 1941, p. 153.

36   *Ep. Metricae*, I, 6, 20.

37   G. Saitta, *Il pensiero italiano nel l'Umanesimo e nel Rinascimento*, Bologna; 1949, pp. 13 f.

38   Lorenzo Valla's works, ed. by W. Schwalm (1928) and by Coleman, Yale University Press, 1932.

39   From the Forward of *De voluptate*, ed. Schwalm. p. 896.

40   *Nicomachean Ethics*, VIII, 15, 1154, B. 26.

41   'Idem est enim natura quod deus, aut fere idem', from *De Voluptate*, I, 13.

42   Saitta, *op. cit.*, p. 259.

43   cf. Bracciolini's *Dailogus contra hypocrosia*.

44   *Della Vita Civile* of Palmieri, ed. by F. Battaglia, Bologna; 1944.

45   cf. E. Walser, *op. cit.*, p. 243. In an article entitled 'Der Renaissance-Humanismus als soziologisches Phänomen', *Geust und Gesellschaft*, Frankfurt; 1948, pp. 92 ff., A. von Martin emphasizes the bourgeois and petty bourgeois origins of many of the humanists. ('Petrarca und Augustin', *AKG*.)

46   Pogio Bracciolini, *De avaritia*, 1429.

47   cf. Poggio's account in a letter to Bruni, 'Epistolario', ed. by Tonelli, I, II to XX.

48   Giovanni da Prato, *Paradiso degli Alberti*.

49   Pier Paolo Vergerio, *de ingenuis moribus* – spirituality of grammar and its educational force are strikingly emphasized in this work.

50   Matteo Vegio, *de educatione liberorum*.

51   C. Neumann, 'Byzantinische Kultur und Renaissance Kultur', p. 36; 'Ende des Mittelalters?', *DVJ*, 1934, pp. 157 ff.

52   J. E. Sandys, *A. History of Classical Scholarship*, Cambridge; 1903, vol. I, p. 418.

53   For a discussion of the sociological and political background of Florentine Platonism, see A. V. Martin, *op. cit.*, pp. 125 ff.

54   On Ficino, see L. Thorndyke, *A History of Magic and Experimental Science*, vol. IV, pp. 562 ff.; Saitta, *op. cit.*, pp. 509 ff. P. O. Kristeller, *The Philosophy*

of Marsilio Ficino. Columbia University Press, 1943, in which Ficino is seen in medieval terms. In G. Saitta's *Marsilio Ficino e la filosofia dell' Umanesimo,* Florence; 1943, the 'modern' features are emphasized.

55 Ficino, *Theologia Platonica,* 1474.

56 Thorndyke, *op. cit.,* IV, pp., 562 f.

57 All this ought not be taken as seriously as 'bourgeois' renaissance enthusiasts and their present-day American descendants have tended to do. It would really be a good idea, especially for intellectual historians, to get rid of the dubious notion of a renaissance. This term, in its various formulations and usages from the ancient world on to the present, causes tremendous confusion, especially when it is applied to the historical and intellectual phenomena of the fifteenth and sixteenth centuries. The discussion on the concept of the renaissance is, however, a very useful and instructive one. The older literature is best summarized by R. Kaufmann '*Der Renaissancebegriff*' ... pp. 3 ff. Before Jakob Burckhardt, who began to use the concept about 1838, Eduard Koloff had already spoken of a Renaissance as an epoch of style. See W. Waetzoldt, *Deutsche Kunsthistoriker,* vol. II, pp. 100 f. On the Italian conception of the renaissance, J. von Schlosser has written several interesting contributions. (J. von Schlosser in *MIOG,* 1929, pp. 50 ff.; 'Praludien', pp. 270 ff.; 'Die Kunsliteratur' especially pp. 167 ff. on the precursors of Vasari.) With regard to German discussion of the problem, see P. Wernle, *Renaissance und Reformation* (1912) pp. 4 ff., the numerous works by Burdach and Piur, and for an attack on Burdach, see P. Joachimsen, 'Vom Mittelalter zur Reformation', *HV,* No. 20, pp. 426 ff. C. Neumann in his article cited above (note 51) correctly underlines the fact that 'in all of Ranke's works, the conception and the term Renaissance simply does not occur'. (p. 150.) See L. Olschki's article in the *DVJ* of 1929, pp. 329 ff. There has also, of course, been much discussion of Jakob Burckhardt. See on this point the articles by A. Neumayer *DVJ.* 1929, pp. 120 ff. and C. Neumann in the *HZ,* No. 150, pp. 485 ff. Werner Kaegi has recently edited Burckhardt's letters and written a splendid biography (Bask; 1947) Huizinga has written two important articles in which he criticizes the 'inflation' of the concept of the Renaissance; these are to be found in his *Wege der Kulturgeschichte,* pp. 61 ff. and his 'Das Problem der Renaissance' (*Parega,* Basle; 1945). Recently there was an exceedingly interesting discussion of the idea of the renaissance in the 4th volume of the *JHI,* 1943, in which, among others, H. Baron, E. Cassirer, P. O. Kristeller, F. R. Johnson and Dana B. Durand made valuable contributions.

58 L. Olschki, *op. cit.,* pp. 271 ff.

59 P. O. Kristeller, *op. cit.*

60 E. Cassirer, 'Giovanni Pico della Mirandola. A Study in the History of Renaissance Ideas', *JHI,* vol. III, 1942, pp. 123 ff. and 319 ff.

61 A. Janner, 'Individualismus und Religiosität in der Renaissance', *DVJ,* No. 13, 1935.

62 Pico della Mirandola, 'Conclusiones Magicae'. sec. pr. op. 9, op. 105.

63 Ironically, it was that very blurred quality of his ideas which gave them their peculiar force and influence on later generations, especially on the Cambridge School up to Shaftesbury, and German thought up to Winkelmann. cf. E. Cassirer, *JHI,* III, 1942, p. 345.

64 Galeotto Mario de Narni, *De incognitis Vulgo*, ed. and selected by M. Frezza, Naples; 1948.
65 Giovanni Pontano, *De magnanimate*.
66 ..., *De Obedientia*, V, p. 38, cf. Landino's *Questiones Camaldulenses*.
67 cf. Pontano's *De Prudentia* in which virtue is seen as a reaction to external pressure.
68 *Opera di Tito Livio de Frulovisi*, ed. by C. W. Previté-Orton, London; 1932.
69 On Piccolomini, see Saitta, *op. cit.*, pp. 335 ff.
70 *Piccolomini's Briefwechsel*, ed. by R. Wulkan, 1909, p. 487.
71 See Letter 105, *ibid.*
72 *Ibid.*, letters to the German and Hungarian Princes.
73 H. B. Gutman, 'The Medieval Content of Raphael's School of Athens' *JHI*, vol. II, 1941, pp. 453 ff.
74 Ph. Hiltebrandt, *op. cit.*, pp. 240 ff. and 270 ff.
75 On Marsili, see Saitta, *op. cit.*, pp. 132 ff.
76 Published in the *Rivista Contemporanea*, 1862.
77 L. Thorndyke, *op. cit.*, pp. 183 ff.
78 Spini, *Introduzione al Savonarala*, Belfagur; 1948, vol. III, pp. 414 f. E. Garin, 'Girolamo Savonarola', *Schweizer Monatshefte*, vol. XXXII, September 1953, pp. 359 ff.
79 cf. Savonarola's *Trattato circa il reggimento e governo della città di Firenze*.
80 V. de Caprariis, *Francesco Guicciardini, dalla politica, alla storia*, Bari; 1950, p. 12.
81 E. Voegelin, 'Machiavelli's Prince: Background and Formation', *The Review of Politics*, vol. XIII, April 1951, pp. 142 ff. R. Koenig, *Nichola Machiavelli – zur Krisenanalyse einer Zeitwende*, Zürich; 1941.
82 cf. *Ricordi politici e civili*, No. 236 and L. Olschki, *op. cit.*, p . 335 ff.
83 L. von Muralt, *Machiavellis Staatsgedanke*, Basle; 1945, pp. 125 ff, 147 ff.
84 E. Walser, *op. cit.*, pp. 202 ff., and Kaegi's introduction, p. xii. On the 'ethos of Machiavelli', see von Muralt, *op. cit.*, pp. 67 ff.
85 cf. his letter of 16 April 1527, to Vettori.
86 Machiavelli's *Discorsi*, I, II c. Guicciardini's *Ricordi*, I, 1.
87 J. H. Randall, *The Development of scientific method in the School of Padua*, pp. 177 ff. E. Troilo, *Averroismo e Aristotelismo padovano*, Padua; 1939.
88 On Alberti: Saitta, *op. cit.*, pp. 393 ff. L. Olschki, *Die Literatur der Technik und der angewandten Wissenchcaften bis zur Renaissance*, Heidelberg; 1919, vol. I, pp. 45 ff. W. Sombart, *Der Bourgeois*, Munich; 1923; Sombart exaggerates Albertini's importance to support his own argument.
89 Alberti, *Della Pittura*, p. 45.
90 On Paccioli, cf. Olschki, *Die Literatur der Technik*, I, pp. 151 f.
91 cf. Vossler, *Die göttliche Komödie*, vol. I, 1, pp. 227 ff.
92 Luca Paccioli, *Divina Proportione, opera a tutti gl' ingegni perspicacie curiosi necessaria*, Venice; 1509.
93 There is a wealth of material on Leonardo. The older literature is ably summarized in W. von Seidlitz's *Leonardo da Vinci, Der Wendepunkt der Renaissance*, new edition, Vienna; 1935, pp. 424–556. There are also P. Valéry, *Divers Essais sur Léonard da Vinci*, Paris; 1931, R. Bayer, *Léonard de Vinci, la Grace*, Paris; 1933. M. Brion, *Génie et Destinée, Léonard de Vinci*, Paris;

1952. Suggestive studies have been made by P. Mesnard, *Léonard de Vinci et la philosophie difficile*; A. Valensin, *Le Sourire de Léonard*; J. Riverain, *Vues sur Léonard, peintre*; and P. Humbert 'Léonard de Vinci, Savant?' *Etudes*, July/August 1952, pp. 23–61. The famous old work of P. Duhèm, *Etudes sur Léonard da Vinci*, 4 vols., Paris; 1908–13, must be used with great caution, but the richness of the material on early and late medieval sources and connections in Leonardo's work makes it useful.

94 cf. Olschki, *Literatur der Technik*, I, pp. 396 ff. on Leonardo's obscenities in the *Codex Atlanticus*.

95 L. Venturi, 'Leonardo da Vinci', *Schweizer Monatshefte*, April 1952, vol. XXXII, p. 38.

96 *Ibid.*, p. 38.

97 cf. W. von Seidlitz, *The Codex Atlanticus*, Ill. 43, and Nos. 12276, 21351; 121.792; 12284 in the Windsor Castle Collection.

98 Compare his studies on the technique of flying (*Codex Atlanticus*) on the human larynx, 'projectiles and archery', the hanged Bandini (1476, Bayonne, Musée Bonaat). The studies of the head and designs for Machines. (Ink drawing, 1478, Uffizi Gallery) and the fingernails of the angel in the 'Annunciation' (Uffizi Gallery).

99 J. Riverain, *op. cit.*, p. 57.

100 L. Olschki, *Literatur der Technik*, p. 349.

101 R. Richter, *The Literary works of Leonardo da Vinci*, London; 1883.

102 L. Olschki, *Literatur der Technik*, p. 412.

CHAPTER 13

Key to abbreviations used in these notes:

C.R. — Corpus Reformatorum   T.R. — Tischeden von Luther
Bo.A. — Bonner Luther-Ausgabe   W.A. — Weimarer Luther-Ausgabe
Erl.A. — Erlangen-Luther-Ausgabe

1 'Ego Sum Deus Tuus', T.R., No. 461, pp. 200, 7 ff.

2 F. W. Schmidt, 'Die Frage nach Gott als Frage der Reformation', *Zeitschrift für Theologie und Kirche*, N.F., 1934, vol. XV, p. 8.

3 Karl Eder, 'Reformation und Gegenreformation in Österreich', *Theologisch-praktische Quartalschrift*, No. 100, Part 1, 1952, p. 23.

4 W.A., XV, p. 32.

5 *Ibid.*, 10, 3, and 18. 3.

6 Eder, *op. cit.*, p. 23, cf. W. Dress, *Die Theologie Gersons*, Gütersloh; 1931, pp. 88 ff.

7 Schmidt, *op. cit.*, p. 28; also H. Appel, *Anfechtung und Trost im Spätmittelalter und bei Luther*, Leipzig; 1938.

8 W.A., VIII, pp. 573, ff.

9 Karl Buchheim, 'Luthers Anfechtung', *Hochland*, 1952, vol. XLIV, pp. 301 ff.

10 *Ibid.*, pp. 301 ff.

11 F. Benary 'Via antiqua und via moderna auf den deutschen Hochschulen des Mittelalters mit besonderer Berücksichtigung der Universität Erfurt', Appen-

dix to *Zur Geschichte der Stadt und Universität Erfurt am Ausgang des Mittelalters*, Gotha; 1919, pp. 70 f.

12 Jacques Maritain, *Trois Reformateurs, Luther, Descartes, Rousseau*, Paris; 1925, p. 25.

13 J. Lortz, *Die Reformation in Deutschland*, 2 vols., Freiburg i. Breisgau, 2nd ed. 1941, vol. I, pp. 172 ff.

14 W. Dilthey, *Gesammalte Schriften*, vol. II, 3rd ed., Leipzig-Berlin; 1923, pp. 162 ff.

15 The assumption that Luther read St Thomas is incorrect and based on a false reference: W.A. 42. 486. 29.; see W. Dress, *op. cit.*, p. 83.

16 See J. Maritain, *op. cit.*, pp. 28 ff., on the contrast between 'person and individual'.

17 W.A., 32.92.3.

18 *Ibid.*, 10, vol. II, 107, 8–11.

19 A. V. Müller, *Luther und Tauler*, Bern; 1918.

20 J. Baruzzi, 'Luther interprete de St. Paul', *Revue de theologie et de philosophie*, January–March, 1928.

21 Lenz, *Briefwechsel Landgraf Philipps von Hessen mit Bucer*, vol. I, pp. 373 f.

22 *Theologia Teutsch*, published by H. Mandel, *Quellenschriften zur Geschichte des Protestantismus*, No. 7, Leipzig; 1908, XXII ff. See especially Luther's own introduction to his second edition.

23 *Ibid.*, p. 72. An interesting attack on the people, who were actually most affected by it. It parallels Luther's attack on the same people.

24 *Ibid.*, p. 23.

25 *Luthers Briefwechsel*, 'An Melancthon', 1 August 1521, ed. Enders, vol. III, p. 208.

26 W.A., 23, 141; 24, 330, 142, and 331.

27 Paulus, *Luthers Labensende und der Eislebener Apotheker Johann Landau*, Mainz; 1896.

28 cf. F. W. Schmidt, *op. cit.*, p. 2.

29 Bo.A., IV, 422.

30 cf. G. Jacob, 'Luthers Kirchenbegriff', *Zeitschrift für Theologie und Kirche*, N.F., 15, 1934, pp. 19 ff.

31 'De Servo Arbitrio', W.A., 18, 652.

32 Rudolf Stadelmann, *Vom Geist des ausgehenden Mittelalters*, pp. 246 ff.

33 K. Holl, *Gesammelte Aufsätze zur Kirchengeschichte*, 3rd ed., Tübingen; 1923, pp. 296 ff.

34 Luther's 'Grosser Katechismus', *Quellenschriften zur Geschichte des Protestantismus*, ed. Johann Meyer, Leipzig; 1914, vol. XII, p. 112.

35 *Ibid.*, IX, 10, 97.

36 M. Pensa, *Il pensiero tedesco*, pp. 42 f.

37 *Briefwechsel*, Enders ed., letter of 14 January 1519, I, p. 173.

38 W.A., 12, 119, ff.; 18, 164.

39 *Ibid.*, 40, P. 1, 362/3.

40 *Ibid.*, 365.

41 Erl.A., 16, 142–8.

42 F. Borkenau, 'Deutschland zwischen Ost und West', *Wort und Wahrheit*, 1949, vol. IV, pp. 33 ff.

43 The critical edition is by F. W. Schmidt in the Munich edition of Luther's works, vol. V, 1923.

44 Erasmus of Rotterdam, *Hyperaspistes Diatribe adversus Servum Arbitrium M. Lutheri*, 2 vols., Basle; 1526/7. The citations from Erasmus's 'De libero Arbitrio' are taken from the edition of Johann von Walter, *Quellenschriften zur Geschichte des Protestantismus*, No. 8, and those from Luther's 'De serov arbitrio' from the same series, No. 12, Leipzig; 1910. The 'Hyperaspites' in the Basle edition given above are in two volumes, of which vol. I is not paginated.

45 J. Huizinga, *Erasmus von Rotterdam*, Basle, 1932, p. q73.

46 Erasmus of Rotterdam, *Opus Epistolarum*, 6 vols., ed. by P. Allen, 1906–26.

47 R. Kelsow, *Luther und die Devotio Moderna*, Hamburg; 1936.

48 Allen, *op. cit.*, No. 23, I, 1; No. 117, I, 26; No. 132, I, 7; No. 967, I, 126; No. 337, I, 328; No. 996, I, 10.

49 Erasmus, *Opera*, Leiden, 1703, V, 141 f., IX, 1248, A.

50 J. Hashagen, ' "Die Devotio Moderna in ihrer Einwirkung auf Humanismus, Reformation, Gegenreformation und spötere Ricntungen', *ZKG*, vol. LV, 1936, pp. 523 ff. Hashagen rightly emphasizes that Erasmus did not represent any new sort of 'Christianity of Christ', as Troeltsch, P. Wernle and others have argued. A. Hyma, *The Christian Renaissance: A History of the Devotio Moderna*, 1924, has been unfairly criticized and should be read on this point.

51 Allen, *op. cit.*, No. 384, 1, 33; No. 428; No. 553; No. 534, 1. 61.

52 *Ibid.*, No. 541, 11, 29 ff.; No. 542; No. 566, 1. 34; No. 642 1. 6; No. 643; No. 966, 1. 39; No. 967, 1. 36.

53 Huizinga, *op. cit.*, pp. 53 ff.

54 There is no greater proof of the historical greatness of Erasmus than the repetition of the accusations against him by both Catholic and Protestant historians. Erasmus has been thoroughly misunderstood by friend and foe alike. An example can be found in such a sensitive and competent Catholic theologian as Joseph Lortz. Like many scholars, Lortz seems to be so fascinated by Luther and so unimpressed by the greatness and enormous problems of political humanism that he allows himself to be carried to this extreme criticism of Erasmus: 'Not only will he not, he cannot draw the last consequences. This leads not only to a tragic flow, but also to a powerless and thoroughly unsympathetic and dangerous attitude.' *Die Reformation in Deutschland*, vol. I, p. 127.

What are the facts? Erasmus refused, in fact, to draw the consequences of the others on the right and the left. He saw clearly where (yesterday as today) such ideas inevitably lead: religious war, civil strife, terror, absolutism and chaos. For whom was Erasmus's attitude 'dangerous'? Only for himself and his followers. Everything positive, constructive, fruitful for the future was begun by Erasmians, or by people whose spirits he essentially influenced: the theology and philosophy of Melancthon and orthodox Lutheranism, as well as the vital definitions of Trent about cooperation between God and man, grace and freedom.

In addition, to his book on Erasmus, Huizinga delivered a famous memorial speech in Basle in 1936, which closed with this memorable sentence: 'The world-historical moment through which we are living is once again the hour of Erasmus.' (J. Huizinga, 'Gedenkrede im Baseler Münster', *Parerga*, Basle, 1945, pp. 65 ff.). In the shadow of the same hour, Stefan Zweig wrote his Erasmus study. The year was 1934.

55 K. Eder, *op. cit.*

56 J. von Walther ed., *op. cit.*, p. 17.

57 'De servo Arbitrio', *W.A.*, 18, 666 A.

58 J. von Walther ed., *op. cit.*, pp. 37 ff., 41 ff.

59 *Ibid.*, 25.

60 *Ibid.*, 76.

61 *Ibid.*, 80.

62 *Ibid.*, 82.

63 *Ibid.*, 90.

64 J. Maritain, *op. cit.*, p. 40, and p. 21.

65 *Hperaspites*, vol. II, pp. 193–4.

66 *Ibid.*, pp. 200 f.

67 *Ibid.*, p. 196.

68 *Ibid.*, p. 220.

69 *Ibid.*, p. 360.

70 *Ibid.*, p. 451. Erasmus again calls Luther a Manichaean, p. 502.

71 *Ibid.*, p. 453.

72 *Ibid.*, p. 235.

73 *Ibid.*, p. 558.

74 J. Lortz, *op. cit.*, vol. I, pp. 302 ff. In the distinction between 'evil' man according to Luther and 'imperfect' man according to Erasmus, the two worlds diverge clearly. One belongs to the radical ecstatic and the other to the civilized humanist, who may be equally religious. Erasmus emphasized this: *Possunt autem imperfectae cognitionis, et imperfectae voluntatis esse multi gradus, quandoquidem neque nostra fides ac voluntas, per quam justificamur, perfecta est in hac vita et tamen dicatur bona voluntas. (Ibid., p. 555).*

75 Urbanus Rhegius, 'Wie man fürsichtiglich und ohne Ärgernis reden soll von den fürnehmsten Artikeln christlicher Lehre', German edition of 1536, ed. by A. Uckelly, *Quellen zur Geschichte der Protestantismus*, No. 6, Leipzig; 1908.

76 J. Lortz, *op. cit.*, I, 310, note 1.

77 K. Holl, 'Luther und die Schwärmer', *Gesammelte Aufsätze*, Tübingen; 1927.

78 See, for example, H. Plessner *Das Schicksal deutschen Geistes im Ausgang seiner bürgerlichen Epoche*, Zürich-Leipzig; 1935. Plessner discusses the political and spiritual consequences of the failure to develop a religious life in the free churches of Germany (pp. 23 ff.) and the way in which the Lutheran Church took from the individual all possibilities to be active in public, political and social life. See vol. IV of the Munich ed. of Luther's works, 1934, for Luther's attitude.

79 Paracelsus, *Sozialethische und Sozialpolitische Schriften*, pub. and ed. K. Goldammer, Tübingen, 1952, especially the introduction.

80 Lortz, *op. cit.*, pp. 310 ff.

81 E. Bloch, *Thomas Münzer als theologe der Revolution*, Munich; 1921.

82 K. Eder, 'Glaubensspaltung und Landstände in Österreich ob der Ems, 1525–1602' p. 117; in addition, A. Scheiblin, 'Reformation und Gegenre-

formation in St. Potten', *Jahrbuch der Gesellschaft für die Geschichte des Protestantismus in Österreich*, No. 67. 1951, p. 109.

83 *Ibid.*, p. 109.

84 On this point, see K. Goldammer, *op. cit.*, pp. 70 ff.

85 Lucas Cranach the Elder, illustrated the position brilliantly in his painting, 'The Prince-Elector Johann Friedrich of Saxony with the Reformers', now in the Toledo Art Museum, Toledo, Ohio. The overly large figure of the Elector has, like a mother hen, gathered his reformers under his wing. There is Luther, Melancthon, Spalatin and Gregor Brück, who was Saxon Chancellor and author of the famous preface to Melancthon's Augsburg confession. (F. Blanke of Zürich has argued that the figure was not Brück but Andreas Osiander. I find myself in agreement with H. Bornkamm of Heidelberg on this point.) Lucas Cranach, who was a family relation both of Luther and of Brück, presents any researches in intellectual history with a remarkable phenomenon: the connection between Mannerism and the crushing of the religious, political, spiritual and artistic freedoms by the victory of princely and partisan confessional absolutism. This relationship obtains both in Protestant and catholic countries. Post-reformation spiritualism and dualism belonged to this phenomenon as an inner component. Neither can imagine, see, conceive or carry out any genuine Sacramentalism. This spiritualism 'discovers' wit and art as a beautifully formed, external structure, to compensate for its sterility.

86 Lortz, *op. cit.*, p. 333.

87 On Denk, see Theodor Kolde, 'Hans Denk und die gottlosen Maler von Nürnberg', *Beiträge zur Bayerischen Kirchengeschichte*, No. 8, 1902.

88 W. Dilthey, *op. cit.*, vol. II, pp. 80 ff. In this essay, 'Weltanschauung und Analyse des Menschen seit Renaissance und Reformation', Dilthey portrays Franck as the hero of intellectual history, the great lonely man, 'lonelier than even Spinoza after him', who dies forsaken like Lessing. On his slender shoulders, Dilthey places Gottfried Arnold, Herder, Hamann, Kant, Goethe, large parts of the Enlightenment and the idealist movement.

89 W. E. Peuckert, *Sebastian Franck, ein deutscher Sucher*, Munich; 1943, pp. 580 ff.

90 *Ibid.*, p. 53.

91 On the relation between Franck and Tauler and the *Theologia Deutsch* see Peuckert, *op. cit.*, pp. 84 ff., and E. Teufel, 'die deutsche Theologie' and 'Sebastian Franck im Lichte der neueren Forschung', *Theologische Rundschau*, vol. XII, 1940.

92 Peuckert, *op. cit.*, pp. 76. 536 ff. and 646 ff.

93 *Ibid.*, pp. 449 ff. cf. R. Kosmos, 'Sebastian Franck und Erasmus von Rotterdam', *Ebelings German Studien*, No. 153, 1934.

94 Peuckert, *op. cit.*, pp. 91, 193 ff.

95 *Ibid.*, pp. 124 ff., W. Oncken, 'Sebastian Franck als Geschichtsschreiber' in *Historische und politische Aufsätze und Reden*, Berlin; 1914, vol. I, pp. 273 ff.

96 Franck, *Paradoxa*, No. 14.

97 Oncken quite rightly emphasized, as Peuckert points out, that 'what Stadel mann has called anarchic. I should describe as aristocratic'. Peuckert, *op. cit.*, p. 598.

98   cf. L. Blaschke, 'Der Toleranzgedanke bei Sebastian Franck', *Blätter für deutsche Philosophie*, II, 1928.
99   cf. his Prefaces of 1534 and 1538 to the *Oermaniae Chronicon*.
100 E. Zilsel, 'Copernicus and Mechanics', *HJI*. No. 1, 1940, pp. 113 ff.
101 For a picture of the German *Gelehrten proletariat*, see A. Steiner 'A Mirror for Scholars of the Baroque', *JHI*, No. 1, 1940, pp. 320 ff.
102 Paracelsus, *Sozialethische Schriften*, ed. K. Goldammer, Tübingen; 1952. As an introduction to the study of Paracelsus, there is the Foreword to his collection of Paracelsus's works by W. E. Peuckert, in *Paraccelsus, Die Geheimnisse – Ein Lesebuch aus seinen Schriften*, Leipzig; 1941. For criticism of Peuckert, see E. Metzke, 'Erfahrung und Natur in der Gedankenwelt des Paracelsus,' *Blätter für deutsche Philosophie*, No. 13, 1939/40, pp. 74 ff.
103 *Paracelsus*, ed. Goldammer, *op. cit.*, p. 44.
104 *Ibid.*, p. 57.
105 *Ibid.*, p. 53.
106 cf. the text in Peuckert, *op. cit.*, pp. 312 ff.
107 E. Metzke, 'Luther und Paracelsus', *Blätter für deutsche Philosophie*, No. 8, 1934, pp. 355 ff.
108 Paracelsus, *Works*, vol. XIV, p. 179.
109 *Ibid.*, XII, p. 479.
110 *Ibid.*, VIII, p. 100.
111 *Ibid.*, I, p. 250.
112 cf. Peuckert, *Paracelsus*, p. 366. E. Metzke, *op. cit.*, pp. 92 ff.
113 The five 'entia' can be found in his early work *Volumen Paramirun*, ed. D. Achelis, Jena; 1928, with important annotation.
114 Paracelsus, *Works*, XII, p. 393.
115 *Ibid.*, IV, p. 534.
116 *Ibid.*, XI, p. 323, and II, p. 288.
117 Metzke, *op. cit.*, p. 83.
118 Paracelsus, *Works*, V, pp. 501 f.; VIII, pp. 284, 350, 364.
119 *Ibid.*, IX, p. 99.
120 *Ibid.*, I, p. 15; II, pp. 65, 179, 184, 224.
121 *Ibid.*, VII, p. 75.
122 *Ibid.*, II, p. 317.
123 *Ibid.*, IV, p. 502.
124 See C. Bauer, 'Die Naturrechtslehre Melancthons', *Hochland*, No. 44, 1952, pp. 313 ff. Also F. X. Arnold, *Zul Frage des Naturrechts bei Martin Luther*, 1937. E. Wolf 'Zur Frage des Naturrechts bei Thomas von Aquin und Martin Luther', *Jahrbuch der Gesellschaft für die Geschichte des Protestantismus in Österreich*, No. 67, 1951, pp. 192 ff. There has been considerable controversy on this point. Arnold believed that he had established a striking agreement on fundamentals between Luther and Aquinas. Wolf, together with J. Heckel, disagreed and pointed to the Ockhamist foundations of Luther's thought and to 'the radical spiritualization of divine law'.
125 Lutheran and protestant thought, including that of Max Weber, consistently seeks to make a radical division between 'values' (as the last secularization of the supernatural world) and 'deeds'. In the scholastic order, rationality and authority are, by contrast, intimately bound up. See S. de Grazia, 'Authority

and Rationality', *Philosophy*, London; 1952, vol. XXVII, No. 101, pp. 99 ff.

126 As in Erasmus's *De Anima*, Strasbourg; 1542.

127 See Dilthey, *op. cit.*, vol. II, p. 186.

128 cf. Zwingli, *De Providentia*: 'Providence is the constant, unchanging rule and order (*administratio*) of all things.'

129 Melancthon *Philosophiae Moralis Epitome* Corp. Ref. XVI, pp. 165 f. and 'Ethicae Doctrinae Elementa' XVI, pp. 21, ff.; XIII, pp. 221 and 346.

130 W. Köhler, *Die Geisteswelt Ulrich Zwinglis*, Gotha; 1920. Köhler believes that Zwingli's *De Providentia* was a 'classical expression of his ancient view of God.'

131 E. Lewalter, *Spanisch-Jesuitische und deutsch-lutherische Metaphysik des 17 Jahrhunderts. Ein Beitrag zur Geschichte der deutsch-iberischen Kulturbeziehungen und zur Vorgeschichte des deutschen Idealismus*, Hamburg; 1935, p. 27.

132 K. Eschweiler, 'Die philosophie der spanischen Spätscholastik auf den deutschen Universitäten des 17. Jahrhunderts', *Spanische Forschungen der Görgesgesellschaft*, vol. I, pp. 251 ff.

133 C. A. Kneller, 'Von der Nachfolge Christi', *Zeitschrift für Aszese und Mystik*, vol. XII, 1937, pp. 40 ff. P. Althaus, *Zur Charakteristik der evangelischen Gebetsliteratur im Reformationsjahrhundert*, Leipzig; 1914; Althaus recognizes the strong Catholic influences.

134 H. Schaeder, *Moskau – das dritte Rom*, Hamburg; 1929, pp. 15 ff.

135 G. Stökl, 'Die politische Religiösität des Mittelalters und die Entstehung des Moskauer Staates', *Saeculum*, II, vol. III, pp. 412 ff.

136 F. Borkenau, *op. cit.*, p. 39.

137 G. Stökl, *op. cit.*, p. 414.

138 F. Borkenau, *op. cit.*, p. 40; see also the opinion of E. Kahler in *Der deutsche Charakter in der Geschichte Europas*, Zürich; 1937, p. 363. He writes: 'The absolutely complete, inner limitlessness and lack of religion of the Germans corresponded to their peculiar external piety, its boundless credulity toward the outside world'. Although Koehler is talking of the medieval German city, it could apply as well to the Lutheran dualism.

139 Certain characteristic features of this Lutheran dualism can be found in the community of Brethren of the Devotio Moderna, in the theology of Ockham, and, above all, of Gerson, whom Luther grudgingly recognized as important. See W. Dress, *op. cit.*, pp. 82 ff. and 167 ff.

140 K. Vietor, 'Luthertum, Katholizismus und deutsche Literatur', *Zeitschrift für deutsche Philologie*, 1949, pp. 133 ff.

141 E. Benz, *Die Ostkirche im Lichte der protestantischen Geschichtsschreibung von der Reformation biz zur Gegenwart*, Freiburg/Munich, 1952, pp. 12 ff.

142 *Ibid.*, p. 20, and p. 384.

143 E. Denissoff, *Maxime le Grec et l'Occident, Contribution al'histoire de la pensée religieuse et philosophique de Michael Trivolis*, Paris and Louvain; 1943. There is a rich bibliography at the beginning of this work.

144 H. Schaeder, *op. cit.*, p. 18 and pp. 59 ff.

145 *Ibid.*, pp. 86 ff.

146 E. Denissoff, *op. cit.*, pp. 197 ff.

147 Erasmus, *Epistola*, ed. Allen, No. 119; J. Huizinga, *op. cit.*, p. 68.

148 E. Denissoff, *op. cit.*, p. 227.

149 *Ibid.*, pp. 241 f.
150 *Ibid.*, p. 277.
151 *Ibid.*, p. 293.
152 Schaeder, *op. cit.*, p. 36.
153 *Ibid.*, 39.
154 *Ibid.*, p. 23.
155 *Ibid.*, p. 31.
156 Schachmatov and others have identified him as Philotheos of Pskov.
157 M. C. Beardsley, 'Dostojevsky's Metaphor of the Underground', *JHI*, vol. III, 1942, pp. 265 ff.
158 On the Judaisers, see G. Stökl, *op. cit.*, pp. 413 ff.
159 E. Denissoff, *op. cit.*, pp. 306 ff.
160 *Ibid.*, p. 317, and p. 360.
161 On Joseph of Volotsk, see E. Stepun, 'Der Cäsaropapismus und die russische Tragödie', *Hochland*, No. 44, 1952, pp. 196 ff. M. Raeff, 'An Early Theorist of Absolutism: Joseph of Volokolamsk', *The American Slavic and East European Review*, vol. VIII, 1949, pp. 77 ff. Also, G. Stökl, *op. cit.*, pp. 412 f.
162 E. Denissoff, *op. cit.*, p. 380.
163 *Ibid.*, p. 384.
164 *Ibid.*, p. 421.
165 *Ibid.*, p. 423 for the original text.
166 T. Kardos, *La Hongrie latine*, Paris; 1946. The humanist movement before and after Luther was intimately associated both with religious reform and national aspirations. Czech courtly humanism and Charles IV led directly to Hus. The Hungarian humanist King, Matthias Corvinus, said in his declaration of war on the Emperor Frederick III that the Emperor was 'an enemy of the Hungarian language and people.' He included in his famous library the Hungarian translation of the Bible by Ladislaus Báthory, the reformer of the Hermits of St Paul. Translation of the Bible into Hungarian was recognized in 1528 as a national deed of the first order.

CHAPTER 14

1 Lambert's studies on the Spanish-Moorish origins and influence on France's Romanesque and Gothic art as cited by Miguel Cruz Hernández, *Saeculum*, III, 1952, p. 368.
2 The last works of Asin Palacios and the relationship between Ibn Masarrah, Ibn Arabi and Dante have been analysed by Cruz Hernandez, *op. cit.*, p. 371.
3 Gonzalez Palencia, *El Arzobispo de Toldeo don Raimondo*, Madrid; 1942.
4 J. M. Doussinague, *El Testamento Politico de Fernando el Catholico*, Madrid; 1950.
5 Erasmus turned against the French nationalism of his friend Bude in a highly characteristic way, beçause he saw the world as a common fatherland of all men. cf. J. Huizinga, 'Wachstum und Formen des nationalem Bewusstseins in Europa biz zum Ende des 19. Jahrhunderts', *Im Banne der Geschichte*, Nijmegen; 1942, p. 163.
6 On the nature of Roman foundations of Spain, see O. Sanchez-Albornoz,

'Proceso de la romanizacion de Espana desde los Escipiones hasta Augusto', *Anales de Historia Antigua u Medievala*, Buenos Aires; 1949, pp. 5 ff.

7   K. Vossler, *Spanien und Europa*, pp. 163 ff.

8   M. Cruz Hernández, *op. cit.*, p. 372.

9   cf. F. Baer, *Die Juden in Christlichen Spanien*, Berlin; 1936, and the great work of José Fernandez Amador de los Rios, *Historia social, politica y religiosa de los Judios de Espana y Portugal*, Madrid; 1875.

10 S. de Madariaga, *Christopher Columbus*, Stuttgart; 1951, pp. 246 ff., and p. 229.

11 *Ibid.*, pp. 154 ff.

12 Ramon Carande, *Saeculum*, III, 1952, p. 385.

13 O. Fessler, 'Die Spanische Volkswirtschaft', *Handbuch der Spanienkunde*, Frankfurt am Main; 1932, pp. 73 ff.

14 A. Schulte, *Geschichte der Grossen Ravensburger Handelsgesellsvhaft, 1380 bis 1530*, 3 vols., Stuttgart; 1923. Modern literature on German economic activity in Spain can be found in H. Hüffer, 'Las Relaciones Hispano-Germanas', *Revista de Estudios Politicos*, vol. XXXVI, 1951, p. 54.

15 For 'orthodox' and 'noble' Spaniards there were only three honourable occupations: *iglesia – o mar o casa reale* – church or sea or royal house. See M. Bataillon, *Erasme et l'Espagne: Recherches sur l'histoire spirituelle du XVIe siècle*, Paris; 1937, p. 15. In 1781 the Academy of the Sciences in Madrid offered a prize for proof that there was nothing dishonourable about useful employment. A. Rühl, *Vom Wirtschaftsgeist im Spanien*, Leipzig; 2nd ed., 1928, p. 14.

16 Salvador de Madariaga, *The Rise of the Spanish-American Empire*, London; 1947, especially pp. 27, 71 ff., and 279 ff.

17 Romon Carande (*op. cit.*, p. 378), cites the studies of Lacroix, Costa and Fairen on the structure of the Moslem right of pasture and on the wandering shepherds in connection with Spain.

18 Even Donoso Cortés saw his people as 'a people of 15 million kings'. See F. Niedermayer in *Saeculum*, III, 1952, p. 454.

19 P. Couturier and Pasteur Delpech, 'La Question Protestante en Espagne', *Unité Chrétienne et tolerance religieuse*, Paris; 1950, pp. 124 ff., and especially pp. 130 f.

20 José Luis Varela in *Saeculum*, III, 1952, pp. 412 ff. on the nature of the picaresque novel.

21 It is important to notice that for a long time Spain was represented abroad first by Jews and later by converted Jews. This applied not only to the Jewish physicians and traders in France, England, and the Low Countries, but also to statesmen and theologians. At the Council of Basle, where Spain made its debut at an all-European forum, the *conversos* were her leading representatives. As another example, one can cite the case of Bartholomew Columbus, Christopher's brother, who tried to interest King Henry VII of England and Charles VII of France in his brother's plans. Se Luis Suarez Fernandez, 'Herencia Medieval de Castilla', *Revista de Estudios Politicos*, vol. XXXV, 1951, p. 139. As Elias Canetti suggested to me in a discussion, this link between the Jews and Spain was still strong even on the eve of the First World War. Levantine Jews told their children and grandchildren about their real native

country – Spain, 400 years after the expulsion, and their eyes were turned more towards Spain than Jerusalem.

22 S. de Madariaga, *Christopher Columbus*, p. 218.

23 Sanchez Alburnoz, quoted in Miguel Cruz Hernandez, *op. cit.*, p. 358.

24 *Ibid.*, p. 358.

25 *Ibid.*, p. 359.

26 *Ibid.*, p. 367.

27 J. Vicens Vives discussed the copious modern Spanish research on Islam in Spain in *Saeculum*, III, 1952, pp. 496 ff. This theme is of great importance today. General Franco began his war with Moors and in 1953 for the first time in the history of Spain a Moorish general was put in charge of an important command on Spanish soil proper.

28 cf. Americo Castro. *Espana en su historia. Christianos, moros y judios*, Buenos Aires; 1948, a chapter of which entitled 'Knightly Orders, Holy War, Tolerance' appeared in German in *Hochland*, June; 1952, pp. 401 ff.

29 A. Mez, *The Renaissance of Islam*, London, 1937; p. 321.

30 See the numerous bibliographical references in F. Niedermayer, 'Zwei Spanien?', *Saeculum*, III, 1952, pp. 455 f. The contrast between the Spanish 'infrastructure', its enduring fundamental folk elements and the artificial governmental and ideological superstructures is well handled.

31 H. Lützeler, 'Die Spanische Kunst', *Handbuch der Spanienkunde*, pp. 276 ff.

32 Miguel Cruz Hernández, *op. cit.*, p. 371.

33 Lützeler, *op. cit.*, p. 310.

34 *Ibid.*, p. 307.

35 W. Beinhauer, *Spanische Umgangsprache*, Berlin/Bonn; 1930; in addition Lützeler, *op. cit.*, p. 314.

36 P. Couturier and Pasteur Delpech, *op. cit.*, p. 131.

37 M. Defourneaux, *Les francais en Espagne en XIe et XIIe siècle*, Paris; 1949, in addition *Rev. de Estudios Politicos*, vol. XXIX, 1950, pp. 270 ff.

38 G. Schreiber, *Deutschland und Spanien, Volkskundliche und Kulturgeschichtliche Beziehungen*, Dusseldorf; 1936, p. 417.

39 On the following M. Bataillon, *op. cit.*, pp. 2 ff.

40 *Ibid.*, pp. 78 ff.

41 'Ego mundi civis esse cupio, communis omnium vel peregrenus magnus Erasmus', *Opus epistularum*, ed. P. S. Allen, Oxford; 1906, and after, Letter No. 1314.

42 çf. M. Bataillon, *op. cit.*, p. 176.

43 *Ibid.*, p. 595.

44 *Ibid.*, p. 573.

45 These reports dating from the first half of the sixteenth century should be compared with that of the Bishop of Malaga, Dr Herrera, published in 1952: two months after the Eucharistic World Congress of Barcelona, celebrated with great pomp and ceremony, he declared that there were localities in Spain which had not seen a priest for ten years.

46 cf. M. Bataillon, *op. cit.*, pp. 181 f.

47 *Ibid.*, pp. 205 ff.

48 *Scripto de S. Ignatio*, I, Mon. hist. S. J., Madrid; 1904, pp. 69 ff. and pp. 598 ff.

49 Karl Rahner, 'Die ignatianische Mystik der Weltfrewudigkeit', *Zeitschrift für Aszese und Mystik*, 12, 1937, p. 134.

50 cf. Hugo Rahner, *Ignatius von Loyola und das geschichtliche Werden seiner Frömmigkeit*, Graz/Vienna; 1947, p. 86.

51 H. Becher, *Die Jesuiten*, Munich; 1951, pp. 186 ff.

52 M. Bataillon, *op. cit.*, p. 340.

53 *Ibid.*, pp. 400 ff.

54 cf. F. Niedermayer, *op. cit.*, p. 463.

55 cf. P. Rassow, *Die Kaiser-Idee Karls V*, Berlin; 1932, and the modern Spanish studies quoted in H. Hüffer in *Revista de Estudios politicos*, vol. XXXVI, 1951. See in addition the issue, 1948, vol. XXVI. cf. also J. M. Parry, *The Spanish Theory of empire in the 16th century*, Cambridge; 1940.

56 cf. to this *Autumn of the Middle Ages*, besides J. Huizinga's old and famous work, also R. Stadelmann, *Von Geist des Ausgehendes Mittelalters*, Halle; 1929.

57 cf. H. Heimpel, 'Karl der Kühne und der burgundische Staat', *Festschrift für Gerhard Ritter*, 1950.

58 J. Huizinga, 'Aus der Vorgeschichte des niederlandischen Nationalbewusstteins', *Im Banne der Geschichte*, pp. 213 ff.

59 Philip II's governess, Eleonora Mascarenhas, for example, had Augustine's *Confessions* translated. A breeze of that feminine religious-humanistic reform culture also blew through the Spanish royal court, as with Marguerite of Navarra and the Italian reform courts between Naples and Gonzaga. Theresa of Avila lived with the Mascarenhas family.

60 Romulo D. Carbia, *Historia de la leyenda negra hispano-americanos*, Madrid; 1944.

61 S. de Madariaga, *The Rise of the Spanish American Empire*, pp. 89 ff. on the later development of the relations of Spaniards to the Indians.

62 R. Ricard, *La Conquête spirituelle du Mexique. Essai sur l'apostolat et les méthodes missionaires des ordres mendicants en Nouvelle Espagne de 1523/4 à 1572*, Paris; 1933.

63 José Ortega y Gasset, *Espana invertebrada*, many translations of which exist.

64 Ramon Menendez Pidal, *Historia de Espana*, Madrid; 1947, I, pp. 215 ff.

65 cf. M. Bataillon, *op. cit.*, p. 529, and S. de Madariaga, 'Envy is the cancer of the Spanish Character', *Christopher Columbus*, p. 169.

66 Vives, *De Institione feminae christianae*.

67 His *Introductio ad veram sapientam*, a collection of sayings for education in the moral life, went through fifty editions among both Catholics and Protestants.

68 A good summary of the Spanish legal thinkers of the sixteenth century, with a tempered comparison of the undeniable differences between Vitoria and Suarez and a view of their significance for Grotius is provided in W. Goldschmidt's, *Francisco Suarez, renovador y innovador de las ciencias del Derecho*, Cordoba; 1951.

69 See the copious modern Spanish literature on Vitoria: in G. Schreiber, *Das Welt-konzil von Trient*, Freiburg; 1951, vol. I, p. XXIIf.

70 A Truyol y Serra, in *Saeculum*, III, 1952, p. 399.

71 C. Gutierrez, *Espanoles en Trento*, Valladolid; 1951, which is based principally on the catalogue of the Spaniards in Trent in Codex 320 of the library of the

Collegio Mayor de Santa Cruz, Valladolid. In addition, see F. Cereceda, 'Ecumenicidad y espanolismo en Trento', *El Concilio de Trento*, Madrid; 1945, and the same author's 'El nacionalismo religioso espanol en Trento', *Hispania*, 5, 1945, pp. 236 ff.

72 M. Grabmann, 'Das Konzil von Trient als Fortschrittsprinzip der katholischen Dogmatik, *Das Weltkonzil von Trient*, ed. G. Schreiber, vol. I, Freiburg; 1951, pp. 357 ff.; E. Stakemeier, 'Trienter Lehrentscheidungen und reformatorische Anliegen', *Ibid.*, pp. 97 ff. and F. Buuck, 'Zum Rechtfertigungsdekret', *Ibid.*, pp. 117 ff.

73 L. Spätling, 'Der Anteil der Fransikaner an Konzil von Trient', *Ibid.*, vol. II, pp. 509 ff.

74 F. Stegmuller, 'Zur Gnadenlehre des spanischen Konilzheologen Domingo de Soto', *Ibid.*, I, pp. 169 ff.

75 The political foundations of this right to resistance are very old in Spain and go back to the Council of Toledo and the Gothic administration of justice. (*Fuero jusgo*.) The Councils became so strong that they could remove kings and elect new ones. Their maxim: *Rey seras si fecieres derecho, et si non fecieres derecho, non seras rey*. ('If you do not create right, you will not be king.') This statement of the *Fuero jusgo* was valid in Aragon until the time of Philip II. See G. Wacker, 'Staat und Gesellschaft in Spanien', in *Handbuch der Spanienkunde*, p. 32.

76 See the literature on the Spanish concept of honour of the sixteenth and seventeenth centuries. K. Vossler, *op. cit.*, pp. 173 ff. For Theresa of Avila's concern over the right of honour of God and man, see P. A. Alkofer, *Sämtliche Schriften der hl. Theresa*, 6 vols., Munich; 1933–41, I, 37; p. 194; VI, p. 251; III, p. 382; V, p. 260. She often had to combat the false mania for honour in her monasteries. *Schriften*, VI, pp. 187 f.; I; pp. 306 f.; VI, p. 74.

77 Karl Rahner, *op. cit.*, pp. 121 ff.

78 Hugo Rahner, *op. cit.*, p. 75.

79 H. Becher, *op. cit.*, p. 87.

80 Ignatius was also against any application of violent physical or moral means against heresy. See *Stimmen der Zeit*, 1927, pp. 72 ff.

81 For the literature on Francis Xavier, see the excellent essay on him by Hugo Rahner, 'Das verlorene Leben', *Der Grosse Entschluss*, No. 8, Vienna; December 1952, pp. 65 ff.

82 *The letters of Francis Xavier 1542–52*, selected and tr. into German by Countess E. Vitzhum, Leipzig; 1939. See especially his letter to John III, the King of Portugal, of 8 February 1545, *Ibid.*, pp. 67 ff., which contains the motto of all great Spanish missionaries: ... the plans of God do not aim at filling your treasures house-with the riches of the Orient and with the gold of the Negro kings, but rather to give Your Highness a chance ...'

83 E. Allison Peers, *Studies of the Spanish Mystics*, vol. II, London, 1927 and 1930, pp. 31 ff. Interesting observation on Osuma and Laredo are contained in a lecture delivered in Madrid, 1 February 1951, by Luis Morales Lliver, *El misticismo de la materia en muestro siglo y el misticismo del espiritu en la epoca de Carlos V*, reported in *Ecclesia*, Madrid; 2 February 1951, Br. 149, 9 ff. On the whole problem, G. Hatzfield, 'Die spanische Mystik und ihre Ausdrucksmöglichkeiten', *DVJ*, No. 10. 1932, pp. 597 ff.

84 cf. M. von Waldberg, *Zur Entwicklungsgeschichte der schöner Seele bei den spanischen Mystikern*, Berlin; 1910.

85 E. Allison Peers, *op. cit.*, vol. I, pp. 32 f., and on Luis de Granada, *Ibid.*, I, pp. 32 ff. and M. Bataillon, *op. cit.*, pp. 635 f.

86 M. Romera-Navarro, 'La Defensa de la lengua espanola', *Bulletin Hispanique* 1929, vol. XXXI, pp. 204 ff.

87 M. Bataillon, *op. cit.*, p. 764.

88 S. Fornieles, *La Espana del siglo XVI. Felipe Il y la Inquisicion*, Buenos Aires; 1951.

89 S. de Madariaga presents a well-grounded judgment of the Spanish Inquisition in Europe and America in *The Rise of the Spanish American Empire*, pp. 142 ff. For the old conception see C. A. Lea, *A History of the Inquisition of Spain*, 4 vols. New York, 1906/7.

90 A. Mager, *Mystik als seelische Wirklichkeit. Eine Psychologie der Mystik*, Graz/Salzburg; 1945, p. 109.

91 See Theresa of Avila, *Schriften*, I, pp. 171 f. Her profound and unshaken faith ties her to Luther, and her songs must be compared with his. On the eve of a religious feast, she sometimes danced, clicked castanets and sang. See *Schriften*, VI, 308, I, p. 17.

92 A. Mager, *op. cit.*, pp. 353 ff.

93 Theresa, *Schriften*, III, pp. 557 and 527 ff., IV pp. 6 ff. and p. 57.

94 On the first page of her account Theresa remarked that her father, unlike most of his contemporaries and social peers, kept no Moorish slaves in the house, 'since these moved him to a great pity', and that he treated a girl slave of one of his brothers like his own child. At seven Theresa wanted to go over to the Moors, in order to become a martyr. All her life she recoiled from (Moorish) Andalusia (Arab 'das andalus' – the wine-country). She revered her brother fallen in the struggle against the Indians as a martyr.

95 Vossler alludes to this somewhat indirectly: 'Man is a setting for spirit.' This connection, however, is dissolved in neo-platonic relations without regard to the trinitarian and christological restriction, Vossler, *op. cut.*, p. 196.

96 Ramon Carande, *op. cit.*, p. 375.

97 In addition L. Pfandl, 'Das spanische Lutherbild des 16. Jahrhunderts', *Hist. Jb.*, 50; 1930.

98 A. Mager, *op. cit.*, p. 45.

99 C. K. Wild, 'Theresianische Mystik', *Zeitschrift für Aszese und Mystik*, 12, 1937, p. 25.

100 A. Mager, *op. cit.*, pp. 31 ff.

101 P. Hippolyte, *Amour et Violence*, pp. 146, p. 189 ff. An excellent study.

102 The posthumous work *Sadilies e illuminados*, by Asim Palacios, quoted by Miguel Cruz Hernández, *op. cit.*, p. 371.

103 For Theresa only Castille was 'The Promised Land'. *Schriften*, III, p. 249 – always in contrast to Andalusia; cf. III, p. 305; p. 402; IV, p. 80.

104 cf. Hugo Rahner, *Der Spielende Mensch*, Einsiedeln; 1952.

105 See the fine paper by Brother M. de Guevarm, 'Von Johannes von Kreuz zu Edith von Stein', *Schweizer Rundschau*, December 1952, pp. 523 f.

106 cf. E. Allison Peers, *op. cit.*, II, pp. 184 ff.

107 Literature on Falconi, *Ibid.*, II, pp. 346 ff.

108 Angel Ganivet, the representative of the generation of 1898, saw in Stoicism *the* natural foundation of Spanish intellectuality and religiosity, and *the* basic feature of the Spanish character. See E. Lerch, 'Spanische Sprach – und Wesensart', *Handbuch der Spanienkunde*, pp. 195 f.

109 O. Brunner, *Adeliges Landleben und europaischer Geist*, Salzburg; 1949, p. 129. Professor Brunner, my honoured teacher, sees in Lipsius's resistance a difference from the thought of stoicism, which I cannot accept.

110 The alliance between the lower class and the Inquisition was also uncommonly important for Spanish South America. See S. de Madariaga, *The Rise of the Spanish American Empire*, p. 343, footnote 17.

111 F. Niedermayer, *op. cit.*, pp. 444 ff.

112 See O. Brunner, *op. cit.*, p. 131, which refers to F. Schaek, Balthasar Gracian and the end of the 'Siglo de Oro'.

113 José Luis Varela in *Saeculum*, III, 1952, pp. 421 ff., reports on the copious modern Spanish polemical literature on the picaresque novel, its character, and its origin.

114 A. Castro, 'Cervantes y la Inquisicion', *Modern Philology*, No. 27, 1930, pp. 427 ff.; by the same author, *El Pensamiento de Cervantes*, Madrid, 1925.

115 For a long time *Don Quixote* was rightly viewed as part of the enlightenment cf. E. Lersch, 'Don Quijote im Spiegel', *Neue Rundschau*, 1916, pp. 1103 ff. in addition Vossler, *op. cit.*, pp. 187 f.

116 Cervantes, *Don Quixote*, II, p. 8, and *Persiles y Segismonda*, II, p. 58.

117 Cervantes, *Don Quixote*, II, pp. 27 and 16.

118 L. E. Palacios presents a noteworthy interpretation of Calderon's much inter-preted *Life is a Dream*, 'La Vie est un songe. Essai sur le sens philosophique du drame de Calderon', *Laval Theologique et Philosophique*, Univ. Laval, Quebec, VII, 1951, pp. 123 ff.

119 See the work of Villasenor, quoted in F. Niedermayer, *op. cit.*, on the very close kinship in thought between the seeming opposite national antagonists: Unamuno and Ortega y Gasset.

120 J. Gebser, *Lorca oder das Reich der Mutter*, Stuttgart; 1949.

121 R. Rauquette, *Etudes*, January 1953, p. 123, a review of the book *Calvin et Loyola*, by A. Favre-Dorsay.

122 Hence it is no accident that Carl Schmitt, the state theorist of the Third *Reich* and the ideologist of the friend-foe theory felt especially drawn to Donoso Cortés. His works are listed in H. Hüffer, *Las Relaciones Hispano-germanas. op. cit.*, p. 71.

123 On the sociological and political problem see Lizuriaga, 'El Analfabetisino en Espana', *Museo Pedagogico*, Madrid; 1926.

124 G. Schreiber, *Deutschland und Spanien*, esp. pp. 17 ff., 136 ff, 437 ff., 458 ff.

125 cf. the literature in H. Hüffer, *op. cit.*, pp. 68 ff.

CHAPTER 15

1 cf. B. Croce, *Storia della eta barocca in Italia*, 2nd ed., Bari; 1946; B. Croce, *La Spagna nella vita italiana durante la Rinascenza*, 3rd ed., Bari; 1940.

2 One of the most difficult problems of European intellectual history, mannerism, must be investigated in these political and social interconnections (Absolutism,

Nicodemism, Counter Reformation). Beginnings have been made by W. Pinder, W. Weissbach, Lili Fröhlich-Bum, H. Hoffmann, M. Hoerner, G. Iven, H. Sedlmayr. For a compilation of the literature, see R. Mühler, *Dichtung der Krise*, Vienna; 1951, in a remarkable essay 'Conrad Ferdinand Meyer und der Manierismus', pp. 147 ff. and 553 f. Further, N. Pevsner, 'Gegen-Reformation and Manierismus', *Rep. f. Kunstwiss*, ed. Waetzold, vol. XLVI, 1925.

3   The text of this important Bull appears in G. Schreiber's *Das Weltkonzil von Trient*, I, pp. 1 ff. cf. in addition ch. XXVII.

4   E. Stakemeier, 'Trienter Lehrentscheidungen und reformatorische Anliegen', *Das Weltkonzil von Trient*, pp. 78 f.

5   Raymond Ruyer, *L'Utopie et les Utopies*, Paris; 1950, pp. 24 ff.; 43 f.; 52 f.; 73, 83 ff. In his investigation of present-day Utopias, Raymond Ruyer has stressed the predilection and enthusiasm of Utopians for purely optical solutions and plans. This arises in part from their confusion of time and optical movement and their inability to accept the nature of history.

6   J. Bonduelle, 'Une ville ou se resserre l'unité', in special issue of *La Vie Spirituelle*, April; 1952; 'La Jérusalem céleste', pp. 340 ff. cf. ib. pp. 367 ff.

7   The tradition of the totalitarian sun-god-king is very ancient: Hammurabi, Alexander, Constantine, Frederick II (since the struggle over investitures emperors and popes fought over the sacral sun-name); the Incas, Louis XIV. The sun sees all, reaches all, watches over all: Campanella realized this principle of Inca ideology in his *City of the Sun*, which he viewed as a model for a 'renovated', world-ruling Catholic Church at whose head stood the pope with the army of St Paul and the 'fleet of St Peter', which educates, forces, and conjures man to peace. The *City of the Sun* already stood in the middle of a series of baroque utopias. Francis Bacon's *New Atlantis* appeared almost at the same time (1620, three years before the *City of the Sun*, published 1623 in Frankfurt). The utopias of Barcley (*Argenis*), G. Winstanley (The Law of Freedom), Harrington's *Oceana*, Restif (*La découverte australe*), Vairasse soon followed. Andreae, the great mediator between Calvinism and Lutheranism in Germany, translated the *City of the Sun*, in Protestant Germany.

8   On Campanella cf. A. Doren *Festschrift für W. Goetz*, 1927, pp. 242 ff.; on relations to imperial baroque; Th. Kvacala, 'Th. Campannella und Ferdinand II', *S.B. d. Ak.*, Vienna; 1908, pp. 157 and 159. Campanella and the baroque must sometime be investigated in connection with those relations of Utopia which A. Doren (*Wünschträume und Wünschzeiten*, Lectures at the Warburg Library, 1924/25, Leipzig/Berlin; 1927) has dealt with, pp. 158 ff.

9   cf. Alberto Savinio's foreword to his edition of T. Campanella's *La Città del Sole*, Rome; 1944, pp. 9 ff. *The City of the Sun* was originally written in Italian and then translated into Latin by Campanella himself. For the importance of the people's language in this respect cf. below on Galileo.

10   L. Olschki, *The Genius of Italy*, pp. 349 ff.

11   D. Cantimori, *Italienische Häretiker der Spätrenaissance*, German ed. W. Kaegi, Basle; 1949.

12   *Ibid.*, p. 178.

13   On the Academy of the Intronati, cf. the literature in Cantimori, *op. cit.*, p. 481, footnote 16.

The Intellectual History of Europe

14 *Ibid.*, p. 309.

15 L. Olschki, *Gesch. der neusprachlichen wissenschlaftlichen Literatur*, Halle; 1927, III, pp. 34 ff. and p. 62.

16 *Timaeus*, 500; *De gener. anim.* 1/2 and IV/1, 4. *De Generatione et Corruptione*, II, 9; *Phys.*, I, 9; *Ennead*, III, 6, 19.

17 Bruno, *de la causa*, pp. 218 ff.

18 J. von Schlosser, *Die Kunstliteratur*, pp. 292 f.

19 We quote from Vasari according to the edition of G. Milanesi, Florence; 1878, *Opere di G. Vasari*, part I–VII.

20 L. Olschki, *The Genius of Italy*, p. 380.

21 See Marcel Reding, *Thomas von Aquin und Karl Marz*, Graz; 1953, for an opinion on the relationship between Aristitle, Aquinas and Marx and on the 'Platonic presuppositions to the historical understanding of Aristotle', as well as on the relation of the *polis*, the city and closed world, to the individual.

22 cf. L. Lange, *Die geschichtliche Entwicklung des Bewegungbegriffes*, 1886.

23 J. H. Randall, 'The Development of scientific method in the school of Padua', *JHI*, I, 1940, p. 203.

24 Olschki, *Gesh. der neusprachlich wiss. Lit.*, III, p. 361.

25 Magic, rhetoric, theology (in the ancient and medieval sense as a natural-philosophical knowledge of God and soul) and jurisprudence, together constituted the 'grand form' of the antique *polis* and its baroque renaissance.

26 This aversion of Galileo is understandable since his own point of departure ws still primarily the idea, the primacy of the 'hypothesis' of pure theory. cf. A. Koyré, *Etudes Galiléennes*, 3 vols., Paris; 1939, and O. Toeplitz, *Entwicklung der Infinitesimalrechnung*, Berlin; 1949. And further the old study by Ernst Mach, 'Theologische, animistische und mystische Gesichtspunkte in der Mechanik', *Die Mechanik in ihrer Entwicklung*, 7th ed., Leipzig; 1912, pp. 429 ff.

27 'Dialogo dei massimi sistemi ... 'Opere, ed. Timpanaro, I, p. 92.

28 cf. R. Russo, 'La politica del Vaticano nella dieta di Ratisbona', *Archivoi storico Italiano Ser. VII*, vol. V, 1926, pp. 25 ff.

29 The Minims (neo-Franciscans) spread Galileo's studies through France and West Europe; cf. R. Dugas, *Histoire de la Mecanique*, Paris; 1950.

30 L. Olschki, *op. cit.*, p. 393.

31 Carpis' words in Italian: *Non mancano in Italia persone pie e dotte che tengono la verità, ma queste non possono nè scrivere nè stampare. – E porto maschera, ma per forza, perchè sanza di quella nessun vomo puo vivere in Italia.* cf. in addition E. Codignola, *Illuministi, Giansenisti e Giacobini nell' Italia del Settecento*, Florence; 1947, p. 188.

32 Conti's letter to G. B. Vico, dated 3 January 1728, was, among others, printed in G. B. Vico's *Principi di una scienza nuova*, pref. P. Viazzi, Milan; 1934, p. 313.

33 P. Browe, *Die Kastration im Mittelalter*, Bresslau; 1924.

34 Modern Italian literature on Jansenism, E. Codignola, *op. cit.*, pp. 288 ff.

35 See interesting studies on this great problem in the *Bulletin de la Societé d'histoire vaudoise*, Piquerol, 1884, ff., from vol. XV; *Bulletino della Societa di Studi Valdesi*, Turin; 1898 ff.

36 cf. P. Alatri, *Profilo storico del cattolocesimo liberale in Italia*, 1st ed., Palmermo; 1950.

37 On Manzoni's Jansenism cf. Codignola, *op. cit.*, pp. 277 ff.

38 Text of the Encyclical *Mirari vos* (in German) in *Mensch und Gemeinschaft in christlichen Schau*, pub. by E. Marmy, Freiburg; Switzerland, 1945, pp. 15 ff.

39 cf. Benedetto Croce, *History of Europe in the Nineteenth Century*, London; 1934 (first English edition).

CHAPTER 16

1 J. Cadier, 'La Tradition Calviniste', *Protestantisme Français*, ed. M. Boegner. Paris; 1945, p. 312.

2 One sees it in Geneva, on and in the old Cathedral, as in all the old 'houses of God' in Calvinist-influenced localities: suddenly the 'house of God' becomes a national place of ceremony, court house (Westminster!), then a museum. Not only the absolutism of the French king, but a deeper instinct, a language-consciousness (that on its side was essentially awakened by Calvinists; Conrart was the ancestor of the Académie Francaise) refused the Calvinist house of God the name of 'Church' and forced the pagan and Old Testament characterization 'Temple'. This was not only a political but an intellectual-historical fact of the first rank to be compared with the refusal of the Father-name to priests in the German language. On Geneva cf. C. Goyau, *Une Ville-Eglise, Genève*, 2 vols., Paris; 1919.

3 H. Bremond, *Histoire litteraire du sentiment religieux en France*, Paris; 1929 ff. I, pp. 13 ff.

4 H. De Man, *Jacques Coeur, der Königliche Kaufmann*, Bern; 1950, p. 132.

5 cf. J. Chambon, *Der französische Protestantismus*, Munich; 1937; pp. 13 ff.

6 J. Bohatec, *Budé und Calvin. Studien zur Gedankenwelt des französichen frühhumanismus*, Graz.; 1950, pp. 472 ff.

7 *Ibid.*, pp. 121 ff.

8 *Ibid.*, pp. 395 ff.

9 *Ibid.*, p. 475

10 *Ibid.*, pp. 294 ff.

11 R. Fédou; 'Histoire et Unité', *Unité chrétienne et tolérance religieuse*, Paris; 1950, p. 36. André Favre-Dorsaz, *Calvin et Loyola, deux Réformes*; Paris/Brussels; 1951, was not just to Calvin. His confessional group-egoism blurs his view of the deep kinship between the two great reformers (cf. the review by R. Rouquette in *Etudes*, January 1953 p. 123).

12 P. Maury, 'La Théologie naturelle chez Calvin', *Etudes sur Calvin et le Calvinisme*, Paris; 1936, p. 267, and J. Cadier, *op. cit.*, p. 314.

13 Th. Preiss, 'Le Témoignage intérieur du Saint Esprit', *Etudes théologiques et religeuses*, July–December 1943, p. 118. In addition, J. Cadier, *op. cit.* p. 314.

14 Even confessional opponents must admit that he is 'one of the great leaders of men' (R. Rouquette, *op. cit.*, p. 123). But also: 'in his conduct he strikingly resembles those great revolutionary chiefs of today who sacrifice everything to the triumph of an arbitrary ideological cause in which they see an absolute truth!'

15 On Calvin and Marx: cf. E. Rosenstock-Huessey, *Die Europäischen Revolu-*

tionen, und der Charakter der Nationen, Stuttgart; 1951, p. 456. R. H. Tawney, *Religion and the Rise of Capitalism*, London; 1938, Pelican ed., p. 120.

16 From J. Gaberel's *Calvin et Rousseau*, Geneva; 1878, down to Charles Maurras and Maritain, the similarity between Calvin and Rousseau has often been analyzed.

17 K. R. Popper, *The Open Society and Its Enemies*, 2 vols., London, 1945.

18 G. de Lagarde, *La Naissance de l'Esprit laique au declin du moyen âge*, 8 vols., Paris; 1934. cf. vol. IV, pp. 108 ff. for a description of the literature.

19 A very instructive example of the rise of such a city through a ruthless political policy is portrayed in E. Coornaert's 'L'Etat et les villes à la fin du Moyen Age. La politique d'Anvers', *Revue Historique*, Paris; 1952, pp. 185 ff.: the rise of Antwerp, one of the administrative centres of Calvinism.

20 H. Pirenne, *Les anciennes Démocraties des Pays-Bas*, Paris; 1910, p. 66.

21 E. Coornaert, *op. cit.*, pp. 185 ff.

22 E. Kahler, *Der deutsche Charakter in der Geschichte Europas*, Zürich, 1937, pp. 484 f.

23 cf. G. Schreiber, *Gemeinschaften des Mittelalters. Recht und Verfassung, Kult und Frömmigkeit*, Munster; 1948.

24 V. Valentin, *Weltgeschichte*, Cologne/Berlin; 1952, pp. 326 f. Valentin himself comes from an old Hugenot family.

25 J. Bohatec, *op. cit.*, pp. 439 ff. In an earlier work, Bohatec stated that Calvin opened a way to modern socialism, *Calvins Lehre von Staat und Kirche*, Breslau; 1937.

26 Veit Valentein, *op. cit.*, pp. 330 ff.

27 J. Romein and A. Romein-Verschoor, *Anherrn der holländischen Kultur*, Bern; 1946, p. 80.

28 cf. e.g. L. Brentano, *Der wirtschaftende Mensch in der Geschichte*, Leipzig; 1923, pp. 204 ff., and pp. 363 ff. On Max Weber's theory of Calvinism: A. Müller-Arnack, *Genealogie der Wirtschaftsstile*, 3rd ed., Stuttgart; 1944, pp. 89 ff., with references to the contraditions between the Lutheran, Calvinist and Catholic economic spirit (*Ibid.*, pp. 107 ff. and 148 ff.). In addition, O. V. Zwiedineck-Südenhorst, 'Weltanschauung und Wirtschaft. Kritisches und Positives zu Müller-Armacks Geneologie der Wirtschaftsstile', *S. B. der Bayer Akad. d. Wiss. Phil. hist. Abt. Heft 2*, Munich; 1942, p. 79 ff., who also cites Bohatec, *Calvins Lehre von Staat und Kirche*, as evidence that the capitalist spirit does not derive from Calvinism. cf. also F. van Gunsteren, *Calvinismus und Kapitalismus*, Amsterdam; 1934; J. B. Kraus, *Scholastik, Puritanismus and Kapitalismus*, Munich; 930; C. Bauer, 'Kirche, Staat und kapitalistischer Geist', *AKG*, No. 21, 1931. R. H. Tawneyr contributed important modifications, corrections and positive additions to Weber's thesis of 1904/5 in his *Religion and the Rise of Capitalism* (first English ed. 1926). H. M. Robertson, *Aspects of the Rise of Economic Individualism*, Cambridge; 1935, with Tawney, Sombart and Pirenne seeks to show the medieval origins of capitalism. C. Lefort in 'Capitalisme et Religion au XVI siècle', *Les Temps Modernes*, April; 1952. pp. 1892 ff., provides a useful criticism of the two English scholars. It is certain that Calvinism successfully fought against one of the most important restraints on the new economic spirit, 'The hindrance of animism' (L. Mumford, *Technics and Civilization*, New York; 1934, pp. 31 ff.),

the magic conditions of the archaic society. The Catholic concept of being for the first time opposed Protestant dualism, which recognized no ultimate connecting (sacral) link between being and appearance, universal matter and spirit. An example of this was the mint controversy between the Lutheran and Catholic Saxons in 1533/5 over the question as to whether the deterioration of a coin and the insufficient metal cover abolished the inner weight of the money. See, in addition, J. Wach, *Sociology of Religion*, Chicago; 1946.

29 cf. H. Rössler, 'Der Calvinismus. Versuch einer Erfassung und Würdigung seiner Grundlagen und Wirkungen', *Bremer Beiträge zur Kultur und Wittschaft*, Bremen; 1951, with copious bibliographical references to the Calvinist intellectual history from the sixteenth to the eighteenth century.

30 Tawney, *op. cit.*, pp. 120 f.

31 Rosenstock-Huessy, *op. cit.*, p. 363.

32 G. Maranon, *Olivares. Der Niedergang Spaniens als Weltmacht*, Munich; 1939, p. 217 – cited in A. Müller-Armack, *op. cir.*, p. 148.

33 cf. C. Lefort, *op. cit.*, p. 1902.

34 L. Mumford, *op. cit.*, pp. 92 ff.

35 A. Müller-Armack, *op. cit.*. pp. 89 ff.

36 *Ibid.*, pp. 240 ff.

37 *Ibid.*, p. 262.

38 L. Mumford, *op. cit.*, pp. 167 ff.

39 On Calvin's Moses-ideal: see Bohatec, *Bude und Calvin*, pp. 463 f.

40 cf. the compilation *La France protestante*, ed. Haagbordier, also P. de Felice and H. Lehr, *Les Protestantes d'autrefois*, 6 vols., Paris; 1898–1901. J. Viénot, *Histoire de la Réforme Française*, 2 vol., Paris; 1926/34. Also P. Lestringant, 'Geographie du Protestantisme francaise', *Protestantisme Française*, edited by M. Boegner, Paris; 1943.

41 André Siegfried, 'Le groupe Protestant Cévenol', *Ibid.*, p. 25.

42 J. Chambon, *op. cit.*, pp. 30 f.

43 *Ibid.*, pp. 51 ff.

44 *Ibid.*, p. 76.

45 R. Fédou, *op. cit.*, p. 55.

46 On Calvin and Rabelais: see Bohatec, *Budé und Calvin*, pp. 214 ff.

47 E. Gilson, *Rabelais franciscain*, (*Les idées et les lettres*), pp. 197 ff. In addition E. Auerbach, *Mimesis*, Bern; 1946, pp. 258 f.

48 On Franciscan optimism and receptivity to Renaissance in the fifteenth and sixteenth century: see A. Gemelli, *Das Franziskanertum*, Leipzig; 1936, pp. 147 ff. and 173 ff.

49 E. Auerbach, *op. cit.*, pp. 262 ff.

50 H. Friedrich, *Montaigne*, Bern; 1949, pp. 117 f.

51 *Ibid.*, pp. 117 f.

52 On Bodin: see W. Dilthey, *Gesammelte Schriften*, II, pp. 145 ff.; H. Friedrich, *op. cit.*, pp. 140 f.; K. Muhs, *Geschichte des abendländischen Geistes*, vol. I, 1950.

53 H. Friedrich, *op. cit.*, pp. 419 ff.

54 *Ibid.*, pp. 150 ff.

55 *Ibid.*, p. 130.

56 On Montaigne's 'verités des faicts' and Lebniz's 'verités de fait', which how-
    ever are subordinated to the eternal verities, see: H. Friedrich, *op. cit.*, p. 167.
57 *Ibid.*, p. 45.
58 *Ibid.*, p. 368.
59 *Essais*, I, 54, p. 304, c. p. 402.
60 H. Friedrich, *op. cit.*, p. 387.
61 *Ibid.*, pp. 105 and 78 f.
62 *Essais*, Book I, ch. III, p. 121.
63 H. Friedrich, *op. cit.*, p. 18.
64 W. Dilthey, *op. cit.*, II, p. 267.
65 Pierre Charron, *De la Sagesse*, II, ch. 5, para, 29.
66 On William of Orange: J. Romein and A. Romein-Verschoor, *op. cit.*, pp.
    43 ff.
67 K. Muhs, *op. cit.*, pp. 196 f.; cf. P. Baasch, *Hollandische Wirtschaftsgeschichte*
    Jena; 1927.
68 W. Dilthey, *op. cit.*, II, p. 79.
69 *Ibid.*, pp. 95 ff.
70 K. Muhs, *op. cit.*, I, p. 197.
71 On Oldenbarnveldt cf. J. Romein and A. Romein-Verschoor, *op. cit.*, pp. 77 ff.
72 On Arminius: J. Cadier, 'La Tradition Calviniste', *Prot. Française*, ed. Goegner
    Paris; 1945, p. 297.
73 On the rise of the idea of religious tolerance see, beside the old works of J.
    Simon (*La Liberté de conscience*, Paris; 1872) and P. Janet (1887), F. Puaux,
    Les Precursuers française de la tolérance au XVIIè siècle, 1881; Bonnet-
    Maury, *Histoire de la liberté de conscience depuis l'Edit de Nantes* ... 1900.
    Also the great work of W. R. Jordan, *The development of religious toleration in
    England*, London; 1936; and D. Cantimori, *Italienische Häretiker der Spät-
    renaissance*, Basle; 1949, pp. 409 ff., with copious bibliographical references.
74 On Grotius, W. Dilthey, *op. cit.*, II, pp. 132 f. and 276 ff., J. and A. Romeim-
    Verschoor, *op. cit.*, pp. 114 ff.
75 L. Mumford, *op. cit.* pp. 116 ff.
76 On glass and the ego: *Ibid.*, pp. 128 ff.
77 P. Chazel, 'Genie Francaise et Protestantisme dans La France contemporaine',
    Protestantisme français, ed. Boegner, pp. 98 ff.
78 J. Chambon, *op. cit.*, p. 113.
79 The reformers of the sixteenth century had felt this tension strongly. Cardinal
    Pole, Machiavelli's first great foe, confessed that the more a man's private life
    conforms to the life of Christ, the less he is fitted to rule in the eyes of men.
    Pope Clement said: *Chi va bonamente vien tratta da bestia* (He who acts
    honourably is treated like a fool). Cited according to L. Brentano, *Der
    wirtschaftende Mensch in der Geschichte*, Leipzig; 1923, pp. 370.
80 J. Chambon, *op. cit.*, pp. 118 f.
81 C. J. Buckhardt, *Richelieu*, Munich; 1941, pp. 470 and 536.
82 *Ibid.*, p. 370.
83 *Ibid.*, pp. 12 f.
84 *Ibid.*, p. 534.
85 *Ibid.*, p. 516.
86 *Ibid.*, p. 240.

87 *Ibid.*, p. 323.
88 *Ibid.*, p. 529.
89 J. Chambon, *op. cit.*, p. 142.
90 The linguistic theory of Port-Royal taught that language is a human invention and that logic is clearly formulated, rational speech. This Jansenist Neocalvinist tradition later flowed into the thinking of the men of the Enlightenment, especially Condillac, and united the two movements in very much the same way that service in Richelieu's campaign to purify the language united the Neocalvinists and the Catholic intelligentsia in the seventeenth century. For a suggestive study of the problem of language in the eighteenth century, cf. H. Friedrich, 'Die Sprachtheorie der französischen Illuminaten des 18. Jahrhunderts, insbesondere Saint-Martins', *DVJ*, 13, 1953, p. 294.
91 G. Moldenhauer, 'Kardinal Richelieus Kulturpolitik', *DVJ*, 13, 1935, pp. 498 ff. cf. literature on the concept of cultural policy. cf. especially Ed. Spranger's article, 'Kulturpolitik' in P. Herre, *Politisches Handwörterbuch*, vol. I, Leipzig; 1923, pp. 1087 f.
92 J. Chambon, *op. cit.*, p. 101.
93 On Père Joseph: C. J. Burckhardt, *op. cit.*, pp. 480 ff.; G. Fagniez, *op. cit.*; L. Dedouvres, *Le Père Joseph de Paris, l'eminence grize*, Paris; 1932. For his spiritual life see: H. Bremond: *Hist. litt.*, II, pp. 168 ff.
94 *Ibid.*, II, p. 180.
95 *Dix Jours*, p. 411, quoted according to Bremond, *op. cit.*, II, p. 191.
96 *Dix Jours*, p. 299.
97 On Mersenne cf. Descartes, *Correspondances*, I, ed. Adam, Paris; 1936, pp. 455 f.; R. Lenoble, *Mersenne ou la naissance du mécanisme*, Paris; 1943, has shown Mersenne's fundamental importance for Descartes and proved him to be the creator of 'mechanism', as an obligatory unitary world-view for philosophers and natural scientists. The retroactive connections of Mersenne in the great tradition of the left spiritualist Franciscans still await disclosure.
98 *Correspondances*, I, pp. 365 ff.
99 On Descartes and the reform of scholasticism see Gilson in his commentary on the *Discours*, p. 133, cf. K. Jaspers, *op. cit.*, p. 114. E. Gilson, *Etudes sur le role de la pensée médiévale dans la formation du système cartésien*, Paris; 1930.
100 His thirst for knowledge, as with Leibniz, brought him into contact with the whole underground of Europe. Beeckman on the journey in 1619 had given him the motto: *ne quid boni in Europa te lateat* (*Correspondances* I, p. 21). This journey, which via Amsterdam led to Copenhagen, Poland, Hungary, Austria, followed with a remarkable exactness the faith of the religious nonconformists, of the Huguenots, the Arminians, Socinians, Enthusiasts, Anabaptists!
101 On Descartes's dream cf. the depth-psychology study of Marie Louise von Franz in vol. III of the *Jung-Studien*, Zürich; 1952.
102 cf. also Descartes (*Correspondences*, IV, p. 379); *J'ai tiré la preuve de l'existence de Dieu de l'idee que je trouve en moi d'un Etre souverainement parfait, qui est la notion ordinaire que l'on en a.*
103 cf. the *Meditationes de prima philosophia*, I, 1641, *principia philosophiae*, 1644 I; and e.g. *Correspondances*, ed. Adam, Paris; 1947, pp. 59 f.
104 On God as the founder of Cartesian clarity and distinction cf. J. Wahl,

Descartes, ed. Adam, Paris; 1937, p. 371. See also D. Mormet, *Histoire de la clarté française*, Paris; 1929.

105 *Correspondances*, I, ed. Adam and G. Milmus, 1936, p. 95; IV, 1947, pp. 330 ff.

106 *Ibid.*, IV, pp. 242 f.

107 *Ibid.*, IV, p. 209 to Colvius, in which he explains the difference between his proposition and the similar one in Augustine, *De Civ. Dei*, ch. 26.

108 *Correspondances*, IV, pp. 330 f.

109 Abroad Descartes set great store on the fact that he was a French nobleman, *Ibid.*, I, p. 458: on Descartes as Seigneur du Perron. On his generosity cf. K. Jaspers, *op. cit.*, p. 107, and on the stoic influences, *Ibid.*, p. 112.

110 *Correspondances*, I, pp. 135 f.

111 L. Pfandl, *Philipp II*, Munich; n.d., pp. 120 ff.

112 Descartes embodied the anxiety of the authentic conservative (authentic conservatives are a rare phenomenon!). Therefore he did not want to attack the state, the constitution, customs, etc., because it is infinitely difficult to reconstruct them, once they are overthrown. *Ouevres*, ed. Adam and Tannéry, VI, p. 14. In addition K. Jaspers, *op. cit.*, p. 111.

113 Descartes, *Oeuvres*, ed. Adam and Tannéry, VI, p. 139.

114 *Correspondances*, I, p. 142.

115 21 April 1641 to Mersenne, *Ibid.*, IV, pp. 336 f.

116 C. Adams, 'Descartes, ses trois notions fondamentales', *Descartes*, Paris, 1937, p. 13.

117 *Oeuvres*, ed. Adam and Tannéry, VII, cf. also K. Jaspers, *op. cit.*, p. 80.

118 His philosophy as a matter of fact was supposed to become that universal language which, together with Mersenne, interested him as a typical project of the Lullian baroque. -

119 History is not needed to grasp eternal truth. (*Oeuvres*, ed. Adam and Tannéry, XI, p. 2, Part 9). A. Koyré (*Descartes*, ed. Adam, 1937, pp. 203 f.) has noted Descartes's deep dislike of concepts of time or motion, unlike Galileo. *Oeuvres*, II, p. 385; III, p. 9, ed. Adam and Tannéry; *Correspondances*, I, 254.

120 K. Jaspers, *op. cit.*, pp. 92 ff. A. Gewirtz, 'Experience and the non-mathematical in the Cartesian method', *JHI*, II, 1941, p. 183, aimed to prove that Descartes adhered fully and completely to empiricism (especially in his *Regulae ad directionem ingenii*). However, he admitted that his whole work was determined in mathematical-logical terms.

121 *Correspondances*, I, p. 431.

122 *Ibid.*, IV, p. 337.

123 cf. K. Jaspers, *op. cit.*, pp. 133 ff.; J. Maritain, *Trois Reformateurs, Luther – Descartes – Rousseau*, Paris; 1925. pp. 73 ff.

124 cf. *Correspondances*, IV, p. 244. The Platonists of Chartres had also tried to work out the nature of the Trinity by studying the properties of the triangle.

125 On Descartes and Pascal: *Ibid.*, IV, pp. 401 f., and the index to Part II.

126 On Pascal cf. ch. 20. The modern literature on Pascal has grown beyond all limits. One of the most interesting recent works is J. Guitton, *Pascal et Leibniz, Etude sur deux types de penseurs*, Paris; 1951, in which Pascal, as the man of experience and of 'seeing' is contrasted with Leibniz as the thinker of the ideal and of logical security. The two thinkers are closely related. Pascal is as close to Leibniz as the latter is to Descartes: their thought rests on a

spiritual method, and is the expression of a spiritual dualism. Through a mathematical theology they all sought to grasp things in a great primal interconnection.

127 cf. H. Platz, *Pascal, der um Gott ringende Mensch*, Dülmen; 1937, p. 133. Like most German treatments, this fine book tends to make Pascal's *Daimon* into something far more harmless than it is. Platz has been strongly influenced by the *Jugendbewegung*, which was fascinated by Pascal's daring dialectic. See also pp. 83 ff.

128 cf. Karl Jaspers, *op. cit.*, pp. 130 f. On the wager recently C. Journet (from totally other points of view), 'Le preambule de l'argument du pari chez Pascal', *Nova et Vetera*, Friburg; 1952, No. 2, pp. 151 ff.

129 P. Burgelin, 'La Piété', *Prot. française, op. cit.*, p. 206.

130 cf. with it what J. Maritain, *op. cit.*, pp. 92 f., says on the Cartesian roots of the deep inhumanity of our modern science.

131 George Sorel demonstrated the Cartesian origins of the dogma of 'progress', cf. J. Maritain, *op. cit.*, p. 121.

132 All the eastern countries between Russia and the West, now 'people's democracies', ought to be studied for this interconnection, the strange mixing of Calvinism and Catholicism (*Blatter f. deutsche Philos.* i3, 1939/40, pp. 290 ff.). Both mentalities strengthened the absolutist element and supported the rule of the secular and clerical nobility over the peasants. The country was subjected and sucked dry as mere 'matter'. Peasants in archaic relations, the petty bourgeois, the cities and monasteries floated like islands until the underground erupted and the surface shattered.

CHAPTER 17

1 W. Levison, *England and the Continent in the Eighth century*, London; 1941, p. 173.

2 W. C. Dampier, 'Science', in E. Barker's *The Character of England*, Oxford; 1947, p. 260. I must thank my friend Roland Hill for his advice and assistance in helping me to understand the nature of English spiritual life.

3 In 1447 the House of Commons already consisted of six estates: prelates, clergy and nobility and in the *communitas populosa*, tradesmen, free yeomen, and artisans. This breadth of representation was a consequence of the burden on the Kingdom caused by the French wars, which made the inclusion of broader masses of the people necessary. cf. J. S. Roskell, 'The Social Composition of the Commons in a Fifteenth Century Parliament', *Bulletin of the Institute of Historical Research*, *XXIV*, London; 1951, pp. 152 ff.

4 On the destruction of the old nobility in England from the twelfth to the fifteenth centuries cf. W. Kellinghusen, 'Der Aufstieg der "Governing Class" in England', *Tymbos für W. Ahlmann*, Berlin; 1951, pp. 162 ff.

5 R. West, 'The Character of England', in Barker, *op. cit.*, p. 481.

6 F. M. Stenton, *Anglo-Saxon England*, quoted in Cyril Garbett, *Church and State in England*, London; 1950, p. 35.

7 R. M. Lumiensky, *JHI*, II, 1941, p. 248.

8 Kemp Malone, as supplement to Hans Kohn's 'The Genesis and Character of English Nationalism', *JHI*, I, 1941, pp. 69 ff.

9 On Wycliffe, G. M. Trevelyan, *England in the Age of Wycliffe*, numerous editions, is still the best. cf. Gairdner, *Lollardy and the Reformation*, London; 1908.

10 J. St Flynn, 'The Influence of Puritanism on the political and religious Thought of the English', in W. Haller, *The Rise of Puritanism*, New York; 1938.

11 C. T. Onions, 'The English Language', in Barker, *op. cit.*, p. 296.

12 R. W. Chambers, *Thomas More*, London; 1945, p. 392.

13 *Ibid.*, p. 132.

14 H. Oncken, *SB der Heidelberger Akademie der Wissenschaften*, phil. hist. Klasse; 1922.

15 I have used the latin edition of More's *Utopia*, ed. by V. Michels and Th. Ziegler, Berlin; 1895.

16 Compare this to Herbert of Cherbury's *De Veritate*, of 1624, which was the basis of the English Enlightenment.

17 An interesting investigation of the intellectual foundations and background of 'Utopia' can be found in F. Battaglia, *Saggi sull' Utopia di Tommaso Moro*, Bologna; 1949. There are references to More's relationship to Erasmus, Nicholas of Cusa, Fortescue, Hooker, Locke and Engels. There is also a criticism of Gerhard Ritter's *Machtstaat und Utopia*.

18 G. G. Coulton, 'The Last days of Medieval Monachism', *Five Centuries of Religion*, IV, Cambridge; 1950.

19 L. Borinski, *Englischer Geist in der Geschichte seiner Prosa*, Freiburg; 1951, pp. 3 ff.

20 On the religious wealth of Old England, cf. G. R. Owst, *Preaching in Medieval England*, Cambridge; 1926; L. B. Wright, 'The significance of Religious Writings in the English Renaissance', *JHI*, vol. I, 1940, pp. 59 ff.

21 E. C. Messenger, 'Das Konzil von Trient und der englische Katholizismus', *Das Weltkonzil von Trient*, ed. G. Schreiber, vol. I, pp. 473 ff.

22 V. Sackville-West, 'Outdoor Life', in E. Barker, *op. cit.*, p. 416.

23 Cyril Garbett, *op. cit.*, p. 59.

24 *Ibid.*, pp. 204 ff.

25 A. T. P. Williams, 'Religion', in E. Barker, *op. cit.*, pp. 66 ff.

26 H. Schöffler, *Abendland und Altes Testament*, 2 ed. Frankfurt/Main, 1941, pp. 28 ff., 46 ff. and 73 ff. Particularly significant is Schöffler's observation on p. 33, 'the lower on the social scale a free church community stood, the greater the chance that the Old Testament would be more important than the New.'

27 G. M. Young, 'Government', in Barker, *op. cit.*, p. 101 and Lord Simonds, 'Law', *Ibid.*, pp. 112 ff.

28 Basil Willey, 'Thought', *Ibid.*, pp. 321 f.

29 'To speak of Shakespeare is to touch upon a prayer filled with unexplained riddles'. E. R. Curtius, *Europäische Literatur und Lateinisches Mittelalter*, Bern; 1948, p. 334.

30 On Bacon's economic ideas, cf. R. Maggi, 'su alcuni pensieri economici di Francesco Bacon', *Gionale delgi Economisti e Annali di Economia*, Milan, No. X, 1951, pp. 482 ff.

31 H. Freyer, *Die Politsche Insel*, Leipzig; 1936, pp. 110 ff.

32 I quote from the German edition: Francis Bacon, *Neu-Atlantis*, ed. by R. Walden, Berlin; 1890, pp. 43 f.

33 *Ibid.*, p. 60.

34 Francis Bacon, *Essays*, London; 1902, pp. 19 ff.

35 *Ibid.*, p. 45.

36 *Ibid.*, pp. 139 ff.

37 *Ibid.*, p. 95.

38 *Ibid.*, p. 88.

39 E. Zilsel, 'The Origins of William Gilbert's Scientific Method', *JHI*, I, 1941, pp. 1 ff.

40 F. R. Johnson, 'Gresham College: The Precursor of the Royal Society', *JHI*, I, 1940, pp. 413 ff.

41 M. Orenstein, *The Role of Scientific Societies in the Seventeenth Century*, Chicago; 1938; and Harcourt Brown, *Scientific Organizations in 17th Century France, 1620–1680*, Baltimore; 1934.

42 L. T. Moore, 'Boyle the Alchemist', *JHI*, II, 1941, pp. 61 ff.

43 W. E. Houghton, 'The History of Trade; its Relation to Thought, as seen in Bacon, Evelyn and Boyle', *JHI*, II, 1941, pp. 40 f.

44 M. Freund, *Die Grosse Revolution in England; Anatomie eines Umsturzes*, Hamburg; 1951, p. 26, and pp. 505 ff. for a good review of the literature; see also the interesting and important interpretation of the English Revolution, in E. Rosenstock-Huessy, *Europäische Revolutionen*, pp. 264 ff.

45 M. Freund, *op. cit.*, p. 26.

46 On Laud, see Hugh Trevor-Roper, *Archbishop Laud*, London; 1950.

47 On the enormous significance of political preaching under James I and Charles I, see G. Davies 'English Political Sermons 1603–1640' *The Huntingdom Library Quarterly*, III, 1939/40, pp. 1 ff.

48 K. A. von Müller in a review of M. Freund's *Die Grosse Revolution*, in *Neue Zeitung*, Frankfurt/Main, No. 5/6, I, 1952.

49 On this problematic personality, see S. Reed Brett, *John Pym*, London; 1940; and E. Wingfield Stratford, *King Charles and King Pym*, London; 1949.

50 M. Freund, *op. cit.*, p. 99.

51 cf. H. Schöffler, *Die Anfänge des Puritanismus. Versuch einer Deutung der englischen Reformation*, Leipzig, 1932; H. James, *Social Problems and Policy during the Puritan Revolution*, 1930; P. Newton, *Colonizing Activities of the English Puritans*, 1948. J. St Flynn, *op. cit.*, in Haller, *Rise of Puritanism*.

52 M. Bonn, *Die Englische Kolonisation in Irland*, 2 vols., Berlin; 1906. A documentary account of the organized terror and intimidation used.

53 M. Freund, *op. cit.*, p. 418.

54 *Ibid.*, p. 149.

55 W. Abbot, *Writings and Speeches of Oliver Cromwell*, London; 1937 and after.

56 M. Freund, *op. cit.*, pp. 207, 236, 278.

57 See, G. P. Gooch, *English Democratic Ideas in the Seventeenth Century*, 2nd ed. Cambridge; 1927, pp. 35 ff.; and G. N. Clark, *The Seventeenth Century*, Cambridge; 1927.

58 cf. W. Abbot, *op. cit.*, for Cromwell's speeches.

59 *The Petty Papers*, ed. by the Marquis of Landsdowne, London, 1927, p. 56.

60 Gertrude Huehn, *Antinomianism in English History*, London; 1952.

61 cf. Rosenstock-Huessy, *op. cit.*, p. 295.

62 On the influence of Harrington's ideas in the American States, see Harold Laski, in Gooch, *op. cit.*, p. 305; and R. Ruyer, *L'Utopie et les Utopies*, pp. 180 ff.

63 R. Polin, 'Economie politique au XVIIè Siècle' *Revue Française de Science Politique*, II, 1952, pp. 24 ff.

64 A. Barker, *Milton and the Puritan Dilemma*, Toronto; 1942.

65 Thomas Hobbes, *Behemoth or the Long Parliament*, first ed. based on the manuscript of Ferd. Tönnies, London; 1889.

66 L. Borinski, *op. cit.*, p. 62.

67 J. Sutherland, 'Literature' in Barker, *op. cit.*, p. 317. In science this social and political attitude implied that theory was not a faith but a policy, a direction for action. This is very much the fundamental approach of contemporary American science. cf. J. B. Conant, *Modern Science and Modern Man*, New York; 1943. Conant, who for many years was the manager of one of America's great universities, wants to do away with every difference between science and the thinking of the average man. This is the final stage in the process of secularizing science, a process which led from the cleric to the clerk.

68 John Locke, *Essay Concerning Human Understanding*, II, ch. 28, p. 5.

69 It is worth recalling that there were many versions of the theory of the social contract current in Locke's time. The successors of the Huguenots and the followers of Buchanan saw the contract as a treaty between rulers and ruled, based upon the Old Testament, Roman Law and the Theory of Feudalism. Hooker's disciples in the English High Church saw it as an agreement among members of a society. Hooker incidentally contained almost all of Locke's crucial ideas, especially in those characteristic lapses in logic. In Hobbes's version, the parties make over all their rights irrevocably to an elected sovereign. Halifax, the first utilitarian among the great English political thinkers, declared that the whole idea of a real, historical contract was pure superstition. cf. G. A. Gooch, *op. cit.*, pp. 290 f.

70 For the broad connections and developments in the growth of the idea of tolerance in England, as an interplay of sectarians and nonconformists of every kind, see the monumental work of W. K. Jordan, *The Development of Religious Toleration in England*, 3 vols., London; 1932–8. On the special position of Locke see T. Lyon, *The Theory of Religious Liberty in England, 1603 to 1639*, Cambridge; 1937.

71 L. Brentano, *Der wirtschaftende Mensch in der Geschichte*, Leipzig; 1923, p. 158.

72 Locke's philosophy of law shows how deeply he was rooted in the old English feudal tradition. See E. Roos, *Naturzustand und Vertrag in der Staatsphilosophie Lockes*, Berlin; 1943; also, C. Schmitt, 'Recht und Raum' in *Tymbos für W. Ahlmann*, Berlin; 1951, p. 249.

73 M. Fierz, *Isaac Newton*, Zürich, 1943.

74 L. Brunschwicg, *Les Etapes de la Philosophie Mathématique*, 3rd ed., Paris; 1929, pp. 192 ff.

75 On Newton's deism, see E. Strong, 'Newton and God', *JHI*, XIII, 1952, pp. 147 ff.

76 For a beautiful description of this phenomenology, see F. J. Powicke, *The Cambridge Platonists*, Cambridge; 1926.

77 The Earl of Shaftesbury, *Miscellania*, III, ch. 2.

78 There is still something of the consciousness of identity and the ontological optimism of archaic society, unruffled by fate's blows, in this 'Whatever is is right', just as in the Italian 'tutte le cose son' buone' and in the old Austrian 'mir kann nix q'scheh'n' of the Steinklopferhans of L. Anzegruber.

79 David Hume, *Autobiography*, published as the introduction to the edition by J. McCormack and M. Whiton Calkins, London; 1913, which also included Hume's *An Enquiry concerning Human Understanding* and *A Treatise of Human Nature*.

80 Hume, *An Inquiry etc.*, II, p. 388.

81 *Ibid.*, p. 138.

82 *Ibid.*, p. 175.

83 E. Campbell-Mossner, 'Was Hume a Tory Historian?', *JHI*, II, 1941, pp. 225 ff.

84 L. Stephen, *op. cit.*, II, p. 103.

85 Reason is 'nothing but a wonderful and unintelligible *instinct* in our souls, which carries us along a certain train of ideas, and endows them with particular qualities according to their particular situations and relations.' Hume, *Works*, Oxford, 1874, I, p. 471. 'This reality is to be found only in the ever-varying stream of feelings, bound together by custom, regarded by a "fiction" or set of fictions as implying some permanent set of external or internal relations, and becoming beliefs only as they acquire liveliness'. Via Herder and Schleiermacher, this was the path followed by German romanticism.

86 A splendid description of the rise of the English ruling class can be found in W. Kellinghusen, 'Der Aufsteig der "Governing Class" in England', *Tymbos für W. Ahlmann*, Berlin; 1951, pp. 160 ff.

87 Still extremely readable is L. Brentano's inaugural lecture at the University of Vienna in 1888, 'Die Klassische Nationalökonomie', *Gesammelte Reden und Aufsätze*, Leipzig; 1923, p. 1 ff.

88 Adam Smith, *The Wealth of Nations*, V, ch. 2.

89 For an example of a man of Johnson's circle, who studied the problem of politics, see William Gerard Hamilton, 'Parliamentary Logic and Tactics', 1808 published in *Dokumente des europäischen Rationalismus*, ed. by H. Blomeyer, Basle; 1951. Other valuable texts can be found in G. Grigson, *Before the Romantics, An Anthology of the Enlightenment*, London; 1946.

90 See W. Struck, 'Der Einfluss Jakob Böhmes auf die englische Literatur des 17. Jahrhunderts', *Neue Deutsche Forschungen, Abteilung Englische Philosophie*, Berlin; 1935; for an account of the seventeenth century background to Law's approach to Böhme.

91 William Law, *Works*, London; 1892/3, V, p. 164, and VIII, p. 5.

92 *Ibid.*, VI, p. 130.

93 L. Borinski, *op. cit.*, p. 113.

94 John Wesley, *Works*, XIII, p. 256.

95 John Wesley, *Journals*, III, p. 143.

96 cf. R. F. Wearmouth, *Methodism and the Working Class Movement of England, 1800–1850*, London; 1937. The quotation from L. Stephen, *op. cit.*, II, p. 424.

536 *The Intellectual History of Europe*

97 Edward Gibbon, *Miscellaneous Works*, London; 1814, I, p. 230.
98 Edmund Burke, *Works*, London; 1808, V, p. 173.
99 *Ibid.*, VII, p. 13.
100 *Ibid.*, VI, p. 239.
101 *Ibid.*, VIII, p. 150.
102 *Ibid.*, IV, p. 149.
103 *Ibid.*, VI, p. 211.
104 Paine and Price were particularly important as forerunners of the ideas of Karl
Marx. See H. Weisinger, 'The English Origins of the Sociological Interpretation of the Renaissance', *JHI*, XI, 1950, pp. 321 ff.
105 L. Hogben, *Mensch und Wissenschaft*, German Ed., ed. J. H. Wild, vol. 1,
Zürich; 1948, p. 526.

CHAPTER 18

1 B. Groethuysen, *Die Entstehung der bürgerlichen Welt und Lebensanschauung
in Frankreich*, Halle; 1927, vol. I, pp. 105–9.
2 H. Bremond, *Autor de L'Humanisme. D'Erasme à Pascal*, Paris; 1937, I, pp.
421 ff.
3 Yves de Paris, *Theologie naturelle*, 4 vols., 1633–6.
4 Yves de Paris, *Le gentilhomme chrétien*, p. 174.
5 Yves de Paris, *Theologie naturelle*, II, p. 502.
6 P. Hazard, *La Crise de la conscience européenne*, Paris; 1935, I, pp. 240 ff.
7 H. Bremond, *op. cit.*, III, pp. 159 ff.
8 *Ibid.*, VI, pp. 445 ff.
9 J. Calvet, *Molière est-il Chrétien?* Paris; 1950.
10 cf. B. Groethuysen, *op. cit.*, I, pp. 163 f., 175.
11 cf. A. H. Rowbotham, *Missionary and Mandarin. The Jesuits at the Court of
China*, Berkeley, California; 1942.
12 Couplet, Intorcetta, Herdtrich, Rougemont, *Confucius Sinarum philosophus
sive scientia sinensis*, Paris; 1687. This remarkable work by four Jesuits of the
China Mission was made available to me through the kindness of W. Kaegi,
Basle.
13 cf. B. Groethuysen, *op. cit.*, I, pp. 159 f.
14 J. Chambon, *Der Französische Protestantismus*, Munich; 1937, pp. 125 ff.
15 P. Hazard, *op. cit.*, II, p. 58.
16 Bossuet, *Sermons*, ed. J. Bénigne, Paris, I, pp. 128 f.
17 *Ibid.*, I, pp. 155 ff.
18 *Ibid.*, I, pp. 175 ff. and 189.
19 *Ibid.*, I, p. 247.
20 *Ibid.*, II, p. 784 – *l'étouffer tout entière*.
21 *Ibid.*, II, p. 787.
22 *Ibid.*, I, p. 239.
23 *Ibid.*, I, p. 622.
24 *Ibid.*, II, p. 223 ff., 244 f.
25 Fénelon, *Pages Nouvelles*, ed. M. Langlois, Paris; 1934, pp. 130 ff.
26 *Ibid.*, 'Sermon on March 1, 1692', pp. 201 ff.
27 cf. J. Orcibal, *Louis XIV et les protestantes*, Paris; 1952.

28 André Siegfried, in *Protestantisme Français*, ed. Boegner, Paris; 1945, pp. 23 ff. and 40 ff.

29 P. Chazel, 'Génie francais et Protestantisme', *Ibid.*, p. 80.

30 See his letters of 2 April 1764 to the Marquis of Chauvelin and of 5 April 1765 to d'Alembert.

31 Jean-Jacques Rousseau, *Works*, 13 vols., Paris; 1872; I, p. 38.

32 *Ibid.*, XI, p. 247.

33 Jean-Jacques Rousseau, *La Profession de Foi du Vicaire Savoyard*, critical edition, P. M. Masson, Fribourg/Paris; 1914, pp. 209 f.

34 Rousseau, *Works*, X, p. 130.

35 *Ibid.*, IX, 73, and *La Profession*, p. 395.

36 *La Profession*, p. 353.

37 Rousseau, *Works*, V, pp. 246, 249.

38 Abbé Coyer, *Dissertation pour etre lues; la première sur le vieux mot Patrie; la seconde sur la nature du peuple*, La Haye; 1755.

39 Abbé Sieyès, *Qu'est-ce que le Tiers-Etat?* Paris; 1788, p. 67.

40 Rousseau, *Works*, III, pp. 366 ff.

41 cf. J. C. Talmon, *The Origins of Totalitarian Democracy*, London; 1952.

42 Rousseau, *Works*, V, pp. 303 ff.

43 *Ibid.*, V, p. 348.

44 M. Horkheimer and T. W. Adorno, *Dialektik der Aufklärung*, Amsterdam; 1947, pp. 16 f. and 27.

45 F. Schalk, *Einleitung in die Enzyklopädie der französischen Aufklärung*, Munich; 1936, pp. 45 ff.

46 *Encyclopedie ou dictionnaire raisonné des sciences, des art et des Métier*, 28 vols., Paris; 1751 to 1772.

47 Diderot, *Oeuvres complètes*, 2 vols., ed. J. Assezat, Paris; 1875, pp. 267 ff. cf. P. Mesnard, *Le Cas Diderot, Etude de caracteriologie littéraire*, Paris; 1952.

48 Court de Gébelin, the official representative of the Reformed Church, in his *Monde Primitif*, VIII, p. LXI.

49 This pan-European Enthusiasm ought not to be confused with the Masonic lodges, which, especially in France, had a rather conservative character. See M. Roger Provret, *La Franc-Macconerie sous les lys*, Paris; 1953. He points out correctly: *Les loges n'ont pas tué l'ancien régime, elles sont mortes avec lui.* Freemasons may well have been sucked into the movement of Enthusiasts, like so many members of the aristocracy and upper bourgeoisie were.

50 E. Despois, *Le Vandalisme Révolutionnaire*, Paris; 1868. This iconoclasm had strongly catharist and manichean features, as did so many of the men among the purgers of the radical enthusiastic wing of the revolution. A. Cochin, *Les Sociétés de Pensée et la Démocratie*, Paris; 1920, for the origin of the Jacobin clubs in the philosophical societies of the Low Enlightenment; Crane Brinton, *A Decade of French Revolution, 1789 to 1799*, New York; 1934, for a discussion of Jacobin religion.

51 G. Lenotre, *Le Mysticisme révolutionnaire. Robespierre et La Mère de Dieu*, Paris; 1926.

52 *Ibid.*, p. 38.

53 Striking perspectives of the anti-trinitarian movement are visible in the United States, which was founded by anti-trinitarians. cf. Earl Morse Wilbur, *A*

History of Unitarianism, vol. II 'In Transylvania, England and America', Harvard/London; 1953. The first atomic bomb explosion in Alamogordo, New Mexico (i.e. on the soil of the decadent Spanish late baroque), took place in 1945 under the code word 'Trinity'. A new form of rock was produced which was called 'Trinitit'. Man had begun to recreate the world. See R. Jungk, *Die Zukunft hat schon begonnen*, 2nd ed., Stuttgart; 1952, p. 31.

54 J. C. Murray, 'L'Eglise et la Démocratie totalitaire', *'La Vie Intellectuelle*, Paris; March 1953, pp. 13 ff.

55 A. Cochin, *Le Révolution et la libre pensée*; G. Lefebre, *La Révolution Française* Paris; 1951; M. Mathiez, *Girondins et Montagnards*, Paris; 1930, pp. 109 ff., on terror and Robespierre's social policy.

56 Lenotre, *op. cit.*, p. 108.

57 Pierre de la Gorce, *Histoire religieuse de la Révolution française*, Paris; vol. III, p. 333.

58 Fritz Ernst, *Essays*, III, Zurich; 1946, pp. 7 ff.

59 Ed. Fleury, *Saint-Just et la Terreur*, I, Paris; p. 228.

60 P. H. Simon, 'Portrait de Saint-Just', *Terre Humaine*, Paris; March 1953, pp. 61 ff.

61 M. Göhring, *Geschichte der grossen Revolution*, Tübingen; 1952, II, p. 198.

CHAPTER 19

1 C. Antoni, *Considerazioni su Hegel e Marx*, Naples; 1946, p. 53.

2 cf. K. Holl, 'Die Entstehung von Luthers Kirchenbegriff', *Festschrift für Dietrich Schäfer*, Jena; 1915, pp. 410 ff., 430 f. Friedrich Meinecke, 'Luther über christliches Gemeinwesen und christlichen Staat', *HZ*, vol. CXXI, pp. 1 ff., and 6 ff. Meinecke attacks Holl and emphasizes the conservative and medieval side of Luther's work, as do Sohm, Rieker, K. Müller, Troeltsch. See also J. Oberhof, 'Die Christlichkeit Luthers und der Begriff der Geschichte', *ZKG*, vol. LVII, 1938, pp. 96 ff. Despite some exaggerations, Oberhof rightly points to the a-Christian, Demonic vein in Luther, which ties him to the other heralds of salvation of the underground.

3 H. Plessner, *Das Schicksal deutschen Geistes im Ausgang seiner bürgerlichen Epoche*, Zurich/Leipzig; 1955, pp. 23 f., 50 f.

4 A tremendously important role was played by the proletarianizing of the intellectual workers and the constant uncertainty of their existence in society. cf. Becker, 'Aus dem Gelehrtenproletariat der nachreformatorischen Zeit', *Archiv. für Kulturgeschichte*, 1911; Michels, 'Zur Soziologie der Boheme und ihre Zusammenhänge mit dem geistigen Proletariat', *Conrads Jahrbuch*, 1932; Raucker, *Die Proletarisierung des geistigen Arbeiters*, 1920; M. Scheler, *Wissenssoziologie*, 1929.

5 E. Lewalter, *Spanisch-Jesuitische und deutsch-lutherische Metaphysik des 17. Jahrhunderts*, Hamburg; 1935, p. 14.

6 Th. Haering, 'Cusanus-Paracelsus-Boehme', *Zeitschrift für deutsche Kulturphilosophie*, II, 1936; L. Vicenti, *Angelo Silesio*, Turin; 1931, on renaissance and baroque nature-magic in Germany; D. Mahnke, *Unendliche Sphäre und Allmittelpunkt*, Halle; 1937; Th. Haering, *Das Deutsche in der Deutschen Philosophie*, 1941; E. von Brakken, *Meister Eckhart und Fichte*, 1944; H.

Bornkamm, *Luther und Böhme*, Bonn; 1925; H. Bornkamm, *Eckhart und Luther*, 2nd ed., 1939; L. Bianchi, *Hammann e Herder*, Bologna; 1930.

7   P. Bonnersheim, 'Die Welt Jakob Böhmes', *DVJ*, No. 20, 1942.

8   E. Benz, 'Jakob Böhmes Sprachphilosophie', *Eurphorion*, 1936, pp. 340 ff.; A. Schleiff, 'Sprachphilosophie und Inspirationstheorie im Denken des 17. Jahrhunderts', *ZKG*, No. 57, 1938, pp. 133 ff.

9   E. Benz, 'Die Geschichtsmetaphysik Jacob Böhmes', *DVJ*, No. 13, 1935, pp. 421 ff.

10   F. W. Wentzlaff-Eggebert, *Deutsche Mystik zwischen Mittelalter und Neuzeit*, Berlin; 1944, pp. 213 ff. and 220.

11   Angelus Silesius, *Cherubinischer Wandersmann*, Book I, No. 10.

12   *Ibid.*, No. 13.

13   C. Antoni, *Der Kampf wider die Vernunft*, Stuttgart; 1951, pp. 210 ff.

14   W. Mahrholz, *Der deutsche Pietismus. Eine Auswahl von Zeugnissen, Urkunden und Bekenntnissen aus dem 17. 18. und 19. Jahrhundert*, Berlin; 1921, pp. 15–34.

15   See J. H. Reitz, *Historie der Wiedergeborenen*, Itzstein; 1717, for a wonderful collection of such lives and experiences.

16   H. Stahl, *August Hermann Francke. Der Einfluss Luthers und Molinos auf ihn*, Vol. XVI, Forschungen zur Kirchen- und Geistesgeschichte, Stuttgart.

17   M. Wieser, *Der sentimentale Mensch. Gesehen aus der Welt holländischer und deutscher Mystiker im 18. Jahrhundert*, Stuttgart; 1924, pp. 82 ff.

18   Jochen Klepper, *Der Soldatenkönig und die Stillen im Lande*, Berlin; 1938; and *Der Vater*, Berlin; 1937. Both works present a tremendous and terrifying potrait of the king. The author died, a victim of Nazi terror, in 1944.

19   J. S. Semler, *Lebensbeschreibung*, Leipzig; 1781.

20   K. P. Moritz, *Anton Reiser*, Berlin; 1785.

21   W. Mahrholz, *op. cit.*, p. 9.

22   H. E. Weber, *Reformation, Orthodoxie und Rationalismus*, Berlin; 1937, I, p. 1. See also, H. E. Weber, 'Das innere Leben der altprotestantischen Orthodoxie', *Rechtsgläubigkeit und Frömmigkeit. Das Gespräch der Kirche um die rechte Nachfolge Christi*, ed. H. Asmussen, Berlin; 1938, Part 2, pp. 20 ff.

23   W. Treue, *Illustrierte Kulturgeschichte des Alltags*, Munich; 1952, pp. 188 f.

24   E. Seeberg, *Gottfried Arnold*, Meerane; 1923. The book lacks a treatment of Arnold's wider influence and connections.

25   R. M. Meyer, *Leibniz und die europäische Ordnungskrise*, Hamburg; 1948, pp. 59 f.

26   H. Schmalenbach, *Leibniz*, Munich; 1921; see Leibniz's letter to Ludwig Feller of 1698, in *Otium Hannoveranum*, Leipzig; 1718, p. 211.

27   Leibniz, *Opera*, ed., Erdmann, p. 163 b.

28   H. Hartmann, 'Die Leibniz-Ausgabe der Berliner Akademie', *Blätter für deutsche Philosohpie*, No. 13, 1939/40, pp. 421, 408 ff. See also, O. D. Wiener, 'Leibniz's Project for a public exhibition of scientific inventions', *JHI*, I, 1940, pp. 232 ff. Wiener sees Leibniz in the context of the museum and exhibition interests of the seventeenth century. In 1683, the year the Turks stormed Vienna, the industrial fair was held in Paris. Leibniz had all the talents of a modern world's fair organizer. He wanted to set up an exhibition which would show the masses all the latest developments in science and technology and at

540   *The Intellectual History of Europe*

the same time provide them entertainment through theatres, casinos, varieties and circuses, just like the 'culture parks' of today in Eastern Europe.

29 D. Mahnke, 'Der Zeitgeist des Barock und seine Verewigung in Leibnizens Gedankenwelt', *Zeitschrift für deutsche Kulturphilosophie*, No. 2, 1936, pp. 95 ff.; also by the same author, *Leibnizens Synthese von Universalermathematik und Individualmetaphysik*, Halle; 1925. See also J. O. Fleckstein, *Scholastik, Barock, Exakte Wissenschaften*, Einsiedeln; 1949, pp. 44 ff. This is an extremely important book which has not received the attention it deserves. In it there is a good treatment of Leibniz as the Don Quixote, as Newton called him, of a lost cause.

30 Hugo Rahner, *Der Spelende Mensch*, Einsiedeln; 1952; J. Huizinga, *Homo Ludens*, Basle/Vienna/Cologne; 3rd ed., pp. 171 ff., 236 ff., 290 ff. (English ed., London; 1949).

31 W. Gent, *op. cit.*, p. 49.

32 R. M. Meyer, *op. cit.*, p. 243.

33 D. Mahnke, 'Die Rationalisierung der Mystik bei Leibniz und Kant', *Blätter für deutsche Philosophie*, No. 13, 1939/40 pp. 28 f.

34 W. Dilthey, *Gesammelte Schriften*, III, p. 33.

35 Leibniz, *Correspondence*, Berlin Academy Edition, II, p. 5.

36 Hans M. Wolff, *Die Weltanschauung der deutschen Aufklärung in geschichtlicher Entwicklung*, Bern; 1949, p. 153.

37 R. M. Meyer, *op. cit.*, p. 241.

38 Emmanuel Hirsch, *Geschichte der neueren evangelischen Theologie im Zusammenhang mit den allgemeinen Bewegungen des europäischen Denkens*, vol. I, Gütersloh; 1949, pp. 204 ff.

39 E. Troeltsch, 'Leibniz und die Anfänge des Pietismus', *Gesannelte Werke*, III.

40 A. Pichler, *Die Theologie des Leibniz*, 2 parts, Munich; 1869/70, II, p. 350. This old work is still a useful source.

41 P. Böckmann, *Formgeschichte der deutschen Dichtung*, vol. I, 1949, p. 485.

42 On the Enlightenment, see E. Cossirer, *Die Philosophie der Aufklärung*, Tübingen; 1932; Fr. Brüggemann, 'Der Kampf um die bürgerliche Welt- und Lebenanschauung in der deutschen Literatur des 18. Jahrhunderts', *DVJ*, No. 3, 1925, pp. 94 ff.; Fr. Brüggemann, *Das Weltbild der deutschen Aufklärung*, Leipzig, 1930; Hans M. Wolff, *op. cit.*; Kath. Franz, *Der Einfluss der stoischen Philosophie auf die Moralphilosophie der deutschen Aufklärung*, Giessen; 1940. On the Catholic Enlightenment: S. Merkle, 'Das Menschenbild im Zeitalter des aufgeklärten Denkens', *Das Bild vom Menschen, Festschrift für T. Tillmann*, Düsseldorf; 1934; J. Schmitt, *Der Kampf un den Kathechismus in der Aufklärungsperiode Deutschlands*, Munich; 1935 A. L. Veit, *Des Aufklärungsschriftum des 18. Jahrhunderts und die deutsche Kirche*, Cologne; 1937; Chrysostomus Schreiber, *Aufklärung und Frömmigkeit. Die Katholische Predigt im Deutschen Aufklärungszeitalter*, Munich; 1940; G. Schnürer, *Katholische Kirche und Kultur im 18. Jahrhundert*, Paderborn; 1941. For a positive evaluation of the Catholic Enlightenement, see the Discussion at the Meeting of the Görres-Gesellschaft, Munich; 1951.

43 C. Antoni, *Der Kampf wider die Vernunft*, p. 351.

44 P. Burckhardt, *Geschichte der Stadt Basel*, Basle; 1942, pp. 91, 92 ff. on Isaak

Iselin. The book offers many interesting clues to the process of transfer from pietism to rational enlightemnent and back again.

45 Hans M. Wolef, *op. cit.*, p. 196.

46 F. Valjavec, *Die Entstehung der politischen Strömungen in Deutschland, 1770–1815,* Vienna; 1951, pp. 244 ff.

47 G. E. Lessing, *Werke,* vol. V, pp. 663 ff.

48 M. Pensa, *Il Pensiero Tedesco,* Bologna; 1938, pp. 68 ff.

49 Karl Barth, *Die Protestantische Theologie im 19. Jahrhundert. Ihre Vorgeschichte und Ihre Geschichte,* Zurich; 1949, pp. 208 ff. and 221. Also K. Aners, *Theologie der Lessing-Zeit,* Halle; 1919, a classic in its field.

50 O. Hintze, 'Uber den Calvinismus in Preussen', *HZ,* vol. CXIV, 1931.

51 P. Gaxotte, *Le Grand Frederic,* Paris; 1938; Gerhard Ritter, *Friedrich der Grosse,* 2nd ed., Leipzig, 1942; ed. Spranger, 'Der Philosoph von Sans Souci', *Abhandlung der Berliner Akademie der Wissenschaften,* Berlin; 1942.

52 H. v.d. Gablentz, *Die Tragik des Preussentums,* Munich; 1948, p. 46.

53 O. Forst-Battaglia, 'Friedrich II von Preussen und Polen', *Blick nach. Osten,* 1952, No. 4, pp. 337 ff.

54 K. A. Meissinger, *Roman des Abendlandes,* 8th ed., Leipzig; 1939, p. 198

55 R. Hohn, *Verfassungskampf und Heereseid, der Kampf des Bürgertums um das Heer, 1815–1850,* Leipzig; 1938; and C. Antoni, *Considerazioni su Hegel e Marx,* Naples; 1946, pp. 223 ff.

56 W. Dilthey, *Gesammelte Schriften,* III, p. 179.

57 O. Brunner, *Adeliges Landleben,* Salzburg; 1949, p. 137.

58 See his famous *Versuch über die Eigenliebe.*

59 Frederick's aversion to the underground corresponded to Catherine the Great's dislike for Lavater and the Enthusiasts. See M. Lavater-Sloman, *Katherina und die Russische Seele,* 5th ed., Zurich; 1941, pp. 375 f., 345 ff. and 406 ff. in which her preference for the Western Enlightenment is discussed.

60 Frederick II, *Werke,* XVI, p. 298.

61 A. Berney, 'Uber das geschichtliche Denken Friedrich des Grossen', *HZ,* No, 150, pp. 86 ff.

62 Johann Christoph Edelmann, *Selbstbiogrophie,* written in 1752, first published by C. R. W. Klose in Berlin in 1849. Note the year of publication.

63 On Edelmann in Austria, cf. W. Kühnert, 'Johann Christian Edelmann' *Jahrbuch der Gesellschaft für die Geschichte des Protestantismus in Osterreich,* No. 67, 1952, pp. 25 ff.

63a J. C. Edelmann, *op. cit.,* p. 133.

64 W. H. Bruford, *Germany in the 18th Century; the social background of the Literary Revival,* Cambridge; 1935. This book is still the best although it could use expansion and correction.

65 The first historical and critical edition of Winckelmann's letters has been prepared by W. Rehm and H. Diepolder: J. J. Winckelmann, *Briefe, 1742–59,* Vol. I and following, Berlin; 1952.

66 W. Rehm, *Götterstille und Göttertrauer. Aufsätze zur deutschantiken Begegnung,* Bern/Munich; 1951. A romantic and elegant image of Winckelmann.

67 J. Nadler, 'Winckelmann', *Wissenschaft und Weltbild,* No. 3, 1950, pp. 449 ff. Nadler sees Winckelmann together with Lessing and Hammann as part of a

renaissance of the 'hellenic East' against the Carolingian, Roman West. See also, C. Antoni, *Der Kampf wider die Vernunft*, pp. 64 ff.

68   F. Hamel, *Johan Sebastian Bach, Geistige Welt*, Göttingen; 1951, pp. 50 ff.

69   *Ibid.*, p. 222.

70   H. U. von Balthasar, *Apokalypse der deutschen Seele*, vol. I, 'Der deutsche Idealismus', Berlin; 1937, the chapter on Hamann. cf. Th. Deman, *Socrate e Gesu*, Florence; 1950, pp. 11 ff.

71   Karl Barth, *op. cit.*, p. 283.

72   P. Böckmann, *op. cit.*, vol. I, pp. 598 ff.

73   R. Adam, 'Wesen und Grenzen der organischen Geschichtsauffassung bei Johann Gottfried Herder', *HZ*, vol. CLV, pp. 22 ff.; on Herder's nationalism and national-mysticism, see T. Steinbüchel, *Zerfall des christlichen Ethos im XIX. Jahrhundert*, Frankfurt; 1951, pp. 122 f., 134; K. Pinson, *Pietism as a factor in the rise of German Nationalism*, New York; 1934.

74   J. G. Herder, 'Briefe des Studium der Theologie betreffend', *Werke*, X, p. 7.

75   C. Antoni, *Der Kampf wider die Vernungt*, p. 254.

76   Erich Heintel, 'Glaube und Wissen im kritischen System', *Jahrbuch der Gesellschaft für die Geschichte des Protestantismus in Oesterreich*, No. 67, 1951, p. 139.

77   J. Kant, 'Metaphysik der Sitten', *Werke*, vol. VII, p. 253.

78   Chrysostomus Schreiber, *op. cit.*, p. 34.

79   Karl Barth, *op. cit.*, p. 270.

80   Kant, Article in the *Berliner Monatsschrift*, September 1793.

81   D. Mahnke, 'Die Rationalisierung der Mystik', pp. 56 ff.

82   Kant, *Gesammelte Schriften*, 'Das Opus Posthumum', Berlin; 1936 and 1938, ed. G. Lehmann, vol. XXI, pp. 69, 93, 97; vol. XXII, pp. 82, 93.

83   *Ibid.*, vol. XXI, pp. 8, 40, 116, 140.

84   Kant's letter of 1798, in H. J. Stöhrig, *Kleine Weltgeschichte der Philosophie*, Stuttgart; 1950, p. 366.

85   Friedrich Karl von Moser, *Der Herr und der Diener*, Frankfurt; 1761.

86   F. Valjavec, *op. cit.*, p. 49.

87   See the *AKG*, 1930, pp. 362 ff., and the issue of 1940, pp. 418 ff.

88   R. Minder, *Die Religiöse Entwicklung von Karl Philipp Moritz auf Grund seiner autobiographischen Schriften*, Berlin; 1936.

89   C. Antoni, *Der Kampf wider die Vernunft*, I, pp. 147 ff.; II, pp. 285 ff.

90   Friedrich Meinecke (*Deutsche Katastrophe*, Berlin; 1947) suggests the formation of Goethe communities as the cells for a potential renewal of Germany. See also, L. Hänsel, *Goethe, Chaos und Cosmos, Vier Versuche*, Vienna; 1949. A worthwhile study of the destructive and creative in Goethe; H. Meyer, *Goethe, Das Leben im Werk*, Hamburg; 1950; the problem of Goethe's western attitude, see F. Koch, 'Goethe', *Blätter für deutsche Philosophie*, 1925, as well as his 'Schiller' (1926) and 'Herder' (1927), in the same periodical. Koch discusses the renaissance influences on German classicism.

91   H. Dieckmann 'Diderot's Conception of Genius', *JHI*, II, 1941, pp. 151 ff.

92   Goethe, *Dichtung und Wahrheit*.

93   Letter to S. Boisserée, 1815.

94   Goethe, *Wilhelm Meisters Wanderjahre*, completed in 1829, Book 2, ch. 7.

95   Goethe, 'Das reine Naturphänomen' and 'Der Versuch als Vermittler von

Objekt und Subjekt' in *Schriften zur Naturwissenschaft*, Frankfurt, 1951, III, pp. 285 ff.

96 *Ibid.*, p. 293.

97 Friedrich Heer, *Gespräch der Feinde*, Vienna; 1949. The chapter on Austria gives a fuller treatment of these themes.

98 K. Helleiner, *MIOG*, 1952, pp. 251 ff.

99 See Felix Braun, *Das Muscishe Land, Versuche über Oesterreichs Landschaft und Dichtung*, Innsbruck; 1952.

100 Anna Coreth, *Oesterreichische Geschichtsschreibung in der Barockzeit (1690–1740)*, Vienna; 1950.

101 *Ibid.*, p. 59.

102 H. Sedlmayr, 'Die politische Bedeutung des deutschen Barock', *Gesamtdeutsche Vergangenheit*, Srbik-Festschrift, Munich; 1938. The strong contrast between Protestant church architecture and the Catholic imperial style could well be studied more intensively.

103 Anna Coreth, *op. cit.*, p. 25.

104 Jakob Masen, *Speculum imaginum veritatis occultae*, Vienna; 1650. This remarkable work by the Jesuit, Masen, which numbered 1120 pages went through eight editions.

105 O. Rommel, *Die Alt-Wiener Volkskomödie, Ihre Geschichte vom Barocken Welt-Theater bis zum Tode Nestroys*, Vienna; 1952.

106 Felix Braun, *op. cit.*, pp. 29 ff. A good treatment of the differences between Austrian and German spirituality.

CHAPTER 20

1 M. Heidegger, *Holzwege*, Frankfurt; 1950, p. 91.

2 E. Rothaker, *Mensch und Geschichte*, Bonn; 1950, p. 68. Rothaker suggests that the line from Eckhart to Nietzsche is 'the theme of a history of German philosophy which is still to be written'.

3 The following are works which discuss the spiritual, political and social bases of German thought between 1770 and 1880: G. P. Gooch, *Germany and the French Revolution*, London; 1920; A. Gerbi, *La politica del Romanticismo*, Bari; 1932; K. S. Pinson, *Pietism as a factor in the rise of German Nationalism*, New York; 1934; and Friedrich Meinecke's review of Pinson's book, *HZ*, No. 191, 1935; R. Aris, *History of Political Thought in Germany from 1789 to 1850*, London; 1936; M. Horkheimer, 'Egoismus und Freiheitsbewegung', *Zeitschrift für Sozialforschung*, 1936, V; R. Schneider, *Schellings und Hegels schwäbische Geistesahnen*, Berlin; 1936.

4 For the roots of modern German nationalism and the role of romanticism, cf. F. C. Sell, *Die Tragodie des deutschen Liberalismus*, Stuttgart; 1953, pp. 46 ff., 53 ff., 68 ff.

5 R. Kohler, *Schriften zur Staatsphilosophie*, pp. 60 ff.

6 G. A. Briefs, 'The Economic Philosophy of Romanticism', *JHI*, 1941, III, pp. 279 ff.

7 K. Hildebrandt, *Schelling und die 'deutsche Bewegung'*, p. 65.

8 K. Löwith, *Von Hegel zu Nietzsche*, 2nd ed., Stuttgart, 1950, p. 183. Hegel's

desire for political power is visible in his early letters. cf. Hegel, *Gesamtausgabe* ed. J. Hoffmeister, Hamburg; 1952, vol. I, 'Briefe von und an Hegel, 1785–1812'. In a letter to Niethammer on 8 June 1807, Hegel wrote: 'Publicity is a Divine power. Printed things often seem entirely different than if they were said or done.' cf. Kierkegaard's remarks in his diaries about the perversion and conformism among men who have been influenced by the press and publishing.

9   *Fichte, Nachgelassene Schriften*, ed. H. Jacob, vol. II, '1790–1800'.

10   A. Corno, 'Razionalismo, classicismo e romanticismo in Germania', *Studi Filosofici*, Milan; 1949, X, pp. 161 ff.

11   J. Maria, 'Un escorzo del romanticismo', *Revista de la Universitad de Buenos Aires*, 1949, III, pp. 407 ff.

12   Martin Heidegger, *op. cit.*, p. 247. Heidegger's entire philosophy reflects the fine sensitivity of the shrewd peasant who knows instinctively what is 'in the air' and what the people want to hear. His enthusiastic romanticism has always been carefully and slyly tuned to the political frequencies of the times. A perfect example is his new edition of his Freiburg lecture series of 1935, in which he glorifies strength and professes allegiance to the enthusiastic ideology of the Third *Reich*. Heidegger is a typical modern manager of ideas, who knows exactly what the latest market quotation of each idea is and who uses the trends of the market in ideas ruthlessly to sell them dearly to the seekers and the yearners.

13   E. Susini, *Lettres Inedites de Franz von Baader*, Vienna; 1951, vol. III, p. 253.

14   R. Lauth in *Die Neue Zeitung*, 1–2 November 1952, on J. Bohatec, *Der Imperialismusgedanke und die Lebensphilosophie Dostojewskijs*, Graz/Cologne; 1951.

15   E. Hölzle, 'Der russische Nationalgedanke und die neue Welt', *Zeitschrift für Religion und Gesitesgeschichte*, 1951, III, pp. 336 ff.

16   Friedrich Heer, 'Aus dem unbekannten Jahrhundert', *Die Furche*, Vienna; 21 March 1953.

17   H. Heimsoeth, *Nietzsches Idee der Geschichte*, Tübingen; 1938; E. Benzl *Nietzsches Ideen zur Geschichte des Christentums*, Stuttgart; 1938; Kar, Jaspers, *Nietzsche und das Christentum*, Munich; 1952. Jaspers points out that Nietzsche never had 'the faintest idea that there were depths' in Christian theology.

18   H. de Lubac, *Die Tragödie des Hamanismus ohne Gott*, Salzburg; 1950, p. 240.

19   Rainer Maria Rilke, 'Die Apostel', *Erzählungen und Skizzen aus der Frühzeit*, Berlin; 1928; on the Rilke myth, see *Hochland*, April 1937; May 1940; October 1947, and F. Kemp, 'Der letzte Mythos', *Süddeutsche Zeitung*, 30 November 1945.

20   George Bernanos, 'Les enfants humiliés', *Journal*, 1939/40, Paris; 1949, p. 170.

21   G. M. Gilbert, *The Psychology of Dictatorship*, New York; 1950, and R. Merle, 'Adolf Hitler', *Les Temps Modernes*, June 1951, pp. 2248 ff.

22   Friedrich Heer, 'Joseph Weinheber aus Wien', *Frankfurter Hefte*, August 1953.

23   G. Simmel, *Goethe*, Berlin; 1923, pp. 90 ff.

24   R. Kassner, *Das 19. Jahrhundert*, Erlenbach/Zürich; 1947, p. 121.

25   It would be valuable to undertake a comparison of Freud and Wagner. There are fascinating parallels between Freud's psychoanalytical theory and

Wagner's ideas of the 'Ur-mutter' and 'Erda', wotan and the father complex. See T. W. Adorno, *Versuch über Wagner*, 1950.

26 cf. the arguments of L. Gabriel, H. Haberlandt and W. Daim against Jung in *Wissenschaft und Weltbild*, Vienna; 1953, pp. 49 ff. See also Martin Buber, 'Religion und Modernes Denken', *Merkur*, 1952, VI, pp. 101 ff. See C. G. Jung, *Psychologie und Religion*, Zürich; 1942, p. 111, where Jung reveals that his gnostic god is the realization of the 'identity of God and man'.

27 Friedrich Engels, *Die Lage der arbeitenden Klasse in England*, ed. V. Adoratskij, Vienna/Berlin; 1932.

28 On Engels, still the best work is G. Mayer, *Friedrich Engels*, 2 vols., The Hague 1934. (English ed. tran. G. and H. Highet, ed. R. H. S. Crossman, London; 1936.) It is worth reading a companion work at the same time: Andrew Ure, *The Philosophy of Manufactures; or An Exposition of the Scientific, Moral and Commercial Economy of the Factory System of Great Britain*, London, 1st ed., 1835; 2nd ed., 1861. This is a work of unique hardness and logicality in the defence of a closed world.

29 Friedrich Engels, *op. cit.*, pp. 49 ff.

30 *Ibid.*, p. 236.

31 *Ibid.*, p. 118.

32 Karl Löwith, *op. cit.*, p. 301.

33 P. Bigo, *Marxisme et Humanisme. Introduction à l'Oeuvre économique de Karl Marx*, Paris; 1953. There is no end to the number of works on Marx. I mention in particular: Plenge, *Marx und Hegel*; Marianne Weber, *Fichtes Socialismus und die Marxsche Doktrin*; H. Cunow, *Die Marxsche Geschichts-, Gesell-schagts-, und Staatstheorie*, 2 vols., Berlin; 1920. Fr. Brupacher, *Marx und Bakunin*, Berlin; 1922.

34 Karl Löwith, *op. cit.*, p. 338.

35 Karl Marx, *Werke*, vol. I, pp. 266 ff.

36 Karl Marx, *Das Kapital*, English ed., London; 1909, ch. 1, p. 43.

37 Karl Marx, *Nationalökonomie und Philosophie*, originally written in 1844 in Paris, edited and published, Berlin; 1950, p. 178.

38 *Ibid.*, p. 182.

39 *Ibid.*, pp. 182 f.

40 J. Lacroix, 'Paternité et démocratie', *Esprit*, 1947, pp. 748 ff.

41 *Ibid.*, p. 753.

42 Baron E. Seillière, *J. J. Rousseau*, Paris; 1921, and other works by the same author.

43 A. Dörrer, 'Wandel im tirolischen Volkskörper seit 1900', *Oesterreichische Zeitschrift für Volkskunde*, 1952, pp. 77 ff.

44 Carl von Clausewitz, *Vom Kriege*, Full edition, W. Hahlweg, Bonn; 1952, pp. 95, 509 ff. On Clausewitz, see Hans Rothfels, 'Clausewitz', *Makers of Modern Strategy*, ed. E. M. Earle, Princeton; 1948.

45 M. Heidegger, 'Bauen, wohnen, Denken', *Darmstädter Gespräch*, 1951, pp. 72 ff.

46 R. Kassner, *op. cit.*, p. 271.

47 K. A. Horst, *Ich und Gnade*, Freiburg; 1951, p. 127.

48 Friedrich, E. D. Schleiermacher, *Der Christliche Glaube*, 2 vols., Berlin; 1921.

49 E. Seeberg, 'Luther, Kant, Schleiermacher in Ihre Bedeutung für den Protestantismus', *Festschrift für G. Wobbermin*, ed. F. W. Schmidt, Berlin; 1939, p. 58.

50 *Ibid.*, p. 62.

51 cf. F. Lieb, 'Dostojewskij', *Orient un Occident*, 16th issue, 1934.

52 *Summa Theologica*, 1g. 10. 4. ad 3 et 5. c.

53 R. Guardini, *Das Ende der Neuzeit*, Basle; 1950, p. 138. The cautious confession of Guardini shows how far the Church has gone: 'The cultural patrimony of the Church will not escape the general decay of tradition, and where it survives, it will be shaken by many problems.'

54 R. Vallery-Radot, *Lamennais ou le Prêtre malgré lui*, Paris; 1931. See also, D. Bagge, *Les idées politique sous la Restauration*, Paris; 1953; and W. Gurian, 'Lamennais', *Perspektive*, 1953, No. 3.

55 H. U. von Balthaser, *Schliefung der Bastionen*, Einsiedeln/Cologne; 1952.

56 J. Y. Tigerino, 'Hispanidad y nueva Cristianidad', *Revista de Estudios politicos*, 1952, pp. 149 ff.; L. Palacios, *El mito de la nueva Cristianidad*, Madrid; 1952, II, pp. 51 f.

57 G. A. Wetter, S. J., *Der grosse Entschluss*, Vienna; 1952, p. 286; A. Malraux, 'Das Abenteuer der Kunst', Paris Lecture, 1952; *Der Monat*, 1952, pp. 339 ff. Malraux makes a parallel point about art: 'The Church no longer expects from painting that it deepen the communion of the faithful, but that, instead, it seduce them . . . The same rationalization of art lies behind devotional painting as behind the academic mannerism of the Brothers Caracci . . . The Russian artists (the Soviet painters Gerasimov, Dudnik, etc.) carry on the tradition of devotional painting, that of intelligent, rationalized art.'

58 J. Domenach, *La propagande politique*, Paris; 1950. A fascinating investigation of this process.

59 E. Bachler, 'Ernst Jünger, Idylliker des Nihilismus', *Schweizer Rundschau*, XII, p. 490.

60 J. Rausch, *Ernst Jüngers Optik*, Stuttgart, 1951.
    H. Cämmerer *R. M. Rilkes Duineser Elegien* Stuttgart; 1951.

61 For a wide-ranging discussion of the psycho-therapeutic use of language, see Richard Marx, 'Die Heilung durch das Wort', *Die Neue Zeitung*, 6/7, VI, 1953, who discusses among others the work of Clara Thompson, W. Daim and G. Schmaltz.

62 Ferdinand Ebner, 'Das Wort und die geistigen Realitäten', *Gesammelte Werke*, Vienna; 1952.

63 E. Rosenstock-Huessy, *Der Atem des Geistes*, Frankfurt; 1951.

INDEX

Aachen, 14
d'Abano, Pietro, 158, 163, 239, 303
Abdarrachaman, 71
Abelard of Bath, 106
Abelard, Peter, 7, 20, 89, 107, 112, 180
Acontius, Jacobus, 299
Acton, Lord, 470
Adalbert, 69, 389
Adler, 455
Adolphus, Gustavus, 306
Adrian VI, Pope, 260, 266
Aegidius, 159
Africa, 51, 271
Agape, 39
Agobard of Lyons, 43, 98
d'Ailly, Peter, 192
Akazius, Bishop, 251
Alcaraz, 260
Alanus of Lille, 109, 110, 139, 147
Albert the Great, 146–8, 176, 195
Alberti, 214
Albigensian Wars, 38, 96, 107, 117, 120, 136, 327
Albigensianism, 52, 78, 109, 111, 113, 114. *See also* Catharism
Alchemy, 160
Alcuin, 39, 40, 41, 43, 44, 60, 64, 71, 75
d'Alembert, 402
Alexander III, Pope, 56, 81, 106, 107, 108
Alexander IV, Pope, 147
Alexius, Emperor, 86, 114
Alfarabi, 96
Alfonso, Pedro, 102
Alfonso VI, 102
Alfonso X, 141
Alfred the Great, 46, 349, 353
Algazel, 101, 207
Amalric of Bena, 123
Ambrose, Bishop of Milan, 18
America, 58, 256, 268, 271, 319, 348, 379, 387, 463
Amsterdam, 2, 14, 321, 335

Anabaptists, 173, 221, 230, 232, 234, 292, 295–6, 327, 400, 443, 460
Angeles, Juan de los, 272–3
Angellus, 30
Angles, 33, 35
Anglo-Saxons, 33, 35, 40, 41
Angilbert, 45
d'Anse, Etienne, 113
Anselm of Canterbury, 51
Anselm of Havelberg, 84, 88–91, 92
Antioch, Council of, 17
Antwerp, 124, 318
Aquileia, Patriarch of, 38
Aquinas, Thomas, 3, 74, 102, 105, 141–157, 159, 176, 199, 208, 223, 288, 309, 434
Arabs, 26, 36, 257
Architecture, Austrian baroque, 443, 445
  Gothic, 254
  Modern, 467
  Spanish baroque, 258, 284
Argentarius, Julianus, 29
Arianism, 15 ff., 39
Aristodios, 115
Aristotle, 3, 28, 50, 99, 102, 103, 144, 145, 155, 167, 208, 223, 240, 268, 303, 309, 313, 371, 411
Arius, 15
Arles, Synod of, 18
Armada, The, 272, 280
Arminianism, 333, 363
Arminius, 332–3
Arnauld, Antoine, 310, 345
Arnd, Johann, 412, 429
Arno, Bishop of Salzburg, 44
Arnobius, 13
Arnold, Gottfried, 415, 437, 440, 446, 452
Arnold of Villanova, 135, 138, 158, 161
Arteveld, Jacob, 172
d'Ascoli, Cecco, 239
Asriel ben Menahem, 103

Astrology, 160
Athanasian creed, 39
Augsburg Confession, 409
Augustine, 3, 13, 20–4, 37, 64, 77, 81, 82, 88, 92, 117, 164, 165, 199, 203, 227, 266, 346, 374, 422, 470
Augustus, Emperor, 39
Austria, 96, 442–7, 453–4
Averroes, 99, 103, 104, 106, 140, 142, 146, 208
Avicebron, 102
Avicenna, 50, 71, 96, 99, 106, 207, 208
Avignon, 160, 191

Baader, 54, 451–2
Bach, Johann Sebastian, 428–9
Bacon, Roger, 51, 131, 134, 135–8, 146, 158, 161, 185, 192, 199, 266, 294, 329, 332, 348, 357–8, 380, 401, 417
Ball, John, 173, 185, 191
Balliol College, 185
Barth, Karl, 431, 434, 468
Bartholomew, Saint, massacre of, 325, 345
Basil of Caesarea, 7, 38, 244
Basle, 2, 14, 107
   Council of, 184, 190
Becket, Thomas, 144, 230
Bede, 348
Bellaremin, 271
Benedict XIII, Pope, 187
Benedict XIV, Pope, 311, 397
Benedict of Nursia, 27, 29, 31, 37, 121
Benedictine Rule, 32, 41, 270
Benedictines, 262, 310, 434
Bentham, Jeremy, 351
Bentivenga, 162
Berangar of Tours, 73, 77
Berlin, 14, 454
Bernard of Clairvaux, 72, 85, 89, 107, 112, 119, 120, 142, 164, 178, 203, 317
Bernardines, 262
Bernardino of Siena, 206
Berthold of Mosburg, 158, 176
Berulle, 383
Bessel, Gottfried, 446
Bettina von Bretano, 182
Biandrata, 296, 298
Biringucci, Vanoccio, 302
Blance de Laurac, 120
Blanco, Jose Maria, 283
Blanquerna, 139
Boccaccio, 201, 203–4
Bodin, 107, 327–8
Boethius, 27, 28, 37, 46, 66, 155, 167, 273, 363
Bogomilism, 115–7, 173

Böhme, 54, 238, 377, 411, 415, 451
Bonagratia of Bergemo, 168
Bonaventure, 80, 146, 148, 149, 211
Boniface, 40, 46, 349
Boniface VIII, 158, 159, 199
Boso, 81, 92
Bossompierre, 337
Bossuet, 22, 82, 280, 385, 389–90
Botticelli, 205
Bourbons, 257, 288
Boyle, Robert, 360
Bradwardine, 349
Braga, Synod of, 39
Brecht, 323
British Isles, 26, 36, 38, 40. *See also* England
Broch, 454
Brownshirts, 257
Bruno, 273, 299–300, 331, 343, 360
Bruun, 45
Buber, Martin, 81, 454, 475
Budé, 7, 266, 316
Buonauti, 11, 314
Burckhardt, 48, 296
Burgundy, 119, 123
Burke, 378–9
Byzantine Christianity, 17, 25, 29–31, 241 ff.
Byzantine Empire, 28 ff., 42, 70, 80, 90, 121, 250, 258

Cabalism, 102, 103, 430
Caccini, Tommasso, 304
Caesarius, 38
Calas Case, 394
Calderon, 256, 286–7
Calixtus II, Pope, 86
Callimaco, 210
Calvin, 50, 150, 217, 224, 229, 235, 239, 243, 263, 268, 278, 290, 297, 301, 315 ff., 437
Calvinism, 32, 50, 116, 235, 244, 270, 271, 297, 301, 315 ff., 364, 375, 380, 382, 407, 409, 410, 467, 473
Campanella, 210, 217, 236, 291, 292–4, 299, 309, 317, 332, 338, 343, 360, 400, 417
Cano, Melchor, 261, 273, 274
Capellanus, Andreas, 151
Capitalism, 319–20
Carmelites, 78, 274, 278
Carranza, 267, 274
Cartesianism, 308, 340 ff.
Carthusians, 78, 426
Cassian, 38
Cassiodorus, 27, 28, 29, 31
Castiglione, 262, 263

Catharism, 84, 114, 115-8, 119, 123, 134, 144, 151, 161, 185, 323-4. *See also* Albigensianism
Catherine the Great, 40
Catherine of Medici, 325
Catherine of Siena, 404
Catholicism, 2, 13, 38, 113, 314, 320, 323, 407, 410, 467, 469, 470-1, 473
Cearularius, 73
Celeste, Suor Maria, 303-4
Cervantes, 256, 268
Cesena, Michael, 168
Cevennes War, 393
Charlemagne, 33, 36, 40 ff., 68, 82, 85, 120, 122, 312
Charles I of Austria, 59
Charles I of England, 132, 361, 363
Charles the Bald, 45, 46
Charles the Bold, 265
Charles V of Spain, 254, 260, 264-6, 272
Charron, Pierre, 329-40, 341
Chartres, 108, 139, 145
Chiliasm, 23
    English, 365
    German, 413, 450, 422
    Russian, 366
China, 134, 271, 272, 387, 397, 416
Chrysostom, 186, 188, 244
Cicero, 19, 20, 66, 240, 262, 266
Cino of Pistora, 163
Cisneros, Cardinal, 265-6, 267, 268
Cisneros, Carcia de, 273, 274
Cistercians, 77, 89, 121, 262
City States, Greek, 25
    Italian, 154, 198, 206, 289
'Civitas Dei', 23, 266
Clare of Monteflaco, 162
Clareno, Angelo, 158
Clausewitz, 50, 425, 464
Clement of Alexandria, 7, 12-13, 14, 46, 99, 270
Clement I, Pope, 75
Clement IV, 136
Clement VI, 183
Clonard, 41
Clonmacnoise, 41
Cluny, 36, 64, 71
Coeur, Jacques, 315
Coleridge, 378
Colet, John, 185, 203, 224, 352
Cologne, 107, 108
Columbanus, 41
Columbus, Christopher, 135, 255
Comenius, 266
Communism, 460
Condillac, 13
Condorcet, 369
Condren, 383, 389

Confucius, 50
Conrad II, 70
Constance, Council of, 145
Constantine, 2, 13, 15 ff., 26, 35, 43, 202, 312
Constantino, Dr, 267
Constantinople, 20, 26, 40, 43, 70, 77, 184, 212, 241, 245, 248, 322, 464
Constantius II, 18
Conservatism, 55, 378
Conventuals, 130
Copernicus, 235, 236, 291, 305, 376
Cornhert, 331
Coronel, Dr Luis Nunez, 260
Corpse Synod, 61
Cortes, Donoso, 288
Cosimo, 213
Cotton, Pierre, 271
Counter-Reformation, 170, 183, 262, 273, 283, 284, 289 ff., 323, 361, 392, 443
Court, Pieter de la, 331
Cranmer, Thomas, 354
Crassus, Petrus, 86
Cripps, Stafford, 472
Croce, Bernadetto, 309, 314
Cromwell, 350, 363-7
Crusades, 96, 102, 107, 114, 119, 139
Curione, Celio Secundo, 296-7
Curtis, E. R., 49

Dali, Salvador, 287
Damasus, Pope, 20, 27, 39
Damian, Peter, 72, 74, 111
Daniel the Metropolitan, 250, 251
Dante, 27, 130, 147, 158, 168, 187, 198, 200, 230, 273, 297, 371
Danton, 407
Darwin, 239, 380
David of Dinant, 124, 145
'De Aeternite Mundi', 150
'Decameron', 204
De Chantal, Jeanne Françoise, 20, 78
'De Consolatione Philosophiae', 28
Defoe, Daniel, 376
Deism, 327, 331, 349, 350, 363, 372, 376, 379, 386, 420, 426, 427
Demetrias, 37
De Meung, Jean, 146-7
Demosthenes, 262
Denk, 222, 233
De Noeriis, Hugh, 63
De Sales, Francis, 20, 78
Descartes, 3, 51, 139, 150, 166, 203, 214, 227, 280, 293, 298, 330, 335, 336, 340 ff., 369, 371, 395, 416, 429
Desiderius, 36

Desmarets, 384
De Vecchi, 311
'De Viris Illustribus', 20
Diaconus, Paulus, 75
'Dialogo de Massimi Sistemi', 305
'Dialogues', 33
Diaz, Juan, 267
'Dictatus Papae', 77
Diderot, 292, 330, 372, 403, 406
Dietrich of Freiberg, 158, 176
Dietrich of Neim, 192
Diggers, 366
Dinis of Portugal, 141
Diocletian, 122
Dionysius, 23, 46, 177–8
Dissenters, 378
Dollinger, 470
Dominicans, 63, 111, 121, 123, 140, 145, 151, 170, 251, 258, 262, 284, 310, 325, 472
'Donation of Constantine', 33, 68
Donatism, 11, 22
Dosithius, Bishop, 250
Dostinian, 31
Dostoievsky, 294, 298, 356, 461, 470
Douceline, 134
Duns, 185
Durand, William of, 294
Durandus of Huesca, 121
Dürer, Albrecht, 303
Dury, John, 360–1
Dutch East India Co., 443

Eberhard, Bishop of Bamberg, 43
Ebreo, Leone, 273, 331
'Ecclesiastical History', 17
Eckhart, 3, 14, 102, 140, 147, 154, 158, 166, 172, 174, 175, 176–9, 195, 220, 231, 431, 435, 449
Edelmann, Johann Christoph, 426
'Edict of Tolerance', 15
Einhard, 45
Einstein, 3
Ekbert of Schonau, 80, 82, 84–5, 119
Ekkehard of Aura, 81
Eleanor of Toulouse, 119
Eliot, T. S., 475
Elipand, Bishop of Toledo, 43
Elisabeth of Schonau, 112
Elizabeth, Queen, 299, 354, 359
Elpidius, 39
Elyot, Thomas, 352
Encyclopediasts, 266, 402–4
Engels, Friedrich, 457, 466
England, 122, 203, 225, 269, 273, 283, 288, 295, 299, 300, 319, 323, 330, 333, 348 ff., 400, 421. See also British Isles

English East India Co., 443
'Enlightenment', 137, 141, 196, 206, 235, 270, 295, 311, 315, 326, 331, 347, 350, 382 ff., 412, 419, 425, 426, 431, 432, 434, 439, 447, 474
'Enlightenment, Low', 402–4
'Enthusiasts', 220–2, 229–33, 250, 259, 290, 363, 378, 389, 391, 396, 400, 404, 410, 413, 420, 422, 428, 429, 432, 439–40, 443, 452, 459, 475
Enzinas, Francisco de, 267
Epicureanism, 200, 205
Erasmus, 7, 19, 22, 50, 57, 130, 180, 185, 193, 203, 223–9, 231, 243, 254, 259–61, 263, 266, 273, 282, 298, 326, 330, 332, 341
Eriugena, 3, 15, 45, 46, 71, 73, 123, 142, 149, 158, 164, 165–6, 176, 185, 207, 208
Eschenbach, Wolfram von, 174
Esperanto, 474
d'Etaples, Faber, 203, 224, 316
Ethelbert, King, 33
Eugene III, Pope, 106
Eusebius of Caesarea, 16, 23
Eustochium, 20
Evangelicals, 394
Everard, 352, 366
Existentialism, 165

Fabricius, 21
Falconi, Juan, 281–2
Fascism, 465
Faustus, Abbot of Lerins, 38
Feirafiz, 174
Felix, Bishop of Urgel, 43, 98, 106
Fénelon, 162, 180, 280, 385, 390–2, 397, 407, 415, 436, 449
Ferdinand VII, 258
Ferdinand the Catholic, 254
Ferdinand the Saint, 123, 141
Fichte, 361, 410, 436, 449, 450
Ficino, Marsitio, 207
Fisher, John, 225, 352
Flagellants, 175, 183
Flanders, 41, 61, 123, 126, 172, 267, 318, 319
Florence, 2, 14, 124, 125, 205, 207, 235, 252, 319
Folk culture, 52 ff., 57, 60
Formosus, Pope, 61
Fourier, 292
Fra Dolcino, 133–4
France, 36, 41, 107, 115, 132, 172, 189, 288, 295, 306, 319, 323, 325, 328, 330, 334, 350, 373, 382 ff., 414

France, Southern, 26, 36, 38, 39, 53, 68, 95, 103, 107, 114, 119
Francis I, Emperor, 54, 316, 440
Francis of Assisi, 1, 81, 126–31, 137, 188–9, 203, 218, 235, 252, 270, 276
Franciscans, 52, 87, 111, 113, 114, 125, 138, 140, 145, 148, 151, 165, 170, 176, 188–9, 251, 258, 262, 273, 316, 325–6, 352, 426
Franck, Sebastian, 222, 233–6, 239, 452
Francks, August, 413, 418, 429
Frankfurt, 14, 174
  Council of, 43
Franks, 26, 33, 35, 36, 40, 75
Fraticelli, 81, 92, 136, 181, 212, 239, 252, 292, 308
Frederick I, Emperor, 50, 85, 86, 107, 122
Frederick II, Emperor, 63, 107, 131, 141–143, 151, 201, 401
Frederick the Great, 40, 419, 423–6, 434–5
'Free Thinkers', 116, 125
French Revolution, 1, 58, 169, 257, 311, 312, 336, 347, 361, 362, 379, 392, 406–408, 425, 449, 467, 470
Freud, 454, 455–6
Friedrich Wilhelm I, 413
Friesians, 35
Frulovisi, Tito Livio, 210
Fuggers, 255, 320
Fulda, School of, 45

Galileo, 291, 293, 301–8, 340, 360, 369, 371
Galitzin, Alexander, 451
Gassendi, 350, 416
Gattinara, 260
Gebeno of Eberbach, 88
Gebirol. See Avicebron
Gellert, Christian, 421
Gemelli, Agostino, 129
Geneva, 2, 235, 315, 319
Genoa, 105, 319
Geoffrey of Monmouth, 81
Gerardino of Borgo San Domino, 132
Gerbert, 66, 67, 113
Gerhoh of Reichensberg, 80, 82, 86–7, 112
Germany, 49, 58, 70, 79, 85, 122, 138, 172, 174, 178, 202, 218 ff., 267, 295, 330, 340, 350, 361, 409 ff., 448 ff.
Gerson, 192–3, 273
Ghent, Henry of, 158, 159
Ghibellines, 144, 206
Ghirlandaio, 205

Giacomo da Piacenza, 163
Gibbon, 378
Gide, André, 2, 323, 475
Gilbert, 304, 360
Giorgione, 205
Giotto, 127, 301
Giroi, Alonso, 274
Gnosticism, 9, 10, 12, 99, 430, 471
Godesalc, 46, 60
Godfrey of Fontaine, 158, 159, 174
Godfrey of Viterbo, 81
Goethe, 80, 148, 372, 410, 412, 415, 419, 428, 434, 436, 439–44, 469
Gonzov, Gennadius, 294, 252
Goths, 26, 28, 38, 257
Gott, Samuel, 367
Goya, 257, 281, 288
Gracian, Balthasar, 285
Gracian, Jeronimo, 278, 281
Granada, Luis de, 273
Gregorian Reform, 70 ff.
Gregory I, 16, 27, 29, 31, 32, 37, 41, 87, 121
Gregory II, 19
Gregory VII, 31, 72, 74 ff., 85, 86, 87, 111, 122, 127, 132, 143, 180, 185
Gregory IX, 63, 105
Gregory XII, 187
Gregory XVI, 123, 302, 312
Gregory Nuzianzen, 7, 20
Gregory of Nyssa, 7
Gresham, Sir Thomas, 360
Grocyn, 185
Groote, Geert, 195, 330
Gropius, 466
Grosseteste, Robert, 184
Grotius, Hugo, 331–4, 398
Guelphs, 144, 206
Guevana, 285
Guiccardini, 212
Guilds, 170
Gunderode, 182
Gunther, Bishop of Bamberg, 57
Gunzo of Novara, 66

Hadrian, 39
Hakluyt, Richard, 359
Halevi, Abraham ben David, 103
Halevy, Jahudah, 103
Hamaan, 294, 428–31, 457
'Harmony of the Gospels', 10
Harnack, 11
Harrington, James, 367–8
Hegel, 79, 155, 177, 195, 361, 376, 412, 415, 449, 450, 458
Hegesippus, 9

Heidegger, Martin, 448, 451, 473
Heiric of Auxerre, 45
Heisenberg, 3
Helisachar, 75
Hellenism, 9, 12, 15, 25, 37, 73, 80, 95,
  98, 103, 121, 177, 239
Helmold, 106
Héloïse, 20, 78, 107, 146
Helvetius, 403
Hemerling, Robert, 232, 453
Henry III, Emperor, 71, 78
Henry IV, Emperor, 72, 76, 86, 96
Henry V, Emperor, 86
Henry VII, Emperor, 200
Henry I of England, 102
Henry II of England, 107, 122, 144
Henry VII of England, 348
Henry VIII of England, 352
Henry IV of France, 326, 337
Henry of Navarre, 271, 326
Herberstein, Count, 293
Herbert, Lord Edward, 359
Herder, 249, 252-3, 372, 409, 415, 428,
  431-3, 434, 439, 449
Hermann of Corinthia, 108
Hernandez, Francisca, 261
Herph, 273, 281
Hilary of Poitiers, 18
Hildebrand, 60
Hildegard of Bingen, 55, 80, 82, 87-9,
  112, 119, 138, 175, 178, 196
Hispaniensis, Petrus, 167
Hitler, 232, 348, 393, 405, 451, 453-4,
  456, 473
Hobbes, 101, 151, 317, 332, 340, 343,
  369-70, 416, 426
Hoffman, Daniel, 241
Hoffman, J. A., 420
Holbach, 403
Holderlin, 448, 449
Holkot, Robert, 349
Holland, 319, 333-5, 340
Holy Grail, concept of, 109, 174
Holy Roman Empire, 71 ff., 79, 81, 92,
  440, 443
Homer, 155, 379, 425
Honorius III, 129, 145
Hooker, Richard, 354-5
Hopkins, Gerard Manley, 130
Horace, 20, 26
Hosius, Bishop, 16
Hrotsvith, 65, 76
Hubmaier, 233
Hugh of St Victor, 80, 82-3
Hugo of Digne, 134
Huguenots, 133, 324-6, 327, 333, 337,
  364, 366, 382, 384, 386, 388, 390, 392,
  393

Humanism, Christian, 224
  English, 203, 225, 352, 376
  French, 203, 316, 327
  German, 175, 223, 460
  Italian, 85, 198 ff., 252, 305
  Western, 177, 244, 409
Humbert, 72 ff., 85, 111, 128, 180
Hume, 100, 367, 373-5
Hundred Years War, 144
Hungary, 52, 61, 68, 122, 186, 330
Hus, 69, 134, 170, 172, 184, 185, 186-8,
  191
Hussites, 1, 52, 111
'Hyperaspistes', 226, 227

Ibanez, Blasco, 283
Ibn Pakuda, 102-3
Ibn Sabin, 142
Ibn Suhr, 103
Ignatius of Antioch, 9
Ignatius of Loyola, 50, 245, 255, 256,
  257, 261-2, 269-70, 273, 287, 288, 317,
  340
Illuminati, 132
Illyricus, Flaccius, 252
'Imitation of Christ', 194
'Impossibilia', 150
Independents, 366
India, 134, 246, 265, 271, 272, 348
Industrial Revolution, 375, 464
Innocent III, 78, 106, 111, 120, 121, 125,
  127, 201, 270
Inquisition, 96, 107, 122-3, 136, 138,
  161, 162, 187, 255, 258, 267, 272, 273,
  275, 289
Investiture contest, 77, 80, 84, 173
Ireland, 40, 41, 45, 362, 365
Ireneaus, 9
Isaac the Blind, 103
Isaac ben Melchisedech, 103
Isabella, Queen, 254, 256, 259
Isidore of Seville, 39
Islam, 25, 39, 42, 50, 71, 74, 78, 80, 95 ff.,
  137, 142, 257, 286
Italy, 26, 40, 41, 48, 61, 65, 93, 114, 115,
  125, 126, 132, 154, 173, 198 ff., 235,
  288, 289 ff., 340, 443, 470, 472
Ivan III, 241, 249, 251
Ivan the Terrible, 253

Jacobinism, 332, 380, 400, 405-8, 460
Jacquerie, 173
James I of Aragon, 105
James I of England, 293, 361, 364
James of Viterbo, 159
Jansenism, 243, 286, 301, 310, 311, 323,
  340, 345-7, 382, 385-9, 399, 413, 428,
  442, 446, 451

Japan, 256, 271, 272
Jerome, 7, 19–20, 304
Jerome of Prague, 134, 185, 186
Jerusalem, 15, 43, 114
Jesuits, 81, 225, 270–2, 284, 289, 311, 317, 332, 364, 382, 385, 386–8, 395, 445, 472
Joachim of Flora, 43, 80, 84, 88, 91, 94, 126, 131, 135, 149, 195, 203
Joan of Arc, 1, 133, 164, 170, 173, 184, 187–91, 200, 205, 218, 232, 235, 278, 292, 315
John of Anville, 146
John, Bishop of Jerusalem, 38
John of the Cross, 255, 257, 274, 278–80, 284, 288
John the Deacon, 36
John of Jandun, 158, 163, 168
John VIII, Pope, 36, 61
John XXII, Pope, 159, 160, 168, 174, 183
John of Salisbury, 81, 92, 106, 107, 112, 213
Johnson, Samuel, 376
Joris, David, 296
Joseph II, Emperor, 311, 345, 440, 442
Joseph, Père, 338–9, 384
Joseph of Volotsk, 294
Joyce, 37
Joyce, James, 475
Judaeus, Abraham, 102
Judaism, 11, 17, 29, 50, 102 ff., 185, 249, 255, 256, 529
Julius II, Pope, 211
Jung, 455–6
Junger, 475
Jung-Stilling, Heinrich, 437, 438
'Jus Primae Noctis', 59
Justin, 10
Justinian, 15, 29, 31, 122
Juvenal, 20

Kafka, Franz, 454, 456
Kant, 3, 51, 79, 179, 195, 374, 398, 404, 410, 412, 419, 433–6, 441, 470
Karlstadt, 222, 225, 231
Kempis, Thomas à, 330
Kepler, 304, 371
Kierkegaard, 13, 165, 188, 429, 433, 467
Klages, 299
Knox, John, 235, 336, 364
Knut the Great, 70
Koran, 43, 95, 98, 109, 422
Kotzebue, 441
Krause, 287–8, 475, 476
Kremlin, 252
Krüdener, Mme, 451, 452
Kurbski, Prince Andreas, 253
Kurliateff, Nil, 253

Lamettrie, 13, 403
Lammenais, 470
Lando, Michele, 173
Laredo, Bernardino de, 273
Las Casas, Bartolome de, 254, 265, 268
Las Navas de Tolosa, Battle of, 120
Lateran Council, Fourth, 111
Latimer, William, 185
Latin, 49, 187–8, 204, 214, 249, 274, 474
Latini, Brunetto, 163
Laud, Archbishop, 361, 365
Laura, 20
Law, William, 377
Lawrence, D. H., 323
Lawrence, T. E., 323, 358, 475
Lavater, 440
Leal, Valdes, 257
Le Bougne, Robert, 123
Lebrixa, Antonio de, 254, 259
Leibniz, 50, 55, 67, 79, 139, 140, 154, 195, 416–9, 425, 435, 436, 444, 469
Leidrad of Lyons, 43
Leo the Great, Pope, 35, 121
Leo X, 301, 313
Leo XIII, 158, 473
Leo III, Emperor, 42
Leon, Luis de, 274
Leonardo da Vinci, 211, 214–7, 291, 301
Leopardi, Giacomo, 312, 465
Lerins, 38, 41
Lessing, 421–3, 436
Levellers, 366
'Libellus de Custodi Virginitatis', 20
'Liber de Rectoribus Christianis', 46
'Liber Doctrinae Puerilis', 139
'Liber Pontificalis', 35, 41
Liberalism, 409, 450, 452, 471
Liberius, Pope, 19
'Librii Carolini', 42
'Life of Gregory the Great', 35
Lilburne, John, 366
Linacre, 185
Lipsius, Justus, 282
Locke, 169, 334, 348, 351, 367, 370, 416
Loen, Michael von, 436
Lollards, 173, 175, 185, 349
Lombards, 33, 35
London, 2, 14, 300, 421
Longinus, 174
Lorca, Frederico Garcia, 287
Lothar, Emperor, 89
Louis the Pious, 44, 46
Louis VII, 122
Louis IX, 105
Louis XII, 316
Louis XIII, 336
Louis XIV, 44, 54, 287, 347, 384 ff., 425

Louis xvi, 132
Low Countries, The, 172, 193, 194, 232, 235, 263, 275, 282, 325, 330–1, 334, 346
Luccan, 20, 39
Lucius ii, Pope, 75
Lucius iii, Pope, 122
Ludwig, Emperor, 174, 183
Lull, Raymond, 3, 134, 135, 138–40, 141, 158, 161, 213, 294, 326, 341, 342, 416
Lupus of Ferrières, 45, 48, 60, 71
Luther, 1, 2, 9, 22, 34, 50, 51, 69, 131, 178, 184, 187, 197, 218 ff., 250, 260, 268, 273, 275, 277, 290, 330, 340–1, 345, 354, 409, 412, 426, 433, 437, 469
Lutheranism, 320, 322, 323, 409, 410, 420, 467
Lyons, 2, 113, 267
  Council of, 132

Mach, Ernest, 51, 139
Machiavelli, 31, 101, 198, 210–3, 262, 263, 425
Madariaga, 51
Magellan, 306
Magus, Simon, 22
Maimonides, 102–4, 142
Maintenon, Madame de, 391
Malebranche, 100
Maluenda, 269
Mandeville, 321
Manetti, 208, 213
Manichaeanism, 22, 98, 103, 122, 220, 227, 256, 321, 345, 349, 363, 473
Manrique, Archbishop, 260, 263
Manrique, Redrigo, 266
Manutius, Aldus, 246
Manzoni, 311, 312
Mape, Walter, 57
Marcellinus, Ammianus, 20
Marcion, 11, 115, 151, 453
Marcus of Memphis, 39
Maria Theresa, 52, 423, 440
Marie Antoinette, 62
Maritain, Jacques, 472
Marsilius of Padua, 158, 163–5, 168
Martial, 39
Marx, 3, 155, 239, 317, 361, 415, 425, 448, 457–60, 466
Masaryk, Thomas, 185
Materialism, 378, 457–8
Mathilde d'Orléans, 404
Matteo da Gubbio, 163
Maurice of Nassau, 332
Maurice of Orange, 320–1, 332
Maurice of Spain, 124
Maurras, Charles, 473

Maurus, Rhabanus, 39
Maximian, Bishop, 30
Maximos the Greek, 245–7, 250–3, 259, 298
Mazarin, 335
Mazio, Galeotto, 209
Mazzini, 311
McCulloch, 375
Mechtild of Magdeburg, 172, 175
Medici, Lorenzo, 213
Melanchthon, 219, 224, 226, 229, 231, 240, 244, 252, 262, 269, 409
Mendel, Gregor, 446
Mersenne, Marin, 339, 341, 343, 369
Merton College, 185
Messalians, 115
Mesta, 258
Methodism, 377–8
Michelangelo, 211, 291–2, 301
Migetius, 43
Milan, 2, 34, 112, 124, 126, 289
  Council of, 18
Mill, James Stuart, 375, 452
Milton, 286, 368, 376
Miona, 261
Mirecourt, John of, 192, 331
Mirecourt, Nicholas of, 405
Missionaries, 67, 134
Mitterer, Albert, 472
Moerbeke, William of, 157, 159, 177
Mohammed, 95 ff.
Molière, 386
Molina, 271, 415
Molinos, Miguel de, 282, 284
Monasticism, 4, 24, 31 ff., 40–1, 57, 112, 180, 204, 258, 261, 277, 322, 350, 446
Montaigne, 328–9, 341, 428
Montanism, 10, 13
Montano, Dr Arias, 275
Montenegro, 284
Montesquieu, 316, 428, 439, 442
More, Thomas, 185, 236, 259, 263, 266, 292, 326, 350–2 357, 363, 376, 380, 417
Moritz, Karl Philipp, 437–8, 457
Moser, Johann, 436
Moser, Justus, 378–9, 421, 438–9
Moses, Ibn Ezra, 103
Muller, Adam, 449
Mumford, Lewis, 48, 321
Munzer, Thomas, 1, 222, 232–3, 234
Muratori, 310
Murillo, 257
Mussato, Albertino, 163
Mussolini, 454
Mutian, 203, 223
Mysticism, 172, 273, 275, 277–8, 378, 382, 404, 412, 415

Nantes, Edict of, 326, 337, 370, 389–90, 392
Naples, 2, 105, 107, 206, 209, 285, 289, 294
University of, 143
Napoleon, 258
Nationalism, 400, 408, 432, 449, 452, 470
Nazis, 287, 438, 450. *See also* Hitler
Neoplatonists, 14, 21, 46, 99, 102, 157, 270, 435
Neo-Thomism, 471–2
Newman, 470, 471
Newton, 290, 348, 371–2, 377, 416
Nicea, Council of, 42
Nicetas, 89, 90, 115
Nicholas of Amiens, 139
Nicholas of Cusa, 67, 79, 110, 139, 140, 147, 154, 176, 193, 195–6, 207, 208, 224, 231, 235, 316, 326, 330, 332, 341, 342, 417, 435
Nicholas of Lubeck, 252
Nicholas I, Pope, 46
Nicholas of Strasbourg, 176
Nicodemism, 100, 125, 162, 180, 200, 250, 286, 410
Nicole, Pierre, 388
Nietzsche, 3, 10, 137, 177, 188, 276, 285, 299, 361, 407, 410, 439, 448, 451, 452–453, 457, 469
Nivard of Ghent, 112
Nominalism, 167, 170–1, 259, 268
Normans, 61
Notker of Liège, 67
Novalis, 448, 449, 450
Novatian, 27

Occultism, 404
'Oceana', 367
Ockham, 131, 134, 135, 149, 158, 159, 161, 166–71, 185, 192, 239, 348
Ockhamism, 219, 315, 316, 322
Odo of Cluny, 61
Oldenbarneveldt, 332–3
Olivi, Peter John, 132–3, 135, 137, 158, 160, 189
'On Learned Ignorance', 196
Oratorians, 310, 383
Origen, 7, 12, 14, 15, 23, 42, 46, 115, 151, 177, 225, 273
Orosius, 39, 81, 227, 255
Ortiz, Francisco, 261
Osorio, Isabel, 274
d'Osuna, Francisco, 260
Otto of Freising, 23, 79, 80, 81, 82, 84, 88–9, 92
Otto the Great, 20, 50, 61, 65, 66, 71, 78
Otto III, 65, 67–9, 71

Ovid, 26
Oxford, 14, 46, 107, 136, 144, 184–5, 214, 266, 267, 300
Synod of, 123

Paccioli, Luca, 215
Pachomius, 38
Padua, 14, 206, 214, 289, 294, 303
University of, 158
Paine, Thomas, 379
Paleologus, Sophie-Zoe, 241, 294
Palestrina, 310
Pantheism, 208, 243, 471
Papebroch, Daniel, 271
Paracelsus, 51, 138, 147, 160, 215, 234–9, 298, 411
Paris 14, 107, 136–7, 159, 267, 406
Council of, 18
University of, 46, 123, 138, 140, 144–145, 252
Paris, Matthew, 63
Pascal, 13, 32, 51, 100, 203, 280, 310, 336, 340, 343–4, 374, 386, 395, 407
Paul III, Pope, 290, 292, 353
Paul IV, Pope, 273, 274, 302
Paula, 20
Paulicians, 115
'Peace of God' Movement, 64, 71
Peasant revolts, 62
Peasants' War, 225
Peckham, John, 185
Pelagianism, 15, 22, 37, 39, 219–20, 242, 345, 349, 375
Pelagius, 37, 225
Pelagius II, Pope, 33
Penn, William, 348
'Pensées', 344
Persia, 96, 134
Pestalozzi, 441
Peter of Aragon, 121
Peter of Bruys, 119
Peter the Great, 40
Petrarch, 7, 20, 57, 130, 201–3
Pez, Bernhard and Hieronymus, 446
Philip the Fair, 159–60
Philip II of Spain, 274–5
Picasso, 287
Pico, Giovanni, 207, 208, 212, 246
Pieper, Josef, 472
Pietism, 182, 241, 286, 328, 378, 410, 412, 414, 426, 435, 449, 467
Pilgrimage, 52, 58
Pirkheimer, 223, 235
Pisa, 105, 306, 319
Pistoria, Synod of, 57, 311
Pius II, 210–11
Pius V, 324

Pius x, 314
Pius xii, 90
Platina, 210
Plato, 10, 21, 28, 50, 195, 205, 207, 303, 313, 371, 417
Poggio, 198, 203, 205–6
Poland, Partition of, 423
Polycraticus, 108
Pombal, 288
Pontano, Giovanni, 209
Pope, Alexander, 373
Porphyry, 167
Port Royal, 310, 312, 345, 388
Pound, Ezra, 475
Poviet, Peter, 415, 416
Prague, 2, 186
Premonstratensians, 78, 90
Presbyterians, 365
Priestley, Joseph, 378, 380
'Prince, The', 211
Priscillian, 39
Proclus, 157, 176, 177
Protestantism, 42, 259, 269, 283, 295, 324, 325, 336, 389, 393–4, 442, 446, 467, 469, 471, 473
Prudentius, 39
Ptolemy, 303
Ptolinus, 14
Pudens, Cornelius, 35
Pufendorf, 411, 431
Puritans, 352, 353, 364
Pym, 362–4

Quakers, 310, 345
'Querela Pacis', 260
Quesnel, 310, 345
Quevedo, 282
Quidort, Jean, 158
Quietism, 280–2, 378, 390
Quinones, 262
Quintano, Pedro de, 254
Quintilian, 39
'Quodlibetales', 152–3

Rabaut, Paul, 393
Rabelais, 130, 316, 326–7, 338
Raimund, Archbishop, 106, 154
Raphael, 211, 301
Raskolniki, 253
'Rassalas', 376
Ratramaus of Corbie, 45
Ratther of Verona, 66
Ravenna, 29, 30, 43, 58
Recared, 33
Reformation, 171, 172, 183, 184, 272, 299, 318, 359, 379, 388, 436. See also Luther

Reimarus, Samuel, 421–2
Relics, 262–3
Rembrandt, 286, 335
Remigius of Girolami, 159
'Retractiones', 21
Revensburg Trading Society, 255
Rhegius, Urbanus, 229
Rhodes, Cecil, 358
Ricardo, 375
Richard ii, 173
Richelieu, 62, 293, 306, 335–40, 361, 364, 384, 400
Rienzo, Cola di, 198, 200–1, 211, 230
Rilke, 453, 454, 473, 475
Ringseis, 455
Robespierre, 116, 201, 236, 317, 405–7
Roger of Marston, 185
'Roman de la Rose', 146
Romanticism, 182, 244, 283, 378, 408, 412, 449–52, 456, 465
Rome, 12, 14, 20, 26, 32, 34, 40, 41, 43, 61, 90, 122, 136, 200, 206, 211, 289, 291, 306, 312, 314, 428, 473
Rosenberg, Alfred, 299, 432, 469
Rousseau, 62, 72, 162, 164, 179, 235, 315, 330, 335, 372, 378, 382, 394, 398–402, 407
Rupert of Duetz, 80, 82–3, 89, 92, 128
Russia, 51, 70, 96, 120, 134, 241, 244–5, 247–9, 258, 283, 330, 350, 361, 393, 443, 452, 461, 463
Ruysbroek, 273, 281

Sabinian, Pope, 31
Sacconi, Raynier, 125
Sade, Marquis de, 285
Sagredo, 305–6
Saint-Basle de Verzy, Council of, 61
Saint-Just, 405, 407
Saint-Simon, 292
Salcedo, Frances de, 275
Salerno, 103
Sales, Francis de, 267, 280, 329, 382, 383, 399
Salmaticensians, 268–9
Salviate, 305
Salzburg, 62
Sanchez, Francisco, 330
Santayana, George, 283
Saracens, 35, 61, 136
Savonarola, 31, 198, 209, 211–2, 232, 235, 246, 252, 273, 292
Saxons, 33
Scaevola, 21
Schelling, 361, 449, 450
Schiller, 410, 419, 434
Schlegel, 467

Schleiermacher, 467–8
Scholasticism, 84, 107, 132, 136, 144 ff., 177, 239, 244, 254, 274, 315
Schweitzer, 72
Schwenckfeld, 222, 233
Scipio, 21
Scotism, 259
Scotland, 362, 364
Scotus, Duns, 348
Scotus, John. See Eriugena
Sega, 278
Semi-Pelagianism, 38, 44
Semler, Johann, 414
Seneca, 39, 177, 279, 329
Sentimentalism, 414, 433, 436
Sepulveda, Juan Gines de, 254, 264, 269
Sergius III, 36
Shaftesbury, Earl of, 372, 383, 428
Shakespeare, 102, 355–7
Shyreswood, William of, 167
Sigebert of Gembloux, 67
Siger, 102, 146–50, 160, 185, 199, 331, 338
Silesius, Angelus, 412
Silvester, 199
Silvestris, Bernard, 109, 110
Simeon, 70
Simon, Richard, 116, 383, 384
Simony, 180, 185
Simplicio, 305–6
Siquenza, Fray José, 275
Slavery, 47, 265
Smith, Adam, 375–6
'Social Contract', 401
Socinianism, 333, 363, 436
Socinus, Faustus, 297–8
Socinus, Laelius, 296
'Song of Roland', 46, 96
Sophie, Electress of Hanover, 415
Sorski, Abbot Nil, 251
Soto, Doningo de, 268–9
Spain, 15, 26, 33, 36, 38 ff., 40, 41, 51, 58, 68, 71, 78, 95, 103, 107, 114, 123, 139, 254 ff., 289, 295, 320, 334, 342, 350, 357, 373, 414, 461, 471, 472
Spener, Jacob, 413, 429
Spengler, 137
Spinoza, 14, 102, 151, 166, 273, 286, 331, 414, 426
Spirituals, 130–4, 137, 308, 311, 422
Staccia, Pietro, 128
Stael, Madame de, 394
Stedinger, 63, 78
Stendhal, 465
Stephen VI, Pope, 61
Stilicho, 26, 27
Stoicism, 155, 177, 200, 205, 240, 241, 282, 326, 327

Strabo, Walafried, 45
Strafford, 364
Straw, Jack, 173
Sturm, 262
Sturzo Don Luigi, 314
Sufiism, 100, 140, 414
'Summa Contra Gentiles' 152–3
Supremacy, Act of, 349, 352
Suso, 172, 175, 182–3
Swedenborg, 160, 405, 406
Swift, 376
Switzerland, 295, 319, 327, 340
Sylvester, Pope. See Gerbert
'Synonyma', 39
Symmachus, 19

'Tain Bo Cualgne', 41
Tarragona, Synod of, 123
Tartaglia, Nicolo, 302
Tasso, 304
Tatian, 10
Tauler, Johannes, 172, 175, 179–82, 183, 220, 231, 234, 241, 260, 261, 273, 281, 316, 341, 412, 429
Templars, 151, 160, 163, 174, 286, 393
Tertullian, 11, 13, 85, 93, 153, 225, 422
Test Act, 353
Texeda, Fernando de, 283
Theodora, 30, 61
Theodoric, 28, 30, 33, 35
Theodosius, 13, 19, 26, 39
Theodulf of Orleans, 42, 75
'Theologia Germanica', 220–1
Theophano, Empress, 65
Theophilos, 42
Theresa, St of Avila, 20, 50, 256, 273, 274–81, 284, 288, 291, 346, 405, 416, 433
Thierry of Chartres, 108, 195
Thietman, 68
Thirty Years War, 285, 306, 329, 340, 410, 443
Thomas of Celano, 130
Thomasius, Jacob, 411
Thomism, 50, 113, 125, 135, 170, 176, 179, 195, 240, 259, 267, 284, 293, 340, 385, 434, 435, 472
Tindall, 37, 436
Toland, 37, 436
Toledo, 103, 106, 139
Tormes, Lazaro de, 256
Toryism, 378
Toulouse, 2, 14, 103, 117, 122, 327
    Counts of, 119
    Synod of, 122
    University of, 123, 144
Tovar, Bernardino, 261

Trajan, 39
Trent, Council of, 9, 77, 113, 267, 290, 299, 310, 353
Trial by Ordeal, 59
Trosle, Synod of, 61
Turkey, 70, 443, 445
Tychonius, 81, 82
Tyler, Wat, 172, 173, 185, 349

Ubertino of Casale, 162
Ulm, 174
Uniformity, Act of, 353
Unitarians, 299, 363
Urban ii, 86, 114
Urban iv, 132
Urban viii, 305, 335
'Utopia', 350-1

Vadier, 407, 408
Valdes, Alfonso, 254, 262, 263, 264
Valdes, Fernando de, 273, 274
Valdes, Juan, 254, 292
Valentian ii, 19
Valéry, Paul, 475
Valla, Lorenzo, 203, 204-5, 350
Valois, Renée de, 295, 296
Vasari, Giorgio, 300-1, 428
Vega, Lope de, 286
Venice, 2, 105, 126, 206, 267, 289, 319, 327, 399
Vergara, 262
Verona, 34
Vico, G. B., 51, 134, 308-9
Vienna, 14, 17, 57, 59, 426, 444, 454
Villon, 338
Vincent of Lérins, 38, 96
Virgil, 26, 198, 262
Virgil of Salzburg, 45
Virnes, 262
Vitalis, Ordericus, 81
Vitoria, Francisco de, 268
Vitrier, Jean, 224
Vitruvius, 41
Vives, Juan Luis, 236, 264, 266
Vladimir, Prince, 70
Vogelweide, Walter von der, 174
Volapuk, 474
Volotsk, Joseph of, 251
Voltaire, 330

Wagner, Hans Jacob, 446
Waldensianism, 52, 109, 111, 113-4, 116, 119, 123, 126, 134, 167, 185, 295, 313, 323, 392
Waldo, Peter, 113
Walter of Lille, 146
Wandelbert of Prum, 45
Wassili, Archduke, 245, 248
Weber, Max, 319
Wesley, John, 377-8
Westphalia, Peace of, 280, 339, 409
William of Blois, 106
William of Chartres, 108-9
William of Conches, 108
William de la Mare, 185
William of Orange, 332
William of Rubruch, 135
Winckelmann, Johann Joachim, 427-8
Winstanley, 352, 366
Wireker, Nigel, 112
Witches, 1, 160
Witelo, 158
Wittenberg, 252
    University of, 219
Wittgenstein, 475
Wolff, Christian, 420, 425
Worms, Concordat of, 86
Wyclif, 134, 170, 172, 184, 185, 191, 225, 273, 313, 348, 349

Xavier, Francis, 255, 271, 280, 288
Ximenez, Cardinal, 254, 259

Yaroslav the Wise, 70
Ydros, Bernard, 113
York, 40
Yves de Paris, 382-3

Zacharias, Pope, 46
Zasius, 223
Zorastrianism, 98
Zosimus, 38
Zurbaran, 257
Zurich, 174
Zwickau, 232-3
Zwingli, 224, 227, 229, 240, 243, 260, 273